D1151966

WILLS, ADMINISTRATION AND TAXATION LAW AND PRACTICE

Tenth Edition

By

J.S. BARLOW, M.A. (Cantab.), LL.M.
(London), L.Lat.
*Formerly Reader and Deputy Director of Academic Studies,
The College of Law*

PROFESSOR L.C. KING, LL.B. (Bristol),
Dip. Crim. (Cantab.)
*Solicitor (hons); Private Client Practice Head,
The College of Law*

A.G. KING, M.A.
*Solicitor (hons); Head of HR Development,
Clifford Chance LLP*

SWEET & MAXWELL
 **THOMSON REUTERS**

First Edition 1983
Second Edition 1986
Third Edition 1988
Fourth Edition 1990
Fifth Edition 1992
Sixth Edition 1994
Reprinted 1994
Seventh Edition 1997
Eighth Edition 2003
Ninth Edition 2008
Tenth Edition 2011

Published in 2011 by
Sweet & Maxwell Limited of
100 Avenue Road,
London NW3 3PF
Part of Thomson Reuters (Professional) UK Limited (Registered in England &
Wales, Company No 1679046. Registered Office and Address for service: Aldgate
House, 33 Aldgate High Street, London EC3N 1DL)
http://www.sweetandmaxwell.co.uk
Typeset by Interactive Sciences Ltd, Gloucester
Printed and bound in Great Britain by Ashford Colour Printers

No natural forests were destroyed to make this product; only farmed timber was
used and replanted.

A CIP catalogue record for this book is available from the
British Library

ISBN 9780414045958

ACKNOWLEDGMENTS

The publishers and authors wish to thank the following bodies for permission to reprint material from the following sources:

LexisNexis Butterworths: *Encyclopaedia of Forms and Precedents*, 4th edn.
IRIS Laserform material reproduced with the permission of Laserform International Limited, part of IRIS Legal, tel. 0845 815575.

PREFACE TO THE TENTH EDITION

This book was originally written principally for students. However, many practitioners have found it to be a useful first source of reference. The tenth edition has been written with this in mind. We have tried to keep the text reasonably concise while covering all the points which are likely to be needed by most practitioners. It is a sign of the times, however, that the page count creeps up inexorably with each edition.

The book states the law as at April 6, 2011.

J.S. Barlow
L.C. King
A.G. King

CONTENTS

TABLE OF CASES

TABLE OF STATUTES

TABLE OF STATUTORY INSTRUMENTS

CHAPTER ONE

INTRODUCTION: WHAT TO DO AFTER DEATH

When a person dies there are a number of practical steps which must be taken. **1.01** For example, the death must be registered, the funeral arranged and the property of the deceased must be made safe. These matters are usually dealt with by members of the deceased's family or by friends.

The question then arises "Who is to be entitled to the deceased's assets?" It is at this point that a solicitor is most likely to be consulted. It is often assumed that the disposition of property depends entirely on whether or not a deceased made a valid will but in fact the disposition of many substantial assets is not affected by the presence or absence of a will. For example, if a deceased owned a house as a joint tenant with another person then that property will pass automatically to the survivor as a result of the right of survivorship; if the deceased had taken out insurance policies for the benefit of other people the proceeds of such policies will frequently be paid directly to those people; if the terms of the deceased's employment provide for payment of a lump sum on death it is common for the trustees of the scheme to be given a discretion to pay the lump sum to the person or persons they consider appropriate (the employee is entitled to inform the trustees of his or her wishes as to the destination of the lump sum but the trustees have an overriding discretion). These matters are discussed in Ch.21.

The disposition of other assets does, however, depend on whether or not there is a valid will. If there is no valid will then the disposition of property will be determined by the intestacy rules (explained further in Ch.3). If there is a will it is necessary to discover whether or not it is valid. This requires a consideration of whether or not the testator had sufficient mental capacity at the time the will was made and whether the appropriate formalities were complied with (see Ch.2). It is quite possible for a will successfully to dispose of some but not all of the deceased's assets. This may be because the will does not deal with all of the deceased's property or because some of the gifts fail (see Chs 16 and 17). In such cases the disposition of the property is governed partly by the will and partly by the intestacy rules.

It may be difficult to discover whether or not a will exists. If one cannot be found amongst the deceased's papers it is advisable to contact any solicitors consulted by the deceased to discover whether or not a will was deposited with them and to contact the deceased's bank to discover whether or not the deceased had a safe deposit box which might contain it. There is a procedure whereby wills can be deposited during a person's lifetime at the Principal Registry of the Family Division but this is little used. However, it would obviously be worth contacting the Registry if a will is proving difficult to find (there are similar provisions for Scotland and Northern Ireland). There are also commercial organisations which provide a will registration service.

1.02   It is necessary for someone to undertake the task of finding the will and checking whether or not it is valid. It is also necessary for someone to collect in the assets of the deceased, pay the debts and other liabilities of the deceased and then transfer the remaining assets to the persons entitled. In order to collect in the assets a person dealing with the estate will often have to *prove* that they have the authority to deal with the deceased's assets. This is done by producing a grant of representation obtained from the Probate Registry by the person(s) entitled to administer the estate.

Similarly there may be problems when it comes to transferring property of the deceased to the persons entitled. In the case of chattels it will often be sufficient to hand them to the person entitled; many assets (for example, land) are, however, held in the name of the deceased and must somehow be transferred into the name of the new owner if the new owner is to be able to deal with them. A grant of representation enables the person entitled to act on behalf of the estate of the deceased person to transfer property into the name of the new owner.

If the deceased appointed someone in the will to administer their estate, that person is called an executor and obtains a grant of representation called a grant of probate which merely *confirms* that person's authority to act in connection with the estate. If no executor was appointed or if the appointed executor is not willing or able to act the Non-Contentious Probate Rules 1987 set out an order for determining who is entitled to act; such a person is called an administrator and must obtain a grant of letters of administration which *confers* authority to act. Executors and administrators can both be referred to as "the personal representatives" of the deceased.

It will often be necessary to obtain a grant of representation in connection with the administration before assets can be collected in or transferred to beneficiaries. The procedure is explained in Ch.10.

Acting as executor or administrator is a time-consuming task. It is also one that carries with it duties and obligations and if those duties are not properly carried out then there may be personal liability (this is discussed further in Ch.11). Readers may wonder why anyone is ever willing to act as a personal representative. There are a variety of reasons. Solicitors, banks and trust corporations will be willing to act as executors provided the will authorises them to charge for their services; beneficiaries will usually be willing to act since until someone accepts office it may be impossible to distribute the assets; friends or relatives of the deceased appointed as executors may be willing to accept office as a mark of their respect for the deceased and as a way of helping the bereaved.

Chapter Two

IS THERE A VALID WILL?

1. Formalities

Introduction

The formalities required for a valid will are set out in s.9 of the Wills Act 1837, **2.01**
as substituted by s.17 of the Administration of Justice Act 1982. A will which
fails to comply with these formalities is invalid and cannot be admitted to
probate.

The substituted s.9 provides that:

"No will shall be valid unless—

(a) it is in writing, and signed by the testator, or by some other person in his
presence and by his direction; and

(b) it appears that the testator intended by his signature to give effect to the will;
and

(c) the signature is made or acknowledged by the testator in the presence of two
or more witnesses present at the same time; and

(d) each witness either—

(i) attests and signs the will; or
(ii) acknowledges his signature,

in the presence of the testator (but not necessarily in the presence of any other
witness), but no form of attestation shall be necessary."

Different formalities are required in the case of a statutory will for someone who
lacks the mental capacity to make a will for themselves and a privileged testator
may make a valid will informally (see paras 2.11–2.12, below).

"In writing"

A will must be "in writing". The writing may be the handwriting of the testator, **2.02**
any other person, it may be word processed or by any form of printing, or
(presumably) produced by a photographic process. The writing may be in ink,
pencil or produced by any other means which make it visible. However, using a

combination of ink and pencil writing raises a rebuttable presumption that the parts in pencil are deliberative only and they will be excluded from probate in the absence of evidence that the testator intended them to be final.

A will may be made on any material and may be written in any language (or even in code, provided that evidence is available from which the code may be deciphered).

The signature

Signature of the testator

2.03 Any mark made by the testator is a valid signature provided the testator *intended* it to be their signature. Testators should be encouraged to sign with their usual signatures so as to avoid any doubt as to the validity of the signature.

The following have been held to be signatures:

(a) a mark made by a rubber stamp with the testator's name on it (*In the Goods of Jenkins* (1863));

(b) the thumb print of an illiterate (*In the Estate of Finn* (1935)); and

(c) a set of initials (*In the Goods of Savoy* (1851)).

The signature need not consist of a name at all. Thus in *In the Estate of Cook* (1960) a document ending with the words "your loving mother" was admitted to probate on the basis that the testatrix in writing them had intended to refer back to her name which appeared earlier in the document.

The mark relied on as a signature must be complete in the sense that the testator completed as much as they *intended* to be their signature. For example, in *Re Colling* (1972) the testator started to sign his name in the presence of two witnesses one of whom left before he had finished writing. The will was held not to be properly executed since the signature was not completed in the presence of two witnesses. In *In the Goods of Chalcraft* (1948) the testatrix started to sign her name and wrote "E. Chal" before she became too weak to continue. This was held to be a valid signature on the basis that she had decided to end the signature at that point and so the signature was complete.

Signature by another person

2.04 The signature of some person on behalf of the testator is valid provided it is made "in his presence and by his direction". The testator must be present both mentally and physically when the signature is made (see para.2.06, below, for the meaning of "presence").

The person signing at the testator's direction may be any person including one of the witnesses and may sign either with their own name or with the testator's name. (It is best for the person signing to sign their own name and write that they are signing on behalf of the testator, in their presence and by their direction.)

The testator intended by their signature to give effect to their will

The original s.9 required that the signature should be "at the foot or end" of the **2.05** will. This led to a number of cases where probate was refused because the position of the signature did not comply exactly with this description. The Wills Act Amendment Act 1852 was then passed to extend the meaning of "foot or end". However, the excessively complicated wording of that Act forced the courts to make some very narrow distinctions. The substituted s.9 now no longer requires that the signature should be at the foot or end of the will. It is sufficient that "it appears that the testator intended by his signature to give effect to the will".

The exact scope of this requirement is a matter for the court. In *Wood v Smith* (1991) the court accepted that the signature could be at the top. In the same case the court also held that a signature at the top was valid even though written before the rest of the will. This will only, however, be so if the signature and writing of the will were "all part of one transaction". A signature in the margin of a will would probably satisfy the requirement and so probably would a signature on a separate page attached to the beginning or end of the will. A handwritten will which happened to include the testator's name (for example by starting with words such as "This is the will of me John Smith . . . ") might, however, still be refused probate on the basis that the words were not intended as a validating *signature* at all but merely as a description of the testator.

The practice (resulting from the wording of the Wills Act Amendment Act 1852) of admitting part of a document to probate but of refusing to admit the parts which appear physically after the signature in certain circumstances, would seem no longer to be possible. This is because the substituted section contemplates that the signature validates all or none of the will.

A signature on an envelope containing an otherwise unsigned will is valid if it was intended to give effect to the will. However, if the signature was written for some other reason (for example, to *identify* the will) the will is not validly signed.

In *Marley v Rawlings* (2011) a husband and wife had signed each other's will. The court held that the testator had not intended his signature to give effect to the will which he signed.

Signature made or acknowledged in the presence of at least two witnesses

The substituted s.9 (like its predecessor) requires that the testator's signature is **2.06** "made or acknowledged by the testator in the presence of two or more witnesses present at the same time". A signature is made in the presence of witnesses, if they see the testator in the act of signing. The witnesses are not required to look at the signature itself nor need they know that the document is a will. It is not necessary to prove that the witnesses actually saw the act of signing; it is sufficient to show they were in such a position that they *could* have seen.

An acknowledgement of signature can be made by words or by conduct. There is an acknowledgement if the testator, or someone else in their presence, asks the witnesses to sign a document and they see their signature on it. The witnesses need not know that the document is a will. However, they must see the signature or at least have an opportunity of doing so. If the *signature* is covered up there is, therefore, no valid acknowledgement (however, the fact that the rest of the will is covered up does not prevent the acknowledgement being valid). The acknowledgement must be made to two or more witnesses present *at the same time*. A will is not, therefore, valid if an acknowledgement is made by the testator to each witness in the absence of the other.

In *Lim v Thompson* (2009) the court held that a will had not been duly executed as it was a photocopy which had been signed by the testator prior to copying but signed by the witnesses after copying. A photocopy of a will with a photocopied signature of the testator was not a document which was signed by the testator at all.

Witnesses

Attestation

2.07 The substituted s.9 requires that each witness must attest and sign the will or acknowledge their signature in the presence of the testator. They must do so *after* the testator has signed or acknowledged. It is not essential that they should sign in each other's presence although, as we have already seen, they must both be present when the testator signs or acknowledges their signature.

Couser v Couser (1996) provides useful guidance on the meaning of "presence" and "acknowledgment". The testator and first witness had both signed the will before the second witness arrived. The testator informally acknowledged his signature by asking the second witness to sign. The first witness had got up to make coffee and was some distance away although in the same room. She gave no formal acknowledgment of her signature but, throughout the period in which the second witness was signing, kept up a discussion with the testator as to whether or not his will would be valid. The judge held that the second witness had signed in the presence of the first witness because the second witness was clearly in such a position that she could have seen. He also held that her continued discussion of the will amounted to an acknowledgment of her own signature. Thus, the two witnesses had signed or acknowledged after the testator had acknowledged his signature in the presence of both the witnesses.

The signatures of the witnesses must "attest" the will, that is the signature must be placed on the will with the intention of validating the testator's signature and not, for example, for the purpose of merely identifying the will. The signatures may appear anywhere on the will and need not be next to or after the testator's signature.

The testator must be mentally and physically present when the witnesses sign. The testator is not mentally present if, for example, they lapse into a coma before the witnesses have finished signing. The testator need not have actually seen the witnesses sign: they are regarded as physically present if they could have seen them had they chosen to look. (Thus, in *Casson v Dade* (1781) the testatrix signed in her solicitor's office in the presence of two witnesses and then retired to her carriage which was waiting in the street outside. There was no evidence that she saw the witnesses sign but, if she had turned her head, she could have seen them through the windows of the carriage and the office. The will was admitted to probate.)

A witness is not required to know that a testator who had already signed a will had to acknowledge their signature. It is enough that the witness intended to and did sign the will as a witness and that before doing that, they saw and heard the words and deeds which constituted the deceased's acknowledgment of their earlier signature. This was the position in *Kayll v Rawlinson* (2010) where the testator signed in the presence of one witness who also signed; when the second witness arrived the testator said "John has signed it, I have signed it, will you sign it?" The will was held to be properly attested.

Capacity of witnesses

No particular rules are laid down as to who may act as a witness. The sole test **2.08** is whether the witnesses were capable of attesting at the time when they signed. A minor may therefore witness a will although a very young child may not since they would not be capable of understanding the significance of what they were doing. A blind person cannot act as a witness since they cannot have the opportunity to see the signature, similarly a person who is very drunk or of unsound mind would be incapable of attesting.

In choosing witnesses a solicitor should bear in mind that they may be required to give evidence as to due execution. The persons chosen should therefore not be very old or likely to be hard to trace. A beneficiary of the will or a beneficiary's spouse should not be chosen since, although their signature is perfectly valid, they will usually lose their legacy if they witness (Wills Act 1837 s.15, see Ch.16, below). A charging clause is no longer a legacy for these purposes (see Trustee Act 2000 s.18) and so a solicitor can witness a will containing a professional charging clause and appointing as executor the solicitor or a firm in which they are a partner.

Attestation clauses

An attestation clause recites that the proper formalities have been complied with. **2.09** A simple clause might read "Signed by the said [Testator] in our joint presence and then by us in his presence" and would be written next to the testator's signature and immediately above the witnesses' signatures. The value of such a clause is that it raises a presumption of due execution. The presumption is a strong one and in several recent cases the Court of Appeal has stated that the testator and witnesses must be taken to have done what the attestation clause declares they have done unless there is clear evidence to prove that this is not the case.

In *Re Sherrington* (2005) the Court of Appeal allowed the defendant's appeal against the first instance decision that a will was invalid because, inter alia, the witnesses had not been aware that they were being asked to witness a signature. The witnesses claimed that they thought they were signing their names on some sheets of paper. However, their evidence was confused and conflicting. The Court of Appeal said that in the absence of the strongest evidence, the intention of the witness to attest is inferred from the presence of the testator's signature on the will, the attestation clause and the signature of the witness. The Court of Appeal took the same approach in *Channon v Perkins* (2005) where the witnesses initially said that they could not recollect having witnessed the will and, by the time they appeared in court were adamant that they had not signed it, although their signatures appeared beside the attestation clause. The beneficiaries of the will sought to rely on the presumption of due execution. The Court of Appeal repeated that the strongest evidence is required to challenge a will which appears from its face to have been properly executed. Arden L.J. said that simple lack of recollection was insufficient but:

> "evidence from both witnesses that they were nowhere near the place of execution stated in the attestation clause on the particular date would be likely to carry more weight".

In *Kayll v Rawlinson* (2010) Richards J. said (unsurprisingly) that where it was common ground that an attestation clause did not reflect what had actually happened (stating that the testator had *signed* in the presence of both witnesses when the most that had happened was that he had acknowledged) that some evidence of due execution by later acknowledgment, in the presence of both witnesses, was required.

2.10   If there is no attestation clause the registrar, before admitting the will to probate, must require an affidavit of due execution from a witness or, if this is not convenient, from any other person who was present at execution (Non-Contentious Probate Rules 1987 r.12(1)). If such an affidavit cannot be obtained, other evidence (such as an affidavit to show that the signature on the will is in the handwriting of the deceased) will be required (r.12(2)). Rule 12(3) of the Non-Contentious Probate Rules provides that a registrar may accept a will for proof without evidence if they are satisfied that the distribution of the estate is not thereby affected. In other cases where there is no evidence the court may apply the maxim *omnia praesumuntur rite ac solemniter esse acta* and admit the will to probate if it appears to have been signed and witnessed but this will usually require a hearing before a judge and will, therefore, lead to delay and added expense.

Where the will has been signed by another person at the direction of the testator or where the testator is blind or illiterate special forms of attestation clauses are desirable. The clause should make it clear that the testator had knowledge of the contents of the will at the time of execution.

A will does not have to be dated, although it is desirable that it should be to avoid uncertainty as to which of several testamentary documents is the last will. In *Corbett v Newey* (1996), a will was held to be invalid where the testatrix had handed her executed will to her solicitors with a blank next to the date. Her intention was that the will was not to come into effect until certain lifetime gifts had been completed. She wanted her solicitors to date the will when the gifts were complete. However, the court held that the will was invalid because it had not been intended to have immediate effect. It is not possible to execute a will conditionally.

Arrangements for execution

In an increasingly litigious climate it is important for those preparing wills to take **2.11** care over the arrangements for execution. In *Esterhuizen v Allied Dunbar* (1998), a will drafting company was held liable in negligence to a disappointed beneficiary where a will was invalid as a result of having been witnessed by only one person. Longmore J. said:

> "It is in my judgement not enough just to leave written instructions with the testator. In ordinary circumstances just to leave written instructions and to do no more will not only be contrary to good practice but also in my view negligent."

For their own protection solicitors should have in writing an offer in the following terms:

- the client can visit the solicitor's office for execution;

- if the client prefers, the solicitor will visit the client's house with a member of staff; and

- if the client prefers, the client can make their own arrangements.

In *Gray v Richards Butler (Supervision of Execution of a Will)* (2000) a will was invalid because the two witnesses had not been present at the time that the testator signed or acknowledged the will. The case was decided before *Esterhuizen* but was not reported until a later date. Lloyd J. took a different approach to Longmore J. in *Esterhuizen* and found that the solicitor had not been negligent in failing to offer to supervise the execution of the will. He commented that the solicitor's written instructions were "most comprehensive" and that his conduct did not fall short of that required of the "reasonably competent solicitor". It was in his opinion necessary "to bear in mind the very clear terms of the attestation provision of the will".

There was a clear assumption in *Gray* that a solicitor has a duty to examine a will returned post-execution. On the particular facts the court accepted that there was nothing about the will which should have aroused the solicitor's suspicion. It follows though that a solicitor who fails to offer to inspect a will may well be negligent if the will turns out to be wrongly executed. In *Humblestone v Martin Tolhurst Partnership* (2004) the court said that a firm which accepts a will for storage has a duty to inspect it, whether or not it is asked to do so.

When a solicitor is asked to prepare a will for a client it is best, in order to **2.12** avoid problems, to adopt the following procedure wherever possible:

(a) The will is prepared by the solicitor from the client's instructions and explained to them.

(b) The client attends at the solicitor's office and, in the presence of two witnesses, places their signature at the end of the will next to a suitable attestation clause.

   (i) The witnesses must not be beneficiaries or spouses or civil partners of beneficiaries.
   (ii) Even if the solicitor is not a witness they should be present to ensure that the correct procedure is adopted.

(c) The witnesses sign in the presence of the testator (as required by law) and of each other (not required, but useful so that either witness can give evidence as to the other's signature if necessary).

(d) A number of cases have held that, where a will is written on more than one piece of paper, there must be physical contact between the pages at the time of attestation if the will is to be valid. It is doubtful whether this rule survives the enactment of the substituted s.9. However, for the avoidance of doubt as to what has been attested and to prevent accidental loss of parts of the will, all the pages should be securely fastened together.

(e) It is good office practice to keep an attendance note explaining what was done and referring to the addresses of the witnesses so that they can be contacted if necessary to prove due execution.

(f) A copy of the will should be kept and the solicitor should insert on it the names of the testator and witnesses and date of execution. (Such a copy may be admissible to probate if the original is lost, see para.2.38, below.)

If the client wishes to execute the will at home, the solicitor should offer to supervise execution and have a written record that the offer was made and rejected. The solicitor can make a separate charge for the supervision provided this was made clear in the terms of engagement. The will must be accompanied by very clear instructions. (In particular the client should be warned not to allow anyone who is or whose spouse or civil partner is a beneficiary to witness, should be told where to sign, should be told to sign their usual signature in ink and should be told to sign in the presence of the witnesses and before they sign.) There must also be an offer to inspect the will after execution.

If a will is to be executed in hospital the solicitor should bear in mind that in many hospitals medical staff are normally prohibited from witnessing wills by the hospital authorities. If this rule applies it is safer to take witnesses to the hospital than to rely on finding witnesses there (other patients are not suitable since there may be doubt about their capacity and they are likely to be hard to trace if needed to give evidence).

If there is any possibility that the capacity of the testator to make a will may be challenged at a later date it is advisable to try to get a doctor to witness the will and/or to make a written statement as to the testator's mental state on the relevant day. (See para.2.26, below.)

Privileged wills

The form of the will

A will can be made informally by a testator who has privileged status. The will **2.13**
can be made in any form including a mere oral statement. Such a will is known
as a nuncupative will. The only requirement is that the statement made should
show an intention to dispose of property in the event of death even if the person
making it does not know that they are making a will. Such a will is valid even
though made by a minor provided the minor has privileged status.

Privileged status

The right to make a privileged will extends to any soldier on actual military **2.14**
service or mariner or seaman being at sea.

"Soldier" includes a member of the R.A.F. and naval or marine personnel
serving on land. The exact extent of "actual military service" is open to some
doubt. Broadly speaking the term may be said to include activities closely
connected with warfare, whether or not war has been declared and whether or not
the testator has actually arrived at the scene of the fighting. In *Re Jones* (1976)
a soldier serving in Northern Ireland at a time of widespread terrorist activity was
held to have privileged status. Similarly the term "being at sea" cannot be
defined precisely. A seaman on leave who is not in receipt of instructions to join
any particular ship is not "at sea": *Re Rapley (Deceased)* (1983). However, a
mariner is treated as being at sea for this purpose when he is still on land but
under orders to join his ship.

It is the circumstances in which the will was made which are relevant in
deciding whether a person had privileged status, not the circumstances in which
death occurred.

It is the circumstances in which the will was made which are relevant in
deciding whether a person had privileged status, not the circumstances in which
death occurred. See, for example, *Re Servoz-Gavin deceased* (2009) where a
ship's radio officer made oral statements to his cousin about what he wanted to
happen to his property after his death while under orders to join his ship. He died
many years later in a nursing home and his statement of was accepted as a valid
privileged will.

Incorporation of documents

A properly drawn will should be contained in one document so as to avoid doubt **2.15**
as to its contents. If changes are to be made later they may be included in a
codicil (see paras 2.39–2.41, below). However, if desired, an unexecuted document can be incorporated into a will by referring to it in the will. The document
is then admitted to probate as part of the will.

An unexecuted document is incorporated if:

(a) it is in existence at the time of execution of the will (or of a codicil republishing the will);

(b) it is *referred to* in the will as being in existence at the time of execution; and

(c) it is clearly identified in the will.

Document in existence

2.16 Whether a document is in existence at the time of execution is a question of fact. The person who seeks to have it admitted to probate must prove its existence at that time.

Referred to as in existence

2.17 The document must be referred to in the will as in existence at the time of execution. Thus a will which says "I leave £100 to each of the persons named in the list *now* to be found in my desk" satisfies this condition (and the list will be validly incorporated provided it can be shown that it was in fact in existence when the will or confirming codicil was executed). A will which says "I leave £100 to each of the persons named in a list which *I will write* before my death" does not satisfy this condition. Even if the list was made before execution, it will not be admitted to probate as the will refers to its coming into existence at a later date. There are some marginal cases where the wording of the will does not make it clear whether or not the document is extant at the time of execution. In such cases the court will refuse to incorporate the unexecuted document. For example, in *University College of North Wales v Taylor* (1908) probate was refused where the will referred to "any memorandum amongst my papers".

If the will is republished by a codicil an unexecuted document will be incorporated if it is in existence at the time of execution of the codicil and is referred to as being in existence in either the will (which is republished and so speaks from the date of the codicil) or the codicil. *In the Goods of Smart* (1902) demonstrates that this is so, but on the facts of that case probate of the unexecuted document was refused because the will referred to its coming into existence in the future.

The document must be identified

2.18 The unexecuted document is only incorporated if it is identified by the will. The identification must be sufficient to indicate, without ambiguity, what document is referred to.

Practical considerations

2.19 Incorporation of documents by reference should be avoided unless absolutely necessary, both because of the danger of drafting the will in a way which does not properly incorporate them and because of the danger that the document referred to might be lost before the testator dies.

A properly drafted will should make clear whether or not a document referred to is being incorporated. If it does not, the registrar is likely to require any such document to be produced and may call for affidavit evidence as to whether or not the document is incorporated (Non-Contentious Probate Rules 1987 r.14(3)).

Once a document has been incorporated into a will it is treated as an ordinary part of the will and must be filed at the probate registry with the rest of the will. Wills are a matter of public record so that the whole of the will, including the unexecuted document incorporated by reference, is available to the public. There is no point, therefore, in putting sensitive information into a document to be incorporated into the will, with the intention of keeping that information secret.

Pilot Trusts

It is increasingly common for testators to make one or more discretionary trusts **2.20** (often called pilot trusts) during their lifetime to which they transfer a small amount of money (say £10). In their wills they leave substantial amounts to these trusts. Provided the trusts are created on different days, they are not related to each other for inheritance tax purposes and neither are they related to trusts created in the will. The advantage is that inheritance tax anniversary and exit charges will be calculated for each trust on the value of the property held in that trust alone without reference to other trusts and will be based on the settlor's cumulative total at the time that trust was created without reference to subsequent events. See Ch.7 for the calculation of anniversary and exit charges.

It is important that the trusts are properly constituted.

In *Re Jones* (1942) a testator left a legacy to trustees appointed under a declaration of trust for the benefit of [X] made at the same date as the Will or "any substitution therefore or modification thereof or addition thereto which I may hereinafter execute". The gift failed on the basis that the testator was trying to reserve power to alter the gift in the will by a later unexecuted document. In *In Re Edwards' Will Trusts* (1948) a testator left the residue of his estate upon the trusts and subject to the powers and provisions of a lifetime settlement "so far as such trusts and provisions are subsisting and capable of taking effect". The settlement provided that the trust funds were to be held for the benefit of the settlor's wife and children subject to a power for him to appoint the property as he saw fit. He made an appointment after the date of the will. The Court of Appeal held that the gift to the settlement was effective but on the original terms unaffected by the subsequent appointment.

2. Capacity

Age

Persons under the age of 18 cannot make a valid will (Wills Act 1837 s.7 as **2.21** amended by the Family Law Reform Act 1969 s.3(1)(a)) unless they have privileged status. Privileged status is enjoyed by soldiers on actual military service and mariners and seamen at sea (see above—Wills Act 1837 s.11).

On the death of a minor (other than one who has made a privileged will) their estate will be administered under the intestacy rules.

Persons aged 16 and over can, however, make a valid statutory nomination of certain assets provided the nomination is in writing and witnessed by at least one person. For a fuller discussion of nominations see Ch.21.

The mental state of the testator

Testamentary capacity

2.22 The test of testamentary capacity has traditionally been that set out in *Banks v Goodfellow* (1870) according to which a testator only has testamentary capacity if they have "a sound and disposing mind and memory". This requires the testator to understand three things:

(a) *The nature of the act and its effects.* It is not necessary for the testator to understand the precise legal machinery involved in the will so long as they understand its broad effects.

(b) *The extent of the property of which he is disposing.* The testator is not expected to be able to produce a detailed list of every item of property owned. It is sufficient if they have a broad recollection of its extent.

(c) *The claims to which he ought to give effect.* This means that the testator must be able to bring to mind the persons who are "fitting objects of the testator's bounty" (per Sir J. Hannen in *Boughton v Knight* (1873)). It does not of course mean that having done so he must dispose of his property to those people. It is sufficient that he is capable of considering them. In *Battan Singh v Armirchand* (1948) a testator who was very ill in the last stages of consumption left his property to certain creditors stating that he had no living relatives. In fact he had three nephews of whom, the evidence showed, he was very fond. The court said that he clearly lacked testamentary capacity having forgotten the moral claims of his nephews.

In *Key v Key* (2010) Briggs J. accepted that the symptomatic effects of bereavement are capable of being almost identical to that associated with severe depression and can, therefore, mean that someone suffers a temporary loss of capacity. He accepted that it was not possible to point to any "conspicuous inability of the deceased to satisfy one of the distinct limbs of the *Banks v Goodfellow* test". However, taking the evidence as a whole, it was clear that the testator in question was simply unable during the week following his wife's death to exercise the decision-making powers required of a testator—or, at least, those propounding the will had not proved that he was. He admitted that that this was "a slight development of the *Banks v Goodfellow* test, taking into account decision-making powers rather than just comprehension", but considered that advances in the understanding of the mind and, in particular affective disorders justified it.

The Mental Capacity Act 2005 introduced statutory provisions relating to capacity to make decisions. Section 1 provides that for the purposes of the Act a person is:

(a) to be assumed to have capacity until the contrary is established on the balance of probabilities;

(b) not to be treated as unable to make a decision unless all practicable steps to help them to do so have been taken without success; and

(c) not to be treated as unable to make a decision simply because they make an unwise one.

Section 2 provides that a person lacks capacity in relation to a matter if at the **2.23** material time they are unable to make a decision for themselves in relation to the matter because of an impairment of or a disturbance in the functioning of the mind or brain. It does not matter whether the disturbance is permanent or temporary.

Section 3 provides that a person is unable to make a decision for themselves if unable to:

(a) understand the information relevant to the decision;

(b) retain the information relevant to the decision;

(c) use or weigh that information as part of the process of making the decision; or

(d) communicate the decision (whether by talking, using sign language or any other means).

The fact that a person is only able to retain information relevant to the decision for a short time does not prevent them being regarded as able to make the decision.

The information relevant to making a decision includes information about the reasonably foreseeable consequences of:

(a) deciding one way or another, or

(b) failing to make the decision.

A person's capacity to make a will is not dealt with in the Act and so its provisions are not directly relevant. However, the Act will undoubtedly influence the approach of the judiciary to questions of capacity. The *Banks v Goodfellow* test is largely replicated by s.3 of the Act and it seems likely that existing case law will continue to be relevant.

The time at which testamentary capacity is to be judged

2.24 The Mental Capacity Act 2005 makes it clear that the question of capacity under the Act is decision and time specific. The question is "has this person got the capacity to make this particular decision at this particular time?"

This has always been the position in relation to testamentary capacity: the testator has to have capacity to make a will at the time the will is signed and witnessed. However, the rule in *Parker v Felgate* provides a limited exception to the time specific element. Under the rule a will may be valid even though the testator has lost testamentary capacity by the time the will was executed provided:

    (a) the testator had testamentary capacity at the time he gave a solicitor instructions to prepare a will;

    (b) the will was prepared in accordance with those instructions; and

    (c) at the time the will was executed the testator remembered having given instructions for a will to be prepared and believed that the will had been prepared in accordance with those instructions. It was immaterial that the testator did not remember precisely what the instructions were or could not understand the will if it were read to him.

This principle was extended to a will prepared by a solicitor on the basis of his client's own draft (*In the Estate of Wallace, Solicitor of the Duchy of Cornwall v Batten* (1952)). However, because of the possibility of abuse, this principle is applied with caution, if at all, where instructions were relayed to a solicitor through an intermediary (*Battan Singh v Armirchand*). *Clancy v Clancy* (2003)) is a modern example of the rule in application.

The rule was approved by the Court of Appeal in *Perrins v Holland* (2010), an unusual case where the interval between giving instructions and executing the will was 15 months.

Capacity does not have to be perfect

2.25 It is important to remember that the only issue is whether or not the testator has sufficient mental capacity to make a will. It is perfectly possible for a person to be incapable of managing their own property and affairs on a day-to-day basis and yet be capable of making a valid will. This was true before the Mental Capacity Act 2005 and is equally true afterwards given that s.2(1) provides expressly that a person lacks capacity if they are unable to make a decision "in relation to the matter".

Ewing v Bennet (2001) and *Barrett v Kaspryyk* (2000) both illustrate the point that a testator need not have unclouded mental faculties.

The burden of proof

The rule has always been that just as the person propounding a will must *prove* **2.26**
that it was properly signed and witnessed so must they prove that at the time of
execution the testator had testamentary capacity. If the burden of proof was not
discharged the will was not admitted to probate. *Vaughan v Vaughan* (2002) is a
good illustration of the principle. The testatrix was aged 82 and in poor health
having had several strokes. Behrens J. found that there was grave suspicion of
incapacity. He accepted that there was some evidence on both sides. However, it
was for the person putting forward the will to prove capacity and he had not done
so. The effect of the burden of proof was that a person who alleged that a will was
made in a lucid interval had to prove it (see *Brown v Deacy* (2002)).

Traditionally two presumptions have applied:

(a) *Will rational.* If the will appears rational on the face of it there is a
presumption that the testator had testamentary capacity; the will is
therefore admitted to probate unless anyone attacking it can produce
sufficient evidence to rebut the presumption. If the presumption is
rebutted, it is then up to the propounder to prove testamentary
capacity.

(b) *Mental states continue.* Mental states are presumed to continue; thus, if
a person who normally suffers from mental illness makes a will, it is
presumed that they lacked testamentary capacity. It is then up to the
propounder of the will to rebut the presumption by proving that the will
was made in a lucid interval.

It is doubtful whether the presumption of continuance survived the Court of
Appeal decision in *Masterman-Lister v Brutton & Co* (2002). Here the Court
of Appeal held that all adults must be presumed to be competent to manage their
property and affairs until the contrary is proved, and that the burden of proof rests
on those asserting incapacity. Just because there was evidence that as a result of
a head injury sustained in an accident the claimant was incapable of managing his
property and affairs for a time did not mean that the presumption of continuance
applied to future events. Where there is clear evidence of incapacity for a
considerable period then the burden of proof may be more easily discharged, but
it remains on whoever asserts incapacity.

Section 1(2) of the Mental Capacity Act 2005 specifically provides that a
person must be assumed to have capacity unless it is established that they lack
capacity. However, s.1 is stated to apply only for the purposes of the Act and,
therefore, has no direct effect on the burden of proof of testamentary capacity.

Wherever possible objective medical evidence should be obtained. It is dan- **2.27**
gerous to rely on the opinions of friends or family who may be partial but also
may be genuinely unaware of deterioration in the mental abilities of someone
they have known well for many years. In a recent unreported case, *In the Estate
of Ellen Wilkes (Deceased)* (2000), a consultant physician specialising in the care
of the elderly gave expert evidence. He warned against the acceptance at face

value of statements, whether by medical practitioners or others, indicating that the testatrix was mentally well at the relevant times, without some form of objective diagnostic analysis (such as a Mini Mental State Examination).

In the absence of such a test, comments about the testatrix's apparent mental ability are purely subjective. In the consultant's opinion they should be viewed with caution since a person may appear to have intact mental functions despite severe deficits in reality. It is common to encounter elderly people who seem quite well, but do badly in simple objective tests. In the case of a Mini Mental State Examination, he would expect at least 25 out of 30 points for a person with capacity to make a will, but it would be perfectly possible to have a good interaction with a person who only scored 10 points.

However, the Mini Mental State Examination is, itself, not entirely suitable for determining testamentary capacity as it is largely concerned with short-term memory. In *Charles v Fraser* (2010) a consultant psychiatrist found that an elderly lady had lesser testamentary capacity on the basis of such an examination where she had, in fact, forgotten the existence of her many relatives.

Solicitors often feel embarrassed about raising the question of mental capacity with clients. It is best to approach the matter on the basis of avoiding any possibility of an unnecessary challenge at a later date.

Insane delusions

2.28   An insane delusion is a belief in the existence of something in which no rational person could believe and which could not be eradicated from the testator's mind by reasoned argument (*Dew v Clark and Clark* (1826)). A person suffering from such a delusion can make a valid will provided the delusion is on a subject in no way connected with the will (for example, a belief that the testator is pursued by evil spirits). However, if the delusion affects the testator's judgment, either generally or on one point which affects the dispositions made, the testator does not have testamentary capacity. If the delusion affects the whole will (as in *Dew v Clark and Clark* where the testator had an irrational dislike of his daughter as a result of which he left her nothing in his will) probate will be refused to the whole will. If the delusion affects only part of the will then only that part will be excluded from probate (as in *In the Estate of Bohrmann* (1938) where one clause of a codicil was omitted from probate).

In *Sharp v Adams* (2006) the Court of Appeal considered the will of a deceased father who had inexplicably left everything to his employees to the exclusion of his two daughters. He was suffering from advanced multiple sclerosis and on a drugs regime which was likely to impair his brain. The Court of Appeal held that, while the first three elements of the *Banks v Goodfellow* test were satisfied, a fourth (no poisoning of the affections) was not. The trial judge was correct in saying that the justice or otherwise of the testator excluding his daughters from benefit must, as a matter of common sense, have a bearing on the decision, so long as inquiry is directed to the testator's soundness of mind and not to general questions of perceived morality. Leaving the residuary estate to the employees was understandable. Leaving nothing at all to his daughters was not.

In *Kostic v Chaplin* (2007) the testator was suffering from severe delusions believing that there was an international conspiracy of dark forces against him. The conspiracy included his family, friends and professional advisers. He left his substantial estate to the Conservative Party. The court held that his natural affection for his family had been poisoned by his disorder of mind. His delusions had brought about a disposal of property which would not have been made had he been of sound mind.

Practical precautions

A solicitor who has any doubts as to the capacity of a client proposing to make **2.29** a will or any suspicion that lack of capacity may later be alleged, should try to avoid future problems by obtaining medical advice. It is desirable that a medical practitioner examine the testator, preferably at the time the will is signed since the severity of certain mental conditions, for example, senility, vary markedly over relatively short periods of time. Doctors and nurses will normally refuse to witness wills. In such a case ask the doctor or nurse caring for the testator to make a statement as to the mental condition of the testator. A full and careful attendance note should be made by the solicitor or member of the staff present. If possible the note should be made contemporaneously.

It is important that solicitors try to comply with the so-called "Golden Rule" set out in full in Ch.13. In addition to trying to obtain medical approval, the rule requires solicitors to:

(a) discuss any earlier will with the client (and the reasons for changing it); and

(b) take the instructions in the absence of anyone who may stand to benefit or who may have influence over the testator.

It is not always possible to interview clients alone as they will sometimes insist that a companion remains with them. However, practitioners should make sure that they have a clear attendance note establishing that it was the client's wish that the third party remained.

Note, however, that the Golden Rule deals only with the way in which solicitors should conduct themselves as a matter of good practice. It does not suggest that a will is invalid merely because the solicitor has not followed the steps laid down. See *Allen v Emery* (2005).

Statutory wills

Section 16(1) and (2) of the Mental Capacity Act 2005 allows the court to make **2.30** decisions on behalf of a person who lacks capacity to make that decision. Section 18(1)(i) states that the court's powers extend to the execution of a will. Schedule 2(2) provides that the will may make any provision (whether by disposing of property or exercising a power or otherwise) which the person lacking capacity could have made, if capable except that it cannot dispose of immoveable property situate outside England and Wales.

A statutory will must:

(a) state that it is signed by the person for whom it is made (the "testator") acting by the authorised person;

(b) be signed by the authorised person with the name of the testator and their own name, in the presence of two or more witnesses present at the same time;

(c) be attested and subscribed by those witnesses in the presence of the authorised person; and

(d) be sealed with the official seal of the court.

Before the Mental Capacity Act 2005 the court tried to make the will which the person lacking capacity would have made if acting reasonably and on competent legal advice, had they enjoyed a brief lucid interval. In other words it was a case of substituted judgement.

The position is quite different since the Act came into force. Section 1(5) provides that "An act done, or decision made, under this Act for or on behalf of a person who lacks capacity must be done, or made, in his best interests." Section 4 expands on the concept of "best interests" and provides that the person making the decision must consider all the relevant circumstances. In particular s.4(6) provides that:

He must consider, so far as is reasonably ascertainable:

(a) the person's past and present wishes and feelings (and, in particular, any relevant written statement made by him when he had capacity),
(b) the beliefs and values that would be likely to influence his decision if he had capacity, and
(c) the other factors that he would be likely to consider if he were able to do so.

When making a statutory will, it is not immediately apparent how the Court of Protection is to determine the testator's "best interests" since the testator will be dead by the time the will comes into effect. In *Re P* (2009) and *Re M, ITW v Z* (2009) the Court of Protection held that it is in a person's interests to be remembered with affecton by their family as having done the "*right thing*", both in life or by will.

The Court of Protection will not normally make a statutory will on the basis of allegations that the existing will is invalid because this would be to become embroiled in family disputes and trespass on the jurisdiction of the probate court. However, in *Re D, VAC v JAD* (2010) Hogg J. accepted that the overarching consideration, was a judicial evaluation of what is in the protected person's "*best interests*". Given the very strong doubts that had been raised as to the validity of the previous wills, he was willing to order the execution of a statutory will, rather than leaving the testatrix's estate to be eroded by the costs of litigation after herdeath, and her memory to be tainted by the bitterness of a contested probate dispute between her children.

In *Re C. (Spinster and Mental Patient)* (1991) the patient had never been rational. It was held that, in those circumstances, the court should make a will assuming that she would, if rational, have acted "decently in accordance with contemporary standards of morality".

Procedure

Practice Direction F which supplements Pt 9 of the Court of Protection Rules sets out the procedure for an application for a statutory will. A draft will must be approved by the Court of Protection. The applicant then executes the will on behalf of the person lacking capacity and must return the original and two copies to the court for sealing. The court returns the original and one copy to the applicant. In *Re Hughes (Deceased)* (1999) it was accepted that the sealing can take place after the death of the patient. The sealing merely confirms that the statutory will, as executed, conforms to its authorisation. It is not analogous to the signing of the will by a mentally capable testator. **2.31**

A statutory will cannot be made for a minor. Where a minor receives a large damages award, legal advisers should consider what will happen to the funds if the minor dies intestate. It is preferable that such sums should be settled on the minor for life rather than held for the minor absolutely. *Bouette v Rose* (2000) is an example of the unsatisfactory operation of the intestacy rules. The property passed equally to the child's mother, who had cared for her throughout her life, and to the child's father, who had had no contact with her. Fortunately the mother's application under the Inheritance (Provision for Family and Dependants) Act 1975 as a person maintained by the deceased was successful.

3. KNOWLEDGE AND APPROVAL

Presumption

A testator must know and approve the contents of the will (except in the case of a statutory will.) If a testator signs a will having no knowledge of the contents, the will is invalid. The time at which knowledge and approval is required is normally the time of execution of the will. However, in cases where the rule in *Parker v Felgate* applies (see above) it is sufficient if the court is satisfied that the will put forward embodies the instructions given by the testator and intended by him to be carried out (*Perrins v Holland*) (2010). **2.32**

The burden of proof of knowledge and approval lies on the person propounding the will; however, there is normally a rebuttable presumption that a testator who executes a will (particularly if they have read the will or have had the will read over to them) does so with knowledge and approval of the contents.

This presumption does not arise in the following cases:

(a) *In the case of a blind or illiterate testator or where another person signs on behalf of the testator.* In such cases the registrar will require evidence that the testator had actual knowledge of the contents (Non-Contentious Probate Rules 1987 r.13). It is advisable in such a case for the attestation clause to include a statement that the will was read over to and approved by the testator. If it does not, evidence will be required from the witnesses or from some other person present.

(b) *Where there are suspicious circumstances.* If there is evidence of suspicious circumstances, the will is not admitted to probate unless the propounder can prove that the testator did know and approve the contents. The most obvious example of a suspicious circumstance is where the will is prepared by a major beneficiary or close relative of a major beneficiary. In *Wintle v Nye* (1959) the House of Lords expressed the view that:

> "It is not the law that in no circumstances can a solicitor or other person who has prepared a will for a testator take a benefit under it. But that fact creates a suspicion that must be removed by the person propounding the will. In all cases the court must be vigilant and jealous. The degree of suspicion will vary with the circumstances of the case. It may be slight and easily dispelled. It may, on the other hand, be so grave that it can hardly be removed" per Viscount Simmonds.

In *Wintle v Nye* it was held that the gift to the draftsman was not admissible to probate for want of knowledge and approval but that the rest of the will could stand. (Solicitors are subject to special rules of professional conduct in relation to receiving legacies from clients; these are dealt with in para.2.33, below.)

2.33   There have been a number of cases recently where the Court of Appeal has emphasised that in the case of simple wills where the testator has had an opportunity to see the will, the presumption of knowledge and approval will operate.

In *Fuller v Strum* (2002) the Court of Appeal considered a will prepared by a major beneficiary. It stated the general principle that the court's suspicion ought generally to be excited where a party prepares a will under which they take a benefit. The court should not pronounce in favour of that will unless the suspicion is removed. Prima facie, if the person with the burden of proof gives no evidence, the issue will be decided against them. However, the onus imposed on the party propounding the will is normally discharged by proof of capacity and the fact that the testator executed the will. *Additional evidence is not always required where a beneficiary prepares a will.* The preparation of the will is merely a suspicious circumstance of more or less weight depending upon the circumstances.

The circumstances of a particular case may raise such grave suspicion that it can hardly be removed. *Fuller v Strum* was not such a case. The will was short and simple and the testator had had an opportunity to read it.

The Court of Appeal expressly approved the "properly objective" approach of Lloyd J. in *Hart v Dabbs* (2001). The major beneficiary had been instrumental in the preparation of the will. He was arrested on suspicion of murdering the testator but later released for lack of evidence. The will was held valid on the basis that it was a short, simple document and there was no reason to doubt the testator's knowledge and approval: "so long as he read the document he would have had no difficulty taking in its provisions even if someone else prepared it".

In *Re Sherrington* (2005) the trial judge had found that the circumstances were such as to excite the suspicion of the court. The Court of Appeal, while agreeing that there were some surprising features (such as the exclusion of the testator's children from benefit) found that the circumstances were not sufficient to excite suspicion. The Court of Appeal attached particular weight to the fact that the will was short and simple and the deceased had had ample opportunity to read it.

The effect of these cases seems to be to make it harder to sustain a claim of want of knowledge and approval in a case where the will is simple and the testator has had an opportunity to read it.

However, where the testator has not had such an opportunity (see *Franks v Sinclair* (2006)) or intermediaries are involved (*Sifri v Clough & Willis* (2007)) a claim of lack of knowledge and approval is more likely to succeed.

In *Franks v Sinclair* the solicitor who had prepared a rather complicated will read it over to the elderly testatrix. He did not explain the meaning of the various clauses and did not leave a copy of the will with the testatrix. The court held that reading a will over to a client might be sufficient when the terms are straightforward, as in *Fuller v Strum* and *Hart v Dobbs* but not where the clause is complicated. Such a clause requires explanation. The Court of Appeal took a similar approach in *Gill v RSPCA* (2010) where it found that probably the will had been read over to the client without explanation. The client suffered from extreme agoraphobia and anxiety disorder and would have been in such a state of panic in the solicitor's office that she would have been unable to take in the terms of her will. The solicitor sent a draft of the testatrix's will to her house but he also sent a draft of her husband's will and the Court of Appeal determined that, since both drafts were probably sent in one envelope, there was no certainty that the testatrix had ever seen her will. The will was held to be invalid for lack of knowledge and approval.

Mistake

A mistake may mean that the testator had no knowledge or approval of the will **2.34** as a whole (for example, where they execute the wrong will) or of only part of the will (as in *Wintle v Nye*). If a testator includes words in their will having intended to write other words, the words mistakenly included will be omitted from probate; similarly if a testator includes words in their will but do not know or approve them then those words will be omitted from probate. An example of the latter type of mistake occurred in *Re Phelan* (1972). The testator bought three printed will forms and, thinking that every holding of shares had to be dealt with in a separate will, executed three wills in favour of X, each will disposing of a separate shareholding. Each will was executed on the same day and each contained a printed revocation clause. Stirling J. held that as the words of revocation were clearly included in the wills by inadvertence and misunderstanding they could be omitted from probate.

The probate court will not interfere, however, where a testator deliberately selects certain words and includes them in the will, even if it is clearly shown that the testator was mistaken as to their legal effect. Thus in *Collins v Elstone* (1893) a testatrix deliberately included a revocation clause under the misapprehension that it would revoke only a small part of her earlier will. The court held that the revocation clause could not be omitted from the will. The rule is the same where a draftsman prepares a will on behalf of a testator and deliberately selects words being mistaken as to their legal effect; those words will be admitted to probate (*Re Horrocks* (1939)). The probate court has always had power to omit words from probate.

2.35 Prior to the Administration of Justice Act 1982 it did not have any power to insert words even where it was obvious that words had been omitted accidentally. However, s.20 of that Act alters this rule to a limited extent. It provides that if a court is satisfied that a will is so expressed that it fails to carry out the testator's intentions in consequence of:

  (a) a clerical error; or

  (b) a failure to understand his instructions;

it may order that the will be rectified so as to carry out their intentions. If, therefore, a typing error is made in a will, the probate court can order that words included by mistake be omitted and that words omitted by mistake be inserted. Similarly if a solicitor misunderstands their instructions the court can order that the mistake be rectified. In *Wordingham v Royal Exchange Trust Co* (1991) the draftsman omitted a clause containing a power of appointment which it had intended to be included in the will. This was held to be a clerical error and so rectification was ordered. However, if the testator or draftsman is mistaken as to the legal effect of words deliberately selected for inclusion in or exclusion from the will the court cannot interfere. *Bush v Jouliac* (2006) is a nice illustration of the difference between the two. A solicitor drafted a will leaving the testatrix's estate equally between her son and daughter. He had a clear instruction that, should the son predecease his mother, his share was not to pass to his daughter. The solicitor did not include words to exclude Wills Act 1837 s.33 (which gives children of a deceased child the right to the share their parent would have taken). The court held that, had the solicitor been ignorant of the section, rectification would not have been possible. However, the solicitor said in evidence:

> "I can confirm that my error in drafting was not a failure to appreciate section 33 of the Wills Act needed to be expressly excluded, but rather an inadvertent clerical error in failing to insert the necessary words".

Rectification was, therefore, allowed.

In *Marley v Rawlings* (2011) the court refused rectification where a husband and wife had signed each other's will. The error was neither a clerical error nor a failure to understand the testator's instructions.

The remedy is discretionary. See *Grattan v McNaughton* (2001).The evidence of error or misunderstanding must be clear. As Chadwick J. (as he then was) said in *Re Segelman* (1996),

> "the probability that a will which a testator has executed in circumstances of some formality reflects his intentions is usually of such weight that convincing evidence to the contrary is necessary."

Cases in which the court held that there was such convincing evidence include *Price v Craig* (2006), *Hobart v Hobart* (2006) and *Clarke v Brothwood* (2006). In *Bell v Georgiou* (2002) the evidence was not convincing and the court dismissed the application as being based on mere speculation as to the testator's intention.

After the expiry of six months from the date of the grant of representation an **2.36** application for rectification cannot be made except with leave from the court. It is possible to make applications out of time and *Chittock v Stevens* (2000) decided that such applications will be governed by the same guiding principles as applications under the Inheritance (Provision for Family and Dependants) Act 1975 s.4. Personal representatives who distribute after that date will not be liable on the ground that they should have taken into account the possibility of an out-of-time application being made.

An application for rectification may be made to a registrar, unless a probate action has been commenced.

The application must be supported by an affidavit, setting out the grounds of the application, together with such evidence as can be adduced as to the testator's intentions and as to whichever of the following matters are in issue:

(a) the respects in which the testator's intentions were not understood; or

(b) the nature of any alleged clerical error.

Unless otherwise directed, notice of the application shall be given to every person having an interest under the will whose interest might be prejudiced by the rectification applied for and any comments in writing by any such person shall be exhibited to the affidavit in support of the application. (Non-Contentious Probate Rules 1987 r.55.)

A disappointed beneficiary may sometimes have a choice of remedy available; typically the beneficiary may have a possible negligence action against the solicitor who drafted the will as well as a possible action for rectification. In *Walker v Medlicott* (1999) the Court of Appeal stated that, where possible, a claimant must mitigate their damage by bringing proceedings for rectification of the will first. Only if that remedy is unavailable or unlikely to be successful should the claimant consider the negligence action. *Horsfall v Haywards* (2000) was an example of a case where rectification would not have been appropriate. The proceeds of sale of the estate assets had been transmitted to Canada and it appeared very unlikely that the beneficiaries would be able to recover them even if the rectification application was successful.

Special rules relating to solicitors

2.37 Solicitors are subject to special rules of conduct set out in the Solicitors' Code of Conduct 2007. Rule 3.04 states:

> "Where a client proposes to make a lifetime gift or a gift on death to, or for the benefit of:
>
> (a) you;
> (b) any proprietor or employee of your firm; or
> (c) a family member of any of the above
>
> and the gift is of a significant amount, either in itself or having regard to the size of the client's estate and the reasonable expectations of the prospective beneficiaries, you must advise the client to take independent advice about the gift, unless the client is a member of the beneficiary's family. If the client refuses, you must stop acting for the client in relation to the gift."

The following points should be noted:

(1) If the client declines to be independently advised, the solicitor must refuse to draft the will, or any other document by which the gift is to be made. It is not sufficient merely to have the will or other document witnessed by an independent solicitor.

(2) A solicitor must also ensure that the implications of R.3.04 are clear to all members of staff who take instructions from clients, whether or not they are solicitors.

(3) The guidance to R.3.04 says that it is not possible to quantify a "significant" amount since it will vary depending on the particular circumstances of the case. However, in general anything more than a token amount will be considered significant. If more than one gift is made to members of a firm, they should be amalgamated for the purpose of deciding whether the gift is significant.

(4) Where a client wishes to leave a legacy which is not of a significant amount to their solicitor, there is no need for independent advice. However, the solicitor should be satisfied that the client does not feel obliged to make such a gift.

(5) Although R.3.04 allows a solicitor to prepare a will for family members, the guidance says that "extreme caution" should always be exercised in such cases as the risk of conflict is very high. The solicitor should insist on independent advice if the family member is proposing a gift which is "disproportionately large" taking into account the reasonable expectations of others.

(6) A solicitor who receives money or property to distribute for the benefit of others, such as in a secret trust; this is a situation where it is not considered to be a gift for the purposes of R.3.04. However, clear

records should be kept both to confirm the arrangement and to ensure that there is no potential for money laundering.

The draft Code of Conduct 2010 contains similar provisions.

4. Force, Fear, Fraud or Undue Influence

Introduction

If a will is made as a result of force, fear, fraud or undue influence it will not be regarded as the act of the testator and will be refused probate. A person who alleges that a will was made as a result of one of these factors must *prove* it. There are no presumptions to assist in discharging the burden of proof.

2.38

Force or fear

There is little authority on this but obviously if it can be shown that a testator made a will only because they were being injured or threatened with injury, the will cannot be admitted to probate.

2.39

Fraud and undue influence

Fraud is something which misleads a testator. Examples of fraud are making false representations as to the character of others to induce the testator to make or to revoke gifts or to exclude persons from a proposed will. Another example would be obtaining a gift from a testator as a result of pretending to be lawfully married to him. As Lord Langdale said in *Giles v Giles* (1836) it is clear that "a legacy given to a person in a character which the legatee does not fill, and by the fraudulent assumption of which character the testator has been deceived, will not take effect". See also, *In the Estate of Posner* (1953). Undue influence is something which overpowers the volition of the testator without convincing the judgment; a testator may be persuaded but not coerced. It is often difficult to draw the line between zealous persuasion and undue influence; so long as the testator retained real freedom of choice a court will not interfere but, if it can be shown that the testator merely surrendered to intolerable pressure, this will amount to undue influence. The court will more readily find undue influence where a testator was weak (whether mentally or physically).

2.40

In the case of lifetime gifts there is a presumption of undue influence where a donee stands in a fiduciary relationship to a donor, for example, father and child, doctor and patient, solicitor and client, but there is no such presumption in the case of testamentary gifts. This is because many of the relationships which give rise to the presumption in relation to lifetime gifts are precisely the relationships which would lead a testator to want to make a gift by will. Thus, if there is no positive evidence of undue influence there is no question of refusing probate (*Parfitt v Lawless* (1872)). *Re Good, Carapeto v Good* (2002) is a recent example

of the difficulty of proving undue influence. The court accepted that the circumstances gave rise to a legitimate suspicion of coercion. However, the judge felt
that there was insufficient evidence to satisfy him that there had been coercion as
opposed to legitimate persuasion. The case also illustrates the danger of making
an allegation of undue influence which is not substantiated. The unsuccessful
challengers will normally have to pay all the costs on the basis that a person
should not have to pay to clear their own name.

2.41   In *Barclays Bank v Etridge and other appeals* (2001) Lord Nicholls, albeit in
a different context (the correct procedure to be followed by banks where one
party to a marriage is offering the matrimonial home as security for a loan to that
party) considered the obligations of solicitors in cases where there may be undue
influence. He said that a solicitor has to ensure that the client receives a clear
explanation of the nature and consequences of the act in the absence of the person
seeking to benefit. It is not necessary for the solicitor to approve of the transaction. However, in a case "where it is glaringly obvious that the wife is being
grievously wronged . . . the solicitor should decline to act further".

    Killick v Pountney (2000) is an example of a successful allegation of undue
influence. The court emphasised the importance of taking instructions from the
client in the absence of any person who might benefit from the will or exert
influence on the client. Undue influence was also successfully pleaded in *Re
Edwards* (2007) where there was clear evidence that the deceased's son had
poisoned the deceased's mind against the beneficiaries of the original will by
making untruthful accusations against them, causing the deceased to change her
will in his favour.

    The action which the court will take if fraud or undue influence is proved
depends on the effect that the fraud or undue influence produced. If it resulted in
the entire will being made in a particular way the entire will is refused probate;
if it resulted in a legacy being given to a beneficiary that legacy will fail (*Giles
v Giles* (1836); *Kennell v Abbott* (1799)). If a testator was prevented from
revoking a will in favour of X and making one in favour of Y the court may allow
Y to claim that the property should be held by X on trust for him (*Betts v Doughty*
(1879)).

5. LOST WILLS

2.42 If a will has been lost or accidentally destroyed it is possible to obtain probate of
a copy or reconstruction provided an order is first obtained. If, however, a will
which was known to have been in the testator's possession cannot be found after
his death there is a presumption that it was destroyed by the testator with the
intention of revoking it (*Eckersley v Platt* (1866)). This presumption will have to
be rebutted if an order for the proof of a copy or reconstruction is to be
obtained.

    The strength of the presumption will vary depending on the circumstances of
the case. In *Rowe v Clarke* (2005) the court held that "the strength of the
presumption in any given case depends on the character of the custody which the
testator had over the will". In this case the testator had kept his papers in some

disorder and had not attempted to keep the original will secure so the presumption was very weak. There was sufficient evidence to rebut the presumption. Importantly the court also held that the presumption can apply where there is no evidence that the will was not in existence at the date of death. The person claiming revocation does not have to prove non-existence of the will. The presumption was also rebutted in *Nichols v Hudson* (2006) and *Wren v Wren* (2006).

The procedure for obtaining an order is set out in the Non-Contentious Probate **2.43** Rules 1987 r.54. The same procedure is used where probate of an oral will is sought. The order can be made by a district judge or registrar but they can require that the matter be referred to a judge of the Family Division. The application must be supported by an affidavit setting out the grounds of the application, and by such evidence on affidavit as the applicant can adduce as to:

(a)   the will's existence after the death of the testator or, where there is no such evidence, the facts on which the applicant relies to rebut the presumption that the will has been revoked by destruction;

(b)   in respect of an oral will, the contents of that will; and

(c)   in respect of a reconstruction of a will, the accuracy of that reconstruction.

The district judge or registrar may require additional evidence in the circumstances of a particular case as to due execution of the will or as to the accuracy of the copy will, and may direct that notice be given to persons who would be prejudiced by the application.

6. CODICILS

Definition

A testamentary instrument which is executed in the same way as a will and which **2.44** supplements the terms of an existing will (either by adding to it, by amending it or by revoking it in part) is usually referred to as a codicil. A codicil must comply with the same requirements as a will if it is to be admitted to probate. *Her amendments* .

Republication

The execution of a codicil to a will "republishes" the will provided there is some **2.45** indication of an intention to republish. Any reference to the earlier will in the codicil is sufficient to amount to an indication of an intention to republish. When a will is republished it takes effect as if executed at the date of the codicil but with the incorporation of any changes made by the codicil.

Republication may affect the construction of a will both in respect of persons and property. In *Re Hardyman, Teesdale v McClintock* (1925) a will made in 1898 gave a legacy to the "wife of my cousin". The wife died with the result that the gift to her lapsed. The testatrix later executed a codicil to her will (which did not refer specifically to the legacy). This republished the will at the date of the codicil. Since the cousin had no wife living at that date the gift in the will took effect as a gift to the first person the cousin married after the date of the codicil.

In *Re Reeves, Reeves v Pawson* (1928) the testator gave his daughter "my present lease" in certain named property. At the time the will was executed the testator owned a short lease of the property. He later took a longer lease of the same property and then executed a codicil which referred to the will. The daughter was held entitled to the new (long) lease which the deceased owned at the date of the codicil.

If a will is altered before its republication and the alteration is not executed then the republication has the effect of validating the alteration. However, there is a presumption that unexecuted alterations were made after the execution of the codicil so that evidence will be required to rebut the presumption.

The republication of a will by a codicil executed by independent witnesses has the effect of saving a gift to a witness of the original will (who would otherwise be deprived of the gift under Wills Act 1837 s.15). This remains so even if the beneficiary witnesses a later codicil.

Revival

2.46 A *revoked* will can be revived by re-execution of the will or by execution of a codicil to the will showing an intention to revive. A mere reference to the earlier instrument is not sufficient to revive it; there must be words which make it clear that the effect of that document is being confirmed. A will cannot be revived unless it is still in existence. The effect of revival is the same as republication.

The revocation of a will by a codicil is not sufficient to revive an earlier revoked will. Once revoked a will stays revoked unless there is a formal act of revival. For example, a testator makes a will in 1980 and then makes a will in 1981 which revokes the 1980 will. The testator then executes a codicil which revokes the 1981 will. The 1980 will is not thereby revived. The codicil is the only document admissible to probate.

Revocation

2.47 A codicil may expressly revoke an earlier will or codicil in whole or in part. If no express revocation clause is included it will impliedly revoke an earlier instrument to the extent that it is inconsistent with it. Revocation is dealt with in the next section.

7. REVOCATION

Introduction

2.48 The various ways in which wills can be revoked are dealt with in paras 2.52–2.63, below.

Mutual wills

A will is always revocable during the lifetime of the testator (unless they lose **2.49**
testamentary capacity). A will cannot be made irrevocable. If a testator contracts
not to revoke they are still free to do so. However, in that case revocation would
be a breach of contract and the testator's estate would be liable to pay damages.

Equity may intervene under the doctrine of mutual wills to impose a trust on
a testator's property. This occurs where two or more people make wills in agreed
terms and agree that neither will revoke without the consent of the other. The
agreement does not have to be included in the will; it can be oral or in writing,
incorporated into the will or proved by clear and satisfactory extraneous evidence
on the basis of probabilities: *Re Goodchild* and *Re Cleaver (Deceased)* (1981).
See also *Fry v Martin Densham-Smith* (2010) where the Court of Appeal
accepted the trial judge's inference from the surrounding circumstances that an
agreement existed.

If the first to die carries out their part of the agreement equity will regard it as
unconscionable for the survivor to deviate from the agreed terms. Therefore,
equity will impose a trust on the survivor's property. The survivor remains free
to revoke their will but because of the existence of the trust the new dispositions
of the property will be ineffective. In *Thomas and Agnes Carvel Foundation v
Carvel* (2007) the Carvel Foundation was the beneficiary of a mutual will
agreement between Thomas and Agnes Carvel. Thomas died first and when
Agnes died the Foundation was unhappy with the actions of her executor. The
Foundation was unable to remove the executor under s.50 of the Administration
of Justice Act 1985 because only a beneficiary of the will can make such an
application and the Foundation was not the beneficiary of Agnes's will. However,
the survivor of two persons who made mutual wills is a trustee and the trust binds
those who claim under him. Accordingly, Agnes's executor was a trustee. The
Foundation was, therefore, able to apply under s.1 of the Judicial Trustees Act
1896 to remove the unsatisfactory executor/trustee.

The trust is a floating one during the lifetime of the survivor and crystallises **2.50**
on the survivor's death. This means that the survivor is free to deal with the
property during their lifetime and raises some concern as to what happens if the
survivor gives away or dissipates the joint assets. In *Re Cleaver* (1981), Nourse
J. quoted with approval from the judgment of Dixon J. in *Birmingham v Renfrew*
(1937) in which he said:

> "No doubt gifts and settlements, *inter vivos,* if calculated to defeat the intention of
> the compact, could not be made by the survivor and his right of disposition, *inter
> vivos* is, therefore not unqualified."

The doctrine of mutual wills applies only where the first party to die does so
having carried out the agreement. In *Re Hobley (Deceased)* (1997) the first party
to die had executed a codicil revoking one of the gifts in his will. The court said
that it could not attempt to assess the importance of the deviation from the
original agreement. An apparently minor alteration by one testator might have
sentimental importance to the other. The doctrine of mutual wills required any

alteration to have been agreed by both parties. Consequently, the second spouse was not bound by the agreement.

The case of *Re Dale* (1994) confirms that it is not necessary that the testators agree to leave property to *each other*. Equity will intervene to impose a trust on the property of the survivor where the agreement is that each testator shall leave property to a third party, for example, their children. If the surviving testator revokes their will and purports to leave their property (now held on trust for the agreed beneficiary), their will is perfectly valid but their personal representative will take the property subject to a trust in favour of the agreed beneficiaries. Ideally, solicitors should enquire as to the existence of an agreement to leave property in a particular way when taking instructions to change a will and when taking instructions to act in an administration.

In *Goodchild v Goodchild* (1996) the Court of Appeal confirmed the first instance decision that in order for wills to be mutual, there must be clear evidence of mutual intention not to revoke unilaterally. However, the testator's belief that her husband would give effect to what she believed to be their mutual intentions established a moral obligation binding on her husband. The obligation justified a claim by the adult son under the family provision legislation (see para.20.05, below).

2.51 Lack of evidence of agreement that the wills were not to be revoked unilaterally also caused a claim for mutual wills to fail in *Birch v Curtis* (2002). It is clearly essential to include a recital of the agreement where it is intended that the doctrine is to apply. However, where wills are **not** intended to be mutual, it is helpful to include a statement that the parties are free to revoke. It may avoid the waste of costs that arises when unnecessary challenges are made to a will. It would have been particularly useful in *Birch v Curtis* where the court accepted that there was an agreement as to how the surviving husband was to leave his property but no evidence as to whether there was a further agreement not to revoke. In *Charles v Fraser* (2010) the judge was critical of a solicitor who had not recorded the mutual wills agreement. *Healey v Brown* (2002) demonstrates the significance of the Law of Property (Miscellaneous Provisions) Act 1989 s.2 in relation to mutual will agreements. The section provides that an agreement to dispose of land or an interest in land is unenforceable unless in writing and signed by both parties. In *Healey v Brown* husband and wife had made wills which were mutual and which agreed that the survivor was to leave the matrimonial home (held as beneficial joint tenants) to the wife's niece. After his wife's death the husband transferred the house into the joint names of himself and his son from an earlier marriage. It was held that because the agreement between the spouses related to land and was not signed and in writing, the doctrine of mutual wills could not apply. The court held that equity can intervene to impose a constructive trust where, as here, it is unconscionable to provide no remedy. However, a constructive trust of this type is limited to the property received from the promisor and cannot affect property already held by the promisee (see *Re Goodchild* (1996)). The only way in which property already held can be impressed with a constructive trust is where the original owner has consented (as is the case with mutual wills). In this case, therefore, the son held the property half for himself absolutely and half for the niece.

In *Olins v Walters* (2007), however, Norris J. held that s.2 is only relevant where the agreement is *expressed* to relate to land. In *Olins* the deceased's will simply asked her executors to convert her estate (which included land) and then disposed of the proceeds. In these circumstances the lack of a signed document was not fatal.

Marriage or the formation of a civil partnership

Section 18 of the Wills Act 1837 (as substituted by the Administration of Justice **2.52** Act 1982) provides that the marriage of the testator automatically revokes any will made before marriage. Section 18B has exactly the same effect in relation to the formation of a civil partnership. There are, however, three exceptions to this rule:

(1) *Sections 18(3) and 18B(3)*

Where it appears from a will that at the time it was made the testator was **2.53** expecting to be married to or to form a civil partnership with a particular person and that they intended that the will should not be revoked by the marriage or formation of the civil partnership, the will shall not be revoked by the marriage or formation of the civil partnership.

These subsections save a will from being revoked provided that two conditions are satisfied.

    (a) The testator must have been expecting to be married to or form a civil partnership with a *particular* person at the time of execution. A will made by a testator who expected to marry someone soon after making the will but who had not decided whom to marry would, therefore, be revoked by the subsequent marriage of the testator. It is not, however, required that the testator should be engaged to marry at the time when the will is made.

        It must "appear from the will" that the testator is expecting to marry or form a civil partnership with a particular person so that an express statement to that effect should be included. It is probable that in the absence of such a statement a reference to "my fiancee" or "my future civil partner" in the will would satisfy this requirement.

    (b) It must also "appear from the will" that the testator intended that the will should not be revoked by the marriage or formation of the civil partnership. There is no guidance in the Act as to how such an intention is to be shown. It is possible that if the will gives substantially all of the testator's estate to the expected spouse or civil partner this condition might be satisfied. However, it is preferable to include an express statement as to the testator's intention in a professionally drawn will. A suitable clause would be: "I declare that I make this will expecting to be married to [insert name of expected spouse] and that I intend that this will shall not be revoked by my marriage to the said [expected spouse]".

Marriage to or civil partnership with any person other than the person indicated in the will revokes the will.

In *Court and Others v Despallieres* (2009) it was held that a will was revoked by the subsequent formation of a civil partnership because the statement that the will was not to be revoked by "subsequent marriage, Civil Union Partnership nor adoption". The statement did not satisfy the requirements of s.18B, since it was merely a general statement that the will was intended to survive marriage, civil partnership or adoption: it did not show that the deceased expected to form a civil partnership, let alone with a particular person.

(2) *Sections 18(4) and 18B(4)–(6))*

2.54 Where it appears from a will that at the time it was made the testator was expecting to be married to or to form a civil partnership with a particular person and that they intended that *a disposition in the will* should not be revoked by the marriage or formation of the civil partnership:

(a) that disposition shall take effect notwithstanding the marriage or civil partnership; and

(b) any other disposition in the will shall take effect also, unless it appears from the will that the testator intended the disposition to be revoked by the marriage or civil partnership.

In a professionally drawn will the testator's intention should be made clear by the use of a suitable declaration. For example, the testator may wish to give £10,000 to X notwithstanding the formation of a civil partnership. A suitable declaration would be "I give £10,000 to X and declare that this gift is to take effect notwithstanding the formation of my civil partnership with Y".

If the testator wishes any other dispositions to be revoked by the marriage or civil partnership it must "appear from the will" that this is their intention (ss.18(4)(b) and 18B(6)). If the testator includes a declaration that one disposition is not to be revoked by a marriage or formation of a civil partnership and does not make any such declaration in relation to other dispositions, it is arguable that they have shown an intention that those other dispositions *are* to be revoked by the marriage or formation of the civil partnership. An express declaration to that effect should be included in the will for the sake of certainty. For example: "I declare that all the gifts contained in this will other than the gift to X are to be revoked by the celebration of my forthcoming marriage with Y."

An appointment of executors is not a "disposition" nor are administrative provisions (such as an extension to the statutory power of insurance). Such clauses will, therefore, be revoked by marriage or the formation of a civil partnership even though the dispositive parts of the will are saved from revocation in whole or in part by s.18(4) or s.18B(4)–(6). However, if the entire will is saved from revocation by s.18(3) or s.18B(3) it is clear that the non-dispositive clauses remain effective.

(3) Sections 18(2) and 18B(2)

The exercise of a power of appointment by will remains effective notwithstand- **2.55** ing a subsequent marriage or the formation of a civil partnership. In this case the appointment is saved from revocation whether or not the will is expressed to be made in expectation of the marriage or formation of the civil partnership and whether or not the testator was expecting to marry or form a civil partnership when the will was made. The exercise of a power of appointment is not, however, saved from revocation by s.18(2) or s.18B(2) where the property appointed would pass to the personal representatives of the testator in default of appointment.

Divorce or dissolution of a civil partnership

Section 18A of the Wills Act 1837 provides that if a marriage is dissolved or **2.56** annulled by the decree of a court, the will is to take effect as if any appointment of the former spouse as executor or executor and trustee of the will were omitted. This will usually mean that the deceased will die without an executor so that letters of administration with the will annexed will be required but if any person has been appointed co-executor with the former spouse that person will remain entitled to take a grant of probate.

Section 18A also provides that on dissolution or annulment of a marriage any devise or bequest to the former spouse shall pass as if the former spouse had died on that date. If the will contains no substitutional gift the property given to the former spouse will, therefore, fall into residue or if itself a gift of residue will pass on intestacy.

Section 18C makes the same provisions in relation to the dissolution or annulment of a civil partnership.

The provisions of ss.18A and 18C are subject to any contrary intention expressed in the will and the failure of gifts to the former spouse or civil partner is expressly stated to be without prejudice to any claim under the Inheritance (Provision for Family and Dependants) Act 1975 (as to which see Ch.20, below).

It should be noted that ss.18A and 18C apply only to dissolution or annulment decreed by a court. A separation does not, therefore, in any way change the effect of the will of a person who has a spouse or civil partner. A person contemplating separation should always consider making a new will. Furthermore, even when a dissolution or annulment is decreed the only effect is to cause gifts to the former spouse or civil partner to lapse; the will should therefore be reviewed at such time to ensure that it disposes of the property as the testator wishes in view of the changed circumstances.

Re Sinclair (Deceased), Lloyds Bank v Imperial Cancer Research Fund (1985) revealed a problem with s.18A as originally drafted. A testator had left property

to his wife provided she survived by one month. There was then a gift to the
Cancer Research Fund which was expressed to take effect "if my said wife shall
predecease me or fail to survive me for one month . . . ". The testator and his wife
divorced and the gift to her, therefore, "lapsed". The testator then died and his
former wife survived by more than one month. Clearly the wife could not take
the gift but the question arose as to whether the gift to the Fund would take effect
or whether there was an intestacy. The Court of Appeal held the word lapse
means no more than "fail" so that the divorced beneficiary is not deemed to have
died before the testator. The conditional gift to the Fund, therefore, could not take
effect. The residuary gift having failed, the property therefore passed under the
intestacy rules to the testator's brother. The decision in *Re Sinclair* led to the
amendment of will precedents so that substitutional gifts were expressed to take
effect "If the gift to my said spouse shall fail *for any reason* . . . " to allow the
conditional gift to take effect.

2.57   The Law Reform (Succession) Act 1995 removed the problems revealed by *Re
Sinclair*. The Act amended s.18A of the Wills Act so that where a marriage has
been dissolved or annulled the former spouse shall be treated as having died on
the date of the annulment or dissolution. The new provisions dealing with civil
partnership are also worded in this way. This means that a substitutional gift
drafted to take effect "if my spouse predeceases or fails to survive me by [a
specified period]", can now take effect where the marriage is dissolved. It is,
therefore, unnecessary to include the words "or if this gift fails for any other
reason" to cover the possibility of the marriage ending in termination. However,
will drafters may prefer to retain these words to cover the possibility of the gift
in the will failing for any other unforeseen reason—for example, forfeiture. The
writers had wondered whether they were being unduly cautious in suggesting
retaining the words "or fails for any other purpose" to cover the possibility of
forfeiture. However, the decision of the Court of Appeal in *Re Jones (Deceased)*
(1997) was on exactly this point.

The testatrix was killed by her son, Robert, who was convicted of her
manslaughter. Her will left her estate to Robert and if he predeceased her to
"such of my nephews . . . as shall be living at the date of her death".

The gift to Robert could not take effect. Did the estate pass to the nephews
under the terms of the will or did it pass on intestacy? The Court of Appeal held
unanimously that as the event provided for in the will (the predecease of Robert)
had not occurred, the gift over could not take effect. Therefore the estate passed
on intestacy.

The decision in *Re DWS* (2001) was similar. The Court of Appeal said that on
intestacy the substitutional gift to issue of a deceased class member cannot take
effect where a member's interest has been forfeited under the Forfeiture Act
1982. Under the terms of the statutory trusts issue cannot take if the parent is
"living". The principle will apply in the same way where a class member
disclaims an interest. The Civil Law Reform Bill contained provisions to deal
with this and similar problems but, unfortunately, the Bill did not survive "wash-
up" before the General Election in 2010. Changes to the law of the distribution
of estates are at the time of writing being taken forward in a private members'
bill, the Estates of Deceased Persons (Forfeiture Rule and Law of Succession)

Bill. The Bill received its second reading in January 2011. The Ministry of Justice has indicated that it will support the Bill and has assisted with drafting both the Bill and the explanatory notes published with it.

Destruction

A will may be revoked by "burning tearing or otherwise destroying the same by   **2.58**
the testator or by some person in his presence and by his direction with the intention of revoking the same" (Wills Act 1837 s.20). Both an act of destruction and an intention to revoke are required for this type of revocation. Neither alone is sufficient.

"Burning tearing or otherwise destroying"

A physical act of destruction is required so that simply crossing out the wording   **2.59**
of the will or the signature of the testator or writing words such as "cancelled" or "revoked" across the will is insufficient to revoke. For example, in *Cheese v Lovejoy* (1877) the testator wrote "all these are cancelled" on the will and crossed out part of it. He then threw the will away but it was found by a servant who preserved it until the testator's death. The will was held to be valid. Although the testator intended to revoke the will he had done nothing which could be regarded as "burning tearing or otherwise destroying" it. Whether destruction has occurred is a question of degree. For example in *In the Estate of Adams (Deceased)* (1990) parts of the will had been heavily scored through with a ball-point pen. This was held to amount to destruction of those parts. The amount of interference with the will was far greater than mere crossing out.

If the testator destroys part of a will this may amount to revocation of the will as a whole if the part destroyed is sufficiently substantial or important (for example, the attestation clause). However, destruction of part may be treated as revocation of only part where the part destroyed is less important. Thus, in *Re Everest* (1975) the testator cut off certain parts of the will containing trusts of residue. It was held that the rest of the will remained valid. In *Hobbs v Knight* (1838) the testator cut out his signature from the will. This was held to be a revocation of the whole will. In deciding how far the revocation extends the court will hear evidence of the testator's intention. In the absence of such evidence the court will decide on the basis of the state of the will after the destruction. If a testator wishes to revoke a will by destruction, they should ensure that the will is totally destroyed. However, since doubts may arise after death as to the testator's true intention at the time of destruction, it is usually preferable to effect the revocation by means of a further testamentary instrument.

Revocation by destruction is only effective if the testator has completed the intended act of destruction. This is illustrated by the curious case of *Doe d. Perkes v Perkes* (1820) where the testator tore a will into four pieces in the presence of a beneficiary with whom he was angry. He was then restrained from further destruction by a third party and, when his anger had subsided, was heard to say "It is a good job it is no worse"; from this the court inferred that the testator had intended more tearing so the act of destruction was incomplete and the will still valid.

If the destruction is carried out by some person other than the testator, it is only effective if done in their presence and by their direction. A destruction in the absence of the testator or without their direction cannot be ratified by the testator so that their only course is to revoke by a further testamentary instrument.

Intention

2.60   The testator must *intend* to revoke the will at the time of the destruction. Accidental destruction does not, therefore, revoke a will nor does destruction by a testator who thinks the will is invalid (since then their intention is merely to destroy an apparently useless piece of paper).

If a will known to have been in the testator's possession is not found after their death it is presumed that they destroyed it with intention to revoke it. Similarly if a will is found to have been in the testator's possession and is found torn or otherwise destroyed at their death there is a presumption that the testator destroyed it with the intention of revoking it. Either of these presumptions may be rebutted (for example, by evidence that the testator kept their papers with such lack of security that the most likely explanation is that the will was lost, see *Rowe v Clarke* and para.2.42, above).

If a will is destroyed but not revoked (because of lack of intention to revoke or because the destruction was done in the absence of the testator), it remains valid. Probate may be obtained of a copy or reconstruction if the terms can be proved with sufficient certainty (see para.10.02, below).

Conditional revocation

2.61   Where a will is destroyed with an intention to revoke, it is a question of fact whether the revocation is absolute (and therefore immediately effective) or conditional (and therefore only effective if the condition is satisfied). Extrinsic evidence is admissible to prove whether the revocation was conditional.

A common reason for revoking a will is that the testator wishes to make a new will disposing of their property in a different way. If the testator has left the bulk of their property to X they may decide to revoke their will so as to make a new will leaving it to Y. If this is done primarily so as to exclude X from benefit the court will infer that the revocation of the original will was absolute. If on the other hand it can be shown that the testator wanted to benefit Y but would have preferred X to take rather than those entitled on intestacy, the court will infer that the revocation was conditional on the execution of a valid will leaving the property to Y so that X will take unless a new will has been made. This is often referred to as "the doctrine of dependent relative revocation" since the revocation is dependent on the making of the new will. However, there must be some evidence that the testator's intention to revoke was conditional. For example, in *Re Jones* (1976) the testatrix made a will leaving a smallholding to certain beneficiaries. She later told her bank manager that she wished to leave the smallholding to her nephew because of the beneficiaries' attitude to her and because they had acquired their own property. The testatrix died soon after this conversation and the will was found mutilated after her death (the signatures and the gift of the smallholding having been cut out). The court held that the will was not saved from revocation since the testatrix's intention was to revoke whether or not she was able to make a new will.

The fact that a new will is intended is only one of many things which may lead to the inference that revocation was conditional. For example, in *In the Estate of Southerden* (1925) the testator made a will in favour of his wife. He thought that his wife would take all his property on intestacy and so destroyed the will by burning it. Because of the size of the estate the wife was entitled to only part of the testator's property on intestacy; the court held that the will was destroyed conditionally on the wife taking the whole estate. It therefore remained valid as the condition would not be satisfied by revocation of the will.

In *Re Finnemore (Deceased)* (1991) the deceased made three wills. Each made a gift to C and each contained a revocation clause. C's husband witnessed the second and third wills. On the face of it this meant that C could not take because of the Wills Act 1837 s.15 (see paras 16.33–16.38, below). However, the court held that the revocation clauses in the second and third wills were conditional on the validity of the gifts contained in them. The clauses were, therefore, ineffective to revoke the gift in the first will to C. They were, however, effective to revoke the rest of the first and second wills.

A testamentary instrument

A will may be revoked in whole or in part by a later will or codicil or by "some **2.62** writing declaring an intention to revoke the same and executed in the manner in which a will is . . . executed" (Wills Act 1837 s.20).

The clearest way in which a later will may revoke an earlier one is where it contains an express revocation clause. Such a clause should always be included in a new will which deals with the whole of the testator's property. A common form of wording is "I hereby revoke all former wills and testamentary dispositions heretofore made by me". If a codicil is drawn up, great care should be taken with the wording of any revocation clause to ensure that it revokes only those parts of the earlier will which the testator intends to revoke or replace.

Similarly, a revocation clause must be carefully drawn where a client has made a will to deal with foreign property. The revocation clause should be limited to revoking wills dealing with property in England and Wales. Even without express words of revocation a will or codicil revokes an earlier will or codicil to the extent that it is inconsistent with it. Where a client has a will dealing with foreign property any subsequent will should be expressly limited to assets in England and Wales.

The doctrine of conditional revocation may apply to save a will (or part of it) from revocation by a later will or codicil. This applies where the revocation (express or implied) in the later instrument is conditional on the effectiveness of that instrument (see, for example, *Re Finnemore (Deceased)* (1991) (see para.2.61)). If the later will starts with a revocation clause but then disposes of the property in a way which is ineffective (for example, because of ambiguity as to the identity of the beneficiary) the court may construe the revocation clause as conditional so that it will not be admitted to probate.

Revocation by privileged testator

2.63 A testator who enjoys privileged status may revoke a will informally whether the will was made informally or not. A testator who makes a privileged will while a minor may revoke it while still a minor even if they have lost the privileged status before revoking (Family Law Reform Act 1969 s.3). However, it seems that the revocation cannot then be made by an informal document but only by destruction (if there is a written will capable of destruction) or by a formal, attested document.

Alterations and obliterations

2.64 Section 21 of the Wills Act 1837 provides that:

> "No obliteration, interlineation or other alteration made in any will after the execution thereof shall be valid . . . except so far as the words or effect of the will before such alteration shall not be apparent, unless the alteration shall be executed in like manner as hereinbefore is required for the execution of a will . . . ".

An alteration made before execution with the knowledge and approval of the testator is valid. However, an alteration in a will is presumed to have been made after execution except that an alteration which completes a blank space in the will is presumed to have been made before execution. Either of these presumptions may be rebutted by internal evidence from the will itself or by extrinsic evidence (for example, a statement from the draftsman or a witness). Once an alteration is shown to have been made before execution it is admissible to probate as part of the will.

An alteration made after execution of the will which is itself signed by the testator and by at least two witnesses is admitted to probate as it complies with the formalities required by the Wills Act 1837. It follows that an alteration which is witnessed is not valid unless the alteration (or the will as altered) is signed by the testator (see *Re White (Deceased)* (1990)). For the avoidance of doubt, any alteration to a will, even if made before execution, should be attested. It is sufficient if the testator and witnesses of the will put their initials in the margin next to the alteration.

A slightly different problem arises where words are crossed out or otherwise made more difficult to read without the alteration being attested. If the original wording is "apparent" it is admitted to probate, the crossing out being ignored. Wording is regarded as apparent if it can be read by ordinary means such as close inspection through a magnifying glass or by holding the document up to the light.

Where the original wording is not apparent because it has been scratched out, **2.65** covered over or otherwise obliterated it is excluded from probate if the obliteration was made by the testator with an intention to revoke. The effect of obliterating words in this way is that they are revoked.

If the obliteration was made by someone other than the testator or by the testator but without intention to revoke, extrinsic evidence (such as evidence from drafts or copies, infra-red photographs or removal of paper stuck over the words) is permitted to prove the original wording.

Where the testator made the obliteration with a conditional intention to revoke, the court will allow the original wording to be proved by extrinsic evidence and admitted to probate if the condition has not been satisfied. The most likely example of such a conditional intention is that the original wording should only be revoked if substituted wording is admissible to probate. (For example, the will originally says "I give to X the sum of £1,000", the testator obliterates "£1,000" and writes "£1,500" instead—clearly the court can infer that X is to get £1,000 if the substitution of £1,500 is not effective.) If the substitution is ineffective because it has not been executed the court will admit extrinsic evidence to prove the original wording. This is really another example of conditional revocation and the same considerations apply as in the case of conditional destruction (see para.2.61, above).

Chapter Three

INTESTACY

1. Introduction

There are many advantages to be gained by making a will, but the majority of **3.01** people die without having made one, either out of ignorance of the courses of action open to them, or out of a reluctance to contemplate their own deaths, or from a mistaken belief that, for them, a will is pointless. The devolution of certain assets is fixed irrespective of whether there is a will. Thus, property held as joint tenants passes by the right of survivorship and nominated property passes to the nominee (See Ch.21, below).

The problem where there is no will is to determine who is to share in the other assets of the deceased's estate. The answer is to be found in Pt IV of the Administration of Estates Act 1925, as amended, which lays down who is entitled to an intestate's residuary estate (that is, the deceased's assets after the payment of debts and expenses). The Act specifies the entitlements of the deceased's immediate family; the provisions were based on "the average will" filed with the Probate Registry in the years before 1925, although they have been amended since.

While the intestacy rules ensure that the "next-of-kin" share in the estate, the proportions are arbitrary and therefore often unsuitable; inevitably they give no rights to cohabitants, friends or charities who might have benefited had the deceased made a will.

If cohabitants, relatives or dependants feel that the intestacy rules do not make adequate financial provision for them, they may be able to bring a claim under the Inheritance (Provisions for Family and Dependants) Act 1975 s.l(l) which provides that the court is not bound to assume that the intestacy rules make reasonable provision for the next-of-kin—see Ch.20, below.

Where property passes as bona vacantia, it may be possible for a deserving claimant to obtain a payment from the Crown, Duchy of Lancaster or Duke of Cornwall. See para.3.05, below.

2. Total or Partial Intestacy

3.02 For the rules to apply, the deceased must have died either totally or partially intestate.

The deceased dies totally intestate if he or she has either made no will at all, has made an invalid will, has revoked any wills that he or she has made or has made a will which does not effectively dispose of any property.

The deceased dies partially intestate if he or she has left a valid will which disposes of only part of his or her estate. This can happen in two ways:

(a) the deceased may have made a valid will which fails to dispose of the whole estate (for example, because it contains no residuary gift). An example of such a will is one leaving money in a building society account to X but not dealing with the rest of the estate; or

(b) the deceased may have made a valid will which dealt with the whole of his or her estate but the residuary gift may fail in whole or in part (for example, because a residuary beneficiary predeceases the testator and the will does not contain a substitutional gift).

In general the same rules apply whether the deceased died totally or partially intestate. Where there are differences these will be indicated later.

3. Undisposed of Property is held on a Statutory Trust

The general rule

3.03 The Administration of Estates Act 1925 s.33(1) as amended by the Trusts of Land and Appointment of Trustees Act 1996 provides:

> "on the death of a person intestate as to any real or personal estate, such estate shall be held on trust by his personal representatives with the power to sell it."

Section 33(2) provides that:

> "The personal representatives shall pay out of:
>
> (a) the ready money of the deceased (so far as not disposed of by his will, if any); and
> (b) any net money arising from disposing of any other part of his estate (after payment of costs),
>
> all . . . funeral, testamentary and administration expenses, debts and other liabilities . . . and out of the residue of the said money the personal representatives shall set aside a fund sufficient to provide for any pecuniary legacies bequeathed by the will (if any) of the deceased."

Partial intestacy

3.04 The statutory trust imposed by s.33 applies to a partial intestacy as well as to a total intestacy. The provisions of the will take precedence over the intestacy rules. Thus, if the undisposed of property was left on an *express* trust (for example, T leaves "residue on trust to A and B in equal shares" and A predeceases T), the express trust prevails over the statutory trust. This may appear to be a minor point but will be important if the *terms* of the express trust differ from s.33 (for example, by directing payment of inheritance tax attributable to lifetime gifts made by the deceased).

4. ORDER OF ENTITLEMENT UNDER THE INTESTACY RULES

Before considering the detailed rules relating to the entitlements of the beneficiaries it is useful to set out the basic structure of the Administration of Estates Act provisions. First, where there is a surviving spouse or civil partner he or she takes everything unless the intestate also left certain relatives. **3.05**

(a) If the intestate also left issue (that is children, grandchildren and remoter lineal descendants) the spouse or civil partner and issue share the estate provided the issue satisfy the requirements of the statutory trusts.

(b) If the intestate left no surviving issue, but left a surviving parent or parents, the parent(s) and the spouse or civil partner share the estate. The parent(s) take(s) the property absolutely or in equal shares. If no parent survives, but the intestate left a living brother or sister of the whole blood (or their issue) they share the assets with the spouse or civil partner, provided that they satisfy the requirements of the statutory trusts.

(The "statutory trusts" are defined at para.3.18, below.)

If the intestate left no surviving spouse or civil partner, the estate is distributed as follows:

(a) to issue on the statutory trusts, but if none, then to,

(b) parents absolutely (and equally if both are alive), but if none, then to,

(c) brothers and sisters of the whole blood (i.e. the children of the same parents as the deceased) on the statutory trusts, but if none, then to,

(d) brothers and sisters of the half blood (i.e. those who share one parent with the deceased) on the statutory trusts, but if none, then to,

(e) grandparents absolutely and equally if more than one, but if none, then to,

(f) uncles and aunts of the whole blood (i.e. brothers and sisters of the whole blood of one of the parents of the deceased) on the statutory trusts, but if none, then to,

(g) uncles and aunts of the half blood (i.e. those with one parent in common with one of the parents of the deceased) on the statutory trusts, but if none, then to,

(h) the Crown, Duchy of Lancaster or the Duke of Cornwall as "bona vacantia".

Each category must be considered in the order listed above and only if there is *no one* in a particular category is it necessary to consider the next category. Furthermore, since a blood relationship, an adoptive relationship or a relationship under the Human Fertilisation and Embryology Act 2009 is vital under the intestacy rules, the *spouse or civil partner* of a person within one of these categories has no right to share in the estate. Matters relevant to the particular categories are considered below.

Human Fertilisation and Embryology Act 2008

3.06 This act makes significant changes to the legal definition of the term "parent" with important implications for the application of the above rules in several types of case.

First, under s.33, where a woman has carried a child as a result of the placing in her of an embryo or of sperm and eggs she, and she alone, is treated as the mother of that child unless the child is adopted or some other woman is treated as the child's mother under a parental order (as to which see below). Under s.33 the husband of the mother is treated as the child's father unless it is shown that he did not consent to the procedure. Similarly where a woman is artificially inseminated with donor sperm, her husband is the father of the child unless it is shown that he did not consent (s.35).

Secondly, where a woman is not married or where her husband is shown not to have consented, another man may, in certain cases, be treated as the father of the child. The main requirements are that the procedures involved are conducted in the UK by persons licensed to provide them and both parties have given written notice of consent to the man being treated as the father (ss.36–38).

3.07 Thirdly, where a woman is a party to a civil partnership and bears a child as a result of the placing in her of an embryo or of sperm and eggs or as a result of artificial insemination, her civil partner is treated as the other parent of the child unless she is shown not to have consented to the procedure (s.42). Under ss.43–45 another woman may be treated as the second parent subject to the same conditions, mutatis mutandis, as apply to a man under ss.36–38.

Under s.48 a person treated as the mother, father or parent of the child under these provisions is treated as the mother, father or parent *for all purposes* and "reference to any relationship between two people in any enactment, deed or other instrument or document (whenever passed or made) are to be read accordingly". As far as intestacy is concerned this means that the effect of parenthood under the act stretches beyond the child and its parents. For example, a child who is treated as a child of the mother's civil partner will also be treated as the brother or sister of the half blood of the civil partner's other children and the grandchild of the civil partner's parents.

The act also provides for parenthood in cases of surrogacy (ss.54–56). This requires an application to the court for a "parental order" within six months of the birth. The child has to have been carried by a woman who is not one of the applicants. The embryo must have been created with the gametes of at least one of the applicants, the applicants must be a married couple, civil partners or living as partners in "an enduring family relationship", they must be both over 18 and at least one of them must be domiciled in the UK, Channel Islands or Isle of Man. The child must be living with the applicants. The woman who bore the child and any other parent of the child (under this act or otherwise) must consent. The surrogate mother must not have received payment other than for reasonable expenses. Once the order is made the child is effectively treated as adopted by the couple in whose favour the order is made.

5. The Rights of a Surviving Spouse

The spouse's entitlement

The Law Reform (Succession) Act 1995 s.1, introduces a statutory survivorship **3.08** period for spouses and civil partners of intestates dying on or after January 1, 1996. In order to take an interest on intestacy a spouse or civil partner must survive the intestate for 28 days before taking an interest.

The spouse's precise entitlement to the deceased's undisposed-of "residuary estate" depends on whether any other close relatives survived the intestate.

For these purposes, a divorced spouse has no rights in the deceased's estate and for deaths occurring on or after January 1, 1970, neither has a *judicially* separated spouse, since they are treated as already being dead provided the separation is still continuing (Matrimonial Causes Act 1973 s.18(2)). (This is not the case, however, if there is a magistrates' court separation order in effect (see s.18(3)) although no such separation order may be made after the Domestic Proceedings and Magistrates' Courts Act 1978.) A civil partner has no inheritance rights after dissolution of the civil partnership nor after a separation order has been made (see Civil Partnership Act 2004 s.57).

When clients consult a solicitor with a view to obtaining a divorce, judicial separation, dissolution of a civil partnership or separation order, the solicitor should ask the clients whether or not they have made wills. If they have not, the solicitor should advise them to make wills since property will pass under the intestacy rules to the spouse or civil partner if the client dies before the final order (the decree absolute in the case of a divorce and the final order in the case of a dissolution of a civil partnership). If the clients have existing wills, they should review them in the light of the changed circumstances.

In the case of polygamous marriages *Official Solicitor to the Senior Courts v Yemoh* (2010) decided there can be more than one spouse for the purpose of intestacy rules. The deceased had left eight wives and the court held that together they constituted the surviving "spouse". The statutory legacy would, therefore, be divided amongst the various widows. As there were surviving issue one half of the residue was held for the "spouse" for life (see para.3.10, below). The court held that the various wives were to be treated as beneficial joint tenants so that the property subject to life interest was to be held until the death of the last, at which point that half of residue would fall.

Spouse or civil partner alone surviving

3.09 If the intestate left a surviving spouse or civil partner but no issue, parents or brothers or sisters of the whole blood (or their issue), the personal representatives hold *the whole of the estate* on trust for sale for the spouse or civil partner *absolutely*. Remoter relatives such as grandparents or uncles and aunts have no rights to share in the estate.

Spouse or civil partner and issue surviving

3.10 The estate of an intestate who leaves a surviving spouse or civil partner and issue is divided between the spouse or civil partner and the issue. The spouse or civil partner receives:

    (a) The deceased's "personal chattels" absolutely. "Personal chattels" are defined in Administration of Estates Act 1925 s.55(1)(x). They are:

> "carriages, horses, stable furniture and effects (not used for business purposes), motor cars and accessories (not used for business purposes), garden effects, domestic animals, plate, plated articles, linen, china, glass, books, pictures, prints, furniture, jewellery, articles of household or personal use or ornament, musical and scientific instruments and apparatus, wines, liquors and consumable stores, but do not include any chattels used at the death of the intestate for business purposes nor money or securities for money".

        To summarise this long definition, personal chattels are items of personal and domestic use and ornament. This has been held to cover a yacht (*Re Chaplin* (1950)) and a collection of watches (*Re Crispin's Will Trusts* (1975)). In the latter case Russell L.J. said that "cherishing . . . by eye and hand [could bring the watches] within the definition of articles of personal use".

    (b) A "statutory legacy" of £250,000 where death occurs on or after February 1, 2009. The legacy is payable free of tax and costs, together with interest at 6 per cent per annum from death until payment. The costs and interest come from the residue of the estate. In the case of deaths occurring prior to February 1, 2009 lower levels of statutory legacy are payable.

    (c) If there is anything left in the estate after (a) and (b), the spouse or civil partner receives a life interest (i.e. a right to the income until death) in one-half of the residue.

The other half of the residue and the interest in remainder in the trust created for the spouse or civil partner go to the issue on the statutory trusts. The statutory trusts are defined below.

Spouse or civil partner and parent or brother and sister (or their issue) surviving

Where the intestate leaves a spouse or civil partner but no issue, the estate is **3.11** divided as follows if one or more parents of the intestate (or brothers and sisters of the whole blood or their issue) also survive. The spouse or civil partner receives:

   (a)   The "personal chattels" (defined above) absolutely.

   (b)   A statutory legacy of £450,000 where death occurs on or after February 1, 2009. Again the legacy is payable free of tax and costs plus 6 per cent per annum interest. In the case of deaths occurring prior to February 1, 2009 lower levels of statutory legacy are payable.

   (c)   One-half of the residue *absolutely*. In contrast to para.3.10 above, the spouse or civil partner in this case receives the capital and not merely the income from this part of the estate.

The rest of the estate (that is, the other half of any residue) goes to the parent or parents in equal shares absolutely or, if none, to the brothers and sisters of the whole blood or their issue on the statutory trusts (see below).

The special rules applying to spouses and civil partners

Redemption of life interest

Where the intestate is survived by a spouse or civil partner and issue, the spouse **3.12** or civil partner is entitled to a life interest in one-half of the residue of the estate. This means that the spouse or civil partner will receive the income from the trust for sale for life. However, a spouse or civil partner may prefer to receive a capital sum (particularly if the residue is small and so capable of producing only a small income).

Section 47A of the Administration of Estates Act 1925 allows the spouse or civil partner to elect to convert the life interest into a capital sum. The election must be made within 12 months of the grant of representation (the time limit may be extended at the discretion of the court) in writing to the personal representatives (s.47A(6)). If the sole personal representative is the surviving spouse or civil partner, the election is made to the Senior Registrar of the Family Division of the High Court. A complex formula for determining the capital value of the interest is laid down in statutory instruments, the latest of which is the Intestate Succession (Interest and Capitalisation) (Amendment) Order 2008 which came into force on February 1, 2009. Provided the issue are *sui juris* the life interest can be valued by agreement between the spouse or civil partner and issue, thus removing the necessity of complying with the statutory provisions.

The effect of the provision can be seen in the following example. The residue of the intestate's estate, after taking personal chattels and the statutory legacy, is £50,000, and the spouse or civil partner is entitled to a life interest in £25,000. Instead of receiving the income from this, the spouse or civil partner can capitalise the interest using the formula and receive, say, £10,000 in cash. The rest of the estate, after deducting the costs of the capitalisation is held on the statutory trusts for the issue.

If the spouse or civil partner makes this election, no "transfer of value" is made for the purposes of inheritance tax. However, since less of the deceased's estate is treated as passing to the spouse or civil partner, less of the estate is exempt under Inheritance Act 1984 s.18 with the result that more inheritance tax may become payable on the deceased's estate (see Ch.4).

Acquiring the matrimonial home

3.13   If the intestate and the surviving spouse or civil partner were joint beneficial tenants of the dwelling-house in which the surviving spouse was resident at the deceased's death, the property will pass by survivorship to the surviving spouse or civil partner. If, however, the intestate was the sole owner or held a share as a tenant-in-common, the house or the interest as tenant-in-common in the house will be part of the undisposed of property. The surviving spouse or civil partner may wish to acquire the house. This can be achieved in a number of ways.

The Second Schedule to the Intestates' Estates Act 1952 gives a surviving spouse or civil partner the right to *require* the personal representatives to appropriate "any dwelling-house in which the surviving spouse was resident at the time of the intestate's death" in total or partial satisfaction of an absolute and/ or capitalised interest in the estate.

If the dwelling-house is worth more than the absolute entitlement of the spouse or civil partner, the personal representative can still be required to appropriate the dwelling-house but the spouse or civil partner must then pay "equality money" from his or her own resources to make up the difference (Sch.2 para.5(2)). The house is valued at the value at the date of appropriation, not death (*Re Collins* (1975)). If it is a time of rising property values, it is important to advise a client to make such an election quickly.

As with capitalising a life interest, the surviving spouse or civil partner must exercise the right within 12 months of the grant of representation (again subject to the court's power to extend the time limit) by notice in writing to the personal representatives.

3.14   The surviving spouse or civil partner will frequently be a personal representative of the deceased. If the spouse is one of two or more personal representatives then notice must be given to the other(s). The Schedule does not mention the giving of notice where the spouse is the sole personal representative.

A personal representative is in a fiduciary position as regards the estate and like a trustee must not profit from that fiduciary position. The Schedule provides that where the spouse is one of two or more personal representatives the rule that a trustee should not purchase trust property is not to prevent the purchase of a dwelling-house from the estate. The Schedule says nothing of the position where a spouse is a sole personal representative. A spouse who is a sole personal representative and who wishes to exercise the right to take a dwelling-house ought to do one of the following:

(a) secure the appointment of a second personal representative;

(b) obtain the consent of the other beneficiaries (but this is only appropriate if they are of full age and capacity); or

(c) obtain the consent of the court.

The need for such steps is confirmed by the case of *Kane v Radley-Kane* (1998). The case concerned an appropriation by a surviving spouse of shares under Administration of Estates Act 1925 s.41 rather than an election to take a dwelling house. However, the court referred to the right of election under the 1952 Act. It emphasised the fact that the right only exists where the spouse is one of two or more personal representatives and that a sole personal representative would have to take additional steps.

During the 12-month period the personal representatives need to obtain the written consent of the surviving spouse or civil partner if they wish to dispose of the house, unless they have to sell it to raise money for the administration when there is no other asset available.

When a surviving spouse or civil partner chooses to exercise this right, it does **3.15** not matter whether the deceased held the freehold or merely a leasehold interest in the house (except where the lease has less than two years to run). However, in four circumstances set out in Sch.2 paras 2 and 4(2) to the 1952 Act, the consent of the court is required before the spouse or civil partner can exercise the right. Such consent is required if the house:

(a) forms part of a building, the whole of which is comprised in the residuary estate;

(b) is held with agricultural land similarly comprised;

(c) as to the whole or part was used as a hotel or lodging house at the death of the intestate; or

(d) as to part was used for non-domestic purposes at the death of the intestate (which would be the case if, for example, part of the house was used as a shop).

In these circumstances, the court must be satisfied that the exercise of the right will not diminish the value of the other residuary assets nor make them more difficult to sell.

If a surviving spouse or civil partner wishes to avoid an application to the court or if the right of election is unavailable for any other reason (for example, expiry of the 12 months' time limit) it is possible to make use of the ordinary power of appropriation contained in s.41 of the Administration of Estates Act 1925. This power allows personal representatives to appropriate assets in or towards satisfaction of pecuniary legacies or entitlement under the intestacy rules provided the legatee or next-of-kin consents and provided no specific legatees are prejudiced. The power is freely available and the court's consent is not normally required. However, the spouse or civil partner has no right to insist on such an appropriation and so must seek the agreement of the personal representatives.

As with the right of election under the 1952 Act a spouse who is a sole personal representative must take care not to breach the rule against self-dealing. In *Radley-Kane* (1998) the second wife of the intestate acted as the sole administrator, despite the fact that there were children of the intestate, on the basis that the value of the estate was below the limit of her statutory legacy. She appropriated to herself shares in a private company which had been valued for probate purposes at £50,000. Two years after the death she sold the shares for over £1.1m. The court held that the appropriation of assets in satisfaction of a pecuniary legacy due to a personal representative was in clear contravention of the self-dealing rule. The administrator should either have obtained the consent of the beneficiaries or sought directions from the court. The court did, however, accept that an appropriation would be permitted if the assets were equivalent to cash (for example, government stock or quoted shares).

Abolition of hotchpot

3.16 The Law Reform (Succession) Act 1995 s.1(2), abolished the requirement under the Administration of Estates Act 1925 s.49(1)(aa) that surviving spouses bring benefits received by will into account against entitlement on intestacy. Thus, there is no longer any hotchpot requirement for surviving spouses (or civil partners). This applies in respect of deaths on or after January 1, 1996.

6. THE RIGHTS OF ISSUE

General

3.17 As we saw in para.3.05, above, after the surviving spouse or civil partner, the issue are the next category of next-of-kin who share in the deceased's estate. The issue take their share of the estate on the statutory trusts. If a spouse or civil partner survives, the issue take one-half of the residuary estate after the statutory legacy has been deducted as well as an interest in remainder following the life interest of the surviving spouse or civil partner in the other half. If there is no surviving spouse or civil partner then the issue take the whole residuary estate.

The statutory trusts

3.18 The "statutory trusts" are set out in the Administration of Estates Act 1925 s.47. Under this section the property is held equally for the children of the intestate who are either alive or *en ventre sa mere* at the date of the intestate's death. The children who satisfy this requirement have a mere contingent interest unless and until they reach 18 or marry under that age.

If a child dies under 18 and without marrying or forming a civil partnership, the property is dealt with as if that child had never existed.

So far, we have only referred to "children" since it is children who are the primary beneficiaries under this heading. However, if a child predeceases the intestate and that child leaves issue at the date of death, those grandchildren or their issue take *per stirpes* the share which their parent would have taken provided those issue reach 18 or marry or form a civil partnership under that age.

Example 1   **3.19**

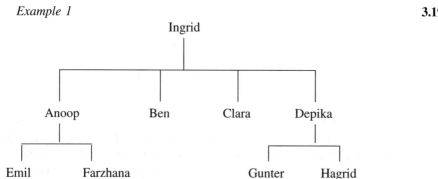

Clara and Depika predeceased Ingrid who died intestate. Anoop, Ben and all the grandchildren are over 18. The estate will be divided into three parts. Anoop and Ben each have vested interests in one-third of the estate. Clara has predeceased the intestate without leaving issue and has no entitlement. Depika has predeceased the intestate but has left issue. Depika's issue divide her share equally between them so that Gunter and Hagrid take one-sixth of the estate each. If Gunter or Hagrid had also predeceased Ingrid but were survived by children, the children would have shared the property that would have passed to their parent provided they satisfied the statutory trusts.

Example 2   **3.20**

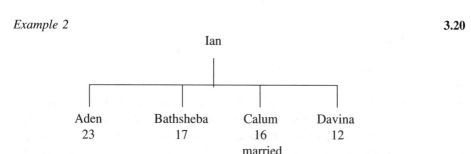

Ian died intestate; all the children survived Ian. Aden and Calum have vested interests immediately on the death of the intestate. If they die before receiving their share of the deceased's property, their share will pass to their estates. Bathsheba and Davina have only contingent interests and, therefore, if either dies without attaining the age of 18 or marrying, her share of the estate will be divided amongst Ian's other children.

3.21   *Example 3*

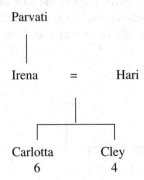

Irena dies intestate, survived by her husband Hari, her two children and her mother, Parvati. Hari, therefore, receives the personal chattels, the £250,000 statutory legacy (plus interest) and a life interest in one-half of the residue. The other half of the residue is held on the statutory trusts for the two children. If either dies unmarried and before reaching the age of 18, the property will be held for the other on the statutory trusts. If both die unmarried and before reaching 18, the estate is dealt with as if they had never existed. Hari will be entitled to a statutory legacy of £450,000 (plus interest) and the residue of the estate will be shared equally by him with Parvati, Irena's mother.

The fact that persons who fail to reach the age of 18 or marry earlier are dealt with as if they had never existed means that property may pass to someone (Parvati, in this example) who appeared to have no entitlement at the moment of death. Furthermore, if Hari and Parvati survive Irena but both die before Carlotta and Cley, Hari and Parvati's estates could both benefit. This is because the property is distributed as it would have been at the date of Irena's death had neither Carlotta nor Cley existed.

Hotchpot

Abolition of hotchpot

3.22   The Law Reform (Succession) Act 1995 s.1(2) abolishes the requirement under the Administration of Estates Act 1925 ss.47(1)(iii) and 49(1)(a) that children and issue bring lifetime advances and benefits received by will into account against entitlement on intestacy. Thus, there is no longer any hotchpot requirement for children or issue. This applies in respect of deaths on or after January 1, 1996.

Adopted, legitimate and illegitimate children

Adopted children

For the purposes of entitlement under an intestacy arising on or after January 1,   **3.23**
1976, s.39 of the Adoption Act 1976 provides that an adopted child is the
legitimate child of its adoptive parent or parents and of no one else. (This rule
applies if the adoption order was made by a court in the UK, the Isle of Man or
the Channel Islands. The same rule applies to certain foreign adoptions.) The
child is thus debarred from claiming on the intestacy of its natural parents and is
treated as a child of the adopting parents. Such a child may therefore be entitled
to take on the intestacy of adoptive grandparents and brothers and sisters.

Legitimated children

Sections 5(1)–(4) and 10(1) of the Legitimacy Act 1976 provide that a legiti-   **3.24**
mated child is entitled to share in a deceased's intestacy as if it had been born
legitimate.

Children whose parents were not married at the time of their birth

In the case of deaths occurring before the coming into force of the Family Law   **3.25**
Reform Act 1987, an illegitimate relationship was not recognised for the purposes of distribution of property on intestacy subject to two limited exceptions.

In respect of deaths occurring after April 4, 1988, the distribution of assets on
intestacy (and otherwise) is to be determined without regard to whether or not the
parents of a particular person were married to each other.

Section 20 of the 1987 Act removes the protection which existed under the old
law for personal representatives who distributed property in ignorance of the
existence of illegitimate claimants. Prima facie, it appears, therefore, that personal representatives should undertake investigations to discover whether or not
there are hitherto unknown relatives of the deceased alive whose parents were not
married. Presumably, however, the protection against claimants of the estate
available generally to personal representatives under the Trustee Act 1925 s.17
and the *Benjamin Order* procedure (see Ch.14, below) extends to cover the
claims of persons whose parents were not married. Moreover, s.18(2) of the
Family Law Reform Act makes special provision for the administration of an
intestate's estate. It provides that where the parents of a child who dies intestate
were not married to each other at the time of that child's birth there is a
presumption that the child has not been survived by *"his father or by any person
related to him only through his father"*. Thus, personal representatives will be
able, in the absence of evidence to the contrary, to distribute on the basis that no
such persons are alive.

Examples

(1) X, whose parents have not married, dies intestate without a spouse or issue. He is known to be survived by his mother but nothing is known of his father or of his father's relatives. X's mother will take the whole estate since the personal representatives are entitled to presume that the father and the father's relatives have predeceased X.

(2) As above, X, whose parents did not marry, has died intestate without a spouse or issue. His mother is dead and the only relative on his mother's side still living is her brother of the whole blood (X's maternal uncle). Nothing is known of X's father or of any of the father's relatives except that the father's brother of the whole blood is known to be alive (X's paternal uncle). X's estate will be divided between the two uncles. X's personal representatives are entitled to presume that the father and father's relatives other than the brother have predeceased X.

Human Fertilisation and Embryology Act 2009

3.26 As we have already seen (para.3.06, above) a child may be treated as the child of one or both parents as a result of the provisions of this act.

7. The Rights of Others

3.27 It should be noted that the other relatives who take on the statutory trusts (that is brothers and sisters of the whole and half blood and uncles and aunts of the whole or half blood) must fulfil the same requirements as issue; that is, they must be living at the intestate's death and reach 18 or marry earlier. A person who predeceases the intestate can be replaced *per stirpes* by their own issue provided they reach the age of 18 marry or enter a civil partnership earlier.

There has never been any hotchpot requirement for other relatives.

8. Bona vacantia

3.28 In the case of property passing as bona vacantia s.46(1)(vi) of the Administration of Estates Act 1925 gives the Crown a discretion to make provision for dependants of the intestate whether they are related to the deceased or not. Similarly the Crown may provide for "other persons for whom the intestate might reasonably have been expected to make provision".

If the intestate died resident within the Duchy of Lancaster or in Cornwall, the Duchy or the Duke of Cornwall respectively take the assets as bona vacantia subject to the same discretions.

The policy and the criteria applied by the Treasury Solicitor in making discretionary grants have been published since December 2002. (See The Treasury Solicitor Bona Vacantia Division, *Guide to discretionary grants in estates cases* (2005), para.31(a).)

When deciding whether to make a discretionary grant, and deciding upon its value, the factors which the Treasury Solicitor considers are:

(1) the size and nature of the estate;

(2) the length and nature of the relationship between the deceased and the applicant;

(3) any legal or moral obligations the deceased had towards the applicant;

(4) the way in which the applicant behaved towards the deceased (including the contribution, if any, made by the applicant to the deceased's welfare); and

(5) any other matter which in the particular circumstances the Treasury Solicitor considers relevant.

These factors are similar to, but not the same as, the considerations to which the court must have regard in exercising its jurisdiction under the Inheritance (Provision for Family and Dependants) Act 1975. There is substantial overlap between the making of discretionary grants and the law of family provision. Where the applicant for a grant is entitled to make a claim under the 1975 Act, it is the Treasury Solicitor's policy to require the applicant to bring proceedings under the Act. This enables the Crown to ensure that all those entitled to claim are party to any compromise that is reached and thereby to minimise the risk of a late and unanticipated claim being made once the estate has been administered. The requirement may, however, be waived so if the estate is modest in size (below £20,000), or if it would not be reasonable to expect the applicant to pursue an application under the 1975 Act (typically on grounds of frailty due to old age or ill health), the Crown may make grants without requiring prior commencement of action.

Potential applicants for a discretionary payment do not have to be eligible to make a claim under the 1975 Act. **3.29**

There may be circumstances where it is advantageous to claim under bona vacantia rather than under the 1975 Act. For example, cohabitants who claim reasonable financial provision under the 1975 Act, can only receive what is reasonable for their maintenance. There is no such restriction on claims under the bona vacantia jurisdiction.

That said, it is rare for estates to be genuinely bona vacantia. Genealogists are so skilled that they will normally be able to trace next of kin.

CHAPTER FOUR

INHERITANCE TAX

1. INTRODUCTION

Definitions

Inheritance tax is, prima facie, payable where there is a *chargeable transfer.* A **4.01** chargeable transfer is defined as "any *transfer of value* which is made to an individual but is not . . . an exempt transfer" (Inheritance Tax Act 1984 (IHTA) s.2(1)). A transfer of value is defined in IHTA 1984 s.3(1) as "a *disposition* made by a person . . . as a result of which the value of his estate immediately after the transfer is less than it would be but for the disposition . . . ". The amount by which the value of the transferor's estate is less as a result of the disposition is the *value transferred* on which inheritance tax is prima facie payable.

Lifetime transfers of value occur as a result of gifts of property or sales at an undervalue. Section 4 of the IHTA 1984 provides that a deceased person is to be treated as if they had made a transfer of value immediately before their death the value of which is equal to the value of their whole estate immediately before death.

The "estate" is the aggregate of all the property to which a deceased person was beneficially entitled immediately before death (IHTA 1984 s.5) apart from certain types of interest in possession (IHTA 1984 s.5(1)(a)(ii)) and excluded property (IHTA 1984 s.5(1)(b)). In fact the charge on death is the most important type of charge as lifetime transfers are normally exempt or potentially exempt (in the latter case they become exempt if the donor survives seven years) unless they are to settlements in which case they are normally immediately chargeable.

The structure of inheritance tax is rather complicated as the outline above will show. This is largely because the tax is a modification of capital transfer tax. Capital transfer tax was a tax on both lifetime and death transfers (with far less extensive exemptions than apply to inheritance tax). The Act which is now called the Inheritance Tax Act 1984 was formerly the Capital Transfer Tax Act 1984. That Act in its unamended form continues to apply to certain transactions entered into before March 18, 1986. References in documents (for example, wills) made before that date to capital transfer tax are taken as references to inheritance tax.

Occasions of charge to inheritance tax

4.02   There are three categories of transfer which can give rise to inheritance tax (exemptions or reliefs may be available to extinguish or reduce a charge—these are dealt with later).

(a) *A transfer on death.* Such a transfer is taxed at the full rates of tax.

(b) *A potentially exempt transfer.* This is defined in IHTA 1984 s.3A as a lifetime transfer of value made on or after March 18, 1986 by an individual, which would otherwise be chargeable, whereby property becomes comprised in the estate of another individual to the extent that it constitutes a gift:

   (i) to another individual;

   (ii) into a disabled trust;

   (iii) made before March 22, 2006 into an accumulation and main-tenance trust or a trust with a qualifying interest in possession; or

   (iv) made on or after March 22, 2006 into a trust for a bereaved minor or young person on the coming to an end of an immediate post-death interest.

The most common example of a potentially exempt transfer is an outright gift to an individual. However, a potentially exempt transfer can arise when the transferor omits to exercise a right (such as by failing to sue on a debt).

The taxation of settlements and trusts is dealt with in Ch.7 but, as we will see there, before March 22, 2006 a transfer of value by an individual into a settlement with an interest in possession was a poten-tially exempt transfer.

A potentially exempt transfer becomes fully exempt if the transferor survives seven years after the transfer. If they die within seven years the transfer becomes chargeable at the rates in force at the date of death (see below for the calculation of tax and the reduction where the transferor survives more than three years).

(c) *A chargeable transfer* made before death. This type of transfer is immediately taxable but at only half the rates which apply on death. If the transferor dies within seven years the transferee becomes taxable at the full rates in force at the date of the death.

As a result of changes introduced by the Finance Act 2006 most lifetime transfers made to settlements on or after March 22, 2006 are chargeable. The only exception is a transfer to a trust for a disabled beneficiary (see Ch.7, below). Lifetime transfers made before March 22, 2006 to settlements were chargeable only if they were to a settle-ment without a qualifying interest in possession which did not qualify as an accumulation and maintenance settlement (see Ch.7, below).

In addition to transfers to settlements, lifetime chargeable transfers can arise in relation to events occurring within settlements without a qualifying interest in possession; for example, anniversary charges and exit charges (see Ch.7, below).

2. The Estate on Death

What is included?

Section 5 of the IHTA 1984 provides that a person's estate is the aggregate of all **4.03** the property to which they are beneficially entitled at the moment before death other than excluded property and certain interests in possession (see IHTA 1984 s.5(1)(a)(ii)). A person who has a general power which enables them, or would if they were sui juris enable them, to dispose of any property as they think fit shall be treated as beneficially entitled to that property. This provision has enabled the Revenue to include in a death estate the whole of a bank account which was held in joint names but which, in reality, was operated for the benefit of only the deceased. See *Sillars v IRC* (2004); *Perry v CIR* (2005); *O'Neill v IRC* (1998). The provision was used in *Kempe v CIR* (2004) to include the proceeds of a life policy which the deceased had designated in favour of family members on the basis that the deceased had the right to change the designation at any time.

The estate at death also includes property subject to a *donatio mortis causa* (a gift made before death in anticipation of death and conditional upon it occurring). Although delivery of the asset or the means of obtaining it will have been made, it will still be treated as part of the deceased's estate for inheritance tax purposes.

Beneficial entitlement does not include property held in a fiduciary capacity. In *Anand v IRC* (1997) bank accounts held in the name of the deceased were held not to be part of the estate because they represented "family money" held by him in a fiduciary capacity as "treasurer".

The deceased's beneficial interest in property passing by survivorship is part of the estate because the deceased was entitled to it immediately *before* the death.

The estate will include the value of the property held in a settlement in which the deceased had an interest in possession if:

(a) the interest was in existence on March 22, 2006; or

(b) the interest is:

    (i) an immediate post-death interest,
    (ii) a transitional serial interest, or
    (iii) a disabled person's interest.

As a result of sub-s.1B (inserted by the Finance Act 2010 to prevent tax avoidance), the estate will include interests in possession to which a person becomes entitled on or after December 9, 2009 where the original transfer was not a transfer of value because it fell within IHTA 1984 s.10 (no gratuitous intent). Settled property will be discussed in Ch.7.

Excluded property

4.04 Excluded property does not form part of the owner's estate on death for inheritance tax purposes so that, in effect, it is exempt from tax. As far as lifetime transfers are concerned the position is slightly more complicated. A lifetime transfer of excluded property is not a chargeable or potentially exempt transfer unless the transfer causes a reduction in value of non-excluded property in which case there is, to the extent of that reduction, a chargeable or potentially exempt transfer as the case may be.

There are three main categories of excluded property:

(a) Reversionary interests in settled property unless, as provided in IHTA 1984 s.48:

   (i) acquired for money or money's worth;
  (ii) vested in the settlor or settlor's spouse; or
 (iii) expectant on a lease for life at a nominal rent;

(b) Most types of property situated outside the UK and owned by a person domiciled outside the UK and some types of property situated in the UK but owned by a person not domiciled in the UK (IHTA 1984 s.6); and

(c) Settled property situate outside the UK provided the settlor was domiciled outside the UK when the settlement was made.

Section 6(1B) of IHTA 1984 provides that a decoration or other award awarded for valour or gallant conduct is excluded property provided it has never been the subject of a disposition for a consideration in money or money's worth.

Liabilities

4.05 Liabilities are taken into account in valuing a transferor's estate to the extent that they were incurred for consideration in money or money's worth or imposed by law (IHTA 1984 s.5) and provided there is no right to reimbursement (IHTA 1984 s.162(1)). In the case of death, the value of the estate for tax purposes is the net amount after deducting debts (and other liabilities incurred for consideration) and liabilities imposed by law (such as a liability to pay damages in tort).

Reasonable funeral expenses can be deducted (IHTA 1984 s.172) including a reasonable sum for mourning for family and servants. The cost of a gravestone or tombstone. Is also deductible. Paragraph IHTM10373 of the IHT Manual states that in deciding what is reasonable HMRC should take account of the deceased's background and profession and may "distinguish between a gravestone and a memorial, which could be a plaque inside a church or a memorial monument. This is because a memorial is not strictly allowable as a reasonable funeral expense". Paragraph 10371 states that deductions claimed should normally be accepted without enquiry unless the expenses seem to be: "wholly unreasonable or large in relation to the estate as a whole, or inconsistent with information on the file."

A mortgage or other liability which is an incumbrance on particular property is taken as reducing the value of that property (rather than the estate generally) so far as that is possible. At first sight this rule might seem unimportant since the whole net value of the estate is taxable anyway but it is relevant where exemptions, such as the spouse exemption (see para.4.23, below), are available.

For example, an estate consists of a house worth £100,000 and £100,000 cash. The house is subject to a mortgage of £10,000. The value of the estate on death is, therefore, £190,000 for tax purposes. If the house is given to the spouse of the deceased and the cash to children an asset worth £90,000 will pass to the spouse and will be exempt (since the mortgage reduces the value of the property given to the spouse). The remaining £100,000 will be regarded as passing to non-exempt beneficiaries and, therefore, chargeable to inheritance tax. If the mortgage reduced the value of the estate generally, an asset worth £100,000 would have passed to the spouse (and been exempt) leaving £90,000 to be regarded as passing to the non-exempt beneficiaries (and chargeable to inheritance tax).

The rule is also significant where the estate includes property eligible for 100 per cent relief. For example, an estate consists of property worth £100,000 eligible for 100 per cent business property relief and £100,000 quoted shares. There is a liability of £100,000. If the liability is charged on the property eligible for relief, it will reduce the value of that property leaving the £100,000 of quoted shares chargeable to tax. If the liability is charged on the quoted shares, none of the estate will be chargeable to tax.

The value of property qualifying for business property relief cannot be increased by charging business debts on non-business property. It is, however, possible to do this in the case of assets qualifying for agricultural property relief.

Unrelieved debts of an insolvent deceased are not deductible from the value of settled property in which the deceased had an interest in possession at the date of death. See *St Barbe Green v IRC* (2005). The same principle applies where property is treated as part of the estate under the reservation of benefit rules.

4.06 The fact that a guarantee in support of a business has been charged over a particular asset does not mean that the asset is a business asset. See *IRC v Mallender* (2001).

Incidental costs of transferring assets are ignored in calculating the value transferred unless they are incurred by the transferee in which case they reduce the value transferred. This rule has no application to transfers on death because the transfer on death (which takes place for tax purposes the moment before death) is an automatic transfer on which no incidental costs can arise.

Where an estate includes property situated outside the UK, an allowance is made against that property for any expense incurred in administering or realising the property which is shown to be attributable to the situation of the property. The allowance cannot exceed 5 per cent of the value of the property.

A liability to pay an insurance company a sum from the death estate in return for a payment from the company is not deductible unless the policy proceeds form part of the death estate.

Section 103 of the Finance Act 1986 provides that a liability consisting of a debt incurred by the deceased or an incumbrance created by them shall not be deductible to the extent that the consideration given for the debt consists of "property derived from the deceased".

Example 1

Mother gives money to son who lends it back to her. On Mother's death the debt owed to the son is not deductible.

The so-called "loan" or nil rate band debt scheme involves a surviving spouse incurring a liability to the estate of the first spouse to die which reduces the value of the survivor's estate on death. This arrangement was very popular before the introduction of the transferable nil rate band as a way of allowing the first spouse to die to make use of their nil rate band while allowing the surviving spouse to have the benefit of the couple's combined assets. Section 103 could cause problems in relation to such schemes.

First, let's look at an example showing the circumstances in which the debt arrangement might be used.

Example 2

First spouse to die (H) gives a nil rate band legacy to a discretionary trust for the benefit of his wife (W) and children and the residue of the estate to W. The estate is £425,000 of which the matrimonial home is £325,000. Instead of the executors using liquid funds to pay the legacy, they transfer all the assets to W and either accept an IOU from the spouse which they then give to the trustees of the nil rate band settlement or transfer the assets to the spouse subject to a charge for the amount due to the trust. W has the use of all the assets and when she dies there is a liability which reduces the value of her estate. The Revenue accepts that the arrangement works when "properly drafted". The will must give the trustees power to accept the debt in lieu of cash and should relieve them from liability if there are insufficient funds to pay off the debt when W dies. The Revenue has said that stamp duty land tax is payable if the surviving spouse gives an IOU but not if the assets are transferred subject to a charge placed on the assets by the personal representatives. The charge must not give the trustees any rights to claim the debt from the spouse personally; their rights must be against the asset only.

Now let's look at the circumstances in which s.103 might present a problem.

Example 3

The facts are as above but some time before H's death W gave H a substantial gift as part of an equalisation of estates exercise. If W incurs a debt in connection with H's estate, the Revenue will argue that s.103 makes the debt non-deductible. They were successful with this argument in the case of *PRs of Phizackerley v HMCR* (2007).

If a couple wants to use the debt arrangement and s.103 may be a problem because one spouse has made gifts to the other, one solution is to leave the residue to the survivor for life so that it is the trustees of the settlement who incur the debt not the spouse. Another possibility is for the executors to charge the assets transferred to W with the debt so that they do not incur the debt. However, s.103 problems will still arise if the house is sold and the trustees then advance funds to W for the purchase of a replacement property. In such a case, provided the trustees have power to do so, they could use the funds available from the repayment of the charge to buy an interest in the replacement property with the surviving spouse.

Since the introduction of the transferable nil rate band, debt arrangements are used much less frequently as the first spouse (or civil partner) to die can leave everything to the survivor and transfer the unused nil rate band to the survivor.

3. THE CALCULATION OF TAX

Two rates of tax

In respect of transfers made before March 15, 1988 the rates of tax were **4.07** "progressive", that is to say, the rate of tax increased as the total of taxable gifts made by the transferor increased. However, in respect of transfers made on or after that date there are only two rates of tax. There is a nil rate band and, once that has been exhausted, tax is charged on further transfers at the rate of 40 per cent. The nil rate band was increased to £325,000 in 2009/2010 and has been frozen at that figure until 2014/15.

Cumulation

In order to establish whether or not the nil rate band has been exhausted in **4.08** respect of a particular chargeable transfer, it is necessary to take into account all previous chargeable transfers made by the transferor within the seven years before the present transfer (IHTA 1984 s.7(1)). This is called the principle of cumulation. The present transfer is added to all the previous transfers in the last seven years and the tax is then calculated as if the present transfer were the highest part of a single transfer equal to all the transfers (including the present one) made within the last seven years. It is therefore taxed at 40 per cent to the extent that it exceeds the nil rate band.

The full rate of 40 per cent applies where the transfer is made on death or was made before death but death follows within *three* years. If the transfer is a chargeable transfer made before death the tax charged at the time of the transfer is at half the full rates (IHTA 1984 s.7(2)). If the transfer is a potentially exempt transfer or a chargeable transfer and death occurs within seven years (but not less than three years) of the transfer, the tax is charged on the value of the transfer (at the date it was made) at the following percentage of the full rates in force at the time of death:

(a) where the transfer is made more than three years but not more than four years before the death, 80 per cent;

(b) where the transfer is made more than four years but not more than five years before the death, 60 per cent;

(c) where the transfer is made more than five but not more than six years before the death, 40 per cent;

(d) where the transfer is made more than six but not more than seven years before the death, 20 per cent.

(IHTA 1984 s.7(4)).

In the case of a *chargeable* transfer made before death the reduction in the rates mentioned above will be available only to the extent that it does not reduce the amount of tax due on that transfer below the amount originally paid on the lifetime transfer. Thus, no refund of tax is allowed.

Examples

4.09

(1) On October 1, 2010 A makes a potentially exempt transfer to B, her nephew, of £455,000. A has made no previous chargeable transfers. The potentially exempt transfer is treated initially as one which will prove to be exempt. No inheritance tax is payable at the time of the transfer. (For the purposes of this illustration and the following ones in this section exemptions and reliefs are ignored.)

If A dies within three years of the transfer, the potentially exempt transfer becomes chargeable and tax will become payable at the full rates in force at the date of death. Thus, assuming that the 2010/11 rates are still in force at the time of the transferor's death, the first £325,000 will be taxed at nil per cent and the remaining £130,000 will be taxed at 40 per cent; a total of £52,000 will be payable.

If A dies more than three years after but within seven years of the transfer, the potentially exempt transfer becomes chargeable but at only a percentage of the full rate in force at the date of the death. Thus, assuming that the 2010/11 rates are still in force at the time of the transferor's death and A's death was within four years of the transfer, tax will be charged at 80 per cent of the full rate, that is:

$$\frac{80}{100} \times £52,000 = £41,600$$

(2) On October 1, 2013 (when the nil rate band is still £325,000) S makes a chargeable transfer to a settlement of £455,000. S has made no other chargeable transfers. As explained in the previous example, tax calculated at the full rate on such a transfer would be £52,000. Since this is a lifetime transfer tax is payable at half that rate so £26,000 will be payable.

(3) Having made the chargeable transfer of £455,000 referred to in the previous example, S dies three years and six months later when the table of rates provides for (say) £355,000 to be taxed at a nil rate and the balance at 40 per cent. The recalculation of tax on the transfer will give a tax figure of:

	Rate		Amount
£ £	%		£
0 – 355,000	0	=	Nil
355,000 – 455,000	40	=	40,000
			40,000

Only 80 per cent of that tax figure of £40,000 is payable since death occurred more than three years after the transfer. Thus,

$$\text{Tax payable on death } \frac{80}{100} \times £40,000 = £32,000$$

Credit must be given for any tax already paid. Thus,

	£
Tax payable on death	32,000
Less: Lifetime tax paid	(26,000)
Extra tax now payable	6,000

If the table of rates on S's death provides for (say) £385,000 to be taxed at a nil rate and the balance at 40 per cent the recalculation would give a tax figure of:

	Rate		Amount
£ £	%		£
0 – 385,000	0	=	Nil
385,000 – 455,000	40	=	28,000
			28,000

Only 80 per cent of that tax figure of £28,000 is payable since death occurred more than three years after the transfer. Thus,

$$\text{Tax payable on death } \frac{80}{100} \times £28,000 = £22,400$$

At the time the lifetime transfer was made £26,000 was paid in tax. No reclaim is, however, permitted so there will simply be no extra tax payable on death.

As we explained briefly above, when deciding which rates of tax are to be charged on a particular chargeable transfer it is necessary to take into account all previous chargeable transfers made within seven years before the present transfer. An illustration may be helpful. For the purposes of this illustration exemptions and reliefs have been ignored.

4.10   *Example*

A is single and has made no previous chargeable transfers. He makes the following lifetime transfers:

May 20, 2009	£100,000 to X, an individual
May 20, 2010	£425,000 to Y, a discretionary trust
May 20, 2015	£130,000 to X, an individual
Dec 20, 2016	A dies, owning £360,000 of assets

Since the 2009 transfer is potentially exempt, it is assumed that it will prove to be an exempt transfer until either seven years expires or the transferor dies within that period. Therefore, no tax is payable in 2009 and the transfer is not cumulated with the chargeable transfer to Y made in 2010. On May 20, 2016 the 2009 transfer actually becomes exempt.

The transfer to Y in 2010 is a chargeable transfer made before death and as such is taxed at half the full rates of tax. Tax will be calculated as follows:

£		£	Rate %		Amount £
0	–	325,000	0	=	Nil
325,000	–	425,000	20	=	20,000

Therefore £20,000 will be payable in 2010.

The 2015 transfer is potentially exempt and so, as with the 2009 transfer, no tax is paid at the time of the transfer.

On A's death in 2016 tax on the 2010 transfer will be recalculated at the full rates in force in tax year 2016/17. Since death has occurred more than six years after the transfer only 20 per cent of the full rates of tax is payable. If this is less than the £20,000 already paid then no refund is available.

As a result of A's death within seven years of the 2015 transfer, it becomes chargeable. In fact death has occurred within three years of the transfer and so tax will be calculated at the full rates in force in tax year 2016/17. As £425,000 of chargeable transfers have already been made the rates appropriate to a transfer from £425,000–£555,000 will be used. Finally, the tax due on the transfer on death will be calculated at the full rates for tax year 2016/17. As £555,000 of chargeable transfers have already been made in the seven years before death, the rates appropriate to a transfer from £555,000 to £915,000 will be used.

Transfer of unused nil rate band between spouses

4.11   On October 9, 2007 the Chancellor announced that where a spouse or civil partner dies on or after October 9, 2007 their personal representatives can claim an increase in their nil rate band for the purposes of the charge to tax on death if his spouse or civil partner died with a proportion of nil rate band unused. The nil rate band of the survivor is increased by the proportion that was unused on the first death. Finance Act 2008 inserted ss.8A–8C into IHTA 1984 to make the necessary amendments. However, the change took effect as from October 9, 2007.

The unused proportion of the nil rate band is normally claimed by the personal representatives who must do so within two years of the end of the month of death or such longer period as HMRC allow (s.8B(1)(a)).

It is irrelevant when the first spouse or civil partner died, whether or not they had any assets at the time of the death and where they were domiciled. What matters is the proportion of the nil rate band unused. The nil rate band of the survivor is increased on death by that proportion.

Example

Fred dies in 2002/03 when the nil rate band was £250,000. He used only half of it. His wife, Janet, died on October 9, 2007 when the nil rate band was £300,000. Janet's personal representatives can claim an additional 50 per cent of the nil rate band in force on Janet's death in addition to Janet's own nil rate band. So, if Janet made no lifetime chargeable transfers, there will be a nil rate band of £450,000 available to her death estate.

The unused proportion of the nil rate band of the first spouse to die can only **4.12** be transferred on death. It is not available against the tax payable on immediately chargeable lifetime transfers.

Example

Assume that Janet in the previous example had made a lifetime chargeable transfer on October 9, 2007 of £600,000 and died on June 9, 2010 (when the nil rate band was £325,000) with a death estate of £525,000, the position would be as follows.

On October 9, 2007 she would have only her own nil rate band available so the first £300,000 of the lifetime transfer would be taxed at 0 per cent and the remaining £300,000 would be taxed at 20 per cent.

When Janet dies on June 9, 2010 her personal representatives will be able to claim an additional £162,500 of nil rate band representing the unused proportion of Fred's nil rate band. This additional nil rate band can be set against the additional inheritance tax payable as a result of her death. Hence, on these figures it will be set against the lifetime transfer rather than the death estate.

There is no benefit to Janet's personal representatives in claiming the transferable nil rate band on these facts because it will be used entirely on the lifetime transfer and none will be available to the death estate. Section 8B(1)(b) provides that if no claim is made by the personal representatives within two years following the end of the month of death, any other person liable for tax chargeable as a result of the death can make a claim. The requirement to wait two years seems pointless and it is thought that HMRC would allow a claim from a lifetime transferee provided the personal representatives confirm that they will not be making a claim.

It is possible to take portions of unused nil rate band from any number of **4.13** previous spouses or civil partners. However, s.8A(6) restricts the additional nil rate band that can be inherited so no death estate can benefit by more than the value of one additional nil rate band.

There is an important planning point here. If a widow and widower marry each other having inherited a full nil rate band from their respective deceased spouses, neither can inherit any further nil rate band from the other. To avoid wasting their inherited nil rate bands they should consider creating nil rate band discretionary trusts in their wills for the benefit of their surviving spouse and issue. Each can transfer assets up to a double nil rate band without a payment of inheritance tax. (Note, however that the trust will have only a single nil rate band available so there will be ongoing anniversary and exit charges calculated on the excess: see Ch.7 for the taxation of settlements).

Section 8C makes provision for the position where tax deferred on the first death (for example in relation to heritage property or woodlands) becomes payable.

4.14   It does not matter how many years ago the first spouse or civil partner died so long as there was unused nil rate band. The nil rate band thresholds for inheritance tax, capital transfer tax and estate duty are available on the HMRC website. In the case of estate duty there was no spouse exemption for most of the life of the tax, so the nil rate band of the first to die may have been exhausted even though the whole estate was left to the surviving spouse. Nor does it matter how much or how little the first spouse to die owned. For example, if Joan dies in 1990 without any assets and her husband, Fred, dies in June 2010, Fred will have his own nil rate band of £325,000 available plus a further £325,000 transferred from Joan.

It is also irrelevant that the first spouse or civil partner died domiciled outside England and Wales. For example, Harry marries Susan, who is domiciled and resident in Australia. He moves to Australia. Susan dies in 2001 leaving everything to Harry. Harry moves back to England in 2005 and dies in 2010 domiciled in England and Wales. Harry's personal representatives can claim Susan's unused nil rate band.

HMRC will require documentation to show that there was a spouse/civil partner and that there was unused nil rate band so personal representatives should obtain certificates of death and marriage together with a copy of any will, IHT account, valuations of assets and details of matters such as lifetime gifts and property assigned by survivorship which reduce the nil rate band available. In the answers to the Frequently Asked Questions available on the HMRC website, HMRC recognises that it may not be possible to obtain all the relevant information where the first spouse died many years ago but clearly in the case of deaths occurring on or after October 9, 2007 it will be important to preserve all relevant information.

Grossing up

The basic principles

4.15   Where inheritance tax is paid by the donor (as it may be in the case of a chargeable transfer made before death), the loss to the donor resulting from the transfer is the value of the gift *plus* the inheritance tax on it. It is on this gross figure that inheritance tax is payable. In such a case the value of the *net* gift is known but in order to calculate the *gross* loss to the estate it is necessary to "gross up" the net gift. Inheritance tax is then calculated on the gross loss to the donor. In order to gross up a net figure, use the formula:

$$\text{Net amount} \times \frac{100}{100 - \text{net}}$$

Example

Andrew has made chargeable transfers which have exhausted his nil rate band. He now makes a chargeable transfer to a discretionary trust of £10,000 and agrees to pay the inheritance tax attributable to the transfer.

The tax payable is calculated by "grossing up" the gift of £10,000 that is by treating the £10,000 as a net amount the tax on which has been notionally deducted. The whole transfer falls within the 40 per cent tax band but as it is a transfer made *before* death tax will be charged at one-half the full rate, that is at 20 per cent. Thus, it can be seen that the gift is 80 per cent of the gross amount transferred.

The gross figure can, therefore, be found by multiplying the net amount by 100 and dividing it by 80.

$$\text{Net} \times \frac{100}{80} = \text{gross}$$

$$\text{i.e. £10,000} = \frac{100}{80} = £12,500$$

The difference between the gross and net amounts is the amount of the tax, i.e. £12,500 − £10,000 = £2,500.

Where inheritance tax is paid by the donee the gross loss to the donor is known and no grossing-up calculation is necessary.

Example

Alan has made chargeable transfers which have exhausted his nil rate band. He now makes a chargeable transfer to a discretionary trust of £10,000; the donee is to pay the inheritance tax attributable to the transfer.

The gross loss to the donor is £10,000. The transfer falls within the 40 per cent band but as it is a transfer made before death, the tax will be charged at one-half the full rate, that is at 20 per cent. The inheritance tax is, therefore:

$$£10,000 \times \frac{20}{100} = £2,000$$

Notice, that in the first example the donee receives £10,000 and the donor loses £12,500 whereas in the second example the donee receives £8,000 and the donor loses £10,000. In the case of lifetime transfers it is, therefore, important for the donor to consider carefully the amount they can afford to transfer and the amount they wish the donee to receive. Where the gift consists of an asset rather than cash, the problem may be particularly serious as neither donor nor donee may have sufficient cash available to pay the inheritance tax. However, if the *donee* is paying the tax it is possible in respect of certain types of property to elect to pay the tax by instalments (see para.4.53, below) and this will mitigate the problem.

Grossing-up is required on lifetime gifts whenever the *donor* pays the tax. The parties may agree that the donee will pay but if the donee fails to do so and the donor in fact pays, grossing-up is required.

Grossing-up is not normally required on the transfer of property forming part of the estate on death. The reason for this is that the tax on death is on the full value of the estate (subject to exemptions) not on the loss to the donor's estate. In very limited circumstances grossing-up is required to calculate the tax on death (see paras 4.53–4.58, below).

Where a potentially exempt or a chargeable transfer has been made and death occurs within seven years, tax may be payable as a result of the death. This is primarily the liability of the donee. As the donee will be paying the tax, the gift to the donee is a gross gift and no grossing-up is required.

Gifts involving more than one tax band

4.16   If a transferor makes a transfer of value part of which is taxed at nil per cent and part of which is taxed at 40 per cent, only the part falling within the 40 per cent tax band needs to be grossed-up.

Gifts within seven years of death—changes in value

4.17   The object of charging the full rates or a proportion of the full rates of tax on death within seven years of a transfer is to prevent donors who know they are about to die from saving tax by making lifetime transfers. It is, therefore, considered appropriate that relief from the extra tax should be given in certain cases where the value of the property transferred has declined between the transfer and the death. The rules which provide this relief are, in detail, very complex but their broad effect is to allow a decline in value of an asset to be deducted from the amount liable to the extra tax where the donee still owns the asset at the donor's death (see IHTA 1984 s.131). Where the asset has been sold before the donor's death by the donee (or their spouse) at a loss in a qualifying sale (which broadly means in a genuine commercial transaction) the decline in value between the date of the gift and the date of sale may be deducted from the amount liable to extra tax. Special rules apply to certain types of property (including land and shares) and no relief is given where the asset was tangible moveable property which had a predictable useful life of 50 years or less immediately before the transfer to the donee.

Section 31 merely reduces the value that is taxed not the value that is cumulated. This means that the cumulative total remains unchanged despite the fall in value of the asset and so there is no reduction in the tax chargeable on the death estate.

Gifts within seven years of death—changes of rate

4.18   When a potentially exempt transfer or chargeable transfer become taxable as the result of death within seven years, the rate of tax chargeable will be the rate in force at the date the gift was made except to the extent that rates have been reduced (IHTA 1984 Sch.2). This is quite a useful tax planning tool since it means that a transferor who fears that rates of tax may rise can make a gift now and guarantee that no increases in the rate of tax will affect the transfer. The transfer will, however, get the benefit of any reductions in rate—a rare example of having your tax cake and eating it.

Gifts with a reservation

The Finance Act 1986 contains special provisions in respect of property subject **4.19** to a reservation. Property is regarded as subject to a reservation where an individual transfers property by way of gift and *either* the donee does not bona fide assume possession and enjoyment within the relevant period *or* at any time in the relevant period the property is not enjoyed to the entire, or virtually the entire, exclusion of the donor. The relevant period is the period ending with the date of death of the deceased and beginning seven years earlier or at the date of the gift if it was made within seven years of the death.

In *Sillars v IRC* (2004) the deceased had put a bank account into the joint names of herself and her two daughters. Her personal representatives argued that only one third of the balance should be included in her estate at death but the Revenue contended successfully that she should be treated as entitled to the whole for inheritance tax purposes. There were two grounds for the decision. First the deceased had a general power or authority to deal with the account as she thought fit and, therefore, the account was part of her estate under IHTA 1984 s.5(2). Secondly, the account was part of her estate under the reservation of benefit rules because the gift was a gift of the chose in action of the whole account and she was clearly not excluded from benefit.

Membership of a class of discretionary beneficiaries will inevitably amount to a reservation of benefit. See *IRC v Eversden* (2002) and *Lyon's PRs v HMRC* (2007).

If a donor dies and there is property which is regarded as subject to a reservation at the date of their death, the property is treated for the purpose of inheritance tax as if it was part of their estate on death.

If property ceases to be subject to a reservation within the "relevant period" **4.20** the donor is treated as making a potentially exempt transfer at that date. This means that tax will be payable on the property which was subject to a reservation if the donor dies within seven years of the property ceasing to be subject to a reservation.

There is clearly the possibility of double charges to tax on the same property.

Example

A transferor gives a country cottage to his son in 2010 stipulating that he retains the right to spend holidays there for three months in the summer for the next four years. He dies in 2015. The initial transfer in 2010 is a PET (arguably the value transferred is reduced because of the transferor's entitlement to occupation). The termination of the right to holidays after four years in 2014 is a PET equal in value of the right to occupation. Because this is a "deemed" PET it cannot be reduced by annual exemptions. When the transferor dies in 2015 both PETs become chargeable.

Had the transferor died before their right of occupation ceased, the continued reservation of benefit would mean that the entire value of the cottage would have been included in his estate for inheritance purposes. Note that the inclusion in the estate is a fiction and is only relevant for inheritance tax purposes. The house would not be treated as part of the transferor's estate for capital gains tax purposes so there would be no uplift in value on the death of the transferor; nor would main residence relief be available on a lifetime disposal.

The Inheritance Tax (Double Charges Relief) Regulations 1987 provide a measure of relief in the case of double charges. They require alternative calculations to be made. It is necessary to consult the Rules carefully since the procedure varies according to the types of transfer involved.

Exceptions to the reservation of benefit rules

4.21 There are exceptions to the reservation of benefit rules. The gifted property must be enjoyed to the entire or *virtually* the entire exclusion of the donor so de minimis benefits can be ignored. The Revenue's views on what amounts to de minimis are set out in Revenue Interpretation 55 (November 93). Under the Finance Act 1986 ss.102A(3), 102B(3)(b) and Sch.20 para.6(1)(a) the reservation of benefit rules do not apply to an interest in land or enjoyment of a chattel if the donor provides full consideration. The consideration must be full throughout the relevant period so rent review clauses should be included in any agreement.

In the case of land, there will be no reservation of benefit if a donor has to go into occupation because there has been an unexpected change in circumstances and, as a result of old age or infirmity or otherwise, the donor is unable to maintain themselves (Finance Act 1986 Sch.20 para.6).

Section 102B of the Finance Act 1986 contains two "get outs" from the reservation of benefit rules where the donor makes a gift of an undivided share in land.

(a) There is no reservation of benefit where the donor makes a gift of a share in land; the donor and donee both occupy the land; and the donor receives no benefit connected with the gift other than a negligible one (s.4). This exception is designed to cover the situation where, for example, an elderly parent gives an interest in the family home to an adult child and both occupy the property. It is fatal if the whole house is given away or if the child moves out. In both cases the requirements of the section are not fulfilled and the reservation of benefit rules will apply (unless the donor can pay full consideration for the occupation). The donee must not pay more than a fair share of the running costs or the donor will receive a benefit. The section replaces an earlier, more restricted, exception based on a statement made in parliament in 1986 when the reservation of benefit rules were first introduced.

(b) There is no reservation of benefit where the donor makes a gift of a share in land and does not occupy the land (s.3). This exception would apply where the donor gives away let land and continues to enjoy the rental income.

The reservation of benefit rules are very troublesome to taxpayers who are trying to enjoy their assets while reducing their exposure to inheritance tax and there have been a number of ingenious attempts to capitalise on loopholes in the legislation.

Taxpayers have largely been successful in court but have then found the loophole blocked by legislation.

(a) Section 102(5) of the Finance Act 1986 provides that the reservation of benefit rules have no application where there is a disposal to a spouse which is exempt under IHTA 1984 s.18. In *IRC v Eversden* (2003) the Court of Appeal held that if a gift is exempt *at the time it is made,* the reservation of benefit rules cannot have any application at a later date. The duration of the proprietary interest gifted to the spouse is irrelevant. This meant, for example, that a wife could settle property on her husband for life but subject to an overriding power of appointment in favour of a class of beneficiaries including herself. After a short period (say six months) the trustees could terminate the husband's interest so that the discretionary trusts came into effect. The reservation of benefit rules would not apply to the trusts following the husband's life interest. This loophole was closed in relation to disposals made on or after June 20, 2003. A new s.102(5B) provides that the effect of the spouse exemption is limited to the period that the spouse retains an interest in possession. If the interest is terminated, the settlor is treated as making a disposal immediately after the spouse's interest comes to an end. Hence, if H gave W a terminable life interest followed by discretionary trusts and W's interest is terminated, H will be treated as making a transfer on discretionary trusts and the spouse's interest in possession will be ignored.

(b) In *Ingram v IRC* (1999) Lady Ingram successfully divided her interest in property into a 20-year lease and a freehold reversion. The reversion was transferred to trustees to hold for the benefits of persons other than Lady Ingram. Lord Hoffman said that decided cases show that while the legislation prevents a man having his cake and eating it, there is nothing to stop him from *"carefully dividing up the cake, eating part of it and having the rest"*. The House of Lords accepted that a contemporaneous lease and gift of freehold was possible without creating a reservation of benefit.

The effect of the decision was reversed by very narrowly targeted legislation. Section 102A of the Finance Act 1986 provides that a donor will be treated as making a gift with a reservation if they:

(i) makes a gift of an interest in land; and

(ii) retains a "significant" right or interest in the land.

A right or interest is not "significant" if the donor pays full consideration for it nor if the interest was obtained at least seven years before the gift.

Taxpayers continued to develop ways round the reservation of benefit rules. For example, there are no provisions in Finance Act 1986 s.102 for tracing cash. Hence a taxpayer could give cash to a donee who would use the cash to buy property. The donor could benefit from the property without reserving a benefit.

4.22 Section 84 and Sch.15 of the Finance Act 2004 introduced an entirely new charge to income tax where a person gives away assets and enjoys benefits derived from those assets. The rules apply from 2005/06 and only catch benefits not within the reservation of benefit rules and the exceptons to them. Taxpayers who are liable to pay the pre-owned assets charge can opt out of that regime and into the IHT reservation of benefit provisions (Finance Act 2004 Sch.15 paras 21(2), 22(2) and (3)) by making an election.

The election must be made (using Form IHT 500) on or before the relevant filing date which is January 31 of the year of assessment that immediately follows the first year in which the taxpayer would otherwise be chargeable (unless they can show a reasonable excuse—Sch.15 para.23(3)). Once made, the election can be withdrawn or amended by the taxpayer but only before the relevant filing date (Sch.15 para.23(5)). It cannot be withdrawn by the taxpayer's PRs.

4. VALUATION OF PROPERTY

General rules

4.23 On a lifetime transfer the loss to the donor or on death the value of the estate will depend on the valuation of particular items of property.

Section 160 of the IHTA 1984 provides that:

> " . . . the value at any time of any property shall for the purposes of inheritance tax be the price which the property might reasonably be expected to fetch if sold in the open market at that time; but that price shall not be assumed to be reduced on the grounds that the whole property is to be placed on the market at one and the same time".

The market value of any property is a question of fact. If property is actually sold within a short period after death on the open market the price received will be evidence (though not conclusive evidence) of the market value at the date of death.

The qualification which prohibits the assumption that all the property is to be sold at the same time will not affect valuation in most cases but would be relevant in valuing a large holding of shares in a private company (or even in a public company if the holding was a significant proportion of the share capital).

Valuation on death

4.24 On death it is important that assets are valued at *market* value. The Revenue will normally want to see a statement in a professional valuation that it has been prepared on this basis or a letter instructing the valuer to prepare a valuation on this basis.

The following principles have been developed:

(a) *The sale on the open market is a hypothetical one between a vendor and purchaser*

It is assumed that the hypothetical purchaser would make the proper enquiries but would not appear too eager to buy; they embody the demand at the particular time for the property concerned (see *IRC v Gray (surviving executor of Lady Fox)* (1994)).

(b) *No deduction for notional expenses of hypothetical sale*

The notional expense of the hypothetical sale in the open market cannot be deducted from the open market price. (See Valuation Office Agency Inheritance Tax Manual, section 7.14) The open market value is the *gross* amount payable by a purchaser without deduction of any notional expenses: *Duke of Buccleuch v IRC* (1967) and *Executor of Price deceased v HMRC* (2010).

A partial exception to the "no expenses" rule is that allowance is made for additional costs of administration or realisation actually incurred in respect of foreign assets when valuing an estate on death: IHTA 1984 s.173.

(c) *The buyer is not a speculator*

The hypothetical vendor and purchaser are serious prudent men of business of the kind who buy and sell the asset in question. If in the real world there are no speculators in the kind of asset under consideration, it is not permissible to invent "*a hypothetical willing speculator*" (see *Bower v HMRC* (2008)).

(d) *Effect of restrictions on sale attached to the particular asset*

Restrictions on sale are ignored and the asset is deemed capable of being freely sold. However, the restrictions on a future sale by the purchaser would be taken into account in determining the price which that purchaser would be likely to pay. (*IRC v Crossman* (1937)).

In other words the question is "what would a purchaser have paid to enjoy the rights attached to the property at the relevant date?"

(e) *The hypothetical vendor acts to get the largest price possible*

For this purpose the estate may be divided into units for the purposes of sale or items of property may be lotted together for sale provided that such splitting or joining does not entail undue expenditure of time and effort (see *IRC v Gray (surviving executor of Lady Fox)* (1994) and *Executor of Price deceased v HMRC* (2010)).

(f) *Price which a "special" purchaser may be prepared to pay should be taken into account*

A special purchaser is a person to whom the property has special value and is therefore willing to pay more than an ordinary purchaser. Although the special purchaser is taken into account, there is no certainty that the special purchaser would succeed in buying the property.

Careful valuation on the basis of market value is particularly significant in the case of land. HMRC's guidance to completing IHT 400 states that the valuer should be asked to take into account any development or hope value. It also says that if, when the property is marketed at the valuation price, offers are received in excess of that valuation, this would suggest that the true value is higher.

In the August 2010 "Newsletter for Estates and Trusts Practitioners" HMRC recommended that in such cases taxpayers should "ask the valuer to reconsider and, if appropriate, amend the date of death value, taking into account such things as the length of time since the death and movements in the property market".

The December 2004 IHT Newsletter announced that from January 2005 the Revenue would be "paying close attention" to the values included for household and personal goods. Personal representatives should normally obtain a professional valuation or be able to explain the basis on which they have determined that such assets are valueless.

There may be cases where personal representatives need to obtain a grant of representation urgently and do not have time to obtain a professional valuation. In *Robertson v CIR* (2002) the Revenue demanded a penalty from a taxpayer who had estimated a value at substantially less than the final figure despite the fact that the taxpayer submitted a corrective account and paid the correct amount before the due date for payment. The Revenue argued that the executor had not fulfilled their obligation under IHTA 1984 s.216(3) to make the fullest inquiries that were reasonably practicable in the circumstances. The special commissioner held that the taxpayer had acted perfectly properly and in *Robertson v IRC (No 2)* (2002) he was awarded his expenses on the basis that the Revenue had acted "wholly unreasonably" in connection with the hearing. Subsequently the Revenue issued guidance in *IHT Newsletter* May 2002:

> "In most circumstances we would expect the exact value of property to be given when form IHT 200 is submitted and not merely an estimate. However, we accept that if there is a proven need to obtain a grant urgently personal representatives may find themselves in a position where they think that they need to submit an estimated account of the value of a particular item of property. In such circumstances they should ensure that they have made the fullest enquiries that are reasonably practicable before doing so, and the estimate should be as accurate as possible. The personal representative should, for example, contact the professional who is going to value the property formally to ensure that the estimate is a reasonable one. The Revenue is more than happy to discuss the circumstances of particular cases with personal representatives and their agents."

It is important that taxpayers do follow these instructions. In *Cairns v HMRC* a taxpayer completed the IHT Account on the basis of an estimated valuation but did not describe it as provisional or estimated. HMRC demanded a penalty when the property was sold for an amount substantially in excess of the valuation. The

Special Commissioners agreed that the failure to describe the valuation as an estimate was an error but held that on the facts it was "minor, technical and of no consequence". Clearly, however, it is preferable to avoid arguments with HMRC.

The transfer of value on death is a transfer of all property owned by the deceased *immediately before their death.* However, IHTA 1984 s.171(1) provides that "changes in the value of [the] estate which have occurred by reason of the death . . . shall be taken into account as if they had occurred before the death". The effect of this provision is to take into account changes in the market value of property which *result* from the death. Sometimes this will lead to an increase in the value of the estate, sometimes to a decrease.

For example, if the deceased is the managing director of a private company and owns a majority share holding in it, then the value of the shares may well decline because of the director's death. Such a decline is likely to occur wherever the goodwill of the company is dependent on the personal ability of the deceased and is particularly likely in cases where the deceased has no successor able and willing to continue to run the company's business.

An example of an increase in the value of property resulting from the death of **4.25** the owner is where the deceased owned a life insurance policy on their own life payable to their estate. Clearly, the value of the policy will increase as a result of the death from the surrender value of the policy to its capital value.

It is important to remember that the transfer on death is a transfer of the deceased's "estate", that is property to which the deceased was beneficially entitled (IHTA 1984 s.5). Thus, any item not in the deceased's beneficial enjoyment will not be part of the estate and will not attract inheritance tax. Always look at insurance policies closely to see whether or not they are part of the estate. A policy on the deceased's life owned beneficially by a third party does not form part of the deceased's estate and so no inheritance tax is payable on the proceeds of the policy on their death. Examples of policies not beneficially owned by the deceased are policies taken out under the Married Women's Property Act 1882 or written in trust for a third party.

Section 171 only allows changes in the *market* value of property to be taken into account, it does not allow changes in the value of the property *to the deceased* to be taken into account. For this reason the deceased's share in joint property (which passes to the remaining joint tenant by survivorship) is fully taxable. Although it is true that the value to the deceased's *estate* of the joint property is nil once the deceased is dead, this does not affect the market value of the *property.* However, where the deceased was a co-owner of land, it is normal when valuing the deceased's interest in residential property to allow a 15 per cent discount to reflect the fact that the surviving co-owner will have the right to continue in occupation—see *Wight v Commissioners of the Inland Revenue* (1982). Where the property is a commercial investment this factor is not relevant and the discount should be no more than 10 per cent unless the interest is a minority interest or there are other complicating factors—see *St-Clair Ford v Ryder* (2006). In certain circumstances co-owned property is valued by reference to the related property rules. See para.4.31, below.

Special valuation rules

Quoted shares

4.26 Quoted stocks and shares are normally valued by taking the lower of the two prices quoted in the Stock Exchange Daily Official List for the relevant day and adding to it one-quarter of the difference between the lower and higher prices there quoted (for example, if the Daily List shows 200p/205p the value will be 201.25p for inheritance tax purposes) or if it produces a lower figure by taking a figure halfway between the lowest and highest prices at which bargains were struck on the relevant day. The "relevant day" is the day of death or the last or next trading day before or after death. "Quoted" means listed on a recognised stock exchange (IHTA 1984 s.272).

Unquoted shares

4.27 In the case of shares not listed on the Stock Exchange, although recent bargains will be taken as a starting point, other factors may lead to a different value being adopted (SP 18/80).

The valuation of unquoted shares is factually very difficult but will take into account: the dividend record of the company, the retained earnings (especially where earnings have been retained with a view to increasing the share value), the profitability of the company even if profits have not been used to pay dividends (this is especially relevant where profits have been used to pay high director's fees to a controlling shareholder) and the value of the assets owned by the company (this is especially relevant where the company is likely to be wound up or taken over).

Three special rules apply to the valuation of unquoted shares:

(a) A reduction in value resulting from the death cannot be taken into account if it arises from the fact that the rights attached to the shares are varied as a result of the death (for example, because the articles of the company provide that the shares are then to lose their right to dividend or to vote) (IHTA 1984 s.171(2)).

(b) If the shares are subject to pre-emption rights the market value is to be assessed on the basis that the pre-emption rights do not apply to the hypothetical sale on the open market at the time of death but that they will apply to the hypothetical purchaser (in other words the value is the price which a purchaser would pay knowing that they would be subject to the pre-emption rights in the future). This was established in *IRC v Crossman* (1937) an estate duty case decided on legislation which was in this respect similar to the inheritance tax legislation.

(c) The value on death is calculated on the assumption that a prospective purchaser would have all the information which a prudent prospective purchaser might reasonably require if they were purchasing from a willing vendor by private treaty and at arm's length (IHTA 1984 s.168(1)).

Other assets subject to restrictions on sale

The *Crossman* principle referred to above has been extended to other assets sold **4.28** subject to restrictions. For example in *Alexander v IRC* (1991) a flat which had been purchased by the deceased under the "Right to Buy" scheme was subject to an obligation to repay the discount if sold within five years of its purchase. The deceased died one year after purchase. The Court of Appeal held that the property was to be valued on the basis of the amount a purchaser would pay to stand in the shoes of the deceased, i.e. to obtain the property subject to the obligation of repaying the discount if the property was sold within five years.

There has been a series of cases on the correct valuation of non-assignable agricultural tenancies, e.g. *Baird's Executors v IRC* (1991); *Walton v IRC* (1996). It has been accepted that such tenancies have a value and therefore the question of deciding on the value is simply a matter of evidence. The Court of Appeal in *Walton* confirmed that there are no hard and fast valuation rules. It is incorrect to proceed on the basis that the landlord is a "special purchaser" if in fact the freeholder is not interested in acquiring the tenancy. The taxpayer should be careful in such a case to gather adequate information on the value of the property. In the absence of such evidence from the taxpayer the view of the Revenue will go unchallenged.

Sale within one or four years of death

If quoted shares are sold within one year of death or an interest in land within **4.29** four years of death for less than the value at death, then a reduction of the tax may be claimed in certain circumstances. (See para.12.13, below.)

Commorientes

Section 184 of the Law of Property Act 1925 provides that where two or more **4.30** people die in circumstances such that it is uncertain which of them survived, for the purposes of succession to property the deaths are deemed to occur in the order of seniority so that the elder is deemed to die first. Consequently if the elder has left property to the younger, the younger will inherit that property which will then pass under the terms of the will or intestacy of the younger. (For a detailed discussion of this rule and a limited exception to it, see Ch.16, below.)

However, for inheritance tax purposes, s.4(2) of the IHTA 1984 provides that "where it cannot be known which of two or more persons who have died survived the other or others they shall be assumed to have died at the same instant". Therefore, where two or more persons die and the order of deaths cannot be known a double charge to tax is avoided. If the elder person has left property to the younger it will be taxed as part of the elder's estate (unless an exemption is available) but the younger will not be deemed to have survived for tax purposes and so the property will not be taxed as part of their estate.

Example

A and her son B are killed in a car accident. A's will leaves everything to B. B's will leaves everything to X. It is uncertain whether A or B died first; therefore, for the purposes of succession to property the deaths are deemed to occur in order of seniority and A's property passes to B. B's property (including that which has been inherited from A) then passes to X. For the purposes of inheritance tax, A and B are deemed to die at the same instant. Thus, when calculating inheritance tax payable on B's estate, B's estate is deemed not to include the property received from A.

If A and B in the above example are husband and wife, the whole of A's estate will be exempt as it is passing to a spouse. B's estate is deemed not to include the property inherited from A. A's property is, therefore, not charged to inheritance tax. B will have the benefit of A's unused nil rate band. This is an extremely beneficial result but since it is impossible to guarantee dying in circumstances where s.4(2) would apply, it is difficult to use the provision for effective tax planning. However, when drafting wills for spouses who are agreed on default beneficiaries, it may be preferable not to include a survivorship clause at all or to provide that a survivorship clause is not to apply if the order of deaths is uncertain. This ensures that the benefit of the spouse exemption is retained if deaths occur *commorientes*.

Related property

4.31 Certain assets are more valuable when owned in conjunction with other assets of the same type than when owned individually. For example, a share in a company owned as part of a majority share holding in the company will be more valuable than a share owned as part of a minority shareholding. There is a possibility that spouses might try to avoid inheritance tax by using the spouse exemption to split the ownership of such items between themselves. In order to prevent this, special rules applying to the valuation of "related property" exist. Section 161(2) of the IHTA 1984 provides that property is related to other property owned by the transferor's spouse at the time of the transfer. Property is also related to property which was transferred by the transferor by an exempt transfer to a charity, political party or certain national bodies (as defined by IHTA 1984 Sch.3), and is owned by the charity, etc. at the time of the transfer or has been owned by it within five years before the transfer. This provision is designed to prevent abuse where a person makes an exempt transfer to a charity of property from which they can benefit or which they control.

On a transfer of related property the transferred property and the property related to it are valued according to the rules set out in IHTA 1984 s.161. Shares are valued as a mathematical proportion of the whole shareholding.

Example

A owns 40 per cent of the shares in a private company and A's spouse owns another 30 per cent. If A dies and makes a chargeable transfer of the shares his estate will be taxed not on a 40 per cent holding but on four-sevenths of a 70 per cent holding. This figure is likely to be considerably higher than the value of a 40 per cent holding since a 70 per cent holding usually gives control of the company.

All property held by spouses is related but in most cases the value will not be affected (for example, if each spouse owns a motor car neither car will be more highly valued as the values of the two properties are factually entirely independent). Apart from shares in private companies, the most likely types of property which may be more highly valued because of the related property rule are collections of chattels and property held as beneficial joint tenants or as tenants-in-common.

The case of *Arkwright v CIR* (2004) considered the application of s.161 to an interest in land held as beneficial tenants in common by a husband, who was terminally ill, and his wife. On the husband's death HMRC argued that the husband's interest in the land should be valued in accordance with s.161(4) as a fractional share of the whole. Hence his interest should be valued at 50 per cent of the whole. The Special Commissioner found that whilst that measure was appropriate for separate units of property such as unit trusts or a set of furniture (for example 12 dining chairs), it did not apply to fractions of a single unit such as land. The taxpayers argued successfully that land should be valued in accordance with s.161(1) and (3) under which it is necessary to value the property as a whole (the aggregate value). The deceased's interest and the related property are then valued separately as if they did not form part of the aggregate. Those two values are then used to establish a ratio. That ratio is then applied to the aggregate. If (and only if) the value of the deceased's share in the aggregate is then greater than the value of their separate share, the related value will be substituted. This means that a deceased co-owner's share will only be an exact half of the total where the values of the deceased's property and the related property are identical. Otherwise the value of the deceased's interest will always be more or less than half of the aggregate. The taxpayers contended that when one co-owner was terminally ill, the value of is interest would be less than the value of the healthy co-owner's. This issue was referred to the Lands Tribunal but the case was settled by agreement.

HMRC issued a Revenue and Customs Brief 71/07 stating that it had received legal advice that in some circumstances s.161(4) may, in fact, apply to a fractional share of a single unit and that in future it would apply s.161(4) when valuing shares of land as related property. However, in *Price v HMRC* (2010) referred to their failure in *Arkwright* to establish that s.161(4) applied to jointly owned land and accepted that s.161(1) and (3) applied as explained in *Arkwright*. The question of the valuation of the deceased's interest in the property valued on that basis was referred to the Upper Tribunal (Lands Chamber) if the parties were unable to agree.

When property is valued as related property on death, it is that value which is taxed (unless an exemption applies). However, if that property is sold within three years of death by the personal representatives or a person in whom the property concerned vested immediately after the death in an arm's length sale it can be revalued as if there had been no related property (IHTA 1984 s.176). This may result in a repayment of tax. Such a revaluation is not permitted where the sale is made in conjunction with a sale of the related property.

Apportionment of income attributable to a period falling partly before and partly after death

4.32 In order to calculate the value of the estate for inheritance tax purposes it is necessary to include any income which accrued prior to death even if it is not paid until after death. The pre-death portion of such income is chargeable to inheritance tax and must be shown on the Inheritance Tax Account (if one is required) while the post-death portion is not chargeable to inheritance tax and will not be shown on an Inheritance Tax Account. Income which is *paid* before death and which relates to a period falling wholly or partly *after* death is not apportioned. It is all treated as a capital asset of the estate. A direction in the will that no apportionments of income should be made, while relevant for the purposes of distribution amongst beneficiaries, is entirely irrelevant for the purposes of inheritance tax. The following examples illustrate the way in which types of income may have to be apportioned when calculating the value of the estate for inheritance tax.

Examples

4.33   (a) *Interest.* Interest which has accrued *up to* the date of death on assets such as money in a building society account or deposit bank account is treated as capital and is chargeable to inheritance tax. Interest on such assets which accrues *from* the date of death is treated as income and is not chargeable to inheritance tax.

(b) *Rent.* If the rent is payable in arrear for a period which falls partly before and partly after death it is necessary to apportion the rent. The pre-death portion is included as an asset on the Inheritance Tax Account and is chargeable to inheritance tax, the post-death portion is not.

(c) *Dividends.* Shares maybe valued "cum div." or "ex div.". If they are valued "cum div." this means that the share price has been calculated on the basis that a purchaser buying the stocks or shares would be entitled to the *whole* of the next dividend. The share price is, therefore, increased to compensate the vendor for the loss of that part of the year's interest or dividend that has already accrued. For inheritance tax purposes if the probate valuation is made "cum div." that value is entered on the Inheritance Tax Account and no further reference need be made to the dividend, since the value of the dividend or interest is included in the share price.

As the date for payment of interest or of a dividend approaches companies close their transfer books. This means that if shares are sold after that date the next interest payment or dividend will be sent to the *old* registered owner. If shares are valued after this date they will be valued "ex div.". This means that the basic share price is reduced to compensate the purchaser for the fact that if they buy they will receive no benefit from the next dividend payment. For inheritance tax purposes if the probate valuation is made "ex div." the ex div. price is entered on the Inheritance Tax Account but so is the whole of the dividend payment which will be paid to the estate by the company.

We will see in Ch.6 that for income tax purposes if a dividend is declared after death or interest paid after death for a period which falls partly before and partly after death the whole of such a receipt will be treated as income and will, therefore, be liable to income tax. This could lead to an element of double taxation since the receipt would already have been apportioned and a part of it made chargeable to inheritance tax. There is, therefore, a limited income tax relief (Income Tax (Trading and Other Income) Act 2005 s.669) whereby residuary income is treated as reduced, for the purposes of income tax liability in excess of the basic rate only, by an amount equal to the inheritance tax liability on that income, grossed up at the basic rate.

(d) *Government securities.* A holder of securities receives interest rather than dividends. Just as the price of company shares can be quoted "cum" or "ex div." so the price of securities can be quoted "cum interest" (that is with the right to receive accrued interest) or "ex interest" (that is without the right to receive any of the next interest payment). For inheritance tax purposes if the valuation is "cum interest" that value is entered on the Inheritance Tax Account and no further reference is made to the interest. If the valuation is "ex interest" the capital value of the security and the whole of the next interest payment payable to the estate are included as separate items.

5. EXEMPTIONS

Introduction

Certain transfers are exempt from inheritance tax as a result of the IHTA 1984 **4.34** ss.18–29 and other parts of the inheritance tax legislation. An exempt transfer is not liable to tax nor is it included in the cumulative total of the transferor (so that it does not affect the rate of tax on later transfers). All the exemptions will be considered in this chapter although they are not all relevant on death. The exemptions which are relevant only to transfers made *before* death are included since lifetime gifts are sometimes a suitable (and from the tax point of view beneficial) alternative to disposing of property by will.

The exemption for transfers between spouses and civil partners

This exemption is equally available for lifetime transfers and on death. **4.35**

Section 18 of the Inheritance Tax Act 1984 provides that a transfer of value is exempt "to the extent that the value transferred is attributable to property which becomes comprised in the estate of the transferor's spouse or civil partner . . . ". This means that gifts to the transferor's spouse or civil partner, before death or on death, are completely exempt. The exemption is lost if the gift does not take effect immediately so that a gift by a testator "to my mother for life, remainder to my spouse" is not an exempt transfer. However, the exemption is not lost if the gift is conditional and the condition is satisfied within 12 months of the transfer. Thus, if property is left to a spouse or civil partner, provided they survive for a period of up to 12 months, the exemption will be available provided that the spouse or civil partner survives the specified period. However, there are other considerations which make a survivorship period exceeding six months inadvisable. Such a gift will be treated as creating a relevant property settlement (see Ch.7) and will result in an immediate chargeable transfer from the deceased to the settlement.

The exemption is available for interests created on death even though the gift to the spouse or civil partner is not absolute, provided the interest is immediate. The exemption applies, therefore, if a testator makes a gift by will "to my spouse for life, remainder to my son".

The exemption was available for lifetime transfers made before March 22, 2006 to a settlement in which a spouse or civil partner had an interest in possession as these were treated as a gift "to" the spouse or civil partner. In the case of transfers made on or after that date (apart from those covered by the transitional provisions—see Ch.7, below) the exemption is not available as such settlements are relevant property settlements.

For inheritance tax purposes (unlike income tax and capital gains tax) "spouse" and "civil partner" has a normal meaning so that the exemption is available even though the parties are separated.

4.36 The exemption is only available in full if the spouse or civil partner is domiciled in the UK. If they are domiciled elsewhere only the first £55,000 of transfers to them are exempt.

In *Executor of Holland deceased v IRC* (2003) the special commissioners held that the exemption was limited to married couples and was not available to cohabitees. This was not contrary to the Human Rights Act. Cohabitees are not analogous to married couples and in any event the difference in treatment was objectively and reasonably justifiable. Married persons have mutual rights and obligations relating to maintenance during their lives and after their deaths. These interlocking property rights and obligations justify the special tax treatment of spouses.

In *Burden v UK* (2008) two elderly, unmarried sisters who had lived together their whole lives, for the last 30 years in a house built on land inherited from their parents, complained to the European Court of Human Rights that the lack of a "*spouse*" exemption from IHT amounted to discriminatory treatment in respect of their right to peaceful enjoyment of their possessions. They lost both at first instance and on appeal. The Grand Chamber of the European Court of Human Rights held that the relationship between adult siblings on the one hand and between spouses or civil partners on the other was qualitatively different. The relationships of marriage and civil partnership involve a public undertaking carrying with it rights and obligations of a contractual nature, which set those relationships apart from other types of cohabitation. There had therefore been no discrimination.

Gifts to charities, etc.

Transfers of value are exempt "to the extent that the values transferred . . . are **4.37** attributable to property which is given to charities" (IHTA 1984 s.23). There is no limit to the amount which is exempt under this provision. As with the spouse exemption the gift must be immediate and, if conditional, any condition must be satisfied within 12 months. In addition a gift to a charity must normally be absolute if the exemption is to be available. The relief has been limited to UK charities but in *Persche v Finanzamt Ludenscheid* (2009) the European Court of Justice said that such restrictions were prohibited by the EC Treaty (Nice) art.56. As a result the British Government agreed to extend the exemption to "equivalent" organisations in Europe (the EU and EEA). The organisations will have to demonstrate "equivalencet".

Transfers of value to exempt political parties are entitled to relief in the same way as transfers to charity. A political party qualifies for exemption if it had two members elected to the House of Commons at the last general election or one member if the party's candidates generally got at least 150,000 votes.

Transfers of value to certain national bodies are entitled to relief in the same way as transfers to charities. The IHTA 1984 Sch.13 contains a list of the national bodies to which this rule applies; they include, for example, national museums and art galleries, universities and their libraries, local authorities and government departments.

Transfers of value to non-profit-making bodies (other than charities, political parties and national bodies) are also exempt if the property transferred is within certain specified categories (which may broadly be described as covering scenic, historic or scientifically important land, buildings, books, papers or objects) and the Treasury direct that an exemption is to be available.

Transfers to charities, etc. are only exempt if the money or other property given is to be used exclusively for the purposes of a charity, political party, national or non-profit-making body. The exemptions are not available if "the property or any part of it *may* become applicable for (other) purposes . . . " (IHTA 1984 ss.24(3), 25(2), 26(7)).

The "annual" exemption

This exemption is only available on transfers made *before* death. Section 19 of **4.38** the IHTA 1984 provides for an annual exemption of £3,000. This exemption applies to the first £3,000 of transfers in each tax year (April 6 to April 5 inclusive). This exemption is available in addition to other exemptions so that a transferor can give as much property as they like to their spouse or civil partner and still have the annual exemption available for gifts to others.

To the extent that the annual exemption is not used in a particular year the unused part may be carried forward for one year but no longer. For example, a transferor who made no transfer last year will be entitled to a £6,000 exemption this year. To ensure that the carry forward is limited to one year the exemption of the current year must be used first and only after the whole of that exemption is exhausted can anything brought forward from the previous year be used.

For example, if A transfers nothing in year one, £6,000 of relief will be available in year two. If only £4,000 is transferred in year two this will use up the whole of year two's exemption and £1,000 from year one. Thus, in year three only an exemption of £3,000 will be available.

If more than one transfer is made in a tax year, the annual exemption must be allocated to the first chargeable transfer made in that tax year. If more than one transfer is made on the same day the exemption is apportioned pro rata irrespective of the order in which the gifts are made.

The annual exemption must be allocated to the *first* transfer in a tax year even though that transfer would otherwise be potentially exempt. This means that it is more tax efficient to make a lifetime chargeable transfer earlier in the tax year than a potentially exempt transfer.

Example

Alan has never made any transfers of value. In the tax year 2010/11 he gives £331,000 to Beth and then £331,000 to a discretionary trust. He survives seven years.

The annual exemption must be allocated to the first transfer which is therefore exempt as to £6,000 and potentially exempt as to £325,000; the second transfer is a lifetime chargeable transfer of £331,000. As Alan survives seven years the potentially exempt transfer becomes fully exempt and Alan derives no benefit from the annual exemption.

In addition to the annual exemption, outright lifetime gifts worth up to £250 per donee are exempt (IHTA 1984 s.20). This exemption does not apply to the first part of a gift which exceeds £250. (For example, a donor who gives three people £250 each does not pay any tax and does not use up any of the £3,000 exemption but, if £600 is given to one donee, £600 of the £3,000 exemption is used up.)

Normal expenditure out of income

4.39   The relief for normal expenditure is only available for lifetime transfers. The Inheritance Tax Act 1984 s.21 provides that a transfer of value is exempt to the extent that:

(a) It is made as part of the normal expenditure of the transferor. (It is a question of fact whether this requirement is satisfied. The Revenue will treat expenditure as normal if it is made under a legal obligation (for example, a deed of covenant) or if similar expenditure is, in fact, incurred on a regular basis.)

(b) It is (taking one year with another) made out of income.

(c) It is such that the transferor's usual standard of living is not affected by it.

Bennett v IRC (1995) shows how useful this exemption can be in tax planning.

Mrs Bennett was an elderly widow and the life tenant of a trust which had always produced a very modest income (£300 p.a. approximately). In 1987 the income of the trust increased enormously as a result of the sale of trust assets. Mrs Bennett instructed her trustees to continue to pay her £300 p.a. and to use the surplus income, for which she had no need, to her sons. The trustees paid £9,300 in 1989 to each of the three sons and £60,000 the following year. She then died. The Revenue contended that the transfers were potentially exempt transfers which became chargeable on her death within seven years. The personal representatives contended that they were exempt as normal expenditure out of income.

The court agreed that the transfers were exempt. It said that "normal expenditure" required a demonstration of a settled pattern of giving. This could be demonstrated by a pattern of giving over a period of time or by the individual assuming a commitment.

> "There is no fixed minimum period during which the expenditure should have occurred . . . if the prior commitment or resolution can be shown, a single payment implementing the commitment or resolution may be sufficient . . . the amount of expenditure need not be fixed in amount nor indeed the individual recipient be the same. As regards quantum, it is sufficient that a formula or standard has been adopted by application of which the payment (which may be of a fluctuating amount) can be identified . . . ."

In *McDowall v IRC* (2004) an attorney made a number of gifts to family members from accumulated surplus income which had been placed on deposit. Although the gifts were held to be invalid as being beyond the attorney's powers, the court accepted that the exemption would have applied had the gifts been valid. They were made out of retained income which remained income in character rather than capital; it was identifiably money which was essentially unspent income and which had been placed on deposit, but not invested in any more formal sense.

Gifts in consideration of marriage

This exemption is only available on lifetime transfers. Section 22 of the IHTA **4.40** 1984 provides that a gift in consideration of marriage is exempt to the extent of:

(a) £5,000 if made by a parent of one of the parties to the marriage;

(b) £2,500 if made by a remoter ancestor of one of the parties or by a party to the prospective marriage; and

(c) £1,000 in any other case.

The limits apply to each marriage, not to each donee (so that a parent cannot give £5,000 to his child and £1,000 to his future child-in-law and obtain exemption for £6,000).

Family maintenance

4.41 This exemption is only available on lifetime transfers. Section 11 of IHTA 1984, provides that a disposition is not a transfer of value (and so is effectively exempt) if it is made by one party to a marriage in favour of the other party or of a child of either party and is for the maintenance of the other party or for the maintenance, education or training of the child. In the case of a disposition in favour of a spouse there would usually be an exemption anyway (see para.4.23, above) but the family maintenance exemption applies to ex-spouses and to spouses domiciled outside the UK whereas the normal spouse exemption does not. The exemption for maintenance, etc. of children is normally available only to the parents (including adoptive and step-parents) but where the child is not in the care of its parents it extends to others maintaining the children in certain circumstances.

Section 11(3) provides that dispositions in favour of dependent relatives other than spouses and children are not transfers of value to the extent that they are "reasonable provision for care or maintenance".

In *PRs of Phizackerley v HMCR* (2007) where the Revenue argued that a debt from a surviving spouse to the estate of his wife was not deductible under Finance Act 1986 s.103 because the debt was incurred in consideration of property derived from the deceased, the taxpayer sought to take advantage of s.103(4) which provides that s.103 will not apply if the initial disposition was not a transfer of value. The taxpayer argued that Mr Phizackerley's initial gift of a half interest in the house was not a transfer of value because it fell under s.11 as a disposition for family maintenance. The special commissioner agreed that the ordinary meaning of maintenance was wide enough to cover the transfer of a house or part interest in a house if it relieved the recipient from income expenditure, for example rent. However, the reason married couples normally had for putting their house into joint names, was not to provide for the maintenance of the other party; it was to give the other party security. When a husband put a house in the joint names of himself and his wife during their marriage it was not within the ordinary meaning of maintenance. The disposition had not been for maintenance and the taxpayer's argument failed.

In *McKelvey v RCC* (2008) a taxpayer who was terminally ill gave two investment properties to her elderly mother intending that they would be sold after her death and the proceeds used to pay for residential care for her mother. In fact the properties were never sold as the mother was cared for at home by other family members until her death. HMRC considered the gift to be a potentially exempt transfer made by the daughter within seven years of her death and, therefore, chargeable. The taxpayers contended that the properties were given for maintenance of a dependant and fell within s.11.

The Special Commissioner decided that the question of whether or not the gift was made for maintenance had to be determined at the date the gift was made and that subsequent events were irrelevant. Here, the gift was made for maintenance. The next question was whether the gift was "reasonable" provision for maintenance. Reasonable imported an objective standard. Taking into account the mother's age and the cost of care, the bulk of the gift (£140,500) fell within s.11(3) and was not a transfer of value. The balance (£28,500) was excessive and was, therefore, chargeable.

There is scope for s.11 to be used by single parents (who have no spouse exemption available) to make death bed provision for the maintenance of their children. However, the section requires the provison to be limited to the minority of the child or the termination of full time education or training whichever is the earlier.

Cumulative effect of exemptions

The exemptions referred to above (other than the small gifts exemption) are **4.42** cumulative with each other. After the exemptions have been claimed the transferor is entitled to a certain amount (£325,000 for Tax Year 2010/11) taxed at a nil rate. For example, a transferor who has made no previous gifts and who wishes to benefit their child who is about to be married as much as possible without a potential liability to inheritance tax if they die within seven years could give the following:

	£
Annual exemption from last year	3,000
Annual exemption for this year	3,000
Marriage exemption	5,000
Nil rate band	325,000

The transferor's spouse could make similar provision immediately and both could give further sums of £3,000 annually. Seven years after these gifts the potentially exempt transfer of £325,000 will prove to be exempt and the transferor will be free to make further transfers up to the limit of the then nil rate band without any liability to inheritance tax.

Miscellaneous

The exemption contained in s.154 of the Inheritance Tax Act 1984 ("IHTA") **4.43** applies where a person was a member of the armed forces and was on active service against an enemy (or other service of a warlike nature involving the same risks in the opinion of the Treasury). It provides that there will be no IHT charged on the death estate of a person certified by the Ministry of Defence or the Secretary of State as having died from:

(a) a wound inflicted, accident occurring or disease contracted while on active service; or

(b) a disease contracted at some previous time, the death being due to or
hastened by the aggravation of the disease during active service.

In *Barty-King v Ministry of Defence* (1979) (decided on an earlier section) May
J. said:

"the purpose and nature of the legislation seem to me to require a benevolent
interpretation in favour of the estate of the deceased".

In *Barty-King* the fourth Duke of Westminster had died of cancer in 1967 after
sustaining a wound in 1944 while on active service. May J. held that the proper
question to ask was "whether the wound was a cause of the deceased's death, and
not whether the wound was the direct cause of the death". The exemption only
relates to IHT payable on the death estate (or by concession to the ending of
certain life interests created in the will of persons dying on active service). It does
not relate to any other tax or duty payable by reason of the death, for example,
tax chargeable on a lifetime transfer or when a discretionary trust comes to an
end, in whole or in part, on the death.

In order to claim the exemption it is essential to obtain a certificate. There are
two forms of certificate, a simplified one is available for deaths of currently
serving people where there is no doubt that s.154 is satisfied and one for other
deaths. Paragraph 11291 of HMRC's IHT Manual deals with the procedure for
claiming exemption.

By concession (Extra-statutory Concession F5) the exemption is applicable to
the estates of members of the Police Service of Northern Ireland (or the previous
police authority, the Royal Ulster Constabulary) who die from injuries caused in
Northern Ireland by terrorist activity. The exemption, while infrequently available, is clearly valuable in appropriate cases.

4.44   "Conditional" exemption is available on death and on certain lifetime transfers in respect of assets designated by the Treasury as being of national, scientific,
historic or artistic interest (IHTA 1984 ss.31–35 as amended). Claims must be
made within two years of the transfer of value or such longer period as the Board
may allow (s.30(3BA) inserted by Finance Act 1998). The exemption is only
available if suitable undertakings are given. The taxpayer must undertake to take
reasonable steps to preserve the asset, to secure reasonable access to the public
and to keep objects permanently in the UK. There had been concern that proper
access for the public was not always available. The Finance Act 1998, therefore,
provided that access by prior appointment is not sufficient. There must be
extended access and also greater disclosure of information about items. See
IHTA 1984 s.31(4FA) and (4FB). The exemption is "conditional" on these
undertakings. Tax becomes payable if an undertaking is broken or if there is a
disposal and similar undertakings are not given. Tax will normally become
payable in any event if the asset is sold. Existing undertakings can be varied as
regards extended access and publication by agreement or, where no agreement
has been reached on a variation proposed by the Revenue within six months, by
the direction of a special commissioner. The commissioner must be satisfied that
the proposed variation is "just and reasonable". See *Re A and B's Undertakings*
(2005) for a discussion of the matters it is appropriate to consider.

6. Reliefs

Introduction

A relief may reduce the tax payable on a particular asset in whole or in part if the **4.45**
required conditions are satisfied. A variety of reliefs are available such as quick
succession relief under s.161 of the IHTA 1984 (where a *death* occurs within five
years of a chargeable transfer), relief on the value of growing timber under the
IHTA 1984 ss.125–130 (where within two years of a death an election claiming
relief is made) and, most importantly, reliefs for business and agricultural
property under IHTA 1984 ss.103–114 and ss.115–124A.

Quick succession relief and timber relief are only available on death, not on
transfers made before death.

The reliefs on business and on agricultural property are available on both
lifetime and death transfers. They take effect by means of a percentage reduction
in the value transferred. A reduction in the value transferred will have the effect
of reducing the tax payable. The relief will prevent any charge to tax arising,
where it brings the value transferred within the nil rate band.

The object of these reliefs is to ease the burden of taxation on businesses and
agricultural land. To ensure that taxpayers cannot take unfair advantage of them
there are rules requiring a minimum period of ownership before the relief
becomes available. Further mitigation of the hardship of paying tax out of
business and agricultural property (which might otherwise lead to the forced sale
of such property) is provided by the instalment option (as to which see para.4.48,
below).

Agricultural relief

Agricultural relief is available in respect of "agricultural property". Agricultural **4.46**
property is defined by IHTA 1984 s.115(2) and includes agricultural land and
pasture and certain land and buildings occupied *in association with it* including
such farm-houses, farm buildings and cottages as are of a character appropriate
to the property. The definition has been extended (in the case of transfers made
on or after April 6, 1995) to include land used for short-term coppice.

Farm cottages must have been occupied for the purposes of agriculture.
However an ESC dated February 13, 1995 extends the relief to cottages by
retired farm employees or their surviving spouses in certain circumstances. In
Atkinson v RCC (2010) the tribunal held that a farm cottage had been occupied
by a farming partnership even though the elderly partner who lived in it had been
in residential care for four years before his death, though his possessions
remained in the cottage. The tribunal chairman, Sir Stephen Oliver QC held that
the cottage had been "occupied" by the partnership for parnership purposes
which had initially been the accommodation of one of the partners and then
became the accommodation of his possessions. The tribunal chairman said that
cottages might be used to accommodate employees and that "there is nothing in

the Act that prescribes that the accommodation of such people is to be continuous". HMRC is known to consider that the case was wrongly decided so anyone seeking to rely on it is likely to encounter resistance.

Agricultural relief takes the form of a percentage reduction in the "agricultural value" of the property which is defined as "the value of the property if the property were subject to a perpetual covenant prohibiting its use otherwise than as agricultural property" (s.115(3)). The effect of this definition is that relief is available to the extent of the value of a farm or other agricultural property *as a farm* but any other value attached to it, such as development value, is not relieved (although business property relief may be available on that value—see below).

In the case of charges to tax arising on or after March 10, 1992, the reduction in value is either 100 per cent or 50 per cent.

The percentage reduction in the agricultural value of the property is 100 per cent where the transferor had the right to vacant possession immediately before the transfer or the right to obtain it within 12 months after the transfer (s.116(2)). (100 per cent relief is also available in certain other cases where the transferor has been beneficially entitled to the property since before March 10, 1981 but in this case there is an upper limit of £250,000 on the value which can be reduced by 100 per cent.)

Extra-Statutory Concession F17 has extended 100 per cent relief to cases where the transferor's interest in the property immediately before the transfer either:

(1) carried the right to vacant possession within 24 months of the date of the transfer; or

(2) is notwithstanding the terms of the tenancy valued at an amount broadly equivalent to vacant possession value.

An illustration of (2) would be the type of arrangement in *IRC v Gray* (1994). In this case Lady Fox had granted a tenancy to a partnership in which she was entitled to 97.5 per cent of the profits. The Revenue successfully contended that as she would have been able to offer the reversion and the partnership for sale together, they should be valued as one unit. However, agricultural land subject to such arrangements will now qualify for 100 per cent relief.

4.47 In other cases the relief is 50 per cent (s.116(2)). Where land is owned by joint tenants or tenants in common each of them is deemed to have a right to vacant possession if the interests of all of them together carry that right (s.116(6)). It is obviously desirable to have the right to vacant possession. A landowner who is thinking of granting a tenancy should not grant it for more than a year and a day so that the right to vacant possession within 12 months exists virtually from the very beginning of the tenancy.

The right to agricultural relief only applies if certain requirements are satisfied. First, the transferor must have *occupied* the land for the purposes of agriculture "throughout the period of two years ending with the date of the transfer" or it must have been *owned* by them throughout the period of seven years ending with the date of the transfer and was occupied by them *or another* for the purposes of agriculture throughout that period (s.117). This means that a farmer who buys their own farm qualifies for relief (at 100 per cent) after two years if they continue to occupy it up to the time of transfer. A person who buys a farm and puts in a tenant qualifies for relief (at 50 per cent) only after seven years. A tenant who purchases their farm qualifies for relief (at 100 per cent) immediately if they have been in occupation for two years. Any break in the periods of ownership or occupation is fatal to the availability of the relief.

Special rules apply in relation to the occupation requirement where a farmer moves from one farm to another (s.118), where a farm is owned by the spouse of a former owner, or where there is a transfer within two years of a previous transfer, provided one transfer is on death (s.120).

A transfer of shares in a company which owns agricultural property is eligible for relief to the extent that the value of the shares reflects the agricultural value of land and provided the shareholder is in control of the company. Occupation by the company is deemed to be occupation by the controlling shareholder (s.119).

Milk Quota used to be very valuable. Currently, however supply outweighs demand and the EU intends to abolish Milk Quota at its next review in 2015. Milk Quota is not an interest in land as such, see *Cottle v Coldicotte* (1995) and IHT Manual para.24250. That paragraph states that where an owner uses their land for a dairy farm, the Quota should be valued as part of the land with agricultural relief on the full combined value if the land itself qualifies for relief. Business relief will normally be available as an alternative so the precise nature of the relief and its apportionment is not relevant.

The introduction in 2005 of the Single Payment Scheme for farmers (replacing most existing direct subsidy schemes) means that farmers will not actually have to produce anything to earn subsidies, merely keep their land in good agricultural and environmental condition. Section 117 does not require agricultural land to be in production either continuously or at a specific time. However, it is considered there must be an intention or expectation that the land will be back in production at some time in the future. A landowner who ceases production and merely keeps their land in good agricultural and environmental condition in order to claim the single payment will probably be unable to satisfy the definition of a farmhouse for Inheritance Tax purposes as discussed at para.4.48, below. The payment itself is a separate asset which will not qualify for agricultural property relief but will usually attract business property relief as an asset of the business. The increase in property values over the last few years means that the availability of 100 per cent relief on a farm house is extremely valuable. As a result farm houses have become something of a battle ground between taxpayers and the Revenue.

There have been a number of cases where the Revenue has declined to allow **4.48** relief on farm houses because they have not been occupied for the requisite period or have not been occupied *with* the land. *Starke v IRC* (1995) was an example of a house which was not occupied *with* land. The house was situate with some substantial outbuildings and one or two small areas of enclosed land and, as a result, failed to qualify for relief. *Harrold v IRC* (1996) is an example of a house which was not occupied for the requisite period. The taxpayer had bought a farm and started working it but could not live in the farmhouse which was in a dilapidated state until essential repairs were carried out. The special commissioners found that despite the taxpayer's care for the property and work on it, he was not in occupation until he actually moved in.

It is frequently difficult in practice to determine whether or not a farmhouse is of a character appropriate to the property. *Lloyds TSB as personal representative of Antrobus (Deceased) v IRC* (2002) summarised the relevant principles as follows:

    (1) one should consider whether the house is appropriate by reference to its size, content and layout with the farm buildings and the particular area of farmland being farmed;

    (2) one should consider whether the house is proportionate in size and nature to the requirements of the farming activities conducted on the agricultural land or pasture in question;

    (3) although one cannot describe a farmhouse which satisfies the "character appropriate" test, one knows one when one sees it;

    (4) one should ask whether the educated rural layman would regard the property as a house with land or a farm; and

    (5) one should consider the historical dimension and ask how long the house in question has been associated with the agricultural property and whether there was a history of agricultural production.

Applying these tests the house in question was "of a character appropriate to the property".

Executors of Higginson v IRC (2002) confirmed that there is no single test. In that case the house was of such value that it was the predominant element of the unit. It was a house with farmland going with it (and not vice versa).

The *Antrobus* case was referred to the Lands Tribunal to determine the value of the farmhouse. In the course of its determination of value, the Lands Tribunal expressed the opinion that:

> "A farmhouse is ... the house in which the farmer of the land lives ... . The question is: who is the farmer of the land for the purpose of the definition in section 115(2)? In our view it is the person who lives in the farmhouse in order to farm the land comprised in the farm and who farms the land on a day to day basis. ... We do not think that a house occupied with a farm is a farmhouse simply because the person living there is in overall control of the agricultural business conducted on the land".

It determined that a working farmer would pay 15 per cent less than someone who simply wanted to buy a house with land and let others manage the property (a so-called "lifestyle farmer"). The relief was, therefore, granted on the discounted figure. Taxpayers should, therefore, expect to get relief only on a discounted figure.

More worrying, though, was the suggestion that a farmer had to be a "hands-on" working farmer. Many people thought that the Lands Tribunal approach was wrong. However, in *Arnander v HMRC* (2006) the special commissioner held that:

"the principle that the farmer of the land is the person who farms it on a day-to-day basis rather then the person who is in overall control of the agricultural business conducted on the land is a helpful principle".

The special commissioner held that while it was not fatal to a claim that land was contract farmed by others, on the facts the day-to-day control of farming activities was carried out by a manager and not by the owner of the house in question. The property in question, therefore, could not be a farm house.

The commissioner also held that the house was not of a character appropriate being too large and grand for the comparatively small amount of land being farmed. The commissioner also held that even if the claim had not failed on those grounds, it would still have failed because the property had not been occupied for the purposes of agriculture for the two previous years. The elderly owners were too old and frail in their final two years of ownership to carry out any farming activities. The same point had been fatal in *Rosser v IRC* (2003) where the special commissioner held that a property which had clearly been a farmhouse for many years had changed in the years before death from a farmhouse to a retirement home for the deceased and her husband.

According to *Williams v HMRC* (2005) buildings used for intensive rearing of livestock or fish only qualify for agricultural property relief if they are used as part of a farm. Section 115(2) requires the occupation of the buildings to be ancillary to the agricultural use. This requires there to be a common purpose with the intensive buildings as the "junior partner" in the enterprise.

Claw back of relief on lifetime transfers

Where a transfer is made before death, whether chargeable or potentially exempt, **4.49** and the transferor dies within seven years, the relief is available only if the property originally given or qualifying property representing it has remained as agricultural property in the ownership of the transferee from the date of transfer to the date of death of the transferor. If the transferee dies before the transferor within the seven-year period, relief is only available on the death of the transferee if the same conditions are satisfied. This is more fully discussed in connection with business property relief.

If only a proportion of the property originally given or qualifying property representing it remains in the ownership of the transferee at the date of death, relief is available on the proportion of the property owned at that date (s.124A).

Clawback is discussed more fully in connection with business property relief.

Business property relief

This relief is available in respect of "relevant business property". The relief is a **4.50** reduction in the value transferred by a particular percentage depending on what type of property is being transferred (IHTA 1984 s.104). Relevant business property is property falling into one of the following six categories:

(a) Property consisting of a business or an interest in a business (this includes the interest of a sole proprietor or of a partner in a business) (s.105(1)(a)).

(b) Unquoted securities which alone or with other shares owned by the transferor or with related property gave the transferor control of the company (s.105(b)). A person has control if they control more than 50 per cent of the votes exercisable in the general meeting.

In deciding whether or not one person has control it is not possible to ignore votes attaching to shares held by another person who lacks capacity: *Walding v IRC* (1996). It is sufficient for the transferor to control a majority of shares *immediately before* the transfer. A company may buy back and cancel some shares with the result that after the cancellation a shareholder may have more than 50 per cent of the remaining shares. A transfer by the shareholders at that point will attract 100 per cent relief even if more shares are issued shortly afterwards.

The transfer of one share from an 80 per cent shareholding will attract 100 per cent relief on the transfer of that one share.

(c) Shareholdings in unlisted companies (s.105(1)(bb)). Again it is not necessary for the transfer to cause the transferor to lose control. Unquoted Shares dealt with in or on the Alternative Investment Market (AIM) are unquoted for this purpose.

In the three cases above the relief is 100 per cent.

(d) Shareholdings in listed companies which alone or with other shares owned by the transferor or with related property gave the transferor control immediately before the transfer. Again control is exercising more than 50 per cent of the votes in general meeting. Temporary control will suffice. Relief is available until the size of the holding dips below the crucial point. Where a persons intends to make a number of gifts of shares from such a holding, it is desirable to make the smaller gifts first to try to ensure that control is maintained for as long as possible.

(e) Land or buildings, machinery or plant used immediately before the transfer wholly or mainly for the purposes of a company controlled by the transferor or of a partnership of which they were a member. Notice the distinction between partnerships and companies for this purpose. An asset used by a company will attract no relief if the owner has a minority shareholding whereas an asset used by a partnership will attract relief however small an interest in the partnership the owner of the asset has.

(f) Land or buildings, machinery or plant used immediately before the transfer for the purposes of a business carried on by the transferor and which was settled property in which the transferor had an interest in possession. Perhaps surprisingly no changes were made to the legislation by Finance Act 2006 so it does not matter whether the person with the beneficial interest in possession is treated as the owner of the underlying trust capital or not.

In the three cases above, the relief is 50 per cent.

"Business"

The term "business" includes a profession or vocation but does not include a **4.51** business carried on otherwise than for gain (s.103(3)). It includes an interest at Lloyds and the interest of market makers on the London International Financial Futures and Options Exchange (LIFFE) (Inheritance Tax (Market Makers) Regulations 1993). Agriculture is regarded as a type of business so that business property relief may be available to the extent that agricultural relief cannot be claimed (that is business property relief is available for any non-agricultural value of agricultural property). It used to be thought that business property relief was only available where the taxpayer transferred "a business or an interest in a business" and that no relief was available, for example, on the transfer of a single field or business asset. However, in *Trustees of the Nelson Dance Settlement v HMRC* (2009) the special commissioner held that this was wrong. On a correct reading of all the relevant sections, it was clear that there is no need for the transfer to be *of* a business; all that is required is that the transfer of value is attributable to the *value* of the business. Hence, relief is available on the transfer of single items.

Non-qualifying businesses

Businesses which consist wholly or mainly of dealing in securities, stocks, **4.52** shares, land or buildings or of holding investments are specifically excluded from relief (s.105(3)). Some commercial landlords have attempted to argue that they are entitled to relief because they are in active management of the land rather than mere passive landlords. On the whole, such arguments have met with little success. See *Powell v IRC* (1997), *Martin (Executors of Moore) v IRC* (1995) and *Burkinyoung v IRC* (1995). Most recently in *McCall v RCC* (2009) the Court of Appeal denied business property relief to a land owner who had let out her land on a grazing licence. She was simply deriving income from land. A person who derives income from land or a building is to be treated as having a business of holding an investment, notwithstanding that in order to obtain the income they carry out incidental maintenance and management work, find tenants and grant leases. In *McCall* there was no doubt that agricultural property relief was available but that relieves only the agricultural value of the property and the land had substantial development value which could only escape tax if business property relief was available. Notice that the relief is all or nothing. Many businesses carry on a range of mixed activities. Once the business crosses the line and becomes mainly a business carrying out one of the forbidden activities, it loses all relief. Businesses change their activities over time and a business which started out as a trading business may become an investment business and vice versa. See *Executors of Clark deceased v HMRC* (2005). It may be preferable to divide businesses into separate entities so as to guarantee relief on part of the activities rather than gambling on getting relief on the whole range carried on in one single business. Slightly surprisingly *Phillips v HMRC* (2006) held that a company which lent money to other companies owned by the taxpayer was a trading company not an investment company and shares, therefore, qualified for relief.

There have been a number of cases involving the availability of relief on static caravan sites. In *Hall v IRC* (1997) the greater part of the income came from rents and standing charges and it was held that the business was "mainly" that of making or holding investments. In *Furness v IRC* (1999) the taxpayer obtained relief where net profit from caravan sales exceeded that from net rents. In *Weston v IRC* (2000) the High Court confirmed that the question of whether or not a business consisted wholly or mainly of making or holding investments was a question of fact for the Special Commissioners. In *IRC v George (Executors of Stedman) dec'd* (2003) the Court of Appeal took an approach which was sympathetic to the taxpayers saying that it was difficult to see any reason why an active family business should be denied relief merely because a necessary component of its profit making activity was the use of land.

In *Farmer v IRC* (1999) the special commissioner concluded that a business which comprised farming and letting of former farm buildings was one business consisting mainly of farming. The case is interesting because the net profit from lettings exceeded that from farming but that was not conclusive. What was actually relevant was the amount of time spent on the various activities, the allocation of capital employed between the activities and the fact that farming turnover often exceeded turnover from rents.

Brander v RCC (2010) involved a landed estate which carried on a mixture of farming and letting activities. The court confirmed that whether a business consists wholly or mainly of making or holding investments is a question of fact for the decision-maker. The decision-maker is required to look at the business in the round and consider the relative importance of the investment to the business as a whole; that involves looking at the business over a period of time. The decision-maker can have regard to various factors; none of those factors is conclusive, and a factor which is relevant to one business may not be relevant to another. It is not appropriate in every case to compartmentalise the business and attribute activity either to investment or to non-investment as an ancillary activity. On the facts the business fell on the "right" side of the line and relief was available.

The value of the business

4.53 Business property relief is given on the net value of business property (s.110). This is the value after deducting liabilities incurred for the purposes of the business (for other inheritance tax purposes in the case of death liabilities are deducted from *the whole estate* unless charged on particular property). The value of property qualifying for relief cannot be increased by charging business debts on non-business property. The fact that a guarantee in support of a business has been charged over a particular asset does not mean that the asset is a business asset. See *IRC v Mallender* (2001).

Period of ownership

The transferor must have owned the relevant business property throughout the **4.54** period of two years before the transfer (s.107(1)). Property which replaces other relevant business property qualifies for relief even though not owned for two years provided that the aggregate period of ownership exceeds two years in the five years before the transfer. Until the new property has been owned for two years the relief is limited to the value of the original property (s.107(2)). Relief is available on shares owned for less than two years where the new shares are obtained as a result of a company reorganisation and can be identified, under TCGA 1992 ss.126–136, with other shares owned for the requisite period. The TCGA provisions require the new shares to be issued in proportion to the existing holding, for example as a rights issue or bonus issue. For an illustration see *Executors of Dugan-Chapman (dec'd) v RRC* (2008).

Where a transfer of value of relevant business property is followed by another transfer of the same property, the second owner need not own the property for two years before becoming entitled to the relief provided that the relief was available on the first transfer and one of the transfers was a transfer on death (s.109(1)). The ownership requirement can be a trap as the facts of *Burrell & Sharman v Burrell* (2005) demonstrate. A beneficiary of an accumulation and maintenance trust obtained a qualifying interest in possession which the trustees terminated within two years in order to appoint the property on discretionary trusts. The termination of the interest in possession was immediately chargeable to inheritance tax and because the beneficiary had not fulfilled the two-year ownership requirement business property relief was not available.

A person who received property on the death of their *spouse or civil partner* may aggregate their period of ownership with their own so as to make up a two-year period of ownership (s.108).

When a business (or other relevant business property) has been owned for two years then business property relief is available on its full value at the time of the transfer (at the appropriate percentage). It is not, therefore, necessary to show that particular assets of the business have been owned for two years. However, the value of an asset is excluded from relief if it has not been used wholly or mainly for the purpose of the business throughout the two years before the transfer or throughout the period since it was acquired if later.

Excepted assets

In order to prevent taxpayers "parking" private assets in a business and then **4.55** seeking to obtain business property relief on them, s.112 provides that relief is not available on "excepted assets". There are assets which were neither:

    (a) used wholly or mainly for the purposes of the business concerned throughout the whole of the previous two years; nor

    (b) required at the time of the transfer for future use.

These are alternative requirements. An asset which fulfils either one of the requirements will not be an excepted asset. However, (b) is not available where relief is claimed on an asset used by a company controlled by the transferor or by a partnership of which they are a member. Assets which are excepted do not qualify for relief. However, their existence does not prejudice the eligibility of the rest of the business for relief.

Contract for sale

4.56 Relief is not available if property is subject to a binding contract to sell. It is important, therefore, that partnerships and companies do not require the personal representatives of deceased partners or shareholder to sell their share(s) and the survivors to purchase them. Pre-emption rights and options to purchase do not present the same problems as there is no binding agreement. The Revenue accepts that automatic accruer clauses do not constitute binding contracts for sale. See Law Society's Gazette, September 1996, p.35.

Clawback of relief on lifetime transfers

4.57 As with agricultural relief, where a transfer is made before death, whether chargeable or potentially exempt, and the transferor dies within seven years, the relief is available only if the property originally given or qualifying property representing it has remained as relevant business property in the ownership of the transferee from the date of the transfer to the date of death of the transferor. If the transferee dies before the transferor within the seven-year period, relief is only available on the death of the transferee if the same conditions are satisfied.

    The property must remain relevant business property in the hands of the donee. This may be beyond the control of the donee. For example, a donor with a controlling holding may give a donee 20 per cent of the shares in an unquoted trading company, thus qualifying for 100 per cent relief. A year later the donor may sell the assets of a trading company and decide to keep the cash in the company using the company as an investment company. If the transfer becomes chargeable, the donee will have no relief available because the shares are no longer in a trading company and no longer qualify as relevant business property.

    If only a proportion of the property originally given or qualifying property representing it remains in the ownership of the transferee at the date of death, relief is available on the proportion of the property owned at that date (s.113A).

    In the case of both agricultural and business property relief it is sufficient if "property representing" the original property is in the hands of the donee at the relevant date. There are some rather strange limitations:

(a) The *whole* of the consideration must have been applied on acquiring the replacement property.

(b) The replacement property must be acquired within three years *after* the disposal of the original property. Note that there is no provision as with roll over relief for the replacement property to be obtained *before* the disposal.

(c) The provision applies only to the first replacement and not to subsequent ones.

The December 1994 Tax Bulletin gives guidance on two matters relating to agricultural and business property relief:

(1) If agricultural property is replaced with business property (or vice versa) shortly before the owner's death, the periods of ownership can be amalgamated.

(2) Where the donee of agricultural property has sold the gifted property and replaced it with business property, agricultural property relief is denied by s.124A(1). Consequently s.114(1) does not exclude *business* property relief if the conditions for relief are satisfied. In the reverse situation, a farming business acquired by the donee can be relevant business property for the purposes of s.113B(3)(c).

Timber

A relief is available on the value of growing timber for transfers made on death **4.58** but not for lifetime transfers (IHTA 1984 ss.125–130). The relief is only available if a written election is made within two years of death. Where an election is made no tax is payable on the value of the timber provided that the deceased was either beneficially entitled to the land on which the timber is growing for five years before their death or acquired it otherwise than for consideration in money or money's worth within the five years.

The relief for timber is merely a conditional relief since tax becomes payable on a later sale or lifetime gift of the timber. The tax is payable at the deceased's death rate and treating the value as the highest part of the value of their estate. Tax is paid on the value of the timber at the date of the later disposal, not on its value at the date of death, and is payable by the person entitled to the proceeds of sale or who would be so entitled if the disposal had been a sale.

The effect of this relief is that no tax is payable on timber until it is sold or given away by lifetime transfer; the tax payable is calculated by reference to the estate of the last person to die owning it.

Timber relief is not available where the woodlands qualify for agricultural property relief (short rotation coppice) and commercial woodlands will often qualify for business property relief.

Quick succession relief

4.59   Where a person dies within five years of a transfer to them (whether inter vivos
or on death) a relief commonly called quick succession relief is available (IHTA
1984 s.141). The relief takes the form of a reduction in the amount of tax payable
on death equal to a percentage of the tax paid on the *net* amount of the increase
in the value of the deceased's estate caused by the transfer within five years.
   The percentage relief is:

> 100% if the death is within one year;
> 80% if more than one but not more than two years;
> 60% if more than two but not more than three years;
> 40% if more than three years but not more than four years; and
> 20% if more than four years but not more than five years.

Example

A dies and leaves B £12,500 worth of property. A's estate pays £2,500 in tax. B dies
three years and three months later. The reduction of tax on B's death is 40 per cent
of the tax on the net amount of the increase in B's estate. This can be calculated in
the following way:

$$\frac{\text{net amount}}{\text{gross amount}} \times \text{tax} \times \text{percentage} = \text{Reduction}$$

i.e. in this case:

$$\frac{£10,000}{£12,500} \times £2,500 \times \frac{40}{100} = £800$$

   The reduction produced by quick succession relief is available whether or not
the deceased still owned the property transferred to them within the five years
before death. Where the amount of quick succession relief is more than the
amount of tax to which the deceased would otherwise have been liable, no tax
will be payable on the death (although no reclaim of the excess relief from the
Revenue is possible—the excess may be carried forward to be set off against the
liability of the deceased's beneficiary on their death if it is within five years of
the original transfer to the deceased).

7. Liability for Inheritance Tax on Death

Introduction

4.60   The inheritance tax legislation includes rules to determine who is liable to
account to the Revenue for inheritance tax due as a result of death.
   Where inheritance tax is payable on an estate no grant of representation can be
obtained until the amount due is paid to the Revenue. The Revenue is concerned
with getting the money and s.200(1) sets out four categories of people who are
concurrently "accountable" or "liable" to the Revenue for the inheritance tax
due on death. The Revenue is not concerned with who actually bears the burden
of inheritance tax and it may be that the person who is accountable to the

Revenue for the tax (for example, the personal representative of the deceased) has a right to recover the money paid from individual beneficiaries. The question of where the burden of inheritance tax eventually falls is dealt with at paras 4.63–4.65, below. It is possible for a testator to change the statutory implied rules on where the burden of inheritance tax falls by express direction in the will but the rules on accountability cannot be altered.

Since inheritance tax must normally be paid before the grant of representation is obtained, the persons accountable to the Revenue (for example, the personal representatives) frequently encounter difficulty in realising assets of the estate to raise cash to pay the amount due (See Ch.12, below). It is common for them to borrow money from a bank in order to discharge their liability.

Persons liable for inheritance tax on death (IHTA 1984 s.200(1))

The four categories of persons accountable for inheritance tax on death are set **4.61** out in s.200(1):

(a) The personal representatives of the deceased are accountable for the inheritance tax attributable to any free estate of the deceased. "Free estate" includes property held by the deceased as co-owner (whether as joint tenant or tenant-in-common), property disposed of by *donatio mortis causa* and property disposed of by nomination.

The liability of ordinary personal representatives for inheritance tax is limited to the value of assets which they received or would have received but for their own neglect or default (s.204(1)).

The term personal representative includes an executor *de son tort*, i.e. a person who has made themselves liable as executor by intermeddling in the estate (see Ch.8, below). The liability for inheritance tax of such a person is limited to the value of assets that have come into his hands, *IRC v Stype Investments* (1982).

(b) The trustees of a settlement are accountable for inheritance tax attributable to property comprised in the settlement immediately before the death. Their liability is limited to the value of assets which they received or disposed of or which they have become liable to account for to the beneficiaries and to the extent of any other property available in their hands for the payment of tax or which might have been available but for their own neglect or default (s.204(2)).

(c) Any person in whom property is vested (whether beneficially or not) or who is entitled to an interest in possession is accountable for the inheritance tax attributable to such property. This category includes beneficiaries under a will, persons entitled to property under the intestacy rules, a beneficiary with an interest in possession in property settled after death and a purchaser. A purchaser for money or money's worth of property is not, however, liable where the property is not subject to an HMRC charge (see below, para.4.82).

Liability of such persons is limited to the value of the property (or any property which represents it) (s.204(3)). This is a rather draconian provision for a beneficiary with an interest in possession as the beneficiary is entitled only to income and yet has a liability limited only by the capital value of the property in which they have an interest in possession. The Revenue confirmed in correspondence with the Society of Trust and Estate Practitioners and the Chartered Institute of Taxation on May 8, 2007 that this was the position and that it had no intention of changing it.

(d) Where property was settled prior to death, a beneficiary for whose benefit settled property or income therefrom is applied thereafter is accountable for the inheritance tax attributable to such property. A beneficiary of a discretionary trust would be an example of such a person. Liability is limited to the amount of the property or income received (less any income tax) (s.204(5)).

Where a person makes a gift before death and reserves a benefit in the property, that property will be treated in certain circumstances as part of the donor's estate on death. Where it is so treated, the personal representatives of the deceased are liable for the tax on that property only if the tax remains unpaid 12 months after the end of the month of death. Their liability is limited to the value of assets which they received or would have received but for their own neglect or default.

Liability for additional tax on lifetime gifts

4.62 Where death occurs within seven years of a potentially exempt transfer, inheritance tax may become payable. Where death occurs within seven years of a chargeable transfer extra tax may become payable. In such circumstances the following are liable for the tax or extra tax:

(a) The personal representatives of the transferor (but only to a limited extent—see below).

(b) Any person the value of whose estate is increased by the transfer.

(c) So far as the tax is attributable to the value of any property, any person in whom the property is vested (whether beneficially or otherwise) at any time after the transfer, or who at any such time is beneficially entitled to an interest in possession in the property.

(d) Where by the chargeable transfer any property that becomes comprised in a settlement, any person for whose benefit any of the property or income from it is applied.

A person liable as a trustee is liable only to the extent of property which they have actually received or disposed of or have become liable to account for to the beneficiaries and to the extent of any other property available in their hands for the payment of tax or which might have been so available but for their own neglect or default.

A person liable for tax as a person in whom property is vested or as a person entitled to a beneficial interest in possession in property is liable only to the extent of that property.

A person liable for tax as a person for whose benefit property or income has been applied is liable only to the extent of that property or income (less any income tax).

The personal representatives of the transferor are liable only to the extent that as a result of the limitations of liability relevant to the other categories no one falling within any of the other categories is liable *or* the tax remains unpaid 12 months after the end of the month in which the death of the transferor occurred. In such a case their liability is limited to the value of assets which they received or would have received but for their own neglect or default.

In a case where potentially exempt or chargeable transfers were made within **4.63** seven years of death and inheritance tax is due, personal representatives would be wise to refrain from completely distributing the assets of the estate until satisfied that the tax has been paid. If they do not, they may find themselves personally liable for unpaid tax. This is, of course, easier said than done, as there will often be cases where the personal representatives are unaware of lifetime gifts. Personal representatives may be unaware of their possible liability for additional inheritance tax when they distribute assets to the beneficiaries of the estate. They can obtain indemnities from the beneficiaries but these will be useless if the beneficiary becomes bankrupt. They can try to obtain insurance but this is often difficult or expensive.

Personal representatives who pay inheritance tax on lifetime transfers have no statutory right of recovery against the donees who were primarily liable for the tax. Section 212 of IHTA 1984 gives power to persons liable for tax to sell, mortgage or charge assets to raise money to pay the tax even if the assets are not vested in them. It is important for personal representatives to make full enquiries to establish any lifetime transfers or property subject to a reservation of benefit. There is a letter from the Revenue to the Law Society dated February 11, 1991 which states that the Revenue will not "usually" pursue personal representatives for inheritance tax who:

- "after making the fullest enquiries that are reasonably practicable in the circumstances to discover lifetime transfers, and so

- having done all in their power to make full disclosure of them to the Board of Inland Revenue

- have obtained a certificate of discharge and distributed the estate before a chargeable lifetime transfer comes to light".

The issue of course is "what is reasonably practicable". Personal representatives may well be expected to look at bank statements going back seven years as well as asking friends and family. Those who give misleading information to personal representatives may face a penalty under para.1A of FA 2007 Sch.24.

There is a similar danger for personal representatives in relation to the inheritance tax on property given away during the deceased's lifetime but subject to a reservation of benefit (see para.4.16, above.) The transferee is primarily liable but the personal representatives will become liable if the tax is unpaid after 12 months from the death. Here, though, the personal representatives do have a statutory right of recovery under Inheritance Tax Act 1984 s.211(3). Personal representatives should be particularly careful to check for property subject to a reservation of benefit as a result of the rules on pre-owned assets.

Taxpayers who are liable to pay the pre-owned assets charge (Finance Act 2004 s.84 and Sch.15) can opt out of the regime and into the IHT reservation of benefit provisions within the relevant time limit (Sch.15 para.21). (The donee, who is the person primarily liable for the IHT on the gifted property, has no say in the matter and may not even know that the election has been made).

The election is sent not to the local Inspector of Taxes but to the Pre-Owned Assets Section at Nottingham. The section will inform the local tax office *and record the election*. There will be a check on death for any elections made by the taxpayer with a view to the collection of inheritance tax. It is, therefore. important for personal representatives to try to establish whether or not the deceased made such an election so that the information given to the Revenue is accurate. Once made, the election can be withdrawn or amended by the taxpayer but only before the relevant filing date (Sch.15 para.23(5)). It cannot be withdrawn by the taxpayer's PRs.

8. Burden (or Incidence) of Inheritance Tax

Introduction

4.64   When inheritance tax is due on death, the beneficiaries of the estate will be very concerned to discover on which part of the estate the burden of the tax will fall since this may affect the size of their entitlement. The following example illustrates this.

> *Example*
>
> T leaves a house to A, a pecuniary legacy to B, jewellery to C and the residue of the estate to D. There is substantial inheritance tax to pay. The personal representatives are liable for the inheritance tax and before obtaining a grant of representation must send a cheque for the amount of tax due to the Revenue. The personal representatives may borrow the money from a bank or from a beneficiary or may arrange for a bank or building society to release funds directly to the Revenue. Whichever course they follow, they will have to decide where the burden ultimately falls. If the entire burden falls on residue, D's benefit from the estate will be much reduced; whereas, if the burden is divided proportionately amongst the beneficiares, D will receive rather more but the benefits received by A, B and C will be reduced.

A testator may include an express direction in the will as to whether or not assets are to bear their own tax. In the absence of such a direction there are statutory rules.

Express direction in the will as to burden

The testator may state in the will that certain gifts are to be "free of inheritance **4.65** tax" while others are to bear their own; if such a direction is included it is conclusive and the inheritance tax payable on gifts made "free of tax" will be a testamentary expense paid from the property available to pay other debts of the estate (primarily undisposed of property and residue). Any professionally drawn will should include an express direction as to the burden of inheritance tax since this not only avoids future disputes but leads the testator to consider whether the proposed disposition of property is satisfactory having regard to the burden of inheritance tax. (However, as we shall see in para.4.71, below, a direction that an exempt share of residue is to bear inheritance tax attributable to a non-exempt share of residue must be disregarded.)

No express direction in will

In order to remove uncertainties which had arisen, IHTA 1984 s.211 makes **4.66** express provision for the burden of inheritance tax in relation to deaths occurring on or after July 25, 1983. Section 211 provides that where personal representatives are liable for inheritance tax on the value transferred by a chargeable transfer made on death the tax shall be treated as part of the general testamentary and administration expenses of the estate but only in so far as it is attributable to the value of property in the UK which:

(a)   vests in the deceased's personal representatives; and

(b)   was not, immediately before the death, comprised in a settlement.

The provision is subject to any contrary intention shown by the deceased in their will. As we shall see in Ch.15, expenses of the estate (and debts) are paid primarily from undisposed-of property and, if none, from the residue of the estate. Thus, where under s.211(1) inheritance tax is to be treated as a general testamentary and administration expense, the burden of it falls primarily on the undisposed-of property and on the residue. Section 211(3) provides that:

> "where any amount of tax paid by personal representatives on the value transferred by a chargeable transfer made on death does not fall to be borne as part of the general testamentary and administration expenses of the estate, that amount shall, where occasion requires, be repaid to them by the person in whom the property to the value of which the tax is attributable is vested".

The effect of s.211(3) is that whenever personal representatives are liable to pay inheritance tax (as they are on all of the deceased's free estate and on settled land which devolves on them), they have a right to recover it from the particular beneficiary receiving the property to which it relates *unless* the tax is a general, testamentary and administration expense under s.211(1); that is *unless* the property to which the inheritance tax is attributable was situate in the UK, vested in the personal representatives and was not comprised in a Settled Land Act settlement immediately before the death. As a result of s.211(3) the personal representatives can recover from the particular beneficiary concerned (subject to contrary intention) inheritance tax attributable to:

(a) non-UK property,

(b) property not vesting in the personal representatives (that is, joint property passing by survivorship, property subject to a nomination or to a *donatio mortis causa*), and

(c) property which was immediately before the death comprised in a Settled Land Act settlement.

(The personal representatives will only have accounted for inheritance tax in respect of trust property where the property was settled land devolving on them. They are not *liable* for inheritance tax in respect of other types of trust property and so will not generally be involved in the payment or recovery of inheritance tax relating to it.)

Practical problems

4.67 In practice where personal representatives have accounted to the Revenue for inheritance tax for which they were liable they may encounter difficulties in obtaining repayment for the residuary estate from the person in whom the property is vested. The personal representatives should take all possible steps to minimise such difficulties.

If a pecuniary legacy has been left to a legatee and the will declares that the legatee is to bear the burden of inheritance tax attributable to it, the personal representatives should deduct an appropriate amount and pay the net legacy to the legatee. Obviously if an asset is left, rather than cash, no deduction can be made. However, the personal representatives should not vest the asset in the beneficiary until arrangements have been made for reimbursement of the amount due.

If the beneficiary has got possession of the asset (for example, because the property has passed by survivorship) there is nothing the personal representatives can do to prevent problems arising unless other assets due to the beneficiary under the will or intestacy rules are in the hands of the personal representatives. If the personal representatives have got possession of other assets due to the beneficiary they should ensure that all repayments of inheritance tax due to the residuary estate are made before they part with the assets.

Personal representatives have power under s.212 to sell, mortgage or charge property *whether or not it is vested in them* to raise money for tax for which they are liable. It would obviously be difficult to do this where the property is not vested in them but the fact that they have such a sanction may persuade the person in whom it is vested to pay them the amount due.

Apportioning the burden of inheritance tax

4.68 Where the burden of inheritance tax due is to be divided amongst different people, it is necessary to apportion the inheritance tax amongst the various assets comprised in the estate. This can be done in one of two ways. *Either* calculate an average rate of inheritance tax for the estate and apply that rate to the assets each beneficiary is to receive; *or* (more simply) allocate a proportionate part of the total inheritance tax to each beneficiary. The result of the two methods will be identical.

Example

A dies having made chargeable lifetime transfers which leave £300,000 of the nil rate band remaining. Her estate comprises:

		£
Land		500,000
Liquid Assets		300,000

Her will directs that the land is to bear its own tax and is to pass to B, that a pecuniary legacy of £60,000 bearing its own tax is to pass to C, and that residue is to pass to D. No exemptions apply.

Band		*Rate*	
£	£	%	£
First	300,000	nil	nil
300,000 –	800,000	40	200,000
Total Inheritance Tax bill			200,000

The tax must then be apportioned.

Using method 1: Calculate an estate rate

$$\frac{\text{Total Tax}}{\text{Value of Estate}} \times 100 = \%$$

$$\frac{£200,000}{£800,000} \times 100 = 25\%$$

This rate can then be applied to the property bearing its own tax passing to each beneficiary:

B's share of tax burden

$$£500,000 \times 25\% = £125,000$$

C's share of tax burden

$$£60,000 \times 25\% = £15,000$$

The rate will also be applied to the residue passing to D. The residue amounts to £240,000 that is the liquid assets of £300,000 less the £60,000 legacy:

D's share of tax burden

$$£240,000 \times 25\% = £60,000$$

The total tax payable on the whole estate is £200,000.

Using method 2: Allocate a proportion of the total tax to each beneficiary:

B's share of tax burden
$$\frac{£500,000}{£800,000} \times £200,000 = £125,000$$

C's share of tax burden
$$\frac{£60,000}{£800,000} \times £200,000 = £15,000$$

D's share of tax burden
$$\frac{£240,000}{£800,000} \times £200,000 = £60,000$$

The total tax payable on the whole estate is £200,000.

9. TIME FOR PAYMENT

General position

4.69 The tax on a transfer on death is payable six months after the end of the month in which death occurred. The tax on a chargeable transfer made before death is payable six months after the end of the month in which the transfer is made or, if the transfer is made after April 5, and before October 1, at the end of April in the next year. Where tax or extra tax is payable on a lifetime transfer because of the death of the donor it is payable six months after the end of the month of death.

Where tax is paid after the date on which it should have been paid interest is chargeable on it. The rate of interest is prescribed by statutory instrument.

Instalment option

4.70 The inheritance tax on certain types of property may be paid by instalments over a 10-year period in certain circumstances (IHTA ss.227–228).

Transfer on death

4.71   (a) Land of any description (this term is not further defined but clearly freehold and leasehold interests are included).

(b) Shares or securities in a company giving the deceased control of the company immediately before death.

(c) Unquoted shares or securities which did not give the deceased control provided that the Revenue are satisfied that the payment of the tax in one sum would cause undue hardship.

(d) Unquoted shares or securities which did not give the deceased control where at least 20 per cent of the tax payable on the death by the person paying the tax on those shares is either tax on those shares or on those shares and other instalment option property.

(e) Unquoted shares which did not give the deceased control and the value of which exceeds £20,000 at the time of death provided that either:

   (i) they are at least 10 per cent (by nominal value) of all the shares in the company; or

   (ii) they are ordinary shares and are at least 10 per cent (by nominal value) of all the ordinary shares in the company.

(f) A business or an interest in a business including a profession or vocation. Liabilities incurred for the purposes of the business must be deducted in computing what is the value of the business for this purpose (normally liabilities are deducted from the whole rather than from particular assets unless the assets are charged with payment of the liabilities).

"Unquoted" means not listed on a recognised stock exchange. Unquoted shares include those dealt in on the Alternative Investment Market. A person has control for this purpose if they (with the benefit of any shares or securities which are related property) has voting control on all questions affecting the company as a whole (IHTA 1984 s.269).

In cases where business property relief or agricultural property relief is available at 100 per cent the instalment option will be irrelevant. However, the instalment option will be useful in cases where the qualifying ownership period has not been fulfilled or where relief is not available because of the nature of the business.

Lifetime Transfers

Inheritance tax on chargeable transfers made before death may be paid by **4.72** instalments in respect of the same types of property as in the case of transfers on death. However, this relief is only available where the inheritance tax is *paid by the donee*. In the case of tax payable on the value transferred by a potentially exempt transfer which proves to be chargeable (or extra tax payable where the transferee dies within seven years of a chargeable transfer), the instalment option is available only to the extent that one of the following conditions is fulfilled:

(a) the transferee owns the qualifying property throughout the period from transfer until the death of the transferor (or, if earlier, of the transferee);

(b) in the case of property eligible for business or agricultural relief, the transferee has disposed of the original property but has applied the proceeds in acquiring replacement property; or

(c) in the case of unquoted shares the shares remain unquoted up to the date of death of the transferor (or, if earlier, of the transferee).

The instalment option is also available on transfers on the termination of an interest in possession in settled property and when tax becomes payable in the case of settlements without an interest in possession. In the case of woodlands tax, this can always be paid by instalments even if paid by the donor.

Procedure for payment by instalments

4.73 The payment of tax by instalments is only possible where the person paying the tax gives notice in writing to the Revenue that he wishes to pay in that way. (On death notice is given in the IHT 400.) Where the election is made, tax is payable in 10 equal annual instalments. The first instalment is due on the date on which the tax would be due if not paid by instalments (in the case of death six months after the end of the month of death).

The taxpayer may pay off all remaining instalments at any time within the 10 years and must do so if the assets are sold. In the case of tax paid by instalments on non-agricultural land, not comprised in a business, interest on the whole of the outstanding tax is payable and is added to each instalment. In the case of tax paid by instalments on shares (other than shares in investment companies), business or interests in businesses interest is only payable to the extent that an instalment of tax is overdue.

It is common for personal representatives to choose to exercise the option initially even if they feel they may wish to pay off the outstanding amount in one lump sum at a later stage. The reason for considering a temporary exercise of the option is that it reduces the amount of inheritance tax falling due for payment six months after the end of the month of the death and so keeps to a minimum the amount of money which may have to be borrowed to pay the inheritance tax due. Once the personal representatives have obtained the grant of representation, they are able to realise assets of the estate and may then decide (particularly if interest is payable on the amount outstanding) to use the money to pay off any outstanding inheritance tax.

Personal representatives should remember that they remain personally liable for the inheritance tax on the death estate until it has been paid in full. Thus, if they transfer property on which the instalment option has been claimed to beneficiaries, they should consider what steps, if any, they can take to ensure that full payment is made. This may well mean retaining assets as security.

The case of *Howarth's Executors v IRC* (1997) indicates the perils which can exist for the unwary. The deceased's will was proved by her son, H, and his wife, who were both beneficiaries, and by S, an employee of a firm of solicitors, who was not a beneficiary.

The executors elected to pay tax in instalments. The deceased's assets were transferred to the two beneficiaries. Initially instalments were paid by H but these ceased and H was eventually declared bankrupt. The Revenue served notices of outstanding tax and interest of £8,084.71 on the three executors.

The Special Commissioner held that, although H was primarily liable for the payment of tax, the co-executor, S, remained personally liable. He had joined in the election to pay by instalments and had then consented to transfer all the assets to the beneficiaries. In so doing he had taken an obvious risk.

10. Partially Exempt Transfers

Introduction

The transfer of value on death is for inheritance tax purposes one transfer of the **4.74** whole of the deceased's estate. This transfer may be fully taxable, fully exempt or it may be partly taxable and partly exempt (for example, because part but not all of the property is given to a spouse, charity, political party or exempt body). If it is partly taxable and partly exempt IHTA 1984 contains rules for calculating the amount of inheritance tax and as to the burden of tax. These rules can give rise to rather complicated arithmetical computations. Details of the method of calculation vary according to the type of dispositions made. The two types of calculation are dealt with in the next two sub-paragraphs.

"Specific" gifts not bearing their own tax to non-exempt beneficiary residue to exempt beneficiary

For this purpose any gift is "specific" if it is not a gift of residue (IHTA 1984 **4.75** s.42). If a specific gift is not exempt, the tax in respect of it will normally be paid from residue (see paras 4.64–4.66). The specific legatee is treated as having received an amount *net* of tax (IHTA 1984 s.3B) and, therefore, the net gift must be grossed up at the death rate to calculate the amount of the tax borne by residue.

Example

Aidan has made lifetime chargeable transfers which have exhausted his nil rate band and has died with a death estate of £50,000. On his death he gives £12,000 to his son, Sam, and *does not provide that this gift is subject to tax*; Aidan leaves the residue of his estate to his wife. Since the gift of £12,000 is not made to bear its own tax, the tax will come out of exempt residue so grossing-up is required.

£12,000 grossed up at the death rates with a cumulative total which has exhausted his nil rate band is:

$$£12,000 \times \frac{100}{60} = £20,000$$

The tax is the difference between the gross and net gifts.

£20,000 − £12,000 = £8,000

The estate is therefore divided as follows:

	£	£
Tax		8,000
Legacy to Sam		12,000
Residue to widow	50,000	
	(20,000)	
		30,000
		50,000

Residue partly to exempt and partly to non-exempt beneficiaries

4.76   Section 41 states that "notwithstanding the terms of any disposition" none of the tax attributable to residue shall fall on an exempt share of residue. Thus, if residue is left "to pay debts and tax and then to be divided between" an exempt and a non-exempt beneficiary, the share of the non-exempt beneficiary is diminished by tax while the share of the exempt beneficiary is not.

> *Example*
>
> *Ted* dies with a nil cumulative total leaving an estate of £900,000 to be divided equally between son and spouse. The half of the estate passing to the son bears its own tax.

The case of *Re Benham* (1995) caused problems for practitioners. For a discussion of the problems raised by *Benham* see para.4.77, below.

Specific gifts not bearing their own tax to non-exempt beneficiaries residue partly to exempt partly to non-exempt beneficiaries

4.77   In this situation the tax on the "specific" gifts is borne by the whole of the residue unless the will provides otherwise. The tax on the non-exempt part of residue *must* however be borne by that part of the residue only. This is because IHTA 1984 s.41 provides that exempt residue is not to bear the tax on any other part of *residue*. To calculate the tax it is necessary to gross up the specific gift (or gifts) not bearing its own tax as if it were cumulated with any chargeable lifetime transfers but was the only taxable part of the estate on death. This figure is then added to any other parts of the estate which are in fact taxable (i.e. specific gifts bearing their own tax and non-exempt residue) to calculate an "assumed rate" of tax. The specific gift not bearing its own tax is then grossed up again at the assumed rate and the tax on the estate is tax on that figure plus tax on any other non-exempt parts of the estate (e.g. residue).

> *Example*
>
> Tessa dies in Tax Year 2010/11 leaving an estate of £800,000. She has made lifetime transfers which leave £300,000 of her nil rate band available. In her will she gives £315,000 to her daughter, residue to be divided between her husband and her sister. The will contains no directions as to the burden of inheritance tax.
>
> (a)   Gross up the gift to the daughter as if it were the only taxable gift on death. On this assumption £300,000 is within the nil rate band so only £15,000 has to be grossed up at 40 per cent. £15,000 grossed up at 40 per cent is £25,000. The gross legacy is therefore £300,000 + £25,000 = £325,000.
>
> (b)   Calculate the other taxable parts of the estate. Only half of the residue is taxable, the other half is going to the husband (and so is exempt).
>
> (c)   Add the grossed-up legacy and the taxable half of residue to give the taxable estate.

	£
Value of estate	800,000
Less: grossed up legacy	(325,000)
"Residue"	475,000
Half residue	237,000
Tax is therefore payable on:	
Grossed up legacy	325,000
Taxable half of residue	237,500
Taxable estate	562,500

(d) Calculate an assumed rate. This is the rate of tax which would be charged on an estate of £562,500 with £300,000 of nil rate band available. The tax would be:

Band	Rate	
£	%	£
First 300,000	nil	nil
Next 262,500	40	105,000
Inheritance Tax		105,000

The assumed rate would therefore be:

$$\frac{£105,000}{£562,000} \times 100 = 18.67\%$$

(e) Gross up the specific gift not bearing its own tax at the assumed rate:

$$£315,000 \times \frac{100}{100 - 18.67}$$

$$= £315,000 \times \frac{100}{81.33}$$

$$= £387,310.95$$

(f) Tax is now payable on the grossed-up specific gift and half the residue, i.e.:

	£
Value of estate	800,000.00
Less: grossed up legacy	(387,310.95)
"Residue"	412,689.05
Half residue	206,344.52
Tax is therefore payable on:	
Grossed up legacy	387,310.95
Taxable half of residue	206,344.52
Taxable estate	593,655.47

Tax is therefore:

Band	Rate	
£	%	£
First 300,000.00	nil	nil
next 293,655.47	40	117,7462.18
Tax		117,7462.18

The portion of the £117,7462.18 attributable to the specific legacy is borne by the residue as a whole. The balance of the residue is then split into two equal parts and the portion of the £117,7462.18 attributable to the non-exempt residue is borne entirely from the non-exempt part of residue. In apportioning the inheritance tax bill either of the two methods explained in para.4.67 can be used.

Section 41 and *Re Benham's Will Trusts* (1995)

4.78   In *Re Benham* the deceased left the residue of the estate to pay debts and then to pay to those beneficiaries:

> "as are living at my death and who are listed in List A and List B . . . in such proportions as will bring about the result that the aforesaid beneficiaries named in List A shall receive 3.2 times as much as the aforesaid beneficiaries named in List B . . . ".

Some of the beneficiaries were charities and some were not.

The deputy judge hearing the case held that "the plain intention of the testatrix is that at the end of the day each beneficiary whether charitable or non-charitable should receive the same as the other beneficiaries . . . ". He found that this was to be achieved by grossing up the shares of the non-charitable legatees so that *after payment of tax* charitable and non-charitable legatees ended up with the same amount.

The effect was that more of the estate had to be allocated initially to the non-exempt beneficiaries so that after the payment of tax they retained the same net amount that the exempt beneficiaries received. The Revenue received more tax than it would have had the initial division been equal. The exempt beneficiaries received less.

It was not clear whether the case was to be interpreted as of very limited importance turning on the particular words used by the testatrix which demonstrated an intention that residue was to be divided unequally or whether it was to be interpreted as of general application wherever residue was left to be divided "equally" between exempt and non-exempt beneficiaries. There was uncertainty and practitioners and charities were unhappy.

There was an exchange of correspondence between the Revenue and the British Heart Foundation. The charity was concerned that the decision would result in a reduction in the amount of property passing to exempt beneficiaries.[1]

The Revenue's response stated that in their view *Benham* is a decision "primarily concerned with ascertaining the intention of the testatrix and . . . does not directly involve the Inland Revenue". It confirmed that the decision followed from the particular facts of the case and that:

> "if the Will is drafted in 'common form' with a direction to ascertain residue after payment of funeral and testamentary expenses and debts followed by a bequest of that residue, then it is focusing on the ascertainment and division of disposable

---

[1] See *Tax Journal,* September 5, 1996, p.3 and *Private Client Business* 1996, no.5, p.295.

residue rather than on what each beneficiary is to receive. Accordingly a will so drafted would not appear to involve *Benham-style* grossing up computations."

The decision in *Re Ratcliffe, Holmes v McMullan* (1999) alleviated the problems caused by *Re Benham*. In *Re Ratcliffe* the testatrix left her residue after payment of debts, funeral and testamentary expenses to be divided equally between exempt and non-exempt beneficiaries. Blackburne J. was of the view that, on a true construction of the will, the testatrix intended to divide her residue equally before payment of tax between the beneficiaries. The non-exempt beneficiaries then had to pay tax from their share without grossing-up.

He accepted that a will could direct that residue be divided unequally between exempt and non-exempt beneficiaries so that after payment of tax they were each left with the same amount. However, he said that to achieve this result "much clearer wording would be needed than the common form wording actually used". He said that he did not regard *Re Benham* as laying down any principle and, accordingly, did not feel bound to follow it.

There are two problems for practitioners:

(1) How to draft a will in the light of *Benham* and *Ratcliffe?*

(2) How to deal with the administration of an estate where the will contains a standard gift of residue dividing it between exempt and non-exempt beneficiaries?

Will Drafting

This is relatively simple. Ask the testator whether they want their residue to be **4.79** divided equally between the exempt and non-exempt beneficiaries. Explain that the result will be that the non-exempt beneficiary will "end up" with less because their share will be reduced by inheritance tax. The alternative is that the residue is divided unequally. The result of an unequal division is that the initial share of the non-exempt beneficiary is bigger, leaving the two shares of equal size once the tax has been deducted. Obviously more of the estate will be lost in tax since more of it is being given to a non-exempt beneficiary. It is permissible to point out to the testator that the calculation of the gifts after their death will be *extremely* complex.

Once the testator has decided on the type of gifts they want the will must be drafted to give clear effect to their wishes. There are many suitable precedents; the following is taken from Butterworths' Will Probate and Administration Service Form 1A, 22.1.

My trustee shall hold the Trust Fund ON TRUST

(a) as to one share absolutely for my Wife (Husband) *(or give name if not already defined as such)* if she (he) survives me for 28 days.

(b) as to another share (or as to the whole if the preceding gift fails) absolutely for such of my children as are alive at my death (and reach the age of [18]) and if more than one in equal shares PROVIDED that if any child of mine [is already dead or] dies before me [or before reaching that age] but leaves a child or children alive at the death of the survivor of my child and me who reach the age of [18] or marry under that age then such child or children shall take absolutely and if more than one in equal shares so much of the Trust Fund as that child of mine would have taken on attaining a vested interest

AND the shares given by (a) and (b) above shall be such shares as before [after] the deduction of any inheritance tax attributable to them respectively are of equal [or are of values bearing to one another the proportions [2₁] the larger share being that given by [a] [b]].

Administration of an estate

4.80   It is necessary to construe the will to determine the testator's intention. If the will contains a common form residuary gift directing division of residue after payment of debts and inheritance tax, it would seem safe in the light of *Re Ratcliffe* to divide the residue equally before payment of tax. However, if there is any ambiguity or unusual wording, the correct construction may be uncertain. In such a case it would be desirable to get the agreement of the beneficiaries as to the method of division but they may not be united. Probably the only thing to be done in such a case is to point out the cost of litigation if the parties are unable to agree.

Partly exempt transfers and agricultural and business property relief

4.81   Prior to the Finance Act 1986 anomalous results sometimes arose where a partly exempt transfer included property qualifying for agricultural or business property relief. The Finance Act 1986 therefore inserted s.39A to ensure that the reliefs are available in a consistent manner. Section 39A cannot be varied by the terms of a will.

Where there is a specific gift of property qualifying for relief, the relief attaches to that property irrespective of whether the specific beneficiary is an exempt or non-exempt beneficiary (s.39A(2)).

Example

T dies with an estate of £1m including a business worth £600,000 qualifying for 100 per cent relief. T has exhausted his nil rate band. T leaves the business to his wife and the residue to his son. Tax will be payable at 40% on all the assets passing to the son.

Had the business been left to the son, no tax would have been paid on the estate at all. It is clearly more tax efficient to leave property attracting 100 per cent relief to non-exempt beneficiaries.

Note that an appropriation of property on which a relief is available by the personal representatives to a residuary beneficiary is not a specific gift for this purpose. However, the disposition of the estate can be varied by the beneficiaries under IHTA 1984 s.142 to produce a specific gift eligible for relief.

Where property eligible for relief passes as part of the residue of the estate, the relief is allocated pro rata to all the assets transferred (s.39A(3)) using the statutory formula:

$$\frac{R}{U}$$

where R is the value of the estate as reduced by agricultural and business relief less the value of any specific gifts qualifying for relief and U is the unreduced value of the estate less the value of any specific gifts qualifying for relief.

Example

T dies with an estate of £1m including a business worth £600,000 qualifying for 100 per cent relief. T has exhausted his nil rate band. T leaves a pecuniary legacy of £200,000 to his son, specific assets worth £100,000 to his daughter and the residue which includes the business to his wife. Since the business has not been left specifically to anyone the benefit of the relief must be apportioned pro rata through the estate.

R is £1m less £600,000 = £400,000

U is £1m

Thus, the value for inheritance tax purposes of the property transferred will be:

Pecuniary legacy

$$£200,000 \times \frac{£400,000}{£1m} = £80,000$$

Specific legacy

$$£100,000 \times \frac{£400,000}{£1m} = £40,000$$

Residue

$$£700,000 \times \frac{£400,000}{£1m} = £280,000$$

While some of the relief is "wasted" on the gift passing to the spouse, the gifts passing to the son and daughter derive some benefit from the relief.

The effect of s.39A can cause problems where the testator has used a formula clause to pass a legacy to a non-exempt beneficiary "equal to the maximum amount that can pass without payment of inheritence tax". If the residuary estate includes property eligible for relief, the amount passing under such a gift will be increased. If this is not what the testator wants, the will should either leave the property eligible for relief to a specific beneficiary or impose a "cap" on the amount that can pass under the gift, for example, "the legacy is not to exceed the value of the nil rate band in force at my death".

It is rarely certain at the time that a will is drafted whether or not assets will qualify for relief at the date of the death. The nature of a business's trading activities may change or a farmhouse may cease to be occupied for the purposes of agriculture before the death. It is, therefore, normally advisable to leave assets which may be eligible for relief to a discretionary trust. Appointments from such a trust within two years of death will be read back into the will under IHTA 1984 s.144—see para.19.24. Personal representatives will, therefore, be able to decide how best to deal with the business assets once they know whether or not relief is available.

11. Some Particular Problems

Inter-relationship of inheritance tax and capital gains tax

4.82 Capital gains tax, like inheritance tax, is a tax charged on movements of capital assets. It is not payable on death (except in certain circumstances in respect of settled property). However, a lifetime transfer may give rise to capital gains tax liability, as well as to inheritance tax liability. Such liability must be taken into account when deciding between lifetime gifts and gifts on death. To ensure that one tax is not paid on the amount of the other tax two rules apply:

(a) Capital gains tax paid by the transferor is not treated as a loss to the transferor's estate for inheritance tax purposes.

(b) Capital gains tax paid by the transferee reduces the value transferred to inheritance tax purposes.

Example

Ann makes a chargeable lifetime transfer to Bob of an asset acquired for £10,000; the current value of the asset is £20,000. We will assume that capital gains tax is £2,800 (i.e. 28 per cent of the £10,000 gain—this will in fact be the amount of tax if there are no exemptions available and Ann's income is equal to or exceeds the limit for basic rate income tax). We will assume that the rate of inheritance tax is half of 40 per cent. This would be the appropriate rate if the transferor had used up his annual exemption and nil rate band. Remember that the value transferred is grossed up where the transferor pays the inheritance tax.

(a) If transferor pays both taxes:

    (i) Capital gains tax (£2,800) is not a loss to the transferor's estate.
    (ii) Inheritance tax is payable on the grossed-up gift.

        Gross gift for inheritance tax purposes

$$£20,000 \times \frac{100}{80} = £25,000$$

        Inheritance tax = £5,000

		£
(iii) Total cost to transferor:	CGT	2,800
	Gift	20,000
	IHT	5,000
		27,800

Amount added to cumulative total	£25,000
Benefit to transferee	£20,000

(b) If transferee pays both taxes:

    (i) Capital gains tax (£2,800) reduces value transferred to £17,200

     (ii) Inheritance tax is payable on gift (not grossed up) less £2,800 (the capital gains tax)

          Inheritance tax £17,200 × 20% = £3,440

    (iii) Total cost to transferor £20,000

          Amount added to cumulative total £17,200

          Net benefit to transferee £13,760

(c)   If transferor pays inheritance tax and transferee pays capital gains tax:

     (i) Capital gains tax (£2,800) reduces value transferred.

     (ii) Inheritance tax is payable on grossed up amount of gift less capital gains tax:

$$£17,200 \times \frac{100}{80} = £21,500$$

Inheritance tax

$$£21,500 \times 20\% = £4,300$$

    (iii) Total cost to transferor

Gift	£20,000
IHT	£4,300
	£24,300

Amount added to cumulative total	£21,500
Benefit to transferee	£17,200

(d)   If transferee pays inheritance tax and transferor pays capital gains tax:

     (i) Capital gains tax (£2,800) not a loss to transferor's estate

     (ii) Inheritance tax payable on gift (not grossed up)

         £20,000 × 20% = £4,000

    (iii) Total cost to transferor   £22,800

Amount added to cumulative total	£20,000
Benefit to transferee	£16,000

Where capital gains tax hold-over relief is claimed on a gift (see para.5.16, below) a different rule applies to deal with the overlap between the two taxes. The amount of inheritance tax paid on the transfer of value is deducted in computing the donee's chargeable gain on a later disposal by them. Where the donor dies within seven years of the gift the inheritance tax may have to be recalculated. In such a case the transferor's estate is entitled to a refund of capital gains tax paid, if appropriate. However, the deduction is only permitted to the extent that it will wipe out the chargeable gain and so cannot give rise to an allowable loss.

Example   **4.83**

Andy buys a business asset for £18,000 and makes a chargeable lifetime transfer of it to Bella, when it is worth £20,000. Hold-over relief is claimed. We will assume that the rate of inheritance tax is half of 40 per cent. This would be the appropriate rate if the transferor had used up his annual exemption and the nil rate band. We will ignore the possibility of business property relief for the purpose of this calculation. If Andy pays the inheritance tax it will be £5,000 (with grossing-up), if Bella pays it will be £4,000 (without grossing-up).

Bella then sells the business asset for £22,500. Assuming that there are no incidental costs of disposal, the gain according to normal capital gains tax principles would be £4,500 (£22,500 – £18,000 = £4,500) since Bella is allowed to deduct Andy's acquisition cost from his disposal consideration. However, as hold-over relief was claimed the amount of inheritance tax paid on the original transfer can be deducted in computing the gain for capital gains tax purposes.

a) Chargeable gain where B (the donee) paid the inheritance tax:

	£
Gain	4,500
Less	(4,000*)
	500

b) Chargeable gain where A (the donor) paid the inheritance tax:

	£
Gain	4,500
Less	(5,000**)
	Nil

In the above example had the transfer been potentially exempt, no inheritance tax would have been payable at the time of the transfer. Therefore, if Bella had sold the business asset for £22,500 before Andy's death then capital gains tax would have been payable on the full gain of £4,500. Assuming Bella has already exhausted her basic rate income tax band, the capital gains tax would be calculated as follows:

$$28\% \times £4,500 = £1,260$$

However, if Andy then died, say, four-and-a-half years after the transfer to Bella, inheritance tax would become payable at 60 per cent of the full rate. Assuming that Bella paid the inheritance tax there would be no grossing-up and the inheritance tax would be 60 per cent of the full rate of 40 per cent (assuming the rates remain identical to the current rates):

$$60\% \times 40\% \times £20,000 = £4,800$$

The £4,800 of inheritance tax now due would be deducted from the gain of £4,500 and would extinguish it. Thus the capital gains tax already paid could be reclaimed.

Anti-avoidance provisions

4.84 Taxpayers are entitled to arrange their financial affairs so as to avoid paying tax unnecessarily. However, such arrangements may be attacked by the Revenue either under the special inheritance tax provisions relating to "associated operations" rules or under general principles laid down by the House of Lords in cases such as *Ramsay v IRC* (1982) and *Furniss v Dawson* (1984).

Associated operations

4.85 Section 268 of IHTA 1984 provides that where a transfer of value is made by "associated operations" carried out at different times it shall be treated as made at the time of the last of them. "Associated operations" are defined very widely as being:

> "any two or more operations which affect the same property . . . or any two operations of which one is effected with reference to the other or with a view to enabling or facilitating the other to be effected whether effected by the same or different people and whether or not they are simultaneous".

The object of these provisions is to prevent donors avoiding inheritance tax by making artificial arrangements.

Obviously many individuals wish to arrange their financial affairs so as to provide the maximum benefit for members of their family and so as to avoid unnecessary tax; this may well involve arrangements which *could* be regarded as associated. In particular, it is common, where one spouse is much wealthier than the other, for the wealthier spouse to make use of the spouse exemption to transfer assets to the poorer spouse. This enables the poorer spouse to make transfers to the issue of the couple which will attract lifetime exemptions and/or prove to be fully exempt if the donor survives seven years. When the associated operations provisions were discussed in Parliament in 1975 the Chief Secretary to the Treasury said that transfers between spouses would only be attacked in blatant cases where a transfer was made *on condition* that the recipient would at once use the money to make gifts to others.

In *Rysaffe Trustee Co (CI) Ltd v IRC* (2003) a taxpayer had set up a series of £10 pilot trusts on different days to which substantial funds were later transferred. The Revenue sought to charge tax on the basis that there was just one single settlement. A unanimous Court of Appeal rejected the Revenue's arguments. Associated operations are only relevant if in substance there is a single disposition which has been divided into a number of separate "operations". While each transfer was part of one scheme, the transfer of each amount made no reference to the other transfers. Each transfer was effected in the knowledge that the others were being effected as well but that is not the same as effecting transfers "with reference to the other" which is what the section requires.

General principles

In the 1980s there was a strong judicial movement to counter artificial tax **4.86** avoidance schemes. The House of Lords in *Ramsay* said that a court was not required to look at documents or transactions in blinkers, isolated from the context to which it belongs. If it is clear that a document or transaction is intended to have effect as part of a nexus or series of transactions, it can be regarded as such.

Furniss v Dawson set out the conditions required for the application of the so-called Ramsey principle: where a taxpayer achieves a purpose either by using a preordained series of transactions or a single composite transaction and steps are inserted which have no commercial purpose apart from the avoidance of a liability to tax, the inserted steps are to be disregarded for tax purposes.

These decisions caused some unease as being little short of judicial legislation and later cases have tended to limit their effect. While taxpayers should be cautious about embarking on artificial schemes designed to achieve tax advantages, it is true that recently the Revenue has tended to respond to what it perceives as tax avoidance with targeted legislation to close loopholes or even in the case of the pre-owned assets legislation to introduce a new charge to tax.

The Inheritance Tax Avoidance Schemes (Prescribed Descriptions of Arrangements) Regulations 2011 require disclosure of certain new schemes designed to avoid inheritance tax as from April 6, 2011. However, disclosure is only required where the scheme is designed to avoid, reduce or defer the charge to tax arising where property is transferred to a relevant property settlement.

12. CERTIFICATES OF DISCHARGE

4.87   If the Revenue is satisfied that the tax attributable to a chargeable transfer has been or will be paid in instalments they can (and, if the transfer is one made on death, must) give a certificate to that effect (s.239(1)). The effect is to discharge all persons (unless there was fraud or non-disclosure of material facts) from liability for any further claim for tax. It also extinguishes any HMRC charge on property for that tax.

It is possible to obtain a more limited certificate which extinguishes an HMRC charge on property which is to be purchased but which does not discharge any accountable person.

An HMRC charge for unpaid inheritance tax attaches to property other than UK personal property beneficially owned by the deceased before death which vests in the personal representatives.

Where property subject to an HMRC charge is disposed of, that property ceases to be subject to the charge (although the property representing it becomes subject to the charge) if:

(a) in the case of land the charge was not registered; or

(b) in the case of UK personalty the purchaser had no notice of the facts giving rise to the charge.

It frequently happens that adjustments have to be made to the value of the estate during the administration (for example, because estimated figures are finalised). In such a case the personal representatives must submit a corrective account to the Revenue giving full information of all changes in value. Until the personal representatives have obtained a certificate of discharge they cannot safely complete the distribution of the assets comprised in the estate since further tax may become due as a result of adjustments to the value of the estate.

A certificate of discharge does not affect any further tax which becomes payable as a result of the discovery of additional assets or as a result of increases in the amount of property passing to non-exempt beneficiaries.

Where inheritance tax is not paid in full on the death, for example, on timber, on blocked foreign assets and where there is a conditional exemption for heritage property, HMRC will issue a limited certificate expressed to be "save and except" those items.

In April 2007 HMRC announced that handling the many applications for formal clearance certificates was placing a significant strain on its limited resources. It therefore announced that as from April 30, 2007 it would treat its final letter as having the same effect as a formal clearance certificate.

The final letter will provide confirmation that HMRC's enquiries are settled and that either:

- no tax is due;

- all the tax has been paid; or

- all the tax has been paid except for any tax being deferred (e.g. on timber) or being paid by instalments.

CHAPTER FIVE

CAPITAL GAINS TAX

1. INTRODUCTION

The *death* of an individual does not give rise to a liability to capital gains tax **5.01** (save in very limited circumstances where there is settled property). However, capital gains tax may have to be considered in connection with all or any of the following:

    (a) disposals made by the deceased up to the date of death;

    (b) disposals made by the personal representatives after the date of death during the period of administration; and

    (c) disposals made by beneficiaries of assets they have received from the estate.

Before considering these three situations, a brief outline of the capital gains tax system contained in the Taxation of Chargeable Gains Act 1992 is necessary. All references are to that Act unless otherwise stated.

The Finance Act 2008 substantially simplified the calculation of capital gains tax for tax year 2008/09 onwards. The main changes were:

    (a) one single rate of 18 per cent;

    (b) the abolition of indexation and taper relief;

    (c) the abolition of the "kink" test (see para.5.08, below) for assets owned on March 31, 1982 so that, when calculating capital gains tax on the disposal of an asset acquired before that date, the acquisition value will always be taken as the value on March 31, 1982; and

    (d) the introduction of an entrepreneurs' relief.

In tax year 2010/11 further changes were made by the coalition government in the Finance (No 2) Act 2010 which reintroduced differential rates of tax part way through the tax year in an attempt to increase tax revenue. The rate charged on a disposal made on or after June 23, 2010 depends on the level of income of the taxpayer.

2. CAPITAL GAINS TAX GENERALLY

5.02 Capital gains tax is payable when a *chargeable person* makes a disposal of *chargeable assets* giving rise to a *chargeable gain* unless an *exemption or relief* applies. The tax is charged on a "current year basis" by reference to gains made in a "tax year", from April 6 to the following April 5 (officially called a "year of assessment").

Taxable person

5.03 Every person who is resident or ordinarily resident in the UK is potentially liable to capital gains tax. This includes the personal representatives of a deceased person, who are treated as a continuing body of persons with the same residence or ordinary residence as the deceased. "Resident" and "ordinarily resident" have the same meanings as in the Income Tax Acts (s.9).

If an individual is domiciled in the UK, they are liable in respect of gains arising from assets situated anywhere in the world. If the individual is not domiciled in the UK, they are liable on gains arising from assets situated in the UK but not liable on gains arising from assets located outside the UK except to the extent that those gains are remitted to the UK (s.12).

Disposals

5.04 The Act does not provide an exhaustive definition of the term but it is clear that a sale or gift amounts to a "disposal". Furthermore, s.21(2) provides that the term "disposal" covers part disposals. Thus the sale of part of a plot of land is a disposal as is the grant of a lease or an easement. In addition, there are statutory provisions by which certain transactions are treated as disposals (such as the total loss or destruction of an asset or the granting of an option). However, if an asset is disposed of under a contract, the date of disposal is the date of the contract, not the date on which the asset is eventually transferred (s.18(1)). If a contract is conditional the operative date is the date on which the condition is satisfied (s.28(2)).

Chargeable assets

5.05 The definition of *assets* for capital gains tax purposes is set out in s.21(1) which provides that:

> "All forms of property shall be assets for the purposes of this Act, whether situated in the United Kingdom or not, including:
>
> (a) options, debts and incorporeal property generally,

(b) any currency other than sterling, and

(c) any form of property created by the person disposing of it or otherwise coming to be owned without being acquired (such as goodwill in a business)."

All *assets* are *chargeable assets* subject to a few exceptions including sterling and motor cars.

Chargeable gains

The basic rule

A gain arises if the "consideration for disposal" exceeds the "allowable deductions" provided for in the Act. **5.06**

The "consideration for disposal" is the sale price if the asset is sold in an arm's length transaction or the market value if there is a gift or a gift element. The market value is the price which the asset might reasonably be expected to fetch on a sale in the open market. Section 272(2) provides that no reduction in the value can be made by assuming that the assets would be placed on the market at the same time.

Once the "consideration for disposal" has been calculated, the allowable expenditure is deducted to calculate the chargeable gains. The allowable expenditure is defined by s.38(1) and falls into three categories:

(a) Initial expenditure, which is the original purchase price (or market value if the asset was acquired by way of gift) plus incidental costs incurred in acquiring the asset, such as solicitors' fees and stamp duty. If the asset was not acquired by the taxpayer from anyone else (because, for example, it is the goodwill of a business they have set up) the initial expenditure is that wholly and exclusively incurred in providing the asset.

(b) Subsequent expenditure, which is expenditure wholly and exclusively incurred for the purpose of enhancing the value of the asset (the expenditure being reflected in the state or nature of the asset at the time of disposal) and expenditure incurred in establishing, preserving or defending title to, or a right over, the asset.

(c) Incidental costs of disposal such as solicitors' fees, estate agents' fees, the cost of advertising, etc.

There must be excluded from the calculation any sum that is charged to income tax (such as portions of premiums on certain leases which are taxable under Income Tax (Trading and Other Income) Act s.276)) or any expense that is deductible for income tax purposes (such as the cost of *repairs* to an asset as opposed to the cost of improvements).

With regard to the allowable deductions, special rules apply if part only of an asset is disposed of since it would clearly be unfair for the taxpayer to be able to deduct expenditure laid out on the whole asset against the sale price of only part. In these circumstances s.42(2) provides that the allowable expenditure to be deducted from the sale price (or market value if appropriate) of the part sold or given away is found by multiplying the total expenditure on the whole asset by:

$$\frac{A}{A + B}$$

where A is the consideration received for the part disposed of and B is the market value of the part retained.

Example

Terence buys a plot of land for £40,000 (his only allowable expenditure). He sells part for £45,000; the value of the remainder is £15,000. From the £45,000 sale proceeds he can deduct:

$$£40,000 \times \frac{£45,000}{£45,000 + £15,000}$$

$$\text{i.e. } £40,000 \times \frac{£45,000}{£60,000} = £30,000$$

He therefore has a chargeable gain of £15,000.

The indexation allowance

5.07 An indexation allowance to offset the effects of inflation was introduced for disposals made on or after April 6, 1982 (April 1 in the case of companies) The effect of the allowance was to "index link" allowable expenditure so that only "real" profits were potentially taxable on a subsequent disposal. For disposals by individuals, personal representatives and trustees the allowance was abolished for months after April 1998 and taper relief was introduced. The Finance Act 2008 completely abolished the indexation allowance and taper relief but at the same time introduced a much lower rate of tax.

Special rules for assets held on April 6, 1965 and March 31, 1982

5.08 Capital gains tax came into force on April 6, 1965 and tax has never been levied on gains arising before that date.

In March 1988 it was announced that the base date for capital gains tax would be altered. In respect of disposals made on or after April 6, 1988 no tax is levied on gains arising prior to March 31, 1982. Taxpayers are treated as having disposed of assets on March 31, 1982 and as having acquired them at market value at that date (s.55(1)).

Example

A acquires an asset in 1980 for £2,000; on March 31, 1982 it is worth £8,000; on September 1, 1992 he disposes of the asset for £9,000. Ignoring exemptions and the availability of any indexation allowance for the purposes of this example he will be treated as making a chargeable gain of £1,000 (£9,000 – £8,000).

The so-called kink test provided that where a taxpayer disposed of an asset owned at March 31, 1982, the real acquisition value could be taken if it would give a smaller gain or loss (unless the taxpayer has elected to take the 1982 value).

The Finance Act 2008 abolished the kink test for disposals made on or after April 6, 2008 so all assets owned on March 31, 1982 will be deemed disposed of and reacquired on that date.

Taper Relief

Taper relief came into effect on April 6, 1998 and gave relief once assets had **5.09** been held for a minimum period of three years for non-business assets and one year for business assets. The relief increased with each year the asset was owned until, after 10 years of ownership in the case of non-business assets, the maximum relief (60 per cent of the gain being chargeable) was reached.

"Business assets" (as defined in Sch.A1) were treated more generously; from April 6, 2002 only 50 per cent of the gain was chargeable once the asset had been owned for one year, reducing to only 25 per cent for assets owned for two or more years.

Taper relief is not available for disposals made on or after April 6, 2008

Losses

If deducting the allowable expenditure from the sale proceeds or market value of **5.10** the asset shows that the taxpayer has made a loss, it may be set off against all gains made during the current tax year. If this year's gains are insufficient to absorb the whole loss, it may be carried forward and set off against all future gains as they arise. The losses can be carried forward indefinitely until such gains arise (s.2(2)).

It is important to note that in the tax year in which the loss arises, it must be set against that year's gains to reduce them as far as is possible. This is so even if the loss would reduce the gains below the annual exemption limit (£10,100 in 2010/11—see para.5.14, below). However, if there are unabsorbed losses which are carried forward, in the future years they are used only to the extent necessary to reduce the gains of those later years to the level of the annual exemption (s.3(5)).

Example

During the tax year 2009/10, X sells two assets; one disposal gives rise to a gain of £6,000 and the other disposal shows a loss of £8,000. The loss must be set against the gain reducing it to nil and leaving £2,000 unabsorbed loss that can be carried forward to 2010/11.

If X in 2010/11 sells an asset making a gain of £10,600, only £500 of the loss brought forward is used to reduce the gain to £10,100, leaving £1,500 of the unabsorbed loss to be carried forward to 2011/12.

A loss is only allowable in circumstances where, if a gain had been made on the disposal of the asset it would have been a *chargeable* gain. Thus the sale of a private motor car at a loss does not give rise to an allowable loss.

Rates of tax

5.11   For tax years before 2008/09 the rates of capital gains tax applicable to individuals were equivalent to the rates of income tax which would apply if gains were treated as the top slice of income. The rate of tax for disposals made in 2009/10 and up to June 23, 2010 was a flat 18 per cent.

For disposals made by individuals on or after June 23, 2010 the rate remains 18 per cent where total taxable gains *and income* are less than the upper limit of the income tax basic rate band (which is £37,400 for 2010–11). Gains or parts of gains above that limit are taxed at 28 per cent.

Where entrepreneurs' relief is available (see para.5.14, below) the rate is reduced. Losses and the annual exemption can be allocated in the way most beneficial to the taxpayer.

Example

- In 2010–11 X's taxable income is £27,400 and he has no allowable losses.

- In May 2010 X sells an asset and realises a chargeable gain of £17,000.

- In November 2010 X sells another asset, realising a chargeable gain £25,100.

- Neither of the gains qualifies for entrepreneurs' relief.

The May 2010 chargeable gain of £17,000 was realised before the change of rates on June 23, 2010 and is taxable at the old 18 per cent rate. It has no effect on the taxation of later gains and is, in effect, parked.

The later gain may be taxed at 28 per cent so X will choose to set the annual exemption against it to reduce the exposure to tax at the higher CGT rate.

That leaves £15,000 taxable (£25,100 – £10,100). The first £10,000 of the £15,000 is taxed at 18 per cent and the remaining £5,000 is taxed at 28 per cent.

Disposals made by personal representatives and trustees on or after June 23, 2010 are taxed at 28 per cent whatever the level of income.

Exemptions and reliefs

5.12   Certain exemptions and reliefs are available. In some cases they extinguish, and in others they reduce, the taxpayer's liability.

Exemptions

5.13   The main exemptions are:

(a) The taxpayer's only or main residence together with gardens and grounds up to, normally, 0.5 of a hectare (s.222). The property must normally have been the taxpayer's main residence throughout their period of ownership and not have been bought with a view to making a gain on the disposal (s.224(3)). Certain periods of absence are disregarded including:

(i) a period of absence not exceeding three years;
(ii) any period of absence during which the taxpayer was employed, or held an office, all the duties of which were performed outside the UK; and
(iii) a period of absence, not exceeding four years, throughout which the taxpayer was prevented from residing as a result of the situation of their place of work or as a result of their employer requiring them to reside elsewhere, the condition being reasonably imposed to secure the effective performance of their duties.

(The last 36 months of ownership will be disregarded in any event; the taxpayer may still claim full relief whether or not the property was occupied as their main residence during that period—s.223(1).) If the taxpayer occupies more than one residence, they can choose which is to be treated as their main residence by an election made within two years of acquiring the additional property. By concession,

> "relief is also given where personal representatives dispose of a house which before and after the deceased's death has been used as their only or main residence by individuals who under the will or intestacy are entitled to the whole or substantially the whole of the proceeds of the house either absolutely or for life".

"Substantially the whole" means at least 75 per cent. (Extra-statutory Concession D5).

(b) Items of tangible moveable property having a predictable useful life not exceeding 50 years (s.45), such as most yachts.

(c) Chattels where the *consideration* for disposal does not exceed £6,000 (s.262). Marginal relief exists if the consideration exceeds £6,000.

(d) National savings certificates and premium bonds (s.121).

There are other exemptions including:

(a) Damages for personal injuries and betting winnings (s.51).

(b) Interests under trusts, unless the interest was acquired for money or money's worth (s.76).

(c) Gains made on the disposal of certain government securities (s.115(1)).

(d) Decorations for valour unless acquired for consideration in money or money's worth (s.268).

(e) Foreign currency purchased for personal use abroad (s.269).

(f) Life assurance policies and deferred annuity contracts (s.210).

    (g) Works of art in certain circumstances (s.258).

Reliefs

5.14 If the assets disposed of do not come within any of the categories in para.5.12, there may be relief from liability to tax as a result of one of the following:

    (a) The Annual Exemption: The first £10,100 of gains arising on the disposals made during tax year 2008/09 (s.3). Married couples and civil partners are taxed independently on their capital gains and have separate annual exemptions.

    (b) Venture Capital Trusts: In respect of disposals taking place on or after April 6, 1995 gains made on the disposal of shares in an approved Venture Capital Trust are exempt. The shares disposed of must not have been acquired in excess of the permitted maximum. A qualified exemption for shares acquired under the Enterprise Investment Scheme is also available.

    (c) Entrepreneurs' Relief: Sections 169H–169S of the Taxation of Chargeable Gains Act 1992 provide that for disposals made on or after April 6, 2008 an entrepreneurs' relief is available on gains arising on or in connection with disposals of the whole or part of a business up to a certain figure. The effect of the relief is to reduce the effective rate of tax on these gains to 10 per cent instead of 18 or 28 per cent.

        The relief is available under s.169I where an individual makes a disposal of:

        (a) the whole or part of a business owned for at least one year before the disposal,

        (b) assets used in a business where the business ceases to be carried on provided the business was owned for at least one year before the cessation and the disposal is within three years of the cessation, or

        (c) shares in a trading company (or the holding company of a trading group) which was—

            (i) the individual's personal company, and

            (ii) the individual is an officer or employee of the company or a company within the group;

        for at least one year before:

            (i) the disposal,

            (ii) the time when the company ceased to be a trading company (or the holding company of a trading group) and the disposal is within three years of the cessation, or

    (d) the limit for gains on which the relief is available has been increased twice since the relief was introduced and are as follows:

(i) disposals before June 6, 2010: £1m;
(ii) disposals after April 6, 2010: £2m (less any of the previous limit used up); and
(iii) disposals after June 22, 2010: £5m (less any of the previous limits used up).

The relief is not available to personal representatives and is only available to trustees in limited circumstances (see Ch.7, below).

Gains up to the limit are taxed at 10 per cent. Above that the 18/28 per cent rate applies depending on the level of income of the taxpayer. Gains eligible for entrepreneurs' relief are taxed before other gains which means that the gains not eligible for relief are likely to be taxed at 28 per cent.

Business includes a business carried on in partnership.

The relief is available under s.169J where trustees of a settlement dispose of shares in a trading company (or the holding company of a trading group) or assets used in a business which are part of the settlement assets provided certain conditions are fulfilled:

(i) there must be a beneficiary with an interest in possession (other than for a fixed term) in the whole of the settled property or in the business assets disposed of;

(ii) in the case of company shares, the company must for a period of at least one year ending not earlier than three years before the disposal have been the beneficiary's personal company and the beneficiary must have been an officer or employee of the company or a company within the group business; and

(iii) in the case of business assets, the assets must have been used in the business for a period of at least one year ending not earlier than three years before the disposal and the beneficiary must cease to carry on the business on the date of the disposal or within the previous three years.

The relief is available under s.169K where an individual disposes of an asset owned by the individual and used for the purposes of a partnership in which the individual is a partner or a company which is the individual's personal company provided that certain conditions are complied with.

"Personal company" is defined in s.169S(3) as one where the individual holds at least 5 per cent of the ordinary share capital giving at least 5 per cent of the voting rights in the company. Where two or more persons hold shares jointly s.169S(4) provides that each person is to be treated as holding the appropriate proportion of the total holding and associated voting power. So, where a husband and wife own a joint 100 per cent shareholding equally, they are treated as each holding 50 per cent of the shares and votes.

The individual making the disposal (or in the case of trust assets the trustees and beneficiary with the interest in possession jointly) must claim the relief by the second January 31 following the tax year in which the disposal was made.

Letting property, whether residential or commercial, will not qualify as a trade for this purpose. However, HMRC's "HelpSheet 275" states that furnished holiday lettings in the European Economic Area (EEA) will be eligible for tax years 2009/10 and 2010/11.

Selling an asset in isolation will not attract the relief. There must be a disposal of a business or part of a business or the disposal of assets on cessation of a business.

Deferments

5.15 The final group of reliefs are those which have the effect of deferring the payment of tax.

When a transfer is made by way of gift or sale at under-value, the donor and donee may in certain circumstances elect to "hold-over" any gain so that the donee is treated as acquiring the asset at the donor's acquisition value.

When an owner sells certain types of assets, they may elect to "roll-over" any gain into new assets purchased so that the acquisition cost is reduced by the amount of the rolled-over gain. If an election is made either to hold-over or roll-over a gain, the whole of the gain must be held-over or rolled-over. It is not possible to elect to hold-over or roll-over a portion of a gain allowing the balance to be covered by the annual exemption.

While tax can eventually become payable on the "held-over" or "rolled-over" gain, it will not be payable until some time in the future. These reliefs may offer advantages beyond the mere postponement of the payment of tax but the possible advantages differ depending on whether the gain is "held over" on a gift or "rolled over" on a sale.

Hold-over Relief

5.16 Considering "held-over" gains first, the advantages are that:

(a) when tax is paid by the donee in the future it will be paid with money that may have been reduced in value by inflation; and

(b) if the donee dies while owning the property the gain will be effectively extinguished (see para.5.21, below).

There is, however, the disadvantage that the donor will lose the benefit of their annual exemption.

The circumstances in which hold-over relief applies include:

(a) *Transfers between spouses and civil partners.* Any transfer of an asset between a husband and wife or between civil partners who are living together is treated as taking place for such consideration as will give neither a gain nor a loss to the transferor. The effect is that any gain is *automatically* "held-over" into the hands of the new owner (s.58).

(b) *Gifts to charities.* The donor is treated as having made the disposal for a consideration which gives rise to neither a gain nor a loss (s.257). Gains made by charities are normally exempt if applicable and applied for charitable purposes (s.256).

(c) *Business assets.* Where a taxpayer disposes (otherwise than under a bargain at arm's length) of "business assets" a joint election can be made by the transferor and transferee (or by the transferor alone if the disposal is to the trustees of a settlement) that any gain be held-over (s.165). The donee receives no credit for the donor's accrued taper relief. Business assets for this purpose are, broadly, assets used for the purposes of a trade, profession or vocation carried on by the transferor or their personal company (s.165(2)). The term also covers shares, provided the shares are in an unquoted company or in the transferor's personal company.

(d) *Transfers chargeable to inheritance tax.* Where a disposal is made which is chargeable to inheritance tax or would be but for the existence of the annual exemption, a joint election can be made by the transferor and transferee (or by the transferor alone if the disposal is to the trustees of a settlement) that any gain be held-over (s.260(2)). The relief is available only to disposals which are initially chargeable to inheritance tax, and not to those which are initially potentially exempt but which become chargeable as a result of the death of the transferor within the seven years. Chapter 7 deals more fully with chargeable transfers but they are broadly transfers to and from settlements without an interest in possession. Note that a transfer is technically chargeable to inheritance tax even though it is within the transferor's nil rate band (s.262(a)).

(e) *Transfers exempt from inheritance tax.* Where a disposal is made which is exempt from inheritance tax because it is a transfer either to a political party, for the public benefit, to a maintenance fund for historic buildings or of property designated by the Treasury as of outstanding national interest, a joint election can be made by the transferor and transferee (or by the transferor alone if the transfer is to the trustees of a settlement) that the gain be held-over (s.260(2)(b)).

(f) *Transfers from an accumulation and maintenance trust, a trust for a bereaved minor or a trust for a bereaved young person.* Where a beneficiary becomes absolutely entitled to assets from one of these trusts the trustees and beneficiary may jointly elect that any gain be held-over (s.260(2)). Chapter 7 deals more fully with these trusts.

Roll-over Relief

The roll-over relief which is available on the sale of assets offers the same **5.17** advantages and suffers the same disadvantages as hold-over relief. The relief applies:

(a) *On the replacement of business assets.* When a trader sells certain business assets (including land, buildings, plant and machinery) and reinvests the proceeds of sale in new business assets within certain time limits, any gain realised on the sale can be "rolled-over" into the new asset. The effect of this is to reduce the trader's acquisition price of the asset by the "rolled-over" gain (ss.152–159).

(b) *On the incorporation of a business.* If the taxpayer transfers an unincorporated business (and all assets other than cash) as a going concern to a company in exchange for shares, the gain realised on the disposal to the company can be "rolled-over" into the newly acquired shares. The effect is that the shares (subject to certain conditions) are treated as having been acquired for the same value as the assets transferred instead of at market value at the date of the disposal (ss.162 and 162A).

(c) *Deferral relief under the Enterprise Investment scheme (s.150C and Sch.5B).* This deferral relief allows an investor to defer a CGT charge on a gain arising on the disposal of a qualifying EIS investment where the gain is rolled over into another qualifying investment within the qualifying time.

There are a number of conditions which must be satisfied for the investment to be a "qualifying investment". However, the key ones are that the investment must be wholly in cash to subscribe for ordinary, non-preferential shares in a company which qualifies for the purposes of EIS income tax relief and the shares must be issued to fund a "qualifying business activity".

(d) *Reinvestment in a Venture Capital Trust.* Gains on disposals of shares issued before April 6, 2004 can be deferred by matching it against a qualifying investment in a Venture Capital Trust made within a period of 12 months before or 12 months after the chargeable gain (Sch.5C(2)). Gains on disposals of shares in a Venture Capital Trust are exempt up to a permitted maximum.

The date for payment of tax

5.18   Capital gains tax due from individuals and trustees is payable on a current year basis on January 31 following the year of assessment (Taxes Management Act 1970 s.59B as substituted). Interest is charged on tax remaining unpaid after the due date.

If the sale price is paid by instalments over a period exceeding 18 months, the tax can be paid over a similar period (subject to a maximum of eight years) if undue hardship would otherwise be caused (s.180).

Where hold-over relief is not available on a disposal by way of gift (or deemed disposal under s.71(1) or s.72—see Ch.7, below) tax on certain assets can be paid in 10 equal yearly instalments (s.181). An election must be made in writing by the person paying the tax. Payment by instalments is possible only where hold-over relief is *not available* and not where it is available but the taxpayer chooses not to claim it.

The relevant assets are land or an interest in land, any shares or securities which immediately before the disposal gave the person disposing of the shares control of the company, and any shares not giving control and not listed on a recognised stock exchange.

3. The Capital Gains Tax Liability of the Deceased

Prior to the date of death, the deceased may have made disposals which gave rise **5.19** to capital gains tax liability. If this liability has not been discharged prior to the death, the personal representatives must discharge it on the deceased's behalf. The personal representatives calculate tax in accordance with the principles outlined above and will be able to claim, on behalf of the deceased, the benefit of any exemptions or reliefs the deceased could have claimed. Once these exemptions and reliefs have been claimed, the personal representatives will pay tax on behalf of the deceased at the appropriate rate(s).

The deceased may have unrelieved losses in the tax year of death. Section 62(2) provides that such losses can be carried back and set against the gains realised by the deceased in the three tax years preceding the tax year of death, taking later years first. If tax was paid in any of those earlier years, a rebate will be claimed.

If there are still unrelieved losses, these cannot be taken over by the personal representatives to set off against gains they make. If the deceased made a disposal by way of a *donatio mortis causa,* no chargeable gain arises (s.62(5)).

4. The Capital Gains Tax Liability of the Personal Representatives

The position on death

There is no disposal of assets on death. Section 62(1)(a) provides that the assets **5.20** of which a deceased person was competent to dispose shall be deemed to be *acquired* on their death by the personal representatives for a consideration equal to their market value at the date of the death. Since there is a deemed acquisition but no deemed disposal, no capital gains tax liability arises as a result of the death. The same rule applies to a person who takes property held jointly with the deceased.

If the value of a deceased's assets have been ascertained for inheritance tax purposes s.274 requires that value to be the asset's value for capital gains tax purposes. This will then determine the acquisition cost of the personal representatives and of the legatee, if the asset is transferred to a legatee.

This method of valuation can be beneficial to taxpayers where, for example, an asset owned by the deceased receives a high inheritance tax value as a result of the related property rules. However, s.274 only has this result if the inheritance tax value has actually been *ascertained*. The Capital Gains Tax manual states at para.CG32222 that a value is not ascertained where:

- All the assets pass to a surviving spouse or civil partner and the entire estate is exempt.

- All the assets pass to charities, political parties or other persons listed in Sch.3 to IHTA and the estate is thus exempt.

- The estimated value of the estate is well below the threshold on which tax is to be payable and it can be accepted that the estate is non-taxpaying.

- The assets of the estate are all covered by the reliefs for agricultural and business assets in a period when the rates of relief for such assets are 100 per cent.

- Some combination of the above factors and/or other exemptions makes the estate non-taxpaying.

The fact that inheritance *reliefs* are available will not reduce the capital gains tax valuation.

If quoted shares and securities are sold within 12 months from the date of death, at less than market value at the date of death, the personal representatives can elect that, for inheritance tax purposes, the sale price be substituted for the probate value. (See below, Ch.12.) If the reduced value is taken for inheritance tax purposes, it becomes the acquisition price of the personal representatives for capital gains tax purposes as well. The personal representatives cannot keep the original acquisition value for capital gains tax purposes once they have elected for the inheritance tax reduction. If land or an interest in land is sold within four years of death at less than market value at the date of death, the personal representatives can elect that the sale price be substituted for the probate value. The reduced value will become the acquisition value for capital gains tax purposes as it is has been ascertained; see s.274.

Disposals by the personal representatives

5.21 In the course of administering the estate, the personal representatives may have to sell assets. If they do so, they will be liable to capital gains tax calculated on the difference between their acquisition value (the value at the date of death) and the value at the date of the disposal after deducting any losses they have incurred on other disposals. The calculation of liability has been outlined in paras 5.02–5.18. Entrepreneurs' relief is not available to personal representatives.

Prior to April 6, 2008 personal representatives paid capital gains tax at a flat rate of 40 per cent. From that date until June 23, 2010 they paid at a flat rate of 18 per cent. For disposals made on or after June 23, 2010 they pay at a flat rate of 28 per cent.

Where beneficiaries are basic rate taxpayers it may be better for personal representatives to vest assets showing increases in value in the beneficiaries and let them make the disposal, benefiting from the lower rate of tax.

In addition to the normal deductions for incidental selling expenses, personal representatives are entitled to deduct a proportion of the costs of valuing the estate for probate purposes *(IRC v Richards' Executors* (1971)). HMRC publishes a scale of permitted deductions (SP 2/04). However, the personal representatives are free to claim more than the scale deduction where they can show that the actual cost was higher.

The rights of personal representatives to claim exemptions and relief are limited. In the tax year of death, and the two following tax years, the personal representatives can claim the annual exemption £10,100 in tax year 2010/11 (s.3(7)). Thereafter all the gains they realise (other than on assets within para.5.13) are taxable. The only or main residence exemption cannot apply to personal representatives since a continuing body of persons cannot have a residence. However, by concession (ESC D5), if before and after the death, the residence has been used as their only or main residence by individuals who, under the will or intestacy, are entitled to the whole or substantially the whole of the proceeds of sale of the house either absolutely or for life, the exemption can be claimed (see above, para.5.13).

If the personal representatives have made losses on their disposals but have no, or insufficient, gains to set them against, these unabsorbed losses cannot be passed on to the beneficiaries.

Where personal representatives are proposing to sell an asset which has fallen in value since death and have no gains against which the loss can be set, it may be preferable for them to consider vesting the asset in a beneficiary and allowing the beneficiary to sell. Even if the beneficiary has no gains in the current tax year, the loss can be carried forward indefinitely; see para.5.09, above.

Transfers to legatees

For capital gains tax purposes, s.64(2) defines the term "legatee" as including: **5.22**

> "any person taking under a testamentary disposition or on an intestacy or partial intestacy, whether he takes beneficially or as trustee, and a person taking a *donatio mortis causa* shall be treated . . . as a legatee and his acquisition as made at the time of the donor's death".

Section 62(4) provides that when the personal representatives transfer an asset to a legatee under the terms of a will, or the intestacy rules, no chargeable gain accrues to the personal representatives. The personal representatives' acquisition is treated as the legatee's acquisition. The position is the same if the personal representatives appropriate an asset in or towards satisfaction of a pecuniary legacy or a share in residue. Therefore, such transfers cannot give rise to capital gains tax liability if the asset has risen in value since the date of death and neither can the personal representatives have the benefit of a loss where the asset has fallen in value since the date of death.

If the personal representatives vest assets in trustees (even if they themselves are the trustees) the trustees are treated in the same way as legatees and so acquire the asset at market value at the date of death. When the beneficiaries of the trust become absolutely entitled to the trust assets there will be a charge to capital gains tax if the assets have risen in value since the death.

When the personal representatives are deciding which assets to sell and which to vest in beneficiaries, they should take into account their own and the beneficiaries' present and future tax liability. The rate payable by beneficiaries may be lower than the 28 per cent rate payable by the personal representatives.

Personal representatives should be particularly careful when dealing with charities. If the personal representatives sell an asset which shows a capital gain, tax will be paid at the rate of 28 per cent. If the asset is transferred to the charity who then make the sale, the gain is exempt (s.256). It is possible for the personal representatives to appropriate an asset to a charity and then sell on behalf of the charity as a bare trustee. The s.256 exemption will then be available. It is important to have a clear record of the appropriation and the instruction to sell. The Institute of Legacy Management has a fact sheet on this subject available on its website *http://www.ilmnet.org* [Accessed January 2011].

5. THE CAPITAL GAINS TAX LIABILITY OF BENEFICIARIES

5.23 As has already been explained, the legatees, whether they are entitled under a will or the intestacy rules, whether they receive a specific legacy, an asset in satisfaction of a pecuniary legacy or a residuary legacy or whether they are beneficially entitled or are merely entitled as trustees, receive the property at market value at the date of the death.

This means they take the asset with the benefit of any unrealised losses that may have accrued since the death and subject to any unrealised gains that have arisen since that date. They cannot, however, take over any unrelieved losses which the personal representatives realised.

On subsequent disposals by beneficiaries the gain or the loss must be calculated on the basis of the market value at the date of death. A beneficiary who purchases an asset from the personal representatives takes as a purchaser not a legatee. Thus the personal representatives will be liable for any gain between date of death and sale.

6. REPORTING REQUIREMENTS FOR CHARGEABLE GAINS

5.24 For tax returns for tax year 2003/04 onwards it is not necessary for individuals, trustees and personal representatives (in the tax year following death and the following two tax years) to complete the Capital Gains pages of a tax return where the total of disposal proceeds does not exceed four times the annual exemption which applies to individuals provided:

- either the gains do not exceed their annual exemption; or

- there are no allowable losses to be deducted from chargeable gains and there is no CGT liability after any available taper has been deducted.

Disposals of assets from spouse to spouse will not count towards the four times annual exemption limit if they are treated as giving rise to neither a gain nor a loss under s.58(1) because they are "living together". For earlier tax years there was a more limited concession.

CHAPTER SIX

INCOME TAX

In the illustrations given in this chapter, it is assumed (except where the contrary **6.01** is stated) that rates will remain as they are for 2010/11 for all future tax years.

1. INTRODUCTION

Many people regard income tax as the bane of their lives and would be distressed **6.02** to discover that the Revenue can pursue them beyond the grave.

When a person dies, income tax must be considered in respect of three different periods:

(1) the period up to death;

(2) the administration period; and

(3) the period after the completion of administration.

The purpose of this chapter is to consider the rules that apply to these different periods but before looking at the detailed rules, a brief explanation of the types of receipt on which income tax is levied and the methods of calculating the tax is necessary.

2. INCOME TAX GENERALLY

A detailed discussion of the income tax system is beyond the scope of this book. **6.03** Instead we intend merely to make some simple basic points to put the particular rules relevant on death into context.

It is necessary when considering income tax to ask the following questions:

(1) What is income?

(2) What income is taxable?

(3) In what year of assessment will income be taxed?

(4) How is the tax liability calculated?

(5) When is the tax payable?

What is income?

6.04 The first problem that arises is to define the kind of receipt which attracts the charge to income tax. Most people would probably not be able to define income but no doubt would hope to recognise it when they receive it.

As there is no statutory definition of "income", over the years, lawyers have attempted to define the nebulous concept of "income" which is subject to tax. In the case of *London County Council v Att.-Gen.* (1901) Lord MacNaughten said "income tax, if I may be pardoned for saying so, is a tax on income". As a definition this is of little assistance. However, more precise guidelines have developed and it can now be said that the tax is paid on profits of an income nature, as opposed to profits arising on the disposal of a capital asset (although there are cases where capital receipts can be treated as income, such as certain premiums on leases). The distinction between these two types of receipt is, broadly speaking, that to be of an income nature, the receipt should be recurrent.

What income is taxable?

6.05 The charging statute for income tax is the Income Tax Act 2007 ("ITA 2007") as amended by later Finance Acts. The statutes which specify the sources of income subject to income tax are the Income Tax (Trading and Other Income) Act 2005 ("ITTOIA 2005") and the Income Tax (Earnings and Pensions) Act 2003 ("ITEPA 2003").

The most important sources of income taxed under the ITTOIA 2005 and ITEPA 2003 are:

a)   Under ITTOIA 2005:
Part 2 Trading income (so profits from a trade, profession or vocation).
Part 3 Property income (so rents and other profits from receipts from land in the UK).
Part 4 Savings and investment income (so interest, annuities and dividends).
Part 5 Other miscellaneous income (such as other annual income not otherwise charged to tax).

b)   Under ITEPA 2003:
Employment and pensions income.

A few types of income are specified in Pt 6, ITTOIA 2005 as being exempt (for example, scholarship income) and so are tax-free.

Each part of the ITTOIA 2005 and the ITEPA 2003 lays down its own rules for the particular type of income dealt with. For example, the rules as to what expenses can be deducted to determine taxable income vary according to the type of income. The tax year in which the income will be taxed is determined by the basis of assessment relevant to the particular part of the ITTOIA 2005 or the ITEPA 2003.

What is the relevant year of assessment?

Tax is calculated by reference to years of assessment (commonly called "tax years"). A new tax year commences on April 6 each year. The charging statutes lay down the basis of assessment—the current year basis. This requires that tax is assessed in each year on the income of that tax year. **6.06**

How is the tax liability calculated?

General

Section 23 of ITA 2007 provides that there are five main steps necessary to calculate income tax: **6.07**

Step 1: calculate "total income".
Step 2: deduct any allowable reliefs (e.g. interest on a loan qualifying under ITA 2007 s.383).
Step 3: deduct any personal reliefs.
Step 4: calculate tax payable at the appropriate rates on total income less allowable and personal reliefs.
Step 5: add together the sums calculated at (4) above.

What is "total income"?

The taxpayer's "total income" is the aggregate of the taxpayer's income from all sources (after deducting allowable expenses) which is chargeable to income tax. The sources are listed at (2), above. Total income is reduced by reliefs at Steps 2 and 3 to give the net income on which tax is calculated. **6.08**

Total income includes sums received gross (such as trading income) and the grossed up amounts of sums which are received net of tax. Some income is received net of tax. For example, interest from banks and building societies normally has tax deducted at the rate of 20 per cent. Dividends have a tax credit of 10 per cent. Salaries will have tax deducted under the PAYE scheme. Unlike interest and dividends where the tax deducted is always at the same rate, the rate at which tax is deducted under the PAYE system varies depending on the personal circumstances of the employee.

Income tax is calculated on the basis of a person's gross income and so it is necessary to gross up sums received net of tax (credit is then given for the tax paid or tax credit). To gross up a net sum where tax has been deducted, simply multiply the sum actually received by

$$\frac{100}{100 - \text{tax rate}}$$

If tax has been deducted at the rate of 20 per cent and £160 is received net of tax, then the £160 is 80 per cent of the gross figure (20 per cent of the gross figure having already been deducted). To calculate 100 per cent of the receipt, simply divide by 80 to find 1 per cent and then multiply by 100 to find 100 per cent. Follow the same steps whatever rate of tax has been deducted.

Example

A life tenant of a trust fund receives £4,000. Tax at the basic rate of 20 per cent has already been deducted. When calculating the beneficiary's statutory income the interest is grossed up to £5,000.

$$£4,000 \times \frac{100}{100 - 20} = £5,000$$

£5,000 is included in the taxpayer's income tax return as part of gross income.

However, it must be remembered that in the above example £1,000 in tax has already been paid. This sum is a "tax credit" so that, when calculating what tax (if any) is due to the Revenue, an allowance must be made for the £1,000 already paid on behalf of the taxpayer by the trustees.

If a taxpayer with a 20 per cent tax credit is only liable to basic rate tax on the receipt then no additional tax need be sent to the Revenue since the "right" amount of tax has already been paid. If the taxpayer is liable to higher rate tax, additional tax will have to be sent.

If the taxpayer from whom income tax has been deducted is not liable to even basic rate tax (because of their entitlement to reliefs at Step 2 and/or Step 3), they can normally reclaim, from the Revenue, the excess tax already paid on their behalf.

Dividends are treated rather differently. They are received with a 10 per cent tax credit. However, this tax credit is irrecoverable. This means that a person with a very low income who receives a dividend and who is not liable to pay income tax, because their income does not exceed their reliefs, will not be able to recover the 10 per cent tax credit.

What are allowable reliefs deductible at Step 2?

6.09 Certain specified commitments known as allowable reliefs are deducted from total income. These reliefs remove sums from the income tax calculation completely so that the income is not regarded as the taxpayer's. Interest payments on qualifying loans (such as loans to buy an interest in or to lend money to a partnership) are allowable reliefs under s.383 of ITA 2007. Other allowable relefs are set out in s.24 and include payments to trade unions or police organisations and certain payments to pensions.

There are special provisions for gifts to charities which qualify for relief under the gift aid provisions in Ch.2 of Pt 8.

What are personal reliefs deductible at Step 3?

There are a variety of personal reliefs available. The availability of these **6.10** allowances depends not on the type of income or payment involved but on the personal circumstances of the taxpayer. Everyone whose total income from all sources is less than £100,000 is entitled to a personal allowance (£6,475 in 2010/11 and £7,475 in 2011/12). If a taxpayer's total income is over £100,000, the personal allowance is reduced by £1 for every £2 in excess of that limit.

The basic personal allowance is increased in the case of someone over 65 but under 75 (£9,490 in 2010/11 and £9,940 in 2011/12) and increased again for persons aged 75 or over (£9,640 and £10,090). However, the increased allowances are reduced if net income exceeds a certain amount (£22,900 in 2010/11 and £24,000 for 2011/12). There are other allowances, for example, a blind person's allowance (£1,890 in tax year 2010/11 and £1,980 for 2011/12).

Spouses and civil partners are normally treated as separate single people with their own personal allowances. Married couples or civil partners where at least one of the parties to the marriage or civil partnership was born before April 6, 1935 get an additional allowance. Tax relief for the Married Couple's Allowance is given at the rate of 10 per cent. In 2010/11 The married couple's allowance is £6,965 in 2010/11 and £7,295 in 2011/12 for the over 75s, although this is reduced where income exceeds the age allowance limit of £22,900 and £24,000. These allowances reduce where the income is above the income limit—by £1 for every £2 of income above the limit.

What are the rates of tax used at Step 4?

The rates of tax payable depend on the type of income being taxed. Therefore, the **6.11** type of income must first be identified and there are three categories:

> *Non-savings income*: this is not separately defined in ITA 2007 but broadly covers earnings, pensions, taxable social security benefits, trading profits and income from property.

> *Savings income*: defined in ITA 2007 s.18 and broadly bank and building society interest.

> *Dividend income*: defined in ITA 2007 s.19.

Non-savings income is normally received gross apart from earnings which frequently have tax deducted under the PAYE system.

Most interest is received net of basic rate tax. Taxpayers who are not liable to pay tax because their income is too small can reclaim the tax deducted.

Dividends are received with a 10 per cent tax credit which is not recoverable if the recipient is a non-taxpayer. Before amounts which are received net of tax or with a tax credit can be included on the tax return, they have to be grossed up. The gross amount is then included and the taxpayer receives credit for any tax already deducted and for the dividend tax credit.

Section 16 of ITA 2007 sets out the order in which different types of income are taxed. Dividends are to be treated as the highest part of a taxpayer's income, then savings income and finally other income. The non-dividend/non-savings income is, therefore, always taxed first.

The rates charged on dividends are different from those charged on savings and other income.

(1) *Rates charged on non-dividend income*

	2010/11 £	2011/12 £
"Starting rate" of 10%		
(for savings income only)	0–2,440	0–2,560
"Basic rate" of 20%	2,441–37,400	0–35,000
"Higher rate" of 40%	37,401–150,000	35,001–150,000
"Additional rate" of 50%	150,000 and more	150,000 and more

The starting rate is available only on savings income. As savings income is taxed after non-savings income, the starting rate of 10 per cent will not be available where a taxpayer has non-savings income in excess of £2,440.

(2) *Rates charged on dividend income in 2010/11 and 2011/12*
Any grossed up dividend (that is, the dividend plus the 10 per cent tax credit) which falls within the "basic rate" band is taxed at 10 per cent. Any grossed up dividend falling within the "higher rate" band it is taxed at 32.5 per cent (the "dividend upper rate") and any falling within the "additional rate" band is taxed at 42.5 per cent.

Because of the order in which different types of income are taxed, dividends always form the highest portion of a taxpayer's income.

Examples

(1) In 2010/11 Peter has earned income of £100,000 and receives net interest of £16,000 (grossed up this will be £20,000) and a dividend of £900 with a £100 tax credit. The earned income will be the first part of his income. Part of it will not be liable to tax at all because he has a personal allowance. The balance will be taxed partly at the basic rate and partly at the higher rate. The savings income will be taxed next; it will all fall into the higher rate tax band. Peter will be liable to tax at 40 per cent on £20,000 but will have the benefit of the 20 per cent tax already deducted. He will have to pay an additional 20 per cent. The

dividend will be taxed last and will all fall into the higher rate tax band. Peter will be liable to tax at 32.5 per cent on £1,000 but will have the benefit of the 10 per cent tax credit. None of Peter's income falls into the additional rate band.

(2) If Peter had no earnings, the interest would be taxed first. Part of it would escape tax because of the personal allowance; the next £2,440 would be taxed at the 10 per cent starting rate available on savings income and the balance at basic rate. The dividend would be taxed at the dividend ordinary rate. Peter would have no further liability to tax on any of his income and would be entitled to a refund on the portion of interest falling into the starting rate band.

(3) In 2011/12 Thomas receives net interest of £800 (grossed up this will be £1,000) and a dividend of £900 with a £100 tax credit. His personal allowances exceed his income and so he is not liable to pay tax at all. He can recover the tax already paid on the interest but the dividend tax credit is irrecoverable.

An example of a simple calculation of a taxpayer's liability may be helpful.

Example

Alec, who is single and aged 30, has the following income on which he is liable to tax in the year 2010/11.

(a) £45,000 from his solicitor's practice for the tax year.
(b) £10,000 gross director's fees from XYZ Ltd, from which the company has deducted £705 under the PAYE system.
(c) £8,000 from a trust fund paid to him net of basic rate tax.

He has paid £5,000 interest on a £50,000 loan to buy an interest in the firm of solicitors.

His tax liability will be calculated as follows:

	£
Step 1: Calculate Total income	
Practice receipts	45,000
Salary (gross)	10,000
Income from trust fund grossed up	
$£8,000 \times \dfrac{100}{80}$	= 10,000
	65,000
Step 2: Deduct allowable reliefs (interest paid)	(5,000)
Step 3: Deduct personal allowance	(£6,475)
	53,525

Step 4: Calculate tax on net income

All of his income is non-savings income:

	£	£
On first	£37,400 tax at 20%	7,480
On next	£16,125 tax at 40%	6,450
Tax Bill		13,930

However, some tax has already been deducted at source and Alec is credited with this. The trustees of the trust fund deducted £2,000 and XYZ Ltd deducted £705. Therefore, HMRC will require £11,225 direct from Alec.

When is the tax payable?

6.12 The due date for the payment of tax is January 31 following the year of assessment. However, there are two interim payments due on January 31 in the year of assessment and July 31 immediately following that year. Tax under ITEPA 2003 on employment and pension income is deducted before the employee receives it under the PAYE system.

3. INCOME OF THE DECEASED

We will now look at the rules which are particularly relevant to death.

Introduction

6.13 It is the responsibility of personal representatives to deal with the income tax affairs both of the deceased and of the estate during the administration period, to ensure that a full declaration of income, arising before and after the death, is made and that tax, at the appropriate rates, is paid. When performing this duty the personal representatives must make self assessment returns both in respect of the income of the deceased up to the date of death and in respect of the administration period.

The tax due on many estates is either already covered by tax deducted from the income, or so small that it is not worth dealing with under normal Self Assessment procedures. To minimise costs and administrative burdens for personal representatives, the Revenue announced in Tax Bulletin 66 that it would allow tax liabilities to be settled informally by a one-off payment in all cases where the estate was not regarded as "complex". The position is now dealt with in para.7410 of HMRC's Trusts, Settlements and Estates Manual (TSEM) which states that personal representatives may make an informal payment of the total liability for the whole period of administering the deceased's estate if the total tax liability (income tax plus capital gains tax) for the entire administration period is less than £10,000 and the following conditions are met:

- the probate/confirmation value of the estate is less than £2.5m,

- the proceeds of assets sold in any one tax year are less than £250,000, and

- the estate is not regarded as complex, so it can be dealt with without the personal representatives having to complete a Self Assessment return.

Informal payments should normally be made to the office that handled the deceased's tax affairs.

There are a few situations where informal payments are not accepted, for example, where part of the tax due is the recovery of income or capital gains tax wrongly refunded to the taxpayer and repayable under TMA 1970 s.30.

An estate is complex and a self assessment form SA900 will be issued where:

- the tax liability for the whole of the administration period is in excess of £10,000,

- the estate has a value at the date of death in excess of £2.5m, or

- the proceeds of assets sold by the personal representatives in any one tax year exceed £250,000.

The estate is also likely to be regarded as complex if the administration has not been completed within two calendar years from the date of death although there is a discretion in borderline cases (see TSEM para.7376).

If the informal procedure is used there is no time limit and, therefore, no interest on "late" tax and no penalties and there is no need to request formal clearance. However, in cases where self assessment returns are required the time limit for submission of the self assessment form is January 31, following the end of the tax year of death.

Income of the deceased

The personal representatives must ascertain the total income of the deceased for the tax year of death. Only income received or receivable before death is included. Income receivable after death is income of the estate (see para.6.17, below). They will calculate the tax liability in the usual way by deducting any charges on income payable before the death together with a *full* year's personal reliefs, regardless of the date of death. **6.14**

Once the deceased's taxable income has been calculated, the appropriate rates of tax are applied and any extra tax due is paid or a rebate claimed where relevant.

Example

Betty, unmarried, died on May 6, 2010 aged 59 and her personal representatives find her share of the profits from a solicitor's practice taxable in the tax year 2010/11 is £55,000. She received £4,000 interest from a Building Society account. They find that she was entitled to a dividend of £900 from A plc (declared on May 1, 2010) and that a dividend of £385 on shares which she owned in B plc was declared on June 1, 2010.

The dividend from B plc is treated as income of the estate (see para.6.15 below).

The tax calculation is as follows.

	£
Step 1: Calculate Total income	
Practice receipts	55,000
Grossed up interest	
$£4,000 \times \dfrac{100}{80}$	5,000
Grossed up divident	
$£900 \times \dfrac{100}{90}$	1,000
	61,000
Step 2: Deduct allowable reliefs	None
Step 3: Deduct personal allowance	(6,475)
	54,525
Step 4: Calculate tax on net income	

The practice receipts are taxed first. The receipts exceed the starting rate band of £2,440 so none of the savings income will be taxed at the starting rate. Everything except the dividend income will be taxed at the basic or higher rate.

The tax on the practice receipts and interest is:

	£		£
On first	37,400 tax at 20%		7,480.00
On remaining	17,125 tax at 40%		6,850.00
Tax Bill			14,330.00

The dividend income of £1,000 is taxed next and is treated as the highest part of her income. It will be taxed at the dividend upper rate of 32.5 per cent.

$$£1,000 \times 32.5\% = £325$$

Betty has a tax credit for 10 per cent (£100) on the dividend and a tax credit for 20 per cent (£1,000) on the building society interest.

Her personal representatives will, therefore, only have to pay £14,330 less £1,100 = £13,230.

Distinguishing income of the deceased from income of the estate

6.15 The personal representatives must differentiate between the deceased's income and that of the administration period and this is done by ascertaining when the particular receipt arose. This causes few problems when considering salary or profits from a trade or profession since these sources of income will normally cease with the death. However, other types of income which continue to arise after the death, such as rent, interest or dividends, will cause greater problems since they are often attributable to a period which falls partly before and partly after the death.

Income which is *due* before the death is part of the deceased's income (for example, a dividend on shares due and payable on a date before death) even if paid after death. Income which is *due* after the death is income of the estate (for example, a dividend due and payable after death or interest which becomes due and payable on a date after the death). The Apportionment Act 1870 (see below, para.16.53), which provides for the apportionment of income on a day-to-day basis for the purposes of distribution, does not apply for income tax purposes (*IRC v Henderson's Executors* (1931)). A limited income tax relief is available where income received after death has been apportioned for inheritance tax purposes and some of that income has been included as an asset of the estate at death attracting inheritance tax (ITTOIA 2005 s.669).

Practical problems

The income tax liability of the deceased may take a considerable length of time **6.16** to finalise. This is particularly likely to be the case where the deceased was a sole trader or a partner as there may be delays in preparing the accounts on which the tax liability is to be calculated. There may be additional tax due to the Revenue or there may be repayments of tax due to the deceased as the result, for example, of excessive PAYE tax paid by an employer on the taxpayer's behalf. Where personal representatives cannot pay tax until they have obtained a grant of representation, the Revenue will by Concession A17 treat any charge to interest on unpaid tax as running from 30 days after the grant.

The personal representatives are normally required to submit an IHT Account at the latest within 12 months of the death detailing the assets and liabilities of the deceased and showing the amount of inheritance tax due calculated on the basis of the net value of the estate. At the same time they are required to pay any inheritance tax due except where the instalment option is claimed. The value of the estate cannot be accurately determined until all the assets and liabilities are ascertained so any delay in finalising the income tax position of the deceased will prevent the final calculation and payment of inheritance tax due.

Personal representatives are usually anxious to pay inheritance tax promptly, partly because interest starts to run after six months from the end of the month of death but more importantly because they cannot get a grant of representation and therefore cannot start administering the estate until the inheritance tax due has been paid. To prevent delays, personal representatives will frequently estimate the income tax liability of the deceased and pay inheritance tax due on the basis of that estimated figure. When they obtain the final income tax figure, they can if necessary submit a corrective account and make any adjustments to the inheritance tax which prove necessary. In a press release of April 4, 1996, the Revenue announced their willingness to issue self assessment tax returns before the end of the tax year at the request of personal representatives. The Revenue will then give early confirmation if they decide not to enquire into the return.

4. INCOME ARISING AFTER DEATH

As regards the income received by the estate during the "administration period" **6.17** there are special rules. This period starts with the day after the date of death and continues until the completion of the administration of the estate (ITTOIA 2005 s.653). It is generally accepted that completion of the administration occurs on the date the residue is ascertained for distribution. Personal representatives cannot claim any personal reliefs since these are only available to individuals. They can deduct interest on a loan (but not an overdraft) to pay inheritance tax when calculating the taxable income of the estate but only in so far as the loan is to pay tax on personalty vesting in the personal representatives to which the deceased was beneficially entitled. Further, this interest is only deductible for one year. Other expenses incurred by the personal representative in administering the estate are not deductible.

ISAs and PEPs are only tax exempt while the holder is living. However, income which arose on such accounts while the holder was alive is exempt even if it is credited after death.

The rates of tax which personal representatives pay is determined by the type of income they receive. They do not pay tax at the higher rate(s) irrespective of the amount of income they receive. Hence they are only ever liable at the following rates:

> *Dividends*: They only have to pay tax at the rate of 10 per cent on any dividend they receive and so the tax credit they receive with the dividend will discharge their tax liability on that income in its entirety.

> *Interest*: They will pay at the basic rate (20 per cent) unless the non-dividend income does not exceed the limit of the starting rate band (£2,440 for 2010/11 and £2,560 for 2011/12). Interest is normally received net of 20 per cent tax so, if the starting rate is available they will be entitled to a refund of tax. In other cases they will have no further liability.

> *Other income*: They will be assessed to basic rate tax applying the rules relevant to the particular type of income. So, for example, if the deceased was carrying on a business and the personal representatives continue to carry it on (either preparatory to winding it up or to passing it on to beneficiaries), the profits during the administration period form part of the assessable income of the personal representatives as trading income under ITTOIA 2005 Pt 2.

To the extent that income is paid to beneficiaries, further rules are relevant. These differ depending on whether the estate is a UK estate or a foreign estate on the beneficiaries' interests in the estate.

The residence status of the personal representatives determines the status of the estate. If they are all resident in the UK, then the estate is UK resident. The residence status of the deceased is irrelevant. Similarly, if none of the personal representatives is UK resident, then the estate is non-UK resident. If the personal representatives have mixed residence, the residence of the deceased acts as a "tie-breaker". If the deceased was UK resident or domiciled here then all of the estate is UK resident. If not, the estate is non-resident. As with individuals, if the estate is not UK resident, it is only assessable on income arising in the UK (see ITA 2007 s.834 and ITTOIA 2005 s.651).

A beneficiary is charged to income tax on the estate income applicable to their interest, grossed up by reference to the rate at which the personal representatives have paid income tax. Personal representatives are required, if so requested by residuary beneficiaries, to provide a written statement setting out the amounts of income paid to the residuary beneficiary in any year of assessment and the amount of tax and the rates which the amounts are deemed to have borne. This requirement was inserted into the Income and Corporation Taxes Act 1988 ("ICTA") as a new s.700(5) and continues to be in force despite the repeal and re-enactment of much of ICTA as part of the tax rewrite project.

Non-residuary legatees

Non-residuary legatees may be entitled to a specific legacy or to a pecuniary or general legacy. **6.18**

Specific legatees

Income arising from property which is the subject of a specific disposition by will belongs to the beneficiary from the date of death, subject to anything in the will to the contrary. The legacy itself does not give rise to tax liability, being a payment out of capital. But if there is delay in vesting the property in a beneficiary who is absolutely entitled, any income arising to the personal representatives belongs to the beneficiary and if it is paid to them will form part of their estate income. The income received will be grossed up at the appropriate rate and included in the beneficiary's tax return. The beneficiary will have credit for the tax paid by the personal representatives. **6.19**

Suppose there is an income producing asset such as a house which has been let and is producing rental income. The beneficiary only becomes liable to *pay* tax after the personal representatives have made an assent of the asset to the beneficiary. However, the liability relates back to the date of death so the assessments for intervening tax years will be reopened and tax will be reassessed for the years in which the income arose. The beneficiary will have the benefit of the 20 per cent tax paid by the personal representatives. If the beneficiary is a higher (or additional) rate taxpayer, they will have to pay the difference between the 20 per cent deducted and the 40 (or 50) per cent liability. If they are not a taxpayer, then they can reclaim the tax.

A specific legatee of shares will have the benefit of the 10 per cent tax credit. The legatee will be liable to further tax to the extent that the dividend, treated as the highest part of the taxpayer's income, exceeds the threshold for the dividend upper rate but, because the dividend tax credit is irrecoverable, will not be able to recover the tax credit if they are not a taxpayer at all.

Pecuniary and general legatees

Such legatees may be entitled to be paid interest on the value of their legacies (see Ch.16, below). The question of their liability to income tax on such interest then arises. In many circumstances income tax is chargeable on income even if not accepted but in the case of interest, tax is only payable on sums actually received. Thus, if a beneficiary disclaims entitlement to interest payable to them **6.20** on a pecuniary or general legacy or the personal representatives cannot pay it, they are not liable to tax—*Dewar v IRC* (1935) (unless a sum has been specifically set aside to pay the legacy in which case tax must be paid even if the legatee fails to draw the interest—*Spens v IRC* (1970)). If interest is paid to the beneficiary it is taxed as savings income in their hands under (ITTOIA 2005 s.369. Payment will be made gross (i.e. without deduction of any tax).

Residuary beneficiaries

6.21 The rules relating to residuary beneficiaries are themselves sub-divided into those which relate to beneficiaries with:

- limited interests,

- absolute interests,

- discretionary interests, and

- successive interests

in the residue of the estate.

Where there are different interests in different parts of the residue, each part is treated as a separate estate (ITTOIA 2005 s.649(4)). Residuary beneficiaries are charged to tax on their share of the residuary income of the estate.

Broadly speaking the income on which residuary beneficiaries may be taxed is their share of the "aggregate income" of the estate less various deductions set out in ITTOIA 2005 s.666 such as:

- interest (other than interest on unpaid inheritance tax);

- higher rate income tax relief available under ITTOIA 2005 s.669 where income of the estate has been included in the calculation of inheritance tax; and

- management expenses which are properly chargeable to income under the general law (as opposed to under a direction in the will).

Aggregate income is income of the estate which is chargeable to income tax less allowable deductions and excluding income to which a specific legatee is entitled (see ITTOIA 2005 s.664).

Amounts treated as income of the beneficiary are "grossed up" at the basic rate, savings rate or dividend ordinary rate, as applicable for the tax year of receipt. The estate income is then treated as having borne income tax at that rate or rates. In determining the rate applicable it is assumed first that amounts are paid to beneficiaries out of the different parts of the aggregate income of the estate in such proportions as are just and reasonable for their different interests, and then that payments are made from those parts bearing tax at the basic rate before they are made from those parts bearing tax at the dividend ordinary rate (ITTOIA 2005 s.679).

Because payments to a beneficiary of an estate are deemed to be made out of their share of income bearing tax at the basic rate in priority to their share of income bearing tax at the dividend ordinary rate, administration expenses chargeable to income are effectively relieved primarily against dividend income.

Beneficiary with a limited interest

A beneficiary who has an entitlement to income once the residue is ascertained **6.22** but not to capital has a limited interest (ITTOIA 2005 s.650(3)). An example of such a beneficiary is a person who has a life interest in residue.

All sums received by the beneficiary will be liable to income tax in the year of receipt. In the final tax year of the administration, the beneficiary is assessed on all receipts before the end of the administration period plus any amounts payable to them at the end of the administration period (ITTOIA 2005 s.654(3)).

In the case of income received gross, the personal representatives will deduct basic rate tax from the income and pay it to the Revenue on behalf of the beneficiary. In the case of savings and dividend income the personal representatives will themselves have received the income net of tax or with a tax credit and so will not have to make any further deduction. The beneficiary is liable to tax on income received in each tax year. The beneficiary will gross up the income at the appropriate rate and then deduct the tax credits. The personal representatives are treated as paying out income taxed at basic rate first (see para.6.21, above).

Example

Martha is entitled to income for life from her mother's estate. The personal representatives receive various items of income and pay all the income to Martha in tax year 2010/11. Martha is an additional rate taxpayer.

	Gross Receipts	Tax paid/deducted	Net Amounts
	£		£
Rent	4,000	20% paid by PRs £4,000 × 20% = £800	3,200
Interest	6,000	20% tax deducted 6,000 × 20% = £1,200	4,800
Dividend	5,000	10% tax credit £500	4,500

Martha grosses up the receipts

	Net		Gross
Rent	$£3,200 \times \dfrac{100}{80}$	=	£4,000
Interest	$£4,800 \times \dfrac{100}{80}$	=	£6,000
Dividend	£4,500 + 500	=	£5,000

As an additional rate taxpayer, she is liable at 50 per cent on the rent and interest but has the benefit of the tax already paid.

		£
Tax @ 50% on £10,000	=	5,000
Less Tax Paid	=	(2,000)
Tax to pay		£3,000

She is liable at 42.5 per cent on the dividend but has the benefit of the tax credit.

Tax @ 42.5% on £5,000	=	2,125
Less Tax Credit	=	(500)
Tax to pay		£1,625

In the above example had the personal representatives paid only £5,000 to Martha in 2010/11, this would have been treated as a payment of £4,000 of income subject to basic rate tax. The delayed income would be paid to Martha in the following tax year so that she would receive additional income that year. In the case of someone who is an additional rate taxpayer already in both tax years, this is not significant unless the additional rate changes. However, had Martha been a basic or higher rate taxpayer, receiving more income in one tax year might have pushed her into the higher or additional rate band in that tax year. If payment of the income can be spread more evenly the beneficiary may remain below the higher or additional rate threshold. Personal representatives should, if practicable, discuss with the beneficiary the strategy for making payments.

Beneficiary with an absolute interest

6.23 A beneficiary has an absolute interest in residue if the capital is properly payable to them, or would be so payable if the residue had been ascertained (ITTOIA 2005 s.650(2)). Such a beneficiary is entitled to both income and capital; income tax is, of course, only payable on income receipts. Therefore, when a beneficiary receives a cash sum from the estate it is necessary to distinguish income from capital receipts.

All payments to the beneficiary are treated as income up to the level of their "assumed income entitlement" for the tax year in question. Assumed income entitlement is the beneficiary's share of the residuary income for all the years of the administration in which they had the interest less income tax at the appropriate rate and any payments already made to them via ITTOIA 2005 s.665. For the year in which the administration period ends (the "final tax year"), income is treated as arising if the beneficiary has an assumed income entitlement for the year (whether or not any payments are made). Payments to a beneficiary of an estate are deemed to be made out of their share of income bearing tax at the basic rate in priority to their share of income bearing tax at the savings rate.

Example

Personal representatives are administering the estate of Theo who died in January 2011 leaving his residuary estate to Rosa absolutely.

(1) In tax year 2010/11 the personal representatives receive the following:

Gross Receipts		Tax paid/deducted	Net Amounts
	£		£
Rent	1,000	20% paid by PRs	
		£1,000 × 20% = £200	800
Interest	2,000	20% tax deducted	
		2,000 × 20% = £400	1,600
			2,400

They make no payments to Rosa.

(2) In tax year 2011/12 the personal representatives receive the following:

Gross Receipts		Tax paid/deducted	Net Amounts
	£		£
Rent	4,000	20% paid by PRs	
		£4,000 × 20% = £800	3,200
Interest	5,000	20% tax deducted	
		5,000 × 20% = £1,000	4,000
			7,200

They complete the administration and pay £500,000 to Rosa.

(3) In Tax Year 2010/11 Rosa's assumed income entitlement is £2,400. As she receives nothing from the estate, she includes nothing on her tax return.

(4) In Tax Year 2011/12 Rosa's assumed income entitlement is £2,400 + £7,200 = £9,600. All receipts will be treated as income up to that figure. Rosa will include on her tax return:

Net		Gross
$£9,600 \times \dfrac{100}{80}$	=	£12,000

She will have credit for the 20 per cent tax paid on the income received gross by the personal representatives and the 20 per cent deducted from the interest.

The balance of the payment to her is capital and as such is not included in her statutory income.

Again, so far as is practicable, personal representatives should discuss with the residuary beneficiary the strategy for making payments. It may be possible for the beneficiary to avoid paying higher (or additional) rate tax on the estate income in some tax years if payments can be staggered suitably.

Beneficiary with a discretionary interest

A person has a discretionary interest in all or part of the residue of an estate if **6.24** a discretion may be exercised in their favour and (if the residue had been ascertained at the beginning of the administration period) on the exercise of the discretion any of the income of the residue would be properly payable to them (ITTOIA 2005 s.650(3)). The person in whose favour the discretion is exercised is charged income tax on the total payments made in a tax year in exercise of the discretion, grossed up, where appropriate (ITTOIA 2005 s.655).

Successive interests

6.25 Special rules apply to the calculation of estate income where there are two or more successive absolute or limited interests during the period of administration. See ITTOIA 2005 ss.671–676.

Completion of the administration

6.26 HMRC state at para.7418 of the Trusts and Settlements Manual that to help personal representatives settle the tax affairs of the administration period quickly it will, on request, issue a tax return before the end of the tax year in which the administration is completed. This practice is not statutory, but was included in the Budget announcement for Finance Act 2007.

Whether the tax return is issued before or after the end of that tax year, HMRC will, on request, give early written confirmation if they do not intend to enquire into that return. This confirmation does not preclude, subsequent enquiries if it turns out that the return was incomplete or incorrect. Again this practice is not statutory, but was included in the Budget announcement for the Finance Act 2007.

Chapter Seven

TAXATION OF TRUSTS AND SETTLEMENTS

1. Introduction

Where property is held on trust the legal and beneficial interests are often held by **7.01** different people and the Revenue find it convenient and, in some cases necessary, to impose liability on both the trustee and the beneficiary. Where the beneficial interest in property is divided between several people, either at a particular time or successively, special rules are required to ensure that the creation of the settlement cannot be used as a means of saving tax.

Tax definitions of "settlements" for inheritance tax, capital gains tax, and income tax are different and will be considered separately later in this chapter. The definitions for tax purposes are not the same as for other purposes.

Settlements may be created by lifetime transfer, by the intestacy rules or by will.

We will deal with each tax separately for the sake of clarity but it is important to realise that in deciding whether or not to create a settlement each tax must be taken into account. Furthermore, the non-tax consequences of creating a settlement should always be regarded as the first consideration. A gift is unwise, even if it saves tax, if it leaves the settlor or their dependants with insufficient income or capital for their needs.

2. Settlements and Inheritance Tax

For inheritance tax purposes the term "settlement" is defined, by s.43(2) of the **7.02** Inheritance Tax Act 1984, as:

> " . . . any disposition or dispositions of property . . . whereby the property is for the time being—
>
> (a) held in trust for persons in succession or for any person subject to a contingency; or
> (b) held by trustees on trust to accumulate the whole or part of any income of the property or with power to make payments out of that income at the discretion

of the trustees or some other person, with or without power to accumulate surplus income; or

(c) charged or burdened (otherwise than for full consideration . . .) with the payment of any annuity or other periodical payment payable for a life or any other limited or terminable period . . . ."

Section 43(3) adds to the definition a lease for life or lives or for a period ascertainable only by reference to a death which is not granted for full consideration.

It should be noted that a settlement is "any disposition or dispositions of property . . . whereby the property is *for the time being*" held in one of the various ways listed in the definition. Whether or not property is settled must, therefore, be considered each time that a potential charge to tax arises. Property ceases to be settled once it ceases to be held in one of the various ways listed in the definition even though it may still be held by trustees (for example, where they have not yet vested it in a beneficiary who has become absolutely entitled).

Despite suggestions to the contrary in 2006 and 2007 the Revenue has confirmed that it accepts that a bare trust (that is a trust where the beneficiary is entitled to require the transfer of the legal title to themselves) is not a settlement for inheritance tax purposes. The beneficiary of such a trust is treated as an absolute owner.

A statutory trust imposed where property is held by co-owners is not a settlement for inheritance tax purposes. The co-owners are treated as absolute owners.

Examples of inheritance tax settlements include:

(a) Trustees are holding property for "A for life remainder to B" (successive interest, see s.43(2)(a), above).

(b) Trustees are holding property for "A if he reaches 25" (subject to a contingency, see s.43(2)(a), above).

(c) Trustees are holding property "to accumulate the income therefrom for 10 years and then to pay capital to A" (trust to accumulate until the 10-year period expires, see s.43(2)(b), above).

(d) Trustees are holding property "to pay the income therefrom for 10 years from [date] to such of my children as they shall in their absolute discretion from time to time appoint and thereafter to pay the capital to A" (discretion to pay income until the 10-year period expires, see s.43(2)(b), above).

(e) Property is being held by someone subject to the payment of an annuity to someone else and full consideration was not given for the annuity. For example, the will of a testator leaves Blackacre "to my son charged with the payment to X of an annuity of £1,000 per annum for the rest of X's life." In this case there will be a settlement of Blackacre from the death of the testator until the death of X (see s.43(2)(c), above).

3. THE INTEREST IN POSSESSION

It is often important for inheritance purposes to know whether or not a settlement **7.03** has an interest in possession and, if so, whether the interest is a "*qualifying*" interest in possession for inheritance tax purposes. This is because a person with a *qualifying* interest in possession is treated for inheritance tax purposes as owning the underlying trust capital.

A person with a *qualifying* interest in possession in settled property (for example, a life tenant of a will trust) is deemed to own the trust assets beneficially. Hence, the value of the trust assets is aggregated with the free estate of the beneficiary on death and if the beneficiary surrenders or assigns the interest, it is a transfer of value.

A qualifying interest in possession is defined in Inheritance Tax Act 1984 s.49 as:

- an interest in possession created before March 22, 2006,

- a disabled person's interest (see para.7.50),

- a transitional serial interest, (see para.7.18), or

- an immediate post-death interest (see para.7.41).

With the exception of transitional serial interests and trusts for the disabled no new qualifying interests in possession can be created by lifetime transfer on or after March 22, 2006. However, they can still be created on death in the form of immediate post-death interests.

What is an interest in possession?

The term "interest in possession" is not defined in the legislation. However, as **7.04** we shall see the House of Lords in *Pearson v IRC* (1980) has defined it as a "a present right to present enjoyment". In most cases it is clear whether or not there is an interest in possession. A beneficiary who has an immediate right to receive income or to use and enjoy trust property has such an interest. Thus, the life tenant of a settlement usually has an interest in possession. A beneficiary whose right to capital is contingent on reaching a specified age may obtain an interest in possession at an earlier age if the settlement (or Trustee Act 1925 s.31) gives them a right to income at an earlier age. Trustees may have power under the terms of a settlement to give beneficiaries a right to income for specified periods. Conversely in the case of an ordinary discretionary trust no one has such an interest since no one has a *right* to income. There are, however, some marginal cases where the position is less clear.

For example, in *Pearson v IRC* (1980) a trust fund was held for three beneficiaries (all adults) who were entitled to the property subject to powers of appointment and a power to accumulate; they would each receive one-third of the income unless the trustees exercised the power to accumulate or the power of appointment. The House of Lords by a majority of three to two (and overruling the decisions at first instance and in the Court of Appeal) held that there was no interest in possession. The majority held that an interest in possession is one giving "a present right to present enjoyment" and that on these facts there was no such right since the beneficiaries would not receive the income to the extent that the power to accumulate was exercised.

In *Douglas's Trustees v HMRC* (2007) trustees were to pay the deceased's widow the whole of the income of a trust fund or such part of it as they "may consider proper and expedient". Had the settlement said no more, the widow would not have had an interest in possession. However, the trust deed said that the trustees could only withhold income "with the concurrence of" the widow. The addition of these words converted the interest into an interest in possession since the widow would receive all the income unless and until she agreed to give up part of it.

In *Judge (PRs of Walden deceased) v HMRC* (2005) a rather unclear trust deed was held to provide that trustees had power to permit a widow to occupy a property "for such period or periods as they shall in their absolute discretion think fit". On that basis the widow did not have an interest in possession. This case is also interesting because it suggests that in order for trustees to create an interest in possession where one does not already exist, they must do something positive. Mere inactivity will not suffice.

Administrative and dispositive powers

7.05   In theory, a beneficiary with an interest in possession is entitled to trust income as it arises. However, trustees will always have an administrative power to pay management expenses of the trust from that income leaving only the balance for the beneficiary. In *Pearson,* Viscount Dilhorne said that there was a distinction between powers which were merely administrative and powers which were dispositive in their nature. A beneficiary with an interest in possession is entitled to all the net income of the trust once the expenses of the trust have been paid. If the trustees have power to withhold that net income from a beneficiary, there is no interest in possession. The difficulty lies in identifying expenses which are merely administrative. Management expenses clearly fall into that category but what if trustees have power to pay items which would be normally be paid from capital (for example, capital gains tax) from income? There are cases where it will be difficult to draw the line.

Power to allow beneficiaries of a discretionary trust to occupy a dwelling house

7.06   The mere existence of such a power is of no importance. However, if the trustees exercise the power, the Revenue may well argue that an interest in possession has been created. The Revenue's view is set out in Statement of Practice 10/79:

> " . . . if the power is drawn in terms wide enough to cover the creation of an exclusive or joint residence, albeit revocable, for a definite or indefinite period, and is exercised

with the intention of providing a particular beneficiary with a permanent home, the Revenue will normally regard the exercise of the power as creating an interest in possession."

The statement may not stand up to judicial scrutiny but challenging the Revenue is an expensive business.

The statement continues with the following:

"no interest in possession arises on the creation of a lease for a term or a periodic tenancy for less than full consideration."

It is, therefore, open to trustees to grant a lease to a member of the class at less than a market rent and avoid an allegation of an interest in possession.

(Note that principal private dwelling house relief will be available to the trustees under TCGA 1992 s.225 where a beneficiary occupies a trust asset whether as of right under the terms of the trust or as the result of the exercise of a trustees' discretion. See *Sansom v Peay* (1976).)

Will expressing wish that a beneficiary be allowed to reside in a dwelling house

Provided the will expresses a mere wish and confers no rights on the beneficiary, **7.07** there is no interest in possession. However, testators frequently try to protect the position of the beneficiary by directing that the trustees *must* allow the beneficiary to occupy the property. If the beneficiary has a right to occupy, there is an interest in possession.

In *IRC v Lloyds Private Banking* (1998) a wife left her half share in the matrimonial home on trust directing that while her husband:

- was alive,
- wanted to reside in the property,
- kept it in repair, and
- indemnified the trustees against rates, taxes and other outgoings,

her trustees would not:

- make any objection to such residence,
- disturb or restrict it in any way,
- take any steps to enforce the trust for sale on which the property is held, or
- obtain any rent or profit from the property.

Subject to this, the property was held for her daughter absolutely.

The husband was held to have an interest in possession in the property. The terms of the gift elevated him to the status of a sole occupier of the whole property, free from the possibility of a claim that he compensate the daughter for her exclusion or that an application be made to court for sale.

In *Faulkner (Trustee of Adams, deceased) v IRC* (2001) a testator directed in his will that a married couple, H and W, H a (or the survivor of them) should be permitted to live in a house which formed part of his estate for as long as they so wished.

The Special Commissioner agreed with the Revenue that there was an interest in possession. The will did not give any dispositive powers to the trustees to decide whether or not H and W should occupy the property. The trustees had no discretion to refuse any request by H and W that they be permitted to occupy the property. It followed that the will created a settlement in favour of H and W and that H (the survivor of the couple) had an interest in possession at the date of his death.

Co-owner in exclusive occupation

7.08 The Revenue has sometimes suggested that where one co-owner is in sole occupation, that co-owner may have an interest in possession in the whole property. In *Woodhall v CIR* (2000) such an argument failed. The testator left his house on trust for sale with a direction that the sale should be postponed so long as any of his children wished to live there. Until sale the trustees were to permit "all or any of them to occupy". All three of the testator's children lived there for a time but two moved out in the 1950s. The third child (Eric) occupied the property until his death.

The Revenue argued that Eric had had an interest in possession in the whole. Eric's executors argued that he had not had an interest in possession at all because he had had no right to exclusive possession. The Special Commissioner found that Eric and the other surviving child each had an interest in possession, being able to claim to occupy the property jointly. The trustees could not exclude them. Eric's estate, therefore, included half of the value of the property.

Note that trusts for the disabled escape the relevant property regime and can be created on death. However, they can also be created by lifetime transfer so they are dealt with separately at para.7.51.

4. THE SIGNIFICANCE OF FINANCE ACT 2006

7.09 On March 22, 2006 the Chancellor introduced huge changes to the way in which settlements are treated for inheritance tax purposes. The Treasury had formed the view that settlements were being used primarily to escape inheritance tax and was determined to make them less attractive. Their intention was to encourage people to make outright gifts rather than to use trusts. There was concerted opposition from professional advisers and the press who pointed out that trusts are used for all kinds of tax neutral reasons. The Treasury backed down to some extent in relation to settlements created on death but made very few concessions in relation to lifetime settlements. The date, therefore, remains a significant watershed in the tax treatment of settlements.

For settlements created before that date the important question was whether the settlement created did or not have an interest in possession. The two types of settlement were subject to different inheritance tax regimes.

For settlements created on or after March 22, 2006 the important question is whether the settlement is created by lifetime transfer or on death. Settlements created by lifetime transfer are virtually all subject to the regime that previously applied only to settlements without an interest in possession. Settlements created on death are subject to that regime unless they fall into one of the privileged categories.

5. Settlements Created before March 22, 2006

In the case of settlements created before March 22, 2006 the crucial question is **7.10** whether or not the settlement has an interest in possession (see para.7.04, above). This is because the inheritance tax treatment of a settlement with an interest in possession is entirely different from the treatment of a settlement without such an interest.

Classification

Pre-March 22 settlements can be divided as follows: **7.11**

a) *Settlements with a qualifying interest in possession*
Typically such a settlement would be a life interest trust for an adult beneficiary but it is possible to have short-term interests in possession, for example where a beneficiary becomes entitled to income at 18 under the Trustee Act 1925 s.31 before becoming entitled to capital. Before March 22, 2006 it made no difference whether the settlement was created by lifetime transfer or on death.

b) *Relevant property settlements*
Before March 22, 2006 relevant property settlements were those without an interest in possession which did not attract privileged inheritance tax treatment. Typically such a settlement would be a discretionary trust. It could also be a settlement in which beneficiaries had an interest contingent on reaching a specified age which failed to fulfil the requirements for privileged inheritance tax treatment.
The property in such a settlement is referred to in IHTA 1984 s.58 as relevant property and hence such settlements are described as relevant property settlements.

c) *Settlements attracting privileged inheritance tax treatment*
A number of settlements without a qualifying interest in possession attracted privileged inheritance tax treatment; for example trusts for the

disabled, accumulation and maintenance trusts (IHTA 1984 s.71), charitable trusts (IHTA 1984 s.58), employees trusts (IHTA 1984 s.86), and maintenance funds for historic buildings (IHTA 1984 s.77).

Settlements with a qualifying interest in possession

7.12 Section 49 of IHTA 1984 provides that a person with an interest in possession created before March 22, 2006 is treated as being beneficially entitled to the property in which the interest subsists. This is a "qualifying" interest in possession.

Tax arising on creation of a settlement with a qualifying interest in possession

7.13 A transfer to any type of settlement is a transfer of value by the settlor. Assuming that no exemptions apply, the transfer will be either exempt, potentially exempt or chargeable.

The fact that a person with a qualifying interest in possession is deemed to own the trust assets beneficially has a number of inheritance tax implications. Before March 22, 2006 if a settlor created a settlement by lifetime transfer in which they were the first life tenant there was no charge to tax. This was because before the creation they *actually* owned the property beneficially; after the creation they were *deemed* to own it beneficially, so for tax purposes the value of their estate has not gone down.

Similarly, if the settlor's spouse or civil partner was the first life tenant, the creation of the settlement (whether by lifetime transfer or on death) did not give rise to tax because it was spouse exempt.

A settlor who made a lifetime transfer to a settlement in which a non-exempt beneficiary had an interest in possession on or after March 17, 1987 and before March 22, 2006 was treated as making a potentially exempt transfer. Thus, no inheritance tax was payable unless the settlor died within seven years of the transfer. If the settlor dies within that period then the transfer becomes chargeable at the full rates in force at the date of death (subject to the possibility of tapering relief).

Example

On February 5, 2006, Sayeed gave £335,000 to trustees to hold on trust for Arshad for life, and the remainder to Bhopal. No exemptions or reliefs apply. Sayeed's cumulative total was nil. Sayeed dies on February 15, 2011.

No tax was payable on creation as the transfer was potentially exempt. However, on February 15, 2011, when the nil rate band is £325,000, the transfer becomes chargeable. The first £325,000 is within the nil rate band; the remaining £10,000 will be taxed at 40 per cent (with the benefit of tapering relief as Sayeed survived five complete years after making the transfer).

If Sayeed had transferred property to the settlement on death, the property transferred would have been taxed as part of his death estate before being transferred to the trustees of the settlement.

Note that if Sayeed transferred £355,000 to trustees to hold for Arshad for life on or after March 22, 2006, the settlement would be a relevant property settlement and the transfer would be immediately chargeable to inheritance tax.

Chargeable events after creation of settlement with a qualifying interest in possession

Since a person with such an interest in possession is treated as owning the trust **7.14** property (or a proportion of it if they are entitled to part only of the income) it follows that a termination of the interest in possession is taxable as a disposition *of the trust property* by that person. Tax may thus become chargeable:

(a) on the death of the person entitled to the interest;

(b) on an actual disposal of the interest (for example, the beneficiary gives their interest away, surrenders it or sells it); or

(c) on the termination of the interest in any other way (for example, where the interest is determinable at a particular date or on the happening of a particular event, tax will be payable on that day or when that event occurs).

Since the termination of the interest is treated as a transfer of the trust property by the person entitled to the interest, the rate of tax will depend on that person's cumulative total and on whether the termination is on death or during their lifetime, to an individual absolutely or on continuing trusts.

Examples

(1) Trustees of a trust created before March 22, 2006 are holding a trust fund of £300,000 on trust for Larry for life remainder to Roger. Larry dies having made chargeable lifetime transfers in the seven years preceding his death which have exhausted his nil rate band, and owning £150,000 worth of unsettled property. Larry's estate on death is £450,000 (i.e. the trust fund and the unsettled £150,000). The whole £450,000 is subject to tax at 40 per cent. The tax is, therefore, £180,000 (that is £450,000 at 40 per cent). This tax will normally be paid by the trustees of the settlement and the personal representatives in the same proportions that the trust property and the unsettled property bear to the whole estate on death. In this case the trustees will pay two-thirds of the tax and the personal representatives one third.

(2) Trustees of a trust created before March 22, 2006 are holding a trust fund of £500,000 for Anya for life, remainder to Bardolph for life, remainder to Casimir absolutely.

In February 2006 Anya surrenders her life interest so accelerating Bardolph's life interest. Anya makes a potentially exempt transfer of £500,000 to Bardolph.

Note that if Anya does the same thing in January 2011, she will make a lifetime chargeable transfer. Lifetime transfers on continuing trusts on or after March 22, 2006 are lifetime chargeable transfers unless they fall within very limited exceptions.

Where a pre-March 22, 2006 interest in possession comes to an end and at that **7.15** time the life tenant becomes beneficially entitled to the trust property there is no tax to pay. This is because, as we saw at para.7.13, before the interest ends they are treated as owning the trust property, after it ends they actually own it so that for tax purposes there is no loss to their (or anyone else's) estate.

Example

Trustees of a trust created before March 22, 2006 hold property on trust to pay the income to Anup until 25 and thereafter to Anup absolutely. When Anup reaches 25, no tax will be payable.

There is no tax on the termination of a pre-March 22, 2006 interest in possession if the property then reverts to the settlor during the settlor's lifetime or to the settlor's spouse or civil partner during the settlor's lifetime or within two years of their death (IHTA 1984 s.53).

Example

Salazar settles property on Brigitte for life with a reversion to the settlor. No tax is payable when the property reverts to Salazar on Brigitte's death.

7.16   Since a person with a pre-March 22, 2006 interest in possession is deemed to own the trust property absolutely, an advance of capital by the trustees to them does not give rise to tax since they are receiving property which is already treated for the purposes of inheritance tax as their own. An advance of capital to anyone else does give rise to tax since it brings the life tenant's interest in that property to an end.

Various exemptions and reliefs are available on the termination of a pre-March 22, 2006 interest in possession including the following:

(a) The annual exemption of £3,000 (unless already used to exempt other transfers) is available where the termination occurs as a result of a lifetime transfer.

(b) The spouse exemption applies unless the spouse has acquired the reversion for money or money's worth. (For example, settlement to A for life remainder to B—no tax on A's death if A is then married to B. Settlement to A for life remainder to X; B (A's spouse) buys X's reversion and then A dies—tax will be payable.)

(c) Business and agricultural property relief. The relief is available pro-vided the person with the pre-March 22, 2006 interest in possession fulfils the conditions for relief. This can be a problem. See *Burrell v Burrell* (2005) where trustees terminated the interest in possession of a beneficiary of a trust of unquoted shares. The beneficiary was the 18-year-old son of the settlor. The son had acquired an interest in possession at the age of 18 and would have received very substantial dividends. The trustees at the suggestion of the settlor used their powers to terminate the son's interest in possession by appointing the property on discretionary trusts. This was a lifetime chargeable transfer by the son which would give rise to a substantial inheritance tax charge unless business property relief was available. The trustees believed that it was but overlooked the fact that the son had not yet owned the shares for two years and, therefore, the ownership requirement of IHTA 1984 s.106 was not fulfilled.

The exemptions for small gifts and normal expenditure out of income cannot be used in relation to transfers from settlements.

Reversions

A reversionary interest (that is a future interest) in settled property is usually   **7.17**
excluded property and so no tax is payable on a transfer (lifetime or on death) of such an interest. This rule is really just a consequence of the fact that the person with an interest in possession is deemed to own the trust property absolutely.

> *Example*
>
> Property is settled before March 22, 2006 on Lashmi for life remainder to Rohan. No tax is payable on Rohan's remainder interest if Rohan dies or gives away his interest during Lashmi's lifetime.

To prevent tax avoidance a reversionary interest is *not* excluded property (so that tax will be payable on the death of its owner or on a lifetimes transfer by them) in certain special cases, for example where the reversionary interest was purchased.

Transitional serial interests

A beneficiary who had a qualifying interest in possession on March 22, 2006   **7.18**
continues to be treated as being beneficially entitled to the underlying trust assets. The tax treatment on the ending of that interest in possession may be different because it is no longer generally possible to create new qualifying interests in possession. Hence if on the ending of the interest in possession, the property continues to be settled, the new beneficiary will normally not have a qualifying interest in possession.

However, new qualifying interests in possession could be created in the transitional period which for this purpose ran from March 22, 2006 to April 5, 2008. These replacement interests are called transitional serial interests. The person with a transitional serial interest is treated in exactly the same way that any other person with a qualifying interest in possession is treated.

> *Example*
>
> Ben had a life interest in a substantial family trust. On March 22, 2006 he was 72 and did not need the income. The trustees terminated his interest on January 1, 2007 and appointed the fund to his son, Jack, for life. Jack obtained a transitional serial interest and Ben made a potentially exempt transfer to him.

A transitional serial interest normally only arises when it replaces an interest which was in existence on March 22, 2006. In the above example if Jack asked the trustees to terminate his interest in favour of his son, Sam, for life and the trustees did so on January 30, 2008, i.e. before the end of the transitional period. Sam would not have a transitional serial interest; he would have an interest in a relevant property trust and Jack would be treated as having made a lifetime chargeable transfer to that relevant property trust.

There is just one case where a transitional serial interest can arise outside the transitional period. This is where a spouse or civil partner with an interest in possession in existence on March 22, 2006 *dies* and their spouse or civil partner takes an interest in possession following their death. The surviving spouse or civil partner takes a transitional serial interest even though the beneficiary's death occurs outside the transitional period. This is not the case, however, if the replacement interest in possession arises outside the transitional period as a result of a *lifetime* transfer.

Example

Alan has a life interest in a family trust. His interest was in existence on March 22, 2006. In 2020 he marries, appoints his wife a life interest in the settlement on his death and promptly dies. His wife has a transitional serial interest (so that she is treated as owning the capital in the settlement) and so the spouse exemption applies. By contrast if in 2023 he divorces and creates an interest in possession for his wife as part of the divorce agreement: (a) the interest of the wife is not a transitional serial interest, and (b) the continuing trust falls within the relevant property regime. He will be treated as making a lifetime chargeable transfer to the relevant property settlement.

Relevant property settlements

Introduction

7.19   The rules which before March 22, 2006 applied only to non-privileged settlements without an interest in possession are described in this section. As we shall see at paras 7.40 and 7.41, below, these rules now apply to all settlements created on or after that date unless they fall within certain limited exceptions so these rules have become extremely important.

There is no interest in possession in a settlement if no individual has "a present right to present enjoyment" of the trust property (*Pearson v IRC* (1980) see para.7.04, above). A typical example is a discretionary settlement.

Where there is an interest in possession, tax is chargeable once for each individual beneficiary's period of enjoyment of the property. The rules for settlements without an interest in possession are designed to achieve the equivalent of one full tax charge every generation thus establishing rough parity of treatment with other settlements and with circumstances where the property is not settled at all.

The settlement itself is treated as a taxable entity. It has its own cumulative total. It is always taxed at lifetime rates even if the initial creation was on death.

The main feature is the "periodic charge" which is charged on the 10th anniversary of the creation of the settlement. It is charged on "relevant property" defined in s.58 as settled property (other than excluded property) in which there is no qualifying interest in possession.

IHT arising on creation of a relevant property settlement

If the settlement is created by lifetime transfer, it is an immediate chargeable **7.20** transfer and tax will be charged initially at half the death rates. Tax will be charged at the full death rates if the settlor dies within seven years of the transfer, although credit is given for any tax already paid. Tapering relief will be available if the settlor survives three years from the transfer. Grossing up will be required if the settlor pays the tax.

> *Example*
>
> Sam made a lifetime transfer of £400,000 to a discretionary trust on January 1, 2006 when the nil rate band was £275,000. He had made previous lifetime chargeable transfers of £200,000 and had exhausted his annual exemptions. The trust paid the IHT (so no grossing up was required). The tax payable by the trust was 20 per cent on the excess over the available nil rate band, i.e. on £325,000.
>
> $$\frac{20}{100} \times £325,000 = £65,000$$

(Had the transfer been made on death, the property would have been taxed as part of the death estate before being transferred to the trustees of the settlement.)

Where a transfer is made to a discretionary trust, there is no reduction in the amount of tax if the settlor or their spouse is one of the discretionary beneficiaries since a discretionary beneficiary has no interest in the trust property for tax purposes. Furthermore, if the settlor is included in the class of beneficiaries, this will amount to a reservation of benefit leading to a possible charge on their death (see para.7.31, below).

It is necessary for the trustees to know the settlor's cumulative total at the time of the transfer as it will form part of the cumulative total of the settlement for all future transfers. It is beneficial for the future taxation of the settlement if it is created at a time when the settlor has a low cumulative total. The settlor should avoid making other settlements on the same day (other than charitable ones) as they will be classified as "related settlements". The value of the property transferred to the related settlement will be added to the value of the settlement being taxed and will increase the rate of tax paid.

It is only settlements created on the same day which are related. In *Rysaffe Trust Company (Cl) v IRC* (2002) a settlor signed five identical discretionary settlements on the same day. His solicitors dated them on different days. He sent a cheque for £50 to his accountants who credited £10 to each settlement. At a later date he transferred five parcels of shares in the same company to the five trusts. The Revenue argued that the initial creation of the settlements and the subsequent transfers were associated operations and, therefore, there was one settlement not five separate settlements. The taxpayer successfully appealed. As a matter of general trust law there were five separate settlements not one.

Although they were initially identical, they each contained powers of appointment and powers to appoint new trustees so that eventually they might be very different. The associated operations rules were held to be inapplicable.

IHT chargeable after creation of relevant property settlements

7.21 After creation, there are three possible occasions of charge to IHT:

   (a) when property ceases to be "relevant property" between creation and the first 10-year anniversary;

   (b) on each 10-year anniversary; and

   (c) when property ceases to be "relevant property" between 10-year anniversaries.

7.22 *(a) Property ceasing to be relevant property before the first 10-year anniversary.* A charge is imposed on the value of the property ceasing to be relevant property (s.65). Property will cease to be relevant property when the trustees appoint capital to a beneficiary, an "exit" charge. Prior to March 22, 2006 property would cease to be relevant property if the trustees created an interest in possession in some or all of the trust property but after the changes introduced in Finance Act 2006 this ceased to be the case.

The charge is always based on lifetime rates. The actual rate of tax charged is 30 per cent of those rates as applied to a hypothetical chargeable transfer.

Step one is, therefore, to calculate the hypothetical chargeable transfer.

For exits in the first 10 years the hypothetical chargeable transfer is calculated by adding together the following:

   • the value of relevant property in the settlement immediately after commencement;

   • value of subsequent additions (at time added); and

   • value of property in a related settlement (immediately after it commenced; subsequent increases in value are ignored).

Step two is to calculate the tax at lifetime rates on the hypothetical chargeable transfer by joining the table of rates at the point reached by the settlor in the seven years before the creation of the settlement. Other chargeable transfers made on the same day are ignored (s.68(4)). The settlor's cumulative total remains relevant to the rate of tax charged on the settlement throughout its life so as a matter of tax planning settlors should create relevant property settlements at a time when they have a full nil rate band available. No account is taken of any earlier transfers from the settlement.

Step three is to convert the tax calculated into an average rate (equivalent to an estate rate). The relevant property in the settlement is charged to tax at 30 per cent of that average rate. This is referred to as the "settlement rate".

Step four is to calculate what proportion of the settlement rate will be applied to the transfer. One-fortieth of the settlement rate is charged for each complete successive quarter that has elapsed from creation of the settlement to the date of the transfer. This is referred to as the "effective rate". There is no charge if property ceases to be relevant property in the first quarter.

> *Example (continued from 7.20)*
>
> Let us assume that the trustees of the trust created by Sam on January 1, 2006 appointed £30,000 to one of the discretionary beneficiaries on April 1, 2008 when the nil rate band was £300,000.

Step one: Find value of hypothetical transfer—In our example the value of the hypothetical transfer is £400,000.

Step two: Calculate tax at half rates on hypothetical transfer—In our example the settlor's cumulative total was £200,000 at the time the settlement was created. This is added to the amount transferred to give an aggregate transfer of £600,000. The nil rate band in tax year 2007/08 is £300,000 so tax will be charged at 0 per cent on the first £300,000 and 20 per cent on the last £300,000 giving a tax figure of £60,000.

Step three: Convert the tax to an average rate and then take 30 per cent which will be the "settlement rate"

$$\text{Tax} \times 100 = \text{Settlement Rate}$$

$$\text{Value of Settlement}$$

$$\frac{£60,000}{£400,000} \times 100 = 15\%$$

Settlement rate is 30 per cent of 15 per cent, i.e. 4.5 per cent.

Step four: Calculate the "effective" rate by reference to the number of quarters completed since the settlement was created—In our example there are nine completed quarters since the date the settlement was created on January 1, 2006 so we take 9/40 of the settlement rate of 4.5 per cent and apply this to the fall in value of the trust property.

$$\frac{9}{40} \times \frac{4.5}{100} \times £30,000 = £303.75$$

If the tax comes from the trust fund the transfer will have to be grossed up.

(b) The first 10-year anniversary. Tax is charged on the value of the relevant **7.23** property in the settlement immediately before the first 10-year anniversary (s.64). Income only becomes relevant property where it has been accumulated (see SP8/86). Accumulation occurs when the trustees take an irrevocable decision to accumulate it although it can also occur after the expiry of a reasonable time.

Again *step one* is to calculate the value of a hypothetical chargeable transfer. On 10-year anniversaries it is calculated by adding together the following:

- current value of relevant property (this does not include income unless formally accumulated) in settlement immediately after commencement;

- value of property in a related settlement (immediately after settlement commenced); and

- value at the date the settlement commenced of any other property in the settlement which has not subsequently become relevant property.

Normally there will only be property in category one. The other two categories are anti-avoidance measures. Related settlements are included because transfers made on the same day are otherwise ignored and without this provision the settlor could save tax by setting up a number of small settlements instead of one large one. Non-relevant property is included to prevent the trustees switching value between relevant and non-relevant property.

Step two is to calculate the tax at lifetime rates on the hypothetical chargeable transfer by joining the table of rates at the point reached:

- by the settlor in the seven years before the creation of the settlement; plus

- any chargeable transfers made from the settlement in the first 10 years.

Step three is to convert that tax into an average rate and to take 30 per cent of that average rate as the "settlement rate" to be applied to the relevant property in the settlement. As the highest rate of tax at lifetime rates is 20 per cent, the highest possible settlement rate is 30 per cent of that which is 6 per cent. It will be even lower if any of the trust property is eligible for business or agricultural property relief.

Example (continued from para.7.22)

The first 10-year anniversary falls on January 1, 2016. Assume the assets remaining in the trust fund are worth £670,000 on that date and assume the nil rate band has risen to £400,000.

Step one: *Find value of hypothetical transfer*—In our example the current value of relevant property is £670,000.

Step two: *Calculate tax at half rates on hypothetical transfer*—In our example the settlor's cumulative total was £200,000 and £30,000 was appointed from the settlement so transfers to be taken into account are £230,000 leaving £170,000 of the nil rate band available. Tax will be at 0 per cent on the first £170,000 and 20 per cent on the last £500,000, i.e. £100,000.

Step three: *Convert the tax to an average rate and then take 30 per cent which will be the "settlement rate"*

$$\frac{\text{Tax}}{\text{Value of Settlement}} \times 100 = \text{Settlement Rate}$$

$$\frac{£100,000}{£670,000} \times 100 = 14.925\%$$

Settlement Rate is 30 per cent of 14.925 per cent, i.e. 4.477 per cent.

Step four: The settlement rate is applied to the property to be taxed to produce the tax payable

$$\frac{4.477}{100} \times £670,000 = £29,995$$

(c) Property ceasing to be relevant property between 10-year anniver- **7.24**
saries.   Tax is charged on the property ceasing to be relevant property. The rate of tax is a proportion of the effective rate charged at the first 10-year anniversary. The proportion is one-fortieth for each complete successive quarter that has elapsed from the date of the first anniversary to the date of the transfer. There is no charge if property ceases to be relevant property in the first quarter.

Example (continued from para.7.23)

Assume the trustees appoint £200,000 to a discretionary beneficiary on December 1 2018.

Step one: Calculate the property ceasing to be relevant property—In our example the fall is £200,000.
Step two: Calculate the effective rate by reference to the quarters completed since the previous anniversary—There are 11 completed quarters since the last 10-year anniversary so take 11/40 of the settlement rate (4.477 per cent) and apply this to the fall in value of the trust property.

$$\frac{11}{40} \times \frac{4.477}{100} \times £200,000 = £2,462.35$$

If the tax comes from the trust fund the transfer will have to be grossed up.

(d) Subsequent 10-year anniversaries.   The charge is calculated in the same way   **7.25**
that it was calculated on the first 10-year anniversary.

Points to be aware of in connection with the taxation of settlements without an interest in possession

Agricultural and business property relief

Agricultural and business property relief will reduce the value of relevant   **7.26**
property if the trustees meet the conditions necessary for relief.

Importance of review before each anniversary

It will normally be preferable for trustees to appoint capital out of a trust   **7.27**
immediately before an anniversary rather than immediately after one. This is because the charge to tax will then be calculated on the value of the trust property when the trust was created or on the previous anniversary rather than on its current value.

   It is particularly important to review nil rate band settlements before the first 10-year anniversary. Because the property settled was within the settlor's availa-ble nil rate band, all exits in the first 10 years will be taxed at 0 per cent no matter how much the trust property increases in value. On the 10th anniversary the property remaining in the settlement is revalued. Transfers from the settlement in the previous 10 years are cumulated when calculating the rate of inheritance tax to be charged.

Example

Harry died on June 30, 2005 with a nil cumulative total. He left a nil rate band legacy (£275,000) on discretionary trusts for his children and the residue to his wife so no inheritance tax was payable on his death.

By May 2015 the trust fund is worth £900,000.

Before June 30, 2015 the trustees can appoint the whole of the fund to the children and there will be no inheritance tax liability.

If they wait until June 30, 2015 to make the appointment, tax will be calculated on the new value of the fund so there will be a tax liability on everything in excess of the current nil rate band.

There is one case (possibly the result of defective drafting of Inheritance Tax 1984) where appointments should not be made before the first 10-year anniversary. This is where property is settled which qualifies for 50 per cent business or agricultural relief. When calculating the *rate* of tax on an exit before the first 10-year anniversary under s.68, it is necessary to take "the value, immediately *after* the settlement commenced, of the property then comprised in it". Valuing the property immediately after the creation of the settlement for the purposes of calculating the rate of tax means no business or agricultural property relief is available because the property has not been owned for the requisite two-year period. If the property leaves the settlement after the necessary two-year ownership period the value of the property will be reduced by the 50 per cent relief but the rate of tax will remain relatively high for the whole of the first 10-year period. The problem does not arise where relief is available at 100 per cent as the value of the property being charged will be reduced to zero so the rate of tax will be irrelevant. On the 10-year anniversary the 50 per cent relief is taken into account when calculating the rate to be charged under s.66 and subsequent exits in that 10-year period will be a proportion of that rate. It is, therefore, preferable to wait until after the expiry of the first anniversary before making the distribution.

Appointments within three months following creation or within three months of an anniversary

7.28 There is no exit charge if an appointment is made within three months of creation of the settlement or within the first three months following an anniversary (IHTA 1984 s.65(4)).

Additions of property to the settlement by the settlor

7.29 If the settlor adds property to the settlement by means of a chargeable transfer special rules apply (s.67(1)). The special rules do not apply where the transfer is exempt, for example because it is covered by the annual exemption.

Where the rules apply, the calculation of the periodic charge following the addition will be modified. When calculating the tax on the hypothetical chargeable transfer the settlor's cumulative total will be taken as the higher of the totals:

- immediately before creating the settlement plus transfers made by the settlement before the addition; and

- immediately before transferring the added property deducting from this latter total, the transfer made on creation of the settlement and a transfer to any related settlement.

Whenever the modification would result in higher rates of tax, the settlor should consider whether it will be preferable to create a new settlement rather than adding property to an existing one.

Pilot trusts

It is common for settlors to create a number of small trusts on consecutive days **7.30** (typically transferring £10 to each) at a time when they have an unused nil rate band. These lifetime settlements are often referred to as pilot trusts.

Because the settlements are created at a time when the settlor has a full nil rate band, each settlement will have the benefit of a full nil rate band. The settlements are not related to each other because they are created on different days. If the settlor adds property to all the settlements on the same day, the rules on additions do not apply. Provided the settlor still had a full nil rate band available on the date of the transfers, each settlement will have a full nil rate band available from the settlor when calculating anniversary and exit charges.

Additional property added by persons other than the settlor will be treated as creating a separate settlement.

Reservation of benefit

Where a settlor creates a settlement without an interest in possession they may be **7.31** a beneficiary of the settlement (e.g. they are one of the objects of a discretionary trust). In this case they have made a gift "subject to a reservation" and tax may, therefore, be payable *on their death* in respect of that property unless they have been excluded from benefit for seven years before they die. See *IRC v Eversden* (2002) and *PRs of Lyon v HMRC* (2007). When trustees terminate a beneficiary's interest in possession, the beneficiary makes a transfer of value (see para.7.14, above) but would not normally be regarded as making a gift. This gave the possibility of avoiding the gift with reservation rules. Trustees could terminate an interest in possession to create a discretionary trust which would include the original beneficiary in the class of beneficiaries. The original beneficiary would be treated as making a lifetime chargeable transfer but so long as the transfer was limited to the nil rate band, there would be no tax to pay. The beneficiary could benefit from the trust funds which would be outside their estate for inheritance tax purposes. To prevent this useful technique, a new s.102ZA was introduced into the Finance Act 1986. This provides that a person whose interest in possession in property is terminated on or after March 22, 2006 is to be regarded as making a gift of the property in which the interest was terminated.

Settlements with no interest in possession which qualify for privileged treatment

Introduction

7.32 A number of pre-March 22, 2006 settlements attract privileged inheritance tax treatment. We will only consider accumulation and maintenance settlements here. These are settlements which satisfy the requirements of IHTA 1984 s.71 as amended.

The purpose of accumulation and maintenance settlements was to enable a settlor to give property without any tax penalty to young people with conditions attached which prevent them having access to income and/or capital at too young an age. They are settlements without an interest in possession but they are not subject to anniversary charges or exit charges. The creation of an accumulation and maintenance settlement by lifetime transfer before March 22, 2006 was a potentially exempt transfer.

The government formed the view that these settlements were being used to avoid inheritance tax and in 2006 changed the rules that apply to such settlements.

Settlements created on or after March 22, 2006 cannot qualify as accumulation and maintenance settlements. Transitional provisions were made for accumulation and maintenance settlements in existence on March 22, 2006. If the terms on which the beneficiaries took the capital complied with the requirements of the new s.71A, the settlement was converted on March 22, 2006 to a bereaved minor trust (see para.7.41, below).

Settlements which did not qualify as s.71A settlements were allowed to continue as accumulation and maintenance settlements until April 6, 2008. On that date the definition of an accumulation and maintenance settlement contained in IHTA 1984 s.71 changed. Settlements which met the new definition continued as accumulation and maintenance trusts, unless. the terms on which the beneficiaries took the capital complied with the requirements of the new s.71D, in which case the settlement was converted to a s.71D settlement (see para.7.47, below).

Definition in IHTA 1984 s.71

7.33 The amended requirements of s.71 are as follows:

(a) one or more persons will, on or before attaining a specified age not exceeding 18, become beneficially entitled to it;

(b) no interest in possession subsists in it;

(c) the income from it is to be accumulated so far as not applied for the maintenance, education or benefit of a beneficiary (i.e. one of the persons who will become entitled under (a)); and

(d) *either*

(i) not more than 25 years have elapsed since the beginning of the settlement (or later time when it satisfied the three requirements above); *or*

(ii) all of the beneficiaries had a common grandparent (or are the children, widows or widowers of the original beneficiaries who die before achieving the specified age).

Originally the age specified in condition (a) was 25 and it was sufficient for beneficiaries to take an interest in income; they did not need to become entitled to capital. The government felt that this was too generous and as from April 6, 2008 beneficiaries must become entitled to *capital* at or before *18*.

The other elements of s.71 continue unchanged.

Relatively few settlements in existence on March 22, 2006 fulfilled the requirements of the amended sub-section (a). Because of the benefits in retaining privileged status (no anniversary or exit charges) a number of accumulation and maintenance settlements were amended to meet the requirements of the new s.71. Some trustees had powers which enabled them to amend the terms of the settlement and some trustees made applications to court under the Variation of Trusts Act 1958 to allow a variation of the terms of the trust. As a result practitioners will continue to meet accumulation and maintenance settlements for some years to come.

We will consider each of the requirements of the amended s.71 in turn.

(a) Entitlement to the trust property at 18 or some lower specified age. A **7.34** settlement only satisfies this requirement if the beneficiaries *will* be entitled at 18 or some lower specified age. It is not sufficient that a beneficiary *may* be entitled at 18 or some lower specified age. Thus a settlement which gives "capital and income at 18 or on earlier marriage" satisfies the requirement since the beneficiary will get the property at 18 at the latest. A settlement which gives "capital and income on marriage or at 18 whichever is the later" does not satisfy the requirement. Strictly speaking it is impossible to have absolute certainty because death can always prevent a beneficiary becoming entitled. However, the possibility of death intervening is ignored. The section is construed to mean "will, if at all".

The requirement is that "one or more persons" will be entitled at a specified age. The "persons" can include unborn persons. This is useful as it means an accumulation and maintenance settlement can have an open class of beneficiaries. However, s.71(7) provides that the condition is not satisfied "unless there is or has been a living beneficiary". Thus a settlement on "the children of A at 18" is not an accumulation and maintenance settlement if A was childless when the settlement was created. If the settlement were to the children of A and A had a child living at the time that the settlement was made, then the settlement would remain an accumulation and maintenance settlement even if that child were to die since there would then "have been" a living beneficiary.

The possibility that trust funds may go to someone who does not qualify as a beneficiary of the accumulation and maintenance trust is usually fatal to accumulation and maintenance status. Thus, settlements had to be drafted without powers of appointment which, if exercised, could result in entitlement being postponed beyond 18 or in property passing to non-qualifying beneficiaries. In some cases the mere existence of a power will compromise a trust's privileged status even if there is never any exercise of the power.

Thus, the mere *existence* of a power of appointment which will enable trustees to pay capital or income to non-qualifying beneficiaries will cause loss of accumulation and maintenance status.

> *Example*
>
> Prior to March 22, 2006 A set up a trust for the benefit of her grandchildren contingent on them reaching 18 with power for the trustees to appoint capital or income to A's brother (who is now 21). The trust does not qualify for privileged status as there is no certainty that A's children will become entitled.
>
> There would be no problem if the trustees had an overriding power to appoint capital or income amongst A's children as they saw fit while the children were under 18. The power does not infringe the s.71 requirement. It cannot be used to benefit anyone other than the class members and cannot postpone their entitlement.

To avoid the danger of trusts losing privileged status by oversight, such settlements often include a direction that no power shall be exercised in such a way as to prevent the trust qualifying as an accumulation and maintenance trust or to direct that appointments and advances shall not be made to any possible beneficiary who is above the age limit.

In *Lord Inglewood v IRC* (1983) it was accepted that the mere *existence* in a trust of a common form power of advancement did not compromise the privileged status of a trust even though it could be used to postpone the vesting of property in a beneficiary beyond the age limit (then 25). However, the *exercise* of such powers inappropriately may do so. This may provide a useful tax planning tool for trustees of existing accumulation and maintenance settlements which include common form powers of advancement. The trustees may use their powers to amend the age of entitlement to capital to 18 so as to retain privileged status for the settlement. As beneficiaries approach 18 if the trustees are unhappy with the idea of the beneficiary obtaining capital they may use their power of advancement to appoint the property on discretionary trusts for the benefit of the beneficiary and issue. There will be a tax charge at that point on the value of the beneficiary's share but the trust will have benefited from its tax free status in the interim.

For the avoidance of doubt the Revenue confirmed[1] that the payment by trustees of an accumulation and maintenance trust of trust funds direct to a school in payment of school fees will not compromise the privileged status of a trust.

7.35 *(b) No interest in possession.* Once there is an interest in possession in settled property it ceases to be subject to the rules for an accumulation and maintenance

---

[1] See [1996] *Private Client Business* 76.

settlement. However, where there is more than one beneficiary each part of the settled property must be considered separately.

Example

A settlement was created in 2003 for "such of the children of Ann as reach 25"; when the settlement was created Ann has been dead for some time and had left two children, Ben, aged 16, and Colin, aged 10. The whole of the settled property was an accumulation and maintenance settlement for two years. When Ben reached 18 in 2005, he became entitled to half the income under s.31 of the Trustee Act 1925 and, therefore, obtained an interest in possession in half the settled property. The other half of the property remained an accumulation and maintenance settlement. If Ben dies before reaching 25, there will be tax to pay on his half share (since he has an interest in possession).

Note that on March 22, 2006 Ben's half of the fund was not an accumulation and maintenance settlement. He had already acquired an interest in possession. Colin's half was an accumulation and maintenance settlement. On April 6, 2008 the settlement will not fulfil the requirements of the new s.71 and so Colin's half of the fund will be converted into a different type of settlement (see para.7.37 below).

(c) Income to be accumulated so far as not applied for maintenance, etc. The **7.36** income must be either accumulated or used for the maintenance, education or benefit *of the beneficiaries.*

This requirement will not be satisfied if the trustees are given power to apply the income for other purposes (such as maintenance of persons other than the beneficiaries).

(d) Common grandparent or less than 25 years since settlement became an **7.37** *accumulation and maintenance settlement.* This requirement is satisfied where all the beneficiaries are children of the same person or grandchildren of the same person. The common grandparent need not be the settlor. This requirement is also satisfied where the settlement provides for the replacement of beneficiaries who have a common grandparent but die before obtaining a vested right to capital by their own children, widows or widowers.

Example

A settlement "to the children of Jay equally at 18 or if any of them shall die before that age such deceased child's share shall go to the children of such deceased child at 18" will be an accumulation and maintenance settlement.

Where the settlement is not on persons with a common grandparent it can only be an accumulation and maintenance settlement for 25 years. However, tax will become payable at the end of 25 years if the settlement is still an accumulation and maintenance settlement and the beneficiaries did not have a common grandparent. Where tax does become payable the rate is dependent solely on the length of time the property has been in the settlement and is usually much higher than the rate for other settlements with or without an interest in possession. It is, therefore, important, where beneficiaries do not have a common grandparent, to ensure that all property ceases to be subject to the rules for an accumulation and maintenance settlement within 25 years.

Capital gains tax and income tax

7.38 There are no special rules for capital gains tax and income tax in relation to accumulation and maintenance settlements save that hold-over relief may be available under s.260 of the Taxation of Chargeable Gains Act when a benefici-ary becomes absolutely entitled to capital.

What happens to settlements which do not satisfy the requirements of the amended s.71?

7.39 Settlements became relevant property settlements on April 6, 2008 if they did not satisfy the requirements of the amended s.71 (unless they qualified as s.71A or s.71D—see below, paras 7.43 and 7.47). There was no charge to inheritance tax either on ending of the accumulation and maintenance settlement or on its conversion to a new form of settlement. The settlement simply changed its nature.

A settlement which converted to a relevant property settlement becomes liable to anniversary charges and exit charges. Anniversary charges are payable on each 10-year anniversary of the conversion of the original creation of the settlement (not its conversion to a relevant property settlement). There is a reduction in the tax charge for each quarter that the settlement was not a relevant property set-tlement.

Example

Sandip created an accumulation and maintenance settlement on January 1, 2000 with £400,000. There were no related settlements and this was Sandip's first transfer (apart from transfers using up his annual exemptions).

The settlement became a relevant property settlement on April 6, 2008 because it did not satisfy the requirements of the new s.71 (or those of s.71A or s.71D).

The first 10-year charge arose on February 1, 2010 when the funds were worth £500,000 and the nil rate band was £325,000.

Tax was calculated on £500,000 (as explained at para.7.23, above) with a reduction for the number of complete quarters that the property was not relevant property, that is the period January 1, 2000 to April 6, 2008 which is 33 quarters.

The value of the hypothetical chargeable transfer is £500,000. Sandip had a full nil rate band available and the settlement has made no transfers so the tax payable on the hypothetical transfer is 0 per cent on the first £325,000 and 20 per cent on the remaining £175,000 giving £35,000.

The rate to be charged is therefore $30\% \times \dfrac{£35,000}{£500,000} \times 100 = 2.1\%$

$$£500,000 \times 2.1\% = £10,500.$$

This is reduced by $\dfrac{33}{40}$ for the time the property was not relevant so the tax payable is:

$$£10,500 - \left(\frac{33}{40} \times £10,500 \right) = £1,837.50$$

Hence the tax charged on the first 10-year anniversary will in many cases, be substantially less than a full charge.

6. Settlements created on or after March 22, 2006 by Lifetime Chargeable Transfer

All lifetime settlements created on or after March 22, 2006 (with the exception **7.40**
of those for disabled beneficiaries—see para.7.50, below) are treated in the same
way. They are all subject to the relevant property regime described at paras
7.19–7.31, above. It is irrelevant whether or not there is an interest in possession
or whether they are for young beneficiaries.

Examples

All the following settlements created by Sam on March 22, 2006 will be relevant
property settlements. The initial transfer will be a lifetime chargeable transfer by Sam
and the settlements will be subject to anniversary charges and exit charges.

    (1) "To myself for life, remainder to my children absolutely".
    (2) "To my wife for life, remainder to my children absolutely".
    (3) "To my son, Jeff, for life, remainder to his children absolutely".
    (4) "To my children contingent on reaching 25".
    (5) "To my children contingent on reaching 18".
    (6) "To my trustees on discretionary trusts for my children and grandchildren".

However, it does not follow that inheritance tax will actually be payable on the
creation of a relevant property settlement. The initial transfer may be within the
settlor's nil rate band. The property transferred may attract 100 per cent agricultural or business property relief.

Examples

Harry and Wanda want to settle property for their grandchildren. On April 6, 2010
they each transfer £331,000. Neither has made any previous transfers.

    No inheritance tax is payable on the initial transfer because the first £6,000 is
covered by two years' annual exemptions and the balance is within their nil rate
bands.

    No inheritance tax will be payable on transfers in the first 10 years because the rate
will be 0 per cent. No anniversary charge will be payable unless the property has
increased beyond the nil rate threshold.

    In addition they could transfer any property that they had which was eligible for
100 per cent relief.

    After seven years the transfers will fall out of the cumulative totals for Harry and
Wanda and, should they so wish, they can make further transfers.

After creation, all relevant property settlements will be subject to anniversary and
exit charges as explained at paras 7.21–7.25.

7. Settlements created on or after March 22, 2006 on Death

Many settlements created on death will be subject to the relevant property **7.41**
regime. However, on death it is possible to create four types of settlement which
will not be subject to the relevant property regime. These are:

(a) Immediate post-death interests (IHTA 1984 s.49A).

(b) Trusts for bereaved minors (IHTA 1984 s.71A).

(c) Trusts for bereaved young people (IHTA 1984 s.71D).

We will look at each in turn. Note that trusts for the disabled escape the relevant property regime and can be created on death. However, they can also be created by lifetime transfer so they are dealt with separately at para.7.51.

Immediate post-death interests

7.42   To qualify as an immediate post-death interest a person must become beneficially entitled to an interest in possession in created on death and must continue to have such an interest at all times since the death. (IHTA 1984 s.49A).

Any life interest created on death will qualify as an immediate post-death interest and it is irrelevant that trustees may be able to terminate the interest. If the interest does come to an end at any point, for example as a result of the trustees exercising a right to appoint the property elsewhere, then the immediate post-death interest ceases. It cannot restart even if the original beneficiary reacquires the interest in possession.

A survivorship clause is ignored provided it does not exceed six months. The dispositions actually taking effect are treated as if they had had effect from the beginning of the period. An immediate post-death interest can arise as a result of a post-death variation under IHTA 1984 s.142 or of an appointment from a will trust within two years of death before an interest in possession has arisen under IHTA 1984 s.144 because in both cases the interest will be treated as arising on death as a result of the reading back effect of the two sections.

A person with an immediate post-death interest is treated as if beneficially entitled to the underlying trust property (as explained in relation to pre-March 22, 2006 settlements with a qualifying interest in possession at para.7.12 et seq). There are no anniversary or exit charges. Instead the property is aggregated with the beneficiary's own estate on death. If the interest comes to an end before death, the beneficiary will be treated as making a lifetime transfer of value. The type of transfer depends on whether the property passes to someone absolutely entitled in which case there is a potentially exempt transfer (to the extent that the transfer is not exempt) or whether the property passes on trust in which case there is a lifetime chargeable transfer.

Example

(1) Terri leaves property to Lara for life, remainder to Raj absolutely. When Lara dies, the trust property is aggregated with her free estate in order to calculate the inheritance tax payable on her death.

(2) Terri leaves property to Lucy for life, remainder to Rohan absolutely. If Lucy surrenders her lifetime interest, the trust property will pass to

Rohan absolutely. Lucy will make a potentially exempt transfer. If, however, she was married to Rohan, the transfer would be exempt.

(3) Terri leaves property to Larry for life, remainder to Linda for life, remainder to Rocco. If Larry surrenders his life interest, he will make a lifetime chargeable transfer, not a potentially exempt transfer, because the transfer is on continuing trusts.

Trusts for bereaved minors

What is a trust for a bereaved minor?

A trust for a bereaved minor is one which satisfies the conditions set out in IHTA **7.43** 1984 s.71A.

(1) The trust must be created by will or on intestacy for the deceased's own child (the bereaved minor).

(2) The bereaved minor must on or before attaining 18 become entitled to the settled property, any income arising from it and any income that has already arisen and been accumulated.

(3) While the bereaved minor is living and under 18:

   (a) any capital applied must be applied for the benefit of the minor, and
   (b) the bereaved minor must be entitled to all the income arising from the settled property or no such income may be applied for any other person.

(Condition 1 does not have to be satisfied in the case of an accumulation and maintenance settlement converted on March 22, 2006.)

Where a settlement satisfies the s.71A requirements, there are no anniversary charges and s.71B(2) provides that there is no exit charge when:

(a) the bereaved minor becomes entitled to capital at 18 (or earlier),

(b) the bereaved minor dies before becoming entitled to capital, or

(c) capital is advanced to the bereaved minor.

Example

Mandy, who is divorced, dies intestate on April 30, 2008 leaving three children aged 4, 3 and 2. Her estate is £900,000. The children will be entitled to the capital at 18. If they all fail to reach 18 the property held on the statutory trusts will pass to Mandy's father.

(1) There will be no anniversary charge on April 30, 2018.
(2) There will be no exit charge as and when each beneficiary reaches 18 and becomes entitled to a share of the capital.
(3) There will be no exit charge if capital is advanced to a child before 18.

(4) If all the children die before 18 and the property passes to Mandy's father, there will be no exit charge.

Points on s.71A

7.44   The power to advance capital under s.32 of the Trustee Act 1925 allows trustees to advance capital for the "benefit" of a beneficiary. "Benefit" is a wide word and could include settling capital for the beneficiary and close family members. This would seem to conflict with the requirement that capital must be applied for the bereaved minor. However, s.71A(4) makes specific provision for this problem. It provides that a settlement can still satisfy the capital condition if s.32 applies or if the terms of the settlement widen the statutory power to allow up to the whole of the beneficiary's interest to be advanced.

This means that if the trustees are unhappy at the prospect of a beneficiary becoming entitled to capital at 18, they can use their power of advancement to settle the beneficiary's share on continuing trusts. There will be no exit charge but the property will then be held on relevant property trusts so thereafter there will be anniversary and exit charges.

As was the case for accumulation and maintenance settlements (see para.7.32, above) the word "will" does not require absolute certainty. Death can prevent the beneficary taking an interest. The word should be read as meaning "will, if at all".

Notice that these trusts are very restricted. A grandparent cannot create a s.71A trust for a grandchild.

A will may leave property to the testator's children contingent on reaching 18 with a substitutional gift to a grandchild if a child predeceases; the trust for the children will fulfil the requirements of s.71A but if a grandchild is substituted that part of the settlement will be subject to the relevant property regime.

> *Example*
>
> Trevor dies with an estate of £600,000 which he leaves on trust for his three children, Ann, Ben and Clare contingent on reaching 18 with a substitutional gift to children of a child who predeceases also contingent on reaching 18.
>
> On Trevor's death Ann is 24, Ben died, aged 22, but has left a child, Brady who is aged 2, and Clare is 17.
>
> Ann has a vested interest and is immediately entitled to her share. Clare's interest fulfils the requirements of s.71A; the portion held for Brady is subject to the relevant property regime.

Oddly IHTA 1984 s.71A provides that where the trusts arise *on intestacy*, a substituted grandchild will be a beneficiary of a trust for a bereaved minor. Had Trevor died intestate in the above example, Brady would have been a beneficiary of a trust for a bereaved minor.

7.45   Section 71A is drafted by reference to a single beneficiary called the bereaved minor suggesting that each bereaved minor must become entitled to their own "share" of the trust capital. If this was the correct interpretation, it would be fatal to the status of the settlement for the trustees to have a power to alter the shares of individual beneficiaries to give one more than the other. However, the Revenue issued guidance in June 2007 (available on websites of the Society for Trusts and Estates Practitioners and Chartered Institute of Taxation) which said that this was not the correct interpretation. It is possible to include a power for trustees to appoint capital in unequal shares or even all to one at the expense of another.

Example

Fred died and left £400,000 to trustees to hold for his three children contingent on reaching 18 but with a power for the trustees to appoint capital to the children in such proportions as they see fit, equally in default of appointment. The trustees decide to appoint £300,000 to the youngest child and the rest equally to the two older children. Despite the power to vary the shares of the beneficiaries this settlement fulfils the requirements of s.71A.

However, according to the Revenue guidance the power must not permit the trustees to vary the share of a child who has *already* reached 18. The Revenue also takes the view that once a child has been excluded from benefit, even revocably, the power cannot afterwards be used to benefit the excluded child. In the Revenue's view it is not possible under the s.71A regime for someone who is not currently benefiting to become entitled in the future. Trustees should therefore consider carefully before excluding a child from benefit or making a revocable appointment of all the trust funds to one child. The mere possibility of trustees exercising the power in this way will not affect the status of the settlement. The mere existence of the powers does not prejudice the status of the settlement.

To prevent problems the power of appointment should be limited in the following way:

"PROVIDED that no such appointment shall be made and no such appointment shall be revoked so as to either diminish or to increase the share (or the accumulations of income forming part of the share) of or give a new share (or new accumulations of income) to a child who at the date of such appointment or revocation has reached the age of 18 nor to benefit a child who has been excluded from benefit as a result of the exercise of the power."

Capital gains tax and income tax

Note there is no special treatment for capital gains tax or income tax except that   **7.46** when a beneficiary becomes absolutely entitled as against the trustees, holdover relief is available under TCGA 1992 s.260.

Trusts for bereaved young people

What is a trust for a bereaved young person?

Many people regard an age of 18 as too young for entitlement to capital. As a   **7.47** result of public criticism of the very restricted trusts afforded privileged treatment for inheritance tax the government amended the Finance Bill 2006 at a late stage and introduced a new s.71D into the 1984 Act. This allows entitlement to capital to be deferred beyond the age of 18 while still offering some inheritance tax privileges. However, the privileges are more restricted than those available to a trust for a bereaved minor.

The following conditions set out in s.71D must be satisfied:

(1) The trust must be created by will for the deceased's own child (B).

(2) B must at or before 25 become entitled to the settled property, any income arising from it and any income that has already arisen and been accumulated.

(3) While B is living and under 25:

(a) any capital applied must be applied for the benefit of B; and
(b) B must be entitled to all the income arising from the settled property or no such income may be applied for any other person.

(Condition 1 does not have to be satisfied in the case of an accumulation and maintenance settlement converted on April 6, 2008.)

As was the case with trusts for a bereaved minor a settlement can still satisfy the capital condition if s.32 applies or if the settlement widens the statutory power to allow up to the whole of the beneficiary's interest to be advanced.

Where a settlement satisfies the s.71D requirements, there are no anniversary charges and s.71E(2) provides that there is no exit charge when:

(a) a beneficiary becomes entitled to capital at 18 (or earlier);

(b) a beneficiary dies before becoming entitled to capital; or

(c) capital is advanced to a beneficiary before 18.

If the capital remains settled after the age of 18 there will be an exit charge on any of the above events but it will only be calculated for the period from 18 to the exit.

Example

Adele dies and leaves property on trust for her two children contingent on reaching 25. If the trustees appoint the capital to the children at or before 18, there will be no charge to inheritance tax. If the trustees appoint capital to the first child at 21 there will be a charge for the period 18–21 and if they appoint to the second child at age 25, there will be a charge for the period 18–25.

The calculation of the exit charge is similar to the calculation of an exit charge in the first 10 years of a relevant property settlement. However, it is based on the value of the property originally settled not on the value of the property at the time the beneficiary becomes entitled to capital (s.71F(9)). Hence the charge may be calculated on the basis of a value which differs substantially from the value of the property at the date of the exit.

Example

Assume that Adele in the previous example died on July 9, 2006 and that the property she left to her two children contingent on reaching 25 was worth £400,000. Her first child reached 18 on May 12, 2008. The trustees decided to allow the trust to continue but on August 19, 2012 they appoint that child his share of capital (now worth £300,000).

The settlement rate is calculated on the basis of the property originally settled (£400,000). Assume that the nil rate band remains £325,000. Tax is calculated at 20 per cent on the balance above the nil rate band and 30 per cent of the resulting rate will be applied to the appointment of capital.

Assumed chargeable transfer = £400,000 − £325,000 = £75,000

Tax on £75,000 × 20% = £15,000

Effective rate $= \dfrac{£15,000}{£400,000} \times 100 \times 30\% = 1.125\%$

$$£300,000 \times 1.125\% = £3,375$$

However, there is a reduction because tax is only chargeable for the number of complete quarters in the period from the day that the beneficiary attained 18 and ending with the day before the chargeable event (from May 12, 2008 to August 18, 2012). In this example the number of complete quarters is 17, so the amount of tax under s.71F(3) is :

$$£3,375 \times \frac{17}{40} = £1,434.37$$

Points on s.71D

As was the case for accumulation and maintenance settlements the word "will" **7.48** does not require absolute certainty. Death can prevent the beneficiary taking an interest. The word should be read as meaning "will, if at all".

Settlements satisfying the s.71D requirements can only be created by parents. The existence of a substitutional gift to issue of the testator's child will not prevent the settlement qualifying as a s.71D trust. However, if the substitution takes effect, the substituted beneficiary will be a beneficiary of a relevant property trust not a s.71D trust.

Section 71D is drafted by reference to a single beneficiary referred to as "B". However, the Revenue guidance issued in July 2007 (referred to at para.7.44, above) takes the same approach in relation to s.71D settlements as to s.71A settlements. Trustees can have a power to appoint capital unequally amongst the beneficiaries without affecting the status of the settlement. As with s.71A settlements the power must not be exercisable in favour of a child who has reached 25 and the trustees must not make an appointment to a beneficiary who has been excluded.

Most people making wills who want to benefit their children without paying continuing IHT charges will probably choose a s.71D settlement in preference to a s.71A one. The trustees of a s.71D settlement are free to advance the trust funds to the beneficiaries at 18 if they choose. This will mean no charges to IHT. If, however, the beneficiary is too immature to deal with the funds at 18, the trustees

can allow the settlement to continue until 25. There will be an exit charge at that
point.

If the trustees are still doubtful as to the maturity of the beneficiary they could
apply any power of advancement they may have to settle the trust funds on
discretionary trusts for the benefit of the beneficiary. The same exit charge will
be payable as if the property went to the beneficiary absolutely. There will be
subsequent anniversary charges and an exit charge but this may be worthwhile if
the beneficiary cannot be trusted to deal sensibly with the funds.

Capital gains tax and income tax

7.49   Note there is no special treatment for capital gains tax or income tax except that
when a beneficiary becomes absolutely entitled as against the trustees, holdover
relief is available under TCGA 1992 s.260.

Accumulation and maintenance settlements converted into s.71d trusts

7.50   Accumulation and maintenance settlements which did not fulfil the requirements
of the amended s.71 of IHTA 1984 (see para.7.37, above) on April 6, 2008 will
normally be converted into a relevant property settlement. However, they can
qualify as s.71D trusts despite the fact that they may have been created by
lifetime transfer and may not be for the settlor's own children. See IHTA 1984
s.71D(3) and (4). The beneficiaries must become entitled to capital at or before
25.

The Revenue takes the view that in order to fulfil the requirements of s.71D the
class of beneficiaries must be closed (see Guidance issued in June 2007). This is
because in the case of an ordinary s.71D trust created for the deceased's own
children, the class must, by definition, be closed.

So if, for example, an existing accumulation and maintenance settlement in
favour of the settlor's grandchildren provides that the class closes only when the
eldest becomes 25 and the trust currently benefits only two existing grandchildren, aged 8 and 9, in order to qualify as a s.71D settlement, the terms of the
trust must be amended to exclude any future born beneficiaries.

8. SETTLEMENTS FOR THE DISABLED

7.51   A settlement for the disabled can be created by lifetime transfer or on death. It
is one:

(1) which is created for:

(a) the benefit of a beneficiary who is "disabled" within the meaning
of IHTA 1984 s.89;

(b) the settlor's own benefit at a time when the settlor is suffering
from a condition that it is reasonable to expect will lead to the

settlor becoming "disabled" within the meaning of IHTA 1984 s.89 (a "self-settlement"); and

(2) where the property transferred into the settlement is held in one of the ways set out in s.89B:

    (a) During the life of a disabled person, no interest in possession in the settled property subsists; and not less than half of the settled property which is applied during the disabled person's life must be applied for his benefit (s.89(2) and s.89B.

    (b) The settlement is a self-settlement within s.89A, and

        (i) during the life of the settlor no interest in possession in the settled property subsists,

        (ii) any settled property applied during the settlor's life can only be applied for his benefit, and

        (iii) any power to terminate the trusts during the settlor's life can only be exercised to give the settlor or another person an absolute entitlement to the settled property, or to create a disabled person's interest within (a) or (c).

    (c) The disabled person becomes entitled to an interest in possession on or after March 22 2006.

    (d) The settlement is a self-settlement within s.89A, and

        (i) the settlor was beneficially entitled to the property immediately before transferring it into settlement,

        (ii) the transfer was on or after March 22, 2006, and

        (iii) any of the settled property applied during the settlor's life must be applied for the settlor's benefit.

Broadly speaking a person is disabled within the meaning of s.89 if they are incapable, by reason of mental disorder within the meaning of the Mental Health Act 1983, of administering their property or managing their affairs, or in receipt of an attendance allowance or disability living allowance by virtue of entitlement to the care component at the highest or middle rate.

Where the conditions are satisfied the disabled person is treated as beneficially entitled to a qualifying interest in possession in the settled property. The effect is that property can be settled but will escape anniversary and exit charges. No inheritance tax will be payable until the disabled person dies when it will be treated as part of their estate for inheritance tax purposes. A settlement falling within s.89B(1)(c) and created on death would be an immediate post-death interest were it not for the fact that s.49A specifically excludes a trust for the disabled from the definition of an immediate post-death interest. This is presumably so that all trusts for the disabled are treated together for inheritance tax purposes.

The creation of a settlement for a disabled beneficiary by lifetime transfer will be a PET in so far as not exempt.

9. Capital Gains Tax and Settlements

7.52 The basic structure of capital gains tax was explained in Ch.5. In this section we will consider the possible liability to capital gains tax, in relation to disposals of trust assets or interests in a trust, of:

> (a) the settlor,
>
> (b) the trustees, and
>
> (c) the beneficiaries.

The Capital Gains Tax legislation draws distinctions between settlements which are UK resident and those which are non-resident. In this book, we will only consider the rules applicable to the former.

"Settled property" is defined, by Taxation of Chargeable Gains Act 1992 s.68, as any property held on trust other than property to which Capital Gains Tax Act s.60, applies.

The property excluded from the definition of settled property by s.60 is assets held by a person:

> (a) as nominee for another person;
>
> (b) as trustee for another person absolutely entitled as against the trustee. Such a bare trust often arises where property has been held on trust for a life tenant who has recently died and the trustees are holding the property while arranging to vest it in the remainderman. Another example of such a bare trust is where the trustees are preparing to transfer the assets to a beneficiary who has satisfied a contingency. The test for deciding whether a person is absolutely entitled as against the trustees is whether they have the exclusive right (subject only to paying the expenses of the trust) to direct how those assets shall be dealt with (s.60(2)). The beneficiary must, therefore, have the right to demand that the assets be handed over to them; or
>
> (c) as a trustee for any person who would be so entitled but for being a minor or other person under disability. Thus, where land has been left to a minor, since a minor cannot hold a legal estate in land, trustees will have to hold the property until the minor reaches 18. If they must satisfy a contingency (such as reaching 18) before they can become absolutely entitled to the property the exception does not apply (*Tomlinson v Glyn's Executor and Trustee Co.* (1970)).

Where the "trust" falls within one of the s.60(1) exceptions, the Taxation of Chargeable Gains Act applies as if the property were vested in the beneficiary and any acts of the nominee or trustee are treated as acts of the beneficiary. Thus, for example, when the trustees transfer assets to the remainderman after the death of the life tenant, no capital gains tax liability can arise.

Property held by two or more persons as joint tenants or tenants in common is not "settled property" provided they are together absolutely entitled to the property.

In 2010/11 trustees of settlements, like individuals, paid capital gains tax at a flat rate of 18 per cent on disposals before June 22, 2010. Disposals on or after that date by trustees are all taxed at a flat rate of 28 per cent irrespective of the level of trust income.

10. CAPITAL GAINS TAX—THE LIABILITY OF THE SETTLOR

Creating a settlement by lifetime transfer

If the settlor transfers assets to trustees (whatever the terms of the settlement), **7.53** this is a disposal. The gain or loss will be calculated in the normal way by deducting from the market value of the assets at the time of disposal, the deductions permitted by the Act (see para.5.06, above). The trustees will in turn acquire the assets at market value at the date of the disposal unless hold-over relief is claimed.

Should the disposal give rise to a loss, that loss can only be set against gains made by the settlor on other transfers to trustees of the same settlement since settlors and their trustees are "connected persons" (TCGA 1992 ss.18(3) and 286).

The potential liability to capital gains tax can arise even if the settlor has an interest as a beneficiary or is a trustee, or the sole trustee, of the settlement (TCGA 1992 s.70). In certain cases hold-over relief may be claimed on the creation of a settlement so that no immediate charge to capital gains tax arises. Hold-over relief is available under s.165 of the 1992 Act where the assets put into settlement are business assets.

Hold-over relief is also available under s.260 of the 1992 Act, regardless of the nature of the assets which are settled, where the creation of the settlement is a chargeable transfer for inheritance tax purposes. Since March 22, 2006 all lifetime transfers to settlements will be chargeable transfers unless to a trust for the disabled. Where hold-over relief is available on the creation of a settlement it is the settlor alone who makes the election for relief, the trustees of the settlement are not required to agree.

Section 169B provides that hold-over relief is not available under either s.165 or s.260 of the 1992 Act if the settlement is settlor interested. Section 169F sets out the situations in which a settlor will be regarded as having an interest for this purpose. A settlor has an interest if settled property could be paid or applied to the settlor or their spouse or civil partner or for their dependant child or if any of them derive a benefit directly or indirectly from the property. A dependant child is one who is under the age of 18 and is unmarried and without a civil partner. "Child" includes stepchild for this purpose. If a settlement becomes settlor interested within six years of the end of the tax year in which the disposal was made, any hold-over relief is lost and capital gains tax becomes payable (s.169C).

Creating the settlement on death

7.54 If the settlement is created on death there will be no disposal and so no capital gains tax liability will arise. The deceased settlor's personal representatives will acquire the assets at their market value at death. This will also be the acquisition value for the trustees.

11. Capital Gains Tax—The Liability of the Trustees

Changes in trustees

7.55 During the "life" of the settlement the persons holding office as trustees may change, whether by reason of death, retirement or removal. Whenever a new trustee is appointed the assets will have to be transferred to the newly constituted body of trustees. Section 69(1) of the TCGA 1992 provides that settlement trustees are a continuing body of persons and disposals to the new trustees do not give rise to capital gains tax liability.

Actual disposals

7.56 The trustees may wish to dispose of items of trust property and replace them with new items. They may wish to sell assets to raise cash, whether to meet expenses or to be able to make a cash advance to a beneficiary. Whatever the reason for the disposal, if the trustees make an actual disposal of trust property they may become liable to capital gains tax.

Whether a gain or loss arises will be determined in the usual way. The trustees can set the exemptions and reliefs they are entitled to claim against any chargeable gains realised. The exemptions and reliefs to which they are entitled include:

(a) The annual exemption which is normally half the exempt amount available to an individual (so that trustees in tax year 2010/11 get £5,050). However, if the settlement is one of a number created by the same settlor the annual exemption is divided equally amongst the settlements subject to a minimum exemption per settlement of one tenth of the annual exemption, so £1,010 for tax year 2010/11. Hence if a taxpayer created 12 settlements, each would have an annual exemption of £1,010.

(b) The principal private dwelling-house exemption given in the TCGA 1992 ss.222, 223, provided the house disposed of has been the only or main residence of a person entitled to occupy it under the terms of the settlement (s.225). Therefore, provided the trustees have been given a power to permit the beneficiary to occupy the house, the exemption will apply, whether the beneficiary is a life tenant or the beneficiary under a discretionary trust (*Sansom v Peay* (1976)).

Note that principal private dwelling-house exemption is not available for disposals on or after December 10, 2003 if the gain includes a gain that was held over on one or more previous disposals. The relief will continue to apply to that part of the gain referable to the period before December 10, 2003. See s.226A of the Act. This is an anti-avoidance provision designed to prevent taxpayers transferring second homes to a trust for the benefit of their children, allowing one child to occupy it as their principal private dwelling-house and then selling and claiming principal private dwelling-house relief.

If a disposal gives rise to a loss the trustees may set that loss against any gains they have made in the year of disposal and may carry forward unabsorbed losses to set against gains made in future years.

Deemed disposals

Persons becoming absolutely entitled as against the trustees

Where a person becomes absolutely entitled to trust property as against the trustees, the TCGA 1992 s.71(1), provides that   **7.57**

> "all assets forming part of the settled property to which he becomes so entitled shall be deemed to have been disposed of by the trustee, and immediately reacquired by him in his capacity as a trustee within section 60(1) . . . , for a consideration equal to their market value".

Any capital gains tax payable is assessed at this point and thereafter the trustee holds as a bare trustee.

Section 71(1) applies where:

(a) the trustees advance assets to a beneficiary (where they are a life tenant or a discretionary beneficiary);

(b) a beneficiary satisfies a contingency and so becomes entitled to all or part of the trust property; or

(c) the settlement comes to an end as a result of the death of the life tenant and the remainderman becomes absolutely entitled to the property. (However, no tax is payable in this circumstance: see below, para.7.58.)

The deemed disposal and reacquisition takes place as soon as the beneficiary becomes absolutely entitled as against the trustees, even though the assets may not be transferred for some time afterwards. Thus, if a person is entitled to property provided they reached the age of 25, on their 25th birthday the trustees are deemed to dispose of the assets as settlement trustees and immediately to reacquire them as bare trustees for the beneficiary. Capital gains tax will be payable if a gain has arisen after taking account of exemptions, reliefs and allowances but there is no further liability when the assets are subsequently vested in the beneficiary.

There are cases where the date of the deemed disposal is unclear. In *Figg v Clarke (I.O.T.)* there was a trust for the children of X who reached 21. In 1964 X had been paralysed from the chest down and was, therefore, incapable of fathering any more children. It was argued that the class closed at that point creating a deemed disposal, rather than on X's death. The court held that this was not so and that the class remained open until X's death. It would be unworkable to have to enquire into the exact date on which a person became incapable of fathering children.

Where property is left contingently to several beneficiaries, beneficiaries who attain a vested interest will not be absolutely entitled as against the trustees unless they are able to call for distribution. They may not be able to do so until the interests of all the beneficiaries have vested. This is because beneficiaries with an entitlement to a share of a trust fund cannot insist on receiving their shares if the effect of distribution would be to damage the interests of other beneficiaries whose interests have not yet vested. Nor can they insist on receiving their shares if the trustees have an express power of appropriation unless the trustees make an appropriation. Until this power is exercised, the beneficiary cannot claim any specific asset and therefore it cannot be said that they are absolutely entitled to a fractional share of everything. In English law, if the settled property is land in England or Wales, the decision of Goff J. in *Crowe v Appleby* (1975) suggests that there is no occasion of absolute entitlement until the final contingency is fulfilled. The land as a whole remains settled property, and any actual disposal of it is a disposal entirely by the trustees. The beneficiary has no right to call upon the trustees to transfer a divided share of the land or to create a tenancy in common.

Reliefs

7.58   Hold-over relief is available in certain circumstances when a beneficiary becomes absolutely entitled as against the trustees. If the settlement is an accumulation and maintenance settlement or a s.71A or s.71D trust at the date the beneficiary becomes absolutely entitled, hold-over relief can be claimed by a joint election of trustees and beneficiary. The relief is also available on a joint election by trustees and beneficiary where there is a transfer by the trustees which is chargeable to inheritance tax; for example, an appointment of assets from a discretionary trust.

Entrepreneurs' relief is available to trustees in limited circumstances. Taxation of Chargeable Gains Act 1992 s.169J provides that there must be a "qualifying beneficiry" and the trustees must dispose of "settlement business assets".

A qualifying beneficiary is one with an interest in possession in the whole of the settled property, or the part of it which includes the settlement business assets being disposed of. Relief is not available if the interest in possession is for fixed term.

"Settlement business assets" are:

(a) company shares, or

(b) assets (other than investment assets) used or previously used for the purposes of a business, which are part of the settled property. Where the disposal is of shares the company must be a trading company and the qualifying beneficiary's "personal company" (as defined in s.169S). In addition the qualifying beneficiary must be an officer or employee of the company. Where the disposal is of assets, they must have been used for a period of at least one year ending not earlier than three years before the disposal.

The lifetime limits which apply to individuals also apply to trustees. See para.5.14, above.

Death of person with qualifying interest in possession where settlement ends

Where a beneficiary with a qualifying interest in possession who is treated as **7.59** owning the underlying trust capital (for example because the interest is an immediate post-death interest or an interest in existence on March 22, 2006) dies and on their death, the remainderman becomes absolutely entitled to the settled property, there is a deemed disposal and reacquisition but no chargeable gain arises (see s.73(1)(a) of the 1992 Act). This is in accordance with the general principle that death does not give rise to capital gains tax and so the remainderman has the benefit of a tax-free uplift in the base value of the settled property.

If the trustees have accrued losses from earlier transactions that they have been unable to set off against chargeable gains, s.71(2) provides that those losses are to be treated as if they accrued to the person becoming absolutely entitled, and not to the trustees.

Death of person with qualifying interest in possession where the settlement continues

Where a beneficiary with an interest in possession who is treated as owning the **7.60** underlying trust capital (for example because the interest is an immediate post-death interest or an interest in existence on March 22, 2006) dies and on their death, the settlement continues, there is a deemed disposal and reacquisition at market value of the assets but no chargeable gain accrues on the disposal (subject to tax becoming payable on gains held-over when assets were transferred to the trustees). See s.72(1) of the 1992 Act.

Thus, if property is held on trust for persons in succession, for example "to A for life, remainder to B for life, remainder to C absolutely" and A's interest is an immediate post-death interest, on A's death there is a deemed disposal and reacquisition. However, no tax is payable on accrued gains unless gains were held-over when the trustees were originally given the assets. The trustees acquire the assets as trustees for B at the market value at the date of A's death.

During B's lifetime, the settlement will be a relevant property settlement unless B is A's spouse or civil partner and acquires a transitional serial interest (see para.7.18).

Death of a beneficiary of a relevant property settlement

7.61 Where a beneficiary of a relevant property settlement dies, there are no capital gains tax implications unless a beneficiary becomes absolutely entitled as a result of the death.

> *Example*
>
> Cassandra transfers assets to a lifetime settlement in 2007. The trustees are to hold the trust assets for Lamia for life and then for Roxanne. Lamia's death will not give rise to a deemed disposal and reacquisition because she is not treated as owning the underlying trust assets.
>
> If following her death, the property is held for Roxanne for life, her death will have no capital gains tax implications whatsoever. If on her death the property passes to Roxanne absolutely, there will be a deemed disposal and reacquisition.

12. CAPITAL GAINS TAX—THE LIABILITY OF BENEFICIARIES

7.62 If a beneficiary is entitled to an interest in settled property, no chargeable gain arises on the disposal of the interest unless it was acquired by the beneficiary (or a predecessor in title) for consideration in money or money's worth, other than consideration consisting of another interest under the settlement (s.76(1)). Thus, if a life tenant sells their interest, no gain arises but the purchaser may face a tax liability on any subsequent disposal.

If the beneficiary is entitled under one of the types of trusts within s.60 of the TCGA 1992 (i.e. broadly speaking where they are the beneficiary of a bare trust—see above, para.7.51), they are treated as if the assets were vested in them and so any disposals made by the trustees are taxed as if the beneficiary had disposed of the property. This means that the normal rules for calculating capital gains tax liability will apply and exemptions, reliefs and allowances the beneficiary is personally able to claim will be available; losses realised by the trustees can be used by the beneficiary (s.71(2)). Furthermore, if the disposal by the trustees is to the beneficiary themselves then there is no capital gains tax liability.

13. SETTLEMENTS AND INCOME TAX—INTRODUCTION

7.63 In Ch.6 we considered the general rules for the taxation of income and the particular rules that apply when a person dies. We saw that it is the personal representatives' responsibility to pay any outstanding income tax liability of the deceased and to pay tax on income that arises in the course of administering the estate. Once the administration period is complete the personal representatives' liability ceases.

If the beneficiaries have absolute interests in the residue, the capital of the residue will be transferred to them (see para.6.23, above, for the income tax rules applying in these circumstances). However, if the will creates any type of trust which is to continue after the administration period the property will be vested in trustees and special tax rules will apply.

Will trusts are basically taxed in the same way as other trusts but since the settlor is dead when the trust becomes operative, the special anti-avoidance provisions relating to settlements contained in Ch.5 of the Income Tax (Trading and Other Income) Act 2005 (income treated as the settlor's where the settlor has retained an interest or where income is paid to minor children of the settlor who are neither married nor in a civil partnership) cannot apply.

Trust income is taxed in two stages. The trustees are liable to tax on all the income of the trust (the rate depends on the type of trust). Beneficiaries who are entitled to income or who receive income from the trust are then assessed to tax. They may be charged further tax or have tax refunded to them, depending on their particular circumstances.

14. INCOME TAX—LIABILITY OF TRUSTEES

General principles

The income of trustees is calculated in the same way as for an individual by applying the rules set out in Ch.3 of Pt 2 of the Income Tax Act 2007. In calculating this figure, the trustees may deduct permitted expenses. **7.64**

Thus, if the trustees are carrying on a trade, the income derived from the trade is assessed in accordance with the provisions of the Income Tax (Trading and Other Income) Act 2005 and they can deduct allowable business expenses. However, they cannot deduct the expenses of managing the trust itself (*Aikin v MacDonald's Trustees* (1894)). Having calculated the income of the trust the trustees are liable to pay income tax at the basic or dividend ordinary rate on *all* of the rest of the income without the deduction of any personal reliefs (which are only available to "individuals" and for these purposes trustees are not "individuals"). The starting rate is only available to individuals.

Trustees are not liable to higher rate tax regardless of the amount of the income. However, trustees of some types of trust are liable at the trust or dividend trust rate. See para.7.64, below.

If income is paid directly to the beneficiary from its source, it is taxed in the hands of the beneficiary without the trustees paying tax (such a situation would arise where, for example, trustees ask a tenant of land owned by the trust to pay the rent to the beneficiary or where interest is mandated to the beneficiary).

If the trustees receive income net of tax, the tax credit will satisfy their liability to tax.

Example

Trustees receive the following income and have trust management expenses of £90 which are properly attributable to income:

Received—Net	Gross £
Gross rental income	1,000
£400 Interest net of 20% tax $400 \times \dfrac{100}{80}$	500
£270 Dividend with 10% tax credit $270 \times \dfrac{100}{90}$	300

The trust management expenses do not reduce the income tax liability of the trustees. Trustees are liable to income tax on all the income of the trust. However, because the expenses reduce the income available to the beneficiary, expenses which are properly chargeable to income will reduce the beneficiary's liability to tax. In the case of settlements where a beneficiary has a right to income, "properly" includes expenses whose final incidence falls on income by virtue of the terms of the trust deed. (See Income Tax Act 2007 s.500(2) and para.7.64 below.)

The trustees' liability to tax on the interest and dividend is already satisfied by the tax deducted from the interest and the dividend tax credit. They only have a liability to pay tax on the income received gross. They will pay tax at 20 per cent on the gross rental income leaving £800.

The trustees will pay the trust management expenses of £90 from the net income in their hands. They will pay the net trust income to the beneficiary and must provide a certificate of deduction of income tax at the appropriate rates. The beneficiary will receive the trust income net of tax at basic and dividend ordinary rate and net of expenses.

Liability of trustees of accumulation and discretionary trusts

7.65   Section 479 of the Income Tax Act 2007 requires trustees who have income:

(a) which must be accumulated; or

(b) is payable at the discretion of the trustees or any other person,

to pay tax at the trust or dividend trust rate on trust income in excess of the first £1,000.

For tax year 2010/11 the trust rate is 50 per cent and the dividend trust rate is 42.5 per cent (see Income Tax Act 2007 s.9). Thus, a discretionary trust which receives interest will receive it net of 20 per cent tax; the trustees will then have to pay a further 30 per cent on the grossed up income. A discretionary trust which receives dividends will receive a tax credit of 10 per cent; the trustees will then have to pay a further 32.5 per cent on the gross dividend.

However, the first £1,000 of trust income is not liable to the special trust rates. Where a trust receives income of different types, Income Tax Act 2007 s.491

provides that income which would be charged at basic rate is to be allocated to the £1,000 band before dividend income.

Example

A trust has the following income:

Received—Net	Gross £
£1,600 Interest net of 20% tax $$1,600 \times \frac{100}{80}$$	2,000
£90 dividend income received with 10% tax credit $$90 \times \frac{100}{90}$$	100

The first £1,000 of interest will be taxed at 20 per cent; the balance of the interest will be taxed at 50 per cent (with credit for the 20 per cent tax already deducted). The dividend income will all be taxed at the dividend trust rate of 42.5 per cent (with credit for the 10 per cent tax credit).

The trust and dividend trust rate are not payable:

(a) where a beneficiary has a right to income;

(b) where income is treated as that of the settlor;

(c) on income of a charitable trust; or

(d) on income properly used for trust expenses (Income Tax Act 2007 s.484).

By comparison with individuals who only pay tax at 50 per cent if their taxable income exceeds £150,000, the trust rate of tax starts at a very low figure. There is, therefore, an incentive to set trust expenses against income rather than capital wherever possible. Expenses "properly" chargeable to income are those so chargeable as a matter of general law and not those made chargeable to income by the trust instrument (*Carver v Duncan* (1985)). In *Carver v Duncan* the House of Lords held that the general rule was that:

"income must bear all ordinary outgoings of a recurrent nature, such as rates and taxes, and interest on charges and incumbrances. Capital must bear all costs, charges and expenses incurred for the benefit of the whole estate."

This was confirmed by the Court of Appeal in *HMRC v Clay's Trustees* (2007) where the taxpayers had contended that expenses which were for the benefit of the whole estate should be apportioned. However, the Court of Appeal did concede that apportionment of an expense is possible if it can be shown that an identified part of an expense is for work carried out for the benefit of the income beneficiaries alone. The onus of showing that an element of an expense relates to income rests on the trustees and in the absence of time records and minutes of what was considered at each trustees' meetings, it will be almost impossible to establish a basis for apportionment.

7.66   Section 486(1) of the Income Tax Act 2007 provides the order in which expenses are to be set against income for the purposes of the trust or dividend trust rate. This is first against income chargeable to the dividend trust rate, then the trust rate.

When calculating liability to the trust or dividend trust rate, the trust management expenses are grossed up (at basic or dividend ordinary rate). The reason for this is that the trust and dividend trust rates are only chargeable on income which can be accumulated or is payable at the discretion of the trustees or some other person. The income which can be accumulated is the trust income *after* the trust expenses have been paid. The expenses are grossed up to reflect the fact that they were paid from taxed income.

The trust and dividend trust rates are applied to "income". Thus, they would not be applied to sums treated as income under particular provisions. However Income Tax Act 2007 s.481 expressly provides that the trust and dividend trust rates are to apply to certain sums treated as income which are listed in s.482 (e.g. to sums received on company buy backs). The application of these rules on expenses can be seen in the following example.

Example

A discretionary trust has the following income:

	Received—Net	Gross £
£1,600 Interest net of 20% $£1,600 \times \dfrac{100}{80}$		2,000
£90 dividend income received with 10% tax credit $£90 \times \dfrac{100}{90}$		100

It has spent £120 on allowable trust management expenses. The expenses are set first against the gross dividend income. The portion of expenses to be set against the gross dividend income is grossed up at 10 per cent and exhausts it.

	£
Dividend	100
Less First slice of Expenses grossed up $£90 \times \dfrac{100}{90}$	(90)
	—

have to be grossed up
   So £90 of the expenses grossed up at 10 per cent
   is set against the £100 of gross dividend income and exhausts it. The balance of the expenses (£120 − £90 = £30) is set against the expenses

	£
Interest	2,000

Less Balance of Expenses grossed up

$$£30 \times \frac{100}{80}$$ (37.50)

Balance of income available 1,962.50

Having deducted the expenses it is then necessary to calculate tax at the appropriate rates on the remaining £1,962.50 of trust income. The first £1,000 of interest is taxable at the basic rate of 20 per cent. The £962.50 of interest left is taxable at the trust rate but has already borne 20 per cent tax so the trustees need only pay a further 30 per cent.

Income	Gross	Tax at trust rate	Tax already paid at basic rate	Balance of tax payable
	£	£	£	£
Interest	1,000	—	200.00	—
Interest	962.50	481.25	192.50	288.75
Total	1,962.50			288.75

The income available for distribution to the beneficiaries is, therefore the income after expenses and is £1,962.50 less £200 and £481.25 which amounts to £1,281.25.

Trustees' liability under Income Tax Act 2007 s.496

Section 494 of the Income Tax Act 2007 provides that trustees who make a **7.67** discretionary payment to a beneficiary are to be treated as making a payment all of which has borne tax at the trust rate (50 per cent). They will provide beneficiaries with a certificate of deduction of income tax at 50 per cent (s.495). To the extent that the beneficiaries are not 50 per cent taxpayers, they can recover the tax treated as paid from HMRC.

The trustees will not have paid 50 per cent tax on the first £1,000 of income nor on income liable to the dividend trust rate. There is, therefore, a mismatch between the tax treated as paid by the trustees and the tax actually paid.

Section 496 of the Income Tax Act 2007 provides that the trustees will be assessed to tax on the difference between the tax treated as paid and the tax actually paid. This may be satisfied by tax credits available in the tax pool. The tax pool consists of tax actually paid by the trustees plus any recoverable tax credits. Prior to April 6, 1999 dividends from UK companies were paid with a recoverable tax credit of 20 per cent. From that date the tax credit was reduced to 10 per cent and is irrecoverable. Dividend tax credits, therefore, no longer enter the tax pool. Trusts which have been in existence for many years and which have accumulated income will have substantial tax pools. Others may have little or nothing in their tax pool. Trusts with no tax pools will have to satisfy any s.496 liability from trust funds. Trustees need to take their liability to tax under s.496 into account when deciding how much to distribute to beneficiaries.

Example

The trustees of the ABC and the XYZ Trust each receive dividends of £9,000 with irrecoverable tax credits of £1,000. The ABC trust has substantial tax credits; the XYZ trust does not. In each case the £10,000 of gross income is taxed as follows:

(a) The first £1,000 is taxed at the dividend ordinary rate of 10 per cent (£1,000).
(b) The remaining £9,000 is taxed at 42.5 per cent (£3,825).
(c) The total tax payable is therefore £3,825 but there is a reduction of £1,000 for the tax credit.
(d) The trustees, therefore, pay £2,825 to HMRC.
(e) They have available for distribution £6,175.

Whatever the trustees distribute to the beneficiaries will be treated as having borne tax at 50 per cent and will be grossed up in the hands of the beneficiaries at that rate. If the trustees distribute all the available income to a beneficiary, they will be treated as paying the beneficiary:

$$£6,175 \times \frac{100}{50} = £12,350$$

The tax treated as paid will be 50 per cent of £12,350 which is £6,175. The beneficiary will have a credit for that amount of tax. To the extent that the beneficiary is not a 50 per cent taxpayer, they can recover the tax treated as paid from HMRC.

As the trustees have only paid £3,825, they have an additional liability under s.496 of £2,350. The ABC trust can satisfy this from the tax pool but the XYZ trust will have to use capital. If the trustees wish to meet the additional liability from the dividend income of the current year, they cannot distribute all of the £6,175. They should only distribute 50 per cent of the cash dividend received as follows:

Distribution to beneficiary:

$$£9,000 \times 50\% = 4,500$$

The trustees made a cash payment to HMRC of £2,825 and so from the £9,000 received, they will be left with £6,175. The beneficiary will be treated as receiving:

$$£4,500 \times \frac{100}{50} = £9,000$$

with tax paid at the rate of 50 per cent (£4,500).

The trustees will be liable for the difference between the tax treated as paid at 50 per cent on the £9,000 (i.e. £4,500) and the £2,825 actually paid which amounts to £1,675. They have this amount available.

7.68   Where the trustees of accumulation and discretionary trusts choose to distribute all available dividend income and have no unused additional tax credits in the "tax pool", they will pay an effective rate of tax in excess of 50 per cent. This excessive rate used to be a real disadvantage for accumulation and discretionary trusts. The problem could be alleviated by giving beneficiaries a right to income but before the Finance Act 2006 this would have given the beneficiary a qualifying interest in possession for inheritance tax purposes. The trust property would have been aggregated with the beneficiary's own estate on death and the lifetime termination of the interest in possession would have been a transfer of value.

Since the introduction of the Finance Act 2006 this problem has disappeared. Trustees cannot create qualifying interests in possession. As a result they are free to give beneficiaries rights to income and terminate those rights as often as they like without any inheritance tax consequences.

15. INCOME TAX—LIABILITY OF BENEFICIARIES

Beneficiary with a right to income

A beneficiary with a right to trust income is entitled to all the trust income less **7.69** trust expenses. The income paid to the beneficiary retains its original nature and is included on the beneficiary's tax return under the appropriate heading grossed up at basic or dividend ordinary rate. The beneficiary is entitled to require a certificate of deduction of income tax at the appropriate rate under Income Tax Act 2007 s.495.

When calculating the tax liability the beneficiary is assessed on the income calculated in accordance with the rules appropriate to the source of the income (*Baker v Archer-Shee* (1927)). Most trust income will be derived from sources which would provide savings or dividend income in the hands of an individual. However, some trusts may derive their income from property or from a trade carried on by the trustees.

If the gross trust income from a trade is £10,000 and there are allowable trading expenses for tax purposes of £2,000, the trustees are taxable on the net profit of £8,000, which is the trust income from the trade. The beneficiary is entitled to the income of the trust (not to the gross receipts). The trust income is £8,000 not £10,000, so the beneficiary is assessed to tax on £8,000. If the net profit after allowable trading expenses is £8,000 and the trustees can claim £3,000 capital allowances for tax purposes, the beneficiary's income for tax purposes is reduced by £3,000 to £5,000. If the trustees have trading or rental losses that they can use against trading or rental income in any year to reduce the trust's taxable income, the beneficiary's taxable income for that year is consequently reduced.

How to decide whether a beneficiary has a right to income

A beneficiary who has a right to trust income is taxed on the income when it **7.70** arises irrespective of whether or not it is paid over to them. Such a right arises when the beneficiary has a vested interest in the income of the trust. A direction to accumulate income will not destroy a vested interest in it provided the accumulated income *must* be paid to the beneficiary or to the estate of the beneficiary at some time.

Three examples of trusts where beneficiaries have vested interests in the income are where the beneficiary has:

(a) A life interest in a trust fund, for example "to A for life". (However, if A is under 18 and s.31 of the Trustee Act applies there will be no right to income and A will effectively have only an interest contingent on reaching 18.)

(b) A right to income conferred by s.31 of the Trustee Act (for example, where a beneficiary has an interest in the capital of the fund contingent on reaching an age greater than 18 and has reached 18).

(c) A vested interest in accumulating income, for example "to A but the income to be accumulated for 10 years and then paid to A or A's estate". A has no right to receive the income immediately but it is certain that A or A's estate will receive it in 10 years' time.

Trust management expenses

7.71 A beneficiary with a right to receive income is assessed to tax on all the income of the trust to which they are entitled less expenses properly chargeable to income. For income tax purposes this is all the trust income net of tax at basic or dividend ordinary rate less trust management expenses properly chargeable to income.

Section 500(2) of the Income Tax Act 2007 provides that in the case of settlements where a beneficiary has a right to income "properly" includes expenses whose final incidence falls on income by virtue of the terms of the trust deed. This is in contrast with discretionary and accumulation trusts, where Income Tax Act 2007 s.484 specifically excludes provisions in the trust deed.

So if a trust deed allows the trustees to pay what are normally capital expenses out of income, those expenses reduce the measure of the beneficiary's income. If a trust deed allows trustees to pay what are in general trust law income expenses out of capital, again the trust deed has priority over general trust law.

Section 503(2) of the Income Tax Act 2007 provides the order of set-off for trust management expenses to reduce the income of a beneficiary with a right to income. The order of set-off of is the same as that used for accumulation/discretionary trustees. Expenses are set first against income taxed at the dividend ordinary rate, then income taxed at basic rate.

Example

This is the same example we used at para.7.64, above, where the trust had expenses properly attributable to income of £90 and the following income:

Received—Net	Gross £
Gross rental income	1,000
£400 Interest net of 20% tax $400 \times \dfrac{100}{80}$	500
£270 Dividend with 10% tax credit $270 \times \dfrac{100}{90}$	300

The trust expenses will be treated as paid first from the dividend income which will be reduced to £180.

The beneficiary's gross income will be:

Received—Net	Gross £
Gross rental income	1,000
Dividend with 10% tax credit $180 \times \dfrac{100}{90}$	200

The beneficiary will include each category of income on the appropriate section of the income tax return because the income retains its original nature. If the beneficiary is a higher or additional rate taxpayer, they will have to pay the difference between the tax already paid on their behalf and the higher rate tax for which they are liable. If the beneficiary is a basic rate taxpayer they will have no further liability to tax. If the beneficiary is not a taxpayer at all, they will be able to recover the tax paid on the rental income and the savings income but not on the dividend as the dividend tax credit is irrecoverable.

Income and capital

A beneficiary's income is usually based on a share of income chargeable on the **7.72** trustees. However, this does not apply to items that are capital in trust law and only deemed to be income for tax purposes. An example of such an item is a premium for a lease not exceeding 50 years. This is treated as rent (Income Tax (Trading and Other Income) Act 2005 s.276). Deemed rent of the trustees is chargeable on them but is not regarded as the beneficiary's income. This is because, under trust law, it is capital.

If a beneficiary with an entitlement to income receives a payment that is income in their hands, they may be liable to income tax on it even if the trustees make the payment from capital (*Michelham's Trustees v IRC* (1930)).

The case of *Stevenson v Wishart* (1986) is interesting in that the Revenue failed in their contention that regular capital payments for nursing home fees should be treated as income. The position now appears to be that capital payments will not be treated as income payments unless:

(a) they are designed to make income up to a fixed amount or a certain defined level; or

(b) the trust instrument authorises the use of capital to maintain the beneficiary's standard of living.

Beneficiary receiving income from an accumulation or discretionary trust

7.73 A beneficiary whose entitlement to receive income depends on satisfying a contingency or on the trustees exercising a discretion in their favour, has no income tax liability unless and until the trustees make a payment to them.

The income is treated as the income of the trustees who will pay tax as described at para.7.64, above. The most common examples of trusts falling within this category are discretionary trusts and trusts where the income is being accumulated for a person with only a contingent interest in capital.

When trustees exercise their discretion to pay income to a beneficiary, a new source of income comes into existence: trust income. The original source of the income is not relevant. See *Cunard's Trustees v CIR* (1946).

Any payments made to a beneficiary must be treated as part of the beneficiary's income. The receipts of trust income must be grossed up on the beneficiary's tax return at 40 per cent. The beneficiary will have a 40 per cent tax credit and can claim a refund if not a higher rate taxpayer. The following example illustrates these points.

Example

A discretionary trust has the following income:

Received—Net	Gross £
£1,600 interest net of 20% $$1,600 \times \frac{100}{80}$$	2,000
£90 dividend income received with 10% tax credit $$90 \times \frac{100}{90}$$	100

It has spent £120 on allowable trust management expenses. It has £1,281.25 available for distribution. (See para.7.66, above for the calculation.)

The trustees pay the whole amount to one of the beneficiaries, Fred, who has no other source of income.

Fred will gross up the £1,281.25 at 50 per cent:

$$£1,281.25 \times \frac{100}{50} = £2,562.50$$

He will have a certificate of deduction of income tax at 50 per cent from the trustees. As a non-taxpayer he will be able to recover the whole 50 per cent (£1,281.25) from HMRC.

The trustees will have an additional tax liability under Income Tax Act 2007 s.496 for the difference between the tax they paid and the tax Fred has reclaimed.

16. INCOME TAX AND TRUSTEE ACT 1925 S.31

Section 31 of the Trustee Act is not a tax provision. However, since it can affect **7.74** a beneficiary's right to income it can affect the income tax liability of trustees and beneficiaries. Section 31 (see Ch.11 for a full discussion) provides that where there is income available to an minor (whether they have a vested or a contingent interest) the trustees of the trust may at their sole discretion apply the whole or part of such income for or towards the minor's maintenance, education or benefit and, to the extent that they do not, they must accumulate the whole or part of such income.

If, after reaching the age of 18, the beneficiary has not attained a vested interest in such income the trustees *shall* thereafter pay the income (together with any income produced by investments bought with accumulated income) to the beneficiary until the beneficiary either attains a vested interest or dies or until their interest fails.

Once the minor reaches the age of 18 the trustees must decide what is to happen to income that has been accumulated (and therefore capitalised). In all cases, except one, the accumulated income is added to capital and devolves with it. Thus, whoever takes the capital takes the accumulations. The exceptional case is that of an minor with a life interest. If the minor reaches 18 any income which has been accumulated is paid to them. However, if the minor dies before reaching 18 the accumulated income is added to capital and devolves with it. An minor with a life interest, therefore, has no *right* to receive income until they reach the age of 18 (since the trustees may decide to accumulate it) and cannot be certain of ever receiving the accumulations (since they may die before reaching 18).

Section 31 can, therefore, *give* certain beneficiaries a right to income where prima facie they had no such right under the terms of the trust. It can also *prevent* beneficiaries having a right to income which under the terms of the trust they would otherwise have enjoyed.

The effect, if any, of s.31 on income tax liability can be illustrated by examples.

(a) *T's will gives 20,000 shares to A for life (A is aged six)*. If s.31 did not apply, A would have *a right* to receive the income from the shares and the trustees would pay only the dividend ordinary rate. A would include the grossed up income on their income tax return and might be liable to higher rate tax if their circumstances justified it.

However, if s.31 applies the trustees have a discretion whether to apply income for A's benefit and A, therefore, has no *right* to receive current income until they reach 18. They have no right to receive accumulated income unless and until they reach 18. A is, therefore, treated as having an interest contingent on reaching 18. The trustees therefore pay the dividend trust rate on all the income in excess of the first £1,000. A will include income actually applied for their maintenance on their tax return. (Liability to higher rate tax or a right to a rebate may arise depending on A's circumstances.) Once A reaches 18 they will obtain a right to current income. The trustees will then pay no further tax. The tax credit on the dividends will satisfy their liability to tax at the dividend ordinary rate.

(b) *T's will gives 20,000 shares to A if they reach 25 (A is aged six).* If s.31 did not apply A would have no *right* to the income until reaching 25 and the trustees would pay the dividend higher rate on all the income in excess of £1,000. Nothing would be included on A's tax return in respect of the trust income unless the trustees chose to apply income for their benefit.

However, if s.31 applies the above will only be correct *until* A's 18th birthday. From 18 to 25 A will have a right to the income. The trustees will then pay no further tax. The tax credit on the dividends will satisfy their liability at dividend ordinary rate. A will include the grossed up amount in their tax return (grossed up at 10 per cent) and again may be liable to extra tax depending on their circumstances.

17. DEMERGERS AND SCRIP ISSUES

7.75 Demergers can present serious problems for trustees. A demerger is a series of transactions which have the effect and purpose of dividing the trading activities carried on by a single company or group of companies between two or more companies or groups of companies. Section 213 of the Income and Corporation Taxes Act 1988 ("ICTA 1988") and s.192 of TCGA 1992 provide special tax treatment if certain conditions are met. Companies may seek advance clearance under s.215 of ICTA 1988 from the Revenue that proposed transactions will be an exempt demerger. There have been some complex demergers during which companies have divided themselves up. Probably the most complex was the Hanson demerger where four separate holdings were created while the biggest was probably the demerger of Zeneca from ICI.

In a simple direct demerger the company declares a dividend from distributable profits and proceeds to satisfy it with an allocation of shares in the demerged company. It follows that the shares represent income so if they are paid to an interest in possession trust, the life tenant will be entitled to them.

From the point of view of the trust fund the consequences can be very serious. The capital value of the trust fund can be greatly reduced and the life tenant can receive a huge income benefit. The trustees may not be happy with this result. They can sell shares before the demerger but this, being a disposal, may lead to an unwelcome capital gains tax liability.

An indirect demerger includes a further step absent from a direct demerger; at the same time as declaring a dividend, Company A transfers all its shares in Company B to another (wholly separate) holding company ("Company C"). In consideration for this transfer of shares Company C satisfies Company A's dividend by issuing its own shares to the shareholders of Company A.

In *Sinclair v Lee* a testatrix bequeathed shares in ICI plc ("ICI") to her husband for life with the remainder to her son. After her death, ICI resolved to demerge its bioscience activities. In preparation it consolidated its bioscience activities into a wholly owned subsidiary company. ICI proposed to transfer the shares of this subsidiary company to a newly created holding company called Zeneca Group plc ("Zeneca"). Zeneca was then to issue its own paid up shares to ICI shareholders. Sir Donald Nicholls V.C., as he then was, conceded that the line of cases on direct demergers required him to treat the Zeneca shares as income but this was such an unsatisfactory result that he felt able to distinguish the indirect demerger. He held that the ICI transaction was to be characterised, not as a distribution at all, but as a company reconstruction resulting in a single capital asset in the trustees' hands being replaced by two such assets.

The Law Commission said of this decision its Report, Capital and Income in Trusts: Classification and Apportionment, Law Com. No.315 that, while helpful, it had:

> "given rise to an unprincipled distinction between direct and indirect demergers. The formalistic ground for distinction adopted by the Vice-Chancellor enabled him to avoid what he considered to be an 'absurd' result, but did not affect the equally absurd result that arises from direct demergers."

What is the tax position?

The life tenant of a trust is entitled to all income and is therefore entitled to the **7.76** shares. The distribution is exempt from income tax provided the relevant conditions for an exempt distribution are complied with. (For capital gains tax purposes the Revenue now accepts that the shares being income belong to the life tenant so that there is no liability to capital gains tax—*Tax Bulletin*, October 1994.)

Where the trust is a discretionary one the receipt of the shares by the trustees is still an exempt distribution so there is no liability to income tax. (For CGT purposes the shares are treated as part of the trustees' original shareholding.)

If the trustees pay out shares to the beneficiaries there will be a charge to income tax at the trust rate. (There will also be a charge to capital gains tax although hold over relief will be available.) In the case of indirect demergers the issued shares are held as capital of the trust fund.

Stock or Scrip

Dividends

Scrip dividends are dividends which offer shareholders the choice of being paid **7.77** in the form of cash or shares. When a company declares a conventional scrip dividend each shareholder has the option to take the dividend in cash or in additional shares of equal value. Such dividends will almost always be treated as income in the hands of the shareholder whichever option is chosen. They are treated as income by virtue of ICTA 1988 s.249 (rewritten to Corporation Tax Act 2010 ss.1049(1), 1051(2)), and taxable as savings income under Ch.5 of Pt 4 of Income Tax (Trading and Other Income) Act 2005 ss.409–414).

The situation is more complicated when the company declares an "enhanced" scrip dividend. Enhanced scrip dividends give shareholders the option of taking the distribution either in cash or in additional shares of greater value than the cash alternative. If (unusually) the shareholder opts for cash the receipt will clearly be income.

The trustee will usually opt to take the more valuable bonus shares. In this case, the classification of the bonus shares will depend on whether the company intended to capitalise its profits or intended to make a distribution. In the majority of cases, especially where (as is common practice) the company arranges for a third party to offer to purchase the new shares at market value to enable shareholders to realise their cash value immediately, the substance of the arrangement will be such that the shares will be received as income.

However, where the bonus shares are received as capital, it has in some cases been held that the income beneficiary is entitled to a lien over the amount of the cash dividend foregone; in effect, an apportionment of the receipt between income and capital. HMRC's position, set out in Statement of Practice 4/94, is that it currently follows the trustees' decision as to the classification of enhanced scrip dividends for tax purposes, provided that their conclusion is supportable on the facts of their particular case. However, on occasion, the courts have retreated from the strict dichotomy of the general rule and ordered an apportionment of receipts from scrip dividends between income and capital.

CHAPTER EIGHT

GRANTS

1. TYPES OF GRANT

A grant of representation is an order of the High Court. The High Court has **8.01** exclusive jurisdiction to make grants in England and Wales. Since October 1, 1971 the Family Division of the High Court has exercised the jurisdiction to make grants (Administration of Justice Act 1970 s.1(4)). The Chancery Division and the county court have certain powers in probate cases but these do not include a power to make grants; these powers will be considered in Ch.9.

There are three basic types of grant of representation:

(a) a grant of probate;

(b) a grant of letters of administration with will annexed; and

(c) a grant of letters of administration (commonly called a grant of simple administration).

A grant once made serves two main purposes. First, it establishes the authority of the personal representative. Secondly, it establishes either the validity of the deceased's will (in the case of probate or administration with will annexed) or that the deceased died without a valid will (in the case of simple administration).

Certain types of property do not devolve on the personal representatives when their owner dies. This applies to property which is the subject of a statutory nomination, property subject to a *donatio mortis causa*, certain payments from pension funds and insurance policies and, most importantly, property held by the deceased and another person (or persons) as joint tenants in equity. Such property is not included in the grant of representation. The ways in which it is dealt with on death are described in Ch.21 (see paras 21.02–21.15, below).

2. CAPACITY TO TAKE A GRANT

Any person, including an alien, a minor, a corporation, a bankrupt, a convicted **8.02** criminal, or a mentally disordered person may be *appointed* an executor by a will. Similarly any such person may prima facie be entitled to a grant of letters of administration.

However, a minor cannot *take* a grant of representation and therefore the grant is made to an adult for the use and benefit of the minor. Such a grant will usually be limited to the period of incapacity so that the minor may take out a grant on attaining majority. Similar rules apply to mentally disordered persons (that is persons who lack the mental capacity to act as personal representatives).

Where an alien resident outside the jurisdiction, a bankrupt or a criminal is entitled to a grant no special rules apply. However, in each case the court may exercise its discretion to pass over the person entitled and make a grant to some other person entitled (Senior Courts Act 1981 s.116).

After the coming into force of the Family Law Reform Act 1987 the fact that a person's parents were not married to each other at the time of his or her birth is irrelevant for the purposes of succession to property and is therefore irrelevant for the purpose of entitlement to a grant of representation (unless a contrary intention has been expressed in a will left by the deceased). Section 21 of the 1987 Act does provide, however, that a deceased person shall be presumed not to have been survived by any person whose parents were not married to each other at the time of that person's birth (or who is related through such a person). The presumption can be rebutted by evidence to the contrary. This provision is designed to facilitate the administration by making it unnecessary to carry out investigations.

3. GRANT OF PROBATE

The executor appointed by will

8.03 Normally the only person who may obtain a grant of probate is the executor appointed by the deceased in his or her will (or in a codicil validly supplementing or amending the will). An executor is a person appointed by the will to administer the deceased's property. The will may *appoint* any number of executors but not more than four persons may take out a grant in respect of the same part of the estate (power may be reserved to any others—see para.8.10, below).

Since most testators want to choose a person to administer the estate, a properly drafted will should expressly provide for the appointment of an executor; for example, by including a clause which says "I appoint X of [address] to be the executor of this will". The person named should be someone suitable to act as executor and who is willing to take a grant. The appointment may describe rather than name the executor; for example, "I appoint the Vicar of St James's Church in the parish of [...] to be the executor of this will" but such appointments are unwise since they may be ambiguous.

The appointment of an executor may be implied in cases where the will shows an intention that a particular person should perform the functions of an executor even though not expressly described as an executor. Such a person is described as "an executor according to the tenor of the will". For example, in *In the Goods of Baylis* (1865) the will directed that named persons should pay the debts of the estate and then hold the estate on trust for sale for the deceased's children. Lord Penzance held that since the "trustees" were to get in the whole estate, pay the debts and distribute the property the clear intention was that they should act as executors; therefore they were entitled to a grant. The appointment of trustees without a direction that they are to pay the debts of the estate is not sufficient to make them executors according to the tenor (*In the Estate of McKenzie* (1909)).

A firm (for example, of solicitors) may be named as executors. However, since the office is a personal one this is treated as an appointment of all the individual partners in the firm. Great care should be taken with such appointments since in the absence of clear words to the contrary, the partners in the firm at the date on which the will is made (rather than the partners at the date of death) are the executors and they may be unavailable or unwilling to act at the time of the death. (The drafting problems connected with appointment of a firm will be considered in Ch.22.)

Appointment other than by will

A will may validly appoint someone to nominate an executor (in such a case the   **8.04**
person appointed may nominate themselves). Such a provision in a will would seldom be advantageous but, if included, a time limit should be imposed on the making of the appointment.

One executor is always sufficient even where there is a minority or life interest. However, the court has a rarely exercised power to appoint an additional personal representative to act with a sole executor in the administration of the estate (Senior Courts Act 1981 s.114(4)). Such a person is not described as an executor but would seem to have the same powers as an executor.

Under the Administration of Estates Act 1925 s.22, trustees of settled land of which the deceased was tenant for life and which remains settled land after his or her death are deemed appointed executors in respect of the settled land alone. However, in accordance with r.29 of the Non-Contentious Probate Rules 1987, as amended, they will act as administrators not executors.

Under s.50(1)(a) of the Administration of Justice Act 1985 the court may appoint a person to be a personal representative in substitution for an existing personal representative. If the substitute is to act with an existing executor he or she is also an executor, in any other case he or she is an administrator.

Chain of representation (Administration of Estates Act 1925 s.7)

Where the sole or last surviving executor dies before completing the administra-   **8.05**
tion of the estate a grant of letters of administration *de bonis non administratis* may be made to the person entitled under r.20 of the Non-Contentious Probate Rules 1987 (see below, paras 8.34–8.36). Where one of a number of executors dies there is no need for a further grant; the remaining executor or executors having full power to complete the administration.

However, where a sole or last surviving proving executor (other than an executor substituted under s.50(1)(a) of the Administration of Justice Act 1985) dies *having appointed an executor themselves,* the latter, on taking a grant of probate in respect of the executor's estate, automatically becomes the executor of the original testator as well so that a grant of administration to the original estate is not needed (Administration of Estates Act 1925 s.7).

Example

A appoints B to be his executor and B appoints C. On A's death B will become his executor and may take a grant of probate. If B dies having taken a grant but without having completed the administration of A's estate and C takes a grant of probate of B's estate he will automatically become executor of A as well as B.

This is called the chain of representation. There may be more than two links in the chain. To continue the same example, if C appoints D to be his executor and C then dies without completing the administration of the estates and D takes out a grant of probate in respect of C's estate, D will automatically become the executor of A and B as well as of C.

The chain of representation only applies where there is a grant of *probate* to the executor of a person who had taken out a grant of probate themselves in respect of someone else's estate. Thus, the chain of representation is broken (and a grant of administration *de bonis non* is required) where:

(a) an executor dies intestate or without appointing an executor;

(b) an executor dies having appointed an executor but that executor has predeceased; or

(c) an executor dies having appointed an executor but that executor fails to take out a grant in respect of the original executor's estate.

The chain of representation can be said to pass from *proving executor* to *proving executor.* There is, therefore, no chain of representation where no executor has been appointed. For example, A dies intestate, B takes out a grant of letters of administration and then B dies having appointed C to be his executor. C does not become the executor of A.

The appointment of an administrator will usually break the chain of representation. However, a temporary appointment does not do so.

Example

A appoints B to be his executor, B appoints C and dies. C is a minor when B dies. A grant of administration is made in respect of B's estate to D. D does not become A's executor. When, however, C reaches majority he may take out a grant of probate in respect of B's estate. If he does so he will then automatically become A's executor.

Similarly a person who becomes executor through the chain of representation may cease to be executor when someone else takes out a grant of probate in respect of the deceased's estate.

Example

A appoints B and C to be his executors: when A dies B is an adult and C a minor. A grant will be made to B alone but C is said to have "power reserved", i.e. he can take out a grant when he reaches majority. If B dies without completing the administration of A's estate appointing D his executor while C is still a minor, D will become A's executor on taking out probate of B's estate. However, if on reaching 18 C takes out a grant in respect of A's estate, D will cease to be A's executor. This is because the chain of representation can only operate on the death of the *last proving* executor and C has now become a proving executor.

Limited, conditional and substitutional appointments

Most wills appoint one or more persons to act as executor for the whole of the **8.06** deceased's estate and without limit as to time. However, an appointment may be limited, for example an appointment may:

(a) be limited in time (the appointment may, for example, appoint one person until another person reaches the age of majority);

(b) be limited to certain property (for example, one executor may be appointed to deal with the deceased's general estate and another to deal with business property or literary effects); and

(c) be limited as to purpose (for example, to conduct litigation).

Limited grants are dealt with in more detail in paras 8.23–8.32, below.

An appointment may also be conditional. For example, "I appoint A to be my executor provided he is a partner in the firm of A, B and Co at the date of my death."

A will may also validly provide for a substitutional appointment. For example, "I appoint A to be my executor but if he is unable or unwilling to act then I appoint B." B may take out a grant once A has renounced probate or died.

Effect of grant of probate

Conclusive proof of content and execution of will

A grant of probate in respect of a particular will is conclusive evidence as to the **8.07** terms of the will of the deceased and that it was duly executed. If a will is found to be invalid (for example, because it is found not to have been properly executed or a later will is discovered) after a grant of probate, the probate must be revoked (see paras 8.38–8.40, below).

Confirmation of executors' authority

A grant of probate merely confirms the authority of the executor conferred by the **8.08** will. The authority derives from the will. An executor may, therefore, deal with the estate of the deceased without first taking out a grant (see Ch.11, below).

However, a grant is in practice necessary to prove to other people that the executor has authority to deal with the property of the deceased and to pass a good title to any land in the estate.

Executor de son tort

8.09 The term executor *de son tort* means literally executor as a result of his or her own wrong. The expression is unfortunate since the noun is wholly misleading and the adjectival phrase almost as much so. An executor *de son tort* is a person who deals with the estate of a deceased person by intermeddling with it as if he or she were an executor or administrator. Acts which have been held to amount to intermeddling include selling property, paying debts, collecting debts and carrying on the business of the deceased. However, acts of charity, humanity or necessity are not sufficient. Thus, arranging the deceased's funeral, ordering necessary goods for the deceased's dependents and protecting the deceased's property by moving it to a safe place have been held not to amount to intermeddling. In *Pollard v Jackson* (1995) it was held that a tenant of part of the deceased's house, who kept the parts formerly occupied by the deceased clean and who burnt rubbish found there was not an executor *de son tort*. The steps he had taken could not be regarded as characteristic of executorship.

An executor *de son tort* has no authority to act in the estate of the deceased and can obtain no rights by intermeddling. However, a person who is in fact the deceased's executor and who intermeddles loses the right to renounce probate and so can be cited to take a grant (see paras 10.56–10.58, below).

The effect of being an executor *de son tort* is that such a person becomes liable to the creditors and beneficiaries to the extent of the real and personal estate coming into his or her hands as if he or she were an executor (Administration of Estate Act 1925 s.8). He or she is also liable for inheritance tax to the extent of such property.

An executor *de son tort* can bring his or her liability to creditors and beneficiaries to an end by delivering the assets received (or their value) to the lawful executor or administrator before the creditors or beneficiaries bring an action against them.

Power reserved to prove at a later date

8.10 A will may appoint several people to act as co-executors. It is unnecessary for them all to join in taking the grant if they do not wish to. Those who do not take the grant may renounce their rights but if they prefer not to renounce they may have power reserved to them to take the grant at a later date if it proves desirable. Where an application for probate is made and power is to be reserved to some executors to prove at a later date, notice of the application must be given to the non-proving executors. The oath for executors, filed when the application for the grant is made, must state that this notice has been given unless the court otherwise orders (Non-Contentious Probate Rules 1987 r.17(1)). Where the other executors are not named in the will and are partners in a firm of solicitors with the proving executors, the persons to whom power is reserved need not be given notice (r.17(1A)).

4. Grant of Letters of Administration with Will Annexed

Circumstances in which grant is made

A grant of letters of administration with will annexed (also called a grant *cum* **8.11** *testamento annexo)* is made when the deceased has a valid will and a grant of probate cannot be made to an executor. Such a situation arises where the will makes no appointment of an executor, where the executor predeceases, where the executor has validly renounced probate, where the executor is passed over by order of the court and where the executor has been cited but has not taken a grant of probate (see paras 10.54–10.57 for the citation procedure). A grant of administration with will annexed is also made in certain cases where an earlier grant of probate or administration with will annexed has been made but the personal representative appointed by the earlier grant has been unable to complete the administration of the estate (see paras 8.33–8.36, below).

Persons entitled to the grant

Rule 20 of the Non-Contentious Probate Rules 1987 contains a list of the persons **8.12** who are entitled to take out a grant of administration with the will annexed. The list follows the order of entitlement to property under the will. Persons who come earlier in the list will take a grant in preference to those who come later. If there is no executor able and willing to act, the following are entitled:

(i) *Any residuary legatee or devisee holding in trust for any other person.* For example, residue is given to X and Y on trust for A and B. X and Y are the residuary legatees holding on trust and so have the first right to a grant. This is logical since the testator by appointing X and Y as trustees has shown that he or she is willing that they should deal with the property.

(ii) *Any other residuary legatee or devisee (including one for life), or where the residue is not wholly disposed of by the will, any person entitled to share in the undisposed of residue (including the Treasury Solicitor when claiming bona vacantia on behalf of the Crown).* For example, residue is given to A, B, C and D in equal shares; each will be entitled to take the grant. If D predeceased the testator and X was entitled to take the quarter of residue undisposed of, X would be equally entitled to the grant.

There are two provisos to this category:

(a) unless a district judge or registrar otherwise directs, a residuary legatee or devisee whose legacy or devise is vested in interest shall be preferred to one entitled on the happening of a contingency, and

(b) where the residue is not in terms wholly disposed of, the district judge or registrar may, if satisfied that the testator has nevertheless disposed of the whole or substantially the whole of the known estate, allow a grant to be made to any legatee or devisee entitled to, or to share in, the estate so disposed of, without regard to the persons entitled to share in any residue not disposed of by the will.

For example the will says "I leave my home, Blackacre, all its contents and my bank account to my friend X". When the testator dies the property described in the will is substantially everything owned by the deceased. X can take a grant in preference to those family members who would be entitled to take residue under the intestacy rules.

(iii) *The personal representative of any residuary legatee or devisee (but not one for life, or one holding in trust for any other person), or of any person entitled to share in any residue not disposed of by the will.* For example, residue is given to A and B in equal shares; A predeceases the testator and X is entitled to take the half share of residue undisposed of. If X and B both die before taking a grant the personal representatives of either will be entitled to the grant.

(iv) *Any other legatee or devisee (including one for life or one holding in trust for any other person) or any creditor of the deceased.* For example, a house is left to A and £1,000 to B. Either is entitled to the grant unless a registrar otherwise directs. A legatee or devisee whose legacy or devise is vested in interest shall be preferred to one entitled on the happening of a contingency.

(v) *The personal representative of any other legatee or devisee (but not one for life or one holding in trust for any other person) or of any creditor of the deceased.* For example, if A and B in the previous example survive the testator but die before taking a grant the personal representatives of either will be entitled to the grant.

Rule 27(4) and (6) of the Non-Contentious Rules 1987 provides that where two or more persons are entitled in the same degree (i.e. come into the same paragraph above) a grant may be made to any of them without notice to the others (contrast the position with grants of probate, see para.8.10, above) and that disputes between persons entitled in the same degree are to be decided by a district judge or registrar.

Living beneficiaries are to be preferred to the personal representative of deceased beneficiaries entitled in the same degree and adults to minors entitled in the same degree unless a district judge or registrar directs to the contrary (r.27(5)). If the whole estate of the deceased is assigned by the beneficiaries, the assignees have the same right to a grant as the assignors (r.24).

The effect of a grant

Conclusive proof of content and execution of will

A grant of administration with will annexed is like a grant of probate in that it is **8.13** conclusive evidence as to content and execution of the will.

Conferral of authority on administrator

A grant of probate merely confirms the authority of executors. However, a grant **8.14** of letters of administration *confers* authority on the administrator and vests the deceased's property in him. Until the grant is made the property of a deceased who appoints no executor is technically vested in the Public Trustee (Administration of Estates Act 1925 s.9, as substituted). Once made the grant does not relate back to the date of death of the deceased except to the extent that relation back would (at the time of the grant) be beneficial to the estate (see para.11.05, below).

5. GRANT OF SIMPLE ADMINISTRATION

Circumstances in which a grant is made

A grant of simple administration is made when there is no will capable of being **8.15** admitted to probate (or of being annexed to letters of administration).

Simple administration is appropriate in the vast majority of cases where there is a total intestacy. However, if there is an admissible will which does not deal with property (for example, a will merely appointing executors) a grant of probate may be made. Similarly, a will is admissible to probate (or may be annexed to letters of administration) where it purports to deal with property but all the gifts fail.

Persons entitled to take a grant

Rule 22 of the Non-Contentious Probate Rules 1987 contains an order of the **8.16** persons who are entitled to take out a grant of simple administration. The order follows the order of entitlement to the estate on intestacy and says that the persons entitled are, in the order listed and provided that they have a beneficial interest in the estate:

(a) the surviving spouse or civil partner of the deceased;

(b) children of the deceased (and the issue of a child who has predeceased);

(c) the parents of the deceased;

(d) the brothers and sisters of the whole blood of the deceased (and the issue of any brothers or sisters who have predeceased);

(e) brothers and sisters of the half blood of the deceased (and the issue of any who have predeceased);

(f) grandparents;

(g) uncles and aunts of the whole blood (and the issue of any who have predeceased); and

(h) uncles and aunts of the half blood (and the issue of any who have predeceased).

Since a beneficial interest is required the entitlement to a grant depends in part on the size of the estate. For example, if the deceased died leaving a spouse or civil partner but no issue and with an estate of £180,000 (plus personal chattels) the parents (if surviving) or brothers and sisters would not be entitled under this provision since the estate would all go to the spouse or civil partner. They would, however, be entitled if the deceased's estate was £600,000.

Rule 22(2) provides that if no-one is entitled as being in any of the above categories then the Treasury Solicitor may take out a grant when claiming bona vacantia on behalf of the crown.

Rule 22(3) provides that a grant may be made to a creditor of the deceased or to a person who would be entitled to a beneficial interest in the estate if there were an accretion to the estate provided that all those entitled according to r.22(1) and (2) are cleared off. Thus, in the example given above (a deceased with an estate of £180,000 and personal chattels who is survived by spouse or civil partner but no issue) the parents (if surviving) would have a right to a grant if the spouse or civil partner had been cleared off. If the parents have predeceased then the brothers and sisters would have a right to a grant.

The personal representative of a person who survives the deceased but dies before taking a grant is entitled in the same degree as the person whom he represents (r.22(4)). However, unless a district judge or registrar otherwise directs, where a number of persons are entitled in the same degree, a person of full age is to be preferred to the guardian of a minor and a living person is to be preferred over the personal representative of a dead person (r.27(5)). Furthermore, relatives who are entitled to part of the estate are to be preferred to the personal representative of a spouse unless the spouse's estate is entitled to the *whole* of the estate as ascertained at the time of application for the grant.

Example

H dies survived by spouse and children. The spouse dies before obtaining a grant. The spouse's personal representative will be able to take a grant if the estate is not more than £250,000 plus personal chattels but if it is larger then the children will have priority.

Effect of a grant

8.17 The effect of a grant of simple administration is the same as that of a grant of administration with will annexed except that it provides conclusive evidence of intestacy rather than as to the contents and terms of the will.

6. RENUNCIATION

Persons who are entitled to a grant of probate or administration may renounce **8.18** their entitlement unless they have lost the right to renounce. Renunciation is made in writing to the registry. The most convenient way to deal with any renunciation is to submit it with the papers submitted by a person who does wish to take a grant.

An executor accepts office and thereby loses the right to renounce if he or she intermeddles in the estate (the principles are the same as those applying to a person becoming an executor *de son tort* so that the performance of acts of charity, humanity or necessity does not deprive the executor of their right to renounce). A potential administrator does not lose the right to renounce if he or she intermeddles. Both an executor and an administrator lose the rights to renounce if a grant is made in his or her favour.

A renunciation of probate by an executor does not operate as a renunciation of any right to administration which he or she may have unless that right is also renounced (Non-Contentious Probate Rules 1987 r.37(1)). However, a renunciation of administration in one capacity in effect operates to renounce *all* rights to a grant of administration.

Once a renunciation has been made it may only be retracted on the order of a district judge or registrar (r.37(3)). The court will only allow the retraction of a renunciation if it can be shown to be for the benefit of the estate or of the persons interested in the estate (*Re Gill* (1873)).

7. NUMBER OF PERSONAL REPRESENTATIVES

Section 114(1) of the Senior Courts Act 1981 provides that "probate or admini- **8.19** stration shall not be granted . . . to more than four persons in respect of the same part of the estate of a deceased person". This means that if more than four executors are appointed in respect of all or any part of the estate a grant can be made to only four of them. Power may be reserved to the others so that they can take a grant if a vacancy occurs (for example on the death of one of the four who has taken a grant). Similarly if more than four persons are equally entitled to a grant of administration (of either type) the grant cannot be made to more than four. If any dispute arises as to which of more than four persons are to take a grant it is resolved by a hearing before a district judge or registrar (Non-Contentious Probate Rules 1987 r.27(6)).

The minimum number of executors is always one, although the court has a discretion to appoint one or more additional personal representatives to act with the sole executor while there is a minority of a beneficiary or life interest subsisting in the estate (Senior Courts Act 1981 s.114(4)). An application for such an appointment may be made by any person interested in the estate or the guardian or receiver of any such person.

The minimum number of administrators is generally one, unless there is a minor beneficiary or a life interest in the estate where the appointment must normally be made to a trust corporation (with or without an individual) or to not less than two individuals (Senior Courts Act 1981 s.114(2)). However, the court has a discretion to appoint a sole administrator where there is a minority or life interest if it appears to the court "to be expedient in all the circumstances" (Supreme Court Act 1981 s.114(2)).

Where two administrators are necessary they may often be persons who have different entitlements to a grant.

Example

T dies intestate survived by a spouse and children and the estate is sufficiently large for the children to have an interest in it. The surviving spouse is entitled to a grant. A second administrator is required and so an adult child of the deceased may be co-administrator.

There is no requirement in cases of a minority or life interest that the numbers be maintained. Thus, if one of two administrators dies, the survivor can continue alone.

8. SPECIAL RULES AS TO APPOINTMENT OF PERSONAL REPRESENTATIVES

After renunciation

8.20 It may appear from what has been said so far that the choice of executor or administrator is automatic. However, this is far from being the case in all circumstances. The person with the best entitlement to a grant may renounce (see para.8.18, above) in which case the rules are applied as if that person had predeceased the testator. Thus:

(a) if an executor renounces (unless there is another executor willing to act), a grant of administration with will annexed will be made to the person with the best entitlement to a grant under r.20; and

(b) if a person with the best entitlement under r.10 (or r.22 if there is an intestacy) renounces the person next in the list will have a right to a grant.

Passing-over

8.21 The High Court has power under the Senior Courts Act 1981 s.116 to pass over the person entitled to a grant if "it appears . . . to be necessary or expedient to appoint as administrator some person other than [the person entitled to take a grant]". When this power is exercised the court may appoint any person to be the administrator so that it does not necessarily appoint the person with the next best right to a grant or indeed a person with any right. Under s.115(1)(b) the court also has power to grant administration to a trust corporation either solely or jointly with another person.

The power to pass over the person entitled to a grant is discretionary so that no exact rules can be laid down as to when the power will be exercised. However, two types of case may be recognised. First, where the persons entitled request the appointment of their nominee. In *Teague and Ashdown v Wharton* (1871) Lord Penzance held that a mere request was insufficient to enable the court to pass over those entitled since " . . . persons entitled to grants . . . are many of them persons who have no opportunity of knowing their own rights, and are not aware of the dangers that may beset them if they transfer these rights to other persons".

In *Re Potter* (1899) Gorell Barnes J. made a grant at the request of the persons who were entitled to a grant. It should be noted that in that case there were other special circumstances and that in his remarkably short judgment the judge seemed to place reliance on the fact that the appointment was made with the agreement of all the persons *interested* in the estate and not merely with the agreement of the persons entitled to a grant. It would seem, therefore, that the court will not pass over those entitled merely because they request that course.

Secondly, the court may pass over a personal representative who is unsuitable for that office either in general or in the circumstances of the case. For example, in *In the Estate of Crippen* (1911) the deceased had been murdered by her husband; she had died intestate and normally he would have taken her property. He would also have been entitled to take a grant to her estate and, as he was dead, his personal representatives would have taken the grant. However, there is a rule of public policy that a person who slays another loses their entitlement to that person's property (see Ch.16). The husband had, therefore, lost his beneficial entitlement to her estate and so his personal representative was passed over in favour of the wife's next-of-kin.

In *In the Estate of Hall* (1914) an executor who was in prison was passed over. In *Re Hall* (1950) the person entitled to administration was passed over on the ground that she could not be traced. In *In the Estate of Biggs* (1966) an executor had dealt with property in the estate without taking a grant (and was therefore debarred from renouncing probate—see para.8.09, above) but was now unwilling to continue acting despite the fact that he had been ordered to take a grant and that proceedings for contempt of court had been started against him. The court passed him over.

In *A.B. v Dobbs* (2010) the court emphasised that, although the power is discretionary, it should only be exercised in extreme cases such as where the executor is in prison, demented, bankrupt or refuses to act. The intentions of the testator should not be set aside "unless the persons chosen had, more or less, disentitled themselves from carrying out the task".

Finally, the case of *In the Goods of Edwards-Taylor* (1951) shows that the power to pass over is designed to control the appointment of personal representatives and cannot be used for a collateral purpose. In that case there was an application to pass over a beneficiary who was alleged to be mentally and physically immature. The application was made so that she would not be able to get possession of the deceased's estate immediately. The court refused to pass her over since the reason for the application was not concerned with the administration of the estate.

Administration of Justice Act 1985 s.50

8.22 Under s.50(1)(a) the court has power to remove an existing personal representative and appoint a substitute. Under s.50(1)(b) where there are two or more existing personal representatives it can terminate the appointment of one or more of those persons. The jurisdiction under s.50 is contentious business and accordingly is dealt with in the Chancery Division. The application must be made by a beneficiary (*Re Thomas and Agnes Carvel Foundation* (2007)). Three recent decisions illustrate the approach that the court is likely to take. In *Kershaw v Micklethwaite* (2010) the court refused to remove executors where there was a breakdown in relations between them and the residuary beneficiary. Removal under s.50 should only be ordered where the hostility interferes with the administration of the estate. Contrast *Re Steele* (2010) where the court removed an executor because the evidence was that the mistrust between the beneficiaries and the executor was likely to affect the proper administration of the estate even though the executor had been guilty of no wrongdoing. In *Alkin v Raymond* (2010) one of the two executors was a friend and business associate of the deceased. During the course of the administration he invoiced the estate for work done in relation to a property development originally undertaken by the deceased. The beneficiaries disputed the invoice. The court held that it did not "bear scrutiny" and the work was not properly calculated. The court ordered the removal of the executor and of his co-executor who, although not involved in the work or the drawing up of the invoice, had supported him in the dispute with the beneficiaries. The court refused to allow the beneficiaries to take a grant but appointed two neutral individuals to replace the executors.

9. LIMITED GRANTS

Introduction

8.23 Most grants are general in their effect. That is, they give the personal representative authority (or, in the case of probate, confirm their authority) to act for all purposes in the administration of the estate and extend to all the property in the estate without time limit.

There are, however, three ways in which grants may be limited in their effect:

(a) they may be limited in time (for example, "until X reaches majority");

(b) they may be limited to part of the estate (for example, "limited to settled land"); or

    (c) they may be limited as to a purpose, that is they may give the personal representative authority to deal with one particular aspect of the administration (for example, "limited to conducting or defending litigation").

Grants limited as to time

Grants on behalf of minors

A minor cannot take a grant of probate or of administration. Where one of several **8.24** executors appointed by a will is a minor the adult executors may take a general grant of probate immediately. Power is reserved to the minor who may take a grant of double probate on reaching 18 (see para.8.36, below). Where one of several potential administrators entitled in the same degree is a minor the grant will usually be made to the adults in preference to the guardians of the minor (Non-Contentious Probate Rules 1987 r.27(4)).

Where, however, the executors or the persons with the best entitlement to be administrators are all minors it is necessary to make a grant of letters of administration to some other person until the minors reach 18. This type of grant is commonly called a grant *durante aetate minore;* it may be a grant of administration with will annexed or a grant of simple administration. It confers on the administrator a general power to deal with the estate but is limited in time until the minor reaches 18. The grant will usually expire automatically on the minor reaching 18 although it is possible for some other time limit to be fixed (for example, the grant may be effective until the minor himself takes a grant). A grant *durante aetate minore* is made "for the use and benefit of the minor" and is therefore, made to the guardian of the minor (subject to the exceptions mentioned below) rather than to others entitled to the estate of the deceased.

The persons entitled to take a grant *durante aetate minore* under r.32 of the Non-Contentious Probate Rules 1987 (as amended by Non-Contentious Probate (Amendment) Rules 1991, 2004 and 2009) are:

    (a) a parent of the minor who has or is deemed to have parental responsibility under the Children Act 1989 as amended, a guardian appointed under that act or in certain circumstances a step-parent or adoption agency;

    (b) an "appointed" guardian; that is someone appointed by a district judge or registrar under r.32(2) either because there is no one eligible under the rule described above or because the registrar decides to pass over those persons; and

    (c) where there is a minority in the estate so that two administrators are required but there is only one person competent and willing to take a grant under the rules listed above, that person may nominate a second administrator.

A Practice Direction of September 26, 1991[1] details the evidence of entitlement required for applications for grants on behalf of minors.

Mental incapacity

8.25 Where the executors or administrators lack mental capacity to act they *may* in some cases be passed over in favour of other applicants but normally a grant will be made to some other person for the use and benefit of the person suffering incapacity (r.35).

The grant is made in the following order of priority unless the district judge or registrar otherwise directs:

(a) to the person authorised by the Court of Protection to apply for a grant;

(b) where there is no person so authorised, to the lawful attorney of the incapable person acting under a lasting power of attorney or a registered enduring power of attorney; and

(c) where there is no person authorised under para.(a) or (b), above, the grant is to the person or persons entitled to the residuary estate of the deceased. In this case a medical certificate from a doctor who is responsible for the patient is required to prove incapacity.

Unless a district judge or registrar otherwise directs, no grant shall be made under this rule unless all persons entitled in the same degree as the incapable person have been cleared off.

Grants limited as to property

8.26 Where a grant is made limited to certain property, up to four personal representatives may join in that grant and up to four in the grant made in respect of the rest of the estate.

Appointment of executors

8.27 A will may appoint different executors to deal with different parts of the estate. One example of this is an appointment of a literary executor to deal with literary effects and of a general executor to deal with the rest of the estate. The grant of probate taken by the literary executor will be limited to literary effects only. The grant taken by the general executor, if taken before the grant to the limited part of the estate, is described as a grant "save and except" the limited part; if taken after the grant of the limited part it is described as a grant *caeterorum*. There is no practical difference between these two types of grant.

---

[1] [1991] 4 All E.R. 562.

The court's discretion

The court can make a grant limited to part of the estate in exercise of its   **8.28**
discretion under s.116 of the Senior Courts Act 1981. However, the court will not
make such a grant unless there are very exceptional circumstances and will
usually pass over the person entitled to a grant altogether rather than make a
limited grant.

Settled land

The legal title to settled land is vested in the tenant for life not in the trustees of   **8.29**
the settlement. When the tenant for life dies and the settlement continues after his
or her death, a grant limited to settled land is required in order that the settled
land vests in the trustees of the settlement rather than the general personal
representatives.

A grant of letters of administration is made to the trustees at the date of death
or, where they fail to take a grant to the trustees at the date of grant or where no
such trustees take a grant by the deceased's general personal representatives.

Where the property passes to a person absolutely entitled after death of the
tenant for life the settlement comes to an end and the property devolves on the
general personal representatives of the deceased tenant for life. There is, therefore, no need for special personal representatives in such a case (*Re Bridgett and
Hayes Contract* (1928)). Similarly no special personal representatives are needed
where a settlement is *created* by the will of the deceased.

The above rules apply only to strict settlements under the Settled Land Act
1925. Where a person is entitled to a life interest under a trust of land (under the
Trusts of Land Act 1996) or a trust for sale, whether or not of land, the property
is vested in the trustees and continues to be vested in them despite the death of
the life tenant. The trust property does not, therefore, pass to any personal
representative of the life tenant. Where a trust of land is created by will or
intestacy, the general personal representatives will deal with the property and will
vest it in the trustees.

Grants limited as to purpose

Grants ad colligenda bona

The purpose of a grant *ad colligenda bona* is to enable collection and preserva-   **8.30**
tion of the assets in the estate before a general grant is made so that any assets
in danger may be preserved. Since the grant does not extend to distribution of the
estate the will is not annexed to it. There are no particular rules as to who may
apply for the grant; application is made to a district judge or registrar ex parte
(Non-Contentious Probate Rules 1987 r.52(b)).

Although a grant *ad colligenda bona* is usually limited to collecting in the
estate the court may grant power to sell or otherwise deal with the assets so as
to preserve their value.

Grant ad litem

8.31   A grant *ad litem* is made to enable proceedings in court to be begun or continued
on behalf of the estate of the deceased or against it. Any person interested in the
litigation may apply ex parte to a district judge or registrar. Where someone
wishes to bring a claim against an estate for family provision under the Inheritance (Provision for Family and Dependants) Act 1975 the Official Solicitor will
usually be willing to take out a grant *ad litem.*

Grant pendente lite

8.32   Where there is a probate action in relation to an estate (for example, because the
validity of an alleged will is in question), the court may appoint an administrator
pendente lite, that is until the probate action is concluded. Any person who is a
party to the probate action or interested in the estate may apply for the grant to
be made but the grant will usually be made to an independent third party. The
administrator will not usually be given authority to distribute any of the
estate.

10. INCOMPLETE ADMINISTRATION

8.33   In most cases the executor or administrator who first takes out a grant will
complete the administration of the estate. Sometimes, however, the original
personal representative will die or otherwise cease to hold office without completing the administration. In such a case, if there is no chain of representation,
a grant to some other person will be required. This will either be a grant *de bonis
non administratis* or a cessate grant depending on the circumstances. Sometimes
before the administration is completed an executor is added by means of a grant
of double probate. A grant of double probate is made where one or some of a
number of executors have taken a grant with power reserved to others to take at
a later stage and one of those others now obtains a grant.

Grant of administration de bonis non

8.34   A grant *de bonis non administratis* is made to enable the administration of the
estate to be completed following the death or incapacity of *all* the previous
personal representatives or the revocation of the previous grant. (If one of the
personal representatives becomes incapable of acting the grant is revoked and a
further grant is made to the remaining personal representatives; this is not,
however, regarded as a grant *de bonis non.)* Although the name "*de bonis non
administratis*" means "concerning unadministered goods" it is appropriate in
cases where any type of property, including realty, is unadministered.

There are three requirements which must be satisfied before such a grant can
be made:

(i) *The administration is incomplete.* Administration is complete once the debts and legacies have been paid, accounts have been prepared and any land or other assets remaining in the estate have been vested in the beneficiaries by means of assents.

(ii) *There is no remaining personal representative.* A grant *de bonis non* cannot be made following the death of one of a number of executors or administrators since the remaining personal representatives have full power to complete the administration. Similarly a grant *de bonis non* cannot be made following the death of the last surviving executor if he or she has appointed an executor who proves his or her will and so becomes an executor by representation (see para.8.05, above).

(iii) *There has been a previous grant.* A grant *de bonis non* must always follow a previous grant. An original grant is appropriate where an executor has acted without a grant or someone has partly administered the estate without any authority.

A grant *de bonis non* may be a grant of administration with will annexed or a grant of simple administration. The order of priority for taking the grant is governed by Non-Contentious Probate Rules 1987 rr.20 and 22 which were explained above.

Usually the person (or persons) to whom the grant is made will be the person who was entitled to a grant equally with the previous grantee or who was next entitled after them. Where the previous personal representative was entitled to the whole of the estate the grant will usually be made to his or her personal representatives (the rule that living persons are to be preferred to the personal representatives of deceased persons only applies as between persons entitled in the same degree).

Where there is a minority or a life interest in the estate at the time when the application for the grant *de bonis non* is made, two administrators will be required unless the court orders to the contrary or makes a grant to a trust corporation.

Cessate grants

A cessate grant is required where the original grant was limited in time and has **8.35** ceased to be effective because the time has expired. The most common circumstances in which such a grant is required is where a grant of administration (with will or of simple administration) has been made to a guardian "for the use and benefit" of a minor who would be entitled to a grant but for minority. When the minor reaches 18 the limited grant to the guardian automatically ceases to be effective and the minor is entitled to apply for a cessate grant. The cessate grant may be a grant of probate, administration with the will annexed or simple administration depending on the nature of the minor's entitlement.

A cessate grant is also appropriate in other circumstances where a grant is limited in time and the time expires. Thus if a will appoints an executor for life the executor's office ceases altogether on death and so the chain of representation cannot provide the estate with an executor. A cessate grant is then made to any executor appointed in substitution for the deceased executor by the will (for example, the will may have appointed "A for life and thereafter B"). If no substitutional appointment has been made a cessate grant of administration with will is made to the person entitled under r.10. If a grant of simple administration is made for the use and benefit of a minor a cessate grant of simple administration is made to the minor on reaching 18.

A cessate grant is theoretically different from a grant *de bonis non* since it is a general re-grant in respect of the whole estate rather than a limited grant in respect of the unadministered part. However, the practical effect of the two types of grant is the same.

Double probate

8.36 A grant of double probate is made to an executor who applies for a grant after a grant of *probate* has already been made to another executor. There are three types of case in which a grant of double probate is appropriate:

(i) Where one of a number of executors does not wish to take a grant immediately, does not wish to renounce and has not been cited to take or renounce probate, power will be reserved to take a grant later. Such an executor may then apply for double probate at any time.

(ii) Where one of a number of executors is a minor at the time of the original grant of probate to the others, power is reserved automatically and the executor can apply for double probate on reaching 18. If the original grant had been a grant of administration the application would be for a cessate grant not a grant of double probate. Thus where a will appoints several executors of whom some are adults and some minors a grant of probate will be made to the adults immediately and a grant of double probate to the minors on reaching majority. Where a will appoints a minor as the only executor, a grant of administration with will annexed will be made to the guardians of the executor (or to the person entitled to residue if the minor executor was not so entitled) and a cessate grant of probate to the infant on reaching majority.

(iii) Where executors are prevented from taking a grant by the rule which restricts a grant to four persons in respect of any part of an estate (Senior Courts Act 1981 s.114(1)) one of them may apply for a grant of double probate if a vacancy occurs (for example on the death of one of the four proving executors) since power is reserved to them in the original grant.

It should be noted that there is no possibility of double grants of *administration*. A potential administrator who does not prove in the original grant will only be able to take a grant later if a grant *de bonis non* or a cessate grant is needed or if a second administrator is needed because a life interest or minority arises.

When applying for a grant of double probate the oath must set out, in addition to the usual matters, particulars of the former grant. An office copy of the original grant should accompany the application.

11. Circumstances in which No Grant is Required

Since an executor's authority derives from the will rather than the grant of probate, certain steps may be taken without a grant. However, in nearly all circumstances a grant is eventually in fact required so that it can be produced to prove title to the assets of the estate. **8.37**

There are a number of statutory provisions which enable certain assets to be dealt with without production of a grant but they are all concerned with relatively small amounts of property (see para.21.03, below).

12. Revocation of Grants

Jurisdiction

In certain circumstances a grant may be revoked by the Chancery Division (or county court) in contentious cases or by a district judge or registrar of the Family Division in non-contentious cases. **8.38**

Where there is a dispute as to whether a grant should be revoked the case is contentious and every personal representative must be a party to the action. The original grant must be lodged with the court. If there is no dispute as to the need for revocation the case is non-contentious. However, a grant cannot normally be revoked in non-contentious proceedings except on the application of the person to whom the grant was made.

Grounds for revocation

A grant will be revoked if it is subsequently found that it ought not to have been made to the person to whom it was in fact made. This may arise in many ways: for example, where a fraudulent application is made by a person with no right to a grant; where a person thought to have predeceased is subsequently found to be alive and better entitled to a grant than the person to whom the original grant was made; where the grant was made despite the entry of a caveat; where a grant was made even though contentious probate proceedings were pending. **8.39**

A grant will be revoked where a subsequent will is discovered (and in most cases where a subsequent codicil is discovered) or where it is found, after a grant, that the will was invalid or had been revoked before death.

A grant will be revoked where a personal representative becomes mentally or physically incapable, or has disappeared or wishes to retire and the court agrees to this.

A grant will be revoked where the "deceased" is not in fact dead.

Consequences of revocation

8.40   Section 27 of the Administration of Estates Act 1925 protects an original personal representative who makes or permits payments or dispositions in good faith. A person who makes a payment to a personal representative in good faith is also protected. Section 39 of the same Act provides that contracts for sale remain binding on and enforceable by the estate despite the revocation of the grant. Section 37 provides that a conveyance of any type of property remains valid despite revocation of the grant provided the conveyance is to a purchaser who gave valuable consideration in good faith (a conveyance is widely defined in this context and includes almost all dealings with property).

   If property is transferred to the wrong beneficiary under a grant which is later revoked (for example, the property is distributed as on intestacy and then a will is found) the beneficiary is liable to return the asset or to refund its value. The true beneficiary is also entitled to trace the asset or its proceeds and to recover it from the person now in possession so long as it remains identifiable. However, there is no right to trace into the hands of a bona fide purchaser for value without notice.

CHAPTER NINE

PROBATE JURISDICTION

1. JURISDICTION—TERRITORIAL LIMITS

Grants of representation are made by the English courts where property of the **9.01** deceased is situated in England and Wales and either an executor is appointed or such property is disposed of in England and Wales. A will which neither appoints an executor nor disposes of English property is not usually admitted to probate although the court has a discretion to issue a grant in such cases.

2. NATURE OF PROBATE JURISDICTION—CONTENTIOUS AND NON-CONTENTIOUS BUSINESS

Probate jurisdiction is concerned with three things only. First, the decision as to **9.02** whether a document may be admitted to probate or annexed to a grant of administration as a testamentary document; secondly, the decision as to who is entitled to a grant of representation in respect of the estate of a deceased person; and thirdly, the decision to amend or revoke a grant.

Since 1970 probate business has been divided between the Family Division (which deals with non-contentious business), the Chancery Division (which deals with contentious business), the county court (which has concurrent jurisdiction to deal with contentious business where the value of the estate of the deceased does not exceed a limit laid down by rules of court, the present limit is £30,000).

Non-contentious business (which is also called common form business) is defined by the Senior Courts Act 1981 s.128 as:

"the business of obtaining probate and administration where there is no contention as to the right thereto, including—

(a) the passing of probates and administrations through the High Court in contentious cases where the contest has been terminated, and
(b) all business of a non-contentious nature in matters of testacy and intestacy not being proceedings in any action, and
(c) the business of lodging caveats against the grant of probate or administration."

The vast majority of probate cases are non-contentious and are dealt with entirely by the Family Division. Non-contentious probate may involve a hearing before a district judge or registrar; for example, a hearing may be required to decide between persons entitled to a grant in the same degree, or where the court is asked to pass over a person entitled to a grant in favour of some other person.

Where there is a dispute as to what document or documents should be admitted to probate, or as to who is entitled to take out a grant, or as to whether a grant should be revoked, contentious (or solemn form) proceedings may be necessary and will be brought in the Chancery Division or county court. In most cases non-contentious proceedings will begin first and the case will only become contentious when the dispute arises.

A grant of representation in common form does not prevent a probate claim for proof in solemn form from being brought later. Thus if, after the Family Division has granted probate, someone wishes to challenge the validity of the will, they may start contentious proceedings.

Frequently, where there is a dispute, a caveat or citation will be entered but neither of these steps is, of itself, sufficient to start a contentious probate action.

After a probate claim is started, the case remains contentious until the dispute is finally decided by the Chancery Division or the county court. Once the dispute is disposed of, the case becomes non-contentious and so is returned to the Family Division which is responsible for the issue of the grant (the Family Division is the only court which actually makes grants).

3. Financial Limits

9.03 The jurisdiction of the High Court (Family and Chancery Division) is unlimited as to the amount of the estate. The county court has no jurisdiction in non-contentious cases and its jurisdiction in contentious cases is limited to cases where the estate is less than the county court limit at the time of death. (In valuing the estate for this purpose debts, funeral expenses and incumbrances are deducted as is property vested in the deceased as trustee and not beneficially.) The county court with jurisdiction is the one within whose area the deceased was resident at the date of death. Once proceedings have been commenced in the county court the Principal Registry should be informed so that no grant is made in common form in the estate.

4. Probate Jurisdiction and Other Jurisdiction Concerning Wills

9.04 Probate jurisdiction is concerned only with what documents are admissible as testamentary documents and to whom grants should be made. Litigation concerning wills and administration of estates may, however, arise in at least three other ways:

(a) there may be no dispute as to what should be admitted as a testamentary document but a dispute as to what it means (that is, a question of construction may arise);

(b) there may be a dispute as to how the estate should be administered by the personal representatives (so that an administration action becomes necessary); or

(c) there may be a claim against a personal representative who is alleged to have acted improperly (and so may be liable for the *devastavit* which has been committed).

Proceedings in each of these three types of case will usually be brought in the Chancery Division. When a question of construction is before the court, it is bound by the decision of the Family Division (or of the Chancery Division in earlier probate proceedings) as to the wording of the testamentary instrument. Questions of construction are not generally decided in probate proceedings except to the extent that it is necessary for the purpose of the probate action. Thus, it is appropriate for the court to decide, in probate proceedings, who the testator intended to appoint as executor and what parts of earlier wills or codicils have been revoked by a later testamentary document.

5. SOLEMN FORM PROCEDURE

We have already outlined the distinction between common form and solemn form **9.05** probate. We intend to give no more than an outline of the solemn form procedure in the High Court (Chancery Division). (The procedure for obtaining a grant in common form cases is dealt with in Ch.10.) Probate claims are dealt with in Pt 57 of the Civil Procedure Rules 1998 and the Practice Direction Supplemental to Pt 57 which deals with rectification of wills and the removal of personal representatives as well as contentious probate. Part 57 (which was added to the Rules by the Civil Procedure (Amendment No 2) Rules 2001 (SI 2001/1388)) came into force on October 15, 2001.

The action is started by issuing a claim form under Civil Procedure Rules Pt 7 in a Chancery District Registry or Chancery Chambers at the Royal Courts of Justice (or in the county court office if the case is in the County Court). A defendant served with the claim must file an acknowledgement of service within 28 days (or within 28 days of service of the particulars of claim if later). Any testamentary documents in the possession of the claimant must be lodged in the court when the claim form is issued, any in the possession of the defendant must be lodged when they acknowledge service (CPR 57.5).

The claim form must contain a statement of the nature of the interest of the claimant in the estate and of the nature of each defendant's interest (CPR 57.7 (1), (2)). A party who disputes any such statement must say so in the statement of case. Similarly a party claiming that the testator did not know or approve of the contents of the will, lacked capacity or was subject to undue influence or fraud must say so and give particulars of the facts relied upon (CPR 57.7 (3), (4)).

A default judgment cannot be obtained in a probate action. This is because the court has to make a positive decision as to whether the will is valid or not. If service is not acknowledged the claimant can proceed with the action as if it had been acknowledged.

The normal rules about costs contained in CPR 44 apply to probate claims. Thus the court has a discretion as to who pays costs and the amount of costs. The costs are not automatically paid out of the estate. Generally the unsuccessful party will be ordered to pay the costs of the successful party. However, costs are usually paid out of the estate if the real cause of the dispute leading to the litigation was actions taken by the deceased or the residuary beneficiary. Executors who successfully prove a will are entitled to take their own costs out of the estate.

Chapter Ten

OBTAINING THE GRANT (NON-CONTENTIOUS CASES)

1. Probate Jurisdiction

Most non-contentious or common form probate business is dealt with in the **10.01** Principal Registry of the Family Division in London or one of the district registries (most of these district registries have sub-registries attached to them). The judicial officers of the Principal Registry are called district judges and those of the district registries are called registrars. In cases of doubt or uncertainty a district judge or registrar may refer a matter to a judge of the Family Division (Non-Contentious Probate Rules 1987 r.61). Registries do not have "catchment areas"; the choice of registry is governed by convenience and personal preference.

It is not necessary for a personal representative to consult a solicitor. The personal representative can make a personal application at the Principal Registry or at a district registry or sub-registry or at certain local probate offices served from the nearest registry. The procedure is simple and will not be considered here. Under the Non-contentious Probate (Amendment) Rules 2004 banks, building societies, insurance companies and members of bodies approved by the Secretary of State for Constitutional Affairs may also make personal applications without using a solicitor. We are concerned only with the procedure where a solicitor is acting for the personal representative.

2. The Papers Leading to a Grant

The solicitor must send or deliver the following: **10.02**

(a) The Inheritance Tax Account, if required. In cases where a solicitor is acting, the solicitor is required to work out the inheritance tax payable although exceptionally form IHT 400 and the papers that go with it can be sent to the revenue with an explanation of the problem which prevents the calculation of the tax. The procedure for paying the tax in cases where a solicitor is acting is as follows:

1. Three weeks before the solicitor expects to send form IHT400 to the Revenue he or she should apply for a reference and a payslip (this can be done online at *www.hmrc.gov.uk*, or by post using form IHT422). The Revenue will then post to the solicitor details of the reference with a payslip and a pre-addressed envelope.

2. The reference should be written on the top right-hand corner of form IHT400.

3. The payslip and cheque for the tax should be put in the pre-addressed envelope unfolded and unstapled. The envelope should then be sent to HMCR Inheritance Tax, Ferrers House, PO Box 38, Castle Meadows Road, Nottingham, NG1 2BB. If the IHT400 is also being sent to Nottingham the envelope containing the cheque and the payslip can be put inside the larger envelope which contains the IHT400.

If tax is to be paid out of the deceased's bank account or building society account under the Direct Payment Scheme the reference should be written on top of form D20 which gives instructions on how the tax is to be paid in such cases.

(b) The appropriate oath sworn or affirmed by the personal representatives before an independent solicitor.

(c) Probate fees. A crossed cheque made payable to H.M. Paymaster General should be used. The fee is £90. The applicant may also obtain office copies of the grant. Each copy is £1 if ordered with the grant. If ordered later the first copy is £5 and additional copies £1 each.

(d) The will (if there is one) and any codicils to it together with two A4 size copies of the will and any codicils after they have been signed by the personal representatives (as to which see para.10.20, below). The copies must be clear and legible and any faint writing on the originals must be clear. The copies must not be stapled. If the will has been taken apart to be copied it must be put back into the same state and condition that it was in before it was taken apart and a letter must be sent to the registry explaining this and that nothing of a testamentary nature was attached or detached. A photographic copy of the will is normally annexed to the grant of representation by the registry. However, if the registrar considers that the will is unsuitable for photographic reproduction or if it contains inadmissible alterations or other irrelevant matter the registry will require the applicant's solicitor to supply a typewritten engrossment. In such circumstances, as an alternative to an engrossment the registrar has a discretion to allow a facsimile copy produced by photography in certain circumstances including:

(i) where a complete page is, or complete pages are, to be excluded; and

(ii) where the original has been altered but neither re-executed nor republished and there is in existence a photocopy of the original executed document.

If the whole or part of the will has been written in pencil, a copy of the will in which the words which appear in pencil in the original are underlined in red ink must be lodged with the will.

If the original will has been lost or destroyed it may be possible to obtain an order admitting to proof the will as contained in a copy or reconstruction (Non-Contentious Probate Rules 1987 r.54(1)). If the original will is lodged in a foreign court a duly authenticated copy of the will may be admitted to proof without need for an order (Non-Contentious Probate Rules r.54(2)). If the will incorporates standard clauses these need not be produced provided that the forms or clauses are contained in published documents and have previously been lodged with the senior district judge of the principal registry and accepted as sufficient lodgment for these purposes (Practice Direction issued by Senior District Judge Angel, April 10, 1995).

(e) Any affidavit evidence that may be required, for example an affidavit of due execution.

(f) Any renunciation by a person who would have been entitled to a grant in priority to the applicant (see para.8.18, above).

(Items (a), (b) and (e) are considered in more detail later in this chapter.)

Once the appropriate papers have been lodged at the registry all testamentary documents are photographed. Searches are made; one to ensure that no caveat has been entered against the estate and one to ensure that no grant of representation has already been issued. Searches are also made to ensure that no application for a grant has been made in a different registry and that no will has been deposited with the registry.

The papers are examined and if they are in order the grant of representation is prepared. A photographic copy of the will and codicils (if any) is attached to the grant. Grants are usually signed by a Probate Officer under the authority of the President of the Family Division; they are sealed with the seal of the Division. The grant is sent by post to the extracting solicitor together with any office copies which have been requested.

If there are defects in the papers the registry will contact the extracting solicitor so that the queries can be resolved.

3. OATHS

Introduction

Every application for a grant of representation must be supported by an oath. It **10.03** is the government's intention to replace oaths with "statements of truth". No timetable has been set for this reform. The oath is prepared by the solicitor acting for the personal representatives and it must be sworn (or affirmed) by the personal representatives before an independent solicitor.

The oath performs three functions:

(a) It sets out the basis of the applicant's claim to be entitled to take the grant (for example, in the case of an executor it recites the fact that the applicant is the person named as executor in the will).

(b) It requires the applicant to swear duly to collect in the assets of the deceased and administer the estate.

(c) In the case of applications for grants of probate and letters of administration with the will annexed, the oath exhibits and identifies the will and any codicils to it.

The three most common oaths are the oaths leading to a first grant of probate, letters of administration with the will annexed or simple letters of administration. The three oaths are similar but differ in points of detail. Points common to all three oaths are considered first and then points relevant to specific types of oath.

Form of oaths

10.04   The form which the oaths are to take is not laid down so that, provided the applicant swears to or affirms the facts which will lead to a grant in their case any words may be used. Precedents for the three common oath forms are included in the appendix. The following paragraphs refer to the clauses in those precedents.

Points common to all oaths

Affirmation

10.05   An "oath" need not be sworn but can be affirmed. If a person wishes to affirm, the words "make oath and say" which appear twice in the body of the oath can be deleted and replaced by the words "do solemnly and sincerely affirm". The words "sworn by" in the jurat at the end of the form should then be deleted and replaced by the words "affirmed by".

Solicitor's name and address

10.06   The name and address of the extracting solicitor should appear in the top right hand corner of the oath. Correspondence concerning queries will then be sent to the solicitor and not to the personal representatives themselves. It is desirable to add the solicitor's reference immediately afterwards since the reference will then be included on the grant of representation when it is returned by the registry.

The deceased's name

The true and proper name of the deceased must always be given. The true and   **10.07**
proper name of the deceased is normally the name in which the birth was
registered or in the case of a married or divorced woman the surname of her
husband (if she has adopted her husband's name). The true and proper name may
have been changed by:

(a) deed poll; or

(b) habit and repute; however, a name is only regarded as changed by habit
and repute if the former name has been completely abandoned over a
period of time.

A testator may have been known by a name (or names) other than the true and
proper name; such a name is not to be included on the oath unless it is necessary
that the name appear on the grant of representation. It is necessary if the will was
made in a name other than the testator's true and proper name or if property was
owned in a name other than the true and proper name.

An explanation justifying the inclusion of the other name must either be given
in a separate affidavit or, if it can be stated sufficiently concisely, included in the
oath. Examples of such concise explanations are:

1. "That the true and proper name of the deceased was Jane Brown but she
made and duly executed the said will in the name of Jane LeBrun."

2. "That the true and proper name of the deceased was Jane Brown but
certain property, to wit . . . is vested in her in the name of Jane
LeBrun."

In such a case at least one property held in the other name must be specified.

The deceased's address

The address given must have been the usual residential address including post-   **10.08**
code of the deceased at the time of death. In the case of an oath leading to a grant
of probate or letters of administration with the will annexed if the latest testamentary document gives an address different from the last address of the testator that
former address should be given but all other earlier addresses may be ignored.

The dates of birth and death of the deceased

These must be set out as they appears in the certificate of death. In cases where   **10.09**
the precise date of death is uncertain the following wording is used:

"who was known to be alive on . . . and whose dead body was found on . . . "

If a person is believed to be dead but his body has not been found (for example,
because the deceased was aboard a ship which disappeared) the Family Division

can make an order giving leave to swear that the person who is believed to be dead died "on or since" a certain date. The wording of such an order should be repeated in the oath.

Age of the deceased at death

10.10 If the precise age of the deceased is not known the best estimate possible should be given.

Domicile of the deceased

10.11 If the deceased died domiciled in England or Wales this should be recited as "England and Wales" (because England and Wales is one jurisdiction). If there is any doubt as to domicile an affidavit setting out the fact should be filed in support of the oath. The Administration of Estates Act 1971 provides that where a grant of representation is issued in England and Wales, Scotland or Northern Ireland in respect of the estate of a person who died domiciled in one of these countries, the grant will be recognised in the other two countries provided it contains a statement of the deceased's domicile. Thus, if a person dies domiciled in Scotland owning assets in England and Wales, provided the Scots confirmation contains a reference to the domicile of the deceased it will be recognised as the equivalent of an English grant.

Settled land

10.12 Each oath must contain a paragraph relating to land settled before the death of the deceased and continuing settled after their death. If there was no such settled land comprised in the deceased's estate the paragraph is left as printed.

If there was settled land the word "no" must be deleted. Normally such settled land devolves not on the general personal representatives but on the trustees of the settlement who take out a special grant of representation limited to the settled land. Therefore normally in such a case the general personal representatives must qualify the later paragraph by inserting in the appropriate spaces the words "save and except settled land". If, however, the settled land is to devolve on the general personal representatives (for example, where they happen to be the trustees of the settlement) the words "including settled land" must be inserted. Since the Trusts of Land Act 1996 no new Settled Land Act settlement can be created.

The personal representatives swear to collect and get in the real and personal estate and to administer it

10.13 Each oath contains a paragraph which sets out the duties of a personal representative (to collect, get in and administer the estate, etc.). Nothing needs to be done to this paragraph unless the estate included settled land in which case as stated in para.10.12, above, the words "save and except" or "including" settled land must be inserted.

Gross and net estate

Each oath contains a paragraph dealing with the gross and net value of the estate **10.14** *which passes under the grant.* The deponent(s) must swear to the gross and net values. The paragraph contains two alternatives one of which must be deleted:

    (a) "the gross estate passing under the grant does not exceed £   and
        the net estate does not exceed £   , and this is not a case in which
        an Inheritance Tax Account is required", or

    (b) "the gross estate passing under the grant amounts to £   and the
        net estate amounts to £   ".

The deponent is not concerned with the value of any part of the estate which does not pass under the grant. The following property does not pass under the grant: a life interest, a joint property devolving by survivorship, a property which is the subject of a *donatio mortis causa* or nomination. The test is whether the grant is necessary to establish a claimant's right to the property. The *gross* value of such property must be stated because the personal representatives swear that they will duly administer the estate, due administration of the estate includes the payment of debts; therefore, they must swear to gross figures not merely to net ones.

    If the gross estate passing under the grant does not exceed the inheritance tax threshold and the other circumstances are such that no Inheritance Tax Account need be delivered, that is the estate is an "excepted estate" (as defined in para.10.37, below), alternative (a) should be completed. If the recital that this is not a case where an Inheritance Tax Account is required is omitted, the oath will be returned for the recital to be inserted and the oath resworn.

    Where an Inheritance Tax Account is required to be delivered, alternative (b) must be completed with the precise values of the gross and net estate passing under the grant. In para.(b) the figures for gross and net estate passing under the grant are the figures shown in the Inheritance Tax Account.

The jurat

The oath must be sworn by each deponent in the presence of an independent **10.15** Commissioner for Oaths or solicitor. An independent solicitor is one who is not a member of the extracting solicitor's firm. The place and date of swearing must be given precisely; it is not sufficient to give the name of the town. If there is more than one deponent and each swears at a different time, then the name of each should be inserted in a separate jurat. Otherwise the name of the deponent(s) need not be inserted at all; it is sufficient for the jurat to refer to "the above named deponents." The wording of the jurat must be altered if there is to be an affirmation.

Oath for executors

This oath is set out on p.498 of the Appendix. **10.16**

10.17   The first paragraph of the oath for executors should commence with the words "I" or "we" as appropriate. The names, addresses and occupations or descriptions of each of the deponents should be inserted. The order of names should be the same as that given in the will and the order of names given on the oath will be repeated on the grant of representation. Sometimes the deponents wish to vary the order so that a trust corporation or professional person can be named first and in this case a letter of consent signed by the executors may be filed with the affidavit. However, if no such letter is filed the executors are presumed to have consented to the change.

The true and proper name of each of the executors must be given. Since one of the functions of the oath is to explain the basis of the claimant's right to take a grant by identifying him or her as the executor named in the will, it is necessary to give an explanation if the true and proper name differs from the name given in the will. The wording used will vary according to the circumstances:

(a) If the discrepancy is very small it is sufficient to say "in the will called" or if it is a mistake in the spelling "in the will written".

Example

"Jennifer Smith in the will called Jenny Smith."

(b) If a change of name was made by deed poll the date of the deed poll should be recited and the deed itself lodged for inspection.

Example

"Charles Coomb, formerly Charles Crumb who changed my name by deed poll dated the 5th day of December 1982."

(c) If the change of name was made on marriage the previous marital status should be given.

Example

"Jennifer Smith, married woman, formerly and in the will called Jennifer Brown, spinster."

(d) If the change of name was by habit and repute the fact that the former name has been completely abandoned must be recited.

Example

"That I was formerly known as David Button but assumed the name of David Betten on or about the 4th of December 1960 since when I have never used the name of David Button but have always been known as David Betten."

Relationship

10.18   It is quite common for a will to mention a relationship in the appointment of an executor for example, "I appoint my niece Frances Brown".

It is also quite common for testators to make a mistake in such relationships, for example, referring to someone as a niece who is in fact a niece of the deceased's spouse. In such a case the oath must state that the deceased had no relative of that name and degree of relationship and recite such facts as will establish that the deponent was the person intended. If the will simply refers to "my wife" or "my husband" the oath must state that the deponent was the lawful spouse *at the time the will was signed*.

Address

The full, private and permanent address of the deponent must be given. A **10.19** solicitor, or other person administering the estate in a professional capacity may give a professional address only. Other persons may give a business address in addition to a private address but only if it can be shown to be for the advantage of the estate.

"Make oath and say that [I/we] believe the paper writing now produced to and marked by [me/us] to be the true and original last will and testament"

This paragraph performs two functions: **10.20**

(a) it makes the oath binding on the deponents. (If the deponent wishes to affirm, the words "make oath and say" must be altered to "do solemnly and sincerely affirm" here, later in the oath (see below) and in the jurat); and

(b) it identifies the documents which it is desired be admitted to probate. The deponent and person before whom the oath is being sworn must sign their names on each document. The signatures should be placed away from the text, if possible, since if the document is made unsuitable for photographic reproduction the Probate Registry will require an engrossment of the will.

If there are codicils to the will the words "with . . . codicils thereto" must be added to "the true and original last will and testament". If a codicil has been revoked by a later codicil, the earlier codicil must still be proved if it altered the terms of the original will or a previous codicil.

If the original will is unavailable then the word "original" should be deleted. If the original is lodged in a foreign court an official copy (bearing the seal, if any, of the court) must be marked and the oath must refer to "the true last will and testament as contained in a true and official copy thereof". If the original will is lost or destroyed a court order must be obtained allowing probate to be obtained of a copy, draft or reconstruction. The oath must refer to "the true last will and testament as contained in a copy thereof" or " . . . as contained in a completed draft thereof".

"And [I/we] further make oath and say that notice of this application has been given to the executor(s) to whom power is to be reserved"

Rule 27 of the Non-Contentious Probate Rules 1987 provides that notice of an **10.21** application for a grant of probate must be given to any executor to whom power is reserved. The oath for executors must therefore (in cases where power is reserved to an executor) include the paragraph set out above stating that such notice has been given to the executors to whom notice has been given should be named. The district judge or registrar can dispense with the need to give notice if satisfied that to do so is impracticable or would result in unreasonable delay or expense. Application for such dispensation is made by letter. Where a partner (or partners) in a firm of solicitors applies for a grant it is not necessary to give notice to other partners to whom power is reserved unless they are named in the will.

When an executor wishes power to be reserved to them to prove at a later stage it is not necessary to include a statement to this effect in the oath; but the name of such an executor should be written in the margin.

"And [I/we] further make oath and say that [I/we] [am/are] . . . the . . . [executors/executrices] named in the said will"

10.22   If only some of the living executors named in the will wish to take probate the number of such executors should be inserted for example, "we are two of the executors named in the said will."

If some of the executors are dead but all the living executors wish to take probate the living ones should be referred to as "the surviving executors". If only one executor was named in the will such a person is referred to as "the sole" executor.

If some of the proving executors are male and some are female, all should be referred to as "executors". If all are female, they should be referred to as "executrices".

If any executors have renounced probate this need not be referred to in the oath but the instrument of renunciation should be filed with the papers. It is not necessary for persons unwilling to take the grant to renounce. Instead power can be reserved to them to prove at a later date.

The oath for administrators with will annexed

10.23   The oath is set out on p.499 of the Appendix.

Comparison with oath for executors

10.24   This oath is similar to that sworn by executors in that it refers to the will to explain the basis of the deponent's claim to be entitled to administer the estate. It, therefore, has to identify the will in the same way that the oath for executors does. However, the oath must recite that the deponent is the person entitled in priority to take the grant and must explain that persons with prior rights (for example, persons appointed executors in the will) have been cleared off. We will comment only on those parts of the oath which differ from the oath for executors.

"[I/we] ... of ... "

The same details of name, address and occupations or descriptions that are given   **10.25**
in the case of executors must be given for administrators; any discrepancy
between will and oath must be explained. The order in which such names appear
on the oath is determined by the extent of their interest in the estate.

"that ... minority ... life interests in [his/her] estate"

If a minority or life interest exists no matter how small it may be (but see   **10.26**
para.10.29, below, for details of certain permitted deductions that may extinguish
an apparent minority or life interest) the grant will usually have to be made to at
least two individuals or to a trust corporation. Therefore, the oath must state
whether or not there is a minority or life interest.

Clearing off persons with prior rights

The deponent must insert a paragraph explaining that any person with a prior   **10.27**
right has been cleared off. Priority is governed by r.10 of the Non-Contentious
Probate Rules 1987.

   If the will did not appoint executors this must be recited. If the will did appoint
executors the reason why they are not seeking a grant must be stated (for
example, because an appointed executor died without taking a grant). Similarly
the oath must state why any other person with a prior right is not seeking a grant.
The reasons are likely to be:

   (a) death,

   (b) renunciation, or

   (c) failure to appear to citation.

The precise wording of such a recital will vary according to the circumstances,
the following is a specimen:

> "That A, the sole surviving executor and trustee appointed in the will, predeceased
> the deceased [or survived the deceased but has since died without having proved the
> will] and that B, the residuary legatee and devisee for life named in the will, has
> renounced letters of administration with the will annexed and that C, the ultimate
> residuary legatee and devisee, has been duly cited to accept or refuse letters of
> administration with the will annexed. That in default of appearance of the said C to
> the said citation it was ordered by District Judge [...] of this Division on the ...
> day of ... 20 ... that letters of administration with the will annexed be granted to
> [me/us]."

It is common practice for applicants for a grant to file, with the other papers, the
renunciation of any executor or any person having an interest prior to their
own.

It is not necessary to clear off persons entitled in the *same* degree as the applicant. For example, if there are three specific legatees one of whom wishes to take a grant he or she must clear off persons with a *prior* right but not the other two specific legatees.

Recital of deponent's right to grant

10.28   After clearing off any person with a prior right the oath must state the exact capacity in which the applicant claims the grant. If the applicant is claiming as a person entitled under a partial intestacy the relationship (if any) must be given.

> *Examples*
>
> - "One of the residuary legatees and devisees named in the will."
>
> - "One of the specific legatees and devisees named in the will."
>
> - "A brother of the whole blood of the deceased and one of the persons entitled to share in the undisposed of estate of the said deceased."

If the person entitled to the grant is a minor and the applicants are taking a grant for their use and benefit, the oath must recite this and must also show the applicants' authority to take such a grant. Suitable wording would be:

> "That A is the residuary legatee and devisee named in the said will and is a minor, the said A being the age of . . . and that there is no other person appointed or deemed to be appointed guardian of the said minor and that I, C, am the father and statutory guardian of the said minor and I, D, am the person nominated by an instrument in writing dated the . . . day of . . . 20 . . . under the hand of the said C, for the purpose of joining with him in taking a grant of letters of administration with will annexed of the estate of the said deceased."

Similarly if a grant is to be taken out for the use and benefit of a person who lacks the mental capacity to take a grant, the oath should state this and should show the basis of the applicant's right to take the grant; for example, that the applicant is the person authorised by the Court of Protection.

Permitted deductions

10.29   At the end of any oath immediately before the jurat it is always possible to insert additional necessary information. Sometimes it is desired to show details of "permitted deductions" from the value of the estate which may reduce the value of the estate below £250,000 or £450,000. This is done where the effect of such deductions will be to reduce the value of the estate to such an extent that no life interest or minority interest arise in respect of any undisposed of property so that it may be possible for the grant to issue to a sole administrator.

The permitted deductions are:

(a) the value of personal chattels,

(b) debts,

(c) inheritance tax payable from the estate without a right of recovery from any other person or property,

(d) fair and reasonable costs incurred and to be incurred, and

(e) probate fees.

Oath for administrators

The oath is set out on p.500 of the Appendix.   **10.30**

Comparison with oath for executors and oath for administrators with the will annexed

This oath is sworn where the deceased left no valid will. It follows that there is   **10.31**
no will to identify and no need to refer to a will to establish the basis of the deponent's claim. Instead the oath must recite the relationship of the deponent to the deceased and show that all persons with a prior right have been cleared off. Only those parts of the oath which differ from the previous oaths will be commented on.

"[I/We] ... of ... "

The same details of names, addresses and occupations or description that are   **10.32**
given in the case of executors must be given in the case of administrators although obviously in the case of an intestacy there can be no discrepancy between will and oath to require explanation. The order of names is governed by their priority to take a grant. A change can be made at the request of all applicants.

Clearing off persons with prior rights

Immediately after the words "died domiciled in ... intestate" the applicant must   **10.33**
explain in what way persons with prior rights have been cleared off. Priority is governed by the Non-Contentious Probate Rules 1987 r.22. Clearing off is done either by stating that the deceased left no-one in the prior categories set out in r.22 or by stating that there were such people at the time of the intestate's death but they have since renounced their rights, failed to appear to a citation or died without taking a grant. A surviving spouse or civil partner has first claim to a grant so if the intestate left no spouse or civil partner the oath must first state that the deceased died intestate "a bachelor" or "a spinster" or "a widower" or "a widow" or "a single man" or "a single woman".

Any other persons entitled under r.22 are cleared off by stating that the deceased died *without* "issue", or "parent", or "brother or sister of the whole [or half] blood" or "their issue", or "grandparent", or "uncle and aunt of the whole [or half] blood" or "their issue".

If a person with a prior right has renounced, an example of the wording is as follows:

> "died intestate, a widow, without issue or parent (or any other person entitled in priority to share in her estate by virtue of any enactment) leaving B her brother of the whole blood and the only person entitled to her estate surviving her and that the said B has duly renounced letters of administration."

If a person with a prior right has survived the intestate but died before taking a grant, that person's personal representatives can apply for the grant and the wording is as follows:

> "died intestate leaving W his lawful widow and the only person now entitled to his estate surviving him and that the said W has since died without having taken upon herself letters of administration of the said estate."

It is not necessary to clear off persons entitled in the same degree as the applicant. For example, if there are three children of the deceased one child does not need to clear off the other two.

"And further make oath and say that [I am/we are] ... of the deceased"

10.34   The applicant must here show the precise relationship to the deceased and state whether they are "the only person entitled to the estate of the deceased", "one of the persons entitled to share in the estate of the deceased", or "a person who may have a beneficial interest in the estate of the said deceased in the event of an accretion thereto."

A surviving spouse is described as "the lawful husband" or "the lawful widow." Since the Family Law Reform Act 1987 it is no longer necessary to describe a child as either "lawful" or "natural". An adopted child should be described as "lawful adopted". A child of a deceased uncle or aunt can be described as "a cousin german". A surviving civil partner is described as "the lawful civil partner".

If the application is made by a grandchild, nephew or niece or cousin german the oath must recite that the parent through whom the claim is made died in the lifetime of the deceased.

It is not necessary to swear in the oath that those with an *equal* entitlement to a grant have been informed of this application (contrast the oath for executors where such a statement is required).

Permitted deductions

10.35   As with the oath for administrators with the will annexed details of permitted deductions may be shown.

4. Inheritance Tax Accounts and Payment of Tax

Introduction

A grant of representation will not, normally, be issued until the personal repre- **10.36** sentatives have dealt with the question of inheritance tax. An account giving full details of the deceased's estate is required unless the estate is excepted (see below). If any inheritance tax is immediately due it must be paid before the grant can be issued (Senior Courts Act 1981 s.109(1)) as amended by the Finance Act 2004 s.294(1)(a)). The account, where it is required, must generally be delivered within 12 months of the end of the month in which the death occurred or within three months after the applicant begins to act as personal representative if later.

The purpose of the account is to enable the extracting solicitor acting on behalf of the personal representatives to list the deceased's assets and to calculate the inheritance tax liability, if any. HMRC will then check the extracting solicitor's "self-assessment" to tax to determine whether or not it is correct.

It should be emphasised that, unless the estate is an "excepted estate", the account must be delivered whether or not there is any tax to pay either on delivery of the account or at any time in the future. If tax is payable on delivery of the account, the personal representative's solicitor must send a cheque for the tax to the Revenue together with the account. The Revenue retains the account and returns form IHT 421 to the solicitor showing that tax has been paid. Form IHT 421 is lodged with the Probate Registry when the application for the grant is made. If it is discovered at a later date that the Inheritance Tax Account does not reflect the true circumstances of the deceased's estate, a corrective account must be filed within six months of the discovery.

The Revenue will accept computer generated facsimiles of Inheritance Tax Accounts.

"Excepted estates" where no inheritance tax account need be filed

The obligation to file an Inheritance Tax Account does not apply to "excepted **10.37** estates" under the Inheritance Tax (Delivery of Accounts) (Excepted Estates) Regulations 2004 as amended. The person applying for the grant will need to complete form IHT 205 which gives brief details of the estate. What estates are excepted depend on the date of death of the deceased. Details of excepted estates are included in the useful (if rather lengthy) "Guide to completing your Inheritance Tax account" which is available on line at *http://www.hmrc.gov.uk/ inheritancetax/* [Accessed January 2011].

At the time of writing three types of estates are excepted:

- Low value estates.

- Exempt estates.

- Foreign domiciliaries' estates.

Low value estates are estates where there is no tax to pay because the estate is below the inheritance tax threshold. For deaths before April 6, 2011 the nil rate threshold was always a single nil rate band. For deaths on or after that date the threshold can be increased by 100 per cent where the deceased inherited a full nil rate band from a predeceased spouse or civil partner. In the interests of simplicity no increase is allowed where the deceased inherited a portion of a nil rate band. An estate is not excepted for this purpose if it falls below the inheritance tax threshold only because the deceased inherited unused nil rate band transferred from a predeceased spouse or civil partner. The estate must fall below the threshold of a single nil rate band to be excepted. See answers to "Frequently Asked Questions" on the HMRC website. However, an estate below the threshold is not excepted, and so an Inheritance Tax Account is required, if there have been lifetime transfers other than "specified transfers". Specified transfers are gifts of cash, quoted shares and securities and gifts of land to an individual and contents enjoyed with land but not gifts into trusts up to an aggregate amount of £150,000. Similarly an estate is not excepted, even though the total is less than the inheritance tax threshold, if the value of property outside the UK exceeds £100,000 or if the estate includes trust assets in a single trust exceeding £150,000. An estate is not excepted if the deceased benefited from an alternatively secured pension fund or made any gifts with reservation. If the deceased died in the period April 6 to August 5 in any year the relevant threshold is the one for the previous tax year.

Exempt estates are estates where the gross value of the estate was £1,000,000 or less and no tax is payable because the spouse, civil partner or charity exemptions (or a combination of those exemptions) reduce the chargeable estate below the threshold after deduction of liabilities. The same restrictions in relation to the value of foreign property, lifetime transfers, trust assets and pensions apply as in the case of low value estates.

Foreign domiciliaries are estates where UK assets consist only of cash, quoted shares or securities passing by will, intestacy or survivorship with a gross value not exceeding £150,000 and the deceased was never domiciled in any UK jurisdiction.

IHT Form 400

Introduction

10.38   If the estate is not "excepted" from the need to do so, the intending personal representatives will have to complete and deliver form IHT 400. This form can be obtained at *http://www.hmrc.gov.uk* or by telephoning the HMRC. Form 400 and its supplements together form a formidably long document. Form 400 itself consists of 16 basic pages which summarise details of the assets of the estate and the tax calculation. Details of the deceased and of the personal representatives are also included and a declaration as to the accuracy of the form. Depending on the circumstances of the estate, supplementary pages selected from a suite of 21 such documents giving details of particular assets and exemptions are also required.

A probate summary (form IHT 421) sets out details of the estate for probate purposes and, when approved by the HMRC, is used to satisfy the Probate Registry that any tax payable before grant has in fact been paid.

The rules as to calculation of inheritance tax and as to the liability to pay the tax were explained in Ch.4. Form 400 is designed to allow self-assessment of the tax liability taking into account:

(a) the amount of tax payable on the death estate taking into account any lifetime chargeable transfers and any exemptions and reliefs available on death;

(b) the amount of tax payable by the personal representatives on the one hand and trustees of any settlement in which the deceased had an interest on the other hand. (It will be recalled that personal representatives are responsible for the tax on joint property, property given away by a *donatio mortis causa* or nomination and foreign assets even though they do not vest in them and so are not part of the estate for probate purposes); and

(c) the amount of tax payable on delivery of the account as opposed to tax payable by instalments.

The form also allows calculation of the value of the estate for probate purposes.

IHT 400, pp.1–3

The first two pages of IHT 400 consists of details of the deceased and of the **10.39** solicitor who is making the application for the personal representative (personal applications for probate or administration are permitted and are quite common but the procedure for dealing with inheritance tax is then quite different and is not dealt with further in this book) and of the will if any. Page 2 enables the person completing the form to work out what supplementary pages are required to deal with particular types of assets and with any exemptions which are available. If any such pages are required, they should be completed first as they contain information which will be summarised in form IHT 400 itself.

IHT 400, pp.4–5

Page 4 includes details of assets referred to in the will which do not form part of **10.40** the estate, for example, because they have been sold or given away during the lifetime of the deceased. The rest of p.4 and the whole of p.5 is a checklist to enable the person completing the form to decide which of the supplementary schedules are needed in this particular estate.

IHT 400, pp.6–10

10.41 Pages 6 and 7 contain lists of the various assets included in the estate as set out in the various supplementary schedules and on which the personal representatives must pay the tax if any is due. Pages 8 to 10 list deductions from the taxable total arising from liabilities of the deceased, exemptions and reliefs. Page 10 also lists assets which are to be taken into account in calculating tax but on which the personal representatives are not liable for the tax (such as interests in trusts).

IHT 400, pp.11–16

10.42 Page 11 is used to calculate the tax actually payable on the estate. Pages 12 and 13 contain a declaration by the applicants that the form has been correctly completed. Page 14 is a checklist to enable the person completing the form to ensure that all necessary information has been supplied. Finally, room is left at the end of the form for the inclusion of further explanations and information

Reduced Form 400

10.43 Where the estate is not an excepted estate but no tax is payable then a reduced form IHT 400 may be submitted. This is a form of the 400 in which only some of the form has to be completed. Details are included on pp.5 and 6 of "Guide to completing your Inheritance Tax account" "form IHT Notes" available from the HMRC website. The most common type of case where a reduced account can be submitted is where the estate is too substantial to be excepted but all or most of the estate is exempt because it is being given to a spouse, civil partner or charity so that no tax is payable

Further forms

10.44 In addition to the forms already described, other forms may have to be completed.

Corrective accounts and direct payments

10.45 If the information originally provided by the personal representatives proves to be incorrect, whether as a result of a mistake or because they discover additional property or liabilities, a corrective account, Form D4, will have to be sent to the Revenue. If the alteration is trivial, they may dispense with the requirement.

Second or subsequent grants

10.46 If the applicant is applying for a grant of double probate, a cessate grant, or a grant *de bonis non administratis*, Form A-5C is normally used. This form is sent to the appropriate Probate Registry not to HMRC. Otherwise (for example, when a new grant is applied for after the previous grant has been revoked) IHT Form 400 is required.

Late payment, penalties and estimated accounts

A failure to deliver an accurate account within the prescribed time limits may **10.47** lead to the assessment of a penalty. The main provision relating to late delivery of an account is IHTA s.245 which provides for a penalty of £100 plus £60 for each day that the account is late once the case has been referred to the Special Commissioners. The penalty does not apply if there is a reasonable excuse for the failure to comply with the time limit. The Revenue has issued guidance in leaflet IHT 13 as to what may be regarded as a reasonable excuse. The circumstances which will be so regarded are quite limited. They do, for example, include life threatening illness, they do not include ignorance of the law, the difficulty of the case or pressure of time.

Penalties are also imposed by Finance Act 2008 Sch.40 in cases where the account proves inaccurate. In this case the amount of the penalty depends in part on whether the error was deliberate or made without due care and on the amount of the tax which could have been lost to the Revenue if the inaccuracy had not been discovered.

A particular problem arises in cases where a personal representative wishes to avoid delay in obtaining a grant but does not have complete information available. This is well illustrated by the case of *Robertson v IRC* (2002). In that case the testatrix had left part of her property in Scotland to the Church of Scotland which was anxious for a quick sale. The executor submitted an account which dealt fully with most of the property. However, a cottage in Hertfordshire was yet to be valued. An estimated figure was included in the account which turned out to be far too low. A corrective account was submitted almost immediately and the correct amount of tax on the estate was paid within six months of the death (i.e. before the time when the tax would have become due if no account had been submitted). The Revenue were not therefore out of pocket as a result of the inaccurate estimate in the original account. Nevertheless, they imposed a penalty of £10,000 on the basis that the executor had not made "the fullest enquiries reasonably practicable" about the value of the property as required by IHTA s.216(3A). The executor was successful on his appeal to the Special Commissioners on the basis that what he had done was in accordance with accepted practice, the fact that the original figure was an estimate was disclosed and there was no negligence involved. At a later hearing the executor was awarded his expenses of and relating to the hearing on the basis that the Revenue had acted wholly unreasonably.

In the light of the *Robertson* case the Revenue has issued the following guidelines as to how they will deal with such cases in future (in their *IHT Newsletter*—Special Issue May 2002):

> "The Revenue is keen to provide assistance to personal representatives to enable them to fulfil their obligations without incurring penalties. In most circumstances we would expect the exact value of property to be given when form IHT 400 is submitted

and not merely an estimate. However we accept that if there is a proven need to obtain a grant urgently personal representatives may find themselves in a position where they think that they need to submit an estimated account of the value of a particular item of property. In such circumstances they should ensure that they have made the fullest enquiries that are reasonably practicable before doing so, and the estimate should be as accurate as possible. The Personal Representative should, for example, contact the professional who is going to value the property formally to ensure that the estimate is a reasonable one."

5. AFFIDAVIT EVIDENCE

Affidavit of due execution

10.48 Before a will or codicil can be admitted to probate the district judge or registrar must be satisfied that it was duly executed.

If a will or codicil contains an attestation clause, which recites that the proper formalities were complied with, a presumption that the will was duly executed arises. Under the Non-Contentious Probate Rules 1987 r.12(1) if the will contains no attestation clause or the attestation clause is insufficient or where it appears to the district judge or registrar that there is some doubt about the due execution of the will an affidavit is required as to due execution before admitting the will to probate in common form. The affidavit should be from one of the attesting witnesses or, if no attesting witness is conveniently available, from any other person who was present at the time the will was executed. If no such affidavit evidence is obtainable, the district judge or registrar may (under r.12(2)) accept affidavit evidence from any person thought fit to show that the signature on the will is in the deceased's handwriting or on any other matter which may raise a presumption in favour of due execution. The district judge or registrar may require notice of the application to be given to any person who may be prejudiced by the will. If the district judge or registrar after considering the evidence is satisfied that the will was not duly executed he or she must refuse probate and mark the will accordingly.

The maxim *omnia praesumuntur rite ac solemniter esse acta* may assist when actual evidence of due execution cannot be obtained. In certain circumstances it allows the inference to be drawn that the necessary formalities have been complied with.

> "The maxim expresses an inference which may reasonably be drawn when an intention to do some formal act is established; when the evidence is consistent with that intention having been carried into effect in a proper way; but where the actual observance of all due formalities can only be inferred as a matter of probability." Per Lord Lindley L.J. in *Harris v Knight* (1890).

The presumption can only be of use where the appearance of the document in question is consistent with the formalities having been complied with. The presumption applies very strongly where there is a formal attestation clause and less strongly where there is an informal clause or no clause at all. *In the Estate of Denning* (1958) is an example of the application of the presumption in the absence of an attestation clause. The dispositive part of a will, together with the testator's signature, was contained on one side of a piece of paper. On the reverse side two signatures were written in different handwriting, one below the other. Sachs J. applied the presumption and declared that the will was duly executed. He said:

> "that there is no other practical reason why the names should be on the back of the document unless it was for the purpose of attesting the will."

However, the presumption will not apply where the evidence suggests that the "will" was not executed in accordance with the formalities required by law even though the testator intended to execute a will. For example, it will not validate a document where there is only one witness to the testator's signature.

Affidavit as to knowledge and approval

Under r.13 of the Non-Contentious Probate Rules 1987, before admitting to proof **10.49** wills which appears to have been signed by blind or illiterate testators or by another person by the testator's direction or which for any other reason give rise to doubt as to the testator having had knowledge of the contents of the will at the time of its execution, the district judges or registrars must satisfy themselves that the testator had such knowledge. Affidavit evidence may be required for this purpose under the Non-Contentious Probate Rules 1987 r.16.

A solicitor who is present when a will is signed by such persons ought to ensure that the attestation clause states that the will was read over to the testator and that the testator appeared to understand and approve the contents.

Affidavits of alteration, condition and date of execution

The following matters are dealt with in Non-Contentious Probate Rules 1987 **10.50** r.14.

Alteration

If a will appears to contain an unexpected alteration (other than the completion **10.51** of a blank space) the district judge or registrar must require evidence to show whether the alteration was present at the time the will was executed (r.14(1)) and may require affidavit evidence for this purpose (r.16). In the absence of evidence to the contrary the alteration is presumed to have been made after execution. The district judge or registrar may, however, disregard an alteration which is of no practical importance (for example, an alteration to a legacy which has lapsed).

Incorporation

If a will contains a reference to another document in such terms as to suggest that **10.52** it ought to be incorporated in the will, the district judge or registrar may require the document to be produced and may call for such evidence in regard to the attaching or incorporation of the document as he or she may think fit (r.14(3)). Affidavit evidence may be required for this purpose (r.16).

Date of execution

10.53 If there is doubt as to the date on which a will was executed, the district judge or registrar may require such evidence as he or she thinks necessary to establish the date (r.14(4)) and may require affidavit evidence for this purpose (r.16).

Affidavit of attempted revocation

10.54 Any appearance of attempted revocation by burning, tearing or otherwise destroying must be accounted for to the district judge or registrar's satisfaction (r.15) and he or she may require affidavit evidence for this purpose (r.16). It is not desirable to attach anything to an original will since the existence of marks, pin holes, staple holes or clip impressions may suggest that there has been an attempted revocation in which case the district judge or registrar may call for affidavit evidence.

6. CAVEATS

10.55 A caveat is a notice entered at any probate registry by post or in person the effect of which is to prevent a grant of probate or administration being made without notice first being given to the person who enters the caveat, called the caveator (Non-Contentious Probate Rules 1987 r.44).

Once a caveat is entered it is effective for a period starting with the day after the day on which it is entered and ending six months after the day on which it was entered. A caveat may be renewed for an additional six months during the last month of the six-month period and again in the last month of each successive six-month period. The probate registry's own internal procedures ensure that no grant can be made in any registry while the caveat is effective. The caveat must contain the name and address of the deceased, the date and place of death and the name and address for service of the caveator.

Any person interested may issue a "warning" to the caveat under r.44(5). The index to caveats has been kept since August 1, 1988 at the Leeds District Probate Registry and not at the Principal Registry. As a consequence, warnings must be issued either personally, through the post or through the document exchange at Leeds District Probate Registry. The "person warning" must state the nature of his or her interest and the date of the will (if any) in the warning which must then be served on the caveator. The warning must also require the caveator to state the nature of the interest. A person whose application for a grant was blocked by a caveat may issue a warning as a "person interested".

Once the warning has been served on the caveator one of four things will happen depending on what right the caveator is alleging and what steps he or she chooses to take:

(a) *The caveator may withdraw the caveat* (r.44(11)). A caveator is free to withdraw the caveat at any time whether a warning has been issued or not. A caveator who withdraws after receiving a warning must give notice to the person warning. Once the caveat is withdrawn it becomes ineffective and the person warning is free to proceed with the application for a grant (unless, of course, there is another caveat in force).

(b) *The caveator may enter an appearance* (r.44(10)). An appearance should be entered within eight days of the service of the warning on the caveator. If it is not the person warning may thereafter take steps to "warn off" the caveator (see para.(d), below). An appearance can only be entered by a caveator who has an interest contrary to that of the person warning. For example, entry of an appearance would be the appropriate step to take where the caveator claims to be an executor under a valid will and the person warning claims to be entitled to letters of administration on the grounds that the will is invalid. The appearance must be entered at the Leeds District Probate Registry.

Once an appearance has been entered, the caveat remains in force until a district judge (or, where the parties consent to the discontinuance of the caveat, a registrar) otherwise directs (r.44(13)). Often the entry of the appearance will be followed by the commencement of a probate action (although neither the warning nor the entry of the appearance itself amounts to the commencement of such an action). Where this happens the caveat is no longer necessary, since the fact that a probate action has been started has the effect of preventing a grant being made (r.45(3)).

(c) *The caveator may issue and serve a summons for directions* (r.44(6)). This step must be taken within eight days of service of the warning, otherwise the caveator risks being warned off. A summons for directions may only be issued by a caveator who has no interest contrary to that of the person warning. It is, therefore, the appropriate step to take where the caveator is entitled to a grant in the same degree as or a lower degree than the person warning but wishes to show cause why that person should not take a grant (for example, because he or she is unsuitable and the caveator wishes the court to pass him or her over).

After a summons for directions has been issued there will be a hearing before a district judge (or in case of difficulty a High Court judge) who will decide to whom a grant should be made.

(d) *The caveator may do nothing.* In this case the person warning may file an affidavit after the time limit for entering an appearance (eight days) has expired (r.44(12)). The affidavit must show that the warning was served on the caveator. The caveat is then said to be "warned off" and is no longer effective so that the person warning is now free to proceed with an application.

7. CITATIONS

10.56   Citations are documents issued by the principal or district registry which call upon the party cited to show cause why a certain step should not be taken. They are used for a variety of purposes but all are designed to give a remedy where a person actually or possibly entitled to a grant is refusing to take steps to take the grant or to renounce so that others may do so. Although citations were formerly issued in contentious cases they are now only used in non-contentious cases.

There are three types of citation:

(a)   a citation to take probate;

(b)   a citation to accept or refuse a grant (of probate or letters of administration); and

(c)   a citation to propound a will.

Citation to take probate

10.57   An executor may normally renounce the right to take a grant. However, once he or she has "intermeddled" (so as to constitute him or herself an executor *de son tort*) in the estate he or she is no longer free to renounce and so may be cited to take probate. The citation may be issued at the instance of any person interested in the estate but cannot be issued until at least six months after the testator's death nor at any time while proceedings as to the validity of the will are pending (Non-Contentious Probate Rules 1987 r.47(3)). An administrator does not, by intermeddling, lose the right to renounce and so cannot be cited to *take* administration; (an administrator who intermeddles will, however, be liable up to the limit of assets coming into his or her hands as an executor *de son tort*).

Citation to accept or refuse a grant

10.58   A citation to accept or refuse a grant may be issued at the instance of any person who would be entitled to a grant if the person were to renounce (Non-Contentious Probate Rules 1987 r.47(1)). This type of citation is, therefore, used where a person with an inferior right to a grant wishes to force the person or persons better entitled to make up their minds whether to apply or not. Where there are several persons with a superior right they must all be cited before the person with the inferior right can take a grant. Where power has been reserved to a person to take a grant of probate, the proving executor may cite them to take or refuse probate (r.47(2)). In other cases it is not necessary or possible to cite a person with an equal right to take a grant since the court can issue a grant to any of the persons equally entitled.

A citation to accept or refuse a grant may be issued to a person with a right to either a grant of probate (unless they have lost the right to renounce) or letters of administration. A citation of this type may be made at any time after the death of the testator or intestate.

Citation to propound a will

The object of this type of citation is to force the persons interested in the alleged **10.59** will to seek probate of it if they can. The application may be made by any person with a contrary interest (which in effect means a person who is entitled on intestacy or under an earlier will). The citation must be directed to all the persons interested under the alleged will and not only to the executors of it (Non-Contentious Probate Rules 1987 r.48(1)).

An executor of a will who doubts the validity of a later codicil is not entitled to cite the beneficiaries of the alleged codicil to propound it. The proper course is to bring a probate action in which he or she will seek to establish the validity of the will and the invalidity of the codicil.

Procedure on citation

A person (called a citor) who wishes to obtain a citation must first issue a caveat **10.60** (Non-Contentious Probate Rules 1987 r.46(3)). The citor must then swear an affidavit confirming every averment in the citation (r.46(2)) and the district judge or registrar must settle the form of citation before it is issued (r.46(1)). Any will referred to in the citation must be lodged in a registry before the citation is issued unless it is not in the citor's possession and it is impractical to lodge it (r.46(5)). The citation will set out the steps which the court will take if the person cited does not show cause to the contrary.

A citation must normally be personally served on the person cited but other modes of service, including advertisement, may be ordered by the registrar (this will be done, for example, where the difficulty in obtaining the grant has been caused by the disappearance of the person entitled).

A person cited must enter an appearance within eight days of service (r.46(6)). If this is not done the citor may apply for an order for a grant if the citation was a citation to accept or refuse a grant (r.47(5)(a)). Where the person cited was cited to take probate he or she can be ordered to do so within a stated time on failing to enter an appearance (r.47(5)(c)), although the court may exercise its discretion to pass over the person cited (see, for example, *In the Estate of Biggs* (1966), para.8.21, above). If the person cited was cited to propound a will and has failed to enter an appearance, the citor may apply for a grant in common form as if the will were invalid.

Where the person cited does enter an appearance he or she may show cause why the steps contemplated by the citation should not be taken. Alternatively, if he or she is now willing to take a grant an ex parte application to a registrar for an order for a grant (r.47(4)) to him- or herself can be made.

Where power to take a grant has been reserved to an executor, a citation to accept or refuse a grant may be made at the instance of the proving executors (or the person who is executor by representation) against that person.

8. Standing Searches

10.61 An entry of a caveat has the effect of ensuring that notice of an application for a grant is given to the caveator. However, it is an abuse of the process of the court for a person to enter a caveat where there is no dispute as to an issue concerned with a probate matter (such as the validity of a will or a right to a grant of probate or administration). A person who merely wishes to know when a grant is made so as to make a claim against the estate should not therefore enter a caveat. Such a person could, in most cases, enter a citation since a creditor is entitled to a grant of administration on clearing off the beneficiaries. However, it will usually be more appropriate for them to make a "standing search".

A standing search is made by lodging the appropriate form together with the prescribed fee (currently £5) at the principal or district registry or any sub-registry. An office copy of any grant made within 12 months before or six months after the search will then be given to the applicant. The period of search can be extended by further periods of six months on payment of a fee for each extension.

9. Guarantees

10.62 Before 1972 almost all administrators were required to enter into bonds for the due administration of the estate of the deceased. This requirement was repealed by the Administration of Estates Act 1971 and replaced by a much less stringent provision requiring a guarantee in certain limited circumstances and no guarantee or bond at all in most circumstances.

The present law is contained in s.120(1) of the Senior Courts Act 1981 which provides that:

> "... the High Court may ... require one or more sureties to guarantee that they will make good, within any limit imposed by the court on the total liability of the surety or sureties, any loss which any person interested in the administration of the estate of the deceased may suffer in consequence of a breach by the administrator of his duties as such."

The Non-Contentious Probate Rules 1987 (unlike the rules which they replace) do not require guarantees in any particular type of case.

Chapter Eleven

POWERS AND DUTIES OF PERSONAL REPRESENTATIVES

1. Duties of Personal Representatives

Duty to collect assets

The first duty of a personal representative is "to collect and get in the deceased's **11.01** real and personal estate" (Administration of Estates Act 1925 s.25 as amended by Administration of Estates Act 1971 s.9). Once the assets are collected the personal representative must administer the estate by paying debts and legacies and by disposing of the residue (these duties are dealt with in Chs 15, 16 and 18). All duties of personal representatives must be performed with "due diligence". The personal representative must, therefore:

(a) take reasonable steps to collect money due to the deceased (by bringing proceedings if necessary); and

(b) collect the assets as quickly as is practical. (Money which is due to the deceased and which is secured by mortgage or other charge need not be collected immediately unless the security is in danger.)

No absolute rule can be laid down as to what is a reasonable time for collection of assets nor as to what steps must be taken in order to collect assets. In each case the personal representative will only be liable for loss resulting from failure to act if he or she has acted unreasonably.

Proof of title to assets

The personal and real property of the deceased devolves on the personal repre- **11.02** sentatives at death, in the case of an executor or on the making of the grant, in the case of an administrator. This only applies to interests in property which continue notwithstanding the death so that a life interest does not devolve on the personal representatives nor does an interest in joint property (which passes to the remaining joint tenant(s) by right of survivorship). The legal title to property held by the deceased as a trustee devolves on the personal representative if the deceased was a sole trustee but on the remaining trustees if there are any at the time of death. If the deceased owned an interest as a tenant in common in equity, it will devolve on the personal representatives, unless it was a life interest in which case it will cease to exist on death.

An interest held as beneficial joint tenant will not devolve on the personal representatives but will pass by right of survivorship to the surviving joint tenant(s). Property subject to a nomination or *donatio mortis causa* will not devolve on the personal representatives, it can be claimed by the nominee or donee immediately after death.

Insurance policies on the deceased's life written in trust for third parties or taken out under the Married Women's Property Act 1882 are not assets of the estate. Such policies are payable to the trustees on proof of death; a grant of representation is not required. The personal representatives will not be concerned in the collection of the proceeds of such policies (unless there is no trustee named in which case the proceeds will be paid to them—even so the proceeds will still not be assets of the estate). A lump sum payable under a discretionary pension scheme is not an asset of the estate and the personal representatives are not concerned in its collection. The trustees of the pension scheme will pay direct to the person(s) they have selected.

In order to collect the assets which devolve on them, personal representatives will have to prove their entitlement to the people who are in possession of the assets at the time of death. This can be done by production of the original grant of probate or administration or of an office copy of the grant. Office copies can be obtained from the registry on payment of a small fee. Personal representatives should apply for sufficient office copies to enable them to deal with the estate of the deceased promptly—the more items of property included in the estate the greater the number of copies which should be obtained. It is not, however, necessary to have a copy for each item of property. A person in possession of estate assets must hand over the assets on production of the original or office copy grant which they must then return to the personal representatives.

Enforcement of personal representatives' duties

11.03   A personal representative who accepts office (by taking a grant or by acting as executor) is liable for loss resulting from any breach of duty which he or she commits. A breach of duty by a personal representative may consist of mis-appropriating the property of the deceased for his or her own benefit, malad-ministration (such as distributing to the wrong people even though in good faith) or negligence (such as an unreasonable delay in dealing with the collection or distribution of the estate). Any breach of duty by a personal representative is called a *devastavit*.

An action may be brought against the personal representative by a beneficiary or creditor who is not paid in full as a result of a *devastavit* by a personal representative. Personal representatives can protect themselves against certain types of breach of duty in a number of ways (see Ch.14, below). In particular a personal representative cannot be held liable to an adult who has consented to the way in which he or she has performed duties with full knowledge of the circumstances.

Where several personal representatives are appointed each is liable for his or her own breach of duty but not for breaches by a co-executor or co-administrator. However, a personal representative who permits a breach of trust by another personal representative will be liable since he or she has then failed to perform his or her own duty of safeguarding the estate. They may also be liable in negligence (see para.11.04, "Duty of Care", below) if they fail to attend to their duties and thus allow a breach by another personal representative to go unnoticed.

Duty of care

The Trustee Act 2000 provides for a single duty of care which applies to trustees. **11.04**
Section 1 provides:

1. (1) Wherever the duty under this subsection applies to a trustee, he must exercise such care and skill as is reasonable in the circumstances, having regard in particular—

   (a) to any special knowledge skill or experience that he has or holds himself out as having, and
   (b) if he acts as trustee in the course of a business or profession to any special knowledge or experience that it is reasonable to expect of a person acting in the course of that kind of business or profession.

Under s.35 the duties set out in the act apply to personal representatives as well as to trustees.

Schedule 1 provides that the duty applies to personal representatives and trustees when:

1. exercising any power of investment whether conferred by the act (as to which see para.11.22 below) or otherwise (for example under the terms of the will);

2. exercising a power to acquire land;

3. entering into arrangements appointing agents, nominees or custodians (see para.11.20, below) or reviewing such agents' arrangements; and

4. exercising the power to insure (see para.11.11, below).

The statutory definition of the duty of care and when it applies is very similar to the common law position. Schedule 1 para.7 allows exclusion or restriction of the duty (in the case of personal representatives, the exclusion or restriction must be in the will).

2. Powers of Personal Representatives before the Grant

11.05   The authority of an administrator derives from *the grant*. The powers of an administrator before the grant is made are, therefore, very limited. In *Caudle* v *L.D. Law Ltd* (2008) Wynn Williams J. recognised (in an *obiter dictum*) that a person entitled to a grant of letters of administration "has an immediate right to possession of personal property owned by the deceased if it is necessary that he takes possession to safeguard the estate . . . such a person also has the right to take legal action to enforce that right". It should be emphasised that this right is very limited allowing the potential administrator to do no more than preserve the property.

Administrators may not otherwise bring any action before grant and if they purport to do so a later grant does not cure the defect in the original proceedings (*Ingall v Moran* (1944)). A new action must be brought once the grant has been made. In order to protect an estate from wrongful injury in the period between death and the obtaining of the grant the authority of an administrator will relate back for the limited purpose of giving validity to acts done before letters of administration were obtained. However, such relation back occurs only in those cases where the acts done are for the benefit of the estate. The test of whether or not an act is for the benefit of the estate is entirely objective. Thus in *Mills v Anderson* (1984) an "administrator" agreed before the grant to accept on behalf of the estate a sum in full and final settlement of a claim for damages. It later became apparent that the settlement was too low. It was held that there could be no question of the administrator's authority relating back to validate the agreement as it would not be to the benefit of the estate.

An administrator has no power to vest property in any person before obtaining a grant. In the period between death and grant of administration the property of the deceased vests in the Public Trustee (Administration of Estates Act 1925 s.9 as substituted).

The power of an executor derives from *the will* of the deceased and not from the grant which merely confirms their authority. An executor can therefore, in principle, exercise all powers without obtaining a grant. An executor can sue or be sued before obtaining a grant. If an executor brings an action (for example, against a creditor) the action is valid even though no grant has been issued. However, before judgment is entered in his or her favour a grant must be obtained since the court will, at that stage, require proof of authority to act as executor if the action depends on title to act in that capacity.

An executor is also entitled to deal with the collection and distribution of the estate without first obtaining a grant. In practice, collection of assets without a grant may prove impossible since the persons in possession may refuse to hand them over without proof of the executor's title. Similarly, as far as distribution is concerned, a purchaser will require proof of title before paying for assets. A beneficiary in whose favour an assent or conveyance of a legal estate in land is made is entitled to have a notice of the assent or conveyance endorsed on the original grant of representation; thus, the grant will have to be obtained before the assent is made.

Certain assets can be dealt with without the production of a grant (see paras 12.08–12.10).

3. IMPLIED ADMINISTRATIVE POWERS

Introduction

Trustees are given many powers by the Administration of Estates Act 1925, the **11.06** Trustee Act 1925 and the Trustee Act 2000. The powers of "trustees" under these acts are also given to personal representatives. The Trustee Act 2000 came into force on February 1, 2001; it extends the powers of trustees and personal representatives and removes many of the restrictions contained in earlier legislation as well as imposing a statutory duty of care on trustees and personal representatives (see para.11.04, above). The Trustee Act 2000 applies to wills made before as well as after the commencement date.

It is always possible for a testator to exclude an implied power by stating in the will that it is not available to the personal representatives or trustees.

Powers of personal representatives to sell, mortgage and lease

Section 39 of the Administration of Estates Act 1925 (as amended by the Trusts **11.07** of Land and Appointment of Trustees Act 1996) gives the personal representatives very extensive powers. Section 39(1)(i) preserves the common law powers of personal representatives to sell and mortgage personal property included in the estate. In relation to realty they are given (by s.39(1)(ii)) all the functions of a trustee of land under the Trusts of Land and Appointment of Trustees Act 1996. This provision effectively gives them the same powers as an absolute owner.

A receipt given by a personal representative for money, securities or other personal property is a sufficient discharge to the person paying or transferring (Trustee Act 1925 s.14) unless that person acts in bad faith (for example, by purchasing property at a fraudulent undervalue) in which case the transaction is vitiated and a beneficiary or creditor of the estate may have the transaction set aside. If trustees sell land, it is necessary for a receipt to be given by at least two trustees or a trust corporation. However, a sole personal representative may give a good receipt for capital money (Law of Property Act 1925 s.27(2)).

The personal representatives obviously have very wide powers to sell assets and raise money. These powers are necessary since cash is required for a number of purposes in connection with the administration; for example, the payment of funeral, testamentary and administration expenses, inheritance tax, debts and pecuniary legacies. Deciding *which* assets to sell is a complex decision and the personal representatives have to consider a number of matters; for example, which assets have been specifically given to beneficiaries, which assets occur first in the statutory order for property available for payment of debts (see Ch.15, below), which assets will fetch the best price and which assets will attract the least liability to tax for the estate and for the beneficiaries. These matters are discussed more fully in Ch.12.

Power to appropriate

11.08   Section 41 of the Administration of Estates Act 1925 gives the personal representatives power to appropriate any part of the estate in or towards satisfaction of any legacy or interest or share in the estate of the deceased, provided that such an appropriation does not prejudice any specific beneficiary.

> *Example*
> T leaves X a pecuniary legacy of £1,000 and the residue of the estate to Y. The residue includes a clock valued at £750. The personal representatives may let X take the clock in partial satisfaction of the legacy.

An appropriation can only be made by the personal representatives if the appropriate consents are obtained. There are two situations to consider.

(a) *If the beneficiary is absolutely and beneficially entitled to the legacy* the consent required is that of the beneficiary or, if the beneficiary is an infant or mentally incapable of managing his or her own affairs, the consent must be that of the beneficiary's parent or guardian or receiver.

(b) *If the legacy is settled* the consent must be that of the trustees (provided they are not also the personal representatives) or of the person for the time being entitled to the income provided such a person is of full age and capacity. If the personal representatives are the only trustees and there is no person of full age or capacity for the time being entitled to the income then no consents are required. However, in this case the appropriation must be of an investment authorised by law or by the will. This limitation as to the type of property appropriated does not exist in other cases.

The asset is valued at the date of the appropriation, not at the date of death (*Re Collins* (1975)); if the asset is rising in value, therefore, a pecuniary legatee will be anxious that the appropriation be made as quickly as possible. The personal representatives will have to ascertain and fix the value of assets for this purpose as they see fit but must strive to be fair to all beneficiaries. A duly qualified valuer should be employed where necessary. Thus, in *Re Bythway* (1911) it was held that an executrix was not entitled to appropriate to herself shares in an unquoted company at her own valuation.

If the asset is worth more than the legacy to which the beneficiary is entitled it would appear that the power granted by s.41 cannot be exercised since in such a case the asset cannot be said to be appropriated "in or towards satisfaction" of the legacy (*Re Phelps* (1980)). The personal representatives can, however, exercise their power of sale under s.39 of the Administration of Estates Act 1925 to sell the asset to a beneficiary in consideration of a part payment of cash and the satisfaction of the legacy.

Because s.41 requires consent, the Revenue regard appropriation as a "conveyance or transfer on sale" so that any instrument giving effect to the appropriation attracted ad valorem stamp duty (*Jopling v IRC* (1940)). For that reason it was common for wills to provide that the personal representatives need not obtain the consent of a legatee to an appropriation. The Stamp Duty (Exempt Instruments) Regulations 1987 exempt from duty all instruments giving effect to an appropriation in or towards satisfaction of a general legacy executed on or after May 1, 1987. Such instruments must be certified as falling within the appropriate category of the Schedule to the Regulations.

Where a personal representative sells an asset to a beneficiary partly in consideration or satisfaction of a legacy and partly in consideration of an additional cash payment it would appear that ad valorem stamp duty may have to be charged on any instrument effecting the transaction. This is because it cannot be said in such a case there has been an appropriation *in or towards* satisfaction of a legacy. Such a transaction may be regarded as a sale for other tax purposes—for example, capital gains tax (*Passant v Jackson* (1986)).

The Intestates' Estates Act 1952 provides that the surviving spouse or civil partner of a person who dies intestate has a *right* to require the personal representatives to appropriate any dwelling house comprised in the residuary estate in which the spouse or civil partner was resident at the time of the intestate's death in or towards satisfaction of his or her entitlement (see Ch.3). Since the spouse or civil partner can compel the personal representatives to make the appropriation there is no contractual element and ad valorem stamp duty has never been payable. (Sch.1 para.5(2) of the Act gives the spouse or civil partner the right to *require* appropriation even where the house was worth more than the spouse's entitlement, provided equality money is paid).

Power to appoint trustees of a minor's property

When a personal representative vests property in a beneficiary absolutely entitled **11.09** (or person otherwise entitled to assets, for example, a trustee) the personal representative obtains a discharge from liability by means of a receipt signed by the person entitled. In the absence of an express direction to the contrary in the will minors cannot give a good receipt for money or securities nor can their parents, guardian, adult spouse or adult civil partner give one on their behalf (a married minor can give a good receipt for income). It is often said that parents and guardians cannot give a good receipt on behalf of the minor without authority in the will although the Children Act 1989 s.3 defines parental responsibility as including "in particular, the right to receive or recover in his own name, for the benefit of the child, property of whatever description and wherever situated which the child is entitled to receive or recover". Personal representatives who, without authority, pay a child's legacy to a parent, guardian, adult spouse or adult civil partner are in danger of personal liability to account to the minor when the minor attains majority. To overcome this difficulty the Administration of Estates

Act 1925 s.42 gives personal representatives power, where a minor is absolutely entitled to property, to appoint a trust corporation or two or more individuals, not exceeding four (whether or not including one or more of the personal representatives) to be trustees of the property for the minor. The personal representatives may transfer property to the trustees and a receipt signed by those trustees will be a good discharge to the personal representatives. However, the power is not available where the minor merely has a contingent interest. In the absence of express authority the personal representatives will either have to continue holding the property until the minor reaches majority or use one of the alternatives set out in Ch.18 (appropriation, payment into court).

Power to postpone distribution

11.10   Section 44 of the Administration of Estates Act 1925 provides that the personal representatives are not bound to distribute the estate of the deceased before the expiration of one year from death. This does not affect their duty to pay debts with due diligence and simply means that a beneficiary cannot insist on earlier payment of a legacy, even if a testator directed payment within a short period after the death. In a case where such a direction for payment is included in the will a pecuniary or general legatee is merely entitled to interest from the date fixed for payment. (There are also cases where there is a right to interest from the date of death—see Ch.16.) The personal representatives cannot necessarily be compelled to pay a legacy even after the 12-month period has expired although they may thereafter be required to explain the delay and all pecuniary and general legatees (other than contingent ones) will thereafter be entitled to interest at the basic rate payable for the relevant time on funds in court or such other rate as the court shall direct (see para.16.55, below).

Power to insure

11.11   The statutory power of insurance is contained in s.19 of the Trustee Act 1925 as substituted by s.34 of the Trustee Act 2000. The substituted section gives a much wider power to personal representatives than did the original s.19. Personal representatives now have power to insure any property in the estate against risks of loss or damage due to any event and power to pay the premiums out of the estate. The duty of care under s.1 of the Trustee Act 2000 applies to the "exercise of the power to insure".

Power to run a business

11.12   A deceased person may have run a business either as a sole trader, a partner or through the medium of a limited company. The personal representatives of such a person must consider their position in relation to the business and determine what powers and duties, if any, they have.

Sole traders

Where the will is silent the personal representatives have implied power to **11.13**
continue the business *for the purpose of realisation only*, that is to enable it to be
sold as a going concern. Such a period will not usually exceed one year (*Re
Crowther* (1895)). It is preferable to give them express power to continue the
business so long as they see fit (thus avoiding the possibility of a forced sale in
a poor market).

Unless the will makes express provision the personal representatives will only
have authority to use those assets used in the business at the date of the
deceased's death. It may be desirable to give them power to use other assets of
the estate if they see fit.

When the personal representatives have authority to carry on a business they
are personally liable for any debts they incur. However, they are entitled to an
indemnity from the estate. If the business is being carried on for the purpose of
realisation only the right of indemnity may be exercised in priority to all
creditors of the deceased and beneficiaries. If the business is being carried on
under authority given by the will the right of indemnity may be exercised in
priority to beneficiaries but not in priority to creditors of the deceased. The
reason for this is that the beneficiaries are bound by the terms of the will but the
creditors of the deceased are not (unless a creditor has expressly assented to the
carrying on of the business). In this case the indemnity extends only to assets
which the will authorised them to use.

Partnerships and limited companies

Where a partner or shareholder in a limited company dies the personal repre- **11.14**
sentatives of the deceased normally have no power to intervene in the management of the business. Death dissolves a partnership unless, as is usually the case,
the partnership agreement provides otherwise.

A company is a legal person which continues to exist despite the death of
shareholders or directors. In the case of a "one man" company there may,
however, be difficulties in directing its activities once the major shareholder/
director dies.

In either case the personal representatives will be mainly concerned with
ascertaining the beneficial entitlement to the deceased's interest in the business
and, if appropriate, arranging a sale of the interest. It is important that personal
representatives should be aware that a partnership agreement frequently contains
provisions relating to death of partners. For example, many agreements provide
for automatic accruer of a deceased's share of goodwill and/or for the exercise by
surviving partners of an option to purchase the deceased's share in the capital
assets. Similarly the Articles of Association of a company or an agreement
between the shareholders may give other shareholders pre-emption rights or
options to purchase a deceased shareholder's shares. Personal representatives
should discover whether or not such rights exist and should not look only at the
deceased's will.

Power to maintain minors

11.15 Section 31 of the Trustee Act gives trustees (and personal representatives) a power to apply available income for the maintenance, education or benefit of minor beneficiaries.

What happens to income—the general rule

11.16 Where a testator directs that property is to be held on trust for beneficiaries (for example, "to A if A becomes a solicitor"), the question arises of what happens to any income produced by the property after death. If the testator has left express directions, they must be carried out. If not, there are general rules (see Ch.16). We can summarise these rules by saying that most testamentary gifts carry with them the right to intermediate income. This means that income produced by the property is added to capital and devolves with it, so that whoever becomes entitled to the capital also becomes entitled to the intermediate income. Certain gifts do not carry with them the right to intermediate income; the most common example of such a gift is a contingent pecuniary legacy (apart from certain exceptional contingent pecuniary legacies dealt with in Ch.16). A contingent pecuniary legatee is entitled to nothing but the capital (unless there is a delay in payment after the contingency has been fulfilled, in which case the legatee becomes entitled to interest). In such a case if the legacy fund is invested any interest produced is paid to the residuary beneficiary or, if there is none, to the person entitled on intestacy.

The effect of s.31 of the Trustee Act

11.17 Section 31 of the Trustee Act provides that where property is held for a minor beneficiary who is unmarried and not a civil partner and the gift carries with it the right to intermediate income the trustees have a discretion as to what they do with that income, whether the minor's interest is vested or contingent. The trustees are entitled under s.31 to choose to apply the income for the main-tenance, education and benefit of the minor but to the extent that they do not, they must accumulate it. In exercising this discretion they are directed to consider the age and requirements of the minor, the circumstances of the case generally and in particular what other income, if any, is applicable for the same purposes. If they have notice that more than one trust fund is available for those purposes the trustees must so far as is practicable, unless the entire income of the funds is applied or the court otherwise directs, apply only a proportionate part of each trust fund. Accumulated income may be applied during the minority of the beneficiary as if it were income of the current year.

Example

T makes two settlements. T gives his share holding in X Co. to trustees to hold for A if A reaches 25 and his share holding in Y Co. to trustees to hold for B for life, remainder to C. At T's death both A and B are minors. A has a contingent interest, B has a vested interest. The trustees may choose to apply the income from the respective shares for the benefit of A and B but in so far as they do not apply it, they must accumulate it.

Section 31(1) provides that if the minor reaches 18 and still has an interest which is contingent the discretion of the trustees ceases and from that date they *must* pay the income to the beneficiary until the contingency is fulfilled or the gift fails. In the above example, therefore, as soon as A reaches 18 the trustees must pay current income to A until A reaches 25 or dies without fulfilling the contingency. B will be entitled to current income at 18 and until death.

Once the minor reaches 18 (or marries or enters a civil partnership earlier) the trustees must consider what is to happen to income which has been accumulated. Section 31(2) provides that with one exception (dealt with below) such accumulations are to be added to capital and will devolve with it. Thus, if a gift is contingent on reaching 21 the beneficiary will be entitled to both capital and accumulations if they reach 21 but if they do not they will both pass to the person entitled in default.

The exceptional case where accumulations do not devolve with capital is that of a minor with a life interest. Section 31(2) provides that *if* such a minor reaches 18 he or she is entitled to any income that has been accumulated. If he or she fails to reach 18 (or marry or enters a civil partnership earlier), the accumulations will devolve with the capital. The effect is that a minor with a life interest has no right to receive income until reaching 18 (or marries or enters a civil partnership earlier); he or she can neither insist on receiving income as it arises nor can he or she be certain of receiving the accumulations.

Example

T gives his shareholding in Y Co to trustees to hold for A for life remainder to B. A is aged six at the time the settlement comes into effect. Until A reaches 18 the trustees must accumulate the income to the extent that they do not choose to apply it for the benefit of A. If A dies before reaching 18 the accumulated income (together with the shares in Y Co.) will pass to B. If A reaches 18 the trustees must pay the accumulated income to A.

Express clause varying s.31

A professionally drawn will may extend the statutory power of maintenance to **11.18** give the trustees an unfettered discretion (so that, for example, they need not consider other sources of income available to the minor).

Where a gift is contingent on reaching an age greater than 18 (for example, 25) the person drafting the will should consider removing the right to income at 18. One reason for removing the right is that if a beneficiary becomes entitled to income at 18 within two years of the death of the deceased, the entitlement will be read back into the will under IHTA s.144 and will create an immediate post-death interest. If a beneficiary with an immediate post-death interest dies aged between 18 and 25 the value of the trust property will be included in the estate when calculating inheritance tax payable even though the beneficiary had no right to capital (see Ch.7). Another reason for considering removal of the right to income at 18 is that hold-over relief for CGT will not be available when the beneficiary becomes absolutely entitled to capital at 25. If the settlement were to continue until 25 without conversion into an immediate post-death interest then hold-over relief would be available.

Power to advance capital

11.19   Section 32 of the Trustee Act provides that trustees (and personal representatives) have an absolute discretion to apply capital for the advancement or benefit of any person who has either a vested or contingent interest in capital. Property may be advanced under this section to new trustees to be held upon new trusts containing powers and discretions not contemplated by the original instrument.

If a beneficiary with a contingent interest dies after receiving an advance and without fulfilling the contingency the trustees have no right to recover property from the estate of the deceased beneficiary. The section does not apply to land or capital money under a Settled Land Act settlement (it does, however, apply to the proceeds of sale of land held upon trust for sale).

There are three limitations on the statutory power:

(a) The trustees may only advance up to one-half of the beneficiary's vested or presumptive share. (For example, if a settlor gives a trust fund of £30,000 to be divided amongst X, Y and Z provided they reach 25, each has a presumptive share of £10,000. The trustees may advance up to half of £10,000 to each or any of them.) If an advance is made to a person who dies without fulfilling the contingency, the trustees have no right to recover the advance from that person's estate.

(b) Any advance made must be brought into account when the beneficiary becomes absolutely entitled.

(c) Any person with a prior interest (e.g. the right to receive income from the trust property) must consent to the advance.

It is common for a will to include an express clause removing the three limitations and to leave the trustees to exercise an unfettered discretion.

Power to delegate—Trustee Act 2000

11.20   The power of personal representatives to delegate is now contained in Pt IV (ss.11–27) of the Trustee Act 2000. Under s.11 personal representatives may delegate any or all of their "delegable functions" to an agent. The delegable functions are defined as any functions except: decisions as to how or whether assets should be distributed, decisions as to whether fees or payments due should be made out of income or capital of the trust fund, exercise of powers under other enactments or under the will (which must be dealt with under those enactments or in accordance with the terms of the will), the appointment of nominees and custodians (ss.16 and 17, see below). The power to delegate is further restricted in the case of charitable trusts.

More than one agent may be appointed (s.12(2)) but if two or more agents are to exercise the same function they must do so jointly. A personal representative may be appointed as agent but a beneficiary may not be (s.12(1) and (3)). The terms on which the agent is appointed are set by the personal representatives and may include provision for remuneration (s.14(1)). Sub-delegation by the agent, any restriction on the agent's liability and any permission for the agent to act where a conflict of interest might arise are only permitted if "reasonably necessary" (s.14(2) and (3)).

Section 15 imposes special restrictions on the appointment of agents in the case of asset management. Asset management is defined as the investment of assets, and the acquisition and disposal of property (s.15(5)). In these cases the agreement authorising the exercise of the functions must be in writing or evidenced in writing (s.15(1)). The personal representatives must supply the agent with a policy statement giving guidance as to how the asset management functions should be exercised (s.15(2)(a)) and the agreement must require the agent to comply with the policy statement or any replacement of it (s.15(2)(b)).

Section 16 contains provisions which allow personal representatives to appoint nominees to hold property. This power enables personal representatives, for example, to vest shares in a nominee to facilitate management of the investments. Section 17 enables personal representatives to appoint "custodians" to undertake the safe custody of assets, documents or records. A nominee or custodian must be carrying on business as such for these appointments to be made (unless it is a body corporate controlled by the personal representatives).

Section 22 requires personal representatives to keep under review the appointments of agents nominees or custodians and the terms under which they act. Provided that the personal representatives comply with the duty of care in appointing and reviewing agents, nominees and custodians they are not liable for any acts or defaults of the agents nominees or custodians. They would, of course, be liable for their own act in making the appointment or in deciding the terms of appointment if they were negligent in doing so.

In drafting a will the implication of these rules and the restrictions contained in the statutory provisions should be considered. In some cases it may be appropriate to provide for the delegation of all powers of personal representatives not just the "delegable functions" as defined by the Act. It may also be appropriate to dispense with the need for a policy statement, to allow sub-delegation by the agent, restriction on the agent's liability and permission for the agent to act where a conflict of interest might arise whether or not "reasonably necessary". In particular it may be appropriate to allow delegation to a beneficiary.

Indemnity

Section 31 of the Trustee Act 2000 provides that personal representatives are **11.21** entitled to reimbursement from the estate for expenses properly incurred. Similarly, under s.32, they are entitled to reimburse agents nominees and custodians.

Powers of investment

11.22   Part II (ss.3–7) of the Trustee Act 2000 simplifies and liberalises the law relating to investment by personal representatives. Section 3(1) provides that a personal representative "may make any kind of investment that he could make if he were absolutely entitled to the assets" of the estate. This is called the "the general power of investment". It does not include a power to invest in land (but s.8 does contain such a power—see below and loans secured on land are permitted under s.3). In exercising the general power of investment or any other power of investment (such as one provided in the will) personal representatives must, under s.4, have regard to "standard investment criteria". These criteria are the suitability to the estate of the kind of investment chosen and the need for diversification of investments in so far as is appropriate to the circumstances of the estate.

Under s.5 personal representatives must take advice in making and reviewing investments. The advice must be:

> "the advice of a person who is reasonably believed by the [personal representative] to be qualified to give it by his ability in and practical experience of financial and other matters relating to the proposed investment." (s.5(4))

However, under s.5(3) advice need not be taken if the personal representatives "reasonably conclude that in all the circumstances it is unnecessary or inappropriate to do so".

These provisions apply to wills made before as well as after the commencement of the Act on February 1, 2001. The power to invest may be restricted in the will. The overall effect of these provisions is to free personal representatives from the restrictions formerly imposed on them by the Trustee Investment Act 1961. However, the potential liability for negligence is increased where more speculative investments are chosen. It is arguable that a failure to consider making investments could also be a failure to have regard to the "standard investment criteria" and so could also give rise to a claim for negligence. However, it is also arguable that a failure to consider making investments is not an exercise of a power at all and so outside the scope of Pt II altogether.

Power to purchase land

11.23   Section 8 of the Trustee Act 2000 gives personal representatives the power to buy land in the UK (freehold or leasehold) as an investment, for occupation by a beneficiary or for any other reason. The power can be restricted by the will. The general duty of care applies to the exercise of the power.

4. ADMINISTRATIVE POWERS GRANTED BY WILL

11.24   As indicated in the previous section it is common to extend many of the statutory powers of trustees and personal representatives. It is also common to confer on them certain additional powers such as the power to make loans to beneficiaries or to advance capital to a surviving spouse to whom a life interest has been given. These matters are dealt with more fully in Ch.22.

5. RIGHTS OF BENEFICIARIES DURING THE ADMINISTRATION

As we have seen it is the function of the personal representatives to administer **11.25** the deceased's estate by collecting the assets, paying off the debts and liabilities and distributing the estate to the beneficiaries under the will or the intestacy rules. The beneficiaries may wish to know what rights they have against the personal representatives during the administration period.

The right to compel due administration

Beneficiaries have no equitable interest in assets

The assets of the deceased vest in the personal representatives and those assets **11.26** come to the personal representatives "in full ownership without distinction between legal and equitable interests" (*Commissioner of Stamp Duties (Queensland) v Livingston* (1965)). In view of this, until the administration of the estate is complete, the beneficiary, whether under a will or intestacy, can have neither a legal nor an equitable interest in the deceased's assets (*Dr Barnardo's Homes National Incorporated Association v Commissioners for Special Purposes of the Income Tax Acts* (1921)). A personal representative cannot be regarded as holding the assets of the estate on trust for the beneficiaries since, until the administration has been completed, it is impossible to say which assets will be available to the beneficiaries and which will have to be used to pay debts and administration expenses. A trust can only exist where there are "specific subjects identifiable as the trust fund" (*Commissioner of Stamp Duties (Queensland) v Livingston*, above). The effect of this is that the beneficiaries cannot claim the assets until the administration has been completed because until then the beneficiaries cannot be certain of entitlement to any assets. They cannot object simply because the personal representatives sell, or intend to sell, an asset given to them in the will. They can only object if the asset should not be sold because, for example, there is no need to sell the asset in the circumstances.

The beneficiaries' chose in action

Although the beneficiaries have no legal or equitable interest in the deceased's **11.27** assets, they do have a chose in action; that is a right to ensure that the deceased's estate is properly administered. The chose in action can be transmitted to another person, as is illustrated by the case of *Re Leigh's Will Trusts* (1970). In this case the testatrix left "all shares which I hold and any other interest . . . which I may have" in a named company. She did not hold any shares in that company but at the date of her death she was the sole beneficiary of her husband's estate which included shares in that company. It was held that the gift took effect as a gift of her chose in action in her husband's estate.

The position of specific legatees

11.28 While the general rule is that beneficiaries acquire merely a chose in action, in *I.R.C. v Hawley* (1928) it was suggested that a specific legatee takes an equitable interest in the property given under the terms of the will from the date of death, even though the property may be used to discharge the debts and liabilities of the estate by the personal representatives in whom the legal estate will vest.

However, this decision is inconsistent with the personal representatives receiving both the legal and equitable interests, as suggested in *Commissioner of Stamp Duties (Queensland) v Livingston* above. In *Re Hayes' Will Trusts* (1971) Ungoed-Thomas J. said "no legatee, devisee or next of kin has any beneficial interest in the assets being administered". In view of this conflict it seems likely that even a specific legatee will have only a chose in action to ensure due administration.

General administration actions

11.29 Where difficulties arise while the estate being administered, whether because of a problem which the personal representatives have encountered or a dispute arising over the conduct of the administration (for example, where the beneficiaries allege that the personal representatives have committed a *devastavit*) an application can be made to the court to have the difficulty resolved. These proceedings which are intended to ensure that the administration is conducted properly are called "administration proceedings". There are two types of administration proceedings:

(a) actions for general administration of the whole or part of the estate by the court. If the court makes such an order the personal representatives cannot exercise their powers to sell or distribute the assets without the consent of the court. The order stops time running under the Limitation Act for creditors' claims; or

(b) actions for specific relief, such as the determination of one specific problem.

Administration proceedings are not necessarily the result of any wrongdoing. The court's help may be sought by the personal representatives themselves if they are anxious about a particular point; this is particularly likely in the case of an action for specific relief and this is, therefore, dealt with in Ch.14 which is concerned with protection of personal representatives. Alternatively, the beneficiaries may seek the help of the court; this is more likely in the case of a general administration action and, therefore, the rest of this section deals with such actions.

Jurisdiction

The Chancery Division of the High Court has jurisdiction in these matters but the **11.30** following also have jurisdiction:

(a) the county court if the estate does not exceed in amount or value the county court limit (at present £30,000), and

(b) the bankruptcy court if the estate is insolvent.

The parties

The action can be commenced by any personal representative, any beneficiary **11.31** under the will or intestacy or any creditor. All the personal representatives must be made parties to any action; those who consent are made claimants and those who do not are made defendants CPR, 63.

The order for administration

If the whole estate is to be administered under the court's direction the court can **11.32** order that an account be taken of:

(a) property that forms part of the residue of the estate which has come into the possession, either of the personal representatives or of some other person by the order or for the use of the personal representatives;

(b) the deceased's debts and funeral and testamentary expenses. If the deceased died more than six years before the date of the order the court can order that an enquiry be made as to whether any such liability of the deceased remains outstanding;

(c) legacies and annuities; and

(d) any parts of the deceased's estate that have not yet been collected or distributed after enquiries have been made and any charges attaching to such property have been ascertained.

If an instance of wilful default is established against the personal representative, the account may be ordered on the footing of wilful default, that is that the personal representatives account for property which would have come into their possession but for their wilful default.

Once accounts and enquiries have been taken and made, the court will order distribution to the beneficiaries.

As an alternative to making a general order the court can order that:

(a) specific accounts and inquiries be taken and made to deal with particular problems that have arisen; or

(b) the personal representative should produce particular accounts within a stated period of time.

Costs

11.33 The personal representatives are entitled to have their costs paid from the assets of the estate, unless they have acted unreasonably or unless the result of such an order would be to diminish the estate to such an extent that claimants to it would be unfairly prejudiced (*Evans v Evans*). The costs of other parties are in the court's discretion.

Appointing a judicial trustee

11.34 Where the personal representatives cannot administer the estate and are unwilling to incur the expense of an administration action they (or a beneficiary) can apply for a judicial trustee to be appointed. The trustee will be appointed to act either alone or with others and can be appointed to replace the existing personal representatives. Since they are officers of the court, once appointed, they do not need the court's consent to exercise their powers.

Substitution or removal of personal representative

11.35 The High Court has a discretionary power under s.50 of the Administration of Justice Act 1985 on an application made by a beneficiary of an estate (or by or on behalf of a personal representative):

(a) to appoint a substitute to act in place of an existing personal representative; or

(b) where there are two or more existing personal representatives to terminate the appointment of one or more, but not all, of these persons.

6. OTHER REMEDIES OF BENEFICIARIES

Personal action against personal representatives

11.36 When a personal representative accepts office he or she accept the duties of the office. A failure to carry out those duties properly is a *devastavit* for which the personal representative will be personally liable to the disappointed beneficiaries (or next of kin). The court may, however, grant relief either wholly or partly from personal liability to a personal representative for a breach of trust where it appears that a personal representative acted honestly and reasonably and ought fairly to be excused (Trustee Act 1925 s.61).

The right to trace

A beneficiary (or next-of-kin or creditor) has the right to trace and recover **11.37**
property of the estate (or property representing property of the estate) from the
personal representative or from any recipient of it other than a bona fide
purchaser for value (or person deriving title from such a purchaser). The right to
trace is lost where the property of the estate has been dissipated or where tracing
would produce an inequitable result.

> *Example*
>
> X, a personal representative, takes £1,000 belonging to an estate he is administering
> and spends it on a car which he gives to Y. The beneficiaries can recover the car from
> Y. If Y sells the car for £900 to Z, a bona fide purchaser for value, the beneficiaries
> have no right to trace the car into the hands of Z. They can, however, recover the
> £900 from Y. If Y dissipates the £900 by spending it on a holiday the right to trace
> is lost.

In some cases a beneficiary may prefer to rely on tracing rather than on
bringing a personal action against the personal representatives (for example,
where they are anxious to recover a particular asset rather than its value). In some
cases the personal remedy may be valueless (for example, where the personal
representative is bankrupt) so that tracing may be the only effective remedy.

A full discussion of the law on tracing is beyond the scope of this book and the
reader is referred to any standard equity textbook.

A personal action against recipients of assets of the estate

Where all the other remedies of a beneficiary, next-of-kin or creditor have been **11.38**
exhausted a personal action may be brought against a person who has wrongly
received assets of the estate. This was established by the judgment of the House
of Lords in *Ministry of Health v Simpson* (1951). In this case, personal representatives had paid large sums of money to various charities in the mistaken
belief that they were entitled to do so under the terms of the will. The next-of-kin
of the deceased had established that the personal representatives were not so
entitled and had exhausted their personal remedies against the personal representatives. They had been able to trace some of the payments into the hands of
the charities and to recover them. However, some of the charities had dissipated
the money with the result that the right to trace was lost. It was held that the next-
of-kin were able to bring an action against the recipients personally to recover an
amount equal to that which had been wrongly paid to them.

Chapter Twelve

PRACTICAL CONSIDERATIONS DURING ADMINISTRATION

1. Introduction

In previous chapters we have studied the legal rules that are relevant to the **12.01** administration of an estate. When applying the legal rules the circumstances of the estate and of the beneficiaries must be borne in mind. In this chapter we will consider some of the problems which can arise.

2. Raising Money to Pay Debts and Inheritance Tax

Introduction

Before the personal representatives can obtain a grant of representation they will **12.02** need to pay any inheritance tax that is due. However, the problem which faces them is that in order to get access to money in the deceased's bank or building society or to raise money by selling assets they will normally need the grant. They will therefore need to find a way of raising money to pay the tax which does not require a grant of representation.

Borrow money from a bank

One of the most common methods of raising money is to borrow it from a bank. **12.03** The bank may be the deceased's bank or the personal representatives may prefer to approach their own bank.

Banks normally insist on an undertaking being given by the personal representatives to the effect that they will account to the bank from the first realised assets of the estate. If the personal representatives have appointed solicitors to act for them, the bank may require a further undertaking to be given by the solicitors.

In this case the solicitor should obtain the personal representatives' irrevocable authority to give an undertaking.

The disadvantage of borrowing from a bank is that the loan will carry interest. Therefore, irrespective of any undertaking that has been given, the loan should be outstanding for as short a time as possible. It is advisable to arrange the loan immediately before the application for the grant is to be made and, once the grant has been obtained, to use it to realise sufficient assets to repay the debt quickly.

The Income Tax Act 2007 ss.383 and 403 provides that the personal representatives may for the purposes of calculating income tax liability deduct interest paid as a charge on their income to the extent that it is paid on a loan to meet an inheritance tax liability on the delivery of the Inheritance Tax Account, in respect of personal property to which the deceased was beneficially entitled immediately before death and which vests in the personal representatives (or would do so if the property were situated in the UK). Even if the loan satisfies this requirement, the interest is only deductible to the extent that it is paid in respect of a period ending within one year from the making of the loan. Furthermore, the personal representatives must open a separate loan account, and not merely allow the deceased's bank account to become overdrawn. The liability to pay interest may make this method unattractive to personal representatives and to beneficiaries.

Banks releasing funds of the deceased

12.04   An interesting article in *The Law Society's Gazette*,[1] revealed differences in the attitudes of the major banks to releasing funds of the deceased held by the bank. It is clearly always worth contacting the deceased's bank to find out whether they will release funds for this purpose.

Direct payment scheme

12.05   With effect from March 31, 2003 the Revenue agreed a scheme with the British Banker's Association and the Building Societies Association whereby personal representatives can draw on money held in the deceased's accounts to pay inheritance tax due on delivery of IHT 400. The scheme is voluntary so personal representatives should check whether the particular bank or building society is part of the scheme. The procedure is set out in the Guidance Notes to Form IHT423.

Personal representatives must obtain a reference number for the deceased using Form IHT422 before sending the IHT 400. They must complete and sign a separate Form IHT423 for each bank or building society from which they wish to transfer money. They send the completed IHT423 to the relevant institution which will then transfer the sum requested to HMRC. Once HMRC receives notice of the payment it will link the payment to IHT Form 400 and return Form IHT421 to the personal representatives. The whole process will take longer than

---

[1] September 14, 1994.

paying by cheque. However, this should be offset by the saving in time and cost of arranging a loan.

National savings products and british government stock proceeds paid direct to the revenue

Where an estate includes National Savings investments or British Government **12.06** stock on the Bank of England register (for example War Loan, Treasury Stock and Exchequer Stock), it is possible to arrange for the payment of IHT from such products direct to the Revenue without the need to encash them. However, the Revenue itself warns that this process may take up to four weeks. The procedure should, therefore, not be used in cases where a grant is needed urgently.

The first step is to write to the appropriate National Savings Department or, in the case of Government Stock, to the Registrar of British Government Stock (Computershare Investors Services PLC) and stating:

- The value of the deceased's asset at the date of death.
- The National Savings Bank or Bank of England Reference.

The solicitor should send those letters to the Pre-Grant Section of Capital Taxes together with a letter detailing the investments to be used, a completed Inheritance Tax Account and a Form IHT421.

If the amount transferred is sufficient to cover the tax due, HMRC will receipt Form IHT421 and return it so that the solicitor can apply for a grant. If any additional tax is due after the transfer of funds, HMRC will give information as to the amount of the shortfall.

Borrow from a beneficiary

Beneficiaries may object to the personal representatives borrowing money from **12.07** banks to meet the inheritance tax liability since the interest paid will reduce the income from the estate available to them. In many cases, the beneficiaries have to accept the payment as unavoidable but it may be possible to borrow money from a beneficiary interest-free.

Since the loan will facilitate the administration, beneficiaries will often be amenable to such a suggestion, provided they have the money available. This may come from their own resources or from the proceeds of an insurance policy taken out by the deceased and payable direct to the beneficiary. Such a policy may be a Married Women's Property Act 1882 s.11 policy or one written in trust for a particular person. In such cases the insurance company will simply require proof of death, in the form of a death certificate and will not require production of a grant.

If the deceased was a member of a pension scheme and a death in service lump sum is paid by the trustees to a beneficiary on the death, the beneficiary may be willing to use such a sum to make an interest-free loan.

Where easily realisable property (such as money in a building society account) was held jointly with the deceased, the survivor may be willing to lend to the personal representatives out of such property. The beneficiary will be reimbursed from the assets of the estate once the grant has been obtained.

Sale of assets

12.08 An executor's authority derives from the will, whereas an administrator's authority derives from the grant. An executor, therefore, has power to sell assets before a grant of representation is made whereas an administrator has no such power. However, an executor may find that it is, in fact, difficult to sell some types of assets since a prospective purchaser may insist on seeing the grant in order to confirm that the person claiming to be the executor is, in fact, the person entitled to the grant. Moreover, while the executors may be able to sell items of moveable personal property such as clothes, paintings and furniture, such items may not raise sufficient funds. Land cannot be sold without the grant because the purchaser will want to examine the original grant and endorse a memorandum of the sale on the original grant.

Assets handed direct to HMRC

12.09 Generally, inheritance tax is required to be paid by cheque. However, the Revenue has a discretion to accept assets in total, or partial, satisfaction of the tax liability on an estate (IHTA 1984 s.230).

To be acceptable, land must have some kind of amenity value and the public must be able to enjoy reasonable access. Other items which the Secretary of State is satisfied are pre-eminent for their national, scientific, historic or artistic interest are also acceptable.

Sums payable without a grant

Small payments

12.10 Various provisions permit small sums to be paid or transferred on death without the need to produce a grant of representation. In all cases this power is discretionary, not obligatory and orders made under the Administration of Estates (Small Payments) Act 1965 place an upper limit on these payments of £5,000. If the sum due to the deceased is in excess of £5,000 the grant is needed for the *whole amount,* not just the excess over £5,000.

Subject to the £5,000 limit the payment can be made to the person appearing to be entitled to the grant or to be beneficially entitled to the sums in respect of inter alia:

(a) Money held in the National Savings Bank, Trustee Savings Bank, Savings Certificates or Premium Bonds. It should, however, be noted that despite these rules the Director of Savings will, in practice, require sight of a grant if the deceased held more than £5,000 *in total* in the National Savings Bank, Savings Certificates and Premium Bonds. In certain circumstances, the Director of Savings must obtain a statement from the Revenue to the effect that either no inheritance tax is payable or that it has been paid, before they will make the payment without the production of the grant.

(b) Moneys payable on the death of a member of a trade union, an industrial or provident society or a friendly society.

(c) Arrears of salary, wages or superannuation on benefits due to employees of government departments.

(d) Police and firemens' pensions, Army and Air Force pensions.

Schedule 7 para.1 of the Building Societies Act 1986 contains corresponding provisions in respect of moneys invested in a building society. These small payments may be a useful source of funds to pay inheritance tax for personal representatives and may be preferable to seeking loans from beneficiaries.

3. SALE OF ASSETS—WHICH TO SELL?

Introduction

When the personal representatives have to sell assets whether to raise money to **12.11** pay inheritance tax or in the course of administering the estate after the grant has been obtained, they must bear in mind a number of considerations:

(a) the terms of the will,

(b) the wishes of the beneficiaries, and

(c) the tax consequences of selling individual items.

The terms of the will and the wishes of the beneficiaries

When deciding which assets to sell first, the personal representatives must have **12.12** due regard to the statutory order for payment of debts (see Ch.16). Should the personal representatives use the wrong items to satisfy the debts then "marshalling" may be necessary so that the appropriate beneficiary bears the burden of the debt. Therefore, if the will gives specific items of property to beneficiaries these items should not be considered for sale until the other assets in the estate have been exhausted.

When the personal representatives are choosing which assets to sell, the wishes and needs of the beneficiaries should be considered. For example, if the residuary beneficiary wants a valuable antique which has not been specifically dealt with in the will, their wishes should be respected if at all possible.

Future destination of property

12.13   If the terms of the will or the intestacy rules create a trust, the personal representatives should ensure that any property retained is suitable in view of the nature of the trust. The personal representatives should consider the needs of the beneficiaries when deciding whether to retain high income as opposed to high capital growth investments.

The sale of shares

12.14   The sale of shares in a quoted company should cause few problems but if the shares are in an unquoted company it may be less easy to find a market for the shares. In this circumstance, the personal representatives could seek a buyer among the other members of the company. The company itself may be willing to buy the shares under the provisions of ss.690ff of the Companies Act 2006. When a payment is made by the company in these circumstances to the deceased member's personal representatives any profit made on the sale may attract income tax liability (the details of these rules are beyond the scope of this book.)

Clearly, where unquoted shares are concerned, the personal representatives must take professional advice as to the price they should obtain for the shares. They should also be aware of the fact that the company's Articles of Association may contain pre-emption rights.

Tax considerations—inheritance tax

12.15   The sale of assets does not normally affect the amount of inheritance tax payable. However, IHTA 1984 ss.178–198 contains provisions giving relief where certain assets are sold for less than their market value at the date of death.

Relief for sales of shares at a loss

12.16   If "qualifying investments" are sold by the "appropriate person" within 12 months of the death at less than their market value at the date of death, the sale price can be substituted for the market value at the date of death. Depending on the size of the death estate and the deceased's cumulative total, this may lead to a repayment of tax.

"Qualifying investments" are shares and securities which are quoted at the date of death, on a recognised stock exchange or the unlisted securities market and units in authorised unit trusts (IHTA 1984 s.178(1) and Finance Act 1987 s.272). The relief also applies to any such investments held in a settlement of which the deceased was a life tenant.

The "appropriate person" is defined in s.178(1) as "the person liable for tax attributable to the value of those investments or, if there is more than one such person, and one of them is in fact paying the tax, that person". In view of the wording of the definition, it is important that the sale be made by the person who has paid the tax (usually the personal representatives or trustees) if the relief is to be available. For example, if the personal representatives had paid the inheritance tax on quoted shares, they must be the ones to sell those shares. The relief would not be available if the shares were vested in a specific legatee even if the legatee sold the shares at a loss within 12 months.

The loss is calculated by deducting the sale price from the market value of the shares at death. However, the Revenue have the power to substitute the best consideration which could reasonably have been obtained (s.179(1)(b)). Expenses incurred as a result of the sale, such as stockbrokers commission and stamp duty, cannot be used to increase the loss.

Example

On X's death he had made chargeable transfers up to the limit of his nil rate band and had a death estate of £500,000 including shares in a public quoted company worth £3,000. Inheritance tax was paid on the estate. If X's personal representatives sell the holding for £2,500 within 12 months of the death, they can claim relief and so receive a rebate equal to the tax paid on the £500 reduction in value.

If a number of sales of qualifying investments are made within the 12-month period the sale proceeds of all transactions must be aggregated to discover the overall gain or loss. If, overall, a loss has arisen the claim for the relief may be made. If, overall, a gain has been made the Revenue cannot demand extra inheritance tax but no loss relief can be claimed on the particular shares sold at a loss.

Example

The figures for X's estate are the same as for the previous example save that X held shares in three separate public companies, each holding being worth £1,000 at his death. If X's personal representatives sell the three holdings for £500, £750 and £1,250 respectively within 12 months of the death, they must aggregate the three sale prices to calculate the overall loss of £500. It is *not* possible to take account only of the first two sales.

The relief is available whenever a sale is made by the appropriate person within the specified period but, if the sale proceeds are reinvested by the appropriate person in other qualifying investments within two months of the last such sale, the loss relief available will be reduced or extinguished (s.180(1)). This is because the purpose of the reliefs is to give assistance where shares are sold to raise money to pay inheritance tax or other debts. If the sale is to improve the estate's portfolio of investments, the relief will not be available to the personal representatives.

If the sale is to be eligible for the relief, it must occur within 12 months of the death. The operative date is the sale date unless there was a contract to sell in which case, the contract date determines whether the sale qualifies for relief.

A problem existed for personal representatives who found themselves at the end of the 12-month period from death holding shares where the quotation had been suspended. Clearly the personal representatives could not sell the shares and, therefore, no relief was available. However, the Finance Act 1993 s.199 inserted a new s.186B into the IHTA providing that the shares can be treated as sold immediately before the end of the 12-month period for their value at the time.

If qualifying investments held by the appropriate person are cancelled within the period of 12 months from death without being replaced by other shares or securities, they are to be treated as sold by the appropriate person for nominal consideration of £1 (IHTA s.186A).

The inter-relation of inheritance tax loss relief on shares and capital gains tax

12.17   When sales which can potentially give rise to claims within para.12.16 take place, the personal representatives will realise an allowable loss for capital gains tax purposes. If the election for the inheritance tax relief is claimed, however, the sale price becomes the personal representatives' acquisition value for capital gains tax (IHTA 1984 s.187 and TCGA 1992 s.274). The personal representatives will then be treated for capital gains tax purposes as selling for the same amount as the acquisition value and will not be able to claim a capital gains tax loss other than for costs of disposal.

Inheritance tax is chargeable at 40 per cent on the value of the portion of an *estate* exceeding the nil rate band (after cumulation). Since capital gains tax is payable by personal representatives at 28 per cent of the chargeable *gain*, it will always be preferable to claim inheritance tax loss relief unless the amount of the capital gains tax loss is more than the amount by which the nil rate band is exceeded and there are (or are likely to be) future gains against which the loss can be set in excess of any exemption or relief the personal representatives can claim.

Relief for sales of land at a loss

12.18   If the deceased was entitled to an interest in land at the time of death and that interest is sold for less than the market value at death, the personal representatives can claim to have the sale price substituted for the market value at death, provided the sale takes place within four years of death, the operative date being the date of the contract for sale (ss.190–198 of the IHTA 1984). This can lead to a rebate in the way illustrated in para.12.16, above.

As with sales of quoted shares the sale must be by "the appropriate person" which has the same meaning as in para.12.16, above. Furthermore s.196 prevents the claim being made where the sale is to one of the beneficiaries (or to certain persons closely connected to a beneficiary). Section 191 provides that small decreases in value are ignored. Thus, the relief is not available if the reduction in the value of the interest is less than either £1,000 or 5 per cent of its value on death, whichever is the lesser.

The Revenue are given the power to substitute the best consideration that could reasonably have been obtained on the sale if this is higher than the sale price, thereby preventing the personal representatives artificially creating or increasing the loss.

Sections 192 to 195 require certain adjustments to be made which may reduce the amount of loss relief that can be claimed. For example, when the sale proceeds are reinvested in any other interest in land within four months of the last qualifying sale, the relief may be reduced or extinguished. Where several interests in land are *sold* within three years of death, if one is revalued in order to claim loss relief, all the interests sold must be revalued. If any interest has increased in value, there may be more inheritance tax to pay as a result. Care must, therefore, be taken when deciding whether to make the claim in these circumstances since if the personal representatives make an overall *gain,* additional inheritance tax *can* be levied. (This is an important distinction as compared with the position on shares. A disadvantageous claim cannot be withdrawn.)

In the case of sales in the fourth year after death, sales for more than value at date of death are ignored. Exchange of contract is not a "sale". See *Jones (Ball's Administrators) v IRC* (1997).

Where the deceased was a co-owner of land, the personal representatives should consider carefully before making a claim. The discount normally available on co-owned land will be lost if a claim is made to substitute the sale proceeds and the result may be to increase the inheritance tax payable. See IHT Manual, para.33182.

Example

Ann dies owning a half-share of Blackacre as beneficial tenant. Blackacre is valued at £200,000 at the date of Ann's death and the value of her one half-share is discounted by 10 per cent to £90,000. A year after the death, the whole property is sold for £190,000. The sale value of the property for these purposes is an arithmetic half-share of the gross proceeds of sale, £95,000. Any claim is, therefore, disadvantageous as additional inheritance tax would be payable.

The inter-relation of inheritance tax loss relief and capital gains tax

Unlike the provisions which deal with loss relief on the sale of shares, the **12.19** provisions which deal with loss relief on the sales of interests in land contain no section which states expressly that the capital gains tax acquisition value is to be reduced in the event of a claim for inheritance tax loss relief. However, s.274 of the TCGA 1992 provides that where a value has been "ascertained" for inheritance tax purposes, that figure will become the acquisition value for capital gains tax purposes. In cases where land is sold for more than death value but no inheritance tax is payable (e.g. because the property passes to an exempt beneficiary), it would be beneficial to elect to substitute the sale price for capital gains tax purposes. This is not possible, see *Stonor v IRC* (2001).

Tax considerations—capital gains tax

Personal representatives will, prima facie, be liable to pay capital gains tax at 18 **12.20** per cent on gains made on sales of assets. However, as personal representatives are chargeable only on gains arising since death and as relief may be available to exempt gains, in many cases, no capital gains tax will be payable.

If the personal representatives vest assets in the beneficiaries, the beneficiaries will acquire the assets at their market value at the date of death. When the beneficiaries dispose of the assets they will be chargeable on any gains realised by them and entitled to the benefit of any allowable losses realised by them. If the beneficiary is liable to 40 per cent CGT a sale by the PRs may be preferable the personal representatives will not have any capital gains tax liability on such disposals.

If the personal representatives wish to sell assets, they should, when deciding which assets to sell, consider the possibility of a capital gains tax liability arising. They should consider the following factors:

(a) *Will a chargeable gain arise?* The assets may have risen in value since the date of death. However, the personal representatives will be able to claim an annual exemption in the tax year of death and the two following tax years. The amount of this exemption is the same as that available to individuals. Where possible sales of assets which have risen in value during the administration should be spread over two or more tax years so that more than one annual exemption may be claimed.

(b) *Will a loss arise?* A loss must be set off against any gains which the personal representatives realise in the same tax year. To the extent that the loss cannot be set off against gains of the same tax year, it is carried forward and set off against gains made by the personal representatives in future tax years. If the personal representatives are unlikely to make future gains they may wish to consider vesting the loss-making asset in a beneficiary, thus allowing the beneficiary to sell the asset. The beneficiary can then set the loss off against any gain that he may make in the future. If the assets sold are shares or land, the inheritance tax loss relief discussed above should be considered.

(c) *Is it better to sell an appreciating asset or a depreciating one?* Selling an asset that is increasing in value may avoid the payment of tax but equally will deprive the estate of a valuable asset. Selling a depreciating one will give rise to a loss which may lead to a tax saving but the personal representatives must not delay too long before selling since the value of the estate may be unnecessarily reduced. However, it would be foolish to sell if there is any possibility of the asset recovering its value in the near future.

(d) *What are the wishes of the beneficiaries?* When choosing which assets to sell and which to retain, the personal representatives should consult with the beneficiaries to obtain their views. Most beneficiaries will want to ensure that the value of their entitlement is maintained so will advocate selling depreciating assets and retaining appreciating ones. However, a beneficiary with a substantial capital gains tax liability from other disposals might agree to receive a depreciating asset so as to sell it, thus realising a loss that can be set against gains. Similarly beneficiaries with unrelieved losses can have appreciating assets vested in them. These assets can be sold by the beneficiaries, the gains being reduced by their allowable losses.

Where assets are held for a charity, it is likely that the charity will want the asset to be appropriated to it and sold on its behalf as bare trustee. This can result in a saving of capital gains tax as compared to the position where the assets are sold by the personal representatives and the proceeds transferred to the charity. It is important to comply with the necessary formalities. There should be a written appropriation and a record of the instruction to sell. Most major charities are familiar with the necessary steps and many have helpful leaflets. The Institute of Legacy Managers website (*http://www.ilmnet.org.uk* [Accessed January 2011]) has a precedent available. It is well worth talking to charities early in the administration and keeping them informed of developments.

For disposals on or after June 23, 2010 personal representatives pay capital gains tax at 28 per cent (instead of 18 per cent) so it is particularly important that they try to minimise the impact on beneficiaries.

4. GENERAL DUTIES

In addition to the detailed points set out above, the personal representatives must **12.21** bear in mind more general considerations when administering the estate. The personal representatives must ascertain the deceased's debts and liabilities, obtain the grant, pay debts and distribute the assets to the beneficiaries. While administering the estate they must ensure that the value of assets are maintained. This obligation will be discharged in a number of ways. The personal representatives must ensure that when any asset is damaged or falls into disrepair it is repaired. This can be expensive and so they should take out insurance cover. If the deceased had taken out property insurance the personal representatives should as soon as possible after the death notify the insurance company and either have their interest noted on the policy or a fresh policy issued.

For estates which include shares, personal representatives must constantly review their portfolio, taking expert advice as appropriate, and ensuring as far as possible that the portfolio maintains its value. Therefore, the personal representatives must consider selling shares that are dropping in value with a view to replacing them with a better investment. Equally the personal representatives should avoid speculative investments even though they might realise substantial profits. Any investments other than stocks and shares of the deceased should also be looked at criticially.

Finally, the personal representatives should ensure that they complete their task quickly and efficiently by anticipating difficulties before they arise (so far as possible) and not delaying the performance of their duties.

CHAPTER THIRTEEN

DUTIES OF SOLICITORS

1. THE EXTENT OF THE SOLICITOR'S DUTY

The solicitor's duty is to prepare a will which carries out the client's testamentary **13.01** intentions and to take any other steps which are necessary to give effect to those wishes. A failure by the solicitor to draft a will so as to comply with the client's wishes is an especially serious matter since the mistake which has been made is not likely to become apparent until the client is dead or may never be discovered at all. It is too late to correct certain types of mistake once the client is dead. The will (or part of it) may be refused probate on the grounds that the client did not have knowledge and approval of the contents but this will not necessarily ensure that the testator's true wishes are put into effect. Section 20 of the Administration of Justice Act 1982 allows rectification of a will to correct clerical errors or failure to understand the client's instructions but as we saw in Ch.2 this does not enable every type of mistake to be corrected. Even if rectification is possible the mistake will cause considerable delay and expense.

A beneficiary who suffers loss as a result of the failure of the solicitor to carry out his duty is all too likely to sue the solicitor who acted for the testator. In *White v Jones* (1995) the House of Lords held that the solicitor's assumption of responsibility towards his client should be held in law to extend to the intended beneficiary in circumstances where the beneficiary would otherwise have no remedy. The result of this decision has been a proliferation of cases alleging breach of duty on the part of solicitors in relation to the drafting and execution of wills.

Similarly a personal representative may sue solicitors retained to act in the administration of the estate. In *Chappell v Somers and Blake* (2004), the retained solicitors delayed obtaining probate for five years with the result that two properties were left vacant with consequent loss of income. The solicitors were held to be liable to pay damages to the executor for the benefit of the estate even though she had suffered no personal loss. In an obiter dictum the judge said that the beneficiaries could not have sued personally because they were not the clients of the defendant. However, see *Humblestone v Martin Tolhurst Partnership (a firm)* (2004) where a person who would have been a beneficiary but for the solicitors' negligence was able to sue.

2. Duties Relating to the Preparation of the Will

The solicitor must clarify the terms of the retainer

13.02 Any ambiguity will be resolved in favour of the client. In *Gray v Buss Murton* (1999) a trainee solicitor believed that he was being asked to give an opinion as to whether or not a will had been validly executed (which it had). The clients believed that he was advising them on whether the will was effective (which it was not). The firm was held liable to the clients on the basis that it was for the solicitor to establish the extent of the retainer. In *Hurlingham Estates Ltd v Wilde & Partners* (1997) Lightman J. said that in the absence of a retainer limiting liability it was necessary to consider whether the solicitor "should reasonably have appreciated" that the client "needed his advice and guidance" on the tax aspects of the transaction. Any limitation on the retainer would have to be in writing to enable the client to consider it and give informed consent.

The solicitor must prepare the will with reasonable speed

13.03 In *White v Jones* itself solicitors received a letter on July 17 instructing them to prepare a new will but had not prepared the will for execution by the time the testator died on September 14. The firm had to compensate the disappointed beneficiaries.

In *X v Woollcombe Yonge* (2001) a solicitor prepared a will for a terminally ill client within a week but the client died before it was ready. Neuberger J. suggested that seven days would be a sufficiently short period "in most cases" where the client was "elderly or likely to die". In this case the testatrix, although terminally ill, was not expected to die within the next couple of weeks. She was planning to move to a hospice and raised no objection when told that the solicitor would bring the will some time in the following week. The amount of time taken was not unreasonable. However:

> "[w]here there is a plain and substantial risk of the client's imminent death, anything other than a handwritten rough codicil prepared on the spot for signature may be negligent".

Perhaps inevitably this is an area of law where narrow distinctions are made between different sets of facts. For example in *Atkins v Dunn and Baker* (2004), a will was sent to a client for approval but was not returned to the solicitors. They did not send the client a reminder but this was held not to amount to negligence as the client understood the importance of making a new will. In *Humblestone v Martin Tolhurst Partnership (a firm)* (2004), the defendants were instructed to draft a will. The client returned it to them for safe keeping. Although the will was checked when it was returned, the solicitors failed to notice that the client had not signed it. This was not noticed until after the client died. The claimant successfully sued for the legacy he would have received if the will had been valid. The court held that the duty to check the validity of the will extended to the potential beneficiaries as well as to the testatrix.

It is beneficial to agree a time-frame with the client for preparation of the will. This is good practice in itself but, beyond that, may be of assistance if the client dies before the will is ready for execution. The duty owed by the solicitor is to the client and is to produce a legally effective will which carries out the client's intentions. If the solicitor has carried out the terms of the agreement, it will be much more difficult (though not necessarily impossible) for the beneficiaries to allege breach of duty.

Take instructions from the client in person wherever possible

It is possible to take instructions in writing or via the internet but there may be **13.04** problems as a result. There may be misunderstandings as a result of the lack of face to face contact. See *Sifri v Clough & Willis* (2007). It is difficult for the solicitor to assess the client's mental capacity and whether there is any possibility of fraud or undue influence.

Ideally solicitors should not accept instructions from an intermediary. The court was extremely critical of the solicitor in *Richards v Allen* (2001) who accepted instructions from his sister-in-law without ever seeing the testatrix.

Be careful of conflicts of interest. It is common to see married couples together but many solicitors are not happy doing this and there may be tensions partic- ularly in the case of second marriages. In *Hines v Willans* (2002) a solicitor was held liable for breach of duty as a result of acting for a husband to the detriment of the wife whom he had already agreed to represent. He had an appointment to see the wife on the following Monday, but made a will for her husband disinherit- ing her and (at his own suggestion) prepared a notice of severance of the couple's joint tenancy.

Be alert to the possibility of undue influence. If a client expresses a wish to save inheritance tax by making lifetime gifts, is he or she under pressure from one or more of the children? Does the client understand what he or she is doing and what could happen in the future? Make sure everything is confirmed in writing and try to see the client in the absence of family members who may be exerting pressure.

Try to establish that the client has testamentary capacity

Where a solicitor fails to check a testator's capacity and prepares a will which **13.05** later turns out to be invalid, there may be a claim from the estate that it has been reduced by the costs of the dispute. See *Worby v Rosser* (1999) and *Corbett v Bond Pearce* (2001).

It is, therefore, important for practitioners to carry out their duties with regard to capacity.

The so-called "Golden Rule" was developed by Templeman J. (as he then was) in *Kenward v Adams* (1975) and *Re Simpson (Deceased)* (1977). It was referred to with approval in *Buckenham v Dickinson* (1997) and by Rimer J. in *Re Morris (Deceased), Special Trustees for Great Ormond Street Hospital for Children v Rushin and others* (2001).

Templeman J. said:

> "In the case of an aged testator or a testator who has suffered a serious illness, there is one golden rule which should always be observed, however straightforward matters may appear, and however difficult or tactless it may be to suggest that precautions be taken: the making of a will by such a testator ought to be witnessed or approved by a medical practitioner who satisfies himself of the capacity and understanding of the testator, and records and preserves his examination and findings.
>
> There are other precautions which should be taken. If the testator has made an earlier will this should be considered by the legal and medical advisers of the testator and, if appropriate, discussed with the testator.
>
> The instructions of the testator should be taken in the absence of anyone who may stand to benefit, or who may have influence over the testator.
>
> These are not counsels of perfection. If proper precautions are not taken injustice may result or be imagined, and great expense and misery may be unnecessarily caused."

It is often difficult to get medical evidence particularly in urgent cases. Always prepare a full attendance note detailing the steps you took to establish testamentary capacity.

Clients with borderline testamentary capacity are often vulnerable to undue influence. Try to see the client alone. In *Killick v Pountney* (2000) an important factor in the court's decision that there had been undue influence was the fact that the beneficiary had been present for some of the time at the interview.

The House of Lords in *Barclays Bank v Etridge and other appeals* (2001) reviewed the law on undue influence in the context of charging one spouse's interest in the matrimonial home as security for the debts of the other. One practical recommendation made was that the interview with the client must be in the absence of the person benefiting from the transaction. There must be a clear explanation of the nature and consequences of the act. It is then for adult persons of competent mind to decide whether they will do an act. The solicitor does not need to approve of the client's decision. Independent and competent advice does not mean independent and competent approval.

In exceptional cases where it is glaringly obvious that the spouse is being grievously wronged, Lord Nichols said that the solicitor should decline to act further. Many practitioners are concerned that the effect of not acting is merely that the client will be coached better and taken elsewhere by the person exerting the influence. However, in *Powell v Powell* (1900) Farwell J. said that a solicitor "ought not to go on, if he disapproves, simply because he thinks that someone else will do the work if he does not". The "Golden Rule" is merely good practice. Failure to comply with it does not invalidate the will. It simply means that there will be less evidence available in the event of a dispute. See *Sharp v Adam* (2006).

Be clear what property the testator owns and in what capacity

13.06   Clients do not always remember how they own property. In *Chittock v Stevens* (2000) a house was believed to be in joint names but eight months after the death of the husband (partially intestate) it was discovered that it had been in his sole name. It is desirable either to check the basis of ownership or record that the will has been prepared on the basis of the information provided by the client. Resolve any ambiguities or uncertainties with the client.

Joint property is particularly problematic. In *Carr-Glynn v Frearsons* (1998) the testatrix (aged 81) consulted a solicitor to make a will leaving her interest in a property "Homelands" to her niece. She owned the property with her nephew and was uncertain as to whether she owned it as beneficial joint tenant or tenant in common.

Her solicitor prepared a will and advised her that the gift of "Homelands" could not take affect if she held it as a beneficial joint tenant. The solicitor asked if the testatrix wanted her to obtain and check the deeds. The testatrix said that she would do it herself. She did not do so and when she died it was discovered that she had owned the property as beneficial joint tenant.

The Court of Appeal found that the solicitor was in breach of her duty which extended beyond the mere preparation of the will to steps necessary to give effect to the client's testamentary intentions. Many people consider the decision rather harsh but according to the Court of Appeal the solicitor's breach lay in not explaining to the client that she could have served a notice of severance without having to obtain the deeds. Had the solicitor given this explanation, there would presumably have been no liability even if the client declined to serve the notice.

A beneficial joint tenancy also caused a problem in *Re Woolnough* (2002). The firm of solicitors overlooked the fact that serving a notice of severance is just one way of severing a joint tenancy (see para.21.13, below) and did not realise that severance had occurred before death.

There may also be cases where property held in joint names is actually held on a resulting trust for the party who provided the funds. See *Aroso v Coutts* (2002) and *Goodman v Carlton* (2002). Explore the nature of ownership while the client is alive and it is possible to clarify and record it. Note, however, that the House of Lords held in *Stack v Dowden* (2007) that in a domestic context the presumption should be that beneficial ownership follows legal ownership. In a case where property is in the name of one party but another may have an interest (e.g. where one party has moved in with another and has made substantial contributions to the costs of the property) it may be desirable to suggest changes in the legal ownership so that the position is clear. In *Sillett v Meek* (2007) a solicitor who prepared a will was criticised for failing to establish the beneficial ownership of a bank account put into joint names by the deceased shortly before giving instructions for the will.

Does anyone else have an interest in property "owned" by the client as a result of proprietary estoppel?

See *Gillett v Holt* (1998) in which the Court of Appeal confirmed that a promise **13.07** to leave property by will can give rise to a claim in proprietary estoppel. The necessary elements are a promise relied on by the promisor resulting in detriment to the promisee so that it would be unconscionable for equity not to provide a remedy. The promisee will not necessarily receive everything he or she feels entitled to. The Court of Appeal has gone out of its way to emphasise that any award must be proportionate to the detriment suffered, the claims of creditors and of other beneficiaries of the estate. See *Campbell v Griffin and West Sussex County Council* (2001) and *Jennings v Rice* (2002).

Does the client have a general power of appointment?

13.08   If so, it is important to clarify the client's wishes for the trust property. The trust property will pass as part of a general residuary gift where the power has not been expressly exercised. However, it is preferable to exercise the power expressly to avoid later allegations that the client was not aware of the effect of the residuary gift. See *Gibbons v Nelsons (A Firm) & Others* (2000).

The solicitor's role in taking instructions should not be entirely passive

13.09   The solicitor should ensure that the client is not under some misapprehension as to the effect of the solicitor's instructions which if corrected might lead to different instructions. It is not possible to give an exhaustive list of all the points which should be drawn to a client's attention but the following are among the most important:

    (a)   Jointly held property will pass to the surviving joint tenant even if the will says otherwise.

    (b)   If dependants and certain relatives are not provided for family provision claims may be made.

    (c)   Gifts of specific items will be adeemed if the items are sold or changed in substance unless specific provision is made.

    (d)   Unless contrary provision is made most types of gift will lapse (and fall into residue or pass on intestacy) if the donee predeceases. A gift will, however, take effect if the beneficiary survives for even a very short time or is deemed to survive under s.184 of the Law of Property Act 1925. This may not correspond with the client's wishes so that a survivorship clause should be considered.

    (e)   Unless contrary provision is made in the will, a person taking a property charged with a debt takes it subject to that debt (Administration of Estates Act 1925 s.35). Check the testator's wishes in relation to a specific gift of an asset which is (or may be at the time of death) charged with a debt.

          Be particularly careful where there is life assurance linked to the debt. Make sure that there is no ambiguity as to where the proceeds of the policy are going. Normally the testator will want the person who is responsible for the debt to take the benefit of the policy so as to have funds available. This may require careful drafting.

(f) Payments from pension funds and insurance policies may be payable to beneficiaries independently of the terms of the will. In the case of pension schemes where lump sums are payable at the discretion of the trustees of the scheme, it is usually possible for an employee to leave a statement of his wishes for the destination of the sum payable. Such a statement is not binding on the trustees but will be considered by them. A client who has the benefit of such a scheme should be advised to make a statement.

3. DUTIES RELATING TO THE EXECUTION OF THE WILL

The solicitor must offer to oversee the execution of the will

The case of *Esterhuizen v Allied Dunbar* (1998) suggests that a solicitor must make the following offer: **13.10**

- the solicitor will attend the client at home and oversee execution;

- the client can come to the solicitor's office and have execution overseen; or

- if the client prefers he or she can execute the will at home.

If the client executes the will at home the solicitor should send a letter explaining exactly how to execute the will.

The solicitor must offer to check the will after the execution

In *Ross v Caunters* (1980) the solicitor sent the testator a letter with the will saying that attestation was required by "two independent witnesses". When the will was returned to the solicitor, one of the witnesses had the same surname as one of the beneficiaries. The solicitors did not query this. The witness was married to the beneficiary who, therefore, lost her entitlement. Megarry, V.C. found that the solicitor had been negligent because he had failed: **13.11**

- to warn the testator that a spouse of a beneficiary should not witness;

- to check whether the will was properly attested;

- to observe that the attesting witness was the spouse of a beneficiary; and

- to draw this to the attention of the testator.

In *Gray and Others v Richards Butler (A Firm)* (2000) the judge accepted that a solicitor owes a duty to a testator, at execution *and also when the will is returned after execution.* (See also the cases referred to in para.13.03, above)

If instructed to attend a client, keep the appointment

13.12 In *Hooper v Fynmores (A Firm)* (2002) a solicitor prepared a will for an elderly client, in early September 1997, increasing the claimant's share in residue by £40,000. The solicitor who prepared the will wrote to the client asking if he would like him to bring it out for signature.

On September 8 the client was admitted to hospital. On September 10 the claimant left a message with the firm of solicitors explaining that the client had gone into hospital. On September 16 an old friend of the client telephoned the solicitor to say that he was having tests and would be in touch when he was home from hospital. The solicitor considered that he had been "stood down".

The client later arranged that the solicitor would visit him on October 13. However, the solicitor himself went into hospital and cancelled the appointment. He did not arrange a new appointment and did not discuss the possibility of sending a substitute. The client died on October 21 without executing the will. The Court of Appeal found that the solicitor had been negligent.

Initially the solicitor was entitled to rely on the client's instructions relayed through a close and reliable friend postponing action. However, the position changed when the further appointment was made. Solicitors have a duty to satisfy themselves that a delay in executing a will resulting from the cancellation of an appointment will not be disadvantageous to the client. If necessary, the solicitor should appoint a substitute. An appointment with an elderly client in hospital should not to be cancelled unless the client is agreeable to it.

Sometimes clients are unwilling to execute a will. A solicitor is not required to ensure that a client executes a will. There may be circumstances where continuing to press a client could amount to undue influence. It will normally be appropriate to write to clients reminding them that the will has not been executed and asking if they want any alteration to be made.

Do not allow a client to execute will conditionally

13.13 See *Corbett v Newey* (1996) where solicitors allowed the testatrix to sign the will but not date it. Her intention was that it should not come into operation until certain lifetime gifts had been completed. The will was not valid because it had not been executed unconditionally. The solicitors had to compensate the disappointed beneficiaries.

4. DUTIES RELATING TO RECORDS

13.14 Full attendance notes are a solicitor's protection against false allegations. In addition, the discipline of preparing them may also help to avoid a mistake. Courts place a great deal of weight on good contemporaneous notes but are unimpressed by those prepared after the event and particularly those prepared from memory in the knowledge of future litigation (see *Killick v Pountney* (2000)). It is sensible to take instructions for a will in the same form so that important questions are not omitted. Many people find using a checklist helpful.

It is particularly important to clarify in correspondence any limitations imposed on the extent of the service (see para.13.15, below) or on the extent of the solicitor's knowledge of the client's assets (see para.13.06, above).

A solicitor who is present at the execution of a will by a testator who is frail (whether mentally or physically) should always make a full and careful attendance note. (See para.13.05, above.)

After execution the solicitor should "make up" a copy of the will (i.e. write in particulars of the date, signature and witnesses) or take a photocopy for their file. Made-up copies and photocopies are admissible as proof of the terms of the will if the will is lost (see paras 2.42–2.43, above). It is especially important to keep a copy if the will itself is to be kept by the client or deposited elsewhere such as at a bank. The solicitor's filing system must be so arranged that the original will (if kept by the solicitor) and copy can be found many years after execution. Nothing should be attached to an original will since the presence of pin holes or clip impressions may lead to an allegation of attempted revocation in which case affidavit evidence will be required. (See para.10.54, above.)

Where a solicitor has prepared a will which is later disputed, the solicitor is a material witness and must provide all the information available to him as to both the preparation and execution of the will. See *Larke v Nugus* (2000).

5. Duties Relating to General Advice

A solicitor who has agreed to prepare a will for a client is under an obligation to **13.15** take any steps necessary to put the client's testamentary wishes into effect. The solicitor should, therefore, explain any problems, disadvantages and necessary steps. It is possible to limit the terms of the retainer (for example by offering to draft a will but not to offer detailed advice on tax planning without a separate charge) but as we have already seen the obligation is on the solicitor to clarify the terms of the retainer (*Gray v Buss Murton* (1999)).

The solicitor must have written evidence of the retainer to have any hope of success (see *Hurlingham Estates Ltd v Wilde & Partners* (1997)). Writing is required, not merely as evidence of what has been agreed, but so that the client can consider (and discuss with others) the position and its implications independently of the solicitor. Furthermore, even if the client consents, the solicitor will not be able to rely on the consent unless it is informed. In particular the client must understand whether the limitation is one which is reasonable and whether it is necessary for the client to seek advice elsewhere.

A solicitor cannot gain protection from liability by claiming to rely on counsel's opinion. In *Estill v Cowling, Swift & Kitchin* (2000), an estate suffered unnecessary inheritance tax because an inappropriate discretionary trust was established in the testatrix's lifetime.

Arden J. said that solicitors do not abdicate their professional responsibility when they seek the advice of counsel:

"He must apply his mind to the advice received. But the more specialist the nature of the advice, the more reasonable is it likely to be for a solicitor to accept and act on it."

If the solicitor has accepted a general retainer to put the client's testamentary wishes into effect, it may also be appropriate to advise on other methods of disposal such as lifetime gifts and on the possible advantages of taking out insurance policies expressed to be for the benefit of third parties. If the solicitor thinks it necessary the solicitor may also advise the client to obtain expert investment advice. If the solicitor himself gives investment advice he or she must be authorised under the Financial Services and Markets Act 2000.

It is also very important to warn clients that a will should never be regarded as permanent. Changed circumstances should lead to a review of the will (particularly changes in family circumstances such as marriage, separation, divorce, entering into or terminating a civil partnership, the birth of children and changes in financial circumstances such as inheritance of property or retirement). A solicitor who is acting for a client in relation to other matters (such as a divorce) should always suggest the making of a new will if it seems to be desirable. When advising a married client or client in a civil partnership who intends to make a will it is desirable to suggest that the spouse or civil partner also considers making a will so that the dispositions of the estates can be considered together.

Although it is a breach of the rules of professional conduct for a solicitor to tout for business there can be no objection to a solicitor informing existing clients of changes in the law which make it desirable for them to make new wills. However, this may lead to suggestions that the solicitor owes a continuing contractual duty to the clients. See *Hines v Willans* (1997).

A solicitor is not under an obligation to keep a client informed of changes in the law unless the firm has accepted a continuing retainer.

6. SOLICITOR AS BENEFICIARY

13.16   Where a person is a beneficiary of a will which he or she has prepared, positive evidence will be required of the testator's knowledge and approval of the contents of the will (see *Wintle v Nye* (1959)). Where the will is simple and short and the testator has had an opportunity to read it, the court may not require any additional evidence (see *Fuller v Strum* (2000)). The Solicitors' Code of Conduct 2007 r.3.04 directs that a solicitor receiving a benefit from a client must *insist* that the client goes to another solicitor for independent advice and for the drafting of the will. It is not sufficient that the client is merely *advised* to take such advice (see Guidance Notes, paras 56–63). These provisions are likely to be renewed in 2011.

Neither of these rules prevents a solicitor from preparing a will which appoints the solicitor or a partner as an executor even where the will contains a charging clause.

7. Duties of Solicitor Acting for Personal Representatives

Personal representatives will frequently retain a solicitor to act for them in the   **13.17** administration of an estate. The personal representatives are then the solicitor's clients. The beneficiaries or family of the deceased are not. If there is any dispute arising out of the administration the solicitor must be careful not to allow an actual or potential conflict of interest to arise by advising the beneficiaries or family of the deceased while he continues to act for the personal representatives.

It is particularly important that the solicitor reminds the personal representatives that they owe their duty to the estate and not to particular beneficiaries. They should remain neutral if there is a dispute between beneficiaries. Where personal representatives incur costs by acting to further the interests of one set of beneficiaries at the expense of another, they will be penalised by the court. See *Tod v Barton and Royal Society of Chemistry* (2002) and *Breadner v Granville-Grossman* (2001).

The duties of a solicitor in acting for personal representatives include giving advice and taking action in the administration on the clients' behalf. Immediately after the death the solicitor will be called upon to obtain any will of the deceased, advise on its validity and take steps to obtain a grant including the preparation of the appropriate oath and the Inheritance Tax Account (if required). In some cases it will also be necessary to obtain affidavits in support of the application (such as affidavits of due execution).

Once the grant has been obtained the solicitor's duty is to advise the personal representatives on their duties. In particular the solicitor will be required to advise on the collection and realisation of the estate, the payment of debts and the distribution of the estate to the beneficiaries.

In *Cancer Research Campaign v Ernest Brown & Co (A Firm)* (1997) Harman J. reviewed the authorities to decide whether or not executors had an obligation to inform legatees of a gift made to them in advance of distribution. He concluded that they had not on the basis that a legatee has no specific right in any asset in the estate. They have merely a chose in action to compel the proper administration of the estate. The estate may have such heavy debts that there is nothing left for legatees. Solicitors acting for executors could not be under any more extensive liability and so they had no obligation either. This was unfortunate for the legatees in question who would have varied their entitlement to achieve a tax saving had they been informed within the two-year time period.

However, there is no doubt that it is good practice to inform beneficiaries of their interest in an estate. Even the authorities relied upon by Harman J. suggest this.

Difficulties can arise when a solicitor acts for the personal representatives of a disputed will. Simple steps need to be taken in the administration of the estate to secure the assets. If the personal representatives of the disputed will have already obtained a grant and the dispute relates to revocation of the will, they should agree with those seeking to have the grant revoked what steps can be taken. Where no grant has yet been obtained, the best course of action may be for both sides to agree to the appointment of a professional on an interim basis with authority limited to safeguarding the estate. See *Sifri v Clough & Willis* (2007).

Missing beneficiaries cause problems for personal representatives. Solicitors must explain that the duty of the personal representatives is to distribute the estate to those entitled and advise on the possible ways of dealing with the situation arising from missing beneficiaries (see Ch.14, below).

Once the administration is complete the solicitor will prepare (or will supervise the preparation of) the estate accounts prior to the distribution of residue. Solicitors have frequently been criticised for failure to prepare such accounts promptly.

8. DUTIES IN RELATION TO ANTI-MONEY LAUNDERING LEGISLATION

13.18 Solicitors are becoming subject to an increasing burden of regulation in relation to money laundering. The main body of UK law relating to money laundering is contained in the Proceeds of Crime Act 2002 and the Terrorism Act 2000.

What follows is a very brief outline of the relevant legislation. The Law Society has helpful guidance available on its website.

The principal offences

13.19 The Proceeds of Crime Act 2002 creates a single set of money laundering offences applicable throughout the UK to the proceeds of all crimes. It also creates a disclosure regime, which makes it an offence not to disclose knowledge or suspicion of money laundering, but also permits persons to be given consent in certain circumstances to carry out activities which would otherwise constitute money laundering. The Act applies to all solicitors, although some offences apply only to persons within the regulated sector, or nominated officers.

The principal offences are:

- **Section 327—concealing**

    A person commits an offence if he conceals, disguises, converts, or transfers criminal property, or removes criminal property from the UK. Criminal property is property which is, or represents, a person's benefit from criminal conduct, where the alleged offender knows or suspects that it is such.

- **Section 328—arrangements**

    A person commits an offence if he or she enters into, or becomes concerned in an arrangement which he or she knows or suspects facilitates the acquisition, retention, use or control of criminal property by or on behalf of another person.

- **Section 329—acquisition, use or possession**

  A person commits an offence if he or she acquires, uses, or has possession of criminal property otherwise than for full valuable consideration.

A person will have a defence to a principal money laundering offence if he or she:

- makes an authorised disclosure prior to the offence being committed and gains appropriate consent (the consent defence), or

- intended to make an authorised disclosure but had a reasonable excuse for not doing so (the reasonable excuse defence).

Disclosure is made to the firm's nominated officer who will consider whether or not to make disclosure to the Serious Crimes Agency (SOCA).

In addition to the above a person commits the offence of non-disclosure under s.330 if:

- they know or suspect, or have reasonable grounds for knowing or suspecting, that another person is engaged in money laundering,

- the information on which their suspicion is based comes in the course of business in the regulated sector,

- they can identify the person engaged in money laundering or the whereabouts of any of the laundered property, or they believe, or it is reasonable to expect them to believe, that the will may assist in identifying the person or the whereabouts of any of the laundered property, and

- they fail to disclose that knowledge or suspicion, or reasonable grounds for suspicion, as soon as practicable to a nominated officer or SOCA.

There are also "tipping off" offences contained in the Proceeds of Crime Act 2002 as amended and in the Terrorism Act 2000, as amended.

Regulatory Requirements

The Money Laundering Regulations 2007 (the Regulations) repeal and replace **13.20** the Money Laundering Regulations 2003 and implement the third Money Laundering Directive. They set out the administrative requirements in this area. These Regulations impose new requirements in relation to trusts.

Relevant persons

The Regulations apply to all "relevant persons" as defined in reg.3. These **13.21** include solicitors but extend to estate agents, banks and Trust and Company Service providers.

Need for identity checks on customer and beneficial owner

13.22   Relevant persons are required by reg.5 to carry out "customer due diligence" that is to:

(a)   identify the customer and verify the customer's identity on the basis of documents, data or information obtained from a reliable and independent source;

(b)   identify, where there is a beneficial owner who is not the customer, the beneficial owner and take adequate measures, on a risk-sensitive basis, to verify his identity so that the relevant person is satisfied that he knows who the beneficial owner is, including, in the case of a legal person, trust or similar legal arrangement, measures to understand the ownership and control structure of the person, trust or arrangement; and

(c)   obtain information on the purpose and intended nature of the business relationship.

This due diligence has to be carried out according to reg.7 when the relevant person:

(a)   establishes a business relationship;

(b)   carries out an occasional transaction;

(c)   suspects money laundering or terrorist financing; and

(d)   doubts the veracity or adequacy of documents, data or information previously obtained for the purposes of identification or verification.

Who is the beneficial owner?

13.23   Solicitors are used to performing identity checks on new clients but the Money Laundering Regulations 2007 introduce the concept of the "beneficial owner" for the first time. It is defined in relation to a trust in reg.6 and it is fair to say that it is not an easy concept.

The beneficial owner of a trust is:

"(a) any individual who is entitled to a specified interest in at least 25 per cent of the capital of the trust property."

A specified interest is one in possession or in remainder irrespective of whether or not it is defeasible. Hence a default beneficiary with a vested interest has a specified interest no matter how unlikely it is that they will ever take an interest.

"(b) as respects any trust other than one which is set up or operates entirely for the benefit of individuals falling within sub-paragraph (a), the class of persons in whose main interest the trust is set up or operates."

This would include a class of beneficiaries with contingent interests, for example "such of my grandchildren as reach 25". The Regulation only requires an understanding of the class as opposed to the individuals within it but the solicitor would have to investigate to discover whether any of the beneficiaries had obtained a vested interest in at least 25 per cent of the capital.

"(c) any individual who has control over the trust."

"Control" means a power (whether exercisable alone, jointly with another person or with the consent of another person) under the trust instrument or by law to:

(a) dispose of, advance, lend, invest, pay or apply trust property;

(b) vary the trust;

(c) add or remove a person as a beneficiary or to or from a class of beneficiaries;

(d) appoint or remove trustees; and

(e) direct, withhold consent to or veto the exercise of a power such as is mentioned in sub-paragraph (a), (b), (c) or (d).

The definition of control is clearly very wide. However para.5(b) of reg.6 provides that an individual does not have control merely as a result of certain statutory provisions including Trustee Act 1925 s.32 (consent of person with a prior interest to an advancement of capital) and Trusts of Land and Appointment of Trustees Act 1996 s.19(2) (appointment and retirement of trustees at instance of the beneficiaries) nor as a result of the rule in *Saunders v Vautier*. This is obviously a helpful provision but it is limited in effect. It will not apply where the trust instrument has replaced the statutory provision with an express one.

In relation to an estate of a deceased person in the course of administration the beneficial owner is defined as the executor or administrator for the time being. This is helpful as it means that customer due diligence is not required on the beneficiaries of the estate. However, if a continuing trust arises, customer due diligence will be required on the "beneficial owner" at the point when assets are transferred to the trust.

Solicitors are clearly well placed to carry out customer due diligence in relation to trusts and estates. However, the same checks have to be carried out by banks when trustees want to open bank accounts and estate agents when trustees want to buy or sell land. The complexity of the concept of the beneficial owner of the trust is bound to cause problems. Solicitors may wish to provide a pack of information to third parties dealing with the trustees to minimise enquiries, delay and cost. Regulation 17 helpfully provides that relevant persons can rely on customer due diligence carried out by, inter alia, solicitors although they will remain liable.

Ongoing monitoring

13.24 Regulation 8 requires a relevant person to conduct ongoing monitoring of a business relationship. This is defined as:

> (a) scrutiny of transactions undertaken throughout the course of the relationship (including, where necessary, the source of funds) to ensure that the transactions are consistent with the relevant person's knowledge of the customer, the customer's business and risk profile; and
>
> (b) keeping the documents, data or information obtained for the purpose of applying customer due diligence measures up-to-date.

In the context of a trust the reference to the "customer" is odd as the customer is the trustee so, at first sight, a solicitor dealing with a trust company would have to scrutinise the business and risk profile of the trust company. However, when asked the Treasury said that the customer was the trustee but that the trustee's business for this purpose was the business of the particular trust.

Chapter Fourteen

PROTECTION OF PERSONAL REPRESENTATIVES

1. Introduction

Personal representatives are personally liable for any loss arising from a failure **14.01** to carry out their duties. If they have incurred personal liability they may be able to obtain relief in one of three ways.

(a) *The will may contain a relieving provision.* Many wills include a clause limiting the liability of personal representatives to liability for wilful fraud or wrongdoing and giving protection from liability for mistakes made in good faith. In *Armitage v Nurse* (1997) Millett L.J. held that a clause purporting to exclude liability for everything except actual fraud was not repugnant or contrary to public policy. There is a core of obligations that beneficiaries must be able to enforce against trustees in order to give effect to the trust, but these obligations do not include the duties of skill, care, prudence and diligence. However, there is an increasing feeling that such clauses are not normally appropriate for professional trustees who are paid and can insure against the risk of liability. The Law Commission recommended that professional bodies should introduce practice rules to deal with the problem. The Solicitors' Code of Conduct 2007 r.2.07 states that a limitation on liability must be in writing and brought to the attention of the client.

(b) *The court may grant relief under Trustee Act 1925 s.61.* The court has a discretion to grant relief where a trustee "has acted honestly and reasonably and ought fairly to be excused".

For example, this discretion was exercised in *Re Kay* (1897) where a personal representative paid a legacy which appeared small in comparison to the estate at a time when he was unaware of liabilities which exceeded the total value of the estate.

(c) *The beneficiaries may grant a release.* The personal representatives can obtain a release from personal liability from all the beneficiaries affected by the breach. Such a release is only effective where the beneficiaries induced the personal representatives to perform the wrongful act (*Trafford v Boehm* (1746)) or if the beneficiaries are sui juris and fully aware of the breach.

(d) *Limitation.* Where personal representatives have incurred personal liability, they may be able to plead the defence of limitation. Creditors cannot bring an action against personal representatives for non-payment of debts after a period of six years has elapsed from date of distribution of the estate (Limitation Act 1980 s.1). Beneficiaries cannot bring an action against the personal representatives to recover land or personalty after the expiration of 12 years from the date on which the right of action accrued (Limitation Act 1980 ss.13 and 15(1)). No limitation period applies where a personal representative is fraudulent or where the personal representative is in possession of trust property or the proceeds thereof. The limitation period will not start to run against a beneficiary who is under a disability or where there has been fraud, concealment or mistake (Limitation Act 1980 ss.18, 38 and 32).

Personal representatives will obviously be anxious to avoid incurring personal liability. It is possible for them to prevent personal liability ever arising by complying with certain statutory provisions which offer protection. Where a solicitor acts on behalf of personal representatives, the solicitor should endeavour to ensure that they obtain protection. These methods of obtaining protection are considered below.

2. STATUTORY ADVERTISEMENTS (TRUSTEE ACT 1925 s.27)

14.02 Personal representatives who have distributed the assets of the deceased are personally liable to any beneficiaries or creditors for any unpaid debts and liabilities even though they were unaware of them at the time for distribution (*Knatchbull v Fearnhead* (1837)). However they can protect themselves from such liability by advertising for claimants under Trustee Act 1925 s.27.

The advertisements

14.03 Under s.27, the personal representatives may give notice of their intention to distribute the assets of the estate, requiring any person interested to send in particulars of their claim (whether as a creditor or as a beneficiary *Re Aldhous* (1955)) to the personal representatives within a stated time, not being less than two months from the date of the notice. This notice must be brought to the attention of the general public by:

(a) placing an advertisement in the *London Gazette;*

(b) placing an advertisement in a newspaper circulating in the district in which land to be distributed (if any) is situated; and

(c) giving "such other like notices, including notices elsewhere than in England and Wales, as would, in any special case, have been directed by a court of competent jurisdiction in an action for administration". (In an action for administration the court would order the advertisement to be placed in such local or national newspapers as might be appropriate having regard to the circumstances of the case. In cases of doubt, personal representatives should apply to the court for directions as to where to place the advertisements since failure to comply with all the requirements denies them the protection of the section.)

Searches

Section 27(2) provides that personal representatives are not freed: **14.04**

> "from any obligation to make searches or obtain official certificates of search similar to those which an intending purchaser would be advised to make or obtain".

Although this subsection does not list the searches that have to be made the prudent personal representative will make the same searches as a purchaser of land would make in the Land Registry or Land Charges Register, as appropriate, and the local land charges register, as well as searching in bankruptcy against the deceased and any beneficiary receiving assets.

Distributing the estate

Once the time limit on the notices has expired the personal representatives can   **14.05** distribute the estate having regard only to the claims of which they have notice. If a claim is made after distribution by someone of whom they had no notice, the personal representatives are not personally liable. In these circumstances the disappointed claimant must recover the assets from the persons who received them from the personal representatives. So as to avoid delay in the distribution of the estate, these searches and advertisements should be made as early in the administration as possible.

The section does not relieve personal representatives from liability if they have notice of a claim. For example, if they know of a debt they are under an obligation to pay it even though the creditor does not respond to the advertisement. In *MCP Pension Trustees Ltd v AON Pension Trustees Ltd* (2010) trustees had received notice of certain claims but had genuinely forgotten all about them. The trustees claimed that forgetting meant they ceased to have knowledge; and that at that point they ceased to have notice. The section includes no definition of what constitutes notice but the Court of Appeal held that s.27 is only concerned with whether the notice had been received by the time funds were distributed. Once actual notice was given, then in general it would persist and remain notice at the time of distribution. Trustees should, therefore, take particular care to maintain clear trust records so that no claims are overlooked.

A problem with s.27 is that having decided what are the appropriate newspapers, it may prove difficult actually to place the advertisement. For example, in

Re Gess (1942), the deceased was Polish and died in England in 1939. Due to the war, no advertisements could be placed in Polish newspapers. Section 27 was of no assistance to the personal representatives who had to seek a different form of protection (they obtained a *Benjamin Order*—see para.14.10, below).

Contingent liabilities

14.06 Although s.27 gives protection against claims of which the personal representatives have no notice, it gives no protection where personal representatives have distributed the estate with knowledge of a future or contingent liability.

If the personal representatives know that a debt will fall due at some time in the future, they will simply set aside a fund to meet that future liability when the time comes. Contingent liabilities are less easy to deal with. For example the deceased may have guaranteed a debt from a third party; the personal representatives cannot know whether or not the estate will be called upon to honour the guarantee. Similarly, there may be a threat of legal proceedings against the estate; while the personal representatives may suspect that the claimant will not take the matter further they cannot be certain of this. The personal representatives must decide what to do in such a case and there are four courses of action open to them.

First, they can set aside assets from the estate sufficient to meet the contingent liability should it actually arise. This course of action will be unpopular with the beneficiaries since they will only receive the assets once the personal representatives decide the contingent liability can no longer arise (for example when the loan guaranteed by the deceased is paid off or the claimant in the proposed action abandons their claim). It does, however, give the personal representatives total protection provided they have set aside sufficient assets.

Secondly, they can distribute all the assets to the beneficiaries but obtain the beneficiaries' agreement to indemnify the personal representatives if the liability ever crystallises. This will be more popular with the beneficiaries but the personal representatives should be wary since an indemnity is only as financially sound as the beneficiary who gives it. Thus, if the personal representatives distribute assets to a beneficiary who spends the money received on a holiday, an indemnity from that beneficiary will be worthless if they have no other assets. Furthermore, it may not be possible to obtain an indemnity; for example, where a beneficiary is a minor, mentally incapacitated or simply refuses to give one. Even where an indemnity has been obtained from a beneficiary who is financially sound, the inheritance may have been invested in assets which are not easily realisable, for example, a house. In this case calling in the indemnity could cause severe financial hardship, since the beneficiary would have to sell their house to meet their obligation.

14.07 Thirdly, the personal representatives could insure against the liability arising. If cover can be obtained (and it depends very much on the risk involved) the only expense will be the premium on the policy; the assets will pass to the beneficiaries free of any liability as far as they are concerned. Provided the premium is not too high, the beneficiaries are likely to find this the most attractive solution.

Finally, as a last resort the personal representatives can apply to the court for directions. This is obviously an expensive option and personal representatives may wonder if the cost can be justified. However, they should apply where the potential liability is large and insurance cover is not available. In the case of *Re Yorke (Deceased), Stone v Chatway* (1997) Lindsay J. gave guidance on this subject in the context of possible liability in the estates of deceased Lloyd's names. As only a court order can give complete protection it cannot be wrong for executors of Lloyd's Names to insist upon the protection of a court order. In *Re K deceased* (2007) the court held that the same approach should be taken in relation to "stale" claims against the estate where it was unclear whether or not the claims were statute barred. The only way in which the personal representatives could obtain complete protection was to apply to the court for directions. For a fuller discussion see para.14.08, below.

The IHTA 1984 created several problems for personal representatives. Where a person dies within seven years of making a potentially exempt transfer, the lifetime transfer becomes chargeable. The transferee is primarily liable for the tax but the personal representatives of the transferor become liable if the tax remains unpaid for 12 months. There is no obligation to report potentially exempt transfers and such transfers may remain undiscovered until after the personal representatives have distributed the assets. Moreover, the discovery of hitherto unknown lifetime transfers will increase the cumulative total of the transferor at the date of death; this may result in the withdrawal of the nil rate band from all or part of the death estate with a consequent increase in the amount of inheritance tax due.

Personal representatives who are solicitors acting in the course of their practice may be protected by their insurance.

Non-solicitor personal representatives and solicitors who are not acting in the course of their practice have no such protection.

The Revenue issued the following statement published in *The Law Society's Gazette*, March 13, 1991:

> "It may be helpful if I say that the capital taxes offices will not usually pursue for inheritance tax personal representatives who:
>
> - after making the fullest enquiries that are reasonably practicable in the circumstances to discover lifetime transfers, and so
> - having done all in their power to make full disclosure of them to the board of Inland Revenue have obtained a certificate of discharge and distributed the estate before a chargeable lifetime transfer comes to light.
>
> This statement of the board's position is made without prejudice to the application in an appropriate case of s.199(2) of the Inheritance Tax Act 1984.
> I am writing in similar terms to the Law Society of Scotland.
>
> DY Pitts
> Director Capital and Valuation Division, Inland Revenue."

It is clearly important that personal representatives do make adequate enquiries as the above statement only applies where the personal representatives have made "the fullest enquiries that are reasonably practicable in the circumstances". The IHT 400 Toolkit published by HMRC to assist professionals complete the

IHT 400 identifies the omissions of gifts made as a common risk area for personal representatives and advises making careful enquiries.

Deceased Lloyd's Names

14.08 The well publicised problems at Lloyd's meant that many Names were faced with unquantifiable losses. To solve the problems Equitas was created. Names waived their claims against Lloyd's and in return received debt and litigation credits and reinsurance of outstanding open years into Equitas. All business for 1992 and prior years of account was reinsured to close with Equitas upon payment of the appropriate premium.

If the resources of Equitas proved inadequate to meet claims, they could be made against the Names (or their estates). This presented a problem for personal representatives who faced the possibility of personal liability if they distributed the estate without providing for this contingent liability.

The Society of Trust and Estates Practitioners brought the test case *Re Yorke (Deceased), Stone v Chataway* (1997) (referred to in para.14.07, above), hoping that the judgment would remove the need for individual applications to be made for all estates in a similar position. The judgment did not achieve this. It approved the use of Equitas but said that personal representatives would face different levels of risk depending on the circumstances of the case and that they could only obtain full indemnity by applying to court for directions. It was accepted that in appropriate cases, judged to be low risk, personal representatives could take indemnities or rely on insurance.

There is a streamlined form of application available which will be heard by a Master rather than a judge. This is dealt with in Practice Statement, *Chancery Division: Estates of Deceased Lloyd's Names* (2001) which replaced the 1998 Practice Direction.

The Practice Direction contains a specimen witness statement to support the claim form and a specimen draft order although both are likely to need adapting to suit the circumstances of the case.

The risk of liability falling on an estate has been much reduced by two events.

(1) There was a substantial increase in reinsurance cover to Equitas as from March 31, 2006, significantly lowering the risk of default by Equitas.

(2) As from June 30, 2009 all 1992 and prior year non-life business underwritten at Lloyd's by open and closed year Names together with the benefit of substantial reinsurance was transferred to a new company. The transfer binds all policyholders as a matter of UK law meaning that names, and the personal representatives of deceased names, no longer have any liability for 1992 and earlier years of account within the European Economic Area ("EEA"). However the extent to which the Pt VII transfer will be recognised by courts of other overseas jurisdictions in the event that a claim is brought against

a Name in that jurisdiction after the transfer takes effect is uncertain. Therefore personal representatives may still wish to make an application to court.

Bankrupt beneficiaries

There is a risk of personal liability for a personal representative who pays a **14.09** legacy direct to a bankrupt beneficiary rather than the trustee in bankruptcy.

When a trustee in bankruptcy is appointed, all property (which is defined very widely in s.436 of the Insolvency Act 1986) belonging to the bankrupt automatically vests in the trustee in bankruptcy. The statutory definition of "property" includes "things in action". A beneficiary of an estate who is declared bankrupt at a time when the estate is in the process of distribution is entitled to a thing in action - the right to compel due administration of the estate. The benefit of this asset vests in the trustee in the same way as do other assets of the bankrupt. The recent decision *in Raymond Saul & Co v Holden* (2008) confirms that the trustee in bankruptcy is entitled to have the assets comprised in the estate distributed to him even if distribution takes place after the beneficiary is discharged from bankruptcy. Personal representatives should, therefore, consider making a bankruptcy search (see below) before distribution.

If the beneficiary is already bankrupt at the time of the death the thing in action is "after acquired property". The Insolvency Act 1986 s.333(2) requires a bankrupt to give notice to the trustee in bankruptcy of any after acquired property. The trustee in bankruptcy may then claim such property by serving notice on the bankrupt.

Where personal representatives are aware that the beneficiary became bankrupt before the time of the deceased's death, they should insist on seeing the bankrupt's notice to the trustee in bankruptcy. They will then need to confirm whether the trustee in bankruptcy has served or intends to serve notice on the bankrupt. The trustee will normally do so in which case the personal representatives must distribute the property to the trustee.

Where personal representatives are not aware of existing bankruptcy, the position in relation to after-acquired property is not entirely clear. Nineteenth century cases state that someone dealing in good faith with a bankrupt and without notice of the bankruptcy cannot be sued by the trustee in bankruptcy to recover the value of after-acquired property. Section 307(4) of the Insolvency Act 1986 gives protection to persons acquiring property in good faith, for value and without notice of the bankruptcy, but this does not protect personal representatives, as they have not "acquired" the relevant property but have transferred it to the beneficiary. If s.307(4) cannot be relied upon by the personal representatives, they will not obtain a good receipt from the beneficiary and will risk a claim for compensation by the trustee in bankruptcy. See also para.15.40, below.

The prudent course is to carry out a bankruptcy-only search in Form K16 at the Land Charges Department of Her Majesty's Land Registry against the name of each beneficiary to whom it is proposed to make a distribution. Registration in the Land Charges Department remains effective for a period of five years. A search should be made immediately before making a distribution to a beneficiary, since, a search made at an earlier date would not reveal a bankruptcy order made, between the date of the search and the date of the distribution.

3. BENJAMIN ORDERS AND ALTERNATIVES

14.10 The personal representatives will not be protected by Trustee Act s.27 if they are aware of the rights of a claimant but simply cannot find him. In these circumstances the personal representatives can apply to the court for a *Benjamin Order* permitting them to distribute the estate on the basis of a particular assumption.

For example, in the case from which the order took its name (*Re Benjamin* (1902)), the deceased by his will left a beneficiary a residuary gift. The beneficiary disappeared some nine months before the testator died and despite advertisements the beneficiary did not claim his share of the estate. In the circumstances the court permitted the assets to be distributed as if the beneficiary had predeceased the testator. The order may allow the estate to be distributed on some other footing. Thus in an unreported case the estate was distributed on the basis that a child who predeceased the testatrix left no child surviving the testatrix.

In *Re Gess, Gess v Royal Exchange Assurance* (1942), the administrators of a Polish national, who died domiciled in England, were unable to advertise for Polish claimants against the estate because of the outbreak of war. They knew of some debts and applied for permission to distribute the estate. The court held that they could distribute the estate, after setting aside a fund to meet the known Polish liabilities, without making further inquiries or advertisements on the basis that all the debts and liabilities of the estate had been ascertained.

Naturally there must be some factual basis for the assumption set out in the order so that full inquiries must be made by the personal representatives before the court will grant the order. The court will obviously require evidence. An order may be made without the court inquiring further into the circumstances if it is satisfied that the statutory advertisements have proved unsuccessful in tracing the missing person. The making of the order is not conditional on the personal representatives having complied with the requirements of s.27 as to advertisement and searches; the court will decide what, if any, advertisements ought to be made.

If the assumption on which the order was made proves to be wrong, because the supposedly dead beneficiary is shown to be alive, the beneficiary can claim their share of the assets from the other beneficiaries. However, the personal representatives are relieved of personal liability in these circumstances. Once an order is obtained, the personal representatives need take no further steps to protect themselves.

The drawback to applying for a *Benjamin Order* is that it is an expensive procedure. In *Evans v Westcombe* (1999) the court approved the purchase of an insurance policy to cover the possibility of a missing beneficiary returning as an alternative to seeking a *Benjamin Order*. It said that personal representatives, particularly of small estates, should not be discouraged from seeking practical solutions to difficult administration problems without the expense of resort to the court. The court also said that it did not wish to restrict the use of insurance to cases where the personal representative was not beneficially entitled.

Unfortunately the case also demonstrates the weakness of insurance. It may be difficult to quantify the amount to be insured. In *Evans* the missing beneficiary was entitled to half of the residue. The personal representative, therefore, obtained a policy for just over half the value of the estate. She was not advised to consider the possibility of interest. When the missing beneficiary returned, he demanded interest from the date of distribution of the estate. The court agreed that he was entitled to interest but there were no funds available to pay him. On the facts, the court was willing to relieve the personal representative from liability under the Trustee Act 1925 s.61. She had sought legal advice and shown herself willing to follow it and had been unaware of the possibility of interest.

It would have been preferable for the personal representative in *Evans* to have employed genealogists to trace the missing beneficiary. There have been huge improvements in the techniques used by genealogists and it is unusual for them to be unable to trace a missing beneficiary. In any event most insurance companies will now require evidence from genealogists before they will consider insurance. It is normally better practice to use a firm which charges an hourly rate rather than one which takes a contingency fee (typically 30 per cent) from the entitlement of the beneficiary. This is because it is the responsibility of personal representatives to identify and then trace the persons entitled to share in the estate.

The question then arises of whether the costs of the genealogist should fall on the estate generally or on the missing person's share. There is nineteenth century authority that the estate should bear expenses *"incidental to the proper perform-ance of duties of personal representatives as personal representatives"* (*Sharp v Lush* (1879)) and in *Evans v Westcombe* the court approved the cost of insurance falling on the general estate. RSC Order 65 r.14B provided that the costs of inquiries to ascertain the person entitled to a share of the estate should fall on that share unless the court directed otherwise. Order 65 was repealed but a modern court would not necessarily find that the position has reverted to *Sharp*. The just result may be that the costs of ascertaining the beneficiaries entitled to a distinct asset or share of the estate should fall on that asset or share. There is probably a difference between ascertaining how many distinct shares there are (cost to fall on the general estate) and then locating the claimants to a share (cost may properly fall on that share).

The safest course is, however, to ask the court for directions. The best known order is the *Benjamin* order. Alternatively, the court may order that known beneficiaries are entitled to their share of the estate immediately. The practical effect is that the cost of further investigations falls on those who have yet to be traced. (See Civil Procedure Rules, Practice Direction 40A para.7.)

4. ILLEGITIMATE AND ADOPTED BENEFICIARIES

The Family Law Reform Act 1987 abolished the concept of illegitimacy. This **14.11** means that a person may take on the intestacy of a relative even though they, the relative or some person through whom they are related, were born of parents who were not married to each other at any time. Similarly, references to relationships in wills made after April 4, 1988 are, unless a contrary intention appears, construed as including persons whose parents never married or who are related through such persons. The statutory protection previously given to personal representatives who distribute an estate in ignorance of such potential beneficiaries has been withdrawn. However, with respect to intestacy only, a person whose father and mother were not married to each other at the time of their birth is presumed not to have been survived by their father or by any person related to them only through their father unless the contrary is shown.

These rules leave personal representatives in a difficult position.

Inquiries should be made of relatives or others to discover any beneficiaries who may exist, and naturally these inquiries should be conducted with the maximum delicacy and tact. Presumably, if personal representatives advertise under the Trustee Act 1925 s.27 and wait the appropriate period they will obtain the protection of that section. However, they may wish to consider the possibility of insuring against liability and of taking indemnities from the known beneficiaries.

A personal representative is protected if they distribute an estate in ignorance of an adoption of which they do not have notice. Disappointed beneficiaries can claim their share of the estate from the other beneficiaries but not from the personal representatives. The personal representatives, therefore, need take no special steps to protect themselves.

5. The Personal Representatives' Liability in Respect of the Deceased's Leaseholds

General

14.12 On death, a leasehold interest held by the deceased devolves on their personal representatives by operation of law, whether or not they enter into possession of the premises. The nature of their liability for rent or breach of covenants depends on whether their liability is:

    (a) representative, that is deriving from their office; or

    (b) personal, that is arising when they enter into possession of the premises as assignees of the deceased's interest.

Representative liability

14.13 The personal representatives are liable as the deceased's personal representatives for rent due, and any breach committed prior to the death as well as for rent due and breaches committed from death to the expiry, or assignment of the lease (unless the deceased was the original lessee in which case the personal representatives are liable until the expiry of the lease irrespective of any assignment).

In their representative capacity the personal representatives are liable to discharge any liability on a lease to the extent of the assets of the deceased which they have received. If the deceased was an assignee of the lease, the personal representatives can end their liability by surrendering or assigning the lease. If the deceased was the original lessee, assignment will not end their liability. The Trustee Act 1925 s.26, however, protects the personal representatives from further liability once they have assigned (this protection cannot be excluded by the terms of the will). Section 26 as amended provides that the personal representatives will not be liable for a future claim if they do three things.

(a)   satisfy all existing liabilities under the lease which may have accrued and been claimed up to the date of the conveyance to a purchaser or beneficiary;

(b)   where necessary, set apart a fund to meet any future claims that may be made in respect of any fixed and ascertained sum which the lessee agreed to layout on the demised premises, although the period for so doing may not have arrived; and

(c)   assign the lease to a purchaser, legatee, devisee, or other person entitled to call for a conveyance.

Thereafter the personal representatives may distribute the deceased's residuary real and personal estate to or amongst the persons entitled thereto without setting aside a fund to meet any future liability under the lease and the personal representatives will not be personally liable in respect of any subsequent claim under the lease.

The lessor can follow the assets of the estate into the hands of the beneficiaries and claim payment from the assets or their proceeds (s.26(2)).

Personal liability

Personal liability arises when the personal representatives enter into possession, **14.14** whether physically or constructively (for example, by receiving rent from a sub-tenant). The personal representatives are then personally liable for the rent and for any breaches of covenant arising while the lease is vested in them as assignees of the deceased's interest. As the personal representatives are not the original lessees, liability ceases once the personal representatives assign their interest.

Oddly, there are different limits on the extent of the personal representatives' personal liability. For rent, the liability is limited to the amount actually received (or that which with reasonable diligence might have been received) during their period as assignees (*Rendall v Andreae* (1892)). For breaches of other covenants the personal representatives are liable without limit.

The personal representatives have no protection under s.26 against *personal* liability; they should either obtain an indemnity from the beneficiaries or create an indemnity fund from the estate. This fund will be distributed to the beneficiaries once the personal representatives cease to be personally liable, for example, as a result of assigning the lease or termination. Such a fund may be unpopular with the beneficiaries who are likely to prefer an immediate distribution of property. It is, therefore, modern practice to insure against this liability, thus reducing the drain on the estate's assets.

6. LIABILITY FOR ACTS OF AGENTS

14.15   The Trustee Act 2000 s.11 gives trustees and personal representatives wide powers to appoint agents (and nominees and custodians under ss.16 and 17). The appointment can be on such terms as they see fit subject to the limitations contained in ss.14(3) and 20(3). They have to comply with the requirements of s.15 if they wish to delegate their asset management functions.

Section 23 provides that they are not liable for any act or default of the agents, nominees or custodians unless they failed to comply with the statutory duty of care:

(a)   when making the appointment, or

(b)   when reviewing the appointment as required by s.22.

7. THE SIX-MONTH TIME LIMIT

14.16   The Inheritance (Provision for Family and Dependants) Act 1975 s.20 (see Ch.20) gives personal representatives protection provided they wait until the expiry of six months from the grant of representation before distributing the estate, if the court then permits an out-of-time application to be made.

Similarly, if the personal representatives wait for the same period before distributing the estate, they suffer no personal liability if the court then makes an order permitting an out-of-time application to have the deceased's will rectified under s.20 of the Administration of Justice Act 1982. However in neither case are the successful applicants denied the right to recover assets from the beneficiaries who received them from the personal representatives.

Personal representatives are, therefore, wise to wait six months from the grant before distributing the estate.

Where a claim form is issued under the Inheritance (Provision for Family and Dependants) Act 1975 within six months of the date of the grant, claimants have four months under the Civil Procedure Rules in which to serve the form. It is, therefore, arguable that personal representatives should wait ten months from the date of the grant before distributing as the protection of s.20 is only available where the court gives permission for an out of time application. However, it will be exceptionally rare for claimants not to communicate *at all* with personal representatives before serving the claim form. Personal representatives should, therefore, consider all the circumstances before deciding whether or not to delay distribution.

8. Administration Proceedings for Specific Relief

As we have seen if the personal representatives distribute the estate to the wrong **14.17** person or become liable for some expense that was not properly incurred for the benefit of the estate, they are (unless specifically protected) personally liable to make good any loss.

In cases of doubt, prudent personal representatives will apply to the court (Chancery Division or county court where the net estate does not exceed in amount or value the county court limit, at present £30,000).

Applications are made under CPR Pt 64.2. It is possible to apply for a general "administration order". This means that the whole administration is carried out under the direction of the court. This is an expensive and time-consuming process and the court will only make such an order if it considers that the issues between the parties cannot properly be resolved in any other way.

It is much more common to ask the court to determine a specific question. Practice Direction 64A gives the following examples of claims which may be made:

"(1) a claim for the determination of any of the following questions—

   (a)   any question as to who is included in any class of persons having:

      (i)   a claim against the estate of a deceased person;
      (ii)   a beneficial interest in the estate of such a person; or
      (iii)   beneficial interest in any property subject to a trust;

   (b)   any question as to the rights or interests of any person claiming:

      (i)   to be a creditor of the estate of a deceased person;
      (ii)   to be entitled under a will or on the intestacy of a deceased person; or
      (iii)   to be beneficially entitled under a trust;

(2) a claim for any of the following remedies—

   (a)   an order requiring a trustee—

      (i)   to provide and, if necessary, verify accounts;
      (ii)   to pay into court money which he holds in that capacity; or
      (iii)   to do or not to do any particular act;

   (b)   an order approving any sale, purchase, compromise or other transaction by a trustee; or

   (c)   an order directing any act to be done which the court could order to be done if the estate or trust in question were being administered or executed under the direction of the court."

Actions are brought in the Chancery Division by issuing a Pt 8 claim form. All the personal representatives must be made parties and any persons with an interest in or claim against the estate can be made a party if it is appropriate having regard to the nature of the order sought. The trustees will be expected to have canvassed all the adult beneficiaries about the proposed or possible courses of action before applying for directions and to set out the details of the consultation undertaken in their witness statements.

The costs incurred by *all* the parties involved in the action for specific relief are usually paid from the estate or trust fund provided it can be shown that there was a problem which justified the application being made.

The trustees or the party concerned may apply to the court at any stage of proceedings for an order that the costs of any party (including the costs of the trustees) shall be paid out of the fund (a "prospective costs order").

9. ADMINISTRATION OF JUSTICE ACT 1985 s.48

14.18   Where there is doubt as to the construction of a will, s.48 allows the High Court, without hearing any argument, to authorise the personal representatives to act in reliance on a written opinion of a barrister of at least 10 years' standing. The court will not make such an order if there is any dispute as to the construction since it would then be inappropriate to make an order without hearing argument. This provision allows a speedy resolution of difficulties of administration. The order will protect the personal representatives from any action for breach of duty.

Chapter Fifteen

THE PAYMENT OF DEBTS

Personal representatives have a duty to pay the debts of the deceased and must **15.01**
do so with due diligence (*Re Tankard* (1942)). Different rules as to the payment
of debts apply depending on whether an estate is solvent or insolvent.

1. The Solvent Estate

An estate is solvent when the assets are sufficient to pay funeral, testamentary **15.02**
and administration expenses and debts and other liabilities in full. Provided these
can be paid, it is irrelevant that legacies cannot be paid in full. The beneficiaries
of the estate will be concerned to know which assets of the estate will be used in
payment of the debts and which will be available for distribution.

Section 34(3) of the Administration of Estates Act 1925 provides that assets
shall be taken in the order set out in Pt II of the First Schedule to the Act.
However, special rules apply where property of the deceased was charged during
the deceased's lifetime with payment of a debt. This situation will be considered
first.

Debts charged on property

Where a debt has been charged on property of the deceased *during the lifetime* **15.03**
of the deceased (for example, a mortgage debt charged on the deceased's house)
Administration of Estates Act 1925 s.35 provides that such property will be
primarily liable for payment of that debt. Thus, a beneficiary who accepts the
property must accept it subject to the mortgage. The deceased may exclude s.35
by showing a contrary intention in the will, a deed or other document. A charge
is usually expressly created by the deceased but may also arise by operation of
law; for example an Inland Revenue charge for unpaid tax or a charge imposed
by the court on land belonging to a judgment debtor.

The case of *Re Birmingham* (1959) illustrates the difference between a simple
debt and a debt charged on property. T agreed to buy Blackacre from V for
£3,500; contracts were exchanged and T paid a deposit of £350. T died before

completion. In her will T left Blackacre to her daughter, D, and the residue to R. T's solicitors completed the purchase of Blackacre. The court held that D took Blackacre subject to an unpaid vendor's lien for the balance of the purchase price. However, the solicitor's costs were to be paid from the general estate since at the time of T's death they were not charged on Blackacre.

Several properties charged with one debt

15.04 If several properties are charged as security for one debt, each property bears a proportionate part of the debt (s.35(1)) and thus, if each property is given to a different beneficiary, each beneficiary will take his property subject to a charge for a proportionate part of the debt. This is so even if some of the properties are specifically given by the will while some merely pass as part of the residue. In *Re Neeld* (1962) the Court of Appeal said that in such a case the testator is not to be presumed to have thrown the whole debt on to the properties comprised in the residue.

Separate debts

15.05 Where separate properties are charged with separate debts and the debt charged on one property exceeds the value of that property the amount of the deficit will be made up from the deceased's general estate and not from the other charged properties. This will be so even if all the charged properties are given to one beneficiary (*Re Holt, Holt v Holt* (1916)). The only exception is where the testator makes it clear that a gift of several different properties is one gift the whole of which is to be treated as charged with several different debts. In that case the deficit will be made up from the other charged properties (*Re Kensington* (1902)).

The rights of creditors

15.06 Section 35 is only concerned with competition amongst beneficiaries as to the property to be used to pay debts. It does not affect the rights of creditors. A secured creditor may be paid by the personal representatives from the general estate instead of from the charged property; if this happens the doctrine of marshalling will apply as between the beneficiaries so that ultimately the debt falls on the charged property (see below, para.15.23).

Options to purchase

15.07 A testator may give an option to purchase a property in the will. The option may be at an undervalue but even so the person exercising it will be treated as taking the property as a purchaser not as a beneficiary. A purchaser is entitled to have any debt charged on the property paid off from the general estate (*Re Fison's Will Trusts* (1950)) so that they will take the property free from any debt charged on the property.

Contrary intention

Methods of showing contrary intention

Section 35 may be varied if the testator shows a contrary intention. Contrary **15.08**
intention is not shown by a simple direction in the will (or any other document)
that debts be paid from *residue*; such a direction is to be construed as relating
only to debts other than those charged on particular items (s.35(2)(a) and (b)). An
additional indication of intention is required. Thus a gift of specific property *free
from the debt* charged on it will suffice; as will an express direction that a
mortgage or other charge be paid from residue. Less obviously, if a testator
directs that debts be paid from a special fund (*other than residue*) the direction
will be construed as extending to all debts including those charged on specific
items of property.

For example, if a testator has a mortgage debt charged on Blackacre and in
their will directs that:

> "[M]y debts be paid from the proceeds of sale of my shares in X company and the
> residue of my estate be held for A",

all the testator's debts including the mortgage debt will be paid from the proceeds
of sale. If the special fund is insufficient to pay off all debts, any unsatisfied
balance of a charged debt will remain charged on the property and will not be
paid from the general estate (*Re Fegan* (1928)).

A contrary intention need not be referred to in the will. In *Re Ross* (2005) the
deceased made a homemade will which included a gift in the following terms "I
leave devise and bequeath my apartment and contents thereof to my friend Irene
Perrin-Hughes . . . ." At the date of the will the apartment was subject to a
mortgage. The deceased was also paying premiums on an endowment policy
taken out at the same time as the mortgage was arranged and for the same amount
as the mortgage. Towards the end of their life, the deceased had increased their
monthly payments under the policy so as to ensure that there would be sufficient
funds to discharge the mortgage debt. On these facts the judge found that the
deceased intended at the time when he made the will that the gift should be free
of mortgage even though this was not expressly referred to in the will. Consequently s.35 applied.

Taking instructions

A solicitor drafting a will for a client should always inquire whether there are any **15.09**
debts charged on property. If there are, the solicitor should ask whether or not the
client wishes such debts to be paid from the general residue and draft the will
accordingly.

Mortgage protection policies

The most common example of a debt charged on property during the deceased's **15.10**
lifetime is a mortgage. A client who wishes to make a will should be asked about

their mortgage arrangements so that they can consider from what source the mortgage debt is to be paid. It is, however, common for mortgagors to take out a mortgage protection policy. This is a life assurance policy which, on the mortgagor's death, pays either a fixed amount (equal to the original loan) or an amount sufficient to payoff the amount of the loan outstanding at the date of death (i.e. a reducing amount). If the proceeds are to be paid to the estate of the mortgagor they will increase the size of the estate for inheritance tax purposes. The policy may, however, be written in trust for a named beneficiary or assigned to the lender, in which case the proceeds will be paid to that person and will not increase the size of the deceased's estate for inheritance tax purposes.

If two people are buying property jointly they normally each take out such a policy. The terms of the policy may state that the proceeds are to be paid to the surviving joint tenant to the exclusion of the estate of the deceased; if no such statement is included the parties may write each policy in trust for the other. A solicitor, drafting a will, should inquire whether such a policy exists and, if one does, should make sure that the client takes it into account when deciding what directions to leave as to the payment of the mortgage debt.

If the client has bought a house in his or her sole name and has a mortgage protection policy which has not been assigned to the lender, the solicitor should point out the desirability of considering leaving the proceeds of the policy to the person who is taking the property subject to the mortgage, so that there will be funds available to that beneficiary for the discharge of the mortgage debt.

The statutory order for unsecured debts

15.11 The deceased may make express provision for the payment of debts. In the absence of such provision the statutory order of application of assets applies and is set out in Pt II of the First Schedule to the Administration of Estates Act. It is as follows:

(1) Property of the deceased undisposed of by will, subject to the retention thereout of a fund sufficient to meet any pecuniary legacies.

(2) Property of the deceased not specifically devised or bequeathed but included (either by a specific or general description) in a residuary gift, subject to the retention thereout of a fund sufficient to meet any pecuniary legacies, so far as not already provided for.

(3) Property of the deceased given for the payment of debts.

(4) Property of the deceased charged with the payment of debts.

(5) The fund, if any, retained to meet pecuniary legacies.

(6) Property specifically devised or bequeathed, rateably according to value.

(7) Property appointed by will under a general power (including the statutory power to dispose of entailed interests) rateably according to value.

Undisposed of property

Such property may arise where a will does not deal with all the assets of the **15.12**
deceased (i.e. where there is no residuary gift); it may also arise where a
residuary gift fails wholly (i.e. where the residuary beneficiary predeceases the
testator) or partly (i.e. where residue is given to two or more beneficiaries in
equal shares or equally and one or more of the beneficiaries predeceases the
testator, the share of the predeceased beneficiary lapses and passes to the
testator's next-of-kin). Before debts are paid from the undisposed of property a
fund is set on one side for payment of any pecuniary legacies.

Residue

Any general gift of property, that is one which is not comprised in a specific **15.13**
bequest or devise, will be a residuary gift. Thus in *Re Wilson* (1967) T made
some specific and pecuniary legacies and then gave "all my real estate and the
residue of my personal estate". Pennycuick J. held that T's devise of realty fell
within para.(2) despite the fact that there was no prior specific devise.

Before any debts are paid from residue, a fund is set on one side for payment
of pecuniary legacies to the extent that sufficient property was not set aside from
any undisposed of property.

Property specifically given for or charged with payment of debts

Property is specifically *given* for payment of debts where a testator *directs in the* **15.14**
will that it be used for this purpose and leaves no directions as to what is to
happen to any balance left over after the debts are paid, for example, "my debts
are to be paid from the proceeds of my premium bonds".

Property is *charged* with payment of debts when a testator *directs in the will*
that it be used for this purpose and directs that any balance left over after the
debts are paid be given to a particular beneficiary; for example "my debts are to
be paid from the proceeds of sale of my shares in A Co and any balance is to go
to X" or "I give X the proceeds of sale of my shares in A Co subject to payment
of debts". This is quite different from the "charge" referred to in s.35 which
deals with debts charged during the deceased's lifetime on particular assets. In
the case of s.34 the assets were unincumbered *during the deceased's lifetime* and
the charge is imposed by the will.

The retained pecuniary legacy fund

A fund will have been set on one side from the undisposed of property and/or **15.15**
residue to meet pecuniary legacies; if necessary that fund (or part of it) is taken
to pay debts. Pecuniary legacies abate proportionally unless the deceased
directed that certain legacies be paid in priority to the others.

"Pecuniary legacy" is defined widely in s.55(1)(ix) of the Administration of Estates Act to include an annuity, a general legacy and a demonstrative legacy in so far as not discharged out of designated property (for definitions see paras 16.04 and 16.05, below).

Property specifically devised or bequeathed rateably according to value

15.16 The order makes no distinction between devises and bequests; both are equally available.

    (a) *Value* means value to the testator. Thus a mortgage charged on the property would be deducted when calculating the value of the property but a legacy charged on the property by the testator in the will would not (*Re John* (1933)).

        Example

        T owns Blackacre value £10,000 but subject to a mortgage of £4,000. T owns Whiteacre value £10,000. T's will gives Blackacre to B and Whiteacre to W but charges Whiteacre with payment to L of a legacy of £6,000. There are debts to pay of £2,000 (apart from the mortgage) and no other assets. Blackacre had a value to the testator of £6,000 (£10,000 − £4,000). Whiteacre had a value to the testator of £10,000.
        Therefore:

        Blackacre bears 6,000/16,000 × £2,000 = £750 of the debts

        Whiteacre bears 10,000/16,000 × £2,000 = £1,250 of the debts

        In addition Blackacre is charged with payment of the mortgage (unless the will directed otherwise) and Whiteacre with payment of the legacy.

    (b) *Option to purchase.* T's will may give a person an option to purchase property at a stated price. This price may well be at an undervalue in which case the will gives the "purchaser" a benefit. The personal representatives may wonder whether such property is available for payment of debts as if it were a specific gift.

        In *Re Eve* (1956) Roxburgh J. directed that when personal representatives were calculating what property to use for payment of debts they should not regard property subject to an option to purchase as equivalent to a specific gift of that property. They should first calculate whether once the purchase price for the property was paid there would be sufficient assets to meet all the debts of the testator. If there would, the purchaser is free to exercise the option and will purchase the property subject to the option. If there would not, the option cannot be exercised and the personal representatives must take the property and use it for payment of debts. Roxburgh J. concluded that:

        "the property subject to an option is the last to be available for the payment of debts. For, indeed, in so far as the property subject to the option is required for the payment of debts, the option over the property cannot be exercised at all and the benefit of it is totally destroyed by the operation of law".

Property appointed under a general power of appointment

Where the testator has a general power of appointment (that is, a power to **15.17** appoint property to anyone the testator pleases) and exercises the power expressly in the will, such property is taken last for payment of debts.

Section 27 of the Wills Act 1837 provides that where a testator has a general power of appointment which is not exercised expressly in the will it is deemed (subject to a contrary intention in the will) to have been exercised by any general gift contained in the will. Thus, for example, if X has a general power of appointment over Blackacre but makes no mention of the power or of Blackacre in the will a general gift of "all the rest of my property" or "all my realty" would be sufficient to dispose of Blackacre. However, if (as a result of s.27) property is included in a general gift it will be treated as available for payment of debts as part of residue not as property subject to a general power.

Property outside the statutory order

Property subject to a *donatio mortis causa* or to a statutory nomination is **15.18** available for payment of debts but is not mentioned in the statutory order. It would, therefore, be taken after all the other assets were exhausted. According to *Re Eve*, if a testator gives a person an option to purchase property at an undervalue the property subject to the option is taken to pay debts when it is necessary to do so because all other assets are exhausted, and not otherwise. It is, however, impossible to say in what order assets subject to an option to purchase, *donatio mortis causa* or nomination would be taken as between themselves.

Variation of the statutory order

A testator has a right to vary the statutory order. There are two ways in which this **15.19** is commonly done.

A gift of residue "subject to" or "after" payment of debts

If residue is given to several beneficiaries in equal shares and one of those **15.20** beneficiaries predeceases the testator that share of residue lapses and becomes undisposed of property. Undisposed of property is normally taken first for payment of debts and any balance will then be available to the testator's next-of-kin. If, however, the testator directs that residue be taken *after* payment of debts (or gives the residue *subject* to payment of debts) that is construed as an express direction that debts be paid from the whole residue before it is divided into shares. Thus, the living beneficiaries and the testator's next-of-kin will bear a proportionate part of the debt and will, therefore, receive a proportionate share in the balance.

Example

(a) *No contrary intention.* T gives certain specific bequests and leaves the residue to A and B in equal shares. B predeceases T. The estate, after setting aside the specific bequests but before paying debts and other liabilities, amounts to £20,000. Debts amount to £8,000. B's lapsed share amounts to £10,000. The debts will be paid from that lapsed share leaving a balance of £2,000 available to T's next-of-kin. A will take £10,000.

(b) *Contrary intention.* The same situation but T leaves the residue *after payment of debts* to A and B in equal shares. The debts must be paid from the £20,000 before it is divided into shares. £12,000 will be left after payment of debts and A and T's next-of-kin will divide this equally. A will, therefore, take £6,000 and T's next-of-kin will take £6,000.

Property "given for" or "charged with" payment of debts—intention to exonerate residue

15.21 If a testator merely gives property for or charges property with payment of debts this will not in itself be sufficient to vary the statutory order. Such property will merely fall within paras (3) or (4) of the statutory order (i.e. property specifically given or charged with payment of debts) and will, prima facie, be taken after property within paras (1) and (2) of the statutory order (i.e. undisposed of property and residue) is exhausted. However, if the will shows an intention to exonerate the property which would otherwise be taken first, this will vary the statutory order. It has been held that where a will contains a gift of residue to a beneficiary together with a direction that debts be paid from a specified fund this shows an intention to exonerate the residue and the statutory order will be varied.

In *Re James* (1947), for example, the testator charged certain specific property with payment of debts and gave the residue to his wife. Roxburgh J. held that the will showed a clear intention to exonerate the residue and therefore the debts would be paid from the charged property.

Conversely in *Re Gordon* (1940) a testatrix directed that her debts be paid from a sum of £50 and any balance therefrom be paid to a named charity. There was no gift of residue. It was held that the statutory order was not varied as there was no indication of an intention to exonerate other property; therefore, the debts were to be paid from the undisposed of property and the £50 was to be paid in full to the charity.

Presumably any form of words could be used in a will to show an intention to exonerate other property. Thus in *Re Gordon* had T expressly declared that debts were to be paid from the £50 "in exoneration of any undisposed of property" the result would have been different.

Desirability of making express provision for payment of debts

When drafting a will it is desirable to discuss with the testator the possibility of **15.22** making express provision for the payment of debts since this will allow a testator to consider the question of debts and to make his own decision as to the property to be used.

The doctrine of marshalling

If a personal representative takes assets falling within one of the later paragraphs **15.23** in the statutory order to pay debts before assets falling within the earlier paragraphs are exhausted, the creditors will be entirely unconcerned. Creditors merely want payment; the source of the payment is irrelevant to them. A beneficiary, on the other hand, will be very concerned if property which that beneficiary hopes to take is wrongly used to pay debts. Marshalling is a way of adjusting the assets so as to compensate a disappointed beneficiary where a payment has been made from the wrong assets.

> *Example*
>
> X is administering the estate of T. T's will left shares in ABC Ltd (value £2,000) to S and the residue of the estate to R (the residue consists of land worth £20,000). There is a debt of £2,000 to pay. The debt *should* be paid from residue. If X uses the shares to pay the creditor, S will be disappointed. However, S can be compensated from property falling within any of the earlier paragraphs. S is therefore entitled to £2,000 from the residuary assets.

2. INSOLVENT ESTATES

Introduction

An estate is insolvent if the assets are insufficient to pay all the funeral, **15.24** testamentary and administration expenses, debts and liabilities. The beneficiaries of the deceased's will or the deceased's next-of-kin under the intestacy rules will receive nothing and the creditors of the estate will not all be paid in full.

There are three methods of administering an insolvent estate:

1. The most economic and straightforward method is for the deceased's personal representatives to do so under a normal grant of representation. Creditors are entitled to take a grant. If a creditor wants to administer and those entitled in priority will neither renounce nor get on with the job, the creditor can use the citation process to try and clear them off or apply to the registrar to pass them over under the Senior Courts Act 1981 s.116. There is no need for the person appointed to be a qualified

insolvency practitioner (Administration of Insolvent Estates of Deceased Persons Order (SI 1986/1999) art.4(3)).

2. It is possible for the court to take over the administration by making an administration order under CPR Pt 64. This means that the personal representatives act under the direction of the court. The courts are not anxious to undertake such a role and professional advisers rarely consider this route.

3. The other alternative is for the estate to be administered by a trustee in bankruptcy following an insolvency administration order made by the bankruptcy court. Creditors or personal representatives can petition and in either case the order vests the estate in the Official Receiver. Subsequently a trustee in bankruptcy will be appointed. The creditors will normally appoint the trustee in bankruptcy and creditors' committee.

The Administration of Insolvent Estates of Deceased Persons Order 1986 art.4(1) provides that, whether the estate is administered by a trustee in bankruptcy or by the deceased's personal representatives the same rules apply to:

(a) the respective rights of creditors;

(b) provable debts;

(c) the valuation of future and contingent liabilities; and

(d) the priority of debts.

In general, therefore, it does not matter whether the estate is administered by a trustee in bankruptcy or by the deceased's personal representatives.

However, there are certain situations where a trustee in bankruptcy has advantages.

1. Challenging lifetime transactions for the benefit of the estate

15.25 A trustee can challenge transactions:

(a) under the Insolvency Act 1986 s.339 if made at an undervalue within "the relevant time" (two years ending with death or five years if the deceased was insolvent at the time or became so as a result of the transaction: Insolvency Act 1986 s.341 as modified by the Administration of Insolvent Estates of Deceased Persons Order);

(b) under the Insolvency Act 1986 s.423 if made at an undervalue for the purpose of putting assets beyond the reach of creditors; and

(c) under the Insolvency Act 1986 ss.340–342 which have preferred some creditors at the expense of others.

Personal representatives are not entitled to bring proceedings to set aside any preference or transaction at an undervalue; if there are grounds for taking such action, that would be a reason for presenting an insolvency administration petition to allow a trustee in bankruptcy to be appointed and pursue such claims.

2. Disclaiming onerous property

A trustee can disclaim onerous property even if he/she has gone into possession, **15.26** attempted to sell it or in some other way exercised rights of ownership (Insolvency Act 1986 s.315). Onerous property is defined in s.315 as any:

(a) unprofitable contract; and

(b) property in the deceased's estate which is unsaleable or not readily saleable, or is such that it may give rise to a liability to pay money or perform any other onerous act.

For example, therefore, any lease which contains covenants on the part of the tenant can be disclaimed.

3. Dealing with the deceased's dwelling house

Other people may have an interest in assets of the deceased (typically a spouse **15.27** in the matrimonial home). Personal representatives and trustees in bankruptcy can apply to the court for an order for sale. Where the application is first made by the trustee in bankruptcy more than 12 months after the deceased's property vested in them, the court will assume, unless there are exceptional circumstances, that the interests of the creditors outweigh all other considerations (Insolvency Act 1986 s.335A(3)). Where the application is made by personal representatives, there is no such assumption so they may have more difficulty.

There is a limit of three years on the period during which the trustee in bankruptcy can deal with a bankrupt's interest in a dwelling house which is the sole or principal dwelling house of the bankrupt, the bankrupt's spouse, civil partner or a former spouse or civil partner (Insolvency Act 1986 s.283A).

It is possible for personal representatives to apply for the appointment of a trustee in bankruptcy if it becomes apparent that there are reasons justifying it at any stage of the administration.

It is important to consider the position as to payment of professional charges where an estate is insolvent. The rules for ordinary personal representatives have changed as a result of the Trustee Act 2000 s.35(3)(b). A solicitor's charges whether made under an express charging clause or under the statutory power contained in s.28 are no longer regarded as a legacy but as "administration expenses". As such they have priority over the preferential debts listed in the Insolvency Act 1986.

A trustee in bankruptcy can charge for his or her services and again the charges will be administration expenses and have priority over preferential debts.

A solicitor appointed as executor should bear in mind that, although administration expenses have priority, the estate may be too small to cover them.

Therefore, if there is a chance that an estate will be insolvent, it is important to assess the risk before committing a substantial amount of time to the estate. Solicitor-executors, and indeed, other executors, may want to renounce. It is important not to intermeddle in an estate which may be insolvent.

Where personal representatives are administering an estate which is (or may turn out to be) insolvent it is important that they observe the correct order for payment of creditors. This is:

(a) funeral, testamentary and administration expenses, and then

(b) the bankruptcy order.

This order cannot be varied by the testator. If the personal representatives do not follow the statutory order they will incur personal liability for "superior" debts which have been left unpaid. Therefore, if there is any possibility that an estate may be insolvent the personal representatives should observe the statutory order when paying debts.

Where an insolvency order is made, it relates back to the date of death. Hence, payments made between death and the order are void unless ratified by the court (Insolvency Act 1986 s.284, as modified by the Administration of Insolvent Estates of Deceased Persons Order 1986). Solicitors acting in relation to the administration should be careful about running up legal expenses unless they are clearly for the benefit of the estate as the court will not ratify unnecessary expenses. See *Re Vos; Dick v Kendall Freeman* (2006).

Assets and liabilities

15.28 When a living person is declared bankrupt there are special rules of bankruptcy which swell the bankrupt's assets. These rules also apply to an insolvent estate by virtue of the Administration of Insolvent Estates of Deceased Persons Order 1986 (SI 1986/1999). The same Order provides that where a bankruptcy petition is presented and then the debtor dies, the bankruptcy proceedings may continue despite the death of the debtor.

All debts and liabilities, present or future, certain and contingent, liquidated or unliquidated are provable against an insolvent estate. If the value of a liability is uncertain (because it is contingent or for any other reason) its value must be estimated (Insolvency Act 1986). A debt which is statute-barred is not provable where the estate is insolvent.

Availability of joint property

15.29 A Court of Appeal decision (*Re Palmer (Deceased) (A Debtor)* (1994)) held that jointly held property passed to the co-owner on death as usual and was not available to the administrator of the estate.

The effect of this decision was reversed by a new s.412A inserted into the Insolvency Act 1986 by the Insolvency Act 2000 s.12. The trustee in bankruptcy of a deceased insolvent can now apply to the court to recover the value of the deceased's former interest in joint property from the survivor for the benefit of the estate. The trustee in bankruptcy can only make the application where the petition for the insolvency order is presented after April 2, 2001 and within five years from the date of death. When deciding whether or not to make the order the court must have regard to all the circumstances of the case including the interests of the creditors and the surviving joint tenant. Unless the circumstances are exceptional, the court must assume that the interests of the creditors outweigh all other considerations.

Note that the application must be made by a trustee in bankruptcy so, where the deceased was a joint tenant, this will be a reason for creditors to petition for an insolvency administration order appointing a trustee.

Secured creditors

A creditor may have security for a debt; for example a bank may have given a **15.30** loan to the deceased and taken a charge over the deceased's house or other assets as security. Such a creditor has a choice.

(a) The creditor may rely on their security and not prove for their debt at all. This is a safe course provided the security is sufficient to cover the debt.

(b) The creditor may realise the security and if the security is inadequate prove for any balance as an unsecured creditor.

(c) The creditor may value the security and prove for any balance as an unsecured creditor. Care must be taken in such a valuation. If the creditor puts too low a value on the security the personal representatives can insist on redeeming it at that value leaving him to prove as an unsecured creditor for the balance. If they put too high a value on it and proves as an unsecured creditor for the balance, they will prove for an insufficient amount.

(d) The creditor may surrender their security and prove for the whole debt as an unsecured creditor.

In so far as the secured creditor obtains payment by realising the security, they have priority over all unsecured creditors of the estate and receives payment in priority to the funeral, testamentary and administration expenses.

Funeral, testamentary and administration expenses

These are paid in priority to all unsecured debts and liabilities of the deceased **15.31** and are paid in priority to preferred creditors. Where an estate is insolvent "reasonable" funeral expenses are likely to be on a lower scale than would be the case with a solvent estate. Personal representatives' charges now rank as administration expenses (Trustee Act 2000 s.35).

Other debts and liabilities

15.32 The Administration of Insolvent Estates of Deceased Persons Order 1986 provides that the bankruptcy order is to apply to the payment of all other debts and liabilities.

The bankruptcy order

15.33 The bankruptcy order is set out in Insolvency Act 1986 ss.328 and 329 and is as follows (after the payment of the expenses of the bankruptcy):

(a) Preferred debts.

(b) Ordinary debts.

(c) Deferred debts.

Within each category the debts rank equally and if the assets are insufficient to meet the debts of one category in full all debts in that category abate proportionally.

Creditors can claim for debts which are contingent, future or the value of which can only be estimated (Insolvency Act 1986 s.382(3)).

Where a trustee in bankruptcy is administering the estate, the trustee must estimate the value of any debt which is uncertain. This is subject to the court's overall supervision. Once estimated by the trustee or by the court, this is the amount which is treated as due (Insolvency Act 1986 s.322(4)).

Where personal representatives are administering the estate, they must estimate the value of the debt. If the other creditors do not accept the valuation, the personal representatives should apply to the court for directions under CPR Pt 64.

Preferred debts include:

15.34 Wages or salary or accrued holiday remuneration owed by the deceased to an employee in respect of the whole or any part of the period of four months before death, such amount not to exceed the limit prescribed by the Secretary of State (currently £800).

If a landlord carries out a distraint on the deceased's goods within three months of death the preferred creditors have a first claim on the goods (or the proceeds of sale). This is to prevent a landlord making use of the special remedy of distraint to obtain payment from the assets of the estate before the preferential creditors. However the landlord is entitled to replace in the order of priority any creditor who is paid as a result of such a claim (Insolvency Act 1986). So to this extent a landlord will get priority over other ordinary creditors.

If the landlord recovers an amount in excess of six months' rent accrued due before death any excess must be held for the estate.

The Tribunals, Courts and Enforcement Act 2007 s.71 will abolish the common law right to distrain for arrears of rent A landlord under a lease of commercial premises will be able to exercise a new (and more limited) statutory right, called commercial rent arrears recovery (CRAR) to enter let premises, take control of goods belonging to the tenant, sell them and recover rent arrears from the proceeds of sale. The new procedure contains the same limits on time and amount as the common law remedy. At the time of writing the relevant provisions are not yet in force.

Ordinary debts

These are all other debts which are not deferred.   **15.35**

Interest

Any surplus remaining after the payment of preferred and ordinary debts shall be   **15.36**
used to pay interest on preferential and ordinary debts from death till payment
(ordinary debts ranking equally with preferential debts for this purpose). The rate
of interest payable is whichever is the greater of:

(a) the rate specified in s.17 of the Judgments Act 1838 at death; and

(b) the rate otherwise applicable to that debt.

Deferred debts

Deferred debts are debts owed in respect of credit provided by a person who   **15.37**
(whether or not the deceased's spouse at the time the credit was provided) was
the deceased's spouse at the date of death. Such debts are payable after the
payment of preferred and ordinary debts and the interest thereon.

Liability for unpaid debts

Personal liability of personal representatives

If a personal representative pays an inferior debt knowing of the existence of a   **15.38**
superior debt, the payment is taken as an admission by the personal representative that they have sufficient assets to pay all debts of which they have notice
which rank in priority to the inferior debt. The personal representative will,
therefore, be personally liable to pay all such debts.

However, they are not personally liable if, without undue haste, they pay an
inferior debt without notice of a superior one. (This is unlike the position of a
personal representative who pays a *beneficiary* without notice of the existence of
a debt of the deceased).

Limited protection

15.39   A personal representative is under a duty to pay all debts in the same category *pari passu* (i.e. proportionately) and has no right to prefer one creditor above others in the same class.

However, under s.10(2) of the Administration of Estates Act 1925 there is limited protection for a personal representative who pays a debt in full at a time when he has no reason to believe the estate is insolvent. A personal representative who makes a payment in such circumstances to a creditor (including himself, unless he took a grant of representation in the capacity of creditor) is not liable to account to other creditors of the same class as the creditor who has been paid, if it subsequently appears that the estate is insolvent.

The section does not protect a personal representative against creditors in a superior category nor does it protect a personal representative who had any reason to believe that the estate was insolvent.

The problem of bankrupt beneficiaries

15.40   A personal representative who pays a legacy direct to a beneficiary who is bankrupt rather than to the trustee in bankruptcy runs the risk of personal liability (see further *Law Society's* Practice Note). When a trustee in bankruptcy is appointed, all property (which is defined very widely in s.436 of the Insolvency Act 1986) belonging to the bankrupt automatically vests in the trustee in bankruptcy: s.306 of the Insolvency Act 1986. A beneficiary of an estate has a chose in action—the right to compel the due administration of the estate. If, therefore, a beneficiary is declared bankrupt during the administration of the estate, the chose in action will vest in the trustee in bankruptcy in the same way as other assets.

The beneficiary may have been automatically discharged from bankruptcy before the personal representatives are ready to distribute but, despite the discharge, the personal representatives must distribute the assets to the trustee not the beneficiary. See *Re Bertha Hemming Deceased, Raymond Saul & Co v Holden* (2008) which confirms this. Only in cases in which the bankrupt has already been discharged from bankruptcy at the time of the death of the testator or the intestate under whose estate the former bankrupt benefits does the trustee in bankruptcy have no claim.

If the beneficiary is already bankrupt when the death occurs, the chose in action is "after acquired property". Section 333(2) of the Insolvency Act 1986 requires the bankrupt to give notice to the trustee in bankruptcy of any property devolving on him. The trustee in bankruptcy is then entitled to claim it by serving notice under Insolvency Act 1986 s.307 on the bankrupt. The personal representatives would then be required to transfer the estate assets to the trustee.

There is no specific protection for personal representatives who distribute in ignorance of a bankruptcy. The safe course is, therefore, to carry out a bankruptcy-only search at the Land Charges Department of HM Land Registry before making a distribution. See also para.14.09, above.

CHAPTER SIXTEEN

LEGACIES AND DEVISES

1. LEGACIES AND DEVISES

A legacy is a gift in a will of personalty; a devise is a gift in a will of realty.   **16.01**

2. CLASSIFICATION OF LEGACIES

Legacies may be classified as specific, general, demonstrative, pecuniary or   **16.02**
residuary. The classification is important because different types of legacy have
different characteristics.

Specific legacies

A specific legacy is a gift of a particular item of property owned by the deceased   **16.03**
at the time of death and distinguished from all other property owned by the
deceased of a similar type.
    Examples of specific legacies are:

> "I give the gold ring I bought in Manchester to X"
> "I give my shares in ABC Ltd to Y."

Specific legacies suffer from the disadvantage that they may fail as a result of the
doctrine of ademption. Ademption means that a specific legacy fails if the
subject-matter has ceased to form part of the deceased's estate at death. This may
be because the property has been sold or has completely changed its substance.
The disappointed beneficiary will receive no compensation from the rest of the
estate. Only specific legacies suffer ademption; therefore when construing a will
the court tends to construe a legacy as general rather than specific where possible
(*Re Rose* (1949)). (For a fuller discussion of ademption, see paras 16.15–16.17,
below.)
    As we saw in Ch.15 specific legacies (and devises) are available for payment
of debts, but only after such items as undisposed of property, residue and any
retained pecuniary legacy fund have been exhausted.

General legacies

16.04   A general legacy is a gift in a will of an item of property which is not
distinguished from property of a similar type. If the deceased does not own
property at the date of death corresponding to the description in the will, the
personal representatives must purchase suitable property using funds from the
estate. In determining from which part of the estate such funds are to be provided
a general legacy is treated as a pecuniary legacy so that the same rules which
apply to the incidence of pecuniary legacies—see paras 16.46–16.50, below—
apply to the incidence of general legacies.
    An example of a general legacy is:

> "I give 100 shares in ABC Ltd to Y."

This is a gift of *any* 100 shares in ABC Ltd. The mere fact that at the time of
making the will the testator owned exactly 100 shares in the company is not
sufficient to turn the legacy into a specific legacy (*Re Willcocks* (1921)). If a
legacy is to be construed as specific there must be a clear indication in the will
itself that the testator is referring to particular property owned at the time of the
will. A general legacy is not liable to ademption but will be taken for payment
of debts before specific legacies. (See para.16.08, below.)

Demonstrative legacies

16.05   A demonstrative legacy is "in its nature a general legacy but there is a particular
fund pointed out to satisfy it" (per Lord Thurlow, *Ashburner v MacGuire*
(1786)).
    Examples of a demonstrative legacy are:

> "I give £100 to X to be paid from my current bank account."

> "I give £100 to Y to be paid out of my National Savings Certificates."

A demonstrative legacy combines the attributes of general and specific legacies.
It is treated as a specific legacy to the extent that the particular fund is in
existence at the date of death and is therefore taken for payment of debts after
general legacies. If, however, the particular fund is not in existence at the date of
death the legacy is not adeemed (as a specific legacy would be). Instead it is
treated as a general legacy and paid from any other property available in the
estate.

Pecuniary legacies

Description

16.06   A pecuniary legacy is a gift in a will of money. Most commonly a pecuniary
legacy is general (for example, "I give £100 to X") but it may be specific (for

example, "I give the £100 I keep in a box under the bed to Y") or demonstrative (for example, "I give £100 to Y to be paid from my current bank account)".

Annuities

An annuity is a pecuniary legacy payable by instalments.   **16.07**

The Administration of Estates Act 1925 s.55(1)(x)

Section 55(1)(x) defines a "pecuniary legacy" for the purposes of the Act. The   **16.08**
expression:

> "[I]ncludes an annuity, a general legacy, a demonstrative legacy so far as it is not discharged out of the designated property, and any other general direction by a testator for the payment of money, including all death duties free from which any devise, bequest or payment is made to take effect."

Thus, a gift of "the £100 I keep in a box under my bed" being a specific legacy is not treated as a pecuniary legacy for the purposes of the Administration of Estates Act; the £100 would, therefore, rank with the other specific legacies for payment of debts.

Availability for payment of debts

In the order of availability of property for payment of debts set out in the   **16.09**
Administration of Estates Act, the fund set on one side for payment of pecuniary legacies is taken fifth, whereas specific legacies (and devises) are taken sixth after the retained fund has been exhausted. If only part of the retained fund is required for payment of debts the various pecuniary legacies will abate proportionally (unless the testator indicated that one legacy was to be paid in priority to the others in which case the indication is binding on the personal representatives).

Residuary legacies

A residuary gift in a will passes the property of the deceased not otherwise   **16.10**
disposed of. It may be a gift of the entire net estate if no other dispositions have been made or it may be a gift of what is left after payment of specific and general gifts. It may be limited to personalty not otherwise disposed of but more usually it will not be so limited and will pass all property whether realty or personalty.

3. DEVISES

A devise is a gift of realty and can be either specific or residuary. If specific it is   **16.11**
subject to the rules on ademption.

4. FAILURE OF LEGACIES AND DEVISES

Introduction

16.12 A gift made in a valid will can fail for a number of reasons. Some of the more important are listed below:

    (a) disclaimer;

    (b) ademption;

    (c) the beneficiary predeceases the testator;

    (d) divorce or the termination of a civil partnership;

    (e) uncertainty;

    (f) the beneficiary witnesses the will;

    (g) the gift is contrary to public policy or for an illegal or immoral purpose;

    (h) the gift is conditional and the condition is not fulfilled;

    (i) the doctrine of satisfaction;

    (j) the gift is induced by force, fear, fraud or undue influence (this has already been considered in Ch.2); and

    (k) the gift infringes the rules against perpetuity or accumulations (a consideration of these rules and their consequences is beyond the scope of this book).

Effect of failure

16.13 Any legacy or specific devise which fails will fall into residue unless the testator has included a substitutional gift. If a residuary gift fails, the property is undisposed of and passes under the intestacy rules to the testator's next-of-kin.

Disclaimer

16.14 No one can force another to accept a benefit under the will. Beneficiaries are free to disclaim any property given by will. However, it is not normally possible to pick and choose—unless the will provides to the contrary, the whole of a gift must be disclaimed or the whole must be accepted; if, however, two entirely separate gifts are made one may be accepted and the other disclaimed. Once a person has accepted any benefit from a gifted property (for example, income from or interest on it) it is too late to disclaim. (It may, however, be possible to vary the terms of the deceased's disposition by a variation agreement.) A fuller discussion of the practical considerations involved in disclaimers and variations will be found in Ch.19, below.

A voluntary disclaimer made during the lifetime of a testator is ineffective (see *Smith v Smith* (2001)). This is because, until the death, a beneficiary has no interest to accept or disclaim; he has a mere expectation of an interest.

Ademption

Introduction

As we saw in para.16.03 and in para.16.11, a specific legacy or devise will fail **16.15** if the subject-matter does not form part of the testator's estate at death. Ademption may occur as a result of sale or destruction of the asset or a change in substance. A disappointed beneficiary has no rights to receive the proceeds of sale where property has been sold nor any rights to the proceeds of any insurance policy where property has been destroyed. There are a number of aspects of the doctrine of ademption which warrant fuller consideration.

A change in substance

A change in substance will cause ademption to take place but a mere change in **16.16** form will not. It is sometimes difficult to decide whether a change is one of substance or of form. In *Re Clifford* (1912), T gave 23 "of the shares belonging to me" in a named company. After the date of the will the company changed its name and subdivided each share into four. Swinfen Eady J. held that the legacy was not adeemed since the subject-matter remained exactly the same although changed in name and form. The beneficiary, therefore, took 92 of the new shares. In *Re Slater* (1907), a testator made a gift of shares in Lambeth Waterworks Company. After the date of the will the company was taken over and amalgamated with other waterworks companies into the Metropolitan Water Board which issued stock to replace shares held in the old companies. The Court of Appeal held that the legacy was adeemed since the new stock was in an entirely different organisation.

In *Re Dorman, Smith v National Childrens Home* (1994) the deceased left the sums contained in a named deposit account to the trustees of a settlement in which she had enjoyed a life interest. These sums represented income of the trust fund which she had received but not spent. After the date of the will these accounts were closed on her behalf and the sums transferred to an account bearing a higher rate of interest (this was done under an enduring power of attorney—see below). The court held that because the accounts were so similar and were funded in the same way there was no change of substance and no ademption.

Effect of republication

If a legacy has been adeemed and the testator afterwards makes a codicil which **16.17** republishes the will, it normally has no effect on the ademption. For example, if T left Blackacre to B, sold Blackacre, then made a codicil republishing the will,

B would still have no rights to the traceable proceeds of sale even if they were identifiable.

However, as a result of the republication the will may be construed in such a way that a gift which would otherwise have been adeemed will be saved. For example, T gives "the house in which I now reside to X." Such a gift is a specific devise and if T sells the house after the date of the will it will be adeemed; if T buys another house X is not entitled to the replacement. However, if T makes a codicil to the will after the purchase of the replacement house, the will is republished as at the date of the codicil and, since the wording used in the gift is wide enough to cover *any* house in which T is residing at the appropriate time, X will be entitled to the replacement house.

A codicil republishing a will can only have the effect of passing a replacement asset if the wording used in the original will is sufficiently wide. If, for example, T gave "the 3 stone diamond ring I bought in London in 1971 to X" and the ring was stolen the gift would be adeemed; if the ring was insured T might use the insurance money to buy an identical three stone ring but even if T made a codicil republishing the will the wording would be too specific to cover the replacement and X would get nothing.

The effect of the doctrine of conversion

16.18   When a vendor enters into a binding contract to sell realty the equitable doctrine of conversion applies so that the vendor is treated from the date of the contract as having an interest in the proceeds of sale rather than in the realty. If T makes a will leaving freehold property, Blackacre, to B and then enters into a binding contract to sell Blackacre, the devise is adeemed from the date of the contract. If T dies between contract and completion B is entitled to any rent or other income Blackacre may produce until completion but B is not entitled to the proceeds of sale, which will fall into residue.

The anomalous rule in *Lawes v Bennett* (1785) can in certain circumstances convert property retrospectively; this may lead to ademption. If T makes a will leaving Blackacre to B and residue to R, later grants an option to purchase Blackacre to O and dies before the option has been exercised, Blackacre passes to B. However, if O subsequently decides to exercise the option this effects a retrospective conversion so that Blackacre is deemed to have been converted into proceeds of sale from the date of T's death. The sale proceeds are therefore paid to R and not to B—B is not, however, required to repay any rents or income received since the date of death.

The rule in *Lawes v Bennett* was extended to a gift of shares subject to an option to purchase in *Re Carrington* (1932). The result was that, when the option to purchase the shares was exercised, the shares were deemed to have been sold as at the date of the testator's death. The gift of shares was treated as adeemed and the proceeds of sale fell into residue.

If the will is made or republished after the date of the grant of the option the testator is deemed to have intended to pass to the beneficiary the property *or* the proceeds of sale so that no ademption will take place even if the option is exercised. The beneficiary will be entitled to the proceeds of sale (*Drant v Vause* (1842)).

Property to be ascertained at date of death

A testator may make a gift of assets to be ascertained at the date of death, for **16.19** example a gift of "all the shares in ABC Co. which I own at my death". Such a gift is not subject to the doctrine of ademption as such, although it will fail if the testator owns no assets corresponding to the description at the date of death.

Problems when drafting a will

The effect of the doctrine of ademption should always be explained to a client **16.20** who wishes to make a bequest or devise of a specific item.

It is possible to include words of substitution so that a testator might give "my shares in ABC Co. or any shares representing that investment at the time of my death." However, such a gift may well create problems for the personal representatives in identifying such shares, particularly if the death occurs some time after the will is made. It may, therefore, be preferable simply to point out to the client the importance of reviewing the will periodically so that it can be changed if an asset specifically given is sold, destroyed or substantially changed.

Alternatively, it may be possible to word the gift so that the precise property is to be ascertained at the date of death (as suggested in para.16.19, above) or to give a pecuniary legacy in substitution for a legacy failing by reason of ademption.

Mental incapacity of donor

The Mental Capacity Act 2005 gives the court and deputies appointed by it wide **16.21** powers to deal with the affairs of mentally incapable persons. There is a danger that assets will be dealt with in a way inconsistent with the wishes of the incapable person as expressed in a valid will made before incapacity. Schedule 2 of the Mental Capacity Act contains provision to ensure as far as possible that ademption of gifts in such a will does not occur. The schedule provides that (in so far as circumstances allow) testamentary beneficiaries shall take the same interest in substituted property as they would have taken in the original property. This makes it unnecessary for a new will to be made by the court.

However, there is no corresponding provision for dealings by the donee of an enduring or lasting power of attorney. The result is that the donee must either check the terms of any will and try to avoid action which will result in ademption or if (as is likely) this is impossible, apply to the court for a statutory will. The dangers of such ademption were illustrated in *Re Dorman, Smith National Childrens Home* (1994), although on the particular facts of the case the court was able to find that ademption had not taken place. In *Banks v National Westminster Bank* (2005), however, the gift of a house sold by the attorney was adeemed.

Beneficiary predeceases testator

Introduction

16.22   In order to take a gift under a will a beneficiary must survive the testator. If the beneficiary predeceases the testator a legacy will lapse and fall into residue or if it is a residuary gift will pass under the intestacy rules. A beneficiary need only survive for a very short period—a minute or a second will suffice.

If a gift is to joint tenants or is a class gift, it will not lapse unless all the joint tenants or members of the class predecease the testator; if one joint tenant or class member survives the testator, that one person takes the whole gift. If a gift is to tenants in common, the share of any tenant who predeceases the testator will lapse.

A testator cannot exclude the doctrine of lapse by declaring that it is not to apply. A testator can, however, include a substitutional gift providing that if the beneficiary predeceases, the property is to pass to another person.

A solicitor should always point out to a client the possibility that a beneficiary may predecease so that the client can consider including a substitutional clause. It is also common to include a survivorship clause in a will. A survivorship clause states that a beneficiary is only to take a benefit under the will if the beneficiary survives the testator for a stated period (usually 28 days). The effect is to prevent a beneficiary who only survives the testator by a very short period from benefiting under the will. The importance of such a clause is obvious when it is remembered that a beneficiary may be *deemed* to survive under the Law of Property Act 1925 s.184 (see para.16.23, below). Without a survivorship clause, the testator's property would pass under the terms of the beneficiary's will or to the beneficiary's next of kin under the intestacy rules. Such a devolution of property might be contrary to the testator's wishes.

Substitutional and survivorship clauses may alter the inheritance tax payable on an estate. Since the introduction of the transferable nil rate band, it is not always advisable to include them in wills made by married couples or civil partners. For a fuller discussion of this topic see Ch.22.

Where the order of deaths is uncertain

16.23   **The statutory presumption.**   It can sometimes happen that there is no evidence as to the order in which people have died, for example where two people die in a car accident. In such a case, s.184 of the Law of Property Act 1925 provides that for the purposes of succession to property the deaths are presumed to have occurred in order of seniority so that the elder is presumed to die first. The section applies equally on intestacy (with one exception which will be considered later).

> *Example*

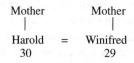

Harold and Winifred both die in a car accident; the order of their deaths is uncertain. They have each made wills leaving all their property to the other. They have no children. Each has a mother who survives.

Harold, being the elder, is presumed to die first. His property therefore passes under the terms of his will to Winifred who is presumed to have survived him. His property forms part of her estate. The gift in Winifred's will to Harold lapses and her estate (which now includes Harold's property) passes to her mother under the intestacy rules. It is unlikely that Harold would have wished his property to pass to Winifred's mother in preference to his own; had he included a survivorship clause in his will his property would not have passed to Winifred and so would not have gone to her mother.

Exceptions to the doctrine of lapse

There are two situations where, despite the fact that a beneficiary has pre-deceased a testator, a gift will not fail.   **16.24**

(a) Gifts in discharge of a moral obligation.

(b) Section 33 of the Wills Act 1837.

Point (a), above, is of comparatively minor importance and can be dealt with briefly; (b), however, warrants a more detailed examination.

Gifts in discharge of a moral obligation

If a testator makes a gift to beneficiary in order to discharge a moral obligation   **16.25** and the beneficiary predeceases the testator the gift will not lapse but will form part of the beneficiary's estate. Examples of gifts which have been held to be in discharge of a moral obligation are a direction to pay a statute-barred debt (*Williamson v Naylor* (1838)) and a mother's direction that the creditors of her deceased son be paid (*Re Leach's Will Trusts* (1948)).

The precise limits of the rule are uncertain and it may be that it applies only to directions to pay debts and not to ordinary gifts (*Stevens v King* (1904)).

Section 33 of the Wills Act 1837

The section.   Section 33(1) (as substituted by the Administration of Justice Act   **16.26** 1982) applies where a testator dies after December 31, 1982. (The rules contained in the original s.33 which applied before 1983 are not dealt with in this book.) The substituted s.33 provides that where:

(a) a will contains a devise or bequest to a child or remoter descendant of the testator; *and*

(b) the intended beneficiary dies before the testator, leaving issue; *and*

(c) issue of the intended beneficiary are living at the testator's death, then, unless a contrary intention appears by the will, the devise or bequest shall take effect as a devise or bequest *to the issue* living at the testator's death.

Section 33(3) provides that such issue take "according to their stock, in equal shares if more than one, any gift or share which their parent would have taken."

Example

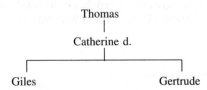

Thomas leaves Catherine a legacy of £20,000 in his will but Catherine predeceases Thomas. Normally the gift to Catherine would fail; however, as a result of s.33 the gift does not fail but passes equally to Giles and Gertrude who take £10,000 each.

Section 33 goes on to provide that no issue shall take whose parent is living at the testator's death and so capable of taking.

Example

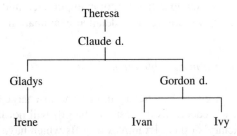

Theresa leaves Claude a legacy of £20,000. Claude and Gordon predecease Theresa. The gift to Claude does not lapse but passes to his issue. Gladys receives one-half (her issue are entitled to nothing as she is still alive); Gordon has predeceased Theresa and therefore his share of £10,000 is divided equally between his issue, Ivan and Ivy, who take £5,000 each.

The section does not make it clear whether, where a gift is contingent, substituted beneficiaries must satisfy the same contingency as primary beneficiaries. Etherton J. in *Ling v Ling* (2002) said that they must.

16.27   Class gifts.   Section 33(2) provides that where:

    (a) a will contains a devise or bequest to a class of persons consisting of children or remoter descendants of the testator; and

    (b) a member of the class dies before the testator, leaving issue; and

    (c) issue of that member are living at the testator's death.

then, unless a contrary intention appears in the will, the devise or bequest shall take effect as if the class included the issue of its deceased member living at the testator's death. Under s.33(3) the issue take *per stirpes* according to their stocks, in equal shares if more than one, the share which their parent would have taken and no issue whose parent is living at the time of the testator's death shall take.

Example

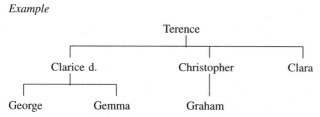

Terence leaves £30,000 to be divided "amongst all my children". Clarice predeceases Terence. Her one-third share (£10,000) will be divided *per stirpes* amongst such of her issue, George and Gemma, as survive Terence. Section 33(3) will apply so that no issue shall take whose parent is living at the testator's death. Therefore Graham will take nothing.

Contrary intention. Both s.33(1) and s.33(2) are expressed to be subject to **16.28** contrary intention. There is, however, some uncertainty as to precisely what constitutes "contrary intention" for this purpose. The original s.33 of Wills Act 1837 stated that it was not to apply when an interest was determinable at or before death. Thus, that section did not save a life interest to a child of the testator who predeceased, nor a gift to a child of the testator as a joint tenant or as a member of a class who predeceased leaving surviving joint tenants or class members; nor did it apply to a gift contingent on an event which had not occurred when the child predeceased. The substituted s.33 does not contain such exclusions and it is not clear whether or not a testator making gifts on such terms thereby demonstrates a contrary intention. If a testator does not wish the issue of a deceased child (or remoter descendant) to take a benefit the safest course is to include a provision stating what is to happen in the event of such predecease. (See the discussion of the new s.33 and will drafting below.)

In *Ling v Ling* (2002) the court had to consider whether or not a will expressed contrary intention. The gift was to children *"living at my death"*. The court held that those words added nothing. They merely stated expressly what would otherwise be implicit, that a class is normally composed of those members, if any, in existence at the death of the testator. To exclude s.33 there would have to be words making it clear that issue were not to be substituted.

Children whose parents were not married and children en ventre sa **16.29** **mere.** Section 33(4) provides that for the purposes of s.33 the illegitimacy of any person is to be disregarded. Thus, a child whose parents were not married can take in the same way as a child whose parents were married. The subsection also provides that a child *en ventre sa mere* is living for the purposes of the section.

The effect of the substituted s.33 on will drafting. As explained above if a **16.30** testator does *not* want s.33 to apply it is desirable for the avoidance of doubt to state in the will what is to happen where a child predeceases. However, even in those cases where a gift to a testator's deceased child (or remoter descendant) *is* to pass to the child's issue, it is desirable to include an express provision to this effect rather than to rely on the section for the following reasons:

(a) If the substitution is set out in the will, a solicitor can be certain that the effect of the statutory provision is brought to the attention of the client; this gives the client the opportunity to request an alternative if the statutory provision does not correspond with their wishes.

(b) If the gift to the testator's child (or remoter descendant) is contingent it is desirable to provide expressly for the possibility that the child might survive the testator but die without fulfilling the contingency leaving issue.

(c) If the gift to the testator's child (or remoter descendant) is contingent it is desirable to state expressly whether or not a substituted beneficiary is to take subject to the same contingency.

In cases where a gift is made to anyone other than a child (or remoter descendant) of the testator (for example "to the children of my brother") an express substitutional gift to issue *must* be included if the testator wants the gift to pass to issue in substitution for a beneficiary who predeceases. Section 33 applies only to gifts to the testator's children (or remoter descendants).

Section applies only where child or issue predecease testator

16.31 If a gift to a child fails for any other reason, for example because of disclaimer or the effect of the forfeiture rule, s.33 does not apply.

Example

Tessa leaves £100,000 to her son, Sam. Sam has two children, Gerry and Gemma. Sam murders his mother in a fit of rage and so forfeits his entitlement under his mother's will. Gerry and Gemma do not replace Sam under s.33 because Sam did not predecease his mother.

The Law Commission recommended in "The Forfeiture Rule and the Law of Succession" (Law Com. No.295) that the harshness of this aspect of the rule should be removed. The Civil Law Reform Bill would have enacted this recommendation (and similar recommendations in relation to disclaimer) but the Bill was lost in the run up to the General Election in 2010. (see below). A private members' bill, the Estates of Deceased Persons (Forfeiture Rule and Law of Succession) is passing through Parliament at the time of writing. The Bill received its second reading in January 2011. The Ministry of Justice has indicated that it will support the Bill and has assisted with drafting both the Bill and the explanatory notes published with it.

Divorce

Wills Act 1837 s.18A as amended by the Law Reform (Succession) Act 1995

As we saw in Ch.2, in cases where a marriage is dissolved or annulled or a civil   **16.32**
partnership is terminated the former spouse is to be treated as having died on the
date of dissolution or annulment. Thus, any gifts made by will to a spouse and
appointments of a spouse as executor will fail.

The effect of the s.18A amendment on will drafting

The fact that the former spouse is to be treated as *dying* on the date of dissolution   **16.33**
or annulment means that the will drafting problems revealed by *Re Sinclair* are
no longer relevant.

A substitutional gift expressed to take effect "if my spouse predeceases or
does not survive me for [a specified period]" will now take effect if the primary
gift to the spouse fails as a result of s.18A.

It is no longer *necessary* to include the words "or fails for any other reason".
However, it is still *desirable* to include such words in case of failure from some
other unforeseen reason—for example, forfeiture. See *Re Jones (Deceased)*
(1997).

In any event it is always desirable to suggest that clients who are contemplating divorce should review their wills and that they should do so as early as
possible since the mere fact of separation (or even a decree of Judicial Separation) will not revoke testamentary dispositions.

Uncertainty

Introduction

If it is impossible to identify either the subject-matter or the objects of a gift, it   **16.34**
will fail for uncertainty.

Uncertainty of subject-matter

Gifts of "some of my best table linen" (*Peck v Halsey* (1726)) or of "a handsome   **16.35**
gratuity" (*Jubber v Jubber* (1839)) have been held to be void for uncertainty. (In
some cases such gifts may now be saved by the Administration of Justice Act
1982 s.21).

A gift may prima facie be of an uncertain amount and yet be capable of
assessment in which case it will not fail. For example, a clause giving a
beneficiary a power to select such items as he wishes is valid; so also is a
direction that a beneficiary enjoy "a reasonable income" from the testator's
properties (*Re Golay* (1965)) since the court can, if necessary, determine what is
a reasonable income.

Uncertainty of objects

16.36   If the beneficiaries are not clearly identified the gift will fail. Thus, a gift to "the son of A" where A had several sons fails for uncertainty (*Dowset v Sweet* (1753)). It is, therefore, important when drafting a will to take care to check the names of individuals and institutions intended to benefit.

   The only case where a gift will not fail for uncertainty of objects is where a testator wishes to make a charitable gift and does not sufficiently identify the charity which is to benefit. The gift will not fail so long as it is clear that the gift is for exclusively charitable purposes. The court will direct a scheme to give effect to the gift. Where there is an error in the name of a charity a cheaper procedure is to apply to the Attorney-General for directions under the Royal Sign Manual.

The beneficiary witnesses the will

The general rule

16.37   Section 15 of the Wills Act provides that a gift made to a beneficiary fails if:

   (a)   the beneficiary witnesses the will; or

   (b)   the spouse or civil partner of the beneficiary witnesses the will.

The validity of the will itself is not affected. The rule exists to ensure that wills are reliably witnessed by independent persons.

Beneficial gifts only

16.38   Section 15 applies only to beneficial gifts. Thus, if a gift is made "to X as trustee to hold for Y" and X or X's spouse witnesses the will the gift does not fail. The gift would fail if Y or Y's spouse witnessed the will.

Subsequent events irrelevant

16.39   It is the time of execution which is important. Subsequent events are irrelevant. Thus, if a witness marries a beneficiary *after* the date of execution of the will the gift remains effective (*Thorpe v Bestwick* (1881)). Similarly, if a gift is to the holder of an office or to a person fulfilling a description the gift will remain effective even though a witness later takes up the office or comes to fulfil the description (*Re Ray's Will Trusts, Public Trustee v Barry* (1936)).

Gift made or confirmed by independently witnessed will or codicil

16.40   A gift will not fail if there is a codicil or will which can be said to confirm the will and which is not witnessed by the beneficiary (or the beneficiary's spouse).

It is not necessary to find any express reference to the gift in the independently witnessed will or codicil. In *Re Trotter* (1899) T made a gift by will to B, a witness; there were two later codicils to the will; B did not witness the first but did witness the second. The court held that, as there was one independently witnessed codicil, the gift to B did not fail.

Secret trusts

If T creates a secret (or half secret) trust in favour of X and X or X's spouse **16.41** witnesses the will, X does not lose his entitlement. This is because X takes under the trust and not under the will (*Re Young* (1951)).

Superfluous attesting witnesses

In the case of a testator dying after May 29, 1968, the Wills Act 1968 provides **16.42** that the attestation of a will by any beneficiaries or their spouses or civil partners is to be disregarded if without them the will is duly executed.

Thus, if a will is witnessed by three people, one of whom is a beneficiary (or spouse of a beneficiary) that person may take a gift in the will; however, if two of the three witnesses (or their spouses) are beneficiaries their signatures cannot be disregarded and neither can take.

If a person (other than the testator) has signed a will, it is presumed that the signature is as a witness. The presumption can be rebutted—for example, by evidence that the signature was to indicate approval of the testator's disposition. If a beneficiary (or spouse of a beneficiary) is able to show that a signature was in such a capacity, there is no question of loss of entitlement.

A charging clause used to be regarded as a pecuniary legacy. However, the Trustee Act 2000 s.28 provides that a charging clause is no longer a legacy for the purposes of the Wills Act 1837 s.15 or for the purposes of abatement of legacies.

This means a solicitor can witness a will containing a charging clause even though the solicitor (or the firm in which the solicitor is a partner) is appointed executor. The right to charge will not be forfeited.

Because a charging clause was regarded as a legacy, it used to be necessary to provide that a solicitor's charges be paid "*in priority to other pecuniary legacies*". This was to prevent them abating with the other pecuniary legacies where the estate was too small to pay all pecuniary legacies in full. As the Trustee Act 2000 s.18 provides that such clauses are no longer legacies, there is no question of abatement and such clauses are unnecessary.

The gift is for an illegal or immoral purpose or contrary to public policy

Such a gift cannot take effect. The principles to be applied in deciding whether **16.43** a gift is illegal, immoral or contrary to public policy are the same as in the law of trusts. The law relating to public policy is not fixed but changes with the passage of time.

In *Gray v Barr* a broad principle of public policy was expressed as being "that no man should be allowed to profit at another person's expense from his own conscious and deliberate crime". Thus, if one person, B, is found guilty of murder of another, T, B cannot take any benefit under the will of T or under the intestacy rules if T dies intestate. Any person claiming from B's estate (for example, B's issue) are also excluded. The Law Commission recommended in "The Forfeiture Rule and the Law of Succession" (Law Com. No.295) that the harshness of this aspect of the rule should be removed (see below).

The rule of public policy will not apply if the killing was carried out while B was insane within the *McNaghten* rules.

There was some doubt as to whether the rule applied to all or only some types of manslaughter.

Re H (Deceased) had suggested that the rule of public policy applied to prevent B taking any benefit if the person has been found guilty of deliberate, intentional and unlawful violence but not otherwise.

However, the majority in *Dunbar v Plant* held that the forfeiture rule applied to all cases of manslaughter. The harshness of applying the forfeiture rule inflexibly to all classes of manslaughter in all circumstances was mitigated by the Forfeiture Act 1982 (see below) which allows relief from forfeiture in certain circumstances. Phillips L.J. said:

> "I can see no reason now for the court to attempt to modify the forfeiture rule. The appropriate course where the application of the rule appears to conflict with the ends of justice is to exercise the powers given by the Act."

In *Dalton v Latham* (2003) (where the claimant was acquitted of murder on the grounds of diminished responsibility but pleaded guilty to manslaughter) Patten J. held that *Dunbar v Plant* (1998):

> "[M]ust now be taken to be a binding statement of the law as to the application of the rule of public policy. It applies to all cases of unlawful killing, including manslaughter by reason of diminished responsibility or by reason of provocation. The only possible exception is where the defendant is found to be criminally insane, which leads to an acquittal".

The same approach was taken in *Land v Land* (2007) despite the fact that an application under the Forfeiture Act was impossible because it was out of time. However. The court allowed the deceased's son to make an application under the Inheritance (Provision for Family and dependants) Act 1975 on the basis that reasonable financial provison had not been made for his maintenance.

The Forfeiture Act 1982 allows the court to offer relief from the harshness of the forfeiture rule. It does not apply where a person has been convicted of murder but applies in any other case where one person has unlawfully killed another (for example, manslaughter) and is precluded by reasons of public policy from taking an interest in property. An offender may apply to the court within three months of the date of conviction (s.2) for an order modifying the forfeiture rule in respect of any beneficial interest which the offender would have acquired from the deceased (but for the forfeiture rule) inter alia:

(a) under the deceased's will or on intestacy;

(b) on a nomination by the deceased; and

(c) as a *donatio mortis causa* (s.2(4)(a)).

An application may also be made where property had been held on trust for any person and as a result of the deceased's death but for the forfeiture rule the offender *would have* acquired an interest in the trust property (s.2(4)(b)).

Section 4(5) of the Act *appears* to provide that where there is more than one interest in property to which the forfeiture rule applies the court may exclude the rule in respect of any *but not all* and where there is one such interest the court may exclude the rule in respect of *part only* of that interest. However, in one of the first applications to come before the court (*Re K* (1985)) Vinelott J. stated that the Act was a private members bill and is not couched in technical language but is intended to be understood by persons other than lawyers specialising in property and trust matters. He said that in his view s.4(5) was intended to enlarge the power of the court by making it abundantly clear that the court is not bound to relieve against the forfeiture rule entirely or not at all but that the court is free if it chooses to modify the effect of the rule to a limited extent. His first instance judgment was approved by the Court of Appeal.

The court must not make an order unless satisfied that the justice of the case requires the forfeiture rule to be modified having regard to the conduct of the offender and of the deceased and to such other circumstances as appear to the court to be material (s.2(2)).

In *Dunbar v Plant* (1998) the Court of Appeal allowed relief from forfeiture to the survivor of a suicide pact in relation to the proceeds of an insurance policy taken out by the survivor's fiance (he had died as a result of the pact). The court held that the survivor had committed the criminal offence of aiding and abetting her fiance's suicide and, therefore, the forfeiture rule applied. However, the Forfeiture Act 1982 s.1(2) allows courts flexibility in applying the rule in cases where public policy demands a more sympathetic approach. Accordingly, she was granted full relief from forfeiture.

No application may be made after the expiry of the three-month period (s.2(3)). This time limit is strict and the court has no discretion to extend it. See *Land v Land* (2007).

A personal representative, who is administering an estate where the deceased was unlawfully killed by another person who would but for the forfeiture rule have received any of the interests in the property set out above, should wait for the expiry of the three months from conviction before distributing such property to others.

Section 3 of the Act provides that the forfeiture rule is not to be taken to preclude any person from making an application under the Inheritance (Provision for Family and Dependants) Act 1975. Such an application can be made if the requirements of *that* Act are complied with. Thus, an applicant must be able to show that the disposition of the deceased's estate effected by the will or by the intestacy rules did not make reasonable financial provision for the applicant (*Re Royse* (1984)). See *Land v Land* (2007).

Re Jones (Deceased) (1997) and *Re DWS* (2000) make it clear that a person whose interest has been forfeited is not to be treated as having predeceased. Hence, a substitutional gift expressed to take effect only if the beneficiary predeceases will not come into effect. If there is an intestacy, the statutory trusts will not apply to allow substitution of issue as issue cannot take if their parent is "living".

For possible changes to the law see para.16.31, above.

Failure of a condition

16.44   If a legacy is conditional on an event or circumstance which at the date of death is impossible or not present, the legacy will fail. However, the court may be able to construe the will in such a way that the legacy is found not to be conditional on the event or circumstance.

In *Watson v National Children's Home* (1995) a testator left half of his estate to one charity and the other half to a second charity conditional on the latter caring for his domestic pets. If the second charity did not agree to do so the residue was to pass entirely to the first charity.

At the time of his death the deceased had no pets. The first charity argued that the gift to the second charity failed because the second charity could not fulfil the condition. The court held that the condition was impossible to fulfil and should be regarded as spent. As such the second charity took the gift absolutely. The clause had to be construed as requiring the charity to care for any of the deceased's pets but if there were none the gift should still pass. If the gift was not construed in this way, it would be deemed ambiguous and extrinsic evidence would be admitted under s.21 of the Administration of Justice Act 1982. The deceased had clearly stated that only if the charity refused to look after his pets should the gift fail.

It may be that a condition attaching to a legacy is void. In *Nathan v Leonard and National Association For Mental Health* (2002) the deceased directed that, if any one of the beneficiaries contested the will, the entire estate was to go to a married couple who were taking two thirds of the residue and who she was anxious to provide for adequately. One of the other residuary beneficiaries made a claim under the Inheritance (Provision for Family and Dependants) Act 1975 for further provision be made for him from the estate. The married couple contended that this brought the forfeiture clause into effect.

There were three issues:

(a)   Was the forfeiture clause void either for repugnancy or because it was contrary to public policy?

(b)   If it was valid, had it been breached?

(c)   If breached, was the gift over to the married couple effective?

The court held that the clause imposing forfeiture was not repugnant. A condition is only repugnant if it is inconsistent with ownership. There is nothing inconsistent about a gift subject to divesting. Inconsistency only arises if the gift purports to limit the incidents of ownership, such as the ability to sell.

Equally, although the condition might well have a strong deterrent effect on a beneficiary who was contemplating making a claim under the Act, that did not in itself make the condition contrary to public policy.

Making an Inheritance Act claim would amount to contesting the will for this purpose and would breach the clause.

However, it was clear that some words had been mistakenly omitted from the final sentence of the codicil. Since it was impossible for the court to say what the omitted words were, the condition failed for uncertainty. The legacies were, therefore, free from the condition.

The doctrine of satisfaction

The equitable presumption of satisfaction is based on the assumption that a **16.45** parent would wish to treat their children fairly and would not wish to make provision for one of their children twice over at the expense of their other children. In appropriate circumstances equity will presume that the second gift satisfies the first. It is merely a presumption and can be rebutted by evidence of the testator's intention.

The presumption of satisfaction has various aspects. We are here concerned with the ademption of a legacy as a result of a subsequent portion. The topic may sound rather outdated but there have been a number of recent cases confirming that the presumption is still active.

A "portion is . . . very broadly speaking, a gift intended to set up a child in life or to make substantial provision for him or her . . . " per Lindsay J. in *Re Cameron (Deceased)* (1999).

It is only lifetime gifts which are classified as "portions" that cause problems in this context. A mere gift is not a portion. There must be an idea of making a permanent provision for the child.

In *Taylor v Taylor* (1875) it was held that paying for the son's entry into Middle Temple, buying him an army commission (after he had given up the idea of law) and buying him a mining business (after he had given up the idea of the army) were all portions. However, other lesser payments including paying his gambling debts were not.

In *Re Cameron* (1999) it was held that it was irrelevant whether the gift was made by the father or the mother (or someone else *in loco parentis*). The gift in *Re Cameron* was actually made *on behalf of* the mother under an enduring power of attorney. Moreover, it was made not to the legatee but to the child of the legatee to cover school fees.

In *Race v Race* (2002) Behrens J. concluded that the rule against double portions can now apply to gifts of land (previously there was some suggestion that it applied only to personalty).

In *Casimir v Alexander* (2002) Hart J. held that the age of the child was irrelevant. The child in question was an old-age pensioner. The gift was a house and thus not a means of assisting her to earn her own livelihood. The gift was capable of being a portion as the key element is the permanent nature of the provision rather than the age or status in life of the donee. However, on the facts, there was sufficient evidence to rebut the presumption. The deceased regarded his daughter as having "earned" the gift through her long years of caring for him and his wife. Moreover, it was a condition of the gift purchase that she would continue caring for her father in the new house. This meant that there was a motive for the lifetime gift which differentiated it from the testamentary gift.

When deciding whether or not a legacy has failed, it is the donor's intention at the time of the later gift that is important not the intention at the time of the will. Even so, if it is apparent at the time a will is made that a testator is intending to make a subsequent gift to one child, it will be sensible for the testator to make a written statement as to his present intention and place it with the will.

5. Incidence of Pecuniary Legacies

Introduction

16.46 Throughout this section the term "pecuniary legacy" is used in the Administration of Estates Act sense to cover a general legacy, an annuity or a demonstrative legacy so far as it is not discharged from the designated property.

If a will gives a pecuniary legacy to a beneficiary, the personal representatives will need to know from which part of the estate they are entitled to take assets to pay the legacy. We saw in Ch.15 that personal representatives have exactly the same problem when deciding which assets are to be used for payment of debts and that there are statutory rules which govern availability of assets for payment of debts. The position with regard to pecuniary legacies is, however, much less certain. This area of the law has been described as "tortuous" and "notoriously obscure" (per Salt, QC, Ch., in *Re Taylor's Estate* (1969)). It is most desirable that anyone drafting a will should avoid any problems of statutory interpretation by stating expressly what property is to be taken for payment of pecuniary legacies.

However, in the opinion of the writers this tortuous area has been simplified by the Law Reform (Succession) Act 1995.

No undisposed of property

16.47 The pre-1926 rules still apply which means that pecuniary legacies are payable from residue. Under the rule in *Greville v Brown*, where a testator gives residue (both real and personal) in one mass to a beneficiary the realty is available to pay pecuniary legacies *but only* in so far as the personalty is exhausted. The precise wording of the gift is irrelevant so long as the testator makes it clear that there is one single gift consisting of both realty and personalty. An example of such wording is "I give all my residue, both real and personal, to X".

Under the rule in *Roberts v Walker* where a testator directs that pecuniary legacies be paid from a mixed fund of realty and personalty, the legacies are payable *proportionately* from both realty and personality. An example of such wording would be "I give my residue, real and personal, on trust for sale to my trustees to use the proceeds to pay my legacies and hold any balance for X".

The question of the extent to which realty is available will only rarely be of any importance.

For example, if residuary realty is given to one person, R, and residuary personalty to another person, P, R will obviously want to insist that legacies be paid exclusively from personalty (P will be equally anxious that realty be made available).

Undisposed of property

The Trusts of Land and Appointment of Trustees Act 1996 amends the Admini- **16.48**
stration of Estates Act 1925 s.33 to read as follows:

> "(1) On the death of a person intestate as to any real or personal estate, that estate shall be held in trust by his personal representatives with the power to sell it.
> (2) The personal representatives shall pay out of—
>
>   (a) the ready money of the deceased (so far as not disposed by his will, if any); and
>   (b) any net money arising from disposing of any other part of his estate (after payment of costs),
>
>   all such funeral, testamentary and administration expenses, debts and other liabilities . . . and out of the residue of the said money the personal representative shall set aside a fund sufficient to provide for any pecuniary legacies bequeathed by the will (if any) of the deceased."

The effect of the amended s.33(2) is, therefore, to make undisposed of property primarily liable for payment of pecuniary legacies. Ready money will be used first but thereafter it is irrelevant whether the undisposed of property is realty or personalty.

Example

T's will leaves a pecuniary legacy of £6,000 to L and the residue to A and B in equal shares. A predeceases T and the gift to him lapses. The estate amounts to £20,000. There are no debts. Since s.33(2) expressly directs that pecuniary legacies be paid from money arising from disposing of *any* part of the estate as to which the deceased was intestate, the pecuniary legacy will be paid from the lapsed share of residue irrespective of whether it is realty or personalty. Therefore B gets £10,000 and A's lapsed share of £10,000 is used to pay L's legacy of £6,000. The balance of £4,000 left after payment of the pecuniary legacy will pass under the intestacy rules to T's next of kin.

Are there any circumstances in which s.33(2) does not apply?

Before the amending of s.33 by the Trusts of Land and Appointment of Trustees **16.49**
Act 1996 it was clear that the direction to pay pecuniary legacies contained in s.33(2) related only to the proceeds of the *statutory* trust for sale imposed by

s.33(1). The statutory trust for sale could not apply if a will imposed an *express* trust for sale because there cannot be two trusts for sale, one statutory and one express, applying to the same property (*Re McKee* (1931)). The express trust took precedence over that imposed by s.33(1). If s.33(1) did not apply then neither did s.33(2) which deals with the proceeds of sale arising under the statutory trust.

> *Example*
>
> A testator died before January 1, 1996 leaving a pecuniary legacy of £6,000 to L and directing that the residue was to be held *on trust for sale* for A and B in equal shares. A predeceased T and the gift to him lapsed. The estate amounted to £20,000.

Since the testator had imposed an express trust for sale on the residue there was no room for a statutory trust for sale to apply to the residue. Thus, s.33(1) did not apply to the undisposed of property and therefore s.33(2) (which dealt only with the proceeds of sale arising from the statutory trust) could not apply. The question then arose of what property was to be used to provide for the payment of the legacy to L. Unfortunately the answer was by no means certain.

There were several conflicting cases—*Re Midgley* (1955), *Re Beaumont's Will Trusts* (1950), and *Re Taylor's Estate* (1969). The better view was that when s.33(2) did not apply, the payment of legacies was still governed by the pre-1926 rules. The result was that legacies were not payable primarily from undisposed of property.

The position may now have been simplified by the Trusts of Land and Appointment of Trustees Act 1996.

It seems to the writers that in the amended s.33 the link between the two subsections is broken. Pecuniary legacies are to be paid from cash in the estate at death or produced by the sale of *any* part of the estate and, therefore, it is irrelevant whether the undisposed of property is held on a statutory or an express trust.

If this interpretation of the new section is correct it removes an area of unnecessary complexity and uncertainty from the administration of estates. Where the will makes no special provision for the payment of pecuniary legacies, they will always be paid from cash either contained in the estate at death or resulting from the disposal of any part of the estate as to which the deceased was intestate.

Will drafting

16.50 Despite the probable simplification of the law it is clearly desirable when drafting wills to state expressly what property is to be used for payment of pecuniary legacies. For example, a testator may leave residue "subject to payment of legacies". It is common for trusts for sale to direct that legacies be paid from residue before division into shares; this is certainly a solution to the problem of uncertainty but it does not necessarily reflect the wishes of testators. Many testators might prefer a direction that, where residue is left on trust, in the event of any share of residue lapsing, pecuniary legacies should be paid from the lapsed share of residue, thus reducing the amount passing under the intestacy rules.

6. Income from and Interest on Legacies and Devises

Introduction

A personal representative cannot be compelled to pay legacies and distribute the **16.51** estates before the expiry of one year from the death (Administration of Estates Act 1925 s.44). Even in a very simple administration there will inevitably be delay between the death and the distribution. Beneficiaries will want to know what rights they have to income or interest in that period.

This part of the chapter is concerned with the rights of a beneficiary:

(a) to receive *income* which has been produced by assets in the period between the death of the testator and the vesting of the assets in the beneficiary; and

(b) to receive *interest* paid from the estate on the value of a pecuniary (or general) legacy in the period between the death of the testator and the payment of the legacy to the beneficiary.

Income

Some assets by their very nature are incapable of producing income (for exam- **16.52** ple, a painting, a ring, a piece of furniture) in which case the question of a beneficiary's right to income is irrelevant. Other assets do, however, produce income (for example, a house which is rented to a tenant, company shares, government stock). We are concerned with the rights of beneficiaries to receive this income. It is necessary to distinguish the following types of gift:

(a) immediate specific gifts;

(b) contingent and deferred specific gifts;

(c) contingent pecuniary legacies;

(d) immediate residuary gifts; and

(e) contingent and deferred residuary gifts.

Immediate specific gifts

A specific legacy or devise which is to take effect immediately carries with it the **16.53** right to any income accruing to the property in the period between the death of the testator and vesting. The beneficiary is not, however, entitled to receive the income *as it arises;* instead, the beneficiary must wait until the personal representatives vest the property in the beneficiary by means of an assent. The assent operates retrospectively to give the beneficiary the right to receive the income which has accrued since the date of death.

An assent can be oral in the case of all assets other than land, for which a written assent is required. An assent indicates that the asset is not required for payment of debts and is available to the beneficiary. (See Ch.18, below.) A specific beneficiary must bear all liabilities relating to the asset after the assent and thus must bear any costs of transporting, insuring or transferring the asset unless there is a direction to the contrary in the will. It is common for a clause to be included in a professionally drawn will directing that such expenses be paid from residue.

Contingent and deferred specific gifts

16.54 An example of a contingent specific gift is "to X if X becomes a solicitor" and an example of a deferred specific gift is "to X after the death of A". Prior to 1925 neither type of gift carried with it the right to receive income. However, s.175 of the Law of Property Act 1925 provides that such gifts do carry with them the right to income (unless the testator has indicated otherwise). Such income will, therefore, be added to the capital and will devolve with it. In the case of will trusts arising under wills executed before April 6, 2010 (the date on which the Perpetuities and Accumulations Act 2009 came into force) or lifetime trusts created before that date income can only be accumulated for so long as the statutory rule against accumulations permits (Law of Property Act 1925 ss.164–166 as amended by the Perpetuities and Accumulations Act 1964 s.13). Thereafter the income will either fall into residue or pass under the intestacy rules. In the case of trusts subject to the 2009 Act there are no statutory restrictions so, unless the will or trust instrument contain restrictions, income can be accumulated throughout the life of the trust.

Contingent pecuniary legacies

16.55 In the absence of an express direction contingent pecuniary legacies do not normally carry interest. Interest is payable from the date of the death in the four situations set out in para.16.62, below.

  If, for example, a testator leaves "£100,000 to my great-granddaughter contingent on her reaching 25" any interest or income produced by the £100,000 will be paid to the residuary beneficiary. This is unlikely to be what the testator would wish so it is preferable to either include an express direction to pay interest or, probably more satisfactory, to provide that the legacy is to be held on trust with appropriate trustee powers for appointment of income and capital.

Immediate residuary gifts

16.56 An immediate residuary gift whether of realty or personalty carries with it the right to income accruing after the testator's death.

Contingent and deferred residuary gifts

16.57 Contingent residuary bequests have always carried the right to income, contingent residuary devises carry the right to such income as a result of the Law of

Property Act s.175. In the absence of contrary direction such income will be added to capital (subject to the rule against accumulations) and will devolve with it.

Section 175 does not mention *deferred* (or deferred, contingent) bequests which are, therefore, subject to the pre-1926 rules and do not carry the right to income. In the absence of a direction to the contrary income will pass to the person entitled to undisposed of property.

There is some uncertainty as to whether a *deferred* residuary *devise* carries the right to income. The better view appears to be that it does with the result that income will be added to capital (subject to the rule against accumulations).

The effect is that probably all residuary gifts carry the right to income apart from deferred (or deferred, contingent) residuary bequests. Examples of such gifts would be "my personalty to X after the death of A" or "my personalty to X after the death of A if X becomes a solicitor".

Apportioning income

It is necessary to consider how the income accruing after death is to be ascer- **16.58** tained and we will, therefore, look at the effect of the Apportionment Act 1870.

In the absence of any direction to the contrary in the will s.1 of the Apportionment Act 1870 provides that:

> "All rents, annuities, dividends and other periodical payments in the nature of income . . . shall, like interest on money lent, be considered as accruing from day to day and shall be apportionable in respect of time accordingly".

Interest is required at common law to be apportioned on a daily basis.

An asset which has been specifically devised or bequeathed may produce income which is paid to the personal representatives after the death of the deceased but which covers a period partly before and partly after the death. The personal representatives will have to decide whether the whole of the income passes to the specific beneficiary or whether it must be apportioned; if it is apportioned that part of the income attributable to the period before death will fall into residue and only that part which is attributable to the period after death will pass to the specific beneficiary.

Example

T leaves shares in ABC Ltd to X and residue to R. A dividend of £365 is declared for a period, 100 days of which precede the death and 265 days of which follow the death. The dividend must be apportioned between X and R. R will get the pre-death income attributable to the 100-day period and X will get the post-death income attributable to the 265-day period.

$$R \text{ will get } \frac{100}{365} \times £365 = £100$$

$$X \text{ will get } \frac{265}{365} \times £365 = £265$$

If the dividend is declared for a period which wholly precedes the death but is not actually paid until after the date of death it will not pass to the specific beneficiary; it will be treated as belonging to the deceased and will, therefore, form part of the residue. If a payment is made *before* death for a period falling partly before and partly after (or even wholly after) the death no apportionment is required and the specific beneficiary is not entitled to claim any portion of the advance payment from the estate. (Apportionments will also be dealt with in Ch.18.)

Apportionments may involve personal representatives in complicated calculations and they are often regarded as more trouble than they are worth. The result is that most professionally drawn wills exclude the need to apportion so that if rents, dividends or other income are paid after death such income will pass entirely to a specific beneficiary even if it did partly relate to a period preceding the death.

The Law Commission recommended in "Capital and Income in Trusts: Classification and Apportionment" (Report No.315) that the rules requiring apportionment be abolished. On March 22, 2010 Bridget Prentice, the then Parliamentary Under-Secretary for Justice, said that the government accepted the recommendations and would consult on the proposed reforms and draft legislation.

Whether the need to apportion has been excluded or whether it applies is of no relevance when it comes to determining the liability of beneficiaries to income tax. Such liability is determined by reference to the income tax rules explained in Ch.6. Similarly the exclusion of the need to apportion has no relevance to the valuation of the estate for inheritance tax purpose. Such valuation is determined by reference to the inheritance tax rules explained in para.4.19, above. The exclusion is only effective for distribution purposes and does not affect the Revenue.

Interest

Introduction

16.59   Interest is paid to a pecuniary legatee (or general legatee or demonstrative legatee if the designated fund has been exhausted) from the time at which the legacy is payable. The interest is to compensate the legatee where payment of the legacy is delayed. The interest is paid from residue and is treated as an administration expense. The testator may make express provision for the payment of interest and order that more or less interest be paid.

Rate of interest

16.60   Where disputes arise as to the administration of an estate, the court has power to order personal representatives to account under CPR 64 and can order the payment of interest. Under CPR, PD40, para.15:

> "interest shall be allowed on each legacy at the basic rate payable for the time being on funds in court or at such other rate as the court shall direct, beginning one year after the testator's death".

It, therefore, appears that in the absence of any express provision in the will this is the rate at which personal representatives should allow interest. There is a useful table on the Court Funds Office website which gives interest rates going back to October 1965. At the time of writing the rate was a derisory 0.3 per cent.

Time for payment

In the absence of any direction to the contrary from the testator, the general rule **16.61** is that a legacy is payable one year from the testator's death (this period is sometimes referred to as the executor's year). It may well be impossible to pay a legacy at the end of the year because of problems with the administration. If the legacy is not paid by the end of that period the legatee becomes entitled to interest from that date.

A testator may specify that a legacy is to be paid at a particular date; for example "£2,000 to X to be paid immediately after my death" in which case interest will be payable from the date specified. Similarly, if a testator directs that a legacy is contingent on the happening of an event or is deferred until a future date interest will be payable not from the end of the executor's year but from the date of the specified event or the future date. However, if a testator directs that a contingent or deferred legacy be severed from the rest of the estate and set aside for the benefit of the legatee it will carry interest from the end of the executor's year.

Four special cases when interest is paid from death

There are four exceptional cases when a pecuniary legacy (or general legacy or **16.62** demonstrative legacy if the designated fund has been exhausted) carries interest from the date of death.

(a) *Satisfaction of a debt.* A legacy to a creditor which is to satisfy a debt carries interest from the date of the death unless the will fixes a later date for payment.

(b) *Legacy charged on realty.* For historical reasons a vested legacy charged on realty carries interest from the date of death, unless the testator fixed a later date for payment.

(c) *Legacy to a testator's minor child.* If a testator gives a legacy to their minor child or to a minor to whom they are in loco parentis the legacy carries interest from the date of death. The rule is an old one designed to provide maintenance for the child; if, therefore, any other fund is designated for its maintenance, the legacy will not carry interest.

Moreover, the rule only applies where the legacy is given to the child directly; interest is not payable from death if the legacy is given to trustees to hold for the child (*Re Pollock* (1943)).

Interest is payable from death if the legacy is contingent on the child reaching full age or marrying earlier but it is probably not so payable if the contingency has no reference to the child's minority (for example reaching an age greater than majority).

(d) *Legacy to a minor with intention to provide maintenance.* If a testator gives a legacy to any minor (not necessarily the testator's own child or a person to whom the testator is *in loco parentis*) and shows an intention to provide for the minor's maintenance it carries interest from death unless the will designates some other fund for maintenance. Unlike the previous rule interest will be carried from death by a legacy contingent on reaching an age greater than majority.

Will drafting

16.63 A person who is drafting a will may prefer to make express provision for the payment of interest rather than leaving personal representatives and beneficiaries to rely on these rather technical rules.

Options to purchase

16.64 A will may give someone the right to purchase an asset of the estate. If the will is silent, the asset is valued at market value at the date of death. See *Re Bliss* (2001). An open market valuation differs from a probate valuation in that it takes into account matters such as a right of occupation granted by will which a probate valuation would ignore. *Re Bliss* also decided that the valuation should not take into account events subsequent to death unless the will directed otherwise. In *Re Bliss* the option to purchase was subject to the right of the deceased's husband to occupy part of the property. A few months after the death and before the option had been exercised, he moved out and indicated that he would not return. The valuation was still to be carried out subject to his right to occupy.

Re Bowles (2003) held that time for the exercise of an option will not be of the essence where the will contains no prescribed consequences for failure to act in time. The testator's will gave a beneficiary the right to buy part of a farm at the amount agreed between the executors and the Revenue. He had to be informed of this right within six months of the testator's death and then had three months to decide whether he wanted to exercise the option. Almost three years after the death agreement had still not been reached with the Revenue. The court held that the time limits were directory in nature and that the beneficiary was entitled to wait until the price was ascertainable. From then he would have a reasonable time to exercise the option. To have found that the time limits were mandatory might have defeated the testator's intention.

Chapter Seventeen

CONSTRUCTION OF WILLS

Entire books have been written on the principles governing the construction of **17.01** wills. One chapter can do no more than give a very brief introduction to some of the more important principles involved. Construction is not a matter of applying a series of rules in a rigid and pre-determined way. The courts are moving towards a more natural and inclusive approach to construction, generally. In *Charles v Barzey* (2002) in the Privy Council, Lord Hoffman said that:

> "the interpretation of a Will is in principle no different from that of any other communication. The question is what a reasonable person, possessed of all the background knowledge which the testatrix might reasonably have been expected to have, would have understood the testatrix to have meant by the words which were used."

In *RSPCA v Sharp & Mason* the Court of Appeal said that the approach to the construction of wills should accord with the approach to the construction of contracts taken by the House of Lords in *Investors Compensation Scheme Ltd v West Bromwich Building Society* (1998):

> "The principle that words should be given their 'natural and ordinary meaning' reflects the commonsense proposition that we do not easily accept that people have made linguistic mistakes, particularly in formal documents. On the other hand, if one would nevertheless conclude from the background that something must have gone wrong with the language, the law does not require judges to attribute to the parties an intention which they plainly could not have had." (Per Lord Lloyd at 115)

Questions of construction are dealt with by the Chancery Division.

1. The Object of the Court is to Ascertain the Testator's Expressed Intention

The basic rule

The object of the court is to ascertain the testator's intention *as expressed in the* **17.02** *will*. In other words the court is simply concerned to determine the meaning of the words written; it will not speculate or conjecture as to what the testator's "real" intention may have been. Thus, in *Re Rowland* (1963) a testator made a will leaving all his property to his wife but in the event of her death "preceding or coinciding" with his own everything was to go to his brother. The testator and his wife were declared dead after a boat on which they were sailing disappeared. The wife was the younger and was, therefore, presumed to have survived her husband. The court declared that the substitutional gift to the brother could not take effect as there was no evidence that the wife's death had preceded or coincided with her husband's; she might have survived him. The husband might well have "really" intended his brother to take in such circumstances but the court was not at liberty to speculate. "The will must be in writing and that writing only must be considered." (per Harman L.J.) Similarly in *Re Jones* (1998) the will gave the testatrix's whole estate to her son with a gift to two nephews if the son predeceased. The son killed the testatrix and so the gift to him was forfeited (see para.16.38, above). The Court of Appeal held that as the son had not predeceased, the nephews could not take. The Court could not speculate as to what the testatrix would have wanted in these circumstances.

Where the wording of a gift is too vague to be given a specific meaning the court cannot rewrite the gift which, therefore, fails for uncertainty (see paras 16.30–16.32, above).

Ordinary words given their ordinary meaning

17.03 If the words used in the will are clear and unambiguous, it is not possible for the court to attribute to them meanings they do not normally bear in order to produce a result which is thought to be more in accordance with the testator's intentions. If, however, such an interpretation gives rise to some obvious absurdity or is manifestly inconsistent with the will read as a whole, the sense of such words may be modified or extended so far as is necessary to avoid the consequences but no further. The mere fact that a disposition seems rather strange is not sufficient to justify departing from the ordinary meaning of words.

Some words have several meanings in which case the court must try and determine in what sense the testator used the word. "Money" is a good example of such a word since it can mean merely notes or coins, can include money "in the bank" or can be used loosely to cover assets in general. The House of Lords in *Perrin v Morgan* (1943) took the view that the word was capable of having a very wide meaning indeed and that courts should carefully consider the context before attributing a narrow meaning to the word (particularly if the result of such an interpretation would be to leave a large part of the estate undisposed).

Technical words must be given their technical meaning

17.04 If a testator uses a technical word or expression, for example "my realty" or "my personalty", such an expression must be given its technical meaning unless the will shows a *very* clear intention to use it in a different sense. Thus, in *Re Cook* (1948) a testatrix in a home-made will left "all my personal estate" to X, there were no other gifts in the will and the greater part of her estate consisted of realty. Harman J. held that the expression "personal estate" was a technical one and must be given its technical meaning despite the fact that doing so meant that the bulk of the testatrix's property passed on intestacy.

In *D'Abo v Paget (No.1)* (2001) a will left property to A for life then on trust absolutely:

> "for the child or other issue of [A] who if the devolution of the said property . . . had been subject to limitations in strict settlement [to A] and his issue would have taken on the death of [A]".

The court held that the use of the words "child or issue" showed that a gift to one person was intended and so the elder daughter alone would take even though strict settlements normally divide the estate between daughters as tenants in common.

The dictionary principle

A testator is free to show that words used in the will are used in an unusual way. **17.05** This may be done expressly, by including a definition clause; for example, a testator may say that wherever they refer to "my monkey" they mean "my son". It is more likely, however, that the will as a whole may suggest that an unusual meaning is attached to one word. Thus, in *Re Lowe* (1890) a testator made a gift "to all my children, apart from X". (X was illegitimate.) At that time the word "children" did not include illegitimate children unless the testator indicated that he wanted it to do so. It was held that the specific exclusion of X indicated that the testator regarded the word "children" as including illegitimate ones, so that all the testator's illegitimate children, apart from X, could take.

Rectification of a will

Section 20 of the Administration of Justice Act 1982 provides that: **17.06**

> "if a court is satisfied that a will is so expressed that it fails to carry out the testator's intentions, in consequence:
>
> (a) of a clerical error; or
> (b) of a failure to understand his instructions,
>
> it may order that the will shall be rectified so as to carry out his intentions".

A fuller discussion of this provision is contained in para.2.34, above.

2. EXTRINSIC EVIDENCE

The general rule

The general rule is that the court construes the words written in the will and will **17.07** not admit extrinsic evidence of the testator's intention. However, there are certain circumstances where extrinsic evidence is admissible.

The first three are long-established; the others were introduced by the Administration of Justice Act 1982.

Where the words used are not apt to fit the surrounding circumstances

17.08 This is sometimes referred to as "the armchair principle".

> "You may place yourself, so to speak, in [the testator's] armchair, and consider the circumstances by which he was surrounded when he made his will to assist you in arriving at his intention," per James L.J., *Boyes v Cook* (1880).

An illustration of this rule is *Thorn v Dickens* (1906) where the testator left "all to mother" but did not have a mother living at the time he made his will; extrinsic evidence of the testator's circumstances was admitted to show that he was in the habit of calling his wife "mother" with the result that she was able to take. Similarly, in *Re Fish* (1893) the testator left property to "my niece, Eliza Waterhouse" but did not have a niece of that name; extrinsic evidence was admitted to show that his wife had a great-niece of that name and it was found that the testator had used the word "niece" in a wide sense so that the great-niece was able to take the gift. In both these cases there was no-one who fitted the description used in the will. If there had been (for example, if in *Thorn v Dickens* the testator's mother had been alive at the time the will was made) then no extrinsic evidence could have been admitted and the apparent beneficiary would have taken. Declarations made by the testator as to their intention are not admissible; only evidence *of the surrounding circumstances* is admissible.

Where there is a latent ambiguity

17.09 A latent ambiguity is one which does not become apparent until an attempt is made to give effect to the dispositions in the will. Thus, if a testator makes a gift of "my motor car" and it turns out that at the time of the will, he owned six cars or, if a testator makes a gift to "my nephew, John Jones" and it turns out that he had several so named, extrinsic evidence *including evidence of declarations made by the testator* as to his intention will be admitted to show which car was intended to be the subject-matter of the gift or which nephew was intended to benefit. If there is no evidence available the whole gift will fail for uncertainty.

An example of a latent ambiguity is *Re Jackson* (1933). The testator made a gift "to my nephew, Arthur Murphy"; he had one illegitimate nephew and two legitimate nephews of that name. At that time illegitimate relationships were ignored unless the will showed a contrary intention. Therefore, had there been only one legitimate nephew that nephew would have fitted the description and would have taken the gift (even if there had been evidence that the testator's intention was that that person should not take). However, as there were two such nephews there was a latent ambiguity and extrinsic evidence, including evidence of the testator's *intention,* was admitted. This evidence showed that, in fact, the testator had intended to refer to the illegitimate nephew and he, therefore, took the gift. In *Pinnel v Anison* (2006) the wording of the will made a gift to "my sister Doreen Hall of [address given]". The deceased had lost contact with his family. He had a sister whose name was Doreen Anison. A woman called Doreen Hall lived at the address given in the will which was in the area where the deceased had spent his childhood. She was, however, not related to the deceased. The gift was clearly ambiguous. Extrinsic evidence showed that the deceased had made amateurish attempts to find his family before making the will. From this the court was able to conclude that he had intended the gift to go to his sister not to Doreen Hall and the will was construed accordingly.

To rebut a presumption of equity

In certain circumstances equity raises presumptions; for example, that a legacy **17.10** from a father (or person in loco parentis) to his child will be adeemed if the father (or person in loco parentis) after the date of the will gives the child an inter vivos portion. These presumptions may be rebutted by extrinsic evidence (including evidence of declarations made by the testator as to their intention).

The Administration of Justice Act 1982

In the case of deaths occurring after December 31, 1982, s.21 provides that **17.11** extrinsic evidence *including evidence of declarations as to the testator's intention* may be admitted to assist in the interpretation of a will in so far as:

(a) any part of it is meaningless,

(b) the language used in any part of it is ambiguous on the face of it, and

(c) evidence other than evidence of the testator's intention shows that the language used in any part of it is ambiguous in the light of the surrounding circumstances.

An example of subsection (b) is a gift of "my money" or "my effects".

Paragraph (c) appears to have extended the existing rules on extrinsic evidence in two ways. First, evidence of surrounding circumstances (though not direct evidence of the testator's intention) can now be admitted to *raise the possibility* that an ambiguity exists, whereas, prior to the 1982 Act, evidence could only be admitted where the words did not fit the surrounding circumstances. Thus, where a testator makes a gift to "my niece, Ann" it would now be possible to admit evidence to show that, although the testator had only one niece called Ann, there was a niece of his spouse also called Ann. Secondly, it is now possible to admit direct evidence of the testator's intention in cases other than latent ambiguity.

In a helpful judgment (*Re Williams, Deceased* (1985)), Nicholls J. stated the principles to be applied when considering the admissibility of extrinsic evidence. He reminded practitioners that the section is merely *an aid* to construction. Thus, evidence may be admitted to show which of several possible meanings a testator was applying to a particular word or phrase (for example "my money", "my effects"). The meaning may be one which without the evidence would not have been at all apparent but so long as the word or phrase is *capable* of bearing that meaning in its context this does not matter. However, it may be that the extrinsic evidence reveals a meaning attached by the testator to a word or phrase which no matter how liberal the approach of the court, the word or phrase cannot bear. The court will not allow extrinsic evidence to vary or contradict the language used in the will since this would amount to rewriting the will for the testator and this can only be done, if at all, under the rectification provisions.

A recent example of s.21 in action is *Harris v The Beneficiaries of the Estate of Margaret Alice Cooper (Deceased)* (2010) the deceased in a homemade will left her house to an old friend (who she also appointed as her executor) and her "money" to "my surviving relatives". Norris J. held that she was clearly using money in a very general sense to cover everything except the house. The next question was who were the surviving relatives? She had never married and had no surviving parent or siblings. Her relatives were, therefore, the offspring of her dead uncles and aunts: their children (who were her first cousins) and then the children and issue of the first cousins (first cousins once and twice removed). There were 29 first cousins once removed but only three surviving first cousins who between them had seven children. The executor who had known the deceased for 64 years before her death said that the only members of her family she talked about were the three known surviving first cousins and that he had always assumed that they were the people the deceased intended to benefit. Norris J. described this evidence as "powerful" and agreed that the first cousins were intended to benefit. He concluded that the reference to "surviving" was intended to provide for the substitution of the childen of any deceased first cousin. However, as all the first cousins survived, they took equally.

3. The Will Speaks from Death

Section 24 of the Wills Act 1837

17.12   Section 24 provides that as regards property every will shall be construed "to speak and take effect as if it had been executed immediately before the death of the testator, unless a contrary intention shall appear by the will". Thus, a gift of "the contents of my house" will pass the contents owned at the date of death, not merely those owned at the date of the will.

Contrary intention

17.13   A will may expressly state that the testator is giving an asset owned at the date of the will. In the absence of an express statement, certain words and expressions are commonly found to show contrary intention.

"My"

If the testator couples the word "my" with a gift of a specific item (for example, **17.14** "my piano") it is possible that the court will construe the gift as a gift of the particular piano owned at the date of the will. Therefore, if the piano is sold or destroyed after the date of the will the gift is adeemed and cannot pass a piano purchased later and owned at the date of the death. However, if the word "my" is coupled with a description of property capable of increase or decrease (for example, "all my shares") there is no contrary intention and the gift will pass any shares owned at the time of death.

"Now" or "at present"

The use of such words will be taken as showing a contrary intention (that is, as **17.15** referring to the date the will is made) if they are an essential part of the description. Thus, in *Re Edwards* (1890) the testator made a gift of "my house and premises where I now reside". After the date of the will he let a part of the property. The court held that the word "now" indicated a contrary intention so that the whole of the property occupied at the time the will was made (including the part subsequently let) passed to the beneficiary, not merely the part occupied at the date of the death.

If, however, the words are regarded as mere additional or superfluous description which has simply become inaccurate by the date of the will the court is unlikely to find that they show a contrary intention. In *Re Willis* (1911) a testator gave "all my freehold house and premises situated at X and known as Y and in which I now reside". After the date of the will he acquired two further plots of land which he enjoyed with the original house. The court held that there was no contrary intention so that the gift was to be construed at the date of death; thus the additional plots were included.

Section 24 has no application to people

Section 24 only applies to property; as regards people a will is construed at the **17.16** date it is made (unless there is a contrary intention).

A gift made "to the eldest son of A" is construed as a gift to the person fulfilling that description at the date the will is made. If that person predeceases the testator the gift fails and does not pass to the eldest surviving son.

It is important to remember that where a will is republished it is construed as if made at the date of the republication.

If a testator makes a gift to a beneficiary who fulfils a particular description (for example, "the wife of X") and to the testator's knowledge no-one fulfils that description at the date of the will the court will construe the gift as one made to the first person to fulfil the description. Once a person has fulfilled the description the gift is construed as a gift to that person even if the description later becomes inaccurate; thus, if in the previous example X and his wife were divorced after the date of the will she would still be entitled to the gift on Y's death, even if X had remarried.

In *Thomas v Kent* (2007) a will contained a gift to the testator's "brothers and sisters in equal shares, the share of any deceased brother or sister to be taken by his or her children in equal shares". At the date of the will the testator had one surviving brother and three surviving sisters. The question arose as to whether the children of a brother who died before the will was made could take under this gift. The Court of Appeal held that they could. As the testator referred to "brothers" (plural) when only one brother was alive showed that he intended the gift to be available to the children of all his siblings whether alive at the time of the will or not. (A further question of whether the children of brothers and sisters could take under the substitutional gift only if alive at the date of the will was remitted to the High Court for further argument.)

Gender Recognition Act 2004

17.17 The purpose of the Gender Recognition Act 2004 is to provide transsexuals with legal recognition in their acquired gender. Legal recognition will follow from the issue of a full gender recognition certificate by a Gender Recognition Panel.

Before issuing a certificate, the Panel must be satisfied that the applicant:

- has, or has had, gender dysphoria,

- has lived in the acquired gender throughout the preceding two years, and

- intends to continue to live in the acquired gender until death.

The effect of legal recognition is that, for example, a male-to-female transsexual person will be legally recognised as a woman in English law for all purposes (s.9(1)).

If a person acquires a new gender, under the act any gender specific reference will be construed as applying to their acquired gender. For example, a reference to "my daughters" would include a person born male who had acquired female gender under the act. However, this provision does not apply to wills made before April 5, 2004.

Protection for trustees and personal representatives

17.18 Under s.17 trustees or personal representatives are relieved from any fiduciary duty to inquire whether a gender recognition certificate has been issued to any person or revoked, even if that fact could affect entitlement to property which they are responsible for distributing. The beneficiary will nevertheless retain their claim to the property and may enforce this claim, e.g. by following the property into the hands of another person who has received it instead.

Powers of the court

Under s.18 the court has power to make orders to deal with the situation where **17.19**
the devolution of property under a will or other instrument is different from what
it would be but for the change of gender.

If, for example, a will left property to *"eldest daughter"* of X, and there is an
older brother whose gender becomes female under the Act, then the person who
was previously the *"eldest daughter"* may cease to enjoy that position. A person
who is adversely affected by the different disposition can apply to the court. The
court, if satisfied that it is just to do so, may make such order as it considers
appropriate in relation to the person benefiting from the different disposition of
the property.

4. PROPERTY SUBJECT TO A GENERAL POWER OF APPOINTMENT

General and special powers of appointment

Instead of making an outright gift of property to a named beneficiary, a testator **17.20**
may give one person a power to appoint property to others. The power may be
entirely unlimited, so that the appointer can appoint to anyone, in which case it
is referred to as a "general" power, or the power may be limited, so that the
appointer can appoint only amongst certain specific people (for example the
children of X), in which case it is referred to as a "special" power of appointment.

A person with a general power of appointment is free to deal with the property
exactly as they please and is therefore for many purposes treated as the owner of
the property subject to the general power of appointment. For example, if a
person exercises such a power by will, the property subject to the power is
available for payment of the deceased's debts (see Ch.15).

Method of exercising a general power of appointment

A testator may make an express appointment by will but this is not essential. **17.21**
Section 27 of the Wills Act provides that, where a testator has a general power
of appointment exercisable by will, it can be exercised by any general devise or
bequest without the necessity for an express reference to the power. A general
devise or bequest is one where the subject-matter is described in a general
manner, for example "all my leasehold land", "all my land in Hampshire" or
"all my shares". If property subject to a general power is to pass under the terms
of such a gift, it must correspond to the general description.

Section 27 is subject to contrary intention. However, the court will not readily
find such an intention. Thus in *Re Jarrett* (1919) the fact that the testator had
made an express appointment in the will which failed was found not to show a
contrary intention and the subject-matter of the power passed as part of the
residue.

The section does not apply if the terms of a general power of appointment require an express reference to the power or the property. Special powers of appointment are not covered by the section and therefore need to be expressly exercised (unless the terms of the power provide otherwise).

5. Special Rules Relating to Children

Adopted children

17.22 The Adoption Act 1976 applies to any adoption order made by a court in the UK, the Isle of Man or the Channel Islands and to certain foreign adoptions. It provides that when construing the will of a testator who dies after December 31, 1975:

> (a) an adopted child is to be treated as the legitimate child of the married couple who adopt it or, if the adoption is by one person, as the legitimate child of that one person (but not as a child of any actual marriage of that person); and

> (b) an adopted child is to be treated as if it were not the child of any person other than the adopting parent(s).

It is immaterial whether the adoption order is made before or after the testator's death. For example, if T gives property "to A for life, remainder to the children of A" any child adopted by A, whether before or after T's death, will be entitled to share in the gift, unless there is any contrary intention shown.

Where a disposition by will depends on the date of birth of a child or children the disposition is to be construed, in the absence of contrary intention, as if:

> (a) the adopted child had been born on the date of the adoption; and

> (b) two or more children adopted on the same date had been born on that date in the order of their actual births.

Example

T makes one gift "to the children of A living at my death" and one gift "to the children of A born after my death". T dies in 2006 and after T's death A adopts a child who was born in 2004. This child is treated as born on the date of the adoption and is therefore not a child living at T's death and cannot take under the first gift. However, it is a child born after T's death and can take under the second gift.

It is expressly provided that these rules do not affect any reference to the *age* of a child. Thus, if T gives property "to the first child of A to reach age 25" and A has a natural child born in 1978 and an adopted child adopted in 1980 at age 12, it is the adopted child who will reach age 25 first and be entitled to the gift. A gift to "the eldest child of A" would probably not be construed as containing a reference to an age so that the general rule would be applied; thus, the adopted child would be treated as born on the date of the adoption and therefore as being younger than the natural child.

Although s.33(1) of the Human Fertilisation and Embryology Act 2008 provides that the woman who carries a child as a result of the placing in her of an embryo or of sperm and eggs is to be treated as the mother of the child, subs.2 provides that this is not the case where the child is adopted by another person. An adoption order will also prevent a man being treated as the father under ss.35 or 36 and a woman being treated as the child's other female parent under ss.42 or 43.

Where a child is born as a result of a surrogacy arrangement, the woman who carries the child is the mother unless a parental order is obtained under Human Fertilisation and Embryology Act 2008 s.54. The effect of such an order is broadly the same as an adoption order. For more detail on when a man or woman is treated as a child's father or other female parent, see paras 3.06 and 3.07.

Children whose parents were not married

In any will or codicil made after April 4, 1988 references to relationships are **17.23** construed without regard to "whether or not the father and mother of either [person], or the father and mother of any person through whom the relationship is deduced, have or had been married to each other at any time" (Family Law Reform Act 1987 s.l(1)). Thus a gift "to my children" includes both legitimate and illegitimate children. A gift "to my grandchildren" includes all the testator's children's children regardless of whether the testator was married at any time and regardless of whether their children were married at any time. The will may show a contrary intention should the testator so wish.

In the case of wills and codicils made after December 31, 1969 and before April 4, 1988, the Family Law Reform Act 1969 s.15 applies. This makes provision the effect of which is similar, in most respects, to the 1987 Act.

6. Class Gifts

The class closing rules

Necessity for such rules

A class gift is a gift of property to be divided amongst persons fulfilling a general **17.24** description (for example "the children of A", "the children of A who reach 18"). The size of any individual's share will depend upon the number of persons who fulfil the description. This makes distributing the property difficult since until A dies it is always possible that the number of persons fulfilling the description will increase. Personal representatives would, therefore, have to wait till A's death before giving any child a share in the property.

To avoid this inconvenient result, certain rules of construction known as "the class closing rules" have been developed; the effect of the rules is to close a class at an artificially early date in order to allow earlier distribution. Beneficiaries who are born after the class has closed lose their entitlement; the unfairness that this may cause is thought to be outweighed by the convenience of allowing early distribution. However, if a testator does not want the class to close early, the rules can always be expressly excluded (subject to the rules against perpetuity). Clear words should be used to exclude the rules. An example of sufficiently clear wording is "to the children of A *whenever born*".

The precise details of the rules vary according to the type of gift (immediate, deferred or contingent) but the principle is that the class closes as soon as there is one beneficiary entitled to immediate distribution.

Throughout this section the word "living" includes a child *en ventre sa mere*.

Immediate class gifts

17.25 An example of such a gift is "to the children of A". If there is any child of A living at the date of the testator's death the class closes and the personal representatives distribute to the class members then in existence (*Viner v Francis* (1789)). No child born after the class has closed can take any interest. If there are no children living at that date, there is no class closing rule applicable and the class will remain open until A dies.

Deferred class gift

17.26 An example of such a gift is "to X for life remainder to the children of A". In this case the property cannot be distributed while X is alive and the class, therefore, remains open until X dies. It will include any children living at the testator's death and any children born thereafter and before the death of X. If any such child dies before the property is actually distributed, their share will be paid to their estate. No child born after the class has closed can take any interest. If there were no children living at the testator's death and none born before X's death, there is no class closing rule applicable and the class will remain open until the death of A.

Contingent class gift

17.27 An example of such a gift is "to the children of A who reach 18". If any child has reached 18 when the testator dies, the class closes at that date and will include any child living at that date who reaches the age of 18. If a child dies without fulfilling the contingency their "share" is divided amongst the other members of the class who fulfil the contingency. If no child has reached 18 at the date of the testator's death, the class remains open until a child reaches 18 and will include any child living at that date who reaches 18. Again if any child dies without fulfilling the contingency their "share" is divided amongst any others who do fulfil the contingency. No child born after the class has closed can take any interest.

Deferred and contingent class gifts

An example of such a gift would be "to X for life, remainder to the children of **17.28**
A who reach 18". In this case the property cannot be distributed whilst X is alive
and the class, therefore, remains open until X's death. It will close at X's death
if any child living at the testator's death has reached 18 and will include any
children living at the testator's death or born since who reach 18. If any child,
living at the testator's death, reaches 18 but dies before distribution the class
closes on X's death and the share of the deceased child is paid to his estate. If no
member of the class has reached 18 at the time of X's death the class remains
open until the first child reaches 18. No child born after the class has closed can
take any interest.

Acceleration of the date for closing a class

If there is a postponed class gift (for example, "to X for life, remainder to the **17.29**
children of Y") it may happen that the prior interest fails, perhaps because the life
tenant predeceases the testator or because the gift to the life tenant is void. In
such a case the gift to the class is accelerated so that it is treated as an immediate
class gift. The class will, therefore, close at the testator's death (if there are any
members then living) and any later born children will be excluded (*Re Johnson*
(1893)).

A life tenant may wish to disclaim or surrender the life tenancy and the
question then arises of whether one person can by voluntarily dealing with their
own interest affect the membership of the class. In *Re Davies* (1957) Vaisey J.
held that where a life tenant disclaimed, the gift to the class would be accelerated
and would close immediately thereby excluding any later born members. However, the decision has been criticised as not reflecting the probable wishes of a
testator; Goff J. refused to follow it in *Re Harker's Will Trusts* (1969) and held
that where a life tenant surrendered her life interest the class would remain open
until her death.

Gifts of a specified amount to persons fulfilling a description

If a testator gives "£1,000 to each of the children of A", it is not a class gift since **17.30**
the amount each child is to receive does not vary according to the number of
persons fulfilling the description. However, problems arise in distributing such a
gift and these problems are similar to the problems which arise in connection
with class gifts. The number of persons fulfilling the description may increase at
any time before A's death and so the personal representatives cannot know how
much money they should retain to cover the possibility of future children being
born. In order that the personal representatives should be able to complete the
distribution without difficulty, there is a rule of construction which provides, in
the absence of a contrary intention, that only persons who are alive at the
testator's death can take; if there is no-one alive at that date fulfilling the
description, the entire gift fails. This is a drastic rule but it enables the personal

representatives to distribute the estate without having to worry about retaining assets to cover a possible future liability.

Class gifts to children of the testator who predecease

17.31 Normally a person who predeceases the testator can take no benefit under a class gift. Section 33 of the Wills Act 1837 as substituted by Administration of Justice Act 1982 s.19 provides that, in the absence of contrary intention, where a class gift is made to children or remoter issue *of the testator* and a member of the class predeceases the testator leaving issue who survive the testator, the issue take *per stirpes* the share which their parent would have taken (see para.16.27, above).

7. DECIDING WHETHER A GIFT IS ABSOLUTE OR LIMITED

Section 22 of the Administration of Justice Act 1982

17.32 Testators who draft wills without professional advice sometimes give property to X and then direct that on X's death what remains should pass to Y. This is because non-lawyers often think that it is possible to give the rights of an absolute owner to persons in succession. The effect of such an attempt depends on the precise words used in the will but may be construed in any of the following ways:

(a) an absolute gift to X, the gift over to Y failing, either as a trust which is void for uncertainty, or because it is repugnant to X's absolute interest;

(b) a life interest to X, with remainder to Y absolutely; and

(c) a life interest to X, with remainder to Y absolutely but subject to X's power to dispose of the capital inter vivos.

Section 22 of the Administration of Justice Act 1982 introduces a presumption where a testator gives property to his spouse in terms which would in themselves give an absolute interest but by the same instrument purports to give *his issue* an interest in the same property, the gift to the spouse is presumed to be absolute despite the purported gift to issue. The presumption applies in the case of deaths occurring after December 31, 1982.

This section is designed to solve the problem of unintended life interests. However, it has no application to gifts other than gifts to spouses and civil partners. The case of *Harrison v Gibson* (2006) shows that even in the case of gifts to spouses there may still be narrow distinctions depending on the exact wording of the will, In that case the wording was "The Bungalow I leave in trust to my wife. On her death the bungalow is to be sold and cash raised is to be equally divided between my children [the names of the children are given]". After the signature the following words were added "no doubt if mum runs into

money problems you can sort something out like selling bungalow". The judge
held that on this wording the terms of the will did not in themselves give an
absolute interest to the spouse so s.22 had no application. He also held that if he
was wrong in that conclusion the wording clearly showed a contrary intention so
that either way a life interest had been created.

The rule in Lassence v Tierney

This rule attempts to reconcile inconsistent provisions in a will.   **17.33**

> "If you find an absolute gift to a legatee in the first instance and trusts are engrafted
> or imposed on the absolute interest which fail either from lapse or invalidity or any
> other reason, then the absolute gift takes effect so far as the trusts have failed, to the
> exclusion of the residuary legatee or next of kin, as the case may be." (*Hancock v
> Watson* (1902))

The rule imputes to T an intention that the absolute gift be modified only so
far as is necessary to give effect to the trusts.

Example

T gives property to A absolutely and later in the will directs that the property given
to A absolutely is to pass, after A's death, to the children of B. If B dies without
children, A (or A's estate) will be entitled to the capital.

The difficulty in such cases is deciding whether or not there was an absolute
initial gift. It is comparatively simple to find such a gift where the testator makes
the absolute gift in the will and engrafts the trust in a later codicil or where, as
in the previous example, there is an absolute gift followed by a later clause
engrafting the trust but difficult questions of construction will arise where a series
of gifts is made in one continuous sentence.

Chapter Eighteen

COMPLETING THE ADMINISTRATION

Once the personal representatives have paid all the debts and liabilities of the **18.01** estate they must vest the available assets in the beneficiaries who are entitled to them and must prepare an account to show the amount of residue available to the residuary beneficiaries.

1. Assents

Position of beneficiaries before assent

As we saw in paras 11.26–11.28, above, a beneficiary (with the possible excep- **18.02** tion of a specific beneficiary) under a will or a person entitled under the intestacy rules has no legal or equitable proprietary interest in any asset comprised in the estate. They merely have a chose in action in the estate (i.e. the right to have the deceased's estate properly administered) and they only obtain rights to assets when the personal representatives indicate by means of an assent that these assets are not required for the purposes of the administration.

Assents in respect of pure personalty

Where there is a will

An executor (and probably an administrator with the will annexed) passes title to **18.03** pure personalty by means of an assent. An assent is an indication from the personal representative that a particular asset is not required for the purposes of the administration. It is not required to be in any particular form; it can be oral (for example, where a personal representative tells a beneficiary that their legacy is ready for collection) or implied from conduct (for example, where a personal representative allows a beneficiary to take possession of an asset). The benefici- ary actually derives title from the will not from the assent; the effect of the assent is merely to activate the gift in the will.

If particular formalities are required to transfer the legal title to an asset, the assent cannot itself pass the legal title. In such a case once the assent has been made the personal representative holds the asset as trustee for the beneficiary until the appropriate formal requirements have been complied with. Most choses (or things) in action require special formalities; money in a Post Office Savings Bank, Trustee Savings Bank or National Savings Certificates require withdrawal or transfer forms; company shares require a share transfer. Although the personal representatives may have themselves registered as members of a company, s.183 of the Companies Act 1985 provides that unless the articles of the company state otherwise, a personal representative may transfer stocks and shares without being first registered. There are no formalities required by law to transfer money from a bank account; a letter of instruction should be sent to the bank manager together with an office copy of the grant of representation.

In the case of a specific legacy (but not a residuary or general legacy) the assent is retrospective to the date of death so that the legatee becomes entitled to income produced by the subject-matter of the gift since the testator's death. Thus, in *I.R.C. v Hawley* (1928) the personal representatives did not make an assent of company shares in favour of a specific legatee for nearly three years after the testator's death. It was held that, because an assent to a specific legacy is retrospective, once the assent had been made the Revenue were entitled to assess the beneficiary to income tax on dividends which had been declared in the intervening years. Similarly, after assent a specific legatee is responsible for the costs of transferring the property. This includes costs of packing, delivering and insuring bulky or delicate chattels and the costs of obtaining a share transfer for company shares.

Many testators would prefer such costs to be paid from residue and it is, therefore, common for an express direction to this effect to be included in a will.

In *Re Clough-Taylor, Coutts & Co v Banks and Others* (2003) an asset specifically bequeathed had been taken by a third party who alleged that the deceased had given it to him during her lifetime. The court held that the executor has no duty to take anything other than normal or routine steps to collect in assets and deliver them to specific legatees. The specific legatee would have to bear the cost of any litigation to recover the asset. The court said it would be helpful—though not strictly necessary—for the executor to assign to the legatee any cause of action it had in relation to the chattel.

Where there is an intestacy

18.04   At common law an administrator had no power to assent in the case of an intestacy (see, W.J. Williams, *Law Relating to Assents* (London: Butterworth & Co., 1947), p.96). Section 36(1) of the Administration of Estate Act 1925 gives administrators as well as executors the power to make title to land (freehold or leasehold) by means of a written assent but it does not mention other property. Administrators must therefore pass title to other property by the method appropriate to the nature of the subject-matter. Chattels, money and bearer securities pass by delivery, shares, stock and debentures by transfer and most other choses in action by assignment.

Assents in respect of land

Administration of Estates Act 1925 s.36

In general a document which is to convey or create a legal estate in land must be **18.05** a *deed* (Law of Property Act 1925 s.52(1)). However, as an exception to this rule, s.36(1) of the Administration of Estates Act gives personal representatives (both executors and administrators) power to *assent* to the vesting of any estate or interest in land (whether freehold or leasehold) in any person entitled (whether beneficially, as trustee or as personal representative of a deceased beneficiary who is entitled to property) *whether by devise, bequest, devolution, appropriation or otherwise.* An assent is a form of conveyance and becomes an essential link in the title of the assentee.

"*Devolution*" covers a person taking under the intestacy rules. The meaning of "*or otherwise*" presents some problems. The other words in the section all refer to transactions which a personal representative would be called upon to effect in the course of the administration of the estate. Probably therefore the words "or otherwise" should be construed ejusdem generis and should not be taken to cover any transaction which is not part of the administration; thus, if a personal representative is selling property or is asked by a beneficiary to transfer the property to a purchaser from the beneficiary the personal representative should not risk using an assent but should use a conveyance. There is in any event little advantage to using an assent in such a case for while it may be a rather shorter document, ad valorem stamp duty is payable on a sale whether an assent is used or whether a conveyance to the purchaser is used.

Form of assent

Section 36(4) of the Administration of Estates Act provides that "an assent shall **18.06** be in writing, signed by the personal representative and shall name the person in whose favour it is given and shall operate to vest in that person the legal title to which it relates; and an assent which is not in writing or not in favour of a named person shall not be effectual to pass the legal estate".

It is clear that an assent of land by a personal representative in favour of another person must comply with the requirements of s.36(4) if it is to pass the legal estate. According to Pennycuick J. in *Re King's Will Trusts* (1964) the same requirements must be complied with where a personal representative wishes to vest land in themselves (whether beneficially or as trustee or as personal representative of another deceased). The reasoning of Pennycuick J. has been criticised by various writers (see R.R.A. Walker, "Personal Representatives Assenting to Themselves" (1964) 80 L.Q.R. 328) but even if the criticisms are justified the provision of a signed, written assent by a personal representative in their own favour is hardly an onerous task and has the merit of avoiding any possible doubt or uncertainty.

It is important to remember that a personal representative is always free to convey land by means of a deed and will often choose to do so (for example, where indemnity covenants are required from the beneficiary).

The effect of an assent

18.07   Section 36(2) of the Administration of Estates Act provides that an assent relates back to the date of death of the deceased unless a contrary intention appears. This is unlike the position in respect of assents of personalty where only an assent to a specific legacy relates back. Thus, a specific or residuary devisee would appear to be entitled to any rents or profits produced by land from the date of death of the deceased.

Protection of purchasers and beneficiaries

18.08   A person in whose favour an assent or conveyance is made may require that notice of the assent is endorsed on the grant of representation at the cost of the estate under s.36(5).

A purchaser will insist that a conveyance from personal representatives contains a statement that the personal representatives have not previously given or made any conveyance or assent in respect of the legal estate. If this statement is incorrect it cannot prejudice the title of any previous *purchaser;* but if there was a previous assent in favour of a *beneficiary* the purchaser will take the legal title in preference to that beneficiary if, and only if, there was no notice of the previous assent endorsed on the grant of representation *and* the purchaser accepted the conveyance on the faith of the statement in the conveyance (s.36(6)).

There is no point in such a statement being included in an assent in favour of a beneficiary since s.36(6)) only protects *purchasers.*

A purchaser has no right to examine a will to ascertain that land was assented to the person actually entitled. However, s.36(7) protects such a person by providing that in favour of a purchaser, unless notice of a previous assent or conveyance has been endorsed on the grant of representation, an assent or conveyance made by a personal representative is "sufficient evidence that the person in whose favour [it] is given is the person entitled to have the legal estate conveyed to him". The section only says that an assent is "sufficient" evidence not "conclusive" evidence; thus, if facts have come to the purchaser's knowledge before completion which indicate that the assent was in fact made in favour of the wrong person, the purchaser cannot rely on the assent (*Re Duce and Boots Cash Chemists (Southern) Ltd's Contract* (1937)).

Protection of personal representatives

18.09   A personal representative will not want to distribute assets until satisfied that all liabilities have been dealt with. Section 36(10) provides that personal representatives may, as a condition of giving an assent or making a conveyance, require security for the discharge of any duties, debts or liabilities to which the property is subject (for example, a mortgage debt or charge for inheritance tax). If reasonable arrangements have been made for discharging such liabilities, however, the personal representative cannot refuse to make the assent to a beneficiary entitled to the property.

If the personal representative is uncertain whether or not land will be required for the payment of liabilities they may under s.43 of the Administration of Estates Act allow a beneficiary to take possession of the land prior to the making of a formal assent. The personal representative can subsequently retake possession of the property and dispose of it if it becomes necessary in the course of the administration.

If the deceased owned land which was subject to covenants for breach of which the personal representatives will remain liable (for example where the deceased was an original lessee or where there have been indemnity covenants) the personal representatives will wish to protect themselves by obtaining an indemnity covenant from the beneficiary. They will therefore have to use a deed when transferring the property to the beneficiary instead of merely an assent.

2. Personal Representative or Trustee

Personal representative for life

A personal representative retains office for life and is not discharged from office **18.10** even when all the debts and liabilities have been paid and all the assets distributed. If there are any subsequent accretions to the estate (for example, if a debt which had been regarded as irrecoverable is paid to the estate or if someone dies leaving a legacy to the deceased which is saved from lapse by one of the exceptions to the doctrine of lapse) the personal representative must distribute such accretions and conversely if legal proceedings are brought or claims made against the estate the personal representatives must deal with them on behalf of the estate.

Comparison with trustees

A personal representative may be a trustee of property left by will or passing **18.11** under the intestacy rules. This may be because:

(a) the testator expressly appointed the personal representative as trustee; or

(b) the testator left property on trust but did not expressly appoint trustees; or

(c) a trust arises under the intestacy rules (although there is some doubt as to whether administrators become trustees in such a case).

Even where a personal representative is not also a trustee there are certain similarities between personal representatives and trustees:

(a) Personal representatives, like trustees, are in a fiduciary position. They must act with the utmost good faith and must not profit from their position.

(b) The provisions of the Trustee Act 1925 apply equally to personal representatives where the context admits.

However, there are also important differences:

(a) The function of a personal representative is to wind up the estate and distribute the assets, whereas the function of a trustee is to hold assets for the beneficiaries.

(b) Executors (and probably administrators) have joint and several authority to deal with *personalty* (they must act jointly if they are to convey *land* although one personal representative can enter into a contract for sale binding on any other personal representatives *Fountain Forestry Ltd v Edwards* (1975)). Trustees must always act jointly.

(c) A sole personal representative may give a good receipt for money for the sale of land whereas at least two trustees (or a trust corporation) are required.

(d) The period of limitation is 12 years against a personal representative but only six years against a trustee.

(e) If a sole personal representative dies without having completed the administration there will either be transmission of office under the chain of executorship or a grant *de bonis non administratis* must be taken out by the person entitled under the Non-Contentious Probate Rules 1987. If, however, a sole or last surviving trustee dies the trust property devolves on the trustee's personal representatives.

(f) A trustee has power to appoint additional or substitutional trustees. A personal representative has normally no power to appoint additional or substitutional personal representatives (although a person entitled to administration may nominate another administrator in certain cases where two administrators are needed because of a minority or life interest).

(g) Personal representatives owe their duty to the estate as a whole, trustees to the individual beneficiaries (*Re Hayes Will Trusts* (1971)).

(h) When personal representatives transfer assets to a "legatee" there is no gain or loss for capital gains tax purposes. The legatee takes over the acquisition value of the personal representatives (together with any expenses of transfer). When a beneficiary of a trust becomes absolutely entitled as against the trustee there is a deemed disposal and may be a charge to capital gains tax. Where the will directs that the personal representatives are to hold on trust, the beneficiary may become absolutely entitled before the personal representatives have assented the assets to themselves as trustees. In such a case the beneficiary takes as legatee and not as trust beneficiary.

In view of such differences it is obviously important where a personal representative is also a trustee to ascertain at what point the personal representative ceases to hold assets as personal representative and starts to hold them as trustee.

Transition from personal representative to trustee

Intestacy

Under the Administration of Estates Act 1925 undisposed of property may have **18.12** to be held on trust either for a spouse for life or on the statutory trusts until a beneficiary achieves a vested interest. There is some doubt as to whether administrators on intestacy ever become trustees in the true sense or whether they continue to hold property as administrators. The better view would seem to be that they do not become trustees. However, Romer J. in the case of *Re Yerburgh* (1928) stated that administrators become trustees as soon as all liabilities have been discharged and the amount of residue to be held on trust has been ascertained. Romer J. went on to state that the administrators ought to mark the moment when residue was ascertained by making an assent to the property vesting in themselves as trustees. It is unclear whether the judge meant that the assent was essential in order to vest the property in the administrators in their capacity as trustees or whether he meant that the assent was merely desirable in practice in order to indicate that the change in capacity had occurred, the change occurring automatically once the residue was ascertained.

Where the will does not appoint the personal representative as trustee

In the case of a specific legacy, once personal representatives have indicated by **18.13** means of an assent that an asset is not required for payment of debts the asset is held on trust for the specific beneficiary (*Re Grosvenor* (1916)).

In the case of residue the position is rather unclear. In *Harvell v Foster* (1954) the Court of Appeal stated that the personal representatives remain liable in their capacity as such for the residue of the estate until it is vested in the beneficiary entitled. If the vesting is delayed (as it may be for example where the beneficiary is a minor and cannot give a good receipt) liability as a personal representative will continue and the personal representatives will not become trustees.

It is difficult to see why, if *Re Yerburgh* is correct, there should be a conversion to trustees in the case of intestacy but not in a case where there is a will.

Where the will appoints the personal representative as trustee

If personal representatives are directed to hold residue on trust there is some **18.14** authority for saying that as soon as liabilities are discharged and the residue ascertained the personal representatives automatically start to hold the property in their capacity as trustees (*Re Cockburn's Will Trusts* (1957)). However, the position is far from clear and there are dicta in *Attenborough v Solomon* (1913) which suggest that the change does not take place automatically but only when the personal representatives assent the property to themselves in their capacity as trustees.

An assent is certainly desirable since it will avoid any doubt as to whether or not a change in capacity has occurred.

3. RECEIPTS AND DISCHARGES

Introduction

18.15 A beneficiary discharges a personal representative from liability by means of a receipt signed by the beneficiary. A residuary beneficiary normally signs the estate accounts.

Pecuniary legacies

18.16 It used to be common for solicitors to ask pecuniary legatees, who wished to receive their legacies in the form of a cheque sent through the post, to sign a receipt in advance. The Law Society's Land Law and Succession Committee considered this practice and on October 14, 1992 stated in the *Gazette* that it considered that:

> " . . . it is no longer reasonable or necessary for legatees and beneficiaries to be asked to sign receipts in advance of payment being made and that such a practice is bound to generate additional correspondence and thus to add unnecessarily to the cost of the administration of the estate."

Precedents for simple forms of receipt for the payment of pecuniary, specific and residuary legacies are available. However, solicitors may find it more convenient to ask the legatee or beneficiary to acknowledge receipt by signing and returning a duplicate copy of the letter accompanying the cheque. In any case, s.3 of the Cheques Act 1957 provides that:

> "An unindorsed cheque which appears to have been paid by the banker on whom it is drawn is evidence of receipt by the payee of the sum payable by the cheque."

So far as residuary beneficiaries are concerned, the solicitor will normally send them copies of the estate accounts (already approved by the personal representatives). The Law Society's Committee recommends sending a cheque at the same time:

> " . . . with a request that the beneficiaries acknowledge payment by signing a receipt either endorsed on the accounts or supplied separately and with the receipt to include, if needed, a discharge to the personal representatives."

Obviously, there may be cases where there has been ill feeling during the administration and the solicitor anticipates that the residuary beneficiary may be difficult. In such a case, the Committee recommends that:

> " ... residuary beneficiaries should be sent in advance copies of the approved accounts and be asked to sign a form of receipt and discharge to the personal representatives on the basis that they will be sent a cheque immediately upon the solicitors receiving the form back signed."

The following form of receipt is a Plain English redraft by Richard Oerton of the form originally produced by the Land Law and Succession Committee. It appeared in "Clarity".

> "THE LATE..........
> The estate accounts show the final sum due to me as £..........
> I approve the accounts and will accept that sum in full satisfaction of all my claims against the estate.
> Please pay it by a crossed cheque in my favour and send it to me by post."

Although it is common to include a discharge to the personal representative in the form of a receipt, it could only be effective if the beneficiaries had been given full and accurate details of all dealings with the estate assets and liabilities.

Minors cannot give a good receipt for money

Unless the will provides otherwise, a minor cannot give a good receipt for money **18.17** (*Re Somech* (1957)). A married minor or minor in a civil partnership can give a good receipt for income but not for capital (Law of Property Act 1925 s.21). It is often said that the parent or guardian of a minor cannot give a good receipt on behalf of the minor without express provision in the will. However, the Children Act 1989 provides that all parents with parental responsibility have the same rights, powers and duties as guardians appointed under the Children Act. These rights are set out in s.3 and include "the right to receive or recover in his own name *for the benefit of the child,* property of whatever description and wherever situated, which the child is entitled to receive or recover".

There may be circumstances where the testator may not be happy to allow the parent or guardian to receive the legacy. It does not appear that the personal representatives would be entitled to withhold the legacy (although the minor's parent may have trouble extracting the money if the personal representative is unwilling to pay it over). The best course is to leave a substantial legacy to trustees to hold for the benefit of the minor and in the case of small amounts to state expressly whether or not the personal representative is to release funds to the parent or guardian.

Under the Administration of Estates Act 1925 s.42 personal representatives have power where a minor is absolutely entitled to a legacy to appoint a trust corporation or at least two individuals (and not more than four) to hold the property on trust until the minor reaches 18. The trustees can give the personal representatives a good receipt. However, s.42 does not apply where the infant's interest is contingent (for example on reaching 18). It does not appear that personal representatives could make such an appointment if the parent or guardian of the minor demanded the legacy.

4. THE EQUITABLE RULES OF APPORTIONMENT

18.18   These rules exist to try to achieve fairness between tenants for life and remaindermen. If residuary personalty is left to persons in succession there is an obligation under the rule in *Howe v Lord Dartmouth* (1802) to sell wasting, hazardous, and unauthorised assets. Pending sale the tenant for life is not entitled to the income from such assets since otherwise they might obtain a benefit from the personal representatives' delay. Instead they are entitled to interest at 4 per cent per annum on the value of the assets. Any surplus income is treated as capital and invested in authorised investments. This rule exists to protect remaindermen.

The rule in *Re Earl of Chesterfield's Trusts* (1883) exists to protect the life tenant. There is an obligation to sell reversionary interests and other non-income producing assets. There will inevitably be some delay before such a sale can be effected and no income is earned during the period. Therefore the proceeds of sale of such assets are not treated as exclusively capital but are apportioned between capital and income under the rule in the *Re Earl of Chesterfield's Trusts*.

Although these rules were originally developed to achieve fairness between the life tenant and the remainderman they lead to extremely complicated calculations and most professionally drawn wills exclude them as a matter of course. Where, as is usually now the case, trustees have wide powers of investment which include power to acquire wasting and non-income producing assets, such assets will be authorised investments and the Rules in *Howe v Lord Dartmouth* and *Re Earl of Chesterfield's Trusts* will have no application. There will, therefore, be no need to exclude them.

There is another type of equitable apportionment known as the *Rule in Allhusen v Whittell* (1867). This rule probably still applies. It is, therefore, advisable to exclude it in wills which create successive interests. This rule provides that where residue is left to persons in succession, debts and other outgoings (such as legacies) are to be treated as paid partly from capital and partly from income accruing to that portion of capital during the period between the testator's death and the payment of the outgoings. The principle is that the life tenant is entitled to income from the net residue after payment of debts and other liabilities but not to income from those assets which are needed for the payment of debts and which, therefore, do not form part of the net residue.

Example

A's will leaves residue to L for life, remainder to R. The personal representatives wish to pay legacies of £11,000 one year after T's death. The estate has produced income at the rate of 10 per cent per annum. The legacies will be treated as paid with £10,000 of capital and £1,000 of income. Thus the net residuary estate will be reduced by £10,000 and the income of the estate will be reduced by £1,000.

Like the other equitable apportionments the rule exists to achieve fairness between life tenant and remainderman. It is, however, usually excluded in professionally drawn wills. If it is not excluded it will affect the capital and income accounts presented to the residuary beneficiaries. The Inland Revenue will ignore any apportionments effected under this rule and will assess the liability of the estate to income tax on all the trust income before apportionments.

5. The Legal Rules of Apportionment

18.19 As explained in para.16.57, above, income is treated as accruing on a daily basis under the common law rules of apportionment of interest and the Apportionment Act 1870. Thus, income received after death must be apportioned if it relates to a period part of which falls before and part of which falls after death.

Most professionally drawn wills exclude the need for such apportionments. If the will creates a trust in favour of a life tenant, the need for apportionments should be expressly excluded on the life tenant's death as well as on the testator's death.

Even if the will does exclude the need for apportionments, the exclusion is only effective for *distribution* purposes. Apportionments will still have to be made to calculate the value of the estate at death for *inheritance tax purposes* (see Ch.4). Moreover, when calculating the liability of the estate to *income tax* no apportionments are made no matter what the will says; any income which is payable after death is treated as income of the estate and not of the deceased even though part or all of the income may be attributable to a period falling before death (however, as we saw in Ch.6 there is an income tax relief available where income has been apportioned and charged to inheritance tax). The position is rather different on the death of a life tenant of a trust. For income tax purposes the Revenue will follow the terms of the trust instrument. If that does not exclude the need for apportionment of income on the death of a life tenant the income tax liability will be apportioned between the life tenant's estate and the person next entitled but if it does exclude the need for apportionment, tax on all income payable after death will be treated as the liability of the person next entitled.

6. Recommendations of the Law Commission

18.20 The Law Commission in its Report Capital and Income in Trusts: classification and apportionment (Law Com. No.315) questioned the need for equitable rules requiring trustees to sell and reinvest in authorised investments when almost all investments are authorised under the Trustee Act 2000 s.3. Furthermore, the Trustee Act 2000 s.4 requires trustees to review trust investments from time-to-time and consider whether they should be varied taking into account the standard investment criteria set out in the Act. The Commission concluded that the obligation to sell imposed by the equitable rules of apportionment should be abolished in relation to future trusts.

So far as the rules of equitable apportionment are concerned, the Commission was rather more hesitant. Whilst agreeing that they are cumbersome, complex and overly technical, they are designed to achieve fairness. Giving trustees a discretion to apportion to achieve a fair result appeared an attractive option but would have had significance tax implications as it would have prevented beneficiaries having a right to receive income. The Commission finally recommended abolition of the equitable rules of apportionment in relation to trusts created or arising in the future.

The Commission also recommended that s.2 of the Apportionment Act 1870 should not apply to trusts created after the commencement of new legislation, unless the terms of the trust expressly state that the section should apply. After the disapplication of the section to trusts, periodic payments such as dividends will accrue to the income beneficiary at the date when they arise.

Bridget Prentice, the then Parliamentary Under-Secretary for Justice, made a statement on March 22, 2010 in which she said of the Law Commission Report:

> "The Government have carefully considered the report and are pleased to announce that they accept the Law Commission's recommendations. It is now intended to consult on these reforms and the proposed draft legislation."

However, at the time of writing no legislation is proceeding.

7. ACCOUNTS

The purpose of accounts

18.21 The personal representatives will prepare a variety of accounts for different purposes. At an early stage of the administration they must complete an Inheritance Tax Account (unless the estate is an "excepted estate" in which case no Account is required). They will also keep records of any income of the estate so that any income tax liability of the estate can be calculated.

In addition, before the personal representatives can complete the administration they must produce estate accounts for the residuary beneficiaries. The purpose of such accounts is to list all the assets of the estate, all the debts, liabilities and expenses that have been paid, all the legacies that have been paid and then to show the balance which is available for distribution to the residuary beneficiaries. The personal representatives will also show how the entitlement of each residuary beneficiary is to be paid. Thus, if the personal representatives propose to pay part of the entitlement in cash and to transfer assets *in specie* to make up the balance this must be explained. The residuary beneficiaries signify their approval of the accounts by signing them and acknowledging receipt of any amount due. This discharges the personal representatives from liability (see para.18.23, below).

The form of the accounts

There are no rules as to the form of estate accounts. However, they *must* be clear **18.22** and easy to understand since their purpose is to convey information to the residuary beneficiaries. An account may be prepared vertically showing assets less liabilities or as a double sided account showing receipts on one side and payments on the other.

An account normally commences with a narrative which sets out such matters as the date of death of the deceased, the date of the grant of representation, a summary of the dispositions made in the will (or of the effect of the intestacy rules), the value of the gross and net estate and any other information relevant to the administration (for example, whether any interim payments have already been made to the residuary beneficiaries, whether it is proposed to transfer assets *in specie* to the residuary beneficiaries). The purpose of such a narrative is to make the account more intelligible to the beneficiaries. In order to cut down the amount included on the account, details of investments may be relegated to separate schedules.

It is usual, except in the case of very small estates, to divide the account into a capital account and an income account. Such a division is essential if a life interest has been created in the residue since one person will be entitled to capital and another to income.

If separate capital and income accounts are prepared it will be necessary, unless the need to apportion has been excluded, to make apportionments of any income received after death which is attributable partly to the period before and partly to the period after death. The former will be shown on the capital account as part of the residuary cash. The latter will be shown on the income account; if the income-producing asset was specifically bequeathed the income will pass to the specific beneficiary, if it was not it will pass as part of the residuary income.

If residuary personalty has been left to one person for life, remainder to **18.23** another, equitable apportionments of certain types of income and of the proceeds of sale of certain types of asset may have to be made for *distribution* purposes. These were discussed in para.18.18, above. If such apportionments of income and capital are made they will obviously affect the entries made in the Estate Accounts. However, it is usual for professionally drawn wills to exclude the need for equitable apportionments.

A simple estate account is set out below.

MRS AMY TESTOR DECEASED

Mrs Amy Testor of the Restwell Nursing Home, Bognor Regis, died on January 4, 2010 at the age of 96.

Probate of her will was granted by the Principal Probate Registry on April 6, 2010 to her daughter, Miss Catherine Testor.

By her will Mrs Testor left £2,500 to each of her two grandchildren, Mr David Kay and Mrs Elizabeth Forbes. The residue was given after payment of debts, funeral, testamentary and other expenses and legacies to Mrs Briony Kay and Miss Catherine Testor. The will excluded the need to apportion income. The personal effects have been taken by Miss Catherine Testor in partial satisfaction of her entitlement at an agreed valuation of £410. Mrs Testor had made chargeable lifetime transfers in the seven years before her death.

Capital Account

	£	£
Investwell Building Society account		181,500
Northern Crest Unit Trust		188,520
Current account		680
Cash in Hand		70
Personal effects—estimated value		410
GROSS ESTATE		371,180
Less debts and other expenses		
Funeral Expenses	1,450	
Solicitors' fees	520	
Arrears at Nursing Home	760	
Inheritance tax	8,000	
		(10,730)
NET ESTATE		360,450
Less Legacies		
Mr D. Kay	2,500	
Mrs E. Forbes	2,500	
		(5,000)
Residue available to beneficiaries		355,450
½ Mrs B. Kay	177,725	
½ Miss C. Testor	177,725	
		355,450

Income Account

	£	£
Income received since death		
Investwell Building Society	700	
Northern Crest Unit Trust	1,800	
		2,500
Less: Interest on bank loan taken out to pay inheritance tax		(100)
Income available to beneficiaries		2,400
½ Mrs B. Kay	1,200	
½ Miss C. Testor	1,200	
		2,400

Note:
Having calculated the entitlement of the two residuary beneficiaries to capital and income it would then, strictly speaking, be necessary to produce an account for each showing how their entitlement is to be made up. However, on these facts each will receive her entitlement in cash (apart from the personal effects valued at £410 which are to go to Catherine Testor) so that the preparation of additional accounts is not essential.

Signature of the accounts

A receipt of a residuary beneficiary is normally given by signing the accounts. **18.24** Such a receipt normally includes an indemnity, for example, "I agree to accept the assets shown in full satisfaction of my entitlement and hereby discharge X as executor and indemnify him against all claims and demands". However, such a release and indemnity is only effective if the beneficiary had full knowledge of all the assets, accounts and dealings.

If a beneficiary persists in a refusal to approve accounts they may commence an administration action for examination of the accounts. If they do not, the personal representatives may pay the outstanding funds into court under the Trustee Act 1925 s.63 as amended by s.36(4) Sch.III of the Administration of Justice Act 1965. However, this involves the estate in extra expense and should not be done unless there is no satisfactory alternative. It will rarely be necessary since a recalcitrant beneficiary will not wish to be deprived of the estate assets indefinitely and will usually either approve the accounts or commence proceedings relatively quickly. If the reason that approval is not forthcoming is that a beneficiary is missing, the personal representatives may have taken steps earlier in the administration to obtain a "Benjamin Order"; if they have not they should consider either obtaining an indemnity from the other beneficiaries or obtaining insurance cover or retaining assets.

A residuary beneficiary who lacks mental capacity will be unable to approve the accounts. A receiver or deputy may have been appointed by the Court of Protection to deal with that person's affairs. In this case the personal representatives should inform the receiver or deputy of the entitlement and act in accordance with their directions. Provided the personal representatives act in accordance with the court's directions they will obtain a good discharge. If no receiver has been appointed then an application should be made to the Court of Protection for the appointment of a deputy. Such an application is normally made by a close relative of the disabled beneficiary. The personal representatives will retain the assets pending the application. However, if the relatives are reluctant to make such an application, the personal representatives will have to consider alternative arrangements such as payment into court under the Trustee Act 1925 s.63.

Chapter Nineteen

POST-MORTEM ALTERATIONS

1. Introduction

The persons entitled to a deceased person's property under the terms of the will **19.01** or under the intestacy rules may not need or want the property left to them. It is sometimes possible for the disposition of a deceased person's estate to be altered after the death. An alteration may achieve a more satisfactory disposition of the property of the deceased and in certain cases may result in a saving of tax. There are a number of ways in which alterations after death to the dispositions of a deceased person's property can be achieved. In this chapter we will consider the following methods:

(a) A "disclaimer".

(b) A "variation".

(c) An order made under the Inheritance (Provision for Family and Dependants) Act 1975.

(d) A "two-year discretionary trust".

(e) A "precatory trust".

In each case we will consider the effect on succession to property and on taxation. We will also look at the right of a surviving spouse or civil partner under the intestacy rules to elect to capitalise their life interest. This is not, strictly speaking, an *alteration* of the intestacy rules merely an application of them. However, the exercise of the right can alter the inheritance tax liability of the estate and it is, therefore, convenient to consider it in this chapter.

2. Disclaimer

The succession effect of disclaimer

It was said as long ago as 1819 that "the law certainly is not so absurd as to force **19.02** a man to take an estate against his will" (per Abbot C.J. in *Townson v Tiekell*

(1819)); the right of disclaimer is long-established. The beneficiary is free to disclaim any property. A person entitled on intestacy is also apparently free to disclaim entitlement under the intestacy rules (*Re Scott* (1975)). A disclaimer is simply a refusal to accept property.

Limitations on the right to disclaim

19.03 The right to disclaim a gift is lost altogether once any benefit from it has been accepted by the beneficiary. This will be the case where, for example, the beneficiary has had the property vested in them or where they have received income from a specific legacy or interest on a pecuniary legacy.

Unless the will provides to the contrary, it is not possible to disclaim part only of a single gift, the entire gift must be given up. If a beneficiary is entitled to two separate gifts, they can disclaim one while accepting the other. Thus a beneficiary given two legacies, one of £1,000, the other of a clock, can disclaim the clock and still accept the money (or vice versa).

The effect of disclaiming

19.04 If a beneficiary disclaims a gift in the will or an entitlement under the intestacy rules, the property passes as if the gift to them had failed. The destination of the disclaimed property thereafter depends on the nature of the gift or entitlement that has been given up.

A will may provide expressly for what is to happen if a gift cannot take effect for any reason. In the absence of express provision the following rules apply. If a non-residuary gift in a will is disclaimed then the property will fall into residue. If a residuary gift is disclaimed, the property passes under the intestacy rules, unless the gift is a class gift in which case it passes to the other members of the class. If it is a gift to joint tenants, it passes to the other joint tenant.

If a gift in a will is disclaimed, this does not prevent the beneficiary receiving the property (in whole or in part) under the intestacy rules. Thus, if a deceased died leaving a spouse and children having by will given his entire substantial estate to his wife, she could disclaim her interest under the will and still share in the property with her children under the intestacy rules, if this distribution is acceptable. If it is not, a "variation" might be more appropriate (see below, para.19.11).

Disclaiming an interest on intestacy will either result in the property passing to the other members of the same class of beneficiaries or, if there are none, to the next category of relatives. Thus, if one of a number of children disclaims, the result is that the others enjoy a larger share of the deceased's estate. The child who disclaims is not treated as having predeceased the testator or intestate and so there is no question of their share passing to their own children by substitution unless there is a will which provides that this should happen. If an only child disclaims, the result is that the deceased's parents or brothers and sisters benefit. See *Re DWS* (2001). Although this was a case on forfeiture the Court of Appeal held that the effect of s.47(1)(i) of the Administration of Estates Act 1925 was that the issue of a child of the intestate could take only if their parent had in fact predeceased the intestate. A child of surviving issue could not take in preference to their parent. If a surviving parent was prevented from taking by disclaimer or disqualification, the intestate's estate should pass, not to their child, but to those entitled if the disclaimer had died without issue.

It can be seen that a disadvantage of disclaimer is that the original beneficiary has no control over the ultimate destination of the property, which must pass under the terms of the deceased's will or the intestacy rules. This may be acceptable to the beneficiary who merely wants to give up their rights to certain property (perhaps because it carries with it onerous covenants or unacceptable conditions), but it will not be acceptable if they want to ensure that someone, other than the residuary beneficiary or next of kin, takes in their place. In the latter case a "variation" would ensure they achieve their wishes.

Note that a direction in a will that property is to pass in a certain way if the beneficiary predeceases, will not take effect if the beneficiary disclaims. The Civil Law Reform Bill contained provisions to deal with this and related problems but the Bill did not survive wash-up before the 2010 General Election.

At the time of writing the changes are being taken forward in a private members' bill, the Estates of Deceased Persons (Forfeiture Rule and Law of Succession) Bill. The Bill received its second reading in January 2011.

Method of disclaiming

There are no statutory provisions governing the method of disclaiming a gift in **19.05** a will or an entitlement under the intestacy rules. It is sufficient for the beneficiary to indicate their intention to the deceased's personal representatives either orally or in writing. Disclaimer can be by informal acts but will not be readily presumed where it is to the advantage of the person to retain the gift. There is a presumption that a person will accept a legacy unless the contrary is proved (see *Cook v IRC* (2002) and the cases cited in *Re Strattons Disclaimer, Stratton v IRC* (1958)). Written notice is, therefore, advisable. A letter stating that the beneficiary does not want the property is sufficient.

The taxation effect of disclaimer

The inheritance tax rules

Under general principles a beneficiary who refuses to accept an entitlement is **19.06** treated as making a transfer of value for the purposes of inheritance tax. Thus, if the beneficiary were to die within seven years of disclaiming, tax would (subject to any exemptions and reliefs available) be payable. If certain conditions are complied with, a disclaimer will not be treated as a transfer of value. Inheritance tax will, instead, be payable as if the deceased had left their property to the person entitled once the disclaimer takes effect. The conditions are set out in Inheritance Tax Act 1984 s.142:

(a) the disclaimer must not be made for consideration in money or money's worth (other than the making of a disclaimer or variation in respect of another disposition);

(b) the disclaimer must be in writing; and

(c) the disclaimer must be made within two years of the death.

Provided these conditions are complied with, no further formalities are required. (In particular, there is no requirement for a statement that s.142 is to apply; as we shall see at para.19.13, below, such a statement is required in the case of a post-death variation.) The property disclaimed will pass to the person next entitled under the terms of the deceased's will (or on their intestacy). The original beneficiary will not be treated as making a transfer of value. If the change of entitlement results in a change in the amount of inheritance tax payable on the deceased's estate (for example, where the spouse exemption becomes available on more or on less of the estate) the personal representatives will recalculate the tax and submit a corrective account to the Revenue.

In some cases the effect of a disclaimer may be to increase tax unnecessarily. For example, the spouse exemption will be lost if the spouse disclaims. In such cases a disclaimer which is not in writing or which is made more than two years after death should be considered. Section 142 will not then apply, the surviving spouse will be treated as making a transfer of value but provided this is potentially exempt and the spouse does survive seven years no tax will be payable. A disclaimer is unilateral. The consent of the personal representatives of the deceased is not required to a disclaimer even if its effect is to increase the tax due.

Section 142(1) refers to the disclaimer of property comprised in the deceased's estate immediately before death "whether passing by will, intestacy or otherwise". As a result of the reference to property passing "otherwise" than by will or intestacy, it is possible to disclaim an interest in joint property passing by survivorship. (Property in which the deceased had merely an interest in possession is not treated as a part of the deceased's estate for the purposes of disclaimer (s.142(5)).)

The Revenue accepts that it is possible for the personal representatives of a dead beneficiary to disclaim on their behalf. See IHT Manual, para.35164. The dead beneficiary must not have accepted any benefit and the disclaimer must be made by both the personal representatives of the dead beneficiary and the beneficiaries of their estate.

Quite apart from s.142 there is power for a person to disclaim an interest in settled property under s.93 of the Inheritance Tax Act. Provided the disclaimer is not made for consideration in money or money's worth, inheritance tax is charged as if the person had never become entitled to the interest. Both life interests and reversionary interests can be disclaimed. The beneficiary must have taken no benefit from the interest. The Revenue accepts that the personal representatives of a deceased life tenant can disclaim (see IHT Manual, para.35165).

The capital gains tax rules

Under general capital gains tax principles a disclaimer will amount to a disposal **19.07**
by the original beneficiary for capital gains tax purposes. However, the Taxation
of Chargeable Gains Act 1992 s.62(6) provides that if certain conditions are
complied with, a disclaimer will not be treated as a disposal. Instead the property
will be treated as if left by the deceased to the person entitled once the disclaimer
has taken effect. As death is not a disposal, no capital gains tax will be payable.
The conditions are identical with those required for inheritance tax relief. No
further formalities are required.

The income tax rules

General principles

There is no statutory provision which makes a disclaimer retrospective for **19.08**
income tax purposes. Therefore, the position with respect to income from the
property disclaimed is governed by the general law. As a disclaimer operates by
preventing a gift from taking effect at all, the disclaiming beneficiary has no
entitlement to income from the disclaimed asset(s). The disclaimer ought, therefore, to prevent the disclaiming beneficiary having any income tax liability.
HMRC have apparently argued that the disclaiming beneficiary's interest
remains intact up to the date of the disclaimer but this seems contrary to principle.

Certainly in relation to pecuniary legacies the position is clear. A pecuniary
legacy carries with it, in certain circumstances, the right to receive interest (see
Ch.16, para.16.58, above). If interest is neither paid nor claimed, there is nothing
for the legatee to be assessed to tax on (*Dewar v I.R.C.* (1935)) unless a fund to
meet the legacy has been set aside (*Spens v I.R.C.* (1970)). A disclaimer can only
be made where no income or interest has been accepted so a legatee who is able
to disclaim will not have any income to be assessed.

Specific legatees and residuary beneficiaries ought to be treated in the same
way as the gifts have never taken effect

The settlement legislation

A disclaimer is a refusal to accept an entitlement rather than a gift of the **19.09**
entitlement to a new beneficiary. This can have an important and beneficial
income tax consequence for parents.

The anti-avoidance legislation contained in Pt 5 Ch.5 of the Income Tax
(Trading and Other Income) Act 2005 provides that a settlor will remain liable
for income tax on income from a settlement in which the settlor, spouse or civil
partner retains an interest and will be liable for income tax on income applied for
their minor children who have neither married nor formed a civil partnership.
The definition of a settlement is wide enough to catch a post-death variation (see
para.19.20, below) but HMRC will apparently normally accept that a disclaimer

is not a settlement on the basis that the property has never been owned by the person disclaiming.

The stamp duty rules

19.10   There is no stamp dity on voluntary dispositions. There will be no stamp duty land tax where, as is normally the case, there is no consideration for the disclaimer. Under para.1 Sch.3 to Finance Act 2003 any land transaction is exempt if made for no consideration.

3. VARIATIONS

The succession effect of variation

19.11   A variation is a direction from a beneficiary to the personal representatives to transfer property to someone other than the original beneficiary. There are no special rules on the form of a variation for succession purposes since it is, in effect, an ordinary lifetime gift. In cases where one or more of the recipients of the property under the variation is providing no consideration, a deed is advisable as the personal representatives may be reluctant to act on the basis of an unenforceable agreement.

For succession purposes, a variation is similar to a disclaimer in that the original beneficiary gives up their rights to receive property under the terms of the will or the intestacy rules but a variation differs from a disclaimer in three material respects:

(a)   A variation is possible even though the original beneficiary has accepted the property, whether by receiving income or by having the property vested in them. It is even possible to vary the deceased's dispositions once the administration of the estate is complete.

(b)   The original beneficiary can make a partial variation of a gift by, for example, giving up part of a gift. (This is not possible in the case of a disclaimer unless the will makes specific provision.)

(c)   The original beneficiary can control the ultimate destination of the property since it passes to whoever they specify. The property does not have to pass under the terms of the deceased's will or the intestacy rules.

Thus, a variation may provide a solution where a person has inherited property which they do not want but which they do not wish to pass to the person next entitled under the deceased's will or the intestacy rules.

Example

Ann dies leaving her residuary estate to her husband Brian. He has no need of it and wishes to give the property direct to his two grandchildren, rather than to his child, Charlotte. A disclaimer will not achieve his aim since if he were to disclaim his interest under the will and his entitlement under the intestacy rules, the property would pass to Charlotte.

In the above example Brian could achieve his aim by making an ordinary lifetime gift to the grandchildren without altering the disposition by the deceased at all. However, this would be a potentially exempt transfer for inheritance tax purposes and a disposal for capital gains purposes which might result in unnecessary payments of tax being made. If he complies with the requirements of the Inheritance Tax Act 1984 s.142 and Taxation of Chargeable Gains Act 1992 s.62(6), he can vary the terms of the will in favour of his grandchildren and can avoid the transaction being treated as his lifetime gift for capital tax purposes.

When choosing between a variation complying with the statutory requirements and an ordinary lifetime gift, tax considerations should be uppermost in the beneficiary's mind since variation is basically a tax concept.

When is a variation concluded?

In *Crowden v Aldridge* (1993) the residuary beneficiaries signed a memorandum **19.12** after the funeral agreeing that the will should be varied in favour of the deceased's housekeeper and stating that each would sign a deed to that effect. When the deed was prepared four of the beneficiaries refused to sign. The court held that the memorandum was a document showing intention to create legal effect and therefore it varied the distribution of the estate as soon as it was communicated to the executors.

The taxation effect of variation

The inheritance tax rules

If an original beneficiary makes lifetime gift of all or part of the property this is **19.13** a transfer of value for inheritance tax purposes. Thus, if they die within seven years of the gift, inheritance tax will be payable (subject to any exemptions and reliefs which may be available). However, Inheritance Tax Act s.142(1) provides that if certain conditions are complied with, a variation will not be treated as a transfer of value. Instead, inheritance tax will be payable as if the deceased had left their property to the substituted beneficiary or beneficiaries. The conditions are:

(a) the variation must not be made for consideration in money or money's worth (other than the making of a disclaimer or variation in respect of another disposition);

(b) the variation must be in writing;

(c) the variation must be made within two years of the death;

(d) the instrument in writing which makes the variation must contain a
     statement by the person or persons making the instrument (and, where
     the variation results in additional tax being payable also by the personal
     representatives) to the effect that they intend s.142(1) to apply to the
     variation. The personal representatives may only refuse to make the
     statement if no or no sufficient assets are held by them as personal
     representatives for discharging the additional tax; and

(e) where additional tax becomes payable as a result of the instrument the
     person or persons making the instrument and the personal representa-
     tives are under a duty to deliver a copy to HMRC and notify them of
     the amount of the additional tax.

Paragraphs (d) and (e) were introduced by the Finance Act 2002 s.120. They
apply to all variations made after July 31, 2002. (The previous provisions
required notice to the Revenue in all cases—even when no extra tax was
payable—but did not require the instrument itself to state that s.142(1) was to
apply.)

As in the case of a disclaimer, any property comprised in the deceased's estate
immediately before death, whether passing by will, intestacy *or otherwise*, can be
the subject of a variation (s.142(1)). It is, therefore, possible to vary the destination of property passing by survivorship.

Section 142(5) provides expressly that a variation agreement will be effective
for inheritance tax purposes whether or not the administration is complete or the
property concerned has already been distributed to the original beneficiary.

The variation is effective for all inheritance purposes so a person who has
varied property will not be regarded as making a gift of that property for the
purposes of the gift with reservation provisions. There is also protection in
para.16 Sch.15 of the Finance Act 2004 to prevent the pre-owned assets rules
applying to post-death variations.

The Revenue take the view that a variation, once made, is irrevocable and that
s.142 will not apply to an instrument redirecting any item that has already been
redirected under an earlier instrument. *Russell v I.R.C.* confirms the Revenue's
view that it is not possible to redirect any item or any part of an item which has
already been redirected under an earlier instrument. A variation, once made,
cannot be amended or corrected unless it the court will rectify the variation to
correct mistakes in the way the transaction had been recorded. See *Martin v
Nicholson* (2004); *Wills v Gibbs* (2007); *Ashcroft v Barnsdale* (2010). It is
possible to have any number of variations in relation to the same estate so long
as they each deal with different assets.

The Revenue has published guidelines setting out the requirements which an
instrument must satisfy to qualify under s.142. They are contained in a letter
published in the Law Society Gazette of May 22, 1985, p.1454 and available at
para.35021 of the Inheritance Tax Manual. The published requirements are that
the instrument must:

- be in writing and must be made by the persons or any of the persons who benefit or would benefit under the dispositions of the property comprised in the deceased's estate immediately before their death;

- be made within two years after the death; and

- clearly indicate the dispositions that are the subject of the instrument, and vary their destination as laid down by the deceased's will or under the law relating to intestate estates, or otherwise.

The effect of the third bullet point is that the variation must refer to the original disposition. In the Revenue's view a document such as a deed of assignment which merely transfers property in fact received by a legatee to a third party without mention of the will does not satisfy this requirement. The third bullet also requires that the destination of the property is varied. However, it is not fatal to a s.142 claim if the property ends up back in the same place that it started so long as the initial destination of the property was varied. Such circular variations often arise in relation to deceased beneficiaries. See para.19.14, below.

Deceased beneficiaries

The beneficiaries of a person who has died may make a variation redirecting that person's entitlement on an earlier death. **19.14**

Example

Jed, who has made no lifetime transfers, dies leaving £100,000 to his brother, Tom, and the rest of his estate to charity. Tom dies six months later leaving his estate of £1m to his sons. The sons can vary Jed's will to leave the £100,000 directly to them instead of to their father.

Paragraph 35042 of the Inheritance Tax Manual says that such a redirection on behalf of a deceased beneficiary does not infringe the requirement to change the destination of the property. However, the Revenue does not consider that it is possible to redirect a life interest after the death of the life tenant. Once the life tenant dies, there is no property in existence that can be redirected. Many people thought this interpretation was wrong but it received judicial support in *Soutters Executry v IRC* (2002). It is possible to disclaim a life interest (see para.19.06, above).

It is possible to vary a will to direct property into the estate of a deceased beneficiary. For example, suppose Fred's first wife died some years ago with an unused nil rate band which Fred inherited. Fred has remarried and has just died leaving assets worth £1m to his children from his second marriage; his second wife died one year earlier leaving her entire estate of £100,000 to the same children. The children can vary their father's will to leave assets to their dead mother to allow her to make use of her nil rate band. The effect is that Fred's estate has the benefit of a double nil rate band (his own and his first wife's). The second wife's estate has her own nil rate band available and, as a result of the variation, has sufficient assets to make use of the full value of the nil rate band.

Whether to have the transfer treated as the deceased's

19.15   A beneficiary (B) will often wish to have the transfer treated as the deceased's since this results in only one possible charge to tax, from the deceased to the new beneficiary; whereas if B makes a lifetime gift there is one charge to B and a risk of a second charge if B dies within seven years of the gift.

However, if B is the spouse of the deceased it may be beneficial not to have the transfer treated as the deceased's since the initial transfer to B is exempt; there is still the risk of a charge if B dies within seven years but this will be at B's rates and tapering relief will be available after three years.

Anti-avoidance

19.16   The Revenue is aware that the driving reason for using post-death variation is the wish to save tax. It is suspicious of arrangements where chargeable beneficiaries will give up benefits under the will in favour of a surviving spouse or civil partner thus gaining the benefit of spouse or civil partner exemption, and the spouse or civil partner then returns the benefits to the original beneficiaries. Paragraph 11032 of the IHT Manual states that HMRC will ask:

> (i)   whether there had been any discussion between the parties before the variation was made about how the benefit redirected to the spouse or civil partner should be dealt with; and
>
> (ii) whether subsequent to the variation the spouse or civil partner has made any transfers to the original chargeable beneficiaries, or is contemplating making any such transfers.

The same result can be achieved if the original beneficiaries vary to create a terminable life interest for the spouse in the expectation that the trustees will terminate some or all of the life interest to transfer capital back to them. In this case the Manual says that the Revenue will ask whether the trustees have already exercised the power of appointment or whether an exercise of it is contemplated.

If the variation creates a terminable life interest, there is an additional problem in s.142(4) of the Inheritance Tax Act 1984. This provides that where a variation results in property being held in trust for a person for less than two years after the death, the disposition of the property that takes effect at the end of the period is to be treated as if it had had effect at the date of the death. In other words the trust drops out. If, therefore, adult children vary the disposition of their father's estate to give their mother an interest in possession lasting 12 months and then to themselves absolutely, the children will be treated as if the gift to them took effect on their father's death. The mother's life interest is disregarded and the desired inheritance tax saving is lost. (If the mother had had a life interest and had died within two years, it would have been her death and not the variation that resulted in the termination of the life interest and sub-s.4 would not have applied. Had the mother had a life interest which the trustees had chosen to terminate within two years, it is probably the variation which results in the termination and so sub-s.4 would apply.)

The capital gains tax rules

Under general principles a redirection of property inherited will amount to a **19.17** disposal by the original beneficiaries for capital gains tax purposes. HMRC draws a distinction between the situation where assets have already vested in the original legatee and situations where they are still vested in the personal representatives. Where the asset has vested in the legatee, they will be treated as making a disposal at market value at the date of the redirection. Tax will be payable if the asset has increased in value by more than the legatee's available annual exemption.

If the asset has not yet vested in the legatee, the Revenue takes the view that the legatee has a chose in action consisting of the right to have the estate duly administered. This chose in action is personal to the legatee and cannot be assigned. However, the legatee can assign the right to receive the proceeds of the chose in action.

If the agreement is for valuable consideration (either under a contract for sale or an agreement to compromise a claim under the Inheritance (Provision for Family and Dependants) Act 1975), the disposal is deemed made at the date of the contract (see Taxation of Chargeable Gains Act 1992 s.28). However, the subject matter remains inchoate until the assets are assented to the legatee at which point the legatee is treated as having acquired the assets and immediately disposed of them to the legatee (see Capital Gains Tax Manual, para.G31970 et seq.).

If there is no valuable consideration for the agreement, it cannot take effect as an assignment of a future chose. Hence, s.28 is irrelevant and there is no disposal until assets vest from the estate in the legatee, normally when the residue is ascertained. As the disposal is a gift, the disposal value will be the market value of the assets at the date of the transfer (see Capital Gains Tax Manual, para.G32010 et seq.).

A legatee who does not want the redirection to be treated as a lifetime disposal can take advantage of s.62(6) of the Taxation of Chargeable Gains Act 1992, which provides that if certain conditions are complied with a variation will not be treated as a disposal. Instead, the property will be treated as if the deceased had left it to the substituted beneficiary or beneficiaries. The conditions are identical to those required for inheritance tax purposes.

The wording of s.142 of the Inheritance Tax Act 1984 and s.62(6) of the Taxation of Chargeable Gains Act 1992 differ in one important respect. Section 142(1) provides that, where the appropriate conditions are complied with, "*this Act* shall apply as if the variation had been effected by the deceased". Section 62(6)(b) provides that "this section shall apply as if the variation had been effected by the deceased". The result is that a variation is retrospective for the purposes of the charge to tax on death contained in s.62 but not for other purposes such as establishing a settlement.

The House of Lord's decision in *Marshall v Kerr* (1994) illustrated the importance of the difference. If a variation creates an offshore settlement, the original beneficiary will be treated as the settlor for the purposes of TCGA 1992 s.86. Section 68C of the Taxation of Chargeable Gains Act 1992 (inserted by the Finance Act 2006) provides expressly that where property becomes settled property in consequence of a variation, the person making the variation is to be treated as the settlor.

The extension of the rules on settlor interested trusts for the purposes of capital gains tax makes this an important point. A settlement is settlor interested if the beneficiaries include their spouse, civil partner or minor children of the settlor who have not married or formed a civil partnership (see TCGA 1992 s.169F). Where a settlement is settlor interested hold-over relief is not available when assets are transferred to the settlement. Hence a parent who varies an entitlement to produce a settlement for the benefit of a class which includes their own minor children will be treated as the settlor for capital gains tax purposes.

Whether to have the disposition treated as the deceased's

19.18 Although the inheritance tax and capital gains tax rules are basically the same, there is no need to have the disposition treated as the deceased's for both taxes. The original beneficiary is free to choose for each tax the method which is most beneficial in order to achieve their ends.

Each case depends on its own facts but, when deciding whether to elect that the disposition be treated as made on death, two points should be borne in mind.

(a) If a loss has arisen since the date of death the original beneficiary may wish to set the loss off against their own gains and so will choose to make a lifetime gift.

(b) It is preferable to treat the gift as a lifetime disposition if the property has *increased* in value by an amount not exceeding the annual exemption from capital gains tax since the beneficiary can take the benefit of the increased acquisition value.

Apart from these circumstances, it is usually preferable to have the disposition treated as the deceased's since no capital gains tax liability arises on death.

The income tax rules

19.19 A variation raises problems with regard to income tax liability since (like disclaimer) there are no statutory provisions making the variation retrospective for income tax purposes. Thus, income arising between the date of death and the date of the variation will be taxed in accordance with the terms of the will (if any) and the rules on the taxation of the income of estates.

Pecuniary legatees are entitled to interest in certain circumstances. However, if interest is neither paid nor claimed, there is nothing for the legatee to be assessed to tax on (*Dewar v I.R.C.* (1935)) unless a fund to meet the legacy has been set aside (*Spens v I.R.C.* (1970)). A specific legatee is entitled to income from the date of death. The legatee will, therefore, be assessed to tax on income arising after the death up to the date of the variation. Income arising after that date will be taxed as income of the new beneficiary unless the settlement provisions apply (see para.19.20, below). Since the original legatee will be assessed to tax on the income from death till the variation, it may be preferable for them to accept the income rather than passing it to the new beneficiary.

So far as residuary beneficiaries are concerned s.671 of the Income Tax (Trading and Other Income) Act 2005 provides that where different persons obtain absolute interests in residue in succession during the administration of the estate, the interest of the later beneficiary is treated as including the interest of the earlier beneficiary for the purpose of calculating their assumed income entitlement. Hence when determining how much has been paid out as income, the personal representatives will take into account all income payments made to the original beneficiaries as well as to the beneficiaries taking under the variation.

The settlement legislation

The anti-avoidance legislation contained in Pt 5 Ch.5 of the Income Tax (Trading **19.20** and Other Income) Act 2005 provides that a settlor will remain liable for income tax on income from a settlement in which the settlor, spouse or civil partner retains an interest in settlement property and will be liable for income tax on income applied for their minor children who have neither married nor formed a civil partnership. A post-death variation will normally amount to a settlement. Parents should, therefore, be careful about making post-death variations in favour of minor children. Where feasible, a disclaimer will be preferable.

Stamp duty and variations

There is no stamp duty on voluntary dispositions. There will be no stamp duty **19.21** land tax where, as is normally the case, there is no consideration for the disclaimer. Under para.1 Sch.3 to the Finance Act 2003 any land transaction is exempt if made for no consideration.

4. INHERITANCE (PROVISION FOR FAMILY AND DEPENDANTS) ACT 1975

The position in relation to orders made under this Act is governed by s.146 of the **19.22** Inheritance Tax Act 1984 which provides that for inheritance tax purposes the provision ordered by the court is treated as if it were the disposition of the deceased. If the tax has to be adjusted in consequence of the court order, the tax underpaid or overpaid does not carry interest from any date earlier than the date of the order (see IHT Manual, para.35203).

The new beneficiary is liable to income tax on income arising after the date of death from property awarded to them.

5. SETTLEMENTS WITHOUT AN INTEREST IN POSSESSION—PROPERTY VESTED WITHIN TWO YEARS OF DEATH

19.23 Some testators wish to leave the ultimate destination of their property flexible so that their personal representatives can look at the circumstances existing at the date of the testators's death and make a distribution which is suitable in the light of those circumstances. This flexibility can be achieved by leaving property on discretionary trusts. It is usual for a testator to leave a letter of intent explaining the person(s) the testator would like to receive a benefit.

Section 144(1) and (2) of the Inheritance Tax Act 1984 provides that where a deceased creates a settlement without an immediate post-death interest in their will and, within the period of two years after their death an event occurs on which tax would be chargeable, no tax shall be charged and the will shall be read as if it provided that on the testator's death the property should be held as it is held after the event.

Example

Terri leaves her entire estate of £1m on discretionary trusts for the benefit of her spouse and children. One year after her death the trustees appoint £400,000 to one of her children and the residue to her spouse. Normally a appointment from a discretionary trust would attract an exit charge but here it does not. Instead the will is read as if it had left "£400,000 to a child and the residue to spouse".

It is not necessary for the terms of the trust to *require* the trustees to exercise their powers of appointment within two years of death. The section applies where the discretion is actually exercised within two years of death as well as to those where the will requires it to be exercised within that period. Because of the relatively low rate of tax on property leaving a discretionary trust (as to which see para.7.21 et seq. above) the trustees may well decide to allow the trust to continue beyond two years.

19.24 There is a trap in the wording of the section. Reading back only occurs if the event is one "on which tax would be chargeable". No inheritance tax is charged on an absolute appointment from a discretionary trust in the first three months following creation so an appointment should not be made until three months after the death—see *Frankland v I.R.C.* (1997) where an appointment of substantial assets to a surviving spouse was made within three months and as a result the spouse exemption was held not to be available.

The Finance Act 2006 introduced new categories of tax-advantaged trusts—immediate post-death interests, trusts for bereaved minors and age 18–25 trusts that can be set up under a person's will. Without express provision, an appointment out of a discretionary will trust would not create one of these new trusts as it would not be an event on which tax would be chargeable.

The Finance Act 2006 therefore amended s.144 to ensure that, where an appointment is made on or after March 22, 2006 on terms that would have created one of the new categories of trust had the provisions been included in the will, those provisions will be read back into the will; see IHTA 1984 s.144(3–6). Oddly, as a result of the wording of the new subsections there is no three-month restriction so the new tax-advantaged trusts can be created within three months of death.

Example

Tamzin leaves her entire estate of £1m on discretionary trusts for the benefit of her spouse and children. One month after her death the trustees appoint £300,000 to her son if he reaches 18 and the balance to her husband for life, remainder to her son. The appointments create an immediate post-death interest for her husband and a s.71A trust for her son. Both are read back into her will.

Had the appointment to her husband been absolute, it would not have been read back into the will.

The event which causes reading back does not have to be an express appoint-   **19.25**
ment. Obtaining a right to income within two years of death can create an immediate post-death interest.

Example

Tariq leaves his entire estate of £1m to such of his children as reach 25, equally if more than one. They are to become entitled to income at 21. Tariq believes that this will create a trust for a bereaved young person under IHTA 1984 s.71D.

When he dies, he has three children: Abe (22), Bea (20), and Chris (16). Abe has an immediate post-death interest which arises on Tariq's death. Bea obtains an immediate post-death interest because she becomes entitled to income within two years of Tariq's death and this is read back into the will. Only Chris has an interest in a bereaved young person's trust. This may not seem very important as all will become entitled to capital at 25 but the tax implications at 25 will be quite different. In the case of Abe and Bea there will be no charge to inheritance tax when they reach 25 as they are already treated as entitled to the trust capital. There will be a charge when Chris becomes entitled to capital based on the length of time the property has remained settled since his 18th birthday. There will be hold-over relief available when Chris becomes entitled to capital as it is a transfer from a trust for a bereaved young person. However, there will be no holdover relief when Abe and Bea become entitled to capital as they do not have interests in a trust for a bereaved young person and neither is the transfer chargeable to inheritance tax.

There are no special capital gains tax rules applicable to s.144 appointments. The exercise of the trustees' discretion is a deemed disposal and re-acquisition by them (see para.7.55, above). The recipient acquires the asset at its market value when the discretion is exercised and not the value at death. As the appointment from the trust is not a transfer chargeable to inheritance tax no holdover relief is available to the trustees.

However, it is often possible to avoid a charge to capital gains tax by making the appointment while the administration of the estate is still continuing. HMRC takes the view (see Capital Gains Tax Manual, para.31432) that if the trustees exercise their power of appointment while the assets are still in the hands of the personal representatives and before the assets have vested in them as trustees, the assets should be treated as passing direct to the appointee under the terms of the will.

The Manual states that the assets appointed should be treated as never becoming subject to the trust. They are treated as though the deceased had intended the assets concerned to pass directly to the legatee rather than into trust. The appointee then takes those assets as legatee and therefore acquires them at probate value like any other legatee.

The normal income tax rules for settlements where no beneficiary has a right to income will apply (see paras 7.63–7.66, above).

19.26　　Section 144 is being used much more since the introduction of the transferable nil rate band (see para.4.11). In the past instead of leaving everything to the surviving spouse, the first spouse to die would often create a nil rate band discretionary trust for the benefit of the surviving spouse and children so as to make use of the first spouse's nil rate band. Now that it is possible to transfer the unused portion of the nil rate band, many families take the view that the discretionary trust is unnecessary. The trustees can appoint the funds to the surviving spouse within two years of death with the following results:

> (a) The appointment will be read back into the will (so long as the *Frankland* trap is avoided—see para.19.23, above) with the result that the spouse exemption will be available on the whole of the estate of the first to die.
>
> (b) The survivor's estate will have the benefit of two nil rate bands.

The trustees do not have to wait until the executors have vested assets in them; they have a chose in action (the right to compel due administration of the estate) and so can appoint their rights under the will to the appointee. There are no particular formalities required by s.144 but obviously the trustees must comply with any requirements of the trust. The trust instrument will usually require powers of appointment to be exercised by deed but may also include power to advance capital which can usually be done more informally, typically by the trustees agreeing to exercise their discretion. It is important that any decision is recorded in writing and that the deed of appointment or record of the decision to advance is preserved. This is because when the survivor dies, their personal representatives will want to claim the additional nil rate band. HMRC will want to see proof that the nil rate band of the first spouse was not used. The first will, of course, created a nil rate band discretionary trust and it is, therefore, essential to have available documents to show that the dispositions in the will were altered.

6. PRECATORY WORDS

19.27　　Where a testator expresses a wish that property left in their will to a beneficiary should be transferred by that beneficiary to someone else, and that beneficiary complies with the wish within two years of the death, IHTA 1984 s.143 provides that inheritance tax is payable as if the deceased had left the property to the eventual recipient. The wish can be included in the will or communicated separately. Such requests are made most commonly in relation to personal chattels.

There are no special capital gains tax rules so the transfer will be treated as a disposal by the original beneficiary. It is likely that there will be no tax to pay as the asset may well not have increased in value by more than the level of the annual exemption. Also in the case of tangible moveable property there is an exception for a disposal of an item or set of items where the disposal consideration is £6,000 or less.

There are no special income tax rules, so income receivable up to the date of transfer will be assessed to tax as part of the original beneficiary's income.

7. Capitalisation of Life Interest by Surviving Spouse

If a surviving spouse capitalises the life interest received under the intestacy rules   **19.28** (see above, para.3.10) this is not a transfer of value for inheritance tax purposes and the spouse is treated as being entitled to the capitalised amount. The capitalisation may, however, lead to more inheritance tax being paid since the spouse exemption will be lost on that part of the capital in which the spouse no longer has any interest.

There are no special capital gains tax or income tax rules.

THE INHERITANCE (PROVISION FOR FAMILY AND DEPENDANTS) ACT 1975

1. INTRODUCTION

A testator is free to leave property in whatever way he or she pleases; no relative **20.01** has a *right* to receive property under the will. However, this principle of testamentary freedom is to some extent eroded by the Inheritance (Provision for Family and Dependants) Act 1975. This Act gives the court limited powers to order financial provision to be made from the net estate of a deceased person for the benefit of certain categories of applicant. Applications under the Act can also be made where a person dies intestate.

If an application is to be successful the following matters must be established:

(a) that certain preliminary requirements are satisfied;

(b) that the application is made within the time limit;

(c) that the applicant falls into one of the five possible categories of applicant; and

(d) that the will or intestacy rules have not made reasonable provision for the applicant.

If these matters are established the court must then decide whether and in what manner to order financial provision for the applicant from the net estate of the deceased (to help the court in its decision there are certain statutory guidelines to be taken into account).

The Act contains certain anti-avoidance provisions under which orders may, in limited circumstances, be made against people who have received property from the deceased before death (see below, paras 20.34–20.44).

2. Preliminary Requirements

20.02   The Act applies only in the case of a deceased who dies domiciled in England and Wales after March 31, 1976 (s.l(l)); earlier legislation (which was narrower in its scope) applies to deaths before that date.

There is no equivalent statute applying to persons who die domiciled in Scotland. (However, under Scots law if a person dies domiciled in Scotland leaving a spouse and issue the spouse is entitled to a one-third share in the whole of the moveable estate of the deceased and the children are entitled to another one-third share. If there is a spouse and no children the spouse's share is increased to one-half. The deceased is free to dispose only of the remaining portion).

Questions of domicile are becoming increasingly frequent. In *Schaffer v Cilento* (2004) the court had to decide whether the playwright Anthony Shaffer had abandoned his domicile of origin and acquired a domicile of choice in Queensland Australia and, if so, whether he had then abandoned that domicile of choice and reacquired a domicile in England and Wales. Lewison J. concluded that he had acquired a domicile of choice and had not abandoned it at the date of his death.

The following points were relevant. To acquire a domicile of choice it is not necessary to show that the intention to make a new home in the new country is irrevocable. The test is whether the person intends to make their home in the new country until the end of their days unless and until something happens to change their mind (*IRC v Bullock* (1976)). A domicile of choice can be lost in the same way that it is acquired. The person must have ceased to reside in the country and have no intention of returning there. The absence of intention must be unequivocal. A person in two minds does not have the necessary absence of intention. The abandonment of a domicile of choice is not to be lightly inferred.

In *Nathaneal, Cyganik v Agulian* (2006) the Court of Appeal emphasised the "adhesiveness" of the domicile of origin. The domicile of origin continues until it is proved that the person intended to make a home permanently or indefinitely in another country. "*Cogent and convincing*" evidence is required to establish a change of domicile and the burden is on the person alleging the change.

3. Time Limits

Normal period

20.03   Application for provision under the Act must normally be made within six months of the date of the first effective grant of representation (s.4). If a grant is revoked because it was wrongly made, the application must be made within six months of the subsequent valid grant (*Re Freeman* (1984)). However, where a limited grant is made time runs only from the making of a full grant. This was decided in the case of *Re Paul Anthony Johnson, (Deceased)* (1987) where a grant limited to pursuing negligence claims was made in 1983. The full grant of probate was made in 1987 and it was held that time ran from the date of the full grant.

In *Re McBroom* (1992) Eastham J. held that it is necessary for a grant of representation to have been taken out to the deceased's estate before an application can be made. However, the earlier case of *Re Searle* (1949) was not cited. In *Re Searle* Roxburghe J. said that the time limit was concerned with applications being too late and not too early. If *McBroom* is correct, it is not possible to have an inheritance claim dealt with immediately after a contested probate application. This is often done in practice and is an efficient method of dealing with intertwined applications.

The court has a discretion to extend the time limit. This discretion is unfettered and the Act itself contains no guidance as to how the court should exercise it. However, in *Re Salmon (Deceased)* (1980) Megarry V.C. suggested six guidelines. These were concisely summarised in *Re Dennis* (1981) as follows:

> "First, the discretion of the court, though judicial, is unfettered. Second, the onus is on the applicant to show special reasons for taking the matter out of the general six month time limit; ... this is not a mere triviality but a substantial requirement. Third, the court has to consider how promptly and in what circumstances the application has been made after the time has expired; one has to look at all the circumstances surrounding the delay. Fourth, the court has to see whether negotiations has started within the six month period. Fifth, one has to consider whether or not the estate has been distributed before the claim has been notified. Sixth, the court has to consider whether refusal of leave to bring proceedings out of time will leave the applicant without recourse against anyone else, ... "

(An example of a person against whom an applicant might have recourse would be a negligent solicitor.)

The list was not intended to be exhaustive and *Re Dennis* itself added a further guideline, "by analogy with applications for leave to defend in summary judgement proceedings, the applicant must show that he has an arguable case, a case fit to go to trial".

In *Re C* (1995) a claim made 18 months after the date of the grant and three years six months after the death was allowed. However, the circumstances were unusual. The applicant was an eight-year-old illegitimate child. The delay was not hers but her mother's. The estate was large so that prejudice to others would be not too great, and finally the chances of a successful claim were high. The *Salmon* guidelines were approved.

In *McNulty v McNulty* (2002) a widow brought a claim four years after death. The reason for the late application was that an asset of the estate which had been valued at £175,000 for probate purposes, was subsequently sold to a building developer for £1,600,000. She had first discovered the increase in value in June 1998 but proceedings were not issued until April 1999. The court said that she could not be criticised for not bringing the claim before June 1998 but that "the matter was treated with inexcusable tardiness between June 1998 and April 1999". However, permission was given for the following reasons:

- she had a strong case on the merits; and

- the estate had not been distributed and as a result there would be no prejudice to the beneficiaries of the will in granting the application.

Practical considerations

20.04   The reason for having such a short time limit is to enable personal representatives to distribute assets without fear of personal liability if a successful application is later made. The Act provides therefore that a personal representative can distribute after the expiry of six months from the date of grant without personal liability even if the court does later extend the time limit (s.20). Where an out of time application is allowed there is power to recover any part of the estate already distributed to the beneficiaries by the personal representatives.

Obviously a cautious personal representative would wait six months before distributing assets; yet in most cases such caution will be unnecessary and may even cause hardship if a beneficiary is in urgent need of finance. A personal representative must therefore carefully consider the circumstances before deciding whether or not to wait for the expiry of the six-month period. The following matters are relevant:

    (a) Since an order for financial provision is made against the *net* estate of the deceased (see below, para.20.32) there can be no objection to paying funeral, testamentary and administration expenses, debts and liabilities before the expiry of the six-month period.

    (b) It will normally be safe to pay a legacy to a beneficiary who is intending to make an application to obtain more (unless there is a risk of applications from other people).

    (c) Since it is unlikely that the court would order provision to be financed out of a very small legacy when the estate is large such a legacy can safely be paid.

    (d) Similarly it will often be safe to distribute assets to a beneficiary who has a strong moral claim particularly if in urgent need.

4. The Categories of Applicant

Section 1(1)

20.05   The following persons may apply to the court for an order in their favour on the ground that the deceased's will or the intestacy rules have not made reasonable provision for them.

20.06   Section 1(1)(a) *The spouse or civil partner of the deceased.*   The applicant must show that there was a subsisting marriage or civil partnership at the time of the deceased's death. This category includes "Spouse", the wife of a polygamous marriage: *Re Sehota, Surjit Kaur v Gian Kaur* (1978).

This category includes a party to a voidable marriage which has not been annulled prior to death. Unusually a person will be regarded as a surviving spouse or civil partner even though the marriage or civil partnership was *void*, provided the applicant entered into the marriage or civil partnership in good faith, unless in the lifetime of the deceased:

(i) the marriage or civil partnership has been dissolved or annulled; or

(ii) the applicant entered into a later marriage or civil partnership.

A judicially separated spouse or a civil partner where a separation order is in place comes into this category but may be barred from making an application by a court order under ss.15 or 15ZA of the Act. See below.

Section 1(1)(b) *A former spouse or civil partner.* A former spouse is a person **20.07** whose marriage or civil partnership with the deceased was dissolved or annulled during the deceased's lifetime by a decree made under the law of any part of the British Islands (the UK, Channel Islands and Isle of Man) or in any country or territory outside the British Islands by a divorce or annulment "which is entitled to be recognised as valid by the law of England and Wales" (s.25).

A former civil partner is a person whose civil partnership with the deceased was during the lifetime of the deceased either dissolved or annulled by an order made under the law of any part of the British Islands, or in any country or territory outside the British Islands by a dissolution or annulment which is entitled to be recognised as valid by the law of England and Wales.

The Act provides, however, in the interests of finality that a former spouse or civil partner may be barred from applying for financial provision by a court order on the granting of a decree of divorce, nullity, or judicial separation (s.15), or dissolution, nullity or separation order (s.15ZA). Moreover, the Court of Appeal observed in *Re Fullard* (1981) that in view of the wide powers of the court to make financial arrangements on divorce, the number of cases in which it would be appropriate for a former spouse to apply under the family provision legislation would be small; an example of such a case might be where the deceased's estate receives the proceeds of a large insurance policy on the deceased's death or where the applicant had been provided for in the divorce proceedings by means of periodical payments rather than by a lump sum.

In *Barrass v Harding* (2001) and in *Cameron v Treasury Solicitor* (1996) the **20.08** Court of Appeal emphasised that, where the parties regard themselves as having settled accounts with the divorce settlement, it will be inappropriate to make a family provision award unless there is some special circumstance. An example of special circumstance would be an assumption of responsibility by one party for the other after the divorce. The following have been held to be insufficient:

- the applicant's "parlous financial circumstances" and poor health in a case where the estate was bona vacantia (*Re Cameron*);

- the substantial value of the deceased's estate (*Barrass v Harding*); and

- the fact that the divorce was pre-1970 at a time when the court had much less extensive powers to redistribute property than it now has (*Barrass v Harding*).

20.09   Section 1(1A) *A person who has lived with the deceased in the same household as husband or wife for two years.*   To be eligible the applicant must not be included in either of the two preceding categories. The deceased must have died on or after January 1, 1996 and during the whole of the period of two years ending immediately before the death of the deceased the applicant must have been living:

(i) in the same household as the deceased; and

(ii) as the husband or wife of the deceased.

Notice that as a result of the wording of the subsection an application is bound to fail if there is any interruption in the two-year period of cohabitation prior to death. For example, where an applicant ceases living with the deceased, then resumes but fails to "clock up" a full two-year period before the death. See *Churchill v Roach* (2003). However, separations brought about by external circumstances, e.g. illness necessitating a stay in hospital or hospice care are irrelevant. In *Re Watson (Deceased)* (1999) exactly this situation arose. The deceased was hospitalised for three weeks prior to death. All parties accepted that the deceased had not ceased to be part of the household. In *Witkowska v Kaminski* (2006) the claimant had been away in Poland for the three months before the deceased's death in England but this was not regarded as a bar to a claim under this section. In *Gully v Dix* (2004) the Court of Appeal held that the trial judge was correct in finding that a three-month absence did not prevent the claimant being a person who had lived with the deceased as his wife for a period of two years ending with his death. It is necessary to look at the settled state of affairs that existed between the parties before the date of death and not the de facto separation between the couple.

It is often difficult to determine whether a couple are living together as husband and wife. In *Re Watson (Deceased)* (1999) the applicant and the deceased had known each other since 1964. She moved into the deceased's house in 1985. They had no sexual relationship after she had moved in although they had had one before. Mr Watson worked and provided most of the funds for the household. The applicant paid her share of the cost of utilities and would be responsible for shopping, cooking and gardening. The court decided that they had lived together as husband and wife.

When making that decision, it is necessary to ask whether, in the opinion of a reasonable person with normal perceptions, it could be said that the two people in question were living together as husband and wife. However, "one should not ignore the multifarious nature of marital relationships". The fact that the couple had an agreement as to who paid for what and who did which jobs did not prevent the arrangement being a marital one. It was also irrelevant that the claimant had another property available to her.

There must be an element of public recognition in the relationship. A marriage and a civil partnership are publicly acknowledged relationships. It is not possible for two persons to live together as civil partners unless their relationship as a couple is an acknowledged one. See *Baynes v Hedger* (2008).

In *Lindop v Agus* (2009) the claimant used her father's address for many purposes. The executors opposed her claim suggesting that this fact showed that the relationship between the claimant and the deceased was not unequivocally displayed to the world as the equivalent of a marital relationship. The court rejected this argument on the basis that there was a stable, sexual relationship between the claimant and the deceased and that she did in fact live with him and largely at his expence.

It was not the intention of Parliament that the Act should apply to same sex partners. When Lord Mackay introduced the Bill, he said: "living as husband and wife appears to us, as the law stands, to apply to partners of opposite sexes and not to partners of the same sex." However, social conditions change and the law changes with them. In *Ghaidan v Mendoza* (2004) the House of Lords decided that a same sex partner was entitled to succeed to a secured tenancy in the same way that a heterosexual cohabitant would have. In *Saunders v Garrett & Others* (2005) a same sex cohabitee was held to be eligible to apply under s.1A of the Inheritance (Provision for Family and Dependants) Act 1975 as a person living as husband or wife of the deceased. The Civil Partnership Act 2004 introduced a new category of applicant for deaths occurring on or after December 5, 2005 (see below).

Section 1(1B) *A person who has lived with the deceased in the same household* **20.10** *as civil partner for two years.* During the whole period of two years ending immediately before the death of the deceased the person must have been living:

    (i) in the same household as the deceased; and

    (ii) as the civil partner of the deceased.

The same points are relevant as for applications under s.1(1A).

Section 1(1)(c) *A child of the deceased.* This category includes a child of a non- **20.11** marital relationship, a legitimated or adopted child and a child *en ventre sa mere.* A child who has been adopted is no longer eligible to make a claim as a child of the *natural* parent (*Re Collins, (Deceased)* (1991)).

There is no distinction between sons and daughters and neither age nor marriage are automatic disqualifications. However, the courts do not look sympathetically at applications by able-bodied adults capable of earning their own living.

In *Re Coventry* (1980), for example, the Court of Appeal quoted with approval the statement by Oliver J. at first instance that

> "applications under the Act of 1975 for maintenance by able-bodied and comparatively young men in employment and able to maintain themselves must be relatively rare and need to be approached . . . with a degree of circumspection".

It used to be said that adult able-bodied children had to show an additional "threshold" requirement of a special obligation owed to them by the deceased (see *Goodchild v Goodchild* (1997)). The Court of Appeal has expressly rejected this in a number of cases (*Re Hancock* (1998); *Re Pearce* (1998); *Espinosa v Bourke* (1999)).

The approach now is that the court will consider all the circumstances in reaching its decision and try to balance all factors. An adult able-bodied child who cannot produce any argument to buttress a claim beyond being badly off is still unlikely to be successful. In *Espinosa v Bourke* the applicant (the deceased's daughter) had behaved badly and had already received some benefit from the deceased during his lifetime. However, this did not outweigh the factors in her favour. These included:

- her poor financial position;

- the substantial size of the estate;

- the fact that the only beneficiary of the will was her son who was at university starting his career without compelling needs;

- the applicant had taken her father into her home and cared for him, at least to a degree, for seven years, thus providing some return for the financial provision he made for her during his lifetime; and

- the deceased had an obligation to the applicant in that he had promised her mother to pass on the mother's share of the paternal grandmother's portfolio of shares to her.

In both *Myers v Myers and Others* (2004) and *Gold v Curtis* (2005) applications by adult children were successful and the court referred to the fact that parents have obligations and responsibilities to their children. However, in *Garland v Morris* (2007) an adult daughter's claim to provision from her father's estate failed despite her poor financial position. Counting against her were the following: the estate was not large, she had inherited from her mother and, to some extent, her misfortunes were of her own making. She had not been in contact with her father for many years before his death.

20.12   Section 1(1)(d) *A person (not being a child of the deceased) who is treated by the deceased as a child of the family in connection with a marriage to which the deceased was a party.*   The concept of "a child of the family" is imported from family law (Matrimonial Causes Act 1973 s.52(1) although under that Act the child must have been treated as a child of the family by *both* parties to the marriage). In *Re Callaghan* (1984) and in *Re Leach (Deceased)* (1985) it was held that applicants were children of the family even though they were adult when the deceased married their parent.

20.13   Section 1(1)(e) *Any person (not being a person included in the foregoing paragraphs) who immediately before the death of the deceased was being maintained wholly or partly by the deceased.*   It is often difficult to decide whether a person is within this category but certain points have been decided in recent cases:

(i) *The meaning of "maintained"*

The starting point is s.1(3) which provides that: **20.14**

> "a person shall be treated as being maintained by the deceased, either wholly or partly, . . . if the deceased otherwise than for full valuable consideration, was making a substantial contribution in money or money's worth towards the reasonable needs of that person".

It has been held that a person is to be regarded as maintained by the deceased *only* if they can bring themselves within s.1(3) (*Re Beaumont* (1980); *Jelley v Iliffe* (1981)). It is obviously difficult to state definitely what amounts to a "substantial contribution" but in *Jelley v Iliffe* the Court of Appeal regarded the provision of rent free accommodation as substantial. In *Re Watson* (1999) the cohabitee applicant had also applied as a person maintained by the deceased on the basis that the deceased had provided her with rent free accommodation. She was not successful in this category. The court found that at the time she lived with the deceased, she had no housing "need" because she had a property of her own available to her. It was irrelevant that by the time of the application the property had become unsuitable for her future needs because she was unable to manage stairs. The question of maintenance has to be determined by reference to the situation prevailing during the life of the deceased.

Once it is established that the deceased was making a substantial contribution, the next problem for a would-be applicant is to show that it was not made for full valuable consideration. It is accepted that consideration may be full and valuable even though not provided under a contract (*Re Beaumont*; *Jelley v Iliffe*).

(ii) *The provision of services can amount to valuable consideration*

The court sometimes has to balance imponderables like companionship and other **20.15** services provided by an applicant against contributions of cash or accommodation provided by the deceased. The court accepts that such services are *capable* of amounting to full valuable consideration (*Re Wilkinson* (1978); *Re Beaumont*; *Jelley v Iliffe*). However, it is a question of fact in each case. The court will normally allow an application to proceed to the later stages of trial unless it is absolutely clear that the services made by the applicant outweigh the contributions made by the deceased to the applicant's maintenance. If, however, it is *clear* that the services amounted to full valuable consideration the application should be struck out at a preliminary stage in order to avoid the costs of further proceedings. In *Bishop v Plumley* (1990) the Court of Appeal stated that a commonsense approach should be adopted "avoiding fine balancing computations involving the value of normal exchanges of support in the domestic sense". The court held that the devoted care and nursing provided by the applicant did not amount to full valuable consideration for the rent-free accommodation of the deceased. The applicant was, therefore, eligible to apply.

In *Re Watson* (1999) the court declined to consider whether or not the applicant's contribution to household expenses and the work she did in the house would have amounted to valuable consideration as it had already found that she had not been maintained. However, it said that it was a difficult point.

(iii) *The meaning of "immediately before the death"*

20.16   Section 1(1)(e) expressly states that the applicant must have been maintained "immediately before the death" of the deceased. Problems have arisen in connection with this phrase. For example, in *Re Beaumont* the deceased had habitually maintained the applicant but had been unable to do so in the few weeks immediately before her death, when she was ill in hospital. Megarry V.C. accepted that the court must look at "the settled basis or . . . general arrangement between the parties" not at "the actual, perhaps fluctuating, variation of it which exists immediately before . . . death".

5. Reasonable Provision

Two standards

20.17   Section 1(2) of the Act sets out two standards for judging whether or not provision is reasonable, one to be applied in the case of a surviving spouse or civil partner (not including a judicially separated spouse or a civil partner where a separation order was in force) and one to be applied in other cases.

The standard for surviving spouses and civil partners

20.18   This is such financial provision as it would be reasonable in all the circumstances for a spouse or civil partner to receive "whether or not that provision is required for his or her maintenance" (s.1(2)(a)). This standard was introduced so that the claim of a surviving spouse to matrimonial assets should be equal to that of a divorced spouse and the court's powers to order financial provision as extensive as in a divorce application.

The court has a discretion to apply this standard where a decree of judicial separation, nullity or divorce has been made within 12 months of death and no order for financial provision has been made (or refused) in the matrimonial proceedings (s.14). The reason is that the applicant would otherwise have no opportunity to obtain a fair share of the matrimonial assets.

The ordinary standard

20.19   This is "such financial provision as it would be reasonable in all the circumstances of the case for the applicant to receive for his *maintenance*" (s.1(2)(b)).

It is difficult to give a precise meaning to the word "maintenance" in this context. It does not mean just enough to enable a person to get by (i.e. mere subsistence) but on the other hand it does not extend to everything which may be regarded as reasonably desirable for their general benefit or welfare. Buckley L.J. suggested in *Re Coventry* (1980) that it could be regarded as "such financial provision as would be reasonable in all the circumstances of the case to enable the applicant to maintain himself in a manner suitable to these circumstances."

The restriction of provision to that required for maintenance is often fatal to applications by non-spouses. In *Re Jennings, (Deceased)* (1994) the applicant was an adult son. At first instance the trial judge found that the applicant had a comfortable standard of living and was unlikely to encounter financial difficulties in the future, providing he maintained his health and his capacity to work. However, he made an award on the basis that the plaintiff reasonably required an amount which would enable him to pay off his mortgage. He identified as a need the fact that the applicant had made no real provision for his pension and observed that the reduction in the mortgage would allow him to provide for his future security.

On appeal Nourse L.J. pointed out that the applicant currently paid the mortgage from his income and had not said that he could not pay his mortgage without further help. "No further financial provision is necessary to enable the plaintiff to discharge the cost of his daily living at the standard appropriate to him".

It is not the purpose of the Act to provide legacies for disappointed beneficiaries but this does not mean that provision for maintenance is limited to income payments. Provision could be by way of a lump sum, for example, to buy a house in which the applicant could be housed, thereby removing one expense from the applicant (*Re Dennis* (1981)).

An objective standard

The court is to decide whether the provision made for an applicant *is* reasonable. **20.20** This is an entirely objective question (*Moody v Stevenson* (1992)). The court is concerned therefore with the facts of the case rather than merely with the facts known to the deceased. If a testator has reasons for making no provision for a relative or dependant it is desirable that they should leave a record of those reasons with the will. The court will consider the reasons given by the testator and in so far as the reasons are good will take them into account; if, however, the testator was mistaken or motivated by malice the reasons will be ignored. In both *Myers v Myers* (2004) and *Gold v Curtis* (2005) the deceased had indicated their reasons for making no provision and in neither case was the court persuaded. It is not advisable to include the reasons in the will itself as a will is a document of public record. In *Re Seagrave (Deceased)* (2007) the court accepted that a claimant's case is likely to be stronger in cases of intestacy than in cases where the deceased has shown an intention as to how the estate is to be divide by making a will. However, the case was decided on a preliminary issue and the existence or non-existence of a will is only one factor to be taken into account.

Under s.3(5) the court will consider changes in the position of beneficiaries and applicants arising after the death of the deceased. In both *Re Hancock* (1999) and *McNulty v McNulty* (2000) the court took into account increases in the value of assets occurring after the death of the deceased. The court will not consider facts which arise between the hearing of the application and an appeal to the Court of Appeal (*Re Coventry*), nor will it consider legally unenforceable assurances given by beneficiaries to an applicant (*Rajabally v Rajabally* (1987)).

Reasonable provision may be nothing. So, for example, the court refused to order any provision in the following cases: in *Re Coventry* for an adult child, in *Rhodes v Dean* (1996) for a cohabitee, and in *Parish v Sharman* (2001) for a surviving spouse.

6. The Court Must Decide Whether and in What Manner to Make an Order (s.3(1))

This is a discretionary matter

20.21   If the court decides that the provision made for the applicant is not reasonable it must then go on to consider whether to exercise its discretion to make an order (and what type of order to make). At both stages the court is directed to consider various guidelines. Some guidelines are common to all applicants while some are limited to a particular category.

The common guidelines

20.22   Under s.3(1) the court will have regard to the following matters:

(a) *The financial resources and needs of the applicant, any other applicant and any beneficiary.* Earning capacity and social security benefits would be relevant here (*Re E* (1966)). The court must balance the resources and needs of all the persons with a claim on the estate. The court should take into account any needs which are reasonably likely to arise. Those needs do not need to be more likely than not but the degree of probability should be taken into account. In *Challinor v Challinor* (2009) the applicant was an adult suffering from Down's syndrome—future increased needs for personal care and physiotherapy were taken into account. In *Barron v Woodhead* (2009) provision of living accommodation for an applicant who would otherwise be homeless was considered particularly relevant. Similarly, in *Moore v Holdsworth* (2010) an award was increased to enable a chronically ill surviving spouse to return to the home she had shared with the deceased during their long marriage. Poor financial circumstances do not guarantee an order (*Garland v Morris*—see para.20.11).

(b) *Any obligations and responsibilities of the deceased towards the applicant or any beneficiary.* The Court of Appeal made it clear in *Re Jennings* (1994) that the obligations and responsibilities must still be operating on the deceased at the date of death. The deceased had abandoned his wife and son (the claimant) when the son was two. He had had no further contact with him and made no provision for him. When the father died, he left nothing to the son, the bulk of the estate going to charity. At first instance the judge construed s.3(1)(d) so as to include legal obligations and responsibilities which the deceased had, but had failed to discharge during the child's minority even though they were long spent and would have been incapable of founding a claim against him immediately before his death. The Court of Appeal said that was a wrong approach. The Act does not "revive defunct obligations and responsibilities." However, in *Myers v Myers* (2004) and *Gold v Curtis* (2005) the court seemed to accept the idea of continuing obligations and responsibilities.

(c) *The size and nature of the estate.* If an estate is large it is frequently relatively easy for the court to make adequate provision for applicants; where the estate is very small, however, it is often impossible to provide adequately for all beneficiaries and applicants. Moreover since the costs of an action normally come out of the estate the action may exhaust a large part of the assets. The courts, therefore, discourage applications in such cases (*Re Coventry*; *Jelley v Iliffe*). In *Re Fullard* (1981) Ormrod L.J. suggested that judges might reconsider the practice of ordering the costs of both sides to be paid out of the estate and look very closely indeed at the merits of an unsuccessful application before ordering the estate to bear the costs. Solicitors should always bear in mind the question of costs when advising clients who wish to make a claim, especially one against a small estate. The Court of Appeal have also exhorted practitioners to inform the legal aid authorities of the likely effects of an application and (a fortiori) an appeal on an estate in cases where legal aid is applied for.

The source of the deceased's assets is often an important consideration. For example, the court is likely to be sympathetic to an application by a child when the deceased parent inherited a large part of their estate from the other parent (as in *Espinosa v Bourke* (1999)).

(d) *Any physical or mental disability of any applicant or any beneficiary.* The availability of state aid, hospital accommodation and social security benefits may be considered (*Re Watkins* (1949)).

(e) *Any other matter*, including the conduct of the applicant or any other person which the court may consider relevant. This obviously gives the court a great deal of freedom. In *Re Snoek (Deceased)* (1983) an award to a spouse was set at a much lower amount than it would otherwise have been as a result of a history of assaults and other abuses in the years before the deceased's death. However, *Barron v Woodhead*

(2009) suggests that only quite extreme conduct by a surviving spouse should lead to a reduced award. In *Espinosa v Bourke* (1999) the applicant's conduct in abandoning her father while she went on extended holidays counted against her as did the applicant's 15-year separation from her father in *Garland v Morris* (2007). In *Re Goodchild* (1997) the applicant's mother had died believing that there was an agreement between herself and her husband to leave their combined estates to their son after the death. The agreement was not enforceable but was regarded as relevant to the Inheritance Act application. In *H v Mitson* (2009) the fact that the deceased had made it clear to the adult daughter that she would receive nothing was important. The court said that it was "not a case of disappointing expectations".

The particular guidelines

20.23   Under s.3(2) without prejudice to the common guidelines the court will also consider additional guidelines in relation to each category.

(a) *The surviving spouse.*   The court will consider:

   (i) the age of the applicant and the duration of the marriage;

   (ii) the contribution made by the applicant to the welfare of the family of the deceased, including any contribution made by looking after the home or caring for the family; and

   (iii) the provision the applicant might reasonably have expected to receive if on the day on which the deceased died the marriage (instead of being terminated by death) had been terminated by a decree of divorce. In *Re Besterman (Deceased)* (1984) the Court of Appeal held that this did not mean that the same provision should be made as if there were a divorce on the day of the death.

The other guidelines must also be taken into account and, in any case, further applications to the court if circumstances change may be made following a divorce whereas this is not possible in the case of a family provision application.

In *Moody v Stevenson* (1992) the Court of Appeal had seemed to suggest that the court should *only* consider the amount a spouse would have been entitled to on divorce. However, the Court of Appeal in *Re Krubert* (1996) stated that this approach was confusing when applied to a small estate. On divorce there were two parties to be considered whereas in a family provision case there was only one and, thus, it might well be reasonable to award the whole estate to a surviving spouse. In *P v G (family provision: relevance of divorce provision)* (2006) the court said:

"The difference between divorce, where there are two surviving spouses to provide for, and death where there is only one, will not infrequently be reflected in greater provision under the Inheritance Act than would have been made on divorce even where the estate is large."

Inevitably changes in divorce law will affect the amount available to spouses under the Inheritance Act. The House of Lords decision in *White v White* (2001) resulted in a change of approach to applications by spouses. In *White* the House of Lords said there should be no bias in favour of the money earner and that a judge would aways be well advised to "check his tentative views against the yardstick of equality of division". As a general guide, equality should be departed from only if, and to the extent that, there was good reason for doing so.

In *Re Adams* (2001) Behrens J. said there was no reason to depart from the **20.24** *White v White* principle of equality. In this case the deceased had been married to the claimant for 54 years and they had had 12 children. The deceased left her the household goods, his personal effects and a legacy of £10,000. The claimant contended that this was not reasonable and wanted to receive the family home. Three of her daughters opposed this. They accepted that the provision made was not reasonable but argued that the house was too large for her. The court held that the question of her needs was irrelevant. She was entitled to receive the family home.

In *Cunliffe v Fielden* (2005) Lord Justice Wall said that in family provision applications caution was necessary when carrying out the *White* cross check with the provision available on divorce:

> "Divorce involves two living former spouses, to each of whom the provisions of section 25(2) of the Matrimonial Causes Act 1973 apply. In cases under the 1975 Act, a deceased spouse who leaves a widow is entitled to bequeath his estate to whomsoever he pleases: his only statutory obligation is to make reasonable financial provision for his widow. In such a case, depending on the value of the estate, the concept of equality may bear little relation to such provision."

In *Aston v Aston* (2007) the court accepted that in a case where a marriage had effectively come to an end before the deceased's death, the divorce fiction would play a large part in determining whether the provision already made for the applicant was reasonable. She had already received more than she would have on divorce and so her application failed.

In *Cunliffe v Fielden* (2005) the court had to consider the significance of a brief marriage. It said there is a clear distinction between brief marriages which end with divorce and those which end with death. A divorce involves a conscious decision by one or both of the spouses to bring the marriage to an end. The premature termination of the marriage is likely to be less important than it would be in the case of a divorce. However, this does not mean that the length of the marriage is irrelevant or that the widow is entitled to one half of the estate. The brevity of the marriage is an argument against equality of division. It is particularly important in the context of assessing housing needs. There is a clear difference between a widow who had been married for many years and who had made an equal contribution to the family of the deceased and a person who had been married for only just over a year and who had made little contribution to the family wealth. While a widow is entitled to have "a reasonable expectation that her life once again as a single woman need not revert to what it was before her marriage" (see *Miller v Miller* (2005)), it may well be inappropriate for her to continue living in the former matrimonial home.

In *Grattan v McNaughton* (2001) a husband left his whole estate to his two children subject to the right of his second wife to occupy the matrimonial home for as long as she remained a widow and did not cohabit. The court found that this was not reasonable provision. It widened the right of occupation by striking out the restrictions on cohabitation and remarriage and permitting her a right of occupation in any substitute property. She also took the residue absolutely subject to legacies of £5,000 to each of the children. In the light of this decision, it is probably necessary to warn a client who wants to include a restriction on cohabitation or remarriage that the restriction may be removed in an Inheritance Act claim.

20.25   (b) *The former spouse.*   Guidelines (i) and (ii) of the surviving spouse guidelines also apply in the case of an application by a former spouse. Guideline (iii) does not apply unless the court has exercised its limited discretion to apply the surviving spouse standard (see above, para.20.18).

Unless there is some special reason, an application by a former spouse who has already received financial provision on the termination of the marriage with a view to a "clean break" will rarely be successful (*Re Fullard* (1981)).

20.26   (c) *A person who has cohabited with the deceased for two years under either s.1(1A) or (1B).*   The court is directed to consider:

    (a)   the age of the applicant and the length of the period during which the applicant lived as the husband or wife of the deceased and in the same household as the deceased; and

    (b)   the contribution made by the applicant to the welfare of the family of the deceased, including any contribution made by looking after the home or caring for the family.

In *Negus v Bahouse* (2008) and *Webster v Webster* (2008) the court held that, as in the case of a spouse, a cohabitee is entitled to have the standard of living enjoyed with the deceased taken into account.

20.27   (d) *A child of the deceased.*   The additional guideline here is the manner in which the applicant was being or in which they might expect to be educated or trained.

20.28   (e) *A person treated by the deceased as a child of the family.*   In addition to the education guideline set out in (d), above, the court is also directed to consider:

    (i)   whether the deceased had assumed any responsibility for the applicant's maintenance and if so the extent to which and the basis upon which the deceased assumed that responsibility and the length of time for which the deceased discharged that responsibility;

(ii) whether in assuming and discharging that responsibility the deceased did so knowing that the applicant was not his own child; and

(iii) the liability of any other person to maintain the applicant.

(f) *A person maintained by the deceased.* The court will consider the extent to **20.29** which and the basis upon which the deceased assumed responsibility for the maintenance of the applicant and to the length of time for which the deceased discharged that responsibility.

It will be noticed that while the category (e) guideline directs the court to consider *whether* the deceased assumed responsibility, the category (f) guideline directs the court to consider *the extent to which* responsibility *has been* assumed. This suggests that a category (f) application can be made only if the deceased assumed responsibility for the applicant's maintenance. In *Re Beaumont* Megarry V.C. accepted this and said that the applicant must be able to point to "some act or acts which demonstrates an undertaking of responsibility"; without such an act an application would fail at the outset. However, in *Jelley v Iliffe*, the Court of Appeal expressly disapproved of this view and stated that the mere fact of maintenance generally raises a presumption that there was an assumption of responsibility; in the absence of evidence to rebut this presumption, therefore, the application can proceed to the later stages. Furthermore, in *Baynes v Hedger* (2009) the court held that a successful claim under s.1(1)(e) requires an assumption of responsibility for maintenance of the applicant by the deceased. In that case the deceased had made payments to the applicant on a number of occasions so that she could pay off debts. This was held to be insufficient for an assumption of responsibility for maintenance.

In *Bouette v Rose* (2000) the Court of Appeal found that a mother had been maintained by her brain-damaged daughter. Robert Walker L.J. then gave a more detailed scrutiny to the question of assuming a moral obligation. He agreed with Megarry V.C. that the contrast in language between the two guidelines was striking. However, he concluded that the category (e) guideline was not adding a new requirement but was merely paraphrasing what is already implicit in s.1(1)(e). In his view *Jelley v Iliffe* makes it clear that the mere fact of one person making a substantial contribution to another person's needs raises a presumption of an assumption of responsibility.

In the end, therefore, the differences in approach are perhaps not that great. All the judges are agreed that an assumption of responsibility is an important element. *Bouette v Rose* and *Jelley v Iliffe* say that it is legitimate to infer such an assumption from the mere fact of maintenance. Megarry V.C. in *Beaumont* said that such an inference might be possible in cases where there was no evidence either way but that the obligation to show the assumption of responsibility would lie on the claimant. If there is no real evidence to suggest that the deceased assumed responsibility for the applicant, it is unlikely that the application will be successful. There is nothing to prevent a testator leaving a statement to the effect that they assumed no responsibility for the applicant or did so only during their lifetime and not after death.

7. Types of Order

The types

20.30 Under s.1(1) the court may make one or more of the following orders:

(a) *Periodical payments.* Such an order may provide for:

(i) payments of a specified amount (for example, £25 per week);

(ii) payments equal to the whole or part of the income of the net estate (for example, one-third of the income from the net estate);

(iii) payments equal to the whole of the income of such part of the net estate as the court may direct to be set aside or appropriated (e.g. the whole income from the deceased's shares in a named company); or

(iv) payments to be determined in any other way the court thinks fit.

Section 2(3) provides that the order for periodical payments may direct that a specified part of the net estate shall be set aside or appropriated for making periodical payments from the income. However, no more may be set aside or appropriated than is sufficient to produce the income at the date of the order.

Periodical payments are for the term specified in the order. In the case of a former spouse the Act provides expressly that an order shall cease to have effect on the remarriage of the former spouse (s.19(2)). In any other case, however, the court must decide the date of termination when it makes the order. Orders for periodical payments may be varied (see below, para.20.33).

Periodical payments are unpopular because they are expensive to provide (requiring trust machinery to operate them) and lack finality. It is more common for the court to order a lump sum.

(b) *Lump sum payment.* A lump sum may be made payable by instalments in which case the number, amounts and dates for payments of the instalments can be varied; apart from that a lump sum order cannot be varied (s.7). A lump sum is obviously appropriate in the case of an application by a surviving spouse but it can also be ordered in the case of other applicants even though they are only entitled to maintenance. Where an estate is very small a lump sum order is particularly useful; indeed it may be the only type of provision which can realistically be made.

(c) *Transfer of property.* The court may order the transfer of a particular asset to an applicant. This may be advisable where a lump sum order would require an improvident sale of assets. Such an order once made cannot be varied.

(d) *Settlement of property.* An order for settlement of property is particularly likely in the case of a minor or a person who is in need of protection. Such a settlement must be drafted with an eye to tax and trust law so that, for example, if a settlement on a minor does not give rise to an interest in possession it should comply with the requirements of an accumulation and maintenance settlement. Such an order, once made, cannot be varied.

(e) *Acquisition of property for transfer or settlement.* The court may order that assets from the net estate of the deceased be used to acquire a specified item (for example, a house) which will either be transferred to or settled on an applicant. Such an order, once made, cannot be varied.

(f) *Variation of marriage settlements.* An ante- or post-nuptial settlement may be varied by the court for the benefit of the surviving spouse of the marriage or the children of the marriage or any person who was treated by the deceased as a child of that marriage. Such an order for variation, once made, cannot be varied.

A provision in a pension scheme allowing an employee to direct benefits to a spouse may be a settlement for this purpose: *Brooks v Brooks* (1996). Even where not directly available as a settlement, pension benefits may still be important as they may increase the resources of other people interested in the estate.

The burden of an order

Any order made by the court may contain such consequential and supplemental **20.31** provisions as the court thinks necessary or expedient for the purpose of securing that the order operates fairly as between one beneficiary of the estate and another. For example, if the court makes a periodical payments order or a lump sum order it may direct which part of the estate is to bear the burden; if the court orders that an asset which had been specifically left to a beneficiary is to be transferred to the applicant the court may vary the disposition of the estate to make alternative provision for the disappointed beneficiary.

"Beneficiary" in this context includes the donee of a statutory nomination or a *donatio mortis causa* or a surviving joint tenant (see para.20.34, below).

Inheritance tax

The court order alters the disposition of the estate of the deceased and is deemed **20.32** to have done so from the date of death of the deceased for all purposes including the payment of inheritance tax (Inheritance Tax Act 1984 s.146). Thus, for example, if an order increases the amount passing to a surviving spouse the chargeable value of the estate for inheritance tax purposes will be reduced whereas if less property passes to a surviving spouse the chargeable value will be increased.

In *Re Goodchild* (1997) the court used its variation powers to order that the testator's will was to be treated as if it had always left £185,000 to trustees to pay the income to the deceased's second wife until her death or until March 1, 1996, whichever was the earlier, and subject thereto for the applicant absolutely. The purpose of the order was to get the benefit of the spouse exemption and avoid the inheritance tax which would have been payable had the property been left directly to the applicant. The parties took the risk of an inheritance tax liability arising on the death of the second wife if she died within seven years of the termination of the interest in possession.

The Court of Appeal expressed some reservations about the use of variation orders under s.1(4) to obtain a tax benefit. However, Morritt L.J. admitted that "if the order made is properly within the jurisdiction of the court the fact that it was sought with the motive of seeking to achieve a better tax position is usually irrelevant". He went on to say that in future, if such an order was sought "the grounds on which it is thought to be authorised by s.1(4) should be clearly demonstrated for the consents and wishes of the parties are not enough".

Interim payments

20.33   The court has power to make an interim order in favour of an applicant if it appears to the court that:

(a)   the applicant is in immediate need of financial assistance but it is not yet possible to determine what order (if any) should be made; and

(b)   property forming part of the net estate of the deceased is or can be made available to meet the needs of the applicant.

Variation of periodical payments order

20.34   The court has limited power under s.6 to vary a periodical payments order. It has no power to vary other orders (apart from the number, amounts and dates for payment of instalments of a lump sum). This is in the interest of certainty.

An application for variation can be made by the original recipient and also, inter alia, by the personal representatives of the deceased, a beneficiary of the estate or a former applicant (s.6(5)). It can be made during the currency of an order or, where the order was to terminate on the occurrence of a specified event, within six months of that event.

Only property already allocated for periodical payments (called "relevant property") can be affected by a variation order. The court cannot order that relevant property be increased (s.6(6)).

The court will consider all the circumstances of the case including any change in matters it considered when making the original order (s.6(7)). It has power to order that periodical payments continue after the occurrence of a terminating event specified in the original order (other than the remarriage of a former spouse where the termination occurs automatically under s.14 and cannot be varied). It can also direct payment of a lump sum or a transfer of property to the applicant from the relevant property.

The variation order can be made in favour of any of the possible applicants. It is not limited to the original recipient (s.6(2)).

8. Property Available for Financial Provision

The net estate

If the court decides to order provision to be made for an applicant such an order **20.35** is made against the "net estate" of the deceased. The net estate is defined by s.25 as comprising:

(a) "All property of which the deceased had power to dispose by his will (otherwise than by virtue of a special power of appointment) less the amount of his funeral, testamentary and administration expenses, debts and liabilities including any inheritance tax payable out of his estate on death".

This will obviously not include insurance policies where the proceeds are payable direct to a beneficiary rather than to the estate of the policyholder as the deceased has no power to dispose of such property.

(b) "Any property in respect of which the deceased held a general power of appointment (not being a power exercisable by will) which has not been exercised".

If the power was exercisable by will the property subject to the power falls into (a) above whether or not the deceased actually exercised it.

(c) Any property nominated by the deceased to any person under a statutory nomination (see Ch.21) or received by any person as a result of a *donatio mortis causa* (see Ch.21) less any inheritance tax payable in respect of such property and borne by the nominee or donee (s.8).

(d) The deceased's severable share of a joint tenancy, but only if the court so orders (see s.9 and para.20.35, below).

(e) Any property which the court orders shall be available as a result of its anti-avoidance powers (see para.20.36, below).

Lump sums payable under discretionary pension schemes and policies written in trust for others are not part of the net estate (though the writing in trust may amount to a disposition for the purposes of s.10).

Joint property

As a result of the right of survivorship a deceased has no power to dispose of the **20.36** interest under a joint tenancy by will. However, under s.9 where the deceased was a joint tenant of any property immediately before death the court may, for the purpose of facilitating the making of financial provision, order that the deceased's severable share of the property (or the value thereof *immediately before death)* shall to such extent as appears to the court to be just in all the circumstances (and after allowing for any inheritance tax payable) be treated as part of the net estate. The discretion only exists in respect of applications made within six months from the date of the grant; there is no power to make such an order in connection with an out-of-time application. If the application for a grant is delayed, an application under s.9 may in fact be made many years after the date of death. See *Dingmar v Dingmar* (2006) in which the Court of Appeal had to decide the value of the deceased's share of a house for the purposes of an application made many years after the death. The Court of Appeal held that s.9 requires a judge to take the proportionate share of the property which would have belonged to the deceased if there had been severance of the joint ownership and to treat the value of that proportion as the share of the property which they were empowered to treat as part of the estate.

Section 9(4) expressly provides for the avoidance of doubt that for the purposes of this section there may be a joint tenancy of a chose in action, for example, the asset represented by a credit balance in a joint bank account.

In *Kourkgy v Lusher* (1981) Wood J. said that the discretion to treat the interest as part of the net estate should be exercised before the court considers whether reasonable provision has been made so that the court can take its availability into account. That is sensible in practice but does not sit well with the limitation that the interest is only to be available if it will facilitate the making of the order.

In *Powell v Osbourne* (1993) the deceased had left his wife and bought a house jointly with a cohabitee. There was a mortgage with a life policy on their joint lives. The benefit of the policy was payable on the death of the first. A decree nisi between the deceased and the applicant had been declared at the date of death. At first instance the judge had ordered the applicant the greater part of the equity of redemption on the house but had said that the policy was not available because the deceased had no beneficial interest, there being no surrender value.

The Court of Appeal said that under s.9 assets had to be valued immediately before death which was the last moment the deceased could have severed. At that moment the policy had a value. This was because it depended for its value on his death. The imminence of his death meant that the value of the policy was the same as on death. The applicant was therefore entitled to a half share of the policy money.

In *Murphy v Holland* (2004), however, the Court of Appeal held that a policy on joint lives was not available under s.9 at all. The terms of the policy made it clear that the deceased had had no interest in the policy immediately before his death. The proceeds of the policy were intended for the exclusive benefit of the survivor. The Court held that this was the ordinary inference to be drawn when a life insurance was effected for a fixed sum without profits, without a surrender value and without an endowment element. However, the individual circumstances of the case will be important. The terms of the policy or the conduct of the parties may displace that ordinary inference.

Anti-avoidance provisions

Introduction

A deceased might attempt to evade the Act either by giving away property inter **20.37** vivos so that the net estate on death is substantially reduced or by entering into a binding contract to leave property by will; the effect of such a contract would be to give the other party to the contract a right to enforce it against the personal representatives, thus reducing the net estate available for family provision. Sections 10 and 11 of the Act enable the court to prevent such evasion; they give power to order a person to satisfy a claim for family provision if they have benefited under an inter vivos disposition or a contract to provide money or other property.

Lifetime Gifts

A disposition is covered by s.10 if it was made: **20.38**

(a) after March 31, 1976 and less than six years before the date of death of the deceased;

(b) with the intention of defeating an application under the Act; and

(c) for less than full valuable consideration.

A "disposition" for this purpose includes any payment of money (including insurance premiums) and any conveyance of property whether or not made by instrument. It does not, however, include any statutory nomination, *donatio mortis causa* or appointment of property under a special power of appointment.

Contracts

A contract is covered by s.11 of the Act if: **20.39**

(a) entered into after March 31, 1976;

(b) the deceased agreed to leave money or other property by will or agreed that money or other property would be paid or transferred to any person from this estate;

(c) the deceased made the contract with the intention of defeating an application under the Act; and

(d) when the contract was made full valuable consideration was not given or promised.

In the case of a contract there is no time limit as there is in the case of inter vivos dispositions.

The intention of defeating an application

20.40 The deceased must have made a disposition or contract with the intention of defeating an application. Section 12 provides that this requirement is satisfied if the court is of the opinion on a balance of probabilities that the deceased's intention (though not necessarily the sole intention) in making the disposition or contract was to prevent an order for financial provision being made or to reduce the amount of the provision which might otherwise be ordered.

In the case of a contract, s.12(2) provides that, if a contract is made for no valuable consideration at all (that is, by way of a deed), there will be a presumption that the deceased's intention was to defeat the application.

The facilitating of financial provision for the applicant

20.41 Even if a disposition is covered by s.10 or a contract is covered by s.11 the court will not use its anti-avoidance powers unless satisfied that to do so will facilitate the making of financial provision.

The powers of the court are discretionary

20.42 If the court is satisfied of the above requirements it may make an order against a donee. However, this is a discretionary matter and in deciding what order (if any) to make the court is directed to consider the circumstances in which the disposition or contract was made, any valuable consideration that was given, the relationship (if any) of the donee to the deceased, the conduct and financial resources of the donee and all the other circumstances of the case (ss.10(6) and 11(4)).

Orders against a donee of a disposition

20.43 The court may order a donee to provide such sum of money or other property as it may specify (s.10(2)). However, there are two limitations:

   (a) if the donee was given money they cannot be ordered to provide more than the money paid to them by the deceased less any inheritance tax borne by the donee in respect of the payment (s.10(3)); and

   (b) if the donee was given property they cannot be ordered to provide more than the value of the property at the date of death of the deceased less any inheritance tax borne by the donee in respect of the payment (s.10(4)). (If they have disposed of the property prior to the deceased's death the limit is the value of the property at the date of disposal).

Order against a "donee" under a contract

20.44 If the personal representatives of the deceased have not transferred money or other property to the donee in accordance with the provisions of the contract, before the date of the application, the court may order them not to make such payment or transfer, or to make no further payment or transfer or to make only a reduced payment or transfer (s.11(2)(ii)). The effect of such an order is to increase the net estate of the deceased available for financial provision.

If the personal representatives of the deceased have already transferred money or property to the donee before the date of the application in accordance with the provisions of the contract, the court may order the donee to provide such sum of money or other property as it may specify (s.11(2)(i)).

The court may only make such orders to the extent that the property transferred under the contract exceeds the value of any consideration given (the property to be valued at the date of the hearing) (s.11(3)).

Order against donee's personal representatives

If a donee has died the court has the same powers against the donee's personal **20.45** representatives under ss.10 and 11 as it would have had against the donee. However, once property has been distributed by the personal representatives the powers of the court cease with regard to that property. The personal representatives will not be liable if they distribute the donee's property without notice of the making of an application under ss.10 and 11 (s.12(4)).

Order against a trustee of the donee

If the deceased transferred property to a trustee or contracted to have property **20.46** transferred to a trustee with the intention of defeating an application, the trustee can be ordered to provide property (s.13(1) and (3)). Section 13 also provides limits on the amount that the trustee can be ordered to repay.

Illustration of use of power

Hanbury v Hanbury (1999) is a good illustration of the court using its anti- **20.47** avoidance powers. The deceased had had no contact with his mentally and physically disabled daughter from the date of the breakdown of his marriage to her mother save that he paid £900 per annum for her maintenance. After legal advice and with the intention of defeating any claim brought on behalf of the daughter he transferred assets into either the joint names of himself and his wife or into her name alone. When he died he left his daughter £10,000 from his estate of £11,981 (apparently calculating that this would be sufficient to prevent a claim).

Sections 9 and 10 were used to recover more than £50,000 of assets from the second wife. Shares in investment trusts (worth £100,000 at the date of death) had been bought in the second wife's name from a joint bank account fed by both parties.

See *Re Dawkins, (Deceased)* (1986) for another example of s.10 in operation.

9. The Choice of Court

The county court

20.48 As a result of the Courts and Legal Services Act 1990, the county court has unlimited jurisdiction (see the County Courts Act 1984 s.15 inserted by the High Court and County Court Jurisdiction Order 1991 (SI 1991/724)). This is in marked contrast to the jurisdiction in normal probate and equity cases which is limited to £30,000.

Proceedings can issue in any county court. London-based practitioners may wish to have proceedings heard in the Central London County Court which has a Chancery Users list. The judges here have a great deal of expertise. However, it is necessary to ask expressly to be put in the Chancery Users list. The matter will not be allocated automatically just because of its nature.

The Family or Chancery Division of the High Court

20.49 An application for an order may be made either in the Chancery Division or in the Family Division. There are no rules limiting the applicant's freedom of choice and a practitioner is, therefore, free to choose whichever Division is more appropriate. Frequently they will be equally suitable so that the practitioner's choice may be governed by personal preference and experience; on occasion, however, one Division may have a particular advantage. For example, it is appropriate to use the Family Division in a case involving the determination of the award a spouse would have got on divorce. The Chancery Division is more suitable where there is a dispute as to the validity of a will which is alleged not to make reasonable financial provision for the applicant (in such a case the probate action can be heard immediately before the family provision application by the same judge with a consequent saving of time and expense), where the true meaning of the will must first be determined under a construction summons or where complicated accounts have to be taken.

Chapter Twenty-One

DISPOSING OF PROPERTY OTHERWISE THAN BY WILL

1. Introduction

It is generally considered to be a "good thing" to make a will. In this chapter we will consider, first, to what extent it is possible to dispose of property on death without a will and, secondly, why solicitors advise clients to make wills. **21.01**

2. Disposition of Property Without a Will

It is important to remember that making a will is not the only means of disposing of property after death. Solicitors advising intending testators should ensure their clients are aware of the other possibilities. **21.02**

Statutory nominations

Where a person is entitled to certain types of investments they can nominate a third party to receive them on their death. In such cases the property will not vest in the nominator's personal representatives on death but will be paid directly to the nominee. The payer will, therefore, want to see the death certificate of the deceased but will not require production of the grant of representation. The nominated property does, however, form part of the deceased's estate for inheritance tax purposes. **21.03**

Nominations were originally designed to allow the poorer members of society to dispose of small amounts of money without the necessity of making a will or of their representatives obtaining a grant. They can be made in respect of deposits in certain Trustee Savings Banks, Friendly Societies and Industrial and Provident Societies up to a limit of £5,000 each. It used to be possible to nominate National Savings Certificates and deposits in National Savings Banks and Trustee Savings Banks but this power was withdrawn as from May 1, 1979 in respect of the latter and May 1, 1981 in respect of the two former (nominations of such property *made* before those dates remain effective).

To be valid, a nomination must be:

    (a) in writing;

    (b) made by a person who is 16 or over; and

    (c) attested by one witness.

Since a will cannot be made by a person who is under the age of 18, a nomination is the only way in which a minor can dispose of property (unless they have privileged status) after death.

A nomination is revoked by subsequent marriage, a later nomination or the death of the nominee before the nominator but it is *not* revoked by a subsequent will. It is therefore important when drafting a will for a client to ascertain whether or not any nominations have previously been made. They are easily overlooked as the paying authority normally holds the nomination form.

Rights under pension schemes

21.04 Pensions is an enormous subject and in a book of this length we can do no more than make a few comments on the most important aspects.

Payments from discretionary schemes

21.05 Many employee pension schemes allow contributors to "nominate" a third party to receive benefits after the contributors' death either in the form of a lump sum or a pension. Where a lump sum is paid it is often the most substantial single asset passing on death and may be used to make a substantial gift to a beneficiary. However, such lump sums are normally only paid when the contributor dies "in service" and therefore the provision for the beneficiary may have to be reconsidered when the contributor ceases to contribute to the scheme (whether on retirement or as a result of changing jobs).

Such a "nomination" is not binding on the trustees of the pension fund being merely an indication of the deceased's wishes, although, naturally, they will usually abide by the expressed wishes of the deceased. This procedure is sometimes referred to as a "nomination" but it is obviously different from the type of nomination referred to in para.21.03, above, where the deceased has an absolute right to the property and is free to deal with it as they like whether after their death or during their lifetime.

These benefits do not form part of the deceased's estate for inheritance tax purposes because the deceased had no control over the destination of the property.

Discretionary schemes must be distinguished from fixed schemes where, for example, the lump sum is paid to the estate of the employee and then under the terms of the employee's will or under the intestacy rules. Here the destination of the property is under the control of the employee and the payment will, therefore, be part of the estate for inheritance tax purposes.

Alternatively secured pensions

From April 5, 2006, a member of a pension scheme, may instead of buying an **21.06** annuity, leave the fund invested and take income from it. Once the member reaches 75, they must either purchase an annuity, or take an alternatively secured pension. Because there is no requirement to draw an income before 75, it would be possible to let the fund grow as a way of passing funds on tax free to dependants after death. The government is determined to stop this happening. If a member with an alternatively secured pension dies with value left in the pension fund at their death, there are special charging provisions under IHTA 1984 ss.151A–151C.

What is left in the fund is treated as part of the taxable estate on death save in so far as it goes to charity or to provide pension benefits for the member's spouse, civil partner, or other dependant. Where the spouse, civil partner, or other dependant has succeeded to such pension benefits and then dies or ceases to be a dependant, and has at that time an unsecured or alternatively secured pension fund, that is then charged to IHT under IHTA 1984 s.151B or 151C. The charge is imposed on what is left after any income tax unauthorised payment charge has been charged on it, and is at the highest marginal rates, i.e. the nil rate band is set off first against the other parts of the deceased's chargeable estate.

The government has announced that it intends to introduce considerable changes to these arrangements. At the time of writing full details are not available but it seems that such schemes will be more flexible and less onerously taxed as from April 6, 2011.

Donatio mortis causa

The requirements for a donatio mortis causa

A *donatio mortis causa* is a lifetime gift which is conditional on death. It has **21.07** some of the attributes of a legacy and some of a lifetime gift. There are four requirements which must be satisfied if a *donatio mortis causa* is to be valid:

(a) *The gift must be made in contemplation of death.*   The death need not be **21.08** imminent so it is, for example, sufficient that a person knows they have a serious illness and cannot live for long. It is irrelevant that death occurs from a super-vening cause (such as an accident or a sudden second illness—*Wilkes v Allington* (1931)) but the gift fails if the donor recovers from the contemplated cause of death. The cause of death need not be an illness as such, contemplation of a dangerous operation is enough.

(b) *The gift must be conditional on death.*   If the donor recovers from the **21.09** contemplated cause of death, the gift will not take effect and the donor will be entitled to regain possession of the property. If, however, the donor dies then the gift to the donee becomes absolute. If there are formal requirements for transfer which need to be complied with in order to complete title then the donee can compel the deceased's personal representatives to complete the transfer.

21.10   (c) *The donor must part with dominion over the property before death.*   Delivery must be made to the donee (or their agent) of the subject matter of the gift or the means of obtaining it. In the case of chattels it is usually readily apparent whether or not this has taken place but in the case of choses in action it is a little more difficult. Since choses in action cannot be physically delivered, there must be delivery of the essential evidence of title which will entitle the possessor to the property given (for example, delivery of National Savings Certificates or bills of exchange).

In both *Sen v Headley* and *Woodard v Woodard* (1991) the deceased delivered a set of keys (in the first case of a house and in the second case of a car) but retained a set himself. In both cases the Court of Appeal held that the retention of the keys did not prevent the donor parting with dominion. In both cases, however, the donor was terminally ill in hospital and could not have made use of the second set of keys unless there had been an unexpected recovery which in any event would have revoked the gift. In *Woodard* it was also argued that the deceased should have handed over the registration document (and possibly the insurance certificate and servicing log book). The Court of Appeal rejected this argument. These items were not documents of title, nor was it essential to hand them over to give the defendant dominion over the car. The handing over would merely have been evidence of the intention to make a gift.

21.11   (d) *The subject-matter of the gift must be capable of passing as a valid donatio mortis causa.*   Most personalty is so capable (for example, chattels, bonds, insurance policies or National Savings Certificates). A cheque drawn by a third party can be the subject of a valid donation but a cheque drawn by the deceased cannot since it is merely an order to the deceased's bank to pay which will be automatically revoked by death: see *Curnock v IRC* (2003) and *Re Owen* (1949).

It has been suggested that shares cannot be the subject of a valid *donatio mortis causa* (*Re Weston* (1902)) but there seems to be no reason in principle why this should be so and indeed the possibility of a *donatio mortis causa* of company shares was accepted in *Staniland v Willott* (1852), although on the facts it was held to have been revoked by the donor's recovery from his illness.

The Court of Appeal held in *Sen v Headley* that, contrary to previous thinking, land is capable of passing by *donatio mortis causa*.

Comparison with legacies

21.12   It is worth noting the more important similarities and differences between legacies and donationes mortis causa.

   (a)   *Similarities*

      (i)   *Lapse.* A *donatio mortis causa* lapses if the donee predeceases the donor. The subject-matter will then form part of the donor's estate on death.

      (ii)   *Tax.* Inheritance tax is payable on the property which is the subject-matter of the *donatio mortis causa* as it is part of the donor's estate on death. A *donatio mortis causa* is, in effect, an incomplete gift so for inheritance tax purposes the property gifted remains part of the estate at death.

  (iii) *Liability for debts.* If the estate of the deceased proves insufficient to pay the deceased's debts then the subject-matter of a *donatio mortis causa* may be taken.

(b) *Differences*

  (i) *No assent.* Normally the personal representatives of the deceased transfer title to beneficiaries by means of an assent. However, since death makes a *donatio mortis causa* absolute, the personal representatives need do nothing unless there are formal requirements which need to be complied with in order to complete the title.

  (ii) *Revocation.* A *donatio mortis causa* is revoked if the donor recovers from the contemplated cause of death or if the donor resumes possession and dominion of the property. It cannot be revoked by a subsequent will.

Joint tenancies

Joint tenancies are extremely important in practice since they are the most **21.13** common way for property to be transferred without a will. Where the deceased was a joint tenant in equity of any property, on death the interest will pass automatically to the surviving joint tenant(s). It will not devolve on the deceased's personal representatives and cannot pass under the terms of the will. This is because it is not possible to sever a joint tenancy by will. However, a joint tenant is free to sever the joint tenancy during his or her lifetime in which case the deceased and the co-owners will hold as tenants-in-common in equity. Such an interest *will* devolve on the deceased's personal representatives and *will* pass under the deceased's will or on intestacy.

Solicitors who are preparing wills for clients should explain to them that jointly-owned property will pass to the survivor no matter how short the period of survivorship may be, despite anything said in the will. For this reason it may be appropriate for a client to sever a joint tenancy. The client is then free to leave the beneficial tenancy-in-common to the survivor *provided the survivor survives* for a stated period.

In *Carr-Glynn v Frearsons* (1998) a client knew she was a co-owner of property but was uncertain whether she was a beneficial joint tenant or tenant in common. Her solicitor explained that the will would be ineffective if she was a beneficial joint tenant unless she severed the joint tenancy but did not explain that it was possible to serve a precautionary notice of severance. The Court of Appeal held that the solicitor was negligent for allowing the testatrix to execute the will not knowing whether or not it would be effective and without suggesting a precautionary notice of severance.

It is important to remember that joint tenancies can be severed without a notice of severance. Section 36(2) of the Law of Property Act 1925 introduced the notice of severance but expressly preserved all the existing methods of severing a beneficial joint tenancy. According to *Williams v Hensman* (1861) there are three methods:

(1) an act of anyone of the persons interested operating upon their own share may create a severance as to that share;

(2) mutual agreement; and

(3) any course of dealing sufficient to intimate that the interests of all were mutually treated as constituting a tenancy in common.

In *Re Woolnough, Perkins v Borden* (2002) a brother and sister, Len and Emmy, owned a property as beneficial joint tenants. They went together to see a solicitor and each made wills leaving the house to the survivor for life and then to their niece, Dorothy, with a substitutional gift to her children. In 1989 Dorothy died and Len made a new will picking out one of Dorothy's three children as his residuary beneficiary. Emmy left her will unchanged. After Emmy's death, Len made a new will leaving everything to charity.

21.14   The issue was whether or not the joint tenancy had been severed by mutual consent before Emmy's death. If it had, only half of the value of the house was in Len's estate. If it had not, he had the whole value of the house. The court found that the making of the two wills leaving the interest of the first to die to the survivor for life was inconsistent with the continuance of the joint tenancy and amounted to severance by agreement. It would not, of course, have amounted to severance had one joint tenant alone made a will dealing with the half share. This is because a will is ambulatory in form and has no effect until death. Clear evidence of mutual agreement will be required: see *Carr v Isard* (2007).

Where, as in *Re Woolnough*, clients want to make wills which are inconsistent with a continuing joint tenancy, it is important that there is clarity as to when the severance takes place. Solicitors should consider preparing a signed agreement or notice of severance without delay.

It may be necessary to establish whether there has already been a severance by mutual agreement:

• when taking instructions for a will from a client who appears to hold the beneficial interest in the whole of an asset as a result of survivorship (like Len in *Re Woolnough*); or

• when administering an estate for a deceased who appears to be a sole surviving joint tenant.

There may also be problems in determining the beneficial interests where two people have bought land without declaring the basis on which the beneficial interests are held. In *Stack v Dowden* (2007) the House of Lords held that, in the domestic consumer context, beneficial entitlement is presumed to be the same as legal title. Hence, a conveyance into joint names indicates both legal and beneficial joint tenancy, unless and until the contrary is proved. In *Adekunle v Ritchie* (2007) John Behrens QC held that the *Stack v Dowden* approach was not limited to cohabiting couples living together in a platonic or sexual relationship. It applied in other domestic cases such as that of mother and son.

Insurance policies

Where a person takes out life assurance, on their death the insurance company **21.15** will pay the assured amount to the deceased's personal representatives. This sum will form part of the death estate and so can potentially attract inheritance tax.

Inheritance tax will not be payable if the death estate falls within the nil rate band or an exemption (such as the spouse exemption) applies. However, even if the property is to be paid to a spouse, the personal representatives will have to wait until a grant is obtained before the insurance company will hand over the money. This delay may be inconvenient at best or financially disastrous for the spouse, at worst.

Rather than have the money channelled through the estate (which will be ill-advised for inheritance tax purposes if the sum is large and the intended beneficiary is not a spouse or a charity), it is better to have the money paid direct to the intended beneficiary.

This can be achieved in one of two ways. First, the assured can make use of the Married Woman's Property Act 1882 s.11. Under this section a policy of life assurance effected by a person on their own life can be expressed to be for the benefit of their spouse, civil partner, children (which includes children of a non-marital relationship) or any of them. This creates a trust in their favour and on the death, the sum assured is paid direct to the trustees of the policy for the benefit of the named beneficiaries. No inheritance tax charge will arise in respect of the assured's estate where policies are written in trust in this way since the assured has no beneficial interest. However, provided the gift is not subject to a contingency, the named beneficiary receives an immediate absolute interest. Therefore, should the beneficiary predecease the assured, the beneficiary's estate suffers tax on the appropriate proportion of the value of the policy. Since the beneficiary has an immediate absolute interest in the policy, the assured is no longer free to surrender or assign the policy.

Since s.11 permits the assured to name their children as beneficiaries, it is advisable to appoint trustees to hold the money until the children reach a suitable age. If such trustees are not appointed, the assured's personal representatives will hold the money as trustees, on trust for the children. Should this situation arise, the sum is still not taxed as part of the assured's estate since the sum does not belong to the estate, it is merely administratively convenient for the personal representatives to hold the property in this way. If the assured wants to benefit someone other than a spouse or children (such as a friend or grandchildren) the policy must be expressly written in trust for them. The trust has the same effect as a s.11 policy. The same result will be achieved by assigning the policy to the named beneficiary.

Where the benefit of a policy is written in trust or assigned, there is a transfer of value of the policy at market value or the total of premiums paid whichever is the greater (IHTA 1984 s.167). If the transferor continues to pay the premiums, each payment will be a transfer of value although they are likely to be exempt under the annual exemption or normal expenditure out of income exemption.

In *Kempe v CIR* (2004) the deceased designated members of his family to take the benefit of a life assurance policy provided by his family. Under the terms of the policy he could change the designation at any time. If no beneficiaries were designated the sum assured passed to his estate. The Revenue successfully argued that the benefit of the policy remained part of his estate at death under IHTA 1984 s.5 because he had a "general power" over the policy which enabled him to dispose of the sum assured as he thought fit.

Enduring and lasting powers of attorney

21.16 Any person may appoint an attorney to deal with their property. However, the power of attorney will automatically end if the person who made the appointment (the donor of the power) becomes mentally incapable. However, the Enduring Power of Attorney Act 1985 provides for the appointment of an attorney whose powers will survive the incapacity of the donor. No new enduring powers of attorney can be made on or after October 1, 2007, although existing enduring powers continue to be valid (whether or not registered before that date).

On or after October 1, 2007 it is possible to make lasting powers of attorney which will survive the incapacity of the donor. Lasting powers cannot be used until registered with the Public Guardian. There are two forms of lasting power of attorney: one authorises the attorney to make personal welfare decisions, the other authorises the attorney to make decisions about property.

A solicitor who is advising a person making a will should consider advising the appointment of an attorney with a lasting power. Where such an appointment is made the attorney may be given power to sell the donor's property, and to a limited extent to give it away, notwithstanding the donor's incapacity. A sale by an attorney of an asset which has been specifically given in the will causes ademption (See *Banks v National Westminster Bank* (2005) and *Re Dorman*). It is sensible for a person making a lasting power to give the attorney a copy of the will or authorise anyone with custody of the will to show the attorney a copy so that the attorney can take the provisions into account so far as possible.

3. LIFETIME PLANNING

Gifts

21.17 As an alternative to leaving property to an intended beneficiary by will, a client can consider making a lifetime gift. Such a gift has the advantage of giving the beneficiary the immediate use of the asset but it has the corresponding disadvantage that the donor will lose the benefit of the property (unless, for example, the gift is to a spouse or civil partner).

Therefore, it is important to ensure that the donor has no need of the property to be given away. A gift of money that will leave the donor with financial problems is pointless as is the gift of an asset that the donor still wants to use. It is quite common for testators to want to leave books, jewellery, fishing tackle, golf clubs and similar items to friends or relatives but they would obviously not wish to make such gifts during their lifetime. While lifetime gifts should always be considered, they are usually only practicable where the donor is fairly wealthy. An additional advantage of lifetime gifts is that they may be useful in saving tax.

Tax considerations

Although tax should never be the first consideration, since lifetime transfers to **21.18** individuals do not attract an immediate inheritance tax liability a lifetime gift will prima facie produce a saving. There is a danger that the donor will die within seven years of the transfer in which case inheritance tax will be charged (subject to tapering relief). It may be wise to insure against the risk of death in this period. The advantage of saving inheritance tax may be outweighed by capital gains tax considerations.

Inheritance tax

Spouses who wanted to provide for the surviving spouse and children in a tax **21.19** efficient manner used to leave property by will to make use of the nil rate band of the first spouse to die—typically by creating a nil rate band discretionary trust for the benefit of spouse and children. This would often require the transfer of assets between spouses to ensure that each spouse had sufficient assets to do this. Since the introduction of the transferable nil rate band on October 9, 2007, this is no longer necessary. If the first spouse to die has not made use of the nil rate band, the proportion unused can be claimed by the personal representatives of the survivor (see para.4.11, above).

However, it may be advisable for cohabiting couples with children to consider making lifetime gifts to ensure that both parties have sufficient assets to make use of their nil rate band. Then in the event of both parties dying at or about the same time they can each leave their estates to their children obtaining the benefit of two nil rate bands. There will not be any tax saving if the couple equalise their estates but the first to die leaves their entire property to the other.

There is an advantage in making potentially exempt transfers of assets which are likely to increase in value over the next few years. Inheritance tax in the event of the transferor's death is calculated on the value of the property at the time the gift is made, not on its value at the time of death. Thus, the value of the property is effectively "frozen" and less inheritance tax will be payable. This value "freezing" will not occur if the donor continues to derive a benefit from the property given away. In such a case the reservation of benefit rules will apply and the property will be treated for inheritance tax purposes as part of the deceased's estate on death (see para.4.11, above).

Grandparents who want to make provision for grandchildren may well consider doing so by lifetime gift in order to make funds available at an earlier date when they may be more useful and to reduce tax payable on their estates on death. Frequently they will prefer to transfer funds to a settlement for the benefit of the grandchildren rather than by outright gift. Such a transfer will be immediately chargeable to inheritance tax but until the amount transferred exceeds the nil rate band, the rate will be nil so this should not be a disincentive. However, there is the risk of dying within seven years in which case the loss of the nil rate band will increase the tax payable on the death estate.

Capital gains tax

21.20 In view of the fact that capital gains tax is not paid on death and the donor acquires the property at its market value at death, lifetime gifts are apparently less advantageous. However, exemptions or reliefs may in many circumstances mean that no capital gains tax is actually payable, so that the gift can be made if other considerations make the disposition advisable.

Business property

21.21 The proprietor of a business should give careful consideration to what provisions they wish to make for the continuation of the business after their death. It will often be necessary to do this by lifetime provision rather than by will. For example, if the business is run through a company, consideration should be given to the possible alteration of the articles so as to provide for the company purchasing its own shares and/or for rights of pre-emption in respect of these shares. If the business is a partnership some provision should be made for succession to the deceased partner's interest by the remaining partners or by the deceased partner's relatives or for the realisation of the value of the interest when the partner dies or retires.

In making such arrangements taxation must be taken into account. It is important, however, that a tax effective disposition should not be made if it conflicts with more general commercial considerations. Business property is favourably treated for tax purposes. A gift of a business or an interest in a business is eligible for inheritance tax business property relief (see paras 4.45–4.52, above) which may in itself produce a large saving in the tax payable. However, planning in advance may produce further savings. Provision may be made in a partnership agreement for automatic accrual of goodwill. This means that when a partner dies their interest in the goodwill passes automatically to the other partners. Clearly this automatic accrual reduces the partner's interest in the goodwill and the value of the estate on death. To the extent that consideration in money or money's worth was given for the accrual clause, the entry into the clause will not be a transfer of value for inheritance tax purposes. There may be some difficulty in showing that consideration was given for such an accrual clause in the case of a family partnership. However, an estate duty case (*Attorney General v Boden* (1912)), which is generally considered still to be relevant, held that an agreement to work for the business is consideration in money or money's worth.

An option granted (for money or money's worth) to purchase goodwill at a fixed price may also give rise to a tax saving. The value of the goodwill to the partner on death is the price that the estate will be paid on the exercise of the option. An agreement that a partner's share *must* be purchased on death is not advisable as the Revenue argues that this contract of sale may disentitle the deceased partner to the business property relief.[1]

The Revenue accepts that automatic accruer clauses (where the share of a deceased partner passes automatically to the surviving partners in return for a payment either on valuation or in accordance with a formula) do not constitute binding contracts for sale and that neither do option arrangements.[2]

If a business is to be run as a company then, when the company is formed consideration should be given to the possibility of providing pre-emption rights. These are rights whereby when one shareholder disposes of shares, or dies owning shares, the other shareholders are given a right to buy at a price fixed by or to be fixed in accordance with the company's articles of association. Such a pre-emption right is an option so that the same considerations apply as in the case of a partner's option to purchase goodwill.

4. WHY MAKE A WILL?

There are a number of reasons why solicitors often advise clients to make wills. **21.22**

To avoid the application of the intestacy rules

As we explained in Ch.3, the property of a person who dies without making a **21.23** will, passes according to a strict legal order. A person who dies intestate, therefore, has no control over who are to be the recipients of their estate and so cannot benefit friends or charities without making a will.

Persons who are married or in a civil partnership will usually want their property to pass to their spouse or civil partner but it is only in the case of small estates that the whole of the estate will necessarily pass in this way under the intestacy rules. If the estate is larger and the deceased is survived by a spouse or civil partner and issue, the spouse or civil partner will take personal chattels, a statutory legacy of £250,000 and only a life interest the spouse or civil partner may be able to capitalise the life interest, a portion of the estate will still go to the children and the spouse may have insufficient funds to maintain an existing standard of living.

While a variation (see Ch.19) may in some cases provide a solution it is clearly more desirable to prevent the problem ever arising. A beneficiary who is under 18 cannot give up an interest in an estate; a parent or guardian cannot do so on behalf of a minor.

The solicitor should, therefore, suggest making a will since otherwise clients cannot ensure that their wishes as to the disposition of their property will be respected. (A solicitor should inform a client that in certain circumstances a

---

[1] Statement of Practice 12/80, October 13, 1980.
[2] See *Law Society Gazette*, September 4, 1996, p.35.

relative or other dependant might be able to claim under the Inheritance (Provision for Family and Dependants) Act 1975.)

Even though a client is satisfied with the general disposition of property under the intestacy rules, if they want to ensure that a particular item is to pass to one of the people specified in the intestacy rules, this can be only done by will. Furthermore, clients may wish to demonstrate expressly that they are happy for their property to pass to the persons who would be entitled under the intestacy rules by making a will in their favour. When making wills for cohabiting couples the solicitor should warn the couple that a subsequent marriage will revoke the will.

Appointment of personal representatives and trustees

21.24   In a will, a testator can make a choice of executors and trustees, whereas on intestacy the personal representatives are determined by r.22 of the Non-Contentious Probate Rules 1987 (see para.8.16, above). If a will is made, it is possible for the testator to choose persons who are suitable and who are likely to be willing to act.

An executor's authority dates from death, whereas an administrator's dates only from the grant of representation; the appointment of an executor may, therefore, facilitate the administration of the estate.

Appointment of guardians

21.25   Testators are often concerned to provide appropriate care for their children. A solicitor should explain that guardians can be appointed in the will. These guardians will normally act after the death of the surviving spouse but can act jointly with the spouse in certain circumstances. It is advisable to include an express appointment since this will ensure that the testator gives thought to whom to appoint. A solicitor should advise a client who proposes to appoint a guardian to consult the prospective guardian as to whether or not they are willing to act. The question of finance for the guardian should be considered. Guardians are dealt with more fully in para.22.23, below.

While it is not necessary to make a will to appoint a guardian it is a convenient place to do it.

Extension of statutory powers

21.26   If a will is made, additional powers can be conferred on personal representatives and trustees which will facilitate the administration. These powers are considered in Ch.22.

Directions as to burial and disposal of body

21.27   If the testator has special wishes as to burial or cremation these can be included in the will. The wishes are not binding as people have no property in their bodies after their death *Williams v Williams* (1882). Although personal representatives will normally want to give effect to the deceased's wishes, they can ignore directions for a lavish or unconventional funeral. In a case where there is no dispute as to the executor's entitlement to act, the executor's decision probably overrides the wishes of close releatives; see *Re Grandison* (1989), although Vinelott J. left open the question of whether the court had the power to override or supplant the executor's decision. In *University Hospital Lewisham NHS Trust v Hamuth* (2006) there was a dispute over the validity of the will. The purported executor proposed to follow the instructions in the will and cremate the body while the family wanted a burial in the family plot. The body was in the mortuary of the NHS trust and Hart J. held that, there being no way of resolving the dispute as to the validity of the will within an acceptable time period, the decision as to the appropriate arrangements for the disposal of the body had to be left to the NHS trust as the person currently in lawful possession of the body.

Some people consider "alternative burials" in woods, fields or gardens. They must obtain the consent of the relevant local authority. One of the most popular alternatives to traditional burials and cremations are those in woodland or nature reserve burial grounds. There are a number of commercial sites opening around the country, promoting eco-friendly funerals and more informal ceremonies. At woodland burial grounds relatives may be able to plant a tree to mark the site either on or near the grave. At nature reserve burial grounds, which can be wild flower meadows or pastures, graves are either unmarked or may be marked by a small wooden plaque that will rot away naturally.

The burial of Princess Diana in the grounds at Althorp drew attention to the idea of being buried at home. However, an interment of this type requires a number of local authority permissions. Relatives will have to take advice from the Environment Agency which has a list of minimum distances from the site of a grave to water, cabling and wells or boreholes. The Department of the Environment, Transport and the Regions says that it is not necessary to apply for planning permission to bury up to two people in a back garden although permission would be required to bury any more. It is possible to apply for a certificate of lawfulness as regards planning law. The result of the application is recorded on a public register. If the application is refused, there is a right of free appeal. There is a requirement to record the burial on the deeds to the property, in accordance with the Registration of Burials Act 1864. A location map must be attached to the deed to confirm the position of the grave and details of the name of the deceased, age, date and place of death should be recorded. This will reduce the potential complication of the Police being called if human remains are discovered during future garden maintenance or building work. There are concerns over the issue of future problems, e.g. who would want to buy a property with a body in the garden, but the prospective buyer has the right to know that someone is buried within the grounds of the property. A certificate for burial issued by the Coroner or Registrar of Birth and Deaths (called the green disposal) will have to be obtained and any other procedural matters of the Registrar satisfied. The detachable section of this certificate needs to be completed and returned to the Registrar by the person who is arranging the burial.

There are a number of organisations which provide advice on secular funerals and "green" burials. See the British Humanist Association website which has publications on secular funerals and provides advice on non-religious funerals. See also the Natural Death Centre website which has a list of natural burial grounds.

Testators may want their organs to be available for donation. A person can give written consent at any time or oral consent during their last illness to the use of organs for therapeutic purposes or for the purposes of medical education or research. (Even without that consent the persons lawfully in possession of the body can authorise the use of organs so long as after making reasonable enquiries, they have no reason to believe the deceased had expressed any objection and have no reason to believe that any surviving spouse or surviving relative will object.) Such directions can be included in the will but it is better for the client to carry a donor card and make sure that family members are aware of their wishes. A mere statement in the will may not be discovered in time to be useful.

Advance decisions or "living wills"

21.28 It is never lawful to take active steps to cause or accelerate death. Even where a person wishes to die, anyone offering assistance will be guilty of complicity in suicide under the Suicide Act 1961 s.2 (see *R. (on the application of Pretty) v DPP* (2002)).

However, in certain circumstances it is lawful to withhold life-sustaining treatment such as artificial feeding and ventilation without which the patient will die (see *Airedale Trust v Bland* (1993)). There is a Practice Note, *Official Solicitor: Vegetative State* (1996), which deals with the procedure to be followed in applications for the withdrawal of artificial feeding and hydration. The Official Solicitor acts on behalf of the patient. Previously expressed advance directives of the patient, in writing or otherwise, will be an important factor.

It is becoming increasingly common for people to want to make advance decisions (commonly referred to as "living wills") stating that in the event of a loss of mental capacity they do not wish to be given medical treatment for any life-threatening illness. Such a statement should not be incorporated into a will but should be kept separately. Close relatives should be informed of the existence and whereabouts of the statement.

Section 25 of the Mental Capacity Act 2005 recognises the validity of an advance decision for the first time. To be valid the advance decision must be applicable to the treatment proposed. The person making it can withdraw it any time (while they have capacity). An advance decision is not applicable to the treatment in question if, inter alia, any circumstances specified in the advance decision are absent, or there are reasonable grounds for believing that circumstances exist which the person making the advance decision did not anticipate at the time of the advance decision and which would have affected their decision had they anticipated them. This might include advances in medical treatment. If, as is usually the case, the decision relates to life-sustaining treatment, the following conditions must be satisfied. The decision must:

(a) be in writing;

     (i) signed by the maker or by another person in their presence and by their direction;

    (ii) the signature must be made or acknowledged in the presence of a witness;

   (iii) the witness must sign to acknowledge in the presence of the maker; and

  (b) state that it is to apply to that treatment even if life is at risk.

The decision will not be valid if the person making it later creates a lasting power of attorney which confers authority on the donee (or, if more than one, any of them) to give or refuse consent to the treatment to which the advance decision relates.

Many organisations have produced living wills. A good example is that produced by the Terrence Higgins Trust.[3] This declares that if the person making the decision is, inter alia, unable to communicate and has an irreversible condition which means they are expected to die in a matter of days or weeks or has brain damage or disease that makes them unlikely ever to recognise or relate to people, they want treatment only to provide comfort and relieve distress, even if this may shorten life.

It is necessary to be very specific in the terms of such a document. In *Re B: Consent to Treatment: Capacity* (2002) Ms B wrote a living will which stated that should the time come when she was unable to give instructions, she wished for treatment to be withdrawn if she was suffering from a life-threatening condition, permanent mental impairment or permanent unconsciousness. As a result of a ruptured blood vessel in her neck she was left paralysed from the neck down.

Her living will was not appropriate to the circumstances of her illness and the medical staff refused to withdraw treatment. She was able to give instructions that she did not wish treatment to continue but the medical staff questioned her mental capacity. The Court of Appeal found that Ms B had possessed the requisite mental capacity to make decisions regarding her treatment and, thus, the administration of artificial respiration by the trust against her wishes had amounted to an unlawful trespass. She was able to withdraw consent to future treatment.

Tax considerations

The possible dispositions that can be made are considered in detail in Ch.22 but the tax advantages to be gained from a carefully drafted will should be drawn to the testator's attention. **21.29**

Private Client practitioners have had a number of significant changes in legislation to deal with in recent years. It is important that they make clear to clients that any will prepared with a view to saving tax needs to be reviewed if there are major changes in tax legislation. It is also important to make clear that

---

[3] Gray's Inn Road, London WC1.

the solicitor is not taking on the responsibility of contacting the client. The solicitor may wish to contact the client as a matter of marketing but it is normally undesirable to have an obligation to do so.

The normal retainer for drafting a will does not extend beyond the preparation of a draft will for the client to consider (see *Atkins v Dunn-Baker* (2004)) but, of course this may be varied by agreement.

Chapter Twenty-Two

PLANNING AND DRAFTING A WILL

1. Introduction

Taking instructions

A solicitor who is asked to prepare a will for a client will usually find that a **22.01** personal interview is necessary. The object of the interview is to obtain, in as short a time as possible, all the information which the solicitor needs in order to prepare the will.

It is often helpful to have a "checklist" for taking instructions so that none of the information required is forgotten and no further correspondence or meetings are required. If the checklist is in the form of a questionnaire it may be possible for some other member of the firm to use it to draft the will if necessary. An example of a simple checklist is included in the Appendix at p.505.

In appropriate circumstances the solicitor should discuss with the client possible action that can be taken during the client's lifetime to arrange financial and business affairs sensibly. In order that advice can be given on taxation and on the suitability of the proposed dispositions, the solicitor should find out what property the client owns and whether there is any property (such as joint property or insurance policies) which will pass independently of the will. The client should also be advised on the effect of any proposed dispositions.

If the testator is married or a civil partner, the solicitor should point out that it is advisable for the testator's spouse or civil partner to make a will at the same time. The reason for this is that thought can then be given to the ultimate destination of their respective estates.

The solicitor who takes instructions from the client should make a written note (on the questionnaire, if used) of the details of the name and address of the testator, the executor(s), and the beneficiaries and where relevant of any testamentary guardian(s) or trustee(s). They should make sure that they have the correct names of the various people mentioned in the will—this is particularly important in the case of institutions, such as charities. Where specific items of property are dealt with in the will, a sufficient description is required so that they can be identified. A draftsman should be careful to avoid errors in description which may cause a gift to fail.

Types of disposition

22.02 Dispositions of property in a will are basically of three types—specific gifts, general legacies and gifts of residue. Testators should be encouraged to think carefully about the purpose of each intended gift. If they want a particular person to have a particular asset, then a specific gift is likely to be suitable (although they should be warned that the gift will be adeemed if the property is sold or changed in nature). If they want a particular person to have a fixed amount of money, then a general (pecuniary) legacy is suitable. A residuary gift is likely to be most suitable for the major beneficiary or beneficiaries of the estate. A residuary gift should always be included in a will so as to avoid the possibility of a partial intestacy. For the same reason the testator should consider the possibility that the residuary beneficiary may predecease them and should consider whether they wish to include a substitutional beneficiary.

The choice of dispositions will largely depend on the testator's family circumstances. The following are among the most common dispositions where a will is made by a married person with children:

22.03 (a) *All to spouse or civil partner.* A will which leaves everything to the testator's spouse or civil partner will ensure that the survivor is provided for as far as possible. However, the testator has no control over the ultimate destination of the property and must trust the survivor to make appropriate dispositions. There is a danger of accidental disinheritance of children where a surviving spouse remarries without realising that marriage automatically revokes an earlier will. If, because of the size of the estate, inheritance tax is a consideration the following points should be borne in mind:

    (i) no tax will be payable on the testator's death (since the spouse or civil partner exemption is available); and

    (ii) before October 9, 2007 the benefit of nil rate band was lost as the estate was exempt from tax. However, the Finance Act 2008 includes provisions which will, in effect, transfer the nil rate band to the surviving spouse or civil partner by increasing that persons nil rate band. Details of the provisions are set out in para.4.11, above.

22.04 (b) *Spouse or civil partner for life remainder to children.* With this type of disposition the testator retains control over the ultimate destination of the property. However, since the survivor is entitled only to the income from the property, they may have insufficient funds available—this problem can be alleviated if the trustees are given power to advance or lend capital to the survivor.

The inheritance tax consequences are virtually the same as in the case of an outright gift (since the survivor has an immediate post-death interest in possession in the settled property and the spouse exemption is therefore available).

22.05 (c) *Legacy to spouse or civil partner, residue to children.* This type of disposition may be appropriate where the testator's spouse or civil partner is independently wealthy but should always be viewed with a certain amount of caution.

Changed circumstances and/or inflation may make the provision for the survivor by means of a legacy quite inadequate in the future. The spouse or civil partner exemption for inheritance tax is lost, except to the extent of the legacy, but in the long run there may be a tax saving because of the effect of equalising estates.

(d) *Legacy to children, residue to spouse or civil partner.* This type of disposi- **22.06** tion has the advantage of making some provision for the children immediately. The legacy should not, of course, be so large as to leave the surviving spouse with insufficient funds.

There may be inheritance tax advantages with this type of gift. The spouse or civil partner exemption is lost to the extent of the legacy. However, there will be no tax payable until the nil rate band is exhausted. Some provision can, thus, be made for the children immediately without an inheritance tax liability.

It is fairly common to give a legacy of "such amount as can pass at the date of my death without payment of inheritance tax". This is often referred to as a nil rate band legacy. It is worded as it is, so that if the deceased has used up some of his nil rate band by the time of death, only an amount equivalent to the unused portion will pass. If the deceased has the benefit of the whole or part of an unused nil rate band of their predeceased spouse or civil partner that amount will be included in the gift. There are two dangers with such a gift:

(a) The size of the nil rate band is likely to fluctuate with successive governments. The gift may turn out to be much larger or smaller by the time the testator dies than was envisaged at the time the will was made. This problem may arise as a result of the introduction of the transferable nil rate band where a gift expressed as a gift of "such amount as can pass at the date of my death without payment of inheritance tax" could pass twice as much as the testator originally intended.

(b) If the estate contains property which attracts 100 per cent business or agricultural property relief, it can pass without payment of inheritance tax. The gift may turn out to be very much larger than was originally envisaged. It may be desirable to impose a maximum limit on the size of the gift.

(e) *Nil rate band discretionary trust, residue to spouse or civil partner.* The **22.07** beneficiaries will include the spouse and civil partner and issue of the testator. So long as the amount passing away from the spouse does not exceed the testator's unused nil rate band at the date of death, there will be no tax to pay on creation and no periodic or proportionate periodic charges. It allows the testator to build into their will a large element of flexibility.

Use of precedents

Precedents are an invaluable aid to good will drafting. Sometimes a precedent **22.08** may be available which is almost exactly what is required but this is unusual. In

all but the simplest cases it is likely that the precedent will have to be substantially amended. Before a precedent can be adapted for use in a particular case
draftsmen must ensure that they understand what the precedent was intended to
do. For example, if a precedent was designed for use where a complicated
settlement is being created it is unlikely to be of much use in drafting a will
which makes a straightforward absolute gift of residue. Old precedents should be
viewed with some caution since they may deal with problems which are no
longer relevant (such as capital transfer tax rules) and may not deal with
problems resulting from new law (such as those arising from amendments to the
inheritance tax system). So that the terminology used in different parts of the will
is consistent, it is best to use precedents from one particular source as far as
possible and to take care when combining two or more precedents.

Wills are traditionally drafted without punctuation. To make reading a little
easier it is usual to divide the will into numbered clauses and to capitalise the
words which explain what the clause is for (so that clauses making gifts usually
contain words such as "I GIVE", clauses appointing an executor usually contains
the words, "I APPOINT" and clauses containing trusts usually contain the words
"UPON TRUST"). Definitions are sometimes very helpful. For example, where
several executors or executors and trustees are appointed the words "hereinafter
together called 'my Executors'" (or "my Trustees") can be included so that
references later in the will can be made to those persons without setting out their
names again. Where there is such a definition, it is good practice to capitalise the
first letter of the word defined so that the reader can see more readily that the
word has been defined (for example, "my Trustee" not "my trustee").

Structure of a will

22.09   A will usually includes the following:

(1) words of commencement,

(2) revocation clause,

(3) appointment of executors (and trustees and guardians if appropriate),

(4) specific gifts (if any),

(5) general legacies (if any),

(6) a gift of residue,

(7) extension of executors' and trustees' powers and declarations, and

(8) attestation clause.

In the rest of this chapter we will consider the drafting of the various parts of the
will.

2. The Formal Parts

Every professionally drafted will should have the words of commencement, a **22.10** revocation clause, a date clause and an attestation clause. For the sake of convenience these "formal parts" are dealt with together in this section.

Commencement

The commencement of the will is intended to identify the person making the will. **22.11** The testator's full name and address should be included. If the testator is known to own property in a name which is different from the full name or to use a name which is not the true and proper name, it is advisable to refer to this fact in the opening words of the will. The reason for this is that after the testator's death it will be clear that the grant of representation should refer to both names.

A commonly used form of wording for the commencement of the will is "This is the Last Will and Testament of me [AB] [(also known as [CD])] of [address] [occupation]". If the will is made in expectation of the testator's marriage or civil partnership, it is necessary to incorporate suitable words (see paras 2.52–2.55, above).

Revocation clause

In Ch.2 we explained that a later will revokes an earlier will to the extent that it **22.12** is inconsistent. If the later will deals with the testator's entire estate, all earlier wills and codicils are revoked. Nevertheless, for the avoidance of any possible doubt, a revocation clause should be included in all professionally drafted wills, even if the solicitor believes the present will to be the only will the testator has ever made.

The revocation clause can be included in the commencement of the will but it is often set out as a separate clause. An appropriate form of wording is "I REVOKE all former wills and testamentary dispositions made by me".

The date clause

The date can be included in the commencement of the will, or at the end **22.13** immediately before the attestation clause. It is more common to include the date at the end.

The date clause may be important in identifying which of a number of wills was the last or in identifying the subject-matter of a gift. The usual form of words is "IN WITNESS of which I have set my hand to this my will the   day of   20..".

The attestation clause

The presence of a correctly drafted attestation clause will in most cases satisfy **22.14** the court that the requirements of Wills Act 1837 s.9 as amended by the

Administration of Justice Act 1982 have been complied with. (As was explained in para.10.48, above, the absence of an attestation clause will lead the registrar to require affidavit evidence to prove due execution under the Non-Contentious Probate Rules 1987 r.12.)

The two most common forms of attestation are as follows:

(a) The Short Form.

> "Signed by the above named [AB] in our joint presence and then by us in [his/hers]."

(b) The Long Form.

> "Signed by the above-named [AB] as [his/her] last will in the presence of us both present at the same time who at [his/her] request in [his/her] presence and in the presence of each other have hereunto subscribed our names as witnesses."

These clauses, implying as they do that the witnesses signed in each other's presence as well as in the presence of the testator, go beyond the strict wording of s.9 as amended but may reduce the possibility of the attestation being challenged after the death.

Where the testator suffers from some disability which would cast doubt on the validity of the will due to the suspected absence of knowledge and approval of the wording of the will, the forms of attestation clause set out above should be amended. The purpose of the amendment is to indicate that the testator did in fact know and approve of the contents of the will.

Thus, if the testator is blind, illiterate or seriously ill the attestation clause should state that the will was read over to the testator and that he or she appeared to thoroughly understand and approve its contents.

If someone signs on the testator's behalf, this fact should be stated in the clause together with a confirmation that the will was signed in the presence of, and at the direction of, the testator. The person signing may sign in their own name or that of the testator.

22.15   Whenever the circumstances are such that, after the testator's death, there may be doubt as to his or her capacity or as to his or her knowledge and approval of the contents of the will, the solicitor should try to be present and should make a full and careful file note. It is desirable that a medical practitioner be asked to prepare a note of the testator's mental and physical state.

Illustrations of such clauses appear below.

(i) *Attestation clause where someone signs on behalf of the testator.*
Signed by me [AB] with the name of the above-named [testator] as [his/her] last will in [his/her] presence and by [his/her] direction and by us as witnesses who in the presence of [AB] and the above-named [testator] and in the presence of each other so subscribed our names.

(ii) *Attestation clause where the testator is blind (and someone signs on behalf of the testator).*

Signed by [AB] with the name of the above-named [testator] as [his/her] last will (the will having been first read over to [him/her] when the said [testator] appeared thoroughly to understand and approve the contents thereof) in [his/her] presence and by [his/her] direction in the presence of us present at the same time who at [his/her] request in [his/her] presence and in the presence of each other have written our names as witnesses.

(iii) *Attestation clause where the testator is illiterate and signs with a mark.*

Signed by the above-named [testator] as [his/her] last will with [his/her] mark [he/she] being unable to read (the will having been first read over to [him/her] by [name] when the [testator] appeared thoroughly to understand and approve the contents of the will) in [his/her] presence and by [his/her] direction in the presence of us present at the same time who at [his/her] request in [his/her] presence and in the presence of each other have written our names as witnesses.

3. EXECUTORS AND TRUSTEES

When taking instructions for the drafting of the will, the testator's wishes must **22.16** be ascertained as to the persons who will administer the estate (the executors) and who will act as trustees of any trust created under the will.

It is often administratively convenient to appoint the same people to hold both offices, a common form of wording being "I APPOINT [AB] of [address and occupation] and [CD] of [address and occupation] to be the executors and trustees of this my will ('my Trustees' which expression shall where the context so admits include the trustees for the time being)". The final words arc required to make it clear that any powers conferred on the trustees are not personal to the original trustees.

Number of executors and trustees

Any number of executors may be appointed but no more than four may take out **22.17** the grant in respect of the same property. One executor will always suffice. However, two are often appointed in case one predeceases the testator or dies before completing the administration. Moreover, if the executors are also to be trustees, it is desirable to appoint two since two trustees (or a trust corporation) are required to give a good receipt for capital money.

The choice of appointees

A testator may appoint an individual, a firm of solicitors, a bank or trust **22.18** corporation. The testator must consider the relative merits of such appointees.

Individuals

22.19   Testators frequently appoint friends or relatives to act as executors. Such an appointment has the advantage of ensuring the administration is completed by someone of whom the testator has personal knowledge and who will not charge for the work done. A disadvantage may be that the appointee lacks expertise but there is nothing to prevent the appointee taking professional advice. However, the need for such advice may mean that the supposed advantage of cheapness is more apparent than real.

The testator has freedom of choice and so can appoint any person to act, including a bankrupt, a criminal, an infant or a person suffering from a mental or physical disability but there are limitations on who can actually take a grant (see para.8.02, above).

Further points must be considered when choosing individuals. The most important points are the appointees' ability to cope with the burdens of the office and their willingness to act. A commercially inexperienced person may find the problems of dealing with a complicated estate excessively onerous.

It may be appropriate to appoint a beneficiary as an executor. The beneficiary will have a personal interest in ensuring the estate is properly administered. However, the possibility of a conflict of interest may arise. If the only executor is a specific legatee, there may be a danger that the interests of the residuary beneficiary will be disregarded. Appointing several individuals may lead to disputes if they are unable to agree on the appropriate steps to be taken when dealing with the assets.

No matter how suitable the appointee may seem to be, if they are older than the testator, there is the probability of the executor predeceasing the testator. In this circumstance a substitutional appointment should be included in the will.

Professional advisers

22.20   The appointment of professional advisers, such as solicitors or accountants, has the advantage of ensuring that the administration is dealt with by experts who, frequently, will have a detailed knowledge of the estate and its assets. Such knowledge, together with their knowledge of estate administration and probate practice, may be invaluable when the estate is complex. The disadvantage of appointing professionals, as compared with individuals, is that the executors will have no personal interest in the estate and will charge for their services.

When appointing solicitors or accountants as executors, although the testator may wish to appoint a particular person to act, problems will arise if that person dies, retires or leaves the firm. For this reason it is usual (subject to the testator's wishes) to appoint the firm to act rather than named individuals. Unless the will says otherwise, an appointment of a firm of solicitors is construed as an appointment of the partners in the firm at the date the will is made. Since partners may die, retire or leave the firm, it is advisable to provide expressly that appointment is of the partners in the firm at the date of death. It is possible that the firm may change its name or amalgamate with another firm and the testator may wish to consider making provision to cover this possibility. It is usual to express the wish that only two of the partners should take the grant but this is not essential.

In the case of a Solicitors' Incorporated Practice (under the Solicitors' Incorporated Practice Rules 2001) care should be taken in drafting to ensure that the individual solicitors who are directors or members of the practice at the time of death are appointed. The practice itself cannot be appointed as it is not a trust corporation.

The appointment is not invalidated if the firm becomes a limited liability partnership. However, it is advisable to make specific provision to include this possibility. An example of a suitable form of appointment is—

> I APPOINT the partners including salaried partners in the firm of [name] of [address] at the date of my death or of the firm which at that date has succeeded to and carries on their practice to be the executors and trustees of this will [("my Trustees")] and in the event of that firm having been incorporated as a limited company at the date of my death then I APPOINT the directors and shareholders at the date of my death to be the executors and trustees of my will [("my Trustees")] and I express the wish that two and two only of the partners shareholders and directors as the case may be shall act as my executors and trustees.

The words "including salaried partners" are included as otherwise it seems only profit sharing partners will be included (at least in the case of a limited liability partnership (*Re Rogers (dec'd)* (2006)). In the case of an incorporated practice the probate registry consider the shareholders to be the equivalent of the partners. The inclusion of the words "the directors" allows members of the firm who are not shareholders to be appointed.

Trust corporations—banks

Instead of or in addition to individuals and professional advisers it is possible to appoint corporations sole or trust corporations, such as the trustee department of one of the leading banks. **22.21**

Banks generally insist that their own standard appointment clause (which incorporates a charging clause) be inserted in the will otherwise they will refuse to act. Such clauses can be readily obtained from any branch. Furthermore, where banks are appointed they often require a sight of the draft will before it is signed.

The banks have scales of charges which the testator may wish to compare with solicitors' fees. The appointment of a corporation may prove expensive since if difficulties arise the corporation may instruct solicitors to act on its behalf with the result that there may be an element of double charging. Trust corporations are unlikely to be willing to carry on the business of the deceased except briefly for the purpose of disposal.

The Public Trustee

The testator can appoint the Public Trustee but the circumstances when the appointment will be appropriate are limited and consent should be obtained in advance. **22.22**

4. Guardians

22.23   Testators with minor children should consider who will have the care of any minor children who survive them. The relevant law is contained in the Children Act 1989 as amended.

A parent with parental responsibility may appoint a guardian. Broadly speaking, a mother has parental responsibility irrespective of her marital status. A father has automatic parental responsibility if he has been married to the mother at any time later than the date of conception. An unmarried father may acquire parental responsibility by becoming registered as the child's father, by court order or agreement with the child's mother (Adoption and Children Act 2002 s.111). An appointment may be made by will or in writing (s.5(5)).

Under s.5(7) and (8) of the Children Act, an appointment by one spouse where the other spouse survives will now not normally take effect until the death of the surviving spouse. If the surviving spouse also appoints a guardian, the two guardians will act together after the death of the surviving spouse.

There is one case where an appointment would take effect immediately despite the existence of a surviving spouse. This is where there is a residence order in force in favour of the deceased parent. For example, H and W have been divorced for five years and there is a custody order in force by which the children live with W; W dies and appoints X as guardian. X will become guardian on W's death and will share parental responsibility with H. A disgruntled surviving parent in such circumstances could apply to the court to have the guardianship terminated (s.6(7)).

An appropriate form of words for an appointment under the Children Act in normal circumstances is

> "I APPOINT [AB] of [address] and [CD] of [address] to be the guardians after the death of my [husband/wife] of any of my children who may then be minors".

If a residence order was in force in favour of the deceased spouse the appointment would be "to act jointly with [my husband/wife]".

When a testator is considering appointing guardians, the appointees should be consulted to ensure that they are willing to act. Where guardians are appointed consideration should be given to the additional expense that the guardians will incur. It is common to make them trustees (either alone or jointly with the professional executors) of a trust fund for the benefit of the children. In such a case the powers of trustees may have to be amended to suit the circumstances.

Although ss.31 and 32 of the Trustee Act 1925 permit the income and capital of a trust fund to be made available for the benefit of the children, testators might wish to make express provision in the will. For example, power could be given to the trustees to allow the trust's capital to be used for the purchase of a larger house for the guardians and the children to live in. The capital could be lent to the guardians at a low rate of interest; alternatively the money could be used to help fund a purchase of the property in the joint names of the guardians and the trust fund.

5. Specific Gifts and General Legacies

Introduction

When drafting specific gifts and general legacies, the draftsman must consider **22.24** both the nature of the legacy and the status of the beneficiary (for example, particular problems may arise where the beneficiary is a charity or a minor).

Specific gifts

A specific gift is one the wording of which distinguishes the gifted property from **22.25** all other property belonging to the testator at the date of death.

Section 24 of the Wills Act 1837

Section 24 provides that, as regards property, the will "speaks from death" unless **22.26** it expresses a contrary intention. The use of the word "my" coupled with a specific item (for example, "my piano") is often construed as showing such a contrary intention. However, if the word "my" is followed by a description of property capable of increase or decrease, this is not usually construed as contrary intention so that, for example, a gift of "my collection of Dresden china" would be construed as a gift of the whole collection at the date of death.

Drafting specific gifts

The solicitor should take great care to ascertain the testator's wishes. The testator **22.27** may wish to give a particular item owned at the date the will is made or may wish to give any item which corresponds to a particular description owned at the date of death.

If the testator wishes to give a particular item owned at the date of the will, the property must be carefully identified. This may be relatively easy where, for example, shares are involved but difficulties can arise where the gift is of personal chattels. Thus, a gift of "my gold ring" may give rise to problems if the testator owned several gold rings. A reference to provenance, a description or an insurance valuation may be helpful in identifying the particular ring given.

When taking instructions, the solicitor should explain to the client that a gift of a particular item owned at the date of the will suffers ademption if the item is sold, destroyed or changed in substance. The result of such ademption is that the beneficiary will get nothing. This may or may not be what the testator wishes.

If the testator wants the beneficiary to receive any item owned at the death corresponding to a particular description, suitable wording should be used. An example of such wording is, "I give to [AB] any motor car which I own at the date of my death".

In some cases, the testator may wish to give a particular item with a provision for a substitutional gift if that item is sold, destroyed or changed in substance. A suggested wording is "I GIVE to [AB] absolutely my grand piano or any other piano which has replaced it and which I own at the date of my death". Such wording is not desirable where there may be several changes between the making of the will and the death (for example, where a testator makes a gift of shares) as it may prove difficult to identify the replacement assets accurately. In such a case it may be preferable for the testator to include a pecuniary legacy to be given in substitution of the original property, if that property is not owned at the date of death.

Power to select

22.28 Specific legacies are often made as a way of passing a "keepsake" to a friend or relative. An outright gift of items of property causes no difficulty but if the testator wishes property to be shared between beneficiaries as they choose then various matters should be considered:

(a) the order of selection if more than one beneficiary has this right;

(b) the insertion of a time limit to avoid the executors' having to wait an unspecified length of time before the beneficiary or beneficiaries make up their minds;

(c) a procedure for resolution of disputes (for example by the executors);

(d) a gift over to a substitutional beneficiary in the event of a beneficiary predeceasing or the beneficiaries failing to choose all the items, as the case may be; and

(e) a limit on the value of items selected.

Mortgage, expenses and inheritance tax

22.29 (a) *Mortgage.* Where a gift is made of property which was charged during the testator's lifetime with a mortgage or other debt the Administration of Estates Act 1925 s.35 provides that the property passes to the beneficiary subject to that debt unless the will provides otherwise. The effect of s.35 should, therefore, be explained to the testator so that if he or she wishes the beneficiary to take the property free of the debt, suitable wording can be included. An example of such wording is "I GIVE to [AB] my leasehold property known as [address] free of all taxes and from any mortgage debt or other charge affecting it which I direct shall be paid out of my residuary estate". The solicitor should remember that in the case of a mortgage, a mortgage protection policy may have been taken out by the testator. The solicitor should, therefore, enquire whether or not such a policy exists so that the testator can give thought to the destination of the estate bearing in mind the existence of the policy (see para.15.10, above).

(b) *Expenses.* Unless the will provides otherwise, specific beneficiaries bear any costs of insuring, packing and transporting of property left to them in a will from the time that the assent is made in their favour. This should be explained to the testator who may not wish a specific beneficiary to bear the costs. This is especially likely where the nature of the gift or the circumstances of the beneficiary would result in high insurance or transportation costs being incurred, which the beneficiary might have difficulty meeting. Contrary provision in the will may ensure that the costs are borne by residue.

(c) *"Free of tax"*. Whenever the disposition of an estate may give rise to an inheritance tax liability, the testator should consider which beneficiaries should bear the burden. Inheritance tax on UK free estate which vests in the personal representatives is usually a testamentary expense borne by undisposed of property (if any) or residue unless the will provides otherwise. The draftsman may consider providing expressly that non-residuary gifts are to be "free of tax" so that the question of burden is brought to the testator's attention. The testator can then consider whether the disposition of the estate is suitable having regard to the burden of inheritance tax.

General legacies

A general legacy is a gift of property which is not in any way distinguished from **22.30** property of the same kind (for example, a gift of "100 shares in ABC Ltd"). If the testator does not own such property at death, the personal representatives will purchase property fulfilling the description. Unless there are special reasons for such a gift, a gift of money is usually more appropriate.

Particular problems arising from pecuniary legacies

Particular problems arise where a pecuniary legacy is given to a minor as, in the **22.31** absence of an express direction, a minor cannot give a good receipt. (This problem was discussed in para.18.17, above).

Problems also arise where a pecuniary legacy is given to an unincorporated association. Such an association has no legal identity separate from its individual members. Therefore, a legacy to such an association is construed as a gift to all the individual members. In the absence of an express provision in the will the personal representative would have to obtain a receipt from each individual member of the association. This would be an onerous and time consuming task and, therefore, it is advisable to provide that the receipt of the person appearing to be the treasurer, bursar or other appropriate officer will be sufficient to give the personal representatives a good discharge. An example of such a clause is:

> "I GIVE free of tax to the [name of club or other institution] of [address] the sum of
> £ . . . with freedom to spend it as income. The receipt of the person who appears to

[my Trustees] to be the treasurer or other proper officer of [name of club or other institution] shall be a good discharge to [my Trustees]."

When drafting a gift to an unincorporated association, the draftsman, having taken appropriate instructions from the testator, should ensure that:

(a) the association is in existence;

(b) the association is correctly identified; and

(c) should the testator so wish, provision is included to cover a change of name, change of objects, the amalgamation of the association with another similar body or the dissolution of the association prior to the testator's death.

Where a gift is left to a charity which ceases to exist during the lifetime of the testator, the gift will not lapse but will be applied *cy-près* provided the testator showed a general charitable intention. If this is in accordance with the testator's wishes, it may be desirable to include words clearly showing a general charitable intent, for example, "To X association for its general charitable purposes". It is important to check whether any particular institution has charitable status.

6. GIFTS OF RESIDUE

22.32 Once the formal parts of the will and any specific or pecuniary legacies have been drafted, it is necessary to consider the drafting of the clause or clauses disposing of residue. The main objective of the draftsman in drafting such clauses is to ensure that the residue of the estate goes to the testator's intended beneficiaries. This will include consideration of whether substitutional beneficiaries should be included in case a primary beneficiary fails to achieve a vested interest and whether a survivorship provision is required. The draftsman should also consider how best to deal with the payment of debts and expenses (which will usually be paid out of residue).

Payment of debts

22.33 The rules as to payment of debts of the estate were considered in Ch.15 where we saw that, unless there is undisposed of property, unsecured debts are, in most circumstances, payable out of residue. This will usually comply with the testator's wishes but, even so, it is usual to make express provision in a professionally drawn will. One way in which this is commonly done is by making the residuary gift subject to the payment of debts and other expenses.

For example, "I GIVE all the residue of my estate (out of which shall be paid my debts, funeral expenses and testamentary expenses) to [AB] of [address]".

Another way in which payment of debts can be provided for is by creating a trust, the first object of which is the payment of debts.

Where a debt of the estate is charged during the deceased's lifetime on specific property it will be payable out of that property unless the will shows a contrary intention (Administration of Estates Act 1925 s.35). Clauses, such as those above which deal with the payment of debts generally, are not sufficient to require charged debts to be paid out of residue. If the intention is that charged debts should be paid out of residue then words such as "including any debts charged on specific property" should be added after the word "debts" in the clauses above.

Payment of pecuniary legacies

The rules as to property available for payment of pecuniary legacies are con-   **22.34** sidered in Ch.16. They are complicated and, in order to avoid possible problems, it is desirable to direct that residue be held on trust for sale and proceeds used to pay debts and legacies. This has the effect of making realty available proportionately with personalty under the rule in *Roberts v Walker*. It also ensures that, in cases where residue has been left to two or more persons equally and one has predeceased (with the result that part of the residue is undisposed of), it is clear that legacies are to be paid before the residue is divided into shares. This avoids the possibility of costly disputes between residuary beneficiaries and the persons entitled to the testator's undisposed of property.

Inclusion of a trust

In some cases a trust of residue should be included. A trust is advisable where the   **22.35** residue is to be divided between two or more beneficiaries or where minors may be entitled to residue. Before the Trusts of Land and Appointment of Trustees Act 1996 an express trust for sale (with power to postpone sale) was generally employed so as to avoid the complication of the Settled Land Act 1925. The trustees of a "trust of land" as defined by the 1996 Act have all the powers of an absolute owner, including sale, so an express trust for sale is no longer necessary. However, if there is no land in the residuary estate, any trust created will fall outside the definition of a "trust of land" with the consequence that the statutory powers will not be available to the trustees. An express trust for sale may, therefore, be considered despite the 1996 Act. If such a trust is included it should include a power to postpone sale. If an express trust for sale is included and the residuary estate does in fact contain land, the trust will be a "trust of land" under the 1996 Act. An alternative approach is to create a trust of residue without a trust for sale but with a power of sale. Again this will be a "trust of land" if there is any land included in the residue. If there is no land then the trustees will be able to exercise their power of sale under the express power of sale in the will.

Personal representatives also have a power to sell the assets of the estate for purposes of administration under the Administration of Estates Act 1925 s.39.

Absolute gift of residue to one person

Where the residue is to be given to one person absolutely, the drafting of the will   **22.36** is quite straightforward. For example "I GIVE the residue of my estate (out of which shall be paid my funeral and testamentary expenses and my debts) to [AB] of [address]." The draftsman should consider whether to make a substitutional gift so as to prevent an intestacy if the intended residuary beneficiary predeceases and whether to include a survivorship clause (see para.22.41, below).

Absolute gift of residue to more than one person

Named beneficiaries

22.37   If the residue is to be divided between two or more persons in equal shares, the following form may be used "I GIVE the residue of my estate (out of which shall be paid my funeral and testamentary expenses and my debts) to [AB] of [address] and [CD] of [address] in equal shares". If the shares are to be unequal the simplest technique is to divide the residue into a suitable number of equal parts and to say how many parts each beneficiary is to get.

Where residue is given "equally" or "in equal shares" and any of the residuary beneficiaries predecease, there will be a partial intestacy. It is, therefore, desirable to add words giving the lapsed share to the surviving beneficiaries or words making a substitutional gift of that share (for example, to the children of the deceased beneficiary). If it is intended that the surviving beneficiaries are to take a larger share suitable wording of the whole clause would be, "I GIVE the residue of my estate (out of which shall be paid my funeral and testamentary expenses and my debts) to such of the following as survive me [by 28 days] and if more than one in equal shares [list names and addresses of beneficiaries]".

Difficulties may arise where some but not all of the beneficiaries are exempt. This is dealt with in para.4.72, above.

Class gifts

22.38   Many gifts of residue to more than one person are gifts to a class of beneficiaries rather than to several named individuals. Most class gifts are gifts to a particular class of relative. The draftsman should explain the class closing rules to the testator and explain that they may artificially exclude certain unborn persons. They should also explain that the exclusion of the class closing rules is possible but may delay final distribution of the estate.

A draftsman should consider carefully whether or not it is desirable to include words expressly limiting class gifts to persons *living at the testator's death*. Where there is an immediate gift to a class (for example, "to my grandchildren") the class closing rules apply (unless excluded). Their effect is that the class will close at the date of the testator's death and will include only those class members living or *en ventre sa mere* at that date (if there are no members living or *en ventre sa mere* at that date the class remains open indefinitely). This is likely to accord with the wishes of most testators since, although it will exclude any later born class members, it does allow the benefits of early distribution. Many precedents state expressly that such gifts are to be limited to persons *living at the testator's death.* These words merely restate the relevant class closing rule but it is desirable to include them to ensure that the testator is aware of the position.

Where a gift to a class is contingent (for example, "to those of my grand-children who reach 18") or deferred (for example, "to X for life and then to my grandchildren") the class closing rules apply (unless excluded). Their effect is, broadly speaking (but see Ch.16 for a fuller discussion), that such a class will remain open until the first class member fulfils the contingency or until the life tenant dies and will include any persons born after the date of the testator's death and before the date of which the class closes. This is likely to accord with the wishes of most testators. Since any distribution is impossible until one person fulfils the contingency or until any life tenant dies, there is no point in closing the class until distribution is possible. If the words *living at my death* are included they limit the gift to persons alive or *en ventre sa mere* at the testator's death and exclude any born thereafter. Unless this is an accurate reflection of the testator's wishes it is desirable not to include the words.

Where a testator wants to keep the class open to include beneficiaries born after the first member has attained a vested interest, it is possible to draft the gift to allow the trustees to distribute the "share" of the first beneficiary and to hold what is left for the remaining class members plus any new additions to the class. (A specimen clause is set out below.)

> "My trustees shall hold the trust fund on trust absolutely for such of my grand-children living at my death **or born afterwards** at any time during their parents' lifetime as reach the age of 18 or marry under that age and if more than one in equal shares PROVIDED that the share in the Trust Fund of any grandchild who has attained a vested interest shall not be diminished by the birth or marriage of or the attainment of 18 by any further grandchildren."

Example

> A testator makes a gift of £600,000 to his grandchildren contingent on reaching 18 in the terms set out above. Three grandchildren, A, B and C are living at the date of death. A reaches 18.
>
> A will take one third of the fund (£200,000) on reaching 18. The class will remain open. If two additional grandchildren, D and E, are born, the trustees will hold the remaining £400,000 on trust for B, C, D and E who will each receive £100,000.

Care should also be taken with the definition of the class so as to avoid any ambiguity and so as to comply with the testator's wishes. If the testator says that they wish to benefit their "cousins", further instructions are needed to establish what degree of relationship is intended. A reference to any class of relative does not include relatives by marriage. Thus, a testator who wishes to benefit "neph-ews and nieces" should be asked whether the nephews and nieces of their spouse are to be included or only their own nephews and nieces (if the spouse's nephews and nieces are to be included in the gift then suitable words must be inserted in the will). Unless contrary provision is made, a reference to any class of relative is deemed to include adopted relatives of the testator but not, for example, stepchildren who have not been adopted. The fact that a person's parents were not married to each other at the time of their birth is irrelevant for the purposes of succession to property unless a contrary intention is expressed in the will.

As with gifts to named beneficiaries the will should make it clear what is to happen to the share of a member of the class who predeceases. A class gift (for example, "to my nieces") is normally construed as a gift to those nieces who survive the testator. There will, therefore, be no question of lapse unless all the members of the class predecease the testator. The testator may wish to include a substitutional clause providing that, if any member of the class predeceases the testator leaving issue who survive the testator, the issue will take *per stirpes* the share which their parent would have taken. In the case of a class gift to *children or issue of a testator*, s.33(2) of the Wills Act 1837, as substituted by the Administration of Justice Act 1982 s.19, provides that such a substitution shall take place unless a contrary intention appears by the will. Despite this provision, it is probably desirable to include express words of substitution so that the matter is brought to the testator's attention and so that there can be no doubt as to his or her wishes. Suitable wording is given in para.22.42, below.

Successive interests in residue

22.39   The testator may wish to create a life or other limited interest in the residue of the estate. In such a case it is best to include an express trust, the first object of which is to pay debts and legacies. The trustees are then directed to pay income to the life tenant and, subject thereto, to hold the balance for the remainderman. For example, "ON TRUST to pay the income thereof to [name of life tenant] during his lifetime and subject thereto ON TRUST for [name of remainderman] absolutely".

The life tenant will frequently be the testator's spouse or civil partner, in which case the testator may wish to ensure that the spouse is entitled to occupy the matrimonial home for life. This can be achieved by making a specific devise of the matrimonial home (so that it is not part of residue). If the matrimonial home is part of residue there will be a trust of land. Section 12 of the Trusts of Land and Appointment of Trustees Act 1996 then gives the beneficiary a right of occupation.

A testator may wish to give the trustees power to advance or lend capital to the life tenant.

Contingent interests in residue

22.40   A gift of residue, whether to a named beneficiary, a number of named beneficiaries or a class and whether immediate or in remainder, may be contingent on the happening of some event or the satisfaction of some condition. (For example, "To such of my children as survive me and reach 18 or marry under that age".) Wherever the gift is contingent the testator should be asked to decide what is to happen to the income pending the satisfaction of the contingency and what is to happen if the contingency is never satisfied. In the absence of any direction to the contrary the provisions of the Trustee Act s.31 (as to which see paras 11.15–11.17, above) will apply in respect of the income. If the contingency is never satisfied, the capital and any income which has been added to it will pass as on an intestacy unless there is a substitutional gift.

The effect of the rule against perpetuities should be considered whenever a contingent gift is made. A gift which would vest outside the perpetuity period is void. The perpetuity period is fixed at 125 years by the Perpetuities and Accumulations Act 2009—no other period may now be specified. Furthermore, the Act and its predecessor (the Perpetuity and Accumulations Act 1964) introduced various provisions which mitigate the severity of the rule against perpetuities. Thus, a gift which might vest outside the perpetuity period will not fail at the outset as it is possible to "wait and see"; it is possible, where necessary to save a gift, to reduce the age at which a gift will vest and/or to exclude members of a class from benefit where otherwise the whole gift would fail. As a result of these provisions problems of perpetuity are much less likely to lead to failure of benefit.

Survivorship clauses

A beneficiary who survives a testator by a very short time or who is deemed to **22.41** survive (under s.184 of the Law of Property Act 1925) will obtain a vested interest in any unconditional gift. Often a testator will want to provide that a beneficiary is not to benefit unless he or she survives for a reasonable period. This can be achieved by means of a "survivorship clause" which provides that the beneficiary is only to take if he or she survives the testator for a specified period, if he or she does not so survive, then a substitutional gift takes effect. Such clauses are particularly common in the case of gifts to spouses or civil partners (this is because the possibility of death in a common accident is greatest in the case of spouses or civil partners).

The advantage of a survivorship clause in such a case is that the testator retains control of the ultimate destination of the property—if there were no such clause then the property would pass on the death of the surviving spouse or civil partner according to the terms of the survivor's will or of the intestacy rules.

A survivorship clause should not be for more than six months since, if it is for longer, a settlement will be created for inheritance tax purposes and there may as a result be an unnecessary charge to tax. If there is a survivorship clause in a will, distribution of the estate cannot begin until the primary beneficiary dies (when the substitutional gift takes effect) or until the end of the period (when the primary beneficiary achieves a vested interest). Owing to the inconvenience of a long delay, it is usual for survivorship clauses to specify a period of 28 days or one month.

In the case of surviving spouses and civil partners the introduction of the transferable nil rate band means that there are circumstances in which for inheritance purposes it is preferable not to have a survivorship clause.

Example

H has £425,000 and W has £125,000. H dies when the nil rate band is £325,000 and W dies two weeks later. Each leaves their property to the other but if the other fails to survive by 28 days to their son, S.

Because of the survivorship clause, H's property passes to S and tax is payable on £100,000. W's passes to S but most of her nil rate band is wasted.

Without a survivorship clause H's property would have passed to W. The tranfer would be spouse exempt. The combined estates would pass from W to S. W would have the benefit of H's transferred nil rate band so no inheritance tax would be payable.

Substitutional gifts

22.42   When a specific or general legacy lapses the subject-matter "falls into residue" and goes to the residuary beneficiary. When a residuary gift fails, there is, prima facie, a partial intestacy. The draftsman should ascertain the testator's wishes as to the disposition of property in the event of a beneficiary predeceasing or failing to survive for a specified period. The testator may prefer to make a substitutional gift rather than have the property pass on intestacy. A suitable clause substituting one beneficiary for another if that other predeceases or fails to survive for a specified period is "I GIVE the residue of my estate to [AB] or if [he/she] shall predecease me or fail to survive for 28 days then to [CD]".

Where the primary beneficiary is the spouse or civil partner of the testator the effect of Wills Act 1837 ss.18A and 18C, must be remembered. A divorce or termination of a civil partnership causes a gift to a spouse or civil partner to fail. If the will gives residue to the spouse or civil partner, the residue will pass as undisposed of property unless a substitutional gift takes effect. Any property which is given by the will to the former spouse or civil partner passes as if they died on the date of the divorce, annulment or termination. A substitutional gift will therefore take effect even though it is expressed to be contingent on the spouse having predeceased or failed to survive for a specified period. (This last point applies only to deaths on or after January 1, 1996.)

Often the most appropriate substitutional beneficiaries are the children of the primary beneficiary. If the gift of residue is to the testator's children, the testator may decide that the property be divided amongst the surviving children or that the share of a deceased child should go to that child's children or remoter issue. If the will is silent, then the Wills Act 1837 s.33 (as substituted) provides that, if a child of the testator predeceases leaving issue who survive the testator, the issue take the share that their parent would have taken.

Despite s.33, it is advisable to include an express substitutional gift so that the testator is given an opportunity to consider whether or not the clause accords with their wishes. (An express substitutional gift is always required if the original gift is to anyone other than a child or issue of the testator.) A suitable clause for a substitution of a child by their own issue on the assumption that there is a trust for sale of residue is:

"[My Trustees] shall hold [my Residuary Estate] ON TRUST for such of my children as are living at my death and if more than one in equal shares PROVIDED THAT if any child of mine dies before me leaving issue living at my death [or born after it who reach the age of 18] such issue shall take by substitution and if more than one in equal shares per stirpes the share of [my Residuary Estate] as that child of mine would otherwise have taken".

(Note that, under this clause issue of a non-marital relationship will take. If the testator wishes to exclude them, express provision must be made.) If desired a further substitution providing for the possibility of the testator dying without any living issue may be included. However, in drafting a substitutional clause unnecessary complications arising from the remote possibility of a large number of potential beneficiaries predeceasing the testator should be avoided by advising the testator of the need to make a new will if circumstances change.

7. ADMINISTRATIVE POWERS

Introduction

As we saw in Ch.11 personal representatives and trustees have various powers **22.43** conferred on them by statute which can be excluded, restricted or extended by the will. It is also possible for the will to confer additional powers on the personal representatives. We will now list and consider some of the more common extensions and additions. The purpose of including such clauses is to facilitate the administration of the estate and of any trust which may arise under the will.

Common extensions to powers of personal representatives

Power to appropriate assets without consent of beneficiary

(a) The personal representatives have a power under s.41 of the Admini- **22.44**
stration of Estates Act to appropriate assets in or towards satisfaction of
a legacy bequeathed by the deceased or interest under the intestacy
rules but must obtain the consent of the beneficiary (or other specified
persons as set out in para.11.19, above).

It is administratively convenient for personal representatives to be
excused from the necessity of obtaining formal consent (even though
they would, no doubt, informally consult with the beneficiaries and
would be under an obligation to exercise their powers in good faith).

A further reason for continuing to give the personal representatives
a power to appropriate without consent is that the Revenue may view
an appropriation with consent as a sale for a variety of tax purposes. It
is, therefore, desirable to ensure that the personal representatives have
both a power to appropriate with consent and without consent enabling
them to choose the most tax effective method. A suitable form of
wording would be: "This power is exercisable in addition to the power
conferred by Administration of Estates Act 1925 s.41".

(b) Since an appropriation is in effect a sale of assets to the beneficiary, any
personal representative who is beneficially entitled to a part of the
estate and who makes an appropriation in their own favour will be
purchasing estate property. There is authority that this is permissible

(*Re Richardson* (1896)) but such a purchase might be attacked subsequently as a breach of the equitable rule that a trustee must not profit from their trust (see, for example, *Kane v Radley-Kane* (1999)). Where personal representatives are beneficially entitled it is, therefore, common to authorise such personal representatives to exercise the power to appropriate in their own favour.

The power to insure contained in Trustee Act 1925 s.19 (as amended by Trustee Act 2000) gives personal representatives and trustees power to insure as if they were absolute owners. Express power is therefore no longer needed.

Power to accept the receipt of parent or guardian on behalf of a minor or of the minor at a specified age

22.45
(a) An unmarried minor not in a civil partnership has no statutory power to give a good receipt for capital or income. A married minor or one in a civil partnership can give a good receipt for income only. The minor's parent, guardian, spouse or civil partner has power under the Children Act to give a good receipt on the minor's behalf (see para.18.17, above). A testator should consider whether it is appropriate to allow the legacy to pass into the hands of the parent or guardian (or spouse or civil partner). If not, the legacy can be left to trustees to hold until the child reaches a suitable age. It is probably good drafting to include a clause in the will authorising the personal representatives to accept the receipt of parent or guardian so that the testator is aware that this will happen.

(b) There is a statutory power under s.42 of the Administration of Estates Act for the personal representatives to appoint trustees to hold a legacy for a minor who is *absolutely* entitled but this does not apply if the minor has only a contingent interest. There is no reason why the testator should not expressly authorise the personal representatives to appoint trustees in such a case.

(c) The testator may authorise the minor to give a good receipt at a specified age, for example, 16.

(d) Alternatively, the will may direct the personal representatives to purchase a suitable investment (perhaps National Savings Certificates) in the name of the minor.

Exclusion of the Apportionment Act 1870 and the common law rules on apportionment

22.46 As we saw in Chs 16 and 18, the Apportionment Act 1870 requires that "rents, annuities, dividends and other periodical payments in the nature of income . . . shall, like interest on money lent, be considered as accruing from day to day" and shall be apportioned accordingly. Interest has to be apportioned under the common law rules. The trouble and expense involved in the calculations is usually thought to outweigh any benefits to the beneficiaries. As a result, in cases where the apportionment of income would otherwise be necessary (that is, where a will gives an income-producing asset to one person, residue to another) the Act and the common law rules are frequently excluded. The effect of exclusion is that all income paid to the personal representatives after death is treated as income of the estate for *distribution* purposes even though some or all of it may be attributable to the period before death.

Power to carry on a business of the deceased

As we saw in Ch.11 the powers of personal representatives to run a business carried on by the deceased as a sole trader are limited. It is, therefore, usual in cases where a testator is a sole trader to provide that personal representatives may: **22.47**

(a)   continue to run the business for as long as they see fit, and

(b)   use such assets of the estate as they see fit.

(A specimen clause is set out below.)

> "I DIRECT that [my Trustees] shall have power to carry on my business of [nature of business] for so long as they in their absolute discretion think fit and they shall have power to use any assets employed in that business at the date of my death together with any assets in my Residuary Estate I DECLARE that my Trustees shall have the same powers to carry on that business as if they were absolute owners of it without being personally liable for any loss that may arise I FURTHER DECLARE that in the event of my business being carried on at a loss my Trustees shall be reimbursed for any loss they suffer from my Residuary Estate."

It is most desirable that a sole trader should consider and make provision for the running of a business after their death, perhaps by taking in partners or by incorporation of the business during their lifetime. Such matters should certainly be discussed when drafting a will for a sole trader. The question of personal representatives should also be carefully considered. It is usually difficult to find a professional person who is willing to accept the office of personal representative where this would involve the running or supervision of a business. Where the business is to be transferred to a beneficiary it may be helpful to appoint that beneficiary either as a general personal representative or as a special personal representative to deal only with the business.

Where a client is a partner in a business or runs a business through the medium of a limited company it is desirable to discuss with the client what provisions if any have been included in the partnership agreement or Articles of Association to deal with death. Matters which should be considered are whether persons surviving the deceased should have options to purchase the interest of a deceased partner/shareholder and what financial arrangements should be made for the dependants of the deceased.

Common extensions to powers of trustees

22.48 These extensions should be considered where a will creates a trust initially (for example by leaving property to a spouse for life) or where a trust may arise if a beneficiary predeceases the testator (for example, "to my spouse absolutely but if he does not survive me by 28 days for such of our children as may reach the age of 25"; even if all the testator's children are over 25 at the time the will is drafted a trust may still arise if a child predeceases and is replaced by issue).

Power to invest

22.49 As we saw in Ch.11 trustees and personal representatives are now given very wide powers of investment. No express power is needed. In rare cases a testator may wish to restrict the power of investment for which purpose a clause could be included in the will.

Power to purchase a house as a residence for a beneficiary

22.50 The Trustee Act 2000 s.8 gives trustees and personal representatives power to buy freehold or leasehold land in the UK including the power to do so "for occupation by a beneficiary" (s.8(1)(b)). An express power would be needed if the personal representatives were to be able to buy a house outside the UK for a beneficiary.

Power to advance capital to beneficiaries with a vested or contingent interest in capital

22.51 We saw in Ch.11 that trustees have a statutory power under s.32 of the Trustee Act 1925 to advance capital to beneficiaries with a vested or contingent interest *in capital*, but that it is subject to the following three limitations:

(a) No more than one half of the beneficiary's vested or presumptive interest can be advanced.

(b) Any advances must be brought into account when and if the beneficiary becomes absolutely entitled.

(c) Any person with a prior interest (for example, the right to receive income from the trust property) must be in existence, of full age and must consent in writing to the advance.

It is common to give the trustees wider powers of advancement by excluding some or all of the limitations listed above and giving them power to advance in their absolute discretion. The case of *Henley v Wardell* (1989) illustrates the need for careful drafting. A will enlarged the powers conferred by s.32 "so as to permit my trustees in their absolute and uncontrolled discretion to advance . . . the whole . . . of any . . . share . . . ". The trustees made advances without the consent of the life tenant arguing that as they had an "absolute" and "uncontrolled" discretion such consent was unnecessary. It was held that the only purpose of the enlargement of trustees' powers was to permit the advancement of "the whole" of a share and that the wording was not sufficient to do away with the need for consents. It is important, therefore, in cases where there is a prior interest and reference is made to enlarging the statutory power expressly to exclude the need for consent. For example, in such a case the clause should include the words:

" ... without the need to secure the consent of any person with a prior interest."

Advances of capital may give rise to inheritance tax in certain circumstances see para.7.14.

A testator may also wish to include an express power authorising trustees to *lend* money to beneficiaries on whatever terms they think fit.

Power to advance capital and make loans to life tenants

The statutory power to advance capital to beneficiaries is only available where **22.52** beneficiaries have an interest in capital. There is no statutory power to advance capital to a life tenant. Neither is there a statutory power to lend capital to a life tenant. A testator, who is proposing to leave property to a person for life, may wish to give the trustees a power to advance or lend capital to the life tenant in case the life tenant finds the income insufficient. This is particularly likely where a testator proposes to leave a life interest to a spouse or civil partner.

Advances and loans to a life tenant with a qualifying interest in possession will have no inheritance tax effect since the life tenant is already treated as the owner of the underlying trust assets. A settlement where the life tenant does not have a qualifying interest in possession is a relevant property settlement and an advance or a loan will trigger an exit charge under IHTA 1984 ss.68 or 69. See paras 7.22 and 7.24, above.

Power to apply income for maintenance, education or benefit of minor beneficiaries

We saw in Ch.11 that trustees have power under the Trustee Act 1925 s.31 to **22.53** apply available income to the maintenance, education or benefit of minor beneficiaries and that to the extent that they do not, such income must be accumulated. If the beneficiary reaches the age of 18 and the interest is still contingent the discretion ceases and the trustees must pay the income to the beneficiary until the interest vests or fails. The testator may wish to remove the right so that the discretion continues.

Section 31(1) provides that the trustees may apply the whole of the income or such part as may in all the circumstances be reasonable; they are required to have regard to the age of the minor and their requirements and generally the circumstances of the case and in particular to what other income, if any, is applicable for the same purpose; where trustees have notice that the income of more than one fund is applicable for these purposes, then so far as practicable unless the entire income of the funds is paid or applied as aforesaid or the court otherwise directs, a proportionate part only of the income of each fund shall be so paid or applied. It may be appropriate to remove the restrictions on the power to apply income by a suitable clause in the will.

Exclusion of the Apportionment Act 1870 and the common law rules on apportionment

22.54   We have already explained in para.22.46, above that it is usual to exclude the need to apportion for the purposes of distribution of the estate on the death of a testator. However, the duty to apportion does not arise only on the death of a testator. If a trust is created in favour of a person for life, the duty arises on the death of the life tenant. Similarly, if there is a trust in favour of those members of a class who fulfil a contingency, a need to apportion arises whenever an additional member joins the class (for example, by birth or whenever an existing member leaves the class either by attaining a vested interest or by dying before reaching a specified age (*Re Joel's Will Trusts* (1967)). It is, therefore, most important that any clause intended to exclude the duty to apportion is drafted sufficiently widely to exclude it not merely on the death of the testator but on any other occasion where it would otherwise apply.

Exclusion of the equitable rules as to apportionment

22.55   We saw in para.18.18, above, that where residuary personalty is left to persons in succession there is an obligation under the rule in *Howe v Lord Dartmouth* (1802) to sell wasting, hazardous and unauthorised assets together with reversionary interests and non-income producing assets; where such an obligation arises the personal representatives will be under a duty to apportion between life tenant and remainderman any income received pending sale from assets in the first category and to apportion the proceeds of the sale of assets in the second category between life tenant and remainderman. Similarly, under the rule in *Allhusen v Whittell* (1867) where residue (real or personal) is left to persons in succession outgoings must be treated as paid partly from capital and partly from the income accruing from that portion of capital from the testator's death to the date of payment of the outgoings. It is extremely common to exclude these rules so as to avoid the need for complex calculations. The rules do not apply on the death of a life tenant and it is, therefore, unnecessary to exclude them on the death of the life tenant. No similar calculations are required for inheritance tax or income tax purposes.

Power to charge

22.56   The general rule is that personal representatives and trustees may not charge for their services in the absence of express provision to the contrary. However, the Trustee Act 2000 s.29 provides an important exception to this rule. Under this section a trust corporation or a person acting in a professional capacity as a personal representative or trustee is entitled to "reasonable remuneration" for any services that they provide to or on behalf of the trust, provided each other personal representative or trustee (as the case may be) gives written agreement to this. If the will itself makes "any provision about the personal representative or trustee's entitlement to remuneration" then s.29 does not apply—the terms of the will take priority.

Despite the statutory provisions, charging clauses should be included in a will which appoints a professional person to be a personal representative both because the approval of other personal representatives will not then be needed and because it will make the position clear to the beneficiaries.

Where provision is made in the will for remuneration to a trust corporation or person acting in a professional capacity, the Trustee Act 2000 s.28 provides that this is not to be regarded as a gift. Consequently, the entitlement to the remuneration will not be void if the professional personal representative witnessed the will nor will it abate if the estate is insufficient to pay legacies. There is now a presumption that provision for payment for services is to include payment in respect of services even if they are services which a lay personal representative could perform personally.

Indemnity

Personal representatives and trustees have a statutory power to indemnify them- **22.57** selves for expenses incurred in carrying out their powers and duties (Trustee Act 2000 s.31). A testator may wish to extend this to provide that they shall not be liable for any loss resulting from improper investment or from any mistake or omission made in good faith. However, it may be thought inappropriate to include such a clause particularly in the case of professional trustees.

Will drafting implications of the Trusts of Land and Appointment of Trustees Act 1996

This Act imposes certain terms on trusts of which practitioners should be aware. **22.58** Section 11 requires trustees of land, so far as is practicable, to consult beneficiaries of full age with an interest in possession when exercising any function in respect of land and so far as it is consistent with the general interest of the trust to give effect to their wishes. The section does not apply if the trust instrument includes a declaration that it should not. It seems desirable to relieve the trustees from *the obligation* to consult by including such a declaration.

Section 12 gives a beneficiary who is beneficially entitled to an interest in possession in land a right to occupy the land if either:

(a) the purposes of the trust include making the land available for their occupation; or

(b) the land is held by the trustees so as to be so available.

"Interest in possession" is not defined in the Act. It has the same meaning as for inheritance tax. Land held by trustees "so as to be available" for occupation by the beneficiary includes land which is suitable for this occupation and is not occupied by someone else (such as a tenant under a lease).

Section 13 goes on to provide that where there is more than one beneficiary entitled to occupy land then the trustees may exclude or restrict the entitlement of one or more (but not all) of the beneficiaries. The trustees may impose conditions on the occupying beneficiary (for example, payment of expenses) and may require the occupying beneficiary to make compensation payments to any excluded beneficiaries or forgo benefits to which they would otherwise be entitled.

These provisions seem unduly complex and are to be avoided if at all possible. When drafting a will it may be desirable to state that "the purposes of the trust do not include making land available for occupation by beneficiaries". The problem is that the testator may wish to give the trustees power to buy land as a residence for a beneficiary. The mere inclusion of such a power might suggest that, despite the declaration, the purposes of the trust did include making land available for occupation (and once the land is purchased it will be "so available" under s.12(1)(b)). (There is of course an arguable distinction between a power and a purpose.)

A further problem is that if the trustees decide to buy land as an investment for the trust, a beneficiary might be able to insist on occupying it under s.12(1)(b) if the property was vacant. The inclusion of a declaration as to the purposes of the trust would then be of no relevance. However, even though a declaration as to purpose will not always be of any help in escaping ss.12 and 13, it may help sometimes and it is difficult to see that it can ever do any harm.

Section 19 allows beneficiaries who are of full age and capacity (i.e. sui juris) and between them absolutely entitled to the trust property to require the trustees to retire and to appoint replacements specified by the beneficiaries. This provision will not apply if the trust instrument says that it should not.

While the prospect of beneficiaries arbitrarily removing and replacing trustees may seem alarming, it is important to look at the matter in context. Beneficiaries who are sui juris can in any event always bring a trust to an end and resettle the property with trustees of their choice. The drawback of so doing is that the termination of the trust will give rise to a potential capital gains tax liability. The s.19 power prevents there being a charge to capital gains tax.

It is likely that for most people the tax advantage will outweigh the concern over the arbitrary replacement of trustees so only rarely will it be appropriate to exclude the s.19 power.

Civil partnership

22.59   The Civil Partnership Act amends many statutes so that the status of a civil partner is in most respects the same as that of a spouse. However, it contains no presumption that terms such as "spouse", "husband", "wife" or "married" in a will or other document are to include civil partner or civil partnership. Express provision must therefore be made if, for example, the testator wishes to include civil partners of their children in a gift or trust or if they wish a gift to take effect on civil partnership as well as on marriage.

Human Fertilisation and Embryology Act (2009)

Section 48(1) of the HFEA provides that where a person is treated as a mother,   **22.60** father or parent of a child under ss.33, 35, 36, 42 or 43 (see para.3.10, above for details) that person is treated as the mother, father or parent of the child *for all purposes*. Subsection 5 provides that references "to any relationship between two people in any enactment, deed or other instrument or document (whenever passed or made) are to be read accordingly". It follows that gifts in a will to "my grandchildren", "my nephews and nieces", "my brothers and sisters" and similar expressions as well as gifts "to my children" will include persons whose relationship arises as a result of the act. If this is not what the testator wants then careful consideration should be given as to how the will is drafted. It may be that a gift, for example, "to my biological grandchildren" would circumvent s.48(1) but this is far from clear as there is a reference to "a relationship". As with many such problems the safest course is to name the beneficiaries where possible.

Section 53(2) provides that "any reference (howsoever expressed) to the father of a child who has a parent by virtue of ss.42 or 43 is to be read as a reference to the woman who is a parent of the child by virtue of that section". This is less likely to give rise to problems in drafting a will but a gift "to my father" would be a gift to the mother's civil partner if she is treated as a parent of the testator under s.42 not to the testator's biological father. In the unlikely event that a gift to the biological father is intended he should be named.

APPENDICES

Introduction

In this appendix we include blank forms of oaths for executors and administrators, a blank Inheritance Tax Account and a checklist for taking instructions in relation to drafting a will.

A1. Blank Forms of Oaths

PR1 – Oath for administrator(s)

IN THE HIGH COURT OF JUSTICE

FAMILY DIVISION

BIRMINGHAM DISTRICT PROBATE REGISTRY

IN THE ESTATE OF   **DECEASED**

I[3][4]

make oath and say that:

1. [5]

    of[6]   deceased

    was born on[7]   and died on

    aged[8]   domiciled in England and Wales.

2. I believe the paper writings now produced to and marked by me to contain the true and original last will and testament[9]   of the deceased.

3. To the best of my knowledge information and belief there was no land vested in the deceased which was settled previously to the death (and not by the will[9]   ) of the deceased and which remained settled land notwithstanding such death.

4. I am[10]   executor named in the said will[9]

5. I will

    (i) collect, get in and administer according to law the real and personal estate of the said deceased;

    (ii) when required to do so by the Court, exhibit in the Court a full inventory of the said estate and render an account thereof to the Court; and

    (iii) when required to do so by the High Court, deliver up to that Court the grant of probate.

6. To the best of my knowledge information and belief the gross estate passing under the grant [does not exceed] [amounts to] [11]£

    and the net estate [does not exceed] [amounts to] [11]£

    [and that this is not a case in which an Inheritance Tax Account is required to be delivered].[2]

7. That notice of this application has been given to[12]

                                                                     the executor

    to whom power is to be reserved.

8. [3][5]

Sworn by the said   ⎫

at   ⎪

this   day of   ⎬

before me   ⎭

Commissioner for Oaths/Solicitor

Notes to PR1

(1) Insert name, address, postcode and DX number (if any) of the solicitors extracting the grant and any reference required.

(2) Delete as appropriate.

(3) Full true name(s) of the executor(s) applying: any difference between this/these names and those appearing in the will (codicil(s)) may be explained by separate statement at the end of the oath or by separate affidavit of identity.

(4) Full permanent address, including postcode: any executor(s) acting in their professional capacity may use their business address.

(5) Full true name of the deceased appearing in the death certificate. If there is any other name by which the deceased was known or in which he/she held any asset this must be given and the reason why it should appear in the grant stated.

(6) Last permanent address, including postcode, of the deceased. If any former address is required to appear in the grant this must be inserted and the reason for its inclusion given.

(7) Insert dates of birth and death as they appear in the death certificate.

(8) Insert age or if not known precisely an approximation e.g. "over 65".

(9) Insert, if appropriate, "and (one) (two) (or as the case may be) codicil(s)".

(10) Insert "the sole" "the surviving" "two of" "three of" or as the case may be.

(11) Insert the gross and net figures from the Inheritance Tax Account or where there is no Account to be delivered, the values the estate does not exceed i.e. the gross value prescribed by the Inheritance Tax (Delivery of Accounts) (Excepted Estates) Regulations, set out in the PREP Form supplied by Laserform. The net value should be the actual net value of the estate rounded up to the nearest £1,000.

(12) Insert the name(s) of any executor(s) having power reserved.

Extracted by:[1]

PR2 – Oath for administrator(s)
IN THE HIGH COURT OF JUSTICE
FAMILY DIVISION
BIRMINGHAM DISTRICT PROBATE REGISTRY
IN THE ESTATE OF

DECEASED

I[3][4]

make oath and say that:

1. [5]

2. of[6]

deceased

3. was born on[7]   and died on
   aged[8]   domiciled in England and Wales intestate[9]
   [and without any other person entitled in priority to share in the estate by virtue of any enactment].[10]

4. A minority and a[2] life interest arises under the intestacy.[11]

5. To the best of my knowledge information and belief there was no land vested in the said deceased which was settled previously to the death of the said deceased and which remained settled notwithstanding such death.

6. I am the lawful[12]
   and one of the persons   entitled to share in the estate of the said deceased.

7. I will
   (i) collect, get in and administer according to law the real and personal estate of the said deceased;
   (ii) when required to do so by the Court, exhibit in the Court a full inventory of the said estate and render an account thereof to the Court; and
   (iii) when required to do so by the High Court, deliver up to that Court the grant of letters of administration.

8. To the best of my knowledge information and belief the gross estate passing under the grant [does not exceed] [amounts to] [13]£
   and the net estate [does not exceed] [amounts to] [13]£
   [and that this is not a case in which an Inheritance Tax Account is required to be delivered].[2]

9. [5]

Sworn by the said

at

this   day of

before me

Commissioner for Oaths/Solicitor

Notes to PR2
(1) Insert name, address, postcode and DX number (if any) of the solicitors extracting the grant and any reference required.
(2) Delete as appropriate.
(3) Full true name(s) of the applicant(s).
(4) Insert full permanent address, including postcode.
(5) Full true name of the deceased appearing in the death certificate. If there is any other name by which the deceased was known or in which he/she held any asset this must be inserted and the reason for its inclusion in the grant given.
(6) Last permanent address, including postcode, of the deceased. If any former address is required to appear in the grant this must be inserted and the reason for its inclusion given.
(7) Insert dates of birth and death as they appear in the death certificate.
(8) Insert age or if this is not known precisely an approximate e.g. "over 65".
(9) Insert the deceased's status at death, e.g. "a widow", "a bachelor" and the necessary clearings in accordance with Rule 22 N.C.P.R. 1987 e.g. "without issue or parent or brother or sister of the whole blood".
(10) Delete words in square brackets where the applicant is the surviving spouse or issue of the deceased.
(11) If either or both such interests arise two applicants for the grant are required.
(12) Delete "lawful" except where application is by the surviving spouse e.g. "lawful widow"; insert the relationship to the deceased e.g. "nephew and niece of the whole blood".
(13) Insert the gross and net values from the Inheritance Tax Account or, where there is no Account to be delivered, the values the estate does not exceed i.e. the gross value prescribed by the Inheritance Tax (Delivery of Accounts) (Excepted Estates) Regulations, set out in the PREP Form supplied by Laserform. The net value should be the actual net value of the estate rounded up to the nearest £1,000.

PR2

Extracted by:[(1)]

PR3 – Oath for administrator(s)
(with will annexed)

IN THE HIGH COURT OF JUSTICE

FAMILY DIVISION

BIRMINGHAM DISTRICT PROBATE REGISTRY

IN THE ESTATE OF   **DECEASED**

I[(3)(4)]

make oath and say that:

1. [(5)(6)]

                                                                                    deceased

    was born on[(7)]   and died on
    aged[(8)]   domiciled in England and Wales.
2. I believe the paper writings now produced to and marked by me to contain the true and original last
    will and testament[(9)]   of the deceased.
3. A minority and a[(2)] life interest arises in the estate.[(10)]
4. To the best of my knowledge information and belief there was no land vested in the deceased which
    was settled previously to the death (and not by the will[(9)]   ) of the deceased and
    which remained settled land notwithstanding such death.
5. [(11)]
6. I am[(12)]
7. I will
        (i) collect, get in and administer according to law the real and personal estate of the said
            deceased;
        (ii) when required to do so by the Court, exhibit in the Court a full inventory of the said estate
            and render an account thereof to the Court; and
        (iii) when required to do so by the High Court, deliver up to that Court the grant of letters of
            administration (with will).
8. To the best of my knowledge information and belief the gross estate passing under the grant [does
    not exceed] [amounts to] [(13)]£
    and the net estate [does not exceed] [amounts to] [(13)]£
    [and that this is not a case in which an Inheritance Tax Account is required to be delivered].[(2)]

Sworn by the said   ⎫
at   ⎪
this   day of   ⎬
before me   ⎪
                         ⎭
Commissioner for Oaths/Solicitor

Notes to PR3
(1) Insert name, address, postcode and DX number (if any) of the solicitors extracting the grant and any reference
required.
(2) Delete as appropriate.
(3) Full true name(s) of the applicant(s).
(4) Insert full permanent address, including postcode.
(5) Full true name of the deceased appearing in the death certificate. If there is any other name by which the deceased was
known or in which he/she held any asset this must be inserted and the reason for its inclusion in the grant given.
(6) Last permanent address, including postcode, of the deceased. If any former address is required to appear in the grant
this must be inserted and the reason for its inclusion given.
(7) Insert dates of birth and death as they appear in the death certificate.
(8) Insert age or if this is not known precisely an approximation e.g. "over 65".
(9) Insert, if appropriate, "and (one) (two) (or as the case may be) codicil(s)."
(10) If either or both such interests arise at least two applicants are required.
(11) Here set out the "clearing off" of the executor(s) by reciting their pre-decease or renunciation.
(12) Here set out the applicant(s) title to apply e.g. "the residuary legatee(s) and devisee(s)". See Rule 20 N.C.P.R. 1987.
(13) Insert the gross and net values from the Inheritance Tax Account or where there is no Account to be delivered the
values the estate does not exceed i.e. the gross value prescribed by the Inheritence Tax (Delivery of Accounts) (Excepted
Estates) Regulations, set out in the PREP Form supplied by Laserform. The net value should be actual net value of the
estate rounded up to the nearest £1,000.

PR3

A2. Checklist for taking instructions

1. *Details of testator*
   (a) Testator's full name
   (b) Any former name(s) or alias(es)
   (c) Address/occupation
   (d) Age (for purposes of tax advice)
   (e) Previous will? If so, what arrangements for revocation?

2. *Value of estate*
   (a) Property owned in testator's sole name
       House(s)
       Contents
       Car
       Jewellery
       Collections (e.g. stamps, coins)
       Cash
       Cash accounts (bank, building society etc.)
       National Savings Products
       Quoted shares
       ISAs, bonds etc
       Unit Trusts etc
       Unlisted shares
       Any other assets
   (b) Property owned with another as beneficial tenants in common
       Include all types of property as in (a) above
   (c) Property owned with another as beneficial joint tenants
       Include all types of property as in (a) above
   (d) Nominations
   (e) Pensions, Superannuation benefits—nominated?
   (f) Insurance policies—MWPA,
                          written in trust,
                          payable to estate
   (g) Trust property
   (h) Foreign property
   (i) Inter vivos gifts to date
   (j) Property likely to be inherited
   (k) Debts charged on property?
   (l) Mortgage protection policy
   (m) Business and Agricultural property

3. *Intended beneficiaries etc*
   (a) Spouse/civil partner/cohabitee—full name/size of estate of spouse etc.
   (b) Children—names/ages/marital status
   (c) Others—names/addresses

N.B. Explain Family Provision legislation particularly if disposition is away from immediate family. Include illegitimate children, children of previous marriage and step-children if any.

4. *Disposition of property*
   (a) Legacies
       (i) specific
       (ii) general
       (iii) free of tax/expenses/mortgage?
   N.B. Explain possibility of ademption of specific gifts.
   (b) Residue
   (c) Age at which beneficiaries are to take. N.B. tax consequences.
   (d) Directions as to substitutional gift where beneficiary predeceases.
       In case of gift to institution directions as to possible change of name, amalgamation, dissolution.
   (e) Provision for payment of debts? Secured debts?

5. *Extension of statutory powers*
   (a) No trust created (remember that a trust may arise where minor beneficiaries take by substitution the share of a deceased parent)
       (i) insurance
       (ii) appropriation
       (iii) receipt clause—infant—unincorporated association
       (iv) exclude Apportionment Act
   (b) Trust created
       as above *plus*
       (i) investment
       (ii) power to buy land
       (iii) maintenance
       (iv) advancement
       (v) loans to beneficiaries
       (vi) exclude legal and equitable apportionments if appropriate
   N.B. Although powers are implied in "trust of land" consider possibility that land will not be included in estate.

6. *Executors/Trustees*
   (a) Choice—explain merits of individuals, solicitors' firms, banks
   (b) Charging clause if appropriate
   (c) Special PR's to deal with special parts of estate, e.g. literary executors
   (d) Name and addresses of intended executors

7. *Guardians*
   (a) Names and addresses
   (b) Willing to act?
   (c) Finance?

8. *Special problems*
   (a) Testator suffering from disability—capacity? Special attestation clause?
   (b) Testator sole trader—special provisions to deal with business?
   (c) Any promises about disposal of property including promises which might lead to promissory estoppel and mutual wills.

9. *Directions as to body, funeral, etc.*

A3. Blank Form IHT 400

 **HM Revenue & Customs**

Inheritance Tax account
IHT400

When to use this form

Fill in this form if:
- the deceased died on or after 18 March 1986, and
- there is Inheritance Tax to pay, or
- there is no Inheritance Tax to pay, but the estate does not qualify as an excepted estate.

The IHT400 Notes, page 1, gives details about excepted estates.

Deadline

You must send this form to us within 12 months of the date of death. Interest will be payable after six months.

The Inheritance Tax (IHT) account

The account is made up of this form and separate Schedules. You will have to fill in some of the Schedules.

To help you get started
- Gather the deceased's papers and the information you have about the deceased's estate. Make a list of the deceased's assets, liabilities, investments and other financial interests and any gifts made.
- Fill in boxes 1 to 28 then work through boxes 29 to 48 of this form to identify which Schedules you will need. If you do not have them all:
   - download them from **www.hmrc.gov.uk/inheritancetax/** or
   - phone the helpline to request them.
- Fill in the Schedules before moving on to complete this form.

IHT reference number

If there is any tax to pay, you will need to apply for an IHT reference number and payslip before you send this form to us. You can apply online at **www.hmrc.gov.uk/inheritancetax/** or fill in form IHT422 and send it to us. Apply for a reference at least two weeks before you plan to send us this form.

Filling in this form

- Use the IHT400 Notes to help you fill in this form.
- Fill in the form in black or blue ink.
- Make full enquiries so you can show that the figures you give and the statements you make are correct.
- If an instrument of variation has been signed before applying for a grant, fill in the form to show the effect of the Will/intestacy and instrument together. *See IHT400 Notes.*

Answer all the questions and fill in the boxes to help us process your form.

Help

For more information or help or another copy of this form:
- go to **www.hmrc.gov.uk/inheritancetax/**
- phone our helpline on **0845 30 20 900**
   - if calling from outside the UK, phone **+44 115 974 3009.**

Deceased's details

1 Deceased's name
Title - enter MR, MRS, MISS, MS or other title

Surname

First name(s)

2 Date of death *DD MM YYYY*

3 IHT reference number (if known) *See note at the top of this form*

4 Was the deceased male or female?

Male ☐   Female ☐

5 Deceased's date of birth *DD MM YYYY*

6 Where was the deceased domiciled at the date of death?

- England & Wales ☐
- Scotland ☐
- Northern Ireland ☐
- other country ☐   *specify country in box below*

See IHT400 Notes for information about domicile.

If the deceased was not domiciled in the UK, fill in
IHT401 now, and then the rest of the form.

If the deceased was domiciled in Scotland at the date of death

7 Has the legitim fund been discharged in **full** following the death? *See IHT400 Notes*

Yes ☐   *Go to box 8*

No ☐   *Please provide a full explanation in the 'Additional information' boxes, pages 15 and 16*

Deceased's details

8 Was the deceased:

- married or in a civil partnership ☐

- single ☐

- widowed or a surviving civil partner ☐

- divorced or a former civil partner? ☐

9 If the deceased was married or in a civil partnership at the time of their death, on what date did the marriage or registration of the civil partnership take place?
DD MM YYYY

☐☐ ☐☐ ☐☐☐☐

10 Who survived the deceased? *Tick all that apply*

- a spouse or civil partner ☐

- brothers or sisters ☐

- parents ☐

- children ☐ number ☐☐

- grandchildren ☐ number ☐☐

11 Deceased's last known permanent address
Postcode

☐☐☐☐ ☐☐☐☐

House number

☐☐☐☐☐

Rest of address, including house name or flat number

12 Was the property in box 11 owned or part-owned by the deceased or did the deceased have a right to live in the property?

Yes ☐   *Go to box 13*

No ☐   *Give details below. For example, 'deceased lived with daughter' or 'address was a nursing home'*

13 Deceased's occupation, or former occupation if retired, for example, 'retired doctor'

14 Deceased's National Insurance number (if known)

☐☐ ☐☐ ☐☐ ☐☐ ☐

15 Deceased's Income Tax or Unique Taxpayer Reference (UTR) (if known)

☐☐☐☐☐ ☐☐☐☐☐

16 Did anyone act under a power of attorney granted by the deceased during their lifetime? This may have been a general, enduring or lasting power of attorney.

No ☐

Yes ☐   *Please enclose a copy of the power of attorney*

Contact details of the person dealing with the estate

For example, a solicitor or executor.

17 Name and address of the firm or person dealing with the estate

Name

Postcode

House or building number

Rest of address, including house name or flat number

18 Contact name *if different from box 17*

19 Phone number

20 DX number and town (if used)

21 Contact's reference

22 Fax number

23 If we have to repay any overpaid Inheritance Tax, we need to know who to make the cheque out to.

Do you want any cheque we send to be made out to the firm or person shown at box 17?

Yes ☐   *Go to box 24*

No ☐   *Give the name(s) here, as you would like them to appear on the cheque*

Deceased's Will

24 Did the deceased leave a Will?

No ☐   *Go to box 29*

Yes ☐   *Go to box 25. Please enclose a copy of the Will and any codicils when sending us your account. If an instrument of variation alters the amount of Inheritance Tax payable on this estate, please also send a copy.*

25 Is the address of the deceased as shown in the Will the same as the deceased's last known permanent address (at box 11)?

No ☐   *Go to box 26*

Yes ☐   *Go to box 27*

26 What happened to the property given as the deceased's residence in the Will?

If the deceased sold the property but used all the sale proceeds to buy another main residence for themselves and this happened more than once, there is no need to give details of all the events. Simply say that the 'residence was replaced by the current property'. In all other cases give details of exactly what happened to the property, and give the date of the event(s).

Items referred to in the Will but not included in the estate

Only fill in boxes 27 and 28 if the deceased left a Will. If not go to box 29.

27 Are you including on this form all assets specifically referred to in the Will?
(For example, land, buildings, personal possessions, works of art or shares.)

No ☐   Go to box 28

Yes ☐   Go to box 29

28 Items referred to in the Will and not included on this form (any gifts should be shown on form IHT403)

Items given away as gifts, sold or disposed of before the deceased's death	Who was the item given or sold to, or what happened to it?	Date of gift, sale or disposal	Value of the item at the date of gift, sale or disposal £	If the item was sold, what did the deceased do with the sale proceeds?

What makes up your Inheritance Tax account – Schedules

To make a complete account of the estate you may need to complete some separate Schedules.
Answer the following questions by ticking the 'No' or 'Yes' box.

29 **Transfer of unused nil rate band**

Do you want to transfer any unused nil rate band from the deceased's spouse or civil partner who died before them?

No ☐   Yes ☐   Use Schedule **IHT402**

30 **Gifts and other transfers of value**

Did the deceased make any lifetime gifts or other transfers of value on or after 18 March 1986? See IHT400 Notes

No ☐   Yes ☐   Use Schedule **IHT403**

31 **Jointly owned assets**

Did the deceased jointly own any assets (other than business or partnership assets) with any other person(s)?

No ☐   Yes ☐   Use Schedule **IHT404**

32 **Houses, land, buildings and interests in land**

Did the deceased own any house, land or buildings or rights over land in the UK in their sole name?

No ☐   Yes ☐   Use Schedule **IHT405**

33 **Bank and building society accounts**

Did the deceased hold any bank or building society accounts in their sole name, including cash ISAs, National Savings and Premium Bonds?

No ☐   Yes ☐   Use Schedule **IHT406**

34 **Household and personal goods**

Did the deceased own any household goods or personal possessions?

No ☐   Yes ☐   Use Schedule **IHT407**

If the deceased did **not** own any household goods or personal possessions or they do not have any value, please explain the circumstances in the 'Additional information' boxes on pages 15 and 16.

35 **Household and personal goods donated to charity**

Do the people who inherit the deceased's household goods and personal possessions want to donate some or all of them to a qualifying charity and deduct charity exemption from the value of the estate?
For example, they may wish to donate the deceased's furniture to a charity shop.

No ☐   Yes ☐   Use Schedule **IHT408**

What makes up your Inheritance Tax account – Schedules continued

36 Pensions

Did the deceased have any provision for retirement other than the State Pension? *For example, a pension from an employer, a personal pension policy (or an alternatively secured pension).*

No ☐   Yes ☐   Use Schedule **IHT409**

37 Life assurance and annuities

Did the deceased pay premiums on any life assurance policies, annuities or other products which are payable either to their estate, to another person or which continue after death?

No ☐   Yes ☐   Use Schedule **IHT410**

38 Listed stocks and shares

Did the deceased own any listed stocks and shares or stocks and shares ISAs (excluding control holdings)?

No ☐   Yes ☐   Use Schedule **IHT411**

39 Unlisted stocks and shares and control holdings

Did the deceased own any unlisted stocks and shares (including AIM and OFEX), or any control holdings of any listed shares?

No ☐   Yes ☐   Use Schedule **IHT412**

40 Business relief, business and partnership interests and assets

Do you want to deduct business relief from any business interests and assets owned by the deceased or a partnership in which they were a partner?

No ☐   Yes ☐   Use Schedule **IHT413**

41 Farms, farmhouses and farmland

Do you want to deduct agricultural relief from any farmhouses, farms or farmland owned by the deceased?

No ☐   Yes ☐   Use Schedule **IHT414**

42 Interest in another estate

Was the deceased entitled to receive any legacy or assets from the estate of someone who died before them and that they had not received before they died?

No ☐   Yes ☐   Use Schedule **IHT415**

43 Debts due to the estate

Was the deceased owed any money by way of personal loans or mortgage at the date of death?

No ☐   Yes ☐   Use Schedule **IHT416**

44 Foreign assets

Did the deceased own any assets outside the UK either in their sole name or jointly with others?

No ☐   Yes ☐   Use Schedule **IHT417**

45 Assets held in trust

Did the deceased have any right to benefit from any assets held in trust (including the right to receive assets held in a trust at some future date)?

No ☐   Yes ☐   Use Schedule **IHT418**

46 Debts owed by the deceased

Do you wish to include a deduction from the estate for debts and liabilities of the following types:
- money that was spent on behalf of the deceased and which was not repaid
- loans
- liabilities related to a life assurance policy where the sum assured will not be fully reflected in the estate
- debts that the deceased guaranteed on behalf of another person?

No ☐   Yes ☐   Use Schedule **IHT419**

47 National Heritage assets

Is any asset already exempt or is exemption now being claimed, on the grounds of national, scientific, historic, artistic, scenic or architectural interest? Or does any such asset benefit from an Approved Maintenance Fund for the upkeep and preservation of national heritage assets?

No ☐   Yes ☐   Use Schedule **IHT420**

If you answered Yes to any of questions 29 to 47, please fill in the Schedule for that asset. The Schedule number is shown at the end of each question.

48 Do you have all of the Schedules you need?

No ☐
- download the Schedules from **www.hmrc.gov.uk/inheritancetax/** or
- phone us on **0845 30 20 900 (+44 115 974 3009** from outside the UK)

When you have all the Schedules you need, fill them in before you go to box 49.

Yes ☐   *Fill in the Schedules now before going to box 49*

Estate in the UK

Use this section to tell us about assets owned by the deceased in the UK. You should include all assets owned outright by the deceased and the **deceased's share** of **jointly owned** assets. You will need to copy figures from the Schedules you have filled in. Any assets the deceased had outside the UK should be shown on form IHT417 and **not** in boxes 49 to 96.

Jointly owned assets

Enter '0' in the box if the deceased did not own any of the assets described.

		Column A	Column B
49	Jointly owned assets (form IHT404, box 5)		£
50	Jointly owned assets (form IHT404, box 10)	£	

Assets owned outright by the deceased

Enter the value of the assets owned outright by the deceased in the amount boxes attached to each question.
Enter '0' in the box if the deceased did not own any of the assets described.

51	Deceased's residence (except farmhouses and jointly owned houses) (form IHT405, box 7). Include the value of jointly owned houses at box 49 and farmhouses at box 68 instead		£
52	Bank and building society accounts in the deceased's sole name (form IHT406, box 1)	£	
53	Cash (in coins or notes) and uncashed traveller's cheques	£	
54	Premium Bonds and National Savings & Investments products (form IHT406, box 5)	£	
55	Household and personal goods (form IHT407, box 6)	£	
56	Pensions (form IHT409, boxes 7 and 15). Include the value of any pensions arrears due at the date of death	£	
57	Life assurance and mortgage protection policies (form IHT410, box 6)	£	
58	Add up all the figures in **Column A** (boxes 50 to 57)	£	
59	Add up all the figures in **Column B** (boxes 49 + 51)		£

Estate in the UK continued

		Column A	Column B
60	Copy the figure from box 58	£	
61	Copy the figure from box 59		£
62	UK Government and municipal securities (form IHT411, box 1), but include dividends and interest at box 64	£	
63	Listed stocks, shares and investments that did not give the deceased control of the company (form IHT411, box 2)	£	
64	Dividends or interest on stocks, shares and securities	£	
65	Traded unlisted and unlisted shares except control holdings (form IHT412, box 1 + box 2)	£	
66	Traded unlisted and unlisted shares except control holdings (see IHT412 Notes)		£
67	Control holdings of unlisted, traded unlisted and listed shares (form IHT412, box 3 + box 4 + box 5)		£
68	Farms, farmhouses and farmland (give details on forms IHT414 and IHT405)		£
69	Businesses including farm businesses, business assets and timber		£
70	Other land, buildings and rights over land (give details on form IHT405)		£
71	Interest in another estate (form IHT415, box 7)		£
72	Interest in another estate (form IHT415, box 9)	£	
73	Debts due to the estate (form IHT416, box 3 total)	£	
74	Income Tax or Capital Gains Tax repayment	£	
75	Trust income due to the deceased – see IHT400 Notes	£	
76	Other assets and income due to the deceased (enter details in the 'Additional information' boxes on pages 15 and 16 of this form if not given elsewhere)	£	
77	Add up all the figures in **Column A** (boxes 60 to 76)	£	
78	Add up all the figures in **Column B** (boxes 61 to 71)		£
79	Gross total of the estate in the UK (box 77 + box 78)	£	

Deductions from the estate in the UK incurred up to the date of death

80 Mortgages, secured loans and other debts payable out of property or assets owned outright by the deceased and shown in **Column B** on pages 6 and 7. For example, a mortgage secured on the deceased's house or a loan secured on a business. Enter the name of the creditor and say which property or asset the deduction relates to and describe the liability.

Name of creditor	Property or asset and description of liability	Amount £
	Total mortgages and secured loans	£

81 Funeral expenses

	Funeral costs	£
	Headstone	£

Other costs (please specify)

	Total cost of funeral	£

82 Other liabilities

Enter any other liabilities that have not been shown in boxes 80 or 81. (For example, outstanding gas and electricity bills, credit card balances or nursing home fees.)

Creditor's name and description of the liability	Amount £
Total other liabilities	

Deductions from the estate in the UK continued

Deductions summary

		Column A	Column B
83	Box 80 figure		£
84	Box 81 + box 82	£	
85	Box 77 *minus* box 84. If the result is a minus figure enter '0' in the box and enter the deficit in box 88	£	
86	Box 78 *minus* box 83. If the result is a minus figure enter '0' in the box and enter the deficit in box 87		£
87	Enter the deficit figure from box 86 (if there is one)	£	
88	Enter the deficit figure from box 85 (if there is one)		£
89	Box 85 *minus* box 87	£	
90	Box 86 *minus* box 88		£
91	Total estate in the UK (box 89 + box 90)	£	

Exemptions and reliefs

92 Exemptions and reliefs deducted from the assets in the deceased's sole name shown in **Column A** on pages 6 and 7
- *see IHT400 Notes*. If you are deducting spouse or civil partner exemption, enter the spouse or civil partner's full name, date and country of birth and their domicile. If you are deducting charity exemption, enter the full name of the charity, country of establishment and the HMRC charities reference, if available.
Do not include exemptions or reliefs on jointly owned assets, these should be deducted on form IHT404, at box 9.

Describe the exemptions and reliefs you are deducting. For example 'cash gift to charity in the Will' and show how the amount has been calculated - please use the 'Additional information' boxes on pages 15 and 16 of this form if you need more space.	Amount deducted £
Total exemptions and reliefs from assets in **Column A**	£

Exemptions and reliefs continued

| 93 | Exemptions and reliefs deducted from the assets in the deceased's sole name shown in **Column B** on pages 6 and 7 – *see IHT400 Notes*. If you are deducting spouse or civil partner exemption enter the spouse or civil partner's full name, date and country of birth and their domicile and/or, if you are deducting charity exemption enter the full name of the charity, the country of establishment and the HMRC charities reference, if available (unless already given at box 92). **Do not include exemptions or reliefs on jointly owned assets, these should be deducted on form IHT404, at box 4.** |

Describe the exemptions and reliefs you are deducting. For example, 'agricultural relief on farm' and show how the amount has been calculated – please use the 'Additional information' boxes on pages 15 and 16 if you need more space.	Amount deducted £
Total exemptions and reliefs from assets in **Column B** £	

94	Box 89 *minus* box 92	£
95	Box 90 *minus* box 93	£
96	Total net estate in the UK, after exemptions and reliefs (box 94 + box 95)	£

Other assets taken into account to calculate the tax

		Column A	Column B
97	Foreign houses, land, businesses and control holdings (form IHT417, box 5)		£
98	Other foreign assets (form IHT417, box 10)	£	
99	Assets held in trust on which the trustees would like to pay the tax now (form IHT418, box 12)		£
100	Assets held in trust on which the trustees would like to pay the tax now (form IHT418, box 17)	£	
101	Nominated assets. Include details of the nominated assets in the 'Additional information' boxes on pages 15 and 16 – *see IHT400 Notes*	£	
102	Box 98 + box 100 + box 101	£	
103	Box 97 + box 99		£
104	Gifts with reservation and pre-owned assets (IHT403, box 17)	£	
105	Assets held in trust on which the trustees are not paying the tax now (form IHT418, box 18)	£	
106	Alternatively secured pension fund(s) (form IHT409, boxes 32 and 42 - only where the date of death is between 06/04/06 and 05/04/07 inclusive)	£	
107	Total other assets taken into account to calculate the tax (box 102 + box 103 + box 104 + box 105 + box 106)	£	
108	Total chargeable estate (box 96 + box 107)	£	

Working out the Inheritance Tax

ℹ️ If there is no Inheritance Tax to pay, you do not need to fill in this page and should go to box 119 on page 12.

If you are filling in this form yourself without the help of a solicitor or other adviser, you do not have to work out the tax yourself; we can do it for you – but first read the following note about paying Inheritance Tax by instalments.

Paying Inheritance Tax by instalments
Instead of paying all of the Inheritance Tax at once you may pay some of it in 10 annual instalments (that is, one instalment each year for 10 years). You can pay by instalments on any assets shown in **Column B** on pages 6 and 7 that have not been sold.

Interest will be payable on the instalments.
The total value of the assets on which you may pay the tax by instalments is box 95 + box 97 + box 99 (if any).

109 Are you filling in the form without the help of a solicitor or other adviser and you wish us to work out the tax for you?

No ☐   *Go to 'Simple Inheritance Tax calculation'*

Yes ☐   *Go to box 110*

110 Do you wish to pay the tax on the amounts shown in box 95 + box 97 + box 99 by instalments?

No ☐   *Go to box 118*

Yes ☐   *If any of the assets in **Column B** have been **sold**, write the total value of those assets here*

£ [   ]

Now go to box 118

Simple Inheritance Tax calculation

You can use the simple calculation in boxes 111 to 117 to work out the Inheritance Tax on the estate as long as the following apply:
• you are paying the tax on or before the last day of the sixth month after the death occurred so no interest is payable
• you want to pay all of the tax now and not pay by instalments on property in Column B (see note above about paying Inheritance Tax by instalments)
• the total of any lifetime gifts is below the Inheritance Tax nil rate band
• you are not deducting double taxation relief on any foreign assets *(see note on IHT400 Calculation)*
• you are not deducting successive charges relief on assets inherited by the deceased in the last five years from another estate on which Inheritance Tax was paid *(see note on IHT400 Calculation)*.

If the simple calculation does not apply to you, you will need to use the form IHT400 *Calculation* to work out the Inheritance Tax due then continue to fill in this form at box 118.

111 Total chargeable value of gifts made by the deceased within the seven years before their death (form IHT403, box 7)   £ [   ]

112 Aggregate chargeable transfer (box 108 + box 111)   £ [   ]

113 Inheritance Tax nil rate band at the date of death
See IHT400 Rates and Tables   £ [   ]

114 Transferable nil rate band (form IHT402, box 20)   £ [   ]

115 Total nil rate band (box 113 + box 114)   £ [   ]

116 Value chargeable to tax (box 112 *minus* box 115)   £ [   ]

117 Inheritance Tax (box 116 x 40%)   £ [   ] · [ ][ ]

Direct Payment Scheme

This is a scheme under which participating banks and building societies will release funds from the deceased's accounts directly to HM Revenue & Customs to pay Inheritance Tax. For National Savings & Investments, see the note on page 14.

| 118 | Do you wish to use the Direct Payment Scheme? |

No ☐

Yes ☐ *Fill in form IHT423 (you will need a separate form for each bank and building society account concerned)*

Declaration

| 119 | I/We wish to apply for the following type of grant (see note 'Grant of representation' in IHT400 Notes to decide on the type of grant) |

- Probate ☐

- Confirmation ☐

- Letters of Administration ☐

- Letters of Administration with Will annexed ☐

- Other (please specify)

[ ]

To the best of my/our knowledge and belief, the information I/we have given and the statements I/we have made in this account and the Schedules attached (together called 'this account') are correct and complete.
Please tick the Schedules you have filled in.

IHT401 ☐	IHT408 ☐	IHT415 ☐
IHT402 ☐	IHT409 ☐	IHT416 ☐
IHT403 ☐	IHT410 ☐	IHT417 ☐
IHT404 ☐	IHT411 ☐	IHT418 ☐
IHT405 ☐	IHT412 ☐	IHT419 ☐
IHT406 ☐	IHT413 ☐	IHT420 ☐
IHT407 ☐	IHT414 ☐	

I/We have made the fullest enquiries that are reasonably practicable in the circumstances to find out the open market value of all the items shown in this account. The value of items in the box(es) listed below are provisional estimates which are based on all the information available to me/us at this time.

I/We will tell HM Revenue & Customs Inheritance Tax the exact value(s) as soon as I/we know it and I/we will pay any additional tax and interest that may be due.

List the boxes in the account that are provisional here.

[ ]

Where Schedule IHT402 has been filled in I/we declare that to the best of my/our knowledge and belief:
- the deceased and their spouse or civil partner were married or in a civil partnership at the date the spouse or civil partner died
- where a Deed of Variation has not been provided there has been no change to the people who inherited the estate of the spouse or civil partner.

I/We understand that I/we may be liable to prosecution if I/we deliberately conceal any information that affects the liability to Inheritance Tax arising on the deceased's death, or if I/we deliberately include information in this account which I/we know to be false.

I/We understand that I/we may have to pay financial penalties if this account is delivered late or contains false information, or if I/we fail to remedy anything in this account which is incorrect in any material respect within a reasonable time of it coming to my/our notice.

I/We understand that the issue of the grant does not mean that:
- I/we have paid all the Inheritance Tax and interest that may be due on the estate, or
- the statements made and the values included in this account are accepted by HM Revenue & Customs Inheritance Tax.

I/We understand that HM Revenue & Customs Inheritance Tax:
- will only look at this account in detail after the grant has been issued
- may need to ask further questions and discuss the value of items shown in this account
- may make further calculations of tax and interest payable to help the persons liable for the tax to make provision to meet the tax liability.

I/We understand that I/we may have to pay interest on any unpaid tax according to the law where:
- I/we have elected to pay tax by instalments
- additional tax becomes payable for any reason.

Each person delivering this account, whether as executor, intending administrator or otherwise must sign on page 13 to indicate that they have read and agreed the statements above.

Declaration continued

Surname

First name(s)

Postcode

House number

Rest of address, including house name or flat number

Signature

Date *DD MM YYYY*

Surname

First name(s)

Postcode

House number

Rest of address, including house name or flat number

Signature

Date *DD MM YYYY*

Surname

First name(s)

Postcode

House number

Rest of address, including house name or flat number

Signature

Date *DD MM YYYY*

Surname

First name(s)

Postcode

House number

Rest of address, including house name or flat number

Signature

Date *DD MM YYYY*

Checklist

For more information look at the relevant page in the IHT400 Notes.

Use the checklist to remind you of:
- the actions you should take, and
- the additional information you should include when sending the Inheritance Tax forms to HM Revenue & Customs Inheritance Tax.

- If the deceased died leaving a Will, provide a copy of the Will, and any codicils.

  No ☐   Yes ☐

- If the estate has been varied in any way and the variation results in either an increase or decrease in the amount of tax, provide a copy of the instrument of variation.

  No ☐   Yes ☐

- Any professional valuation of stocks and shares.

  No ☐   Yes ☐

- Any professional valuation of household effects or personal possessions.

  No ☐   Yes ☐

- Any professional valuation of houses, land and buildings.

  No ☐   Yes ☐

- A copy of any insurance policy (and annuity, if appropriate) where the deceased was paying the premiums for the benefit of someone else and any trust documents if the policy has been written in trust.

  No ☐   Yes ☐

- A copy of any trust deed(s), if the trustees are paying tax at the same time as you apply for the grant.

  No ☐   Yes ☐

- Any evidence of money owed to the deceased, including loan agreements and related trusts or policies and any evidence of the debts being released.

  No ☐   Yes ☐

- A copy of any joint life assurance policy or policy on the life of another person.

  No ☐   Yes ☐

- A copy of any structural survey and/or correspondence with the loss adjuster about any structurally damaged property.

  No ☐   Yes ☐

- If you are deducting agricultural relief, a plan of the property and a copy of the lease or agreement for letting (where appropriate).

  No ☐   Yes ☐

- If you are deducting business relief, a copy of the partnership agreement (where appropriate) and the last two years' accounts.

  No ☐   Yes ☐

- If you are deducting double taxation relief or unilateral relief, provide evidence of the foreign tax, in the form of an assessment of the foreign tax, a certificate of the foreign tax paid and (if available) the official receipt.

  No ☐   Yes ☐

- Any written evidence of debts to close friends or family.

  No ☐   Yes ☐

- Have all executors signed page 13 of this form?

  No ☐   Yes ☐

- If you have calculated your own tax, have you enclosed the calculation with this form and arranged to pay the tax?

  No ☐   Yes ☐

- If you are applying for a grant, have you enclosed form IHT421 *Probate summary?*

  No ☐   Yes ☐

Direct Payment Scheme (if used)

- If you are using the Direct Payment Scheme, have you sent a form IHT423 to each organisation from which funds will be provided? *See IHT423*

  No ☐   Yes ☐

- If you want HM Revenue & Customs Inheritance Tax to call for payment from National Savings & Investments, provide a letter detailing the investments to be used, how much of the tax is to be paid by National Savings & Investments and official letters from the relevant National Savings & Investments office stating the value of those investments.

- If you want HM Revenue & Customs Inheritance Tax to call for payment from British Government stock, provide a letter detailing the investments to be used and how much of the tax is to be paid by Government stock.

For more information on paying by National Savings or British Government stock go to **www.hmrc.gov.uk** or phone the helpline for a copy of the IHT11 *Payment of Inheritance Tax from National Savings or from British Government stock.*

Return addresses and contact details

- If you are applying for a grant in England, Wales or Northern Ireland you should send the forms to our Nottingham office (the DX addresses are for solicitors, practitioners and banks)

HM Revenue & Customs
Inheritance Tax
Ferrers House
PO Box 38
Castle Meadow Road
Nottingham
NG2 1BB
DX 701201 NOTTINGHAM 4

Phone **0845 30 20 900**

- If you are applying for Confirmation in Scotland you should send the forms to our Edinburgh office (the DX addresses are for solicitors, practitioners and banks)

HM Revenue & Customs
Inheritance Tax
Meldrum House
15 Drumsheugh Gardens
Edinburgh
EH3 7UG
DX ED 542001 EDINBURGH 14

Phone **0845 30 20 900**

- If you want to know more about any particular aspect of Inheritance Tax or have specific questions about completing the forms go to **www.hmrc.gov.uk/inheritancetax/**

  Or phone the Probate and Inheritance Tax Helpline on **0845 30 20 900 (+44 115 974 3009** from outside the UK).

- If you need a copy of any of our forms or leaflets you can download them from our website or phone the Probate and Inheritance Tax Helpline to order them.

Additional information

Use this space:
- to explain the circumstances where the deceased did not own any household effects or personal possessions or they do not have any value (box 34)
- to give us any additional information we ask for, including details of:
  - any claim for discharge of legal rights (box 7)
  - other assets and income due to the deceased (box 76)
  - nominated assets (box 101)
  - successive charges relief (IHT400 Calculation, box 10).

Additional information continued

Additional information continued

INDEX

LEGAL TAXONOMY

FROM SWEET & MAXWELL

This index has been prepared using Sweet & Maxwell's Legal Taxonomy. Main index entries conform to keywords provided by the Legal Taxonomy except where references to specific documents or non-standard terms (denoted by quotation marks) have been included. These keywords provide a means of identifying similar concepts in other Sweet & Maxwell publications and online services to which keywords from the Legal Taxonomy have been applied. Readers may find some minor differences between terms used in the text and those which appear in the index. Suggestions to *sweet&maxwell.taxonomy@thomson.com*.